Published by Merrill Publishing Company
A Bell & Howell Information Company
Columbus, Ohio 43216

This book was set in Korinna

Administrative Editor: John Stout
Developmental Editor: Ann Mirels
Production Coordinator: Julie Higgins
Art Coordinator: Vincent Smith
Cover Designer: Brian Deep

Library of Congress Catalog Card Number: 88-63027

International Standard Book Number: 0-675-20797-5

Printed in the United States of America
1 2 3 4 5 6 7 8 9—92 91 90 89

Compensation Administration

SECOND EDITION

Leonard R. Burgess

Merrill Publishing Company
A Bell & Howell Information Company
Columbus • Toronto • London • Melbourne

Dedicated to the memory of John E. Pearson,
former dean of the College of Business Administration
at Texas A&M University

Preface

This book, designed for use with both college undergraduates and graduate level students, stresses a "hands on" approach to the subject of compensation administration. Included are five special features:

- pay and benefits projects;
- job descriptions;
- employee benefits tables;
- end-of-chapter summaries, discussion questions, case studies, and references; and
- a comprehensive glossary.

In addition, pay rates for selected jobs are available in the accompanying Instructor's Manual.

Students learn by doing. In particular, the pay and benefits projects allow them to practice developing pay and benefits manuals for particular organizations. In such a project, students can be assigned any one of five different types of organizations, six different employee groups within the organizations, and six major methods of job evaluation.

The 125 job descriptions in Appendix A give substance to the "how to" information on job analysis and job descriptions in Chapter 5. Students use these descriptions in the pay and benefits projects. Included are 25 descriptions uniquely applicable to the Hay guide chart-profile method of job evaluation. Familiarity with job descriptions is important because job analysis is typically the beginning task in the wage and salary field.

The pay rates, which cover different jobs in specific employee groups, add realism to the projects. Pay rates are separated from other job evaluation data in order to encourage the student to realize that *job worth* as measured in points, for example, is separate and distinct from *market worth* as reflected in job pricing.

The employee benefits tables in Chapter 13 stimulate the student to think about benefit costs for particular employee groups in a specific organization. These tables show in a concise format, both the variety and cost of employee benefits for selected industries.

End-of-chapter supplements are also designed to stimulate student thinking. For example, the case studies provide students an opportunity to apply what was learned in each chapter. The book uses the case method of instruction as practiced at the Harvard Business School, and also gives students a specific role assignment for each case. This encourages them to consider *first* what the problems are, and only *then* to consider alternative solutions.

Discussion questions clarify the ideas and issues in each chapter and stimulate class participation. Summaries provide students with an overview of the chapter, and references enable the more curious students to further pursue those aspects of compensation administration in which they are interested. References also provide resource materials for written assignments and term papers.

In addition to the job descriptions in Appendix A, Appendices B and C include definitions of factors for use with point plans for production workers as well as for clerical, technical, and supervisory workers. The conversion table in Appendix D enables the student to compute hourly, weekly, monthly, and annual rates of pay with ease. Finally, Appendix E covers the grade descriptions used under the federal government's General Schedule.

To help the student understand pay and benefits terms, some of which are rather technical, a glossary has been added to the second edition.

Acknowledgments

Original versions of almost all chapters of the first edition were read aloud to my first wife, Virginia, who died while that edition was still in progress. She contributed to the creative flow of the book with a perceptive eye and a sensitive ear. For later versions of chapters in the first edition, Louise Hyde Reilly played a similar listening role and offered valued comments.

In the development of this second edition, I am grateful to a number of people who provided useful data and insightful suggestions. International pay and productivity comparisons in Chapter 2 were contributed by Karlis Kirsis of World Steel Dynamics. John Farnham of the Toronto office of TPFC made available data showing CEO pay vs. rank and file worker pay for three major nations, and Janet Norwood, commissioner of the Bureau of Labor Statistics, made available to me vital information from the Asian Productivity Association. Data from Jack Stanek of International Survey Research Corporation made possible useful comparisons of Japanese vs. U.S. worker attitudes.

The part of Chapter 2 relating to efforts to make the United States more internationally competitive benefited from several inputs. Jack Batty of General Electric Corporation and Mark Potts of the *Washington Post* contributed information about the Welch regime at GE. Walter H. Read came up with useful insights about IBM's efforts, both as to general management and incentive pay. Hewlitt-Packard Corporation provided valuable executive seminar material relating to its efforts to be internationally competitive.

Chapter 5 on Job Analysis has been strengthened by material on computer aspects from Jack Roose of Wyatt Company and Marsha Roberts of the Bank of America.

In connection with Chapter 12 on Incentive Pay, my thanks go to Barbara Fiss of the Office of Personnel Management for helping me to update the information on U.S. government incentive plans, to the ESOP Association for useful material on Employee Stock Ownership Plans, and to Jill Kanin-Lovers in the New York office of TPFC for a better historical picture of long-range executive incentive plans.

I also owe thanks to Phil McCoury of San Francisco State University for his encouragement in the classroom use of pay and benefits projects, as well as to Dr. Luke T. Chang, President of Lincoln University for his continuing interest in my research activities.

Thanks are especially due to the reference librarian at the Graduate Social Sciences Library of the University of California at Berkeley, to the Government Documents personnel of the Stanford University Library, to the reference librarian at the Hastings Law School Library, and to Senator Allen Cranston for information on the legislative and legal aspects of pay and benefits.

The present edition reflects suggestions for improvements made by several colleagues who reviewed the manuscript: Daniel R. Hoyt of Arkansas State University, Carolyn Wiley of Texas Women's University, Kermit R. Davis, Jr. of Auburn University, Anthony Campagna of Ohio State University, and Pamela Wolfmeyer of Winona State University. Their comments have been extremely helpful.

My special thanks go to Yogenthiran Penambulam whose consultation on the computerized aspects of writing this second edition served me so well.

Leonard R. Burgess

Contents

4. Unions and Inequities in Pay and Benefits   59

5. Job Analysis, Job Descriptions, and Computer Applications   99

6. Overview: Job Evaluation   137

7. Ranking, Predetermined Grading, and Point Methods   153

8. Factor Comparison and Guide Chart–Profile Methods   181

9. Pay and Benefits Surveys   209

13. Employee Benefits 311

14. Pay and Benefits: Executives 337

15. Pay and Benefits: Professionals 363

The Impact of Organizational Hierarchy on the Compensation Administrator

1

Chapter Outline

- The Internal Hierarchy
- The External Hierarchy
- Related Rational Structures
- Incentive Plans
- Unions, Women, Minorities, and Legislative Changes
- Summary
- Case Study—Walker State University

Compensation administrators in typical large American corporations are, like many other corporate executives, buffeted by numerous internal and external forces that restrict their freedom of action. It is nevertheless relevant to single out for special attention the influence on the compensation administrator of organizational hierarchy—both internally and externally.

The Internal Hierarchy

The compensation administrator must operate within a complex internal organizational structure. Despite economic pressures that may encourage reducing the layers of authority, empire building in organizations continues. The compensation administrator has a fair number of staff people who report to him, and in turn he must relate to higher level executives, typically including the vice president of human resources, the president, and/or the chairman, whoever is the company's chief executive officer (CEO). The way the compensation manager deals with these executives and others often depends on the organizational structure. (See Figures 1–1 and 1–2 for typical organization relationships.)

Management in a unionized organization must be structured to handle problems in the pay and benefits area. To illustrate this concept, we shall examine the structure of a consumer goods manufacturing company with worldwide operations employing over 5,000 workers. The key parts of the organization are shown in Figure 1–1.

Reporting to the director of compensation and benefits are three managers—for salary administration, employee relations information systems, and group insurance—as well as a director for employee benefits programs. These officials interact often because their duties are closely related.

The bottom layer of the organizational structure, under the manager of salary administration, includes the entry job of compensation analyst (Figure 1–2). Two of the three compensation administrators have compensation analysts who work closely with them. Other jobs in the section include compensation administrative assistant, a position control specialist, a forms control specialist, and a departmental secretary. The role and activities of the compensation analyst will be explored further in Chapter 5.

```
Chairman & Chief Executive Officer
  Vice President, Employee Relations
    Manager, Administrative Services & Planning
    Director, Organization Development
      Director, Management Development & Training
      Manager, Employee Relations Programs
      Corporate Manager, Professional Employment
      Supervisor, Headquarters Personnel Department
    Director, Corporate Employee Relations
      Director, Labor Relations
      Manager, Employee Relations Research
    Manager, Health & Safety
      Manager, Workers' Compensation
      Corporate Industrial Hygienist
      Corporate Fleet Safety Supervisor
    Director, Compensation & Benefits
      Manager, Salary Administration
      Manager, Employee Relations Information Systems
      Manager, Group Insurance
      Director, Employee Benefits Programs
```

FIGURE 1–1
Employee relations organization for a large manufacturer of consumer goods.

The director of compensation's influence over pay and benefits is hierarchically limited within the organization. Of course, he does have an influence over the pay of those lower down in the structure. But there is a strong tendency for higher-paid people to determine their *own* pay levels.[1]

How much influence on higher pay levels the administrator may have is affected by the personal and power relationships between him and the vice president for employee relations, and in turn between the latter and the CEO. The compensation administrator may strive to provide pay and benefits to attract, hold, and motivate the best people for the organization. But a top executive in the organization who is more *economically* than *humanly* inclined may place serious obstacles in the way of the compensation administrator doing an effective job. Americans have a natural tendency to believe that not only for the compensation administrator but also for the personnel/human resources department the important thing is to keep the employees happy. They often look with skepticism upon the strongly held economic beliefs of top managers. But in a modern competitive world, the economic aspects are too critical to ignore, as will be seen in Chapter 2.

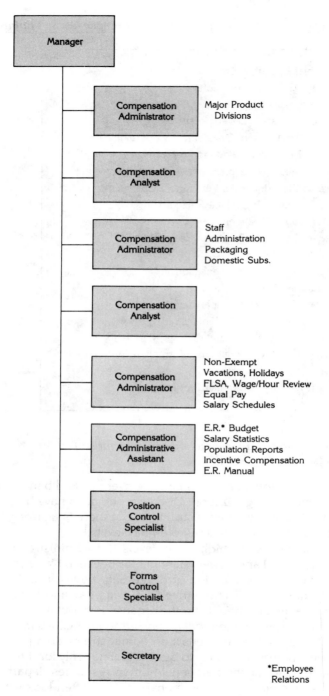

FIGURE 1–2
Salary administration organization chart.

4

The External Hierarchy

Turning now to the external hierarchy, much of the picture is apparent in the interrelationships among company size, the pay of the chief executive officers in the largest corporations, how pay structures are built, and what these structures imply as to the total pay and benefits costs.

Data for the year 1985 show that there is a positive correlation in the United States between company size and the pay (base salaries and cash bonuses) of the CEO. A tenfold increase in sales was accompanied by a doubling of salaries. Absolute levels and ranges from low to high as well as medians for top U.S. executives are worth looking at.

Top Officers in the 100 Largest Manufacturing Companies

The regulations of the Securities and Exchange Commission (SEC) require that companies report pay for officers earning over $40,000 a year in "cash and cash equivalent" forms of remuneration, which consist mostly of salaries, director's fees, and bonuses.[2] The 1986 figures for the three highest paid officers in the 100 largest manufacturing firms are shown in Table 1–1.

The information shown in Table 1–1 is taken from studies conducted by the management consultant firm of Towers, Perrin, Forster & Crosby but is based primarily on information from company annual proxy statements. As can be seen from the table, there is quite a range of figures, extending all the way from $205,000 for the fifth highest paid officer in the "low" company to $1.740 million for the highest paid officer in the "high" company. The median company in this case is the typical company. That is, if you took all the chief executive officers in the 100 largest companies and lined them up from the lowest paid to the highest paid, the officer in the middle would be the one who received $970,000.

TABLE 1–1
*Total cash compensation of top officers among the 100 largest industrial companies in the United States (in thousands of dollars).**

	Low	*Median*	*High*
Chief Executive Officer**	$412	$970	$1740
Second highest paid	254	652	1315
Third highest paid	245	515	1162
Fourth highest paid	231	443	1087
Fifth highest paid	205	402	894

*Includes any award paid in cash either immediately following the close of the year on which the award was based or in installments beginning in that year and continuing for a number of years during active employment (such as cash bonuses paid in the automobile industry).
**Chief Executive Officers were not reported as the highest-paid executives in four companies.
Source: Towers, Perrin, Forster & Crosby, *1987 Top 100 Industrial Executive Compensation Study.* Data are for 1986.

The data in Table 1–1 need to be qualified, however. Smaller corporations do not typically pay their top people at such high rates. Also, the data do not reflect substantial additional employee benefits of various kinds. Finally, these are before-tax figures. The after-tax pay figures would be considerably less, although the differentials would still be substantial. While we shall consider these and other aspects in detail later, it is sufficient here to note that these executive pay data constitute the upper end of the meaningful pay range for almost all jobs in the United States.

Top Officers in the 25 Largest Labor Organizations

In contrast, if we exclude expenses, only two of the highest paid officers in the 25 largest labor organizations made more than $200,000 in salary, as shown in Table 1–2. The typical industry top executive among the 100 largest industrials received $970,000 in total cash compensation compared with $122,400 in salary plus expenses for the typical top labor organization officer.

Now, of course, corporations and unions have different basic purposes—the corporation's bottom line being profitability, while the union's bottom line is the welfare of its membership—so there is no reason to expect the two sets of figures to approximate each other. Nevertheless, while corporations can show large assets and sales, unions can often have a big influence on sizable payrolls, and at least five of the unions can boast of more than a million members. All things considered, should the typical top executive among the largest companies earn 8 times as much as the typical union leader among the 25 largest labor organizations?

The allowances and expenses in the union pay table are roughly comparable in nature (if not in amount) to similar expenses typically claimed by business executives. For example the highest paid officer in the Food and Commercial Workers Union had allowances and other expenses amounting to $87.4 thousand. Such expense information must be reported by labor unions under the Labor Management Reporting and Disclosure Act of 1959. However, the SEC does *not* require the same information from top executives in industry.

CEO's Earnings Versus Average Earnings in Three Nations

If you do not find the contrast of pay between top executives and union leaders a reason to reflect, you should look at the cash executives are paid compared to what average workers earn in the United States, Canada, and Australia, as shown in Table 1–3. The average wage is calculated from government sources assuming a 35-hour work week with all dollar statistics presented in U.S. dollar terms. The executive information is taken from TPF&C's *Worldwide Total Remuneration,* 1987.

The question that must be asked about the results shown in Table 1–3 is whether it is necessary that our top executives earn 11 times what our average

TABLE 1–2

Salaries and expenses of the highest paid officers in the 25 largest labor organizations (in thousands of dollars).

Union	Salary	Allowances, Expenses, etc.	Total	Members (Thou.)
Food & Commercial Workers	200.7	87.4	288.1	1207
Teamsters	242.8	26.8	269.6	1900
Hotel & Restaurant Employees	157.2	52.9	210.1	301
State, County, & Municipal Employees	138.7	28.7	167.4	1100
Laborers	140.3	23.2	163.5	385
Operating Engineers	132.9	28.2	161.1	320
Electrical Workers (IBEW)	132.7	17.3	150.0	791
Machinists	105.1	31.1	136.2	700
Education (NEA)	82.5	44.1	126.6	1700
Steelworkers	72.6	53.3	125.9	731
Paperworkers	114.9	10.9	125.8	240
Plumbers	87.6	35.0	122.6	226
Carpenters	109.2	13.2	122.4	564
Graphic Communications Workers	88.2	30.7	118.9	194
Ladies' Garment Workers	94.7	22.1	116.8	210
Electrical Workers (IUE)	79.8	34.3	114.1	198
Clothing & Textile Workers	83.5	28.8	112.3	314
Postal Workers	72.2	35.4	107.6	255
Autoworkers	77.2	29.8	107.0	1017
Letter Carriers	88.2	7.8	96.0	275
Musicians	71.4	21.5	92.9	201
Communications Workers	72.0	15.6	87.6	515
Government Workers (AFGE)	81.2	3.5	84.7	200
Teachers	61.7	19.5	81.2	610
Service Employees	80.2	0.0	80.2	850

Sources: Financial data are from U.S. Department of Labor and cover 1986. Membership data from the Bureau of National Affairs are for 1985.

workers earn, when only half that spread appears to be satisfactory to Australian executives. And the evidence does not stop with these three nations. Ralph Sorenson, chief executive officer of Barry Wright Corporation, a Massachusetts firm, says in part:

> In U.S. companies, the compensation spread between the lowest and highest paid employees is much greater than in the typical Japanese manufacturing company.[3]

In Chapter 14 we explore pay and benefits for executives in more depth. And in Chapter 13 we shall look at employee benefits in a more general way.

If there is a question as to the justification for wide pay spreads between the top executives in companies and the rank-and-file workers, then we need to look

TABLE 1–3
CEO's cash payments versus average earnings in three nations.

Country	Average Wage Annualized	CEO Total Cash	Multiple of Average Wage
Canada	$20,093	$158,800	7.9
Australia	14,414	79,100	5.49
U.S.	24,170	265,000	10.96

Source: TPF&C, a Towers Perrin Company.

at how pay structures get that way. The answer depends in part on the nature of the pay curve. Are the differentials between the midpoints of pay grades equal dollar intervals, equal percentage intervals, or rising percentage intervals? All three possibilities are actually practiced. These matters are explored in Chapter 10. However, it is relevant here to explore in more detail the actual pay-setting process under one of the three possibilities—that of equal percentage differentials. The president of DuPont made the following frank observation:

> In the DuPont Company, we recognize sixteen positional levels between wage earner and president. Compensation at each of these levels must be sufficiently greater to tempt the man below to make the climb . . . For the progression to be meaningful, it must be on an after-tax basis. If we say an increase of 25% after taxes for each rung of the ladder is reasonable, simple arithmetic pushes gross compensation at the top into stratospheric levels.[4]

The total compensation cost implied by such a pay curve is a function of a mix of factors: taxes, the level at which the percentage differential is set, and the number of layers of authority. Do there have to be sixteen layers of authority? And remember we are talking here only of base pay. What about the additional costs of employee benefits, which tend to be a function of base pay? We shall be looking further in Chapter 2 at the international significance of these hierarchically biased costs.

Related Rational Structures

There are a number of rational, predominantly managerial devices that typically tie in with the organizational hierarchy and tend to bolster the rationale of hierarchical habits. Such devices are job analysis, job evaluation, and performance evaluation. As will be seen in Chapter 10, pay structures, often heavily hierarchically influenced, are typically constructed with pay boxes (whose heights are pay rate ranges and whose widths are often point ranges). Which jobs go into which boxes are determined by job analysis and job evaluation, and how people are paid within these boxes is determined mostly by performance evaluation. Despite the hierarchical relationship, these three processes still have utility, and most people who are critical of them on various grounds still do not have workable alternative proposals. We shall look at these matters in greater depth in Chapters 5, 6, 7, 8, and 11. In passing, it may be noted that the Guide Chart–Profile Method discussed in Chapter 8 appears to be somewhat more hierarchically oriented than other methods of job evaluation.

Incentive Plans

Some incentive plans may be hierarchically related—for example where bonuses to executives tend to be in proportion to salaries paid. But bonuses and other incentive plans seem more related to the idea of pay for performance rather than according to either time served or rank. In Chapter 12, this situation will be explored along with the desirability of lump sum bonuses in lieu of merit salary increases.

Unions, Women, Minorities, and Legislative Changes

The relationship of the compensation administrator to unions, women, minorities, and other outside groups may in some ways be rather structured; and if hierarchical, may be tied in to other than managerial hierarchy. For example, when federal and state legislation and regulations must be followed, any hierarchical influence will tend to be governmental. (See Chapter 3.) And, of course, in unionized situations, the union hierarchy may come into play. However, a strong case can be made that relationships with unions, with women, and with minorities involve situations where hierarchy and structure are far less important than the sensitivity of the compensation administrator to a changing social environment. These matters are discussed in Chapter 4 and in a somewhat related chapter, Chapter 15.

Summary

Compensation administrators are influenced both by internal and external hierarchical structures, which tend to limit their freedom of action. While the compensation administrator and perhaps the vice president for human resources may want to provide pay and benefits to attract, hold, and motivate the best people for the organization, these inclinations vie with top management tendencies to emphasize economic aspects rather than keeping the employees happy.

Externally the hierarchical tendencies are even more evident, and in many ways more critical. The role of hierarchy is reflected in the positive correlation between corporate size in the United States and the pay of our top executives. A comparison of the pay for the top officers in the 100 largest manufacturing companies to the pay of the top officers of 25 labor unions shows enormous differences. We would hardly expect the two groups to have the same levels of pay. But should the typical top executive earn 8 times more than the typical top union leader? One obvious reason for the discrepancy in pay is that unions are not as hierarchically dominated. Their structures have fewer layers, no matter what the size of the union.

The ratio of cash earned by chief executive officers to average employee earnings in the United States is on the order of 11 to 1. This contrasts with only 8 to 1 in Canada and 5 to 1 in Australia. And the Japanese ratio is also reported to be quite low. Differences in hierarchical structure—the number of layers of authority within business organizations—is again an important causative factor. Adding to the direct hierarchical effect is the fact that employee benefits are not included in the comparisons. Many of these tend to be a function of base pay and thus if included would result in even greater international labor cost differences.

Other rational processes including job pricing (especially the differentials between pay grades), job analysis and evaluation, and performance evaluation all tend to reinforce the hierarchical differences. Some critics would like to do away with all such rigidities. But it is unlikely they will be able to eliminate them, in part because there are no real substitutes for these processes.

Incentives (individual, group, or some combination of both) need to be examined as important sources of motivation. The compensation administrator needs to remain continually alert to employee sentiments, not only union views, but also the opinions of women and minorities within and outside of the organization. Remaining aware of legislative enactments, executive orders, and other administrative requirements is necessary but it is not enough.

Major aspects of the problems pointed to here will be further explored in later chapters.

Case Study

Walker State University

Dr. Pyung Park, chief executive officer (CEO) of Walker State University, an old and venerable institution in the Southwest, sat back in his swivel chair in his well-appointed office and gazed at the tall willow trees outside. He wondered whether it was worth it all. He had to keep so many constituencies happy. He had to listen to the views of faculty members, students, former students, the administrative staff, and the state legislature. At that he sat bolt upright. Yes, the annual hassle over the budget had to be contended with once more. It was a task Dr. Park took seriously.

Shortly Mr. Michael Simmons, his chief budget officer, came in with some information on the pay of administrative officers at the university. The two men looked at the column showing the median salaries for administrators in public institutions and at the corresponding actual salaries at Walker State. While both recognized that there were differences in the jobs at State compared with those covered in the national survey, they assumed the data to be comparable for budget purposes. Mr. Simmons laughingly pointed out that both he and the CEO were earning more than the typical academic administrators. But he added that the dean of extension services and the bookstore manager were lagging behind, and several others were earning the median salary as reported in the survey.

Dr. Park remarked with some asperity that he couldn't see the justice of the salary increases voted and signed by the governor a week earlier, which resulted in increases of 8 percent for members of the senate and state assembly and 10 percent for the governor and the lieutenant governor. These hikes, he noted, compared with the across-the-board 4 percent increase which the finance committee of the assembly was now considering for all other state employees. Mr. Simmons pointed out that this decision would not be finalized until after the finance committee hearings the next week, at which Dr. Park would testify concerning the university's needs. Both men understood that the 4 percent limit, if imposed, would apply directly to the administrative salaries, which are carried in the budget as a separate line item. (Employee benefits, another separate line item, were not at issue here.)

The CEO commented that he had talked with a local banker and with some of the faculty in the economics department. The consensus was that the consumer price index was likely to rise about 6 percent over the next year. Dr. Park said he wanted a provision to cover this to be included in the university's budget proposal, and he wondered how much of an increase this would mean in dollars. Other questions bothered him, too. Should they ask for cost-of-living adjustments for administrators who were, according to the survey, now overpaid? In fact, should already overpaid administrators be given even a 4 percent increase? On the other hand, what action should be taken regarding those administrators whose present pay was low compared with the national standard? And should the university go along with the 4 percent limit now under consideration by the committee?

Role Assignment

You are Michael Simmons, chief budget officer of Walker State University. The CEO has asked you to prepare a detailed budget proposal for next year's administrative salaries. You must be prepared to explain the reasoning behind the proposal when it is presented to the assembly's finance committee. For purposes of this case, assume that the salary data for Walker State University constitute the entire administrative salary budget for the current year.

Position	U.S. Public Institutions (Median Salaries)*	Walker State University (Actual Salaries)
Chief executive officer	$107,980	$115,000
Executive vice president	90,100	89,000
Dean, arts and sciences	85,000	85,000
Dean, extension	77,385	45,600
Director, medical center personnel	50,000	55,000
Chief budgeting officer	55,140	65,000
Director, computer center	66,000	66,000
Director, physical plant	63,500	63,500
Director, bookstore	40,700	20,500

*Data for enrollment level of 20,000.
Source: College and University Personnel Association. *The 1987–88 Administrative Compensation Survey.*

Questions for Discussion

1. Assuming you become a compensation manager in a large corporation, what problems do you expect to face within the organization? Discuss.
2. Considering the nature of the typical company organization structure, what other executives within the organization are you likely to have to deal with?
3. How does the pay of top executives in the largest American corporations compare with that of the leaders of the largest American labor organizations? What factors explain the differences?
4. Are top executives in the largest American industrial corporations paid too much, too little, or about right? Discuss.
5. Should labor union leaders be required to make public their allowances and expenses while industry top executives are not

required to do so? Why or why not?
6. The TPFC study shows that for the United States cash earnings for CEOs are roughly 11 times the average wages, while in Australia CEO's earnings are only about 5 times the average. Is such a difference significant? If so, why?
7. Do the number of layers of authority within a large organization have a bearing on differences in levels of pay? Discuss.
8. What are some of the other rational devices used by management that tend to reinforce the effects of hierarchy?
9. Do you think that incentives are an important matter to the compensation manager? Explain.
10. Need the compensation manager be sensitive to a changing social environment, or is that solely the responsibility of others in the organization? Discuss.

Notes

1. See my *Wage and Salary Administration in a Dynamic Economy* (New York: Harcourt, Brace & World, 1968), 12.
2. Other benefits, such as stock options and the like, must also be reported to SEC but are not included in "cash and cash equivalent forms of remuneration." Such benefits will be discussed in Chapter 14.
3. "Competitiveness: 23 Leaders Speak Out." *Harvard Business Review* 65, no. 4 (July–

August 1987): 113.
4. Crawford H. Greenewalt, "Incentives and Rewards," (Second of 1958 McKinsey Foundation Lectures, delivered at the Graduate School of Business, Columbia University on April 22, 1958), 11–12 of mimeographed release. This quote is taken from my *Top Executive Pay Package* (Graduate School of Business, Columbia University and The Free Press of Glencoe, Inc., 1963), 165.

References

Balkin, David B., and Gomez-Mejia, Luis R., eds. *New Perspectives on Compensation*. Englewood Cliffs, NJ: Prentice-Hall, 1987.

Belcher, David W., and Atchison, Thomas J. *Compensation Administration*. 2nd ed. Englewood Cliffs, NJ: Prentice-Hall, 1987.

Bowey, Angela M., ed. *Handbook of Salary and Wage Systems*. 2nd ed. Brookfield, VT: Gower, 1982.

Burgess, Leonard R. *Wage and Salary Administration in a Dynamic Economy*. New York: Harcourt, Brace & World, 1968.

Capelli, Peter. *What People Earn, The Book of Wages and Salaries.* London: Macdonald & Co., 1981.

Cascio, Wayne F. *Costing Human Resources: The Financial Impact of Behavior in Organizations.* Boston, MA: Kent Publishing, 1987.

"Competitiveness: 23 Leaders Speak Out." *Harvard Business Review* 65, no. 4 (July–August 1987): 106–123.

Ellig, Bruce R. *Compensation and Benefits: Design and Analysis.* Scottsdale, AZ: American Compensation Association, 1985.

Henderson, Richard I. *Compensation Management, Rewarding Performance.* 4th ed. Reston, VA: Reston Publishing Co., 1985.

Lawler, Edward E. III. *Pay and Organizational Development.* Reading, MA: Addison-Wesley, 1981.

Milkovich, George T., and Newman, Jerry M. *Compensation.* 2nd ed. Plano, TX: Business Publications, 1987.

Moore, Thomas "Goodbye, Corporate Staff." *Fortune* (December 21, 1987): 65–76.

Rock, Milton L., ed. *Handbook of Wage and Salary Administration,* 2nd ed. New York: McGraw-Hill, 1984.

Schuster, Jay. *Management Compensation in High Technology Companies.* Lexington, KY: Heath, 1984.

Sibson, Robert E. *Compensation.* rev. ed. New York: AMACOM, 1981.

Towers, Perrin, Forster, & Crosby. *Worldwide Total Remuneration.* New York: 1985.

Wallace, Marc J., Jr., and Fay, Charles H. *Compensation Theory and Practice.* Boston, MA: Kent, 1983.

National & International Aspects of Pay and Economic Trends

2

Chapter Outline

- National Trends in Compensation, Gross National Product, and Profits
- International Trends in Compensation and Other Indicators
- Measures to Improve the United States' International Competitiveness
- Summary
- Case Study—Kessler Steel Company

This chapter will deal with both national and international aspects of pay, with the emphasis on the international aspects. We shall be examining in particular the extent to which pay and benefit practices affect the economic competitiveness of the United States in international trade and the steps that could be taken to improve the situation.

But first we shall explore briefly the trends in compensation and related variables in the United States.

National Trends in Compensation, Gross National Product, and Profits

We will discuss trends in base pay here, leaving an analysis of the detailed trends within employee benefits to Chapter 13. Some sectors in the economy are increasing and others are declining in importance. For example, the role of the public sector is increasing relative to the private sector, and the output of services continues to increase compared with the production of goods. Some specific occupations are growing, while others are shrinking. Trends of this sort can have an important influence on the decision-making process with respect to compensation. What has happened to compensation in relation to GNP and profits can be seen in Figure 2–1.

The data in Figure 2–1 were taken from a recent Economic Report of the President. The figures for compensation include not only wages and salaries but supplements to wages and salaries (which means that some but not all of the benefits are included). The data are all expressed in 1982 dollars to remove the effects of inflation.

The vertical scale in this diagram is called a ratio or semilogarithmic scale. The distance from 50 to 100 is the same as from 500 to 1000; that is, a doubling of the numbers takes up the same vertical distance. This type of scale is useful in comparing rates of change for both trends and fluctuations. Of two rising trend lines, the one with the steeper slope shows faster growth. If cyclical change is being examined, the line with the highest peaks and deepest valleys represents the cycle with the greater sensitivity or percentage variability. Both statements are true, no matter what the numbers.

16

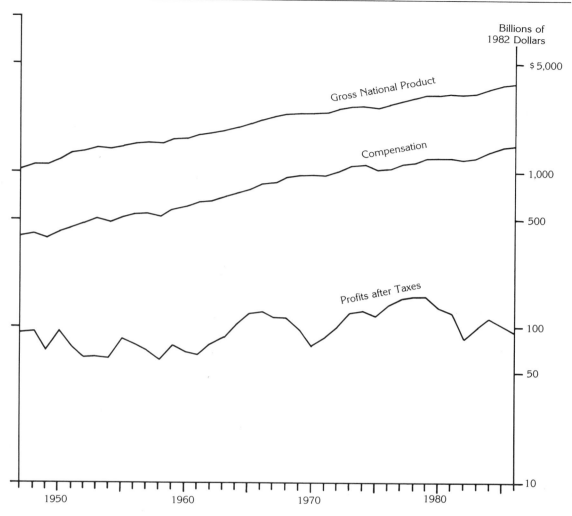

FIGURE 2–1
Trends in compensation, gross national product, and profits after taxes. While trends in the first two indicators are similar, profits show not only a slower upward trend but wider cyclical swings. Source: U.S. Department of Commerce.

Our analysis of the data in Figure 2–1 tells us two things. First, if you use the "eye-squares" method and draw an imaginary line through each of the three series, it will be evident that compensation is increasing at a much more rapid rate than are corporate profits after taxes and at about the same rate as the output of the nation's goods and services as represented by gross national product (GNP). This latter tendency means that the share of labor *and* management in GNP is holding steady. However, profits are much more variable from year to year than the other two factors. This variability has important implications for companies with profit-sharing plans, as will be discussed later in Chapter 12, which deals with incentives.

International Trends in Compensation and Other Indicators

An overall way to look at the international economic picture is to look at the standard of living of different nations. The single most generally accepted measure of standard of living is found by dividing each nation's total output of goods and services or gross national product by the total population of the nation. This is shown in Table 2–1.

As can be seen, the United States continues to have the highest standard of living in the world. However, while this was true in 1985, there is no guarantee that it will remain true in the future. And the extent of our lead is much less than it was at one time. Switzerland, Norway, Canada, and Sweden are not too far behind.

TABLE 2–1
GNP per capita in constant dollars.

Nation	GNP/Capita, 1985
United States	16,700
Switzerland	15,329
Norway	13,369
Canada	13,070
Sweden	11,637
Iceland	11,083
Finland	10,776
Japan	10,776
Australia	10,700
Denmark	10,622
West Germany	10,214
Luxembourg	9,838
France	9,191
Austria	8,622
Netherlands	8,560
United Kingdom	8,000
Belgium	7,096
New Zealand	6,640
Italy	6,205
Ireland	4,746
Spain	4,312
Greece	3,334
Portugal	1,910
Turkey	1,074

Source: U.S. Department of State and OECD.

Compensation, Productivity, and Unit Labor Cost

The data for GNP per capita are subject to possible drastic change in the future as a look at factors that determine our ability to compete in world markets strongly suggests. Under reasonably free competitive conditions, the major operational factors to be considered are compensation, productivity, and unit labor costs.

The following equation summarizes these interrelationships:

$$\frac{\text{Compensation}}{\text{Hours Worked}} \div \frac{\text{Output}}{\text{Hours Worked}} = \frac{\text{Compensation}}{\text{Hours Worked}} \times \frac{\text{Hours Worked}}{\text{Output}} = \frac{\text{Compensation}}{\text{Output}}$$

This is just another way of saying that the hourly wage rate divided by productivity (as measured by output per labor hour) gives us unit labor cost. In other words, where pay increases faster than productivity, the unit labor cost rises.

A brief look at the steel industry can illustrate how labor costs and productivity are actually related. Employment costs per hour and unit labor costs in the steel industry are shown for six major producers in Table 2–2.

The data in the table are for all employees, not just production workers, and the employment costs include employer contributions for employee benefits. As can be seen from the table, the United States had the highest employment cost per hour but had a lower unit labor cost than either West Germany or Japan. However, three other nations all had lower employment costs per hour and also lower unit labor costs. South Korea had both the lowest employment cost per hour and also the lowest unit labor cost. Two further observations are in order about the table: the United States' position compared to West Germany's and Japan's is relatively much more favorable now than it was in 1980, when Japanese and German costs were much lower than those in the United States, and the United States still has a long way to go to be fully competitive in the steel industry.

Other data for manufacturing show rates of change in productivity for Pacific Rim countries. In these comparisons, shown in Table 2–3, productivity was measured in terms of output per employed person rather than output per hour.

TABLE 2–2

Employment costs per hour and unit labor costs for six major steel producers.

Nation	Employment Cost Per Hour	Labor Cost Per Metric Ton of Hot-Rolled Product
West Germany	$23.95	$98
Japan	23.00	92
United States	24.11	89
France	20.35	83
United Kingdom	15.72	58
South Korea	5.03	27.50

Source: World Steel Dynamics. Data are for late 1987.

TABLE 2–3
Manufacturing productivity in U.S. versus six Asian areas: average annual rates of change, 1971–83.

Japan	6.5%
Republic of Korea	5.3
Hong Kong	5.1*
Republic of China (Taiwan)	4.7
United States	2.3**
Singapore	1.7
Malaysia	1.4***

*Period 1971–80. **Reflects Aug. 1987 revision. ***Period ending 1981.
Sources: Asian Productivity Organization and United States Bureau of Labor Statistics.

For the period shown, Japan was increasing its productivity faster than the United States and the other countries. Also, such nations as South Korea, the Republic of China (Taiwan), and Hong Kong—which have relatively lower compensation rates—apparently are on the way to posing a competitive threat to the United States and also to Japan.

Again, we must point out that it is the absolute level of unit labor cost at a given time that determines the relative position of any country in competition with other countries. The absolute level must be stated in constant terms (e.g., U.S. dollars) so that the figures for all countries can be compared.

It must be stressed that *total* cost per unit is just as important as labor cost per unit. However, in many companies or industries compensation costs account for a large share of total costs. In recent years many U.S. firms have sought to offset rising unit costs—and especially rising unit labor costs—by building their newer plants in nations with lower pay and benefit levels while also retaining their efficient manufacturing facilities. To the extent the employees in these plants are foreign nationals, the process has cost many U.S. employees their jobs. However, many new jobs are created for U.S. citizens when Japanese firms, for example, build plants in the United States.

Cultural Differences in Employee Attitudes

In considering what is happening behind these economic figures, it is relevant to consider cultural differences as reflected in employee attitudes towards their employers. A survey investigating these attitudes in different countries is done each year by the International Survey Research Corporation. The data for two nations in 1986 are shown in Figure 2–2.

There are some similarities. Both in the United States and in Japan, employees are generally satisfied with their working relationships, they have a high degree of job satisfaction, and they appear to be happy with their immediate bosses. There are also some differences. The Japanese workers, while dissatisfied with communications, are not nearly as dissatisfied as workers in the United

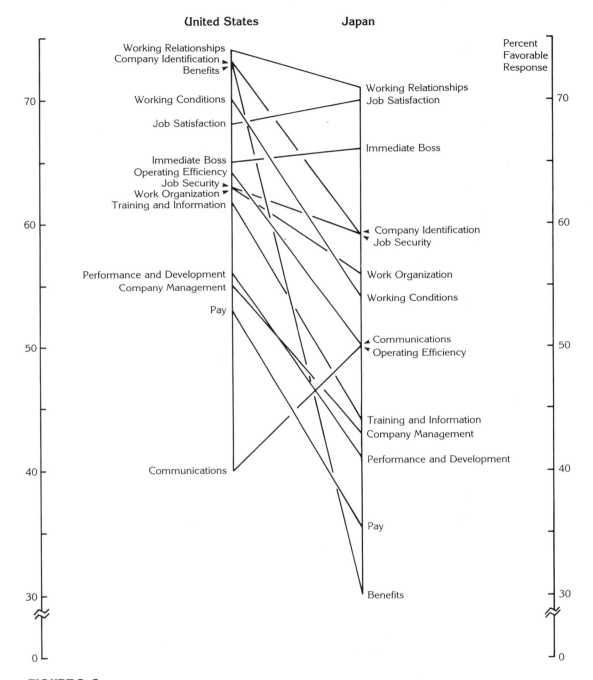

United States   Japan

Percent
Favorable
Response

FIGURE 2–2
*Employee attitudes towards their employers in the United States
and Japan show some similarities but many differences. Source:
International Survey Research Corporation.*

21

States. Perhaps the process of *ringi-do* or bottom-up Japanese style communication has a bearing here. On benefits, the Japanese are terribly dissatisfied while U.S. workers are quite satisfied. Does this mean unions in Japan are headed towards a stronger role and that, conversely, we may put too much emphasis on employee benefits? On pay, apparently American employees, while not terribly happy, are much more so than the Japanese. Is Japanese compensation likely to move ahead more rapidly, given these feelings? Satisfaction with promotion policies (as reflected in performance and development) appears to be greater in the United States than in Japan. Does this arise from greater American emphasis on the individual and less on the group than in Japan? Analysts do not know all the answers, but such questions do suggest a considerable cultural diversity between the United States and Japan. Is the American cultural pattern necessarily the best pattern? There is at least some evidence that Japanese style management can work with American workers. For example,

> when Toyota and General Motors opened their new joint venture at Fremont, California, they cut back the number of job classifications at the plant to four. When GM ran the plant by itself, the United Auto Workers had insisted on more than 80 categories and it took 36.1 hours to assemble a Chevrolet Nova. Today, with the new work rules and Japanese style management, the assembly line turns out better-quality cars in 17.5 hours.[1]

Thus, at least some cultural attitudes appear to be transportable. This fact, together with the unit labor cost data, suggests that we do not have all the answers in the United States and that we need to know more about what has gone wrong with our production techniques.

Quality of Goods and of the Labor Force

Not only the volume of output but its quality in the United States is in question. As one consultant, Carla S. O'Dell, puts it,

> Look at the consumers' rankings of U.S. and Japanese quality. In 1967 Japan ranked tenth; the U.S. was number one. By 1982, the U.S. had dropped to number three and Japan had risen to number one.[2]

Another aspect to consider is the dedication and quality of the work force. Do workers work too few days out of the year? As students, do they study too little? Table 2–4 shows that U.S. students spend less time in school than students in other industrialized nations, while Japanese students put the most days into the school year.

Consider these further points made by O'Dell.

1. Seventy-seven percent of the U.S. students graduate from high school; 94 percent of the Japanese students graduate from high school.

TABLE 2—4
Days in an eighth grader's school year, six nations.

Japan	243
West Germany	210–220*
U.S.S.R.	211
Britain	192
France	185
United States	180

*School holidays in West Germany vary from state to state.
Sources: *U.S. News and World Report,* Jan. 19, 1987, International Association for the Evaluation of Educational Achievement, and Soviet and West German governments.

2. By the time the Japanese student graduates, she has had two more years of math and science than a U.S. student.
3. By the time high school students in Japan graduate, they have the equivalent of four more years of school. In other words, they end up with the equivalent of a college degree.[3]

Another related aspect of the work force is the extent of the national commitment to high technology. Table 2—5 shows how much each of four leading nations spends on nondefense research and development as a share of gross national product.

Hierarchical Influence

In the previous chapter, I pointed to the high ratio of executive pay versus average workers' pay in the United States in contrast to the much lower ratios for other countries. I suggested this arose out of hierarchical thinking and that it probably led to excessive compensation costs. As Ralph Sorenson, CEO of Barry Wright Corporation, puts it

We pay a heavy price for this practice because it raises our total costs and thus puts us at a competitive disadvantage in international markets. Purchases of outside services such as those of lawyers, accountants, consultants, investment bankers, insurance vendors, and purveyors of medical programs run much higher in U.S. manufacturing companies than they do in, say, Japanese or Korean manufacturing companies.[4]

TABLE 2—5
Share of GNP spent on nondefense R & D in 1985.

Japan	2.6%
West Germany	2.5
United States	1.9
France	1.8

Sources: *U.S. News and World Report,* Feb. 2, 1987 and National Science Foundation.

A clear implication of the Sorenson statement is that managements need to reduce layers of authority and pay less to their CEOs.

Availability of Capital and Our National Debt

Another major problem for our international competitiveness centers around the availability of capital. An essential element of the problem is the accumulation of personal savings—something Americans have not been doing recently. According to O'Dell, Japanese save about 18 percent of personal income while U.S. workers save about 6 percent.[5]

The treatment of capital gains under the most recent U.S. tax legislation tends to discourage new investment, while our continued failure to balance our federal budget—and at least as important, the common expectation that this will continue and perhaps even worsen—will tend over the longer run to drive up our interest rates and the capital cost of making new investments. The opposite conditions already prevail in Japan, placing us at a net disadvantage in this regard.[6]

Measures to Improve the United States' International Competitiveness

What can we do about some of these problems? First, we shall consider some of the measures that can be encouraged by compensation managers and by management generally. We shall look at two-tier plans and at various measures taken by IBM and the oil industry. Then we shall consider again the cost of capital.

Two-Tier Plans

During 1985 and 1986, many companies engaged in collective bargaining included two-tier compensation provisions in their contracts. These arrangements provide for permanent or temporary lowering of wages and/or benefits for new employees. A settlement between Eastern Airlines and the Air Line Pilots Association provided for a two-tier system where new employees are paid 20 percent below regular rates for the first 5 years on the job. Another agreement with Delta Airlines also included a two-tier system, but a temporary one. A union official said the company insisted on the provision because its other nonunion employees were already covered by such systems, as well as because of the cost savings. Under the plan, new pilots will be paid at 66 percent of those already on the payroll, again for 5 years, at the end of which time their pay reverts to the upper tier.[7]

Actions Taken by IBM

We will discuss here certain measures taken by IBM to make their company more competitive, including employment reductions in the middle management layers, changes in the work year, and redeployment of the work force. Some other measures relating to incentive bonuses and merit pay, which are also part of the company's strategy, we shall consider in Chapter 12 dealing with incentives.

Reducing the Layers

What IBM has accomplished to reduce the layers of management is shown graphically in Figure 2–3.

The company objective was to reduce the size of staff and the number of managers as one means of remaining competitive worldwide. In doing so, their compensation manager, Walter Read, noted that

> It is possible to decrease the number of people on the payroll and still benefit those involved. A prime example is the retirement incentive, or window program. IBM offered a program in 1986 that added five years to the age and service of eligible individuals. Seminars were offered on such subjects as family adjustment and financial planning. Standard benefits continued, such as the retirement educational assistance program. This gives each retiree and spouse $2500 each to be spent on any class that will make retirement more pleasant . . . Over 15,000 employees worldwide have taken this *voluntary* program.[8]

Redoing the Work Year

Internationally the corporation has seen wide variations in its various business units, reflecting national differences as to length of vacation, number of holidays,

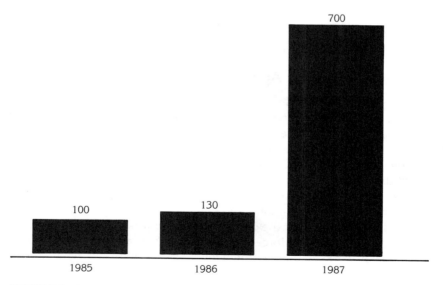

FIGURE 2–3
The number of employees retiring each year at IBM has increased dramatically under the most recent plan. Data are index numbers, with the year 1985 equal to 100. Source: IBM Corporation.

the length of the workweek, overtime limitations, and the amount of paid absence. This variation and pressure in European countries to reduce the length of the workweek posed a productivity problem. In IBM's view,

> While a reduced workweek implies a reduction in overall productivity, we have found approaches to offset this—and to introduce new efficiencies in our business! . . . We focused on annual available hours . . . We were able to work in concert with various national work time patterns to optimize manufacturing processes . . . By redesigning shifts and looking at weekend work, we achieved significant growth in utilization while accommodating a reduction in the workweek.[9]

Redeployment

Still another way IBM sought to increase international competitiveness was by the encouragement of voluntary redeployment of employees to activities that contribute more to the success of the company—a feature characteristic of Japanese firms. As IBM reports,

> We found some changes that needed to be made . . . We needed to spend more time with our customers. We began a back-to-the-field program . . . During 1986 and 1987 we asked headquarters employees and people from some of our manufacturing and development sites to join the marketing and market support teams on a voluntary basis. Just in the U.S. and Canada over 12,000 people signed up for transfers. Of course, the success of these programs depends on having a flexible work force, willing and able to be retrained for new careers.[10]

General Electric's Approach

For close to a decade under the leadership of its chief executive officer, John F. Welch, GE has striven to keep the company in first or second place internationally in each of its major fields of competition. During this period, GE has bought more than 300 businesses or product lines, divested more than 200 others, and invested close to $12 billion in new land and equipment. Company employment at the end of 1987 was 100,000 less than in 1981. As to company employment in the United States, more of the reduction consisted of normal attrition—retirements and the like—than it did of layoffs. The layoffs that did occur made union leaders unhappy, but the company has become internationally more competitive.

While the work force has been reduced and pay and benefit concessions asked of workers, management felt these measures were needed to achieve international competitiveness. Welch states that

> We see our task as . . . aimed at liberating, facilitating, unleashing the human energy and initiative of our people.[11]

One of the primary means of accomplishing this under Welch has been to reduce the hierarchical layers and thus to flatten the organizational structure. This has been done along with broadening the span of management. As Welch puts it,

> In reducing the layers we are trying to get the people in the organization to understand that they can't do everything they used to do. They have to set priorities. The less important tasks have to be left undone . . . We found that with fewer layers we had wider spans of management. We weren't managing better. We were managing *less* and *that* was better.[12]

The result of this was to push decision making farther down in the organization. As Welch states,

> We used to go from the CEO to sectors, to groups, to businesses . . . We now go from the CEO . . . to businesses. Nothing else. There's nothing else there. Zero.[13]

Welch stresses the importance of the reward system, saying that big rewards go for those who do big things but that those who reach for the big concept but fail should not be penalized. Punishing failure, he points out, assures that no one dares.[14]

> Under the GE system as now practiced managers are asked: Are you freer to do more things? Is your job more exciting, more challenging than it was a year ago or two years ago?[15]

Welch also tells this story:

> It is when this freedom reaches *all* the way down through the organization and the energy at the *individual* level is released that truly great things begin to happen. In our Major Appliance business in Louisville a few years ago, people on the assembly line suddenly found two levers in front of them. One lever stopped the line. The other sent a part on its way *only* after an individual was satisfied that it was perfect. The line workers suddenly became the final authority on the quality of their work. The cynics scoffed when this system was proposed, predicting chaos or production at a snail's pace.
>
> Whatever happened? Quality increased enormously and the line ran faster and smoother than ever.[16]

Hewlett-Packard's Approach

Hewlett-Packard believes that it has become more competitive internationally through (1) an increased international presence, (2) a shortened product development cycle, (3) reduced manufacturing costs, (4) increased emphasis on human resource planning, (5) letting customer needs dictate strategy, and (6) use of information systems to create competitive advantage.

The company points out that its investment in information systems involves a network of some 860 HP 3000 minicomputers and 63,000 workstations and terminals to run the business side of a dispersed and decentralized organization. The company's investment in information systems, which includes both companywide and local or shared systems, was around 3.6 percent of net sales in 1987.

A few of the results from the company's efforts to become more internationally competitive (especially through the use of information systems) can be seen in these changes, which took place from 1979 through 1987:

1. Quality has improved. Field failure rates were cut to ⅙ of the 1979 levels.
2. Inventory was reduced from 20.5 percent to 13.8 percent of sales.
3. Accounts receivable were reduced from 58 days to 50 days outstanding.
4. Sales force productivity has increased through a 35 percent increase in customer contact time.[17]

How the Oil Industry Has Become More Competitive

Under the impact of falling prices and reduced demand by major countries, the oil industry has been in a struggle for survival. Some of the actions they have taken include reductions in force, salary reductions, and readjustment of employee benefits.

Reductions in force have included early retirement and layoff programs as well as the use of temporary workers and consultants in place of full-time employees.

Pay reductions have included reductions in working hours with corresponding decreases in salaries, elimination of bonus and incentive plans or introduction of plans based on positive levels of operating performance, across-the-board percent reductions, and staggered percent reductions. Table 2–6 illustrates these.

Employee benefit reductions have included standard cost containment measures on medical benefits such as increasing deductibles, requiring employees to pay higher premiums, requiring second opinions and preadmission testing, using health maintenance organizations or preferred provider organizations, and giving more attention to S–125 plans.

TABLE 2–6
Example of staggered percent reductions.

Salary	Percent Reduction
Up to $20,000	2%
$40,000	6
$50,000	10

The industry has moved to decreasing the amounts of life insurance coverage and requiring the employee to pay all or part of the premium.

On pension plans, actions have included eliminating plans and/or recapturing assets, or combining life insurance/annuity plans.

Stock option plans have been terminated or reissued as companies' stock prices have dropped far below the option price.

Finally, company automobiles and credit cards have been eliminated or substantially reduced in number.[18]

Reducing the Cost of Capital

While high interest rates, partly resulting from lack of action on the national debt, cannot be changed by the compensation administrator, reducing the current national deficits over a period of years, restructuring our taxes to remove the penalty for capital gains, and encouraging personal savings are actions that should be promoted if we are to compete effectively internationally.

Summary

In the United States, compensation, including supplements to wages and salaries, has increased at about the same percentage rate as gross national product. Profits after taxes have not increased as rapidly. But they have shown a far greater percentage fluctuation than have either GNP or compensation. This has a special significance for profit-sharing plans to be discussed in a later chapter.

The most used measure of the standard of living, GNP per capita in constant dollars, still shows the United States in the lead, but the differences between the United States and other nations such as Switzerland, Norway, and Canada are not as great as they were.

Despite our high standard of living serious questions remain in terms of international competitiveness.

In a comparison of unit labor costs in the steel industry it appears that the United States has improved its standing relative to West Germany and Japan since 1980. But France, the United Kingdom, and especially South Korea have much lower unit labor costs than the United States.

Much of this is due to inadequate growth in U.S. productivity. From 1971 through 1983, the annual percentage increase in manufacturing productivity for Japan was almost 3 times that for the United States. Pacific Rim states such as the Republic of Korea, Hong Kong, and the Republic of China (Taiwan) all show rates of productivity increase well in excess of the U.S. figure.

There are cultural differences in employee attitudes towards their company managements, but these differences should not blind us from seeing that Japanese style management apparently works for American workers in the United States.

Product quality in the United States has also suffered compared to some other nations. Some of the decline in quality may be traceable to an inadequately educated work force. For example, a six-nation comparison showed that Japan, West Germany, the U.S.S.R., and France all have longer school years than the United States. A related cause may be that not enough of GNP is spent on non-defense research and development. Our percentage is higher than that in France but lower than in Japan or West Germany.

Other problems affecting U.S. competitiveness are a savings rate in the U.S. of about one third that of Japan as well as less favorable capital costs than Japan.

Central to our competitiveness problems appears to be the high ratio cited earlier of U.S. CEO pay to the average workers' pay compared to the similar multiple for other nations. This ratio points to the problem of hierarchy and the resulting excessive unit labor costs.

What actions can be taken? Other than incentive plans, which are treated in a later chapter, possible actions include reducing top executive pay levels, two-tier pay plans, employment reductions in middle management layers (often induced by special retirement provisions), redeployment of people within the organization to achieve more flexibility and productivity, scaling back some employee benefits or having the worker pay a larger share of the costs, greater use of cafeteria benefit plans (which involve greater employee choice of benefits),[19] and the elimination of unnecessary executive perquisites.

Other measures that would help include encouraging savings, removing penalties on capital gains, and reducing our national debt to help keep capital costs down.

Case Study

Kessler Steel Company

The Kessler Steel Company, a medium-sized manufacturer of steel, has operations in five states. Its headquarters are located in Comstock, a small town in Ohio, It sells its products to metal fabricators in the auto industry and the container industry, as well as to machinery manufacturers and firms in the heavy construction field.

Heinz Dietrich, chairman of the board and chief executive officer, stared out of the window of his office as he looked out at the dingy smokestacks of the Comstock Plant. He was contemplating the future course of his company.

About five years ago the company had been forced to shut down one of its plants because it could not operate the obsolete facilities and still sell the output from this plant at a profit. A few employees were successfully relocated within the company, but there also had been some layoffs. In general Kessler's costs had been running somewhat higher than the industry average, and its profits were leaner. However, there had been no losses in recent years.

One reason for this was Heinz Dietrich himself. He paid close attention to the control side of his business. Yet, his was a nonunion plant. He had a reputation of being tough but fair. He was popular with his employees and for a while served as mayor of the city of Comstock, a post to which he had been twice reelected. He also had favorable relations with the financial world. The current financial position of the company was strong, and he was confident that he could raise money for any needed expansion.

In recent years West Germany, Japan, France, the United Kingdom, and South Korea had become increasingly competitive with the United States, a situation that disturbed President Dietrich. Meanwhile, in response to this and other aspects of world markets in many industries, Congress had been active. In fact, a bill that would impose more restrictive tariffs and quotas on steel (as well as other products) had passed the House with more than the two-thirds vote needed to override a possible presidential veto. A bill with almost identical provisions had passed the Senate but by a few votes less than the two-thirds vote needed to override. The final outcome remained in doubt.

Dietrich walked back to his desk and reread once more the letter from the president of a steel company near Pusan, South Korea. It was a proposal for a joint venture between Kessler Steel and Kwangju Steel, which would involve the construction of a new plant in South Korea.

Going through Dietrich's mind was another possibility. Perhaps what was really needed was to tighten up on executive salaries (he realized he might have to set an example and cut his own too) and to involve his employees in some kind of profit-sharing plan. If so, he was uncertain as to what kind of a plan would be most effective.

The president, after giving the situation further thought, concluded that he had four alternatives: (1) continue present policies and await the result of favorable protective legislation from Congress assuming that either the president would sign the bill or that a possible veto would be overridden, (2) cut costs including executive salaries and put in an incentive profit-sharing plan to spur productivity and cut operating costs, (3) go ahead with the joint venture proposed by Kwangju Steel, or (4) seek out a joint venture with a Japanese firm—an outside possibility because there was no specific proposal in the offing.

Abruptly President Dietrich reached for the telephone—time, he thought, to get something moving.

Role Assignment

You are Sandra Simonetti, manager of compensation and benefits. The president has called you in and asked for your opinion. He outlined to you the four options discussed in the case. What do you recommend and why?

Questions for Discussion

1. What has happened to the trend in profits after taxes compared with the trend for gross national product?

2. Which has shown the greater variability—profits after taxes or compensation? What are the implications of this for compensation policy?

3. Which factor has shown the fastest rate of growth over the years—compensation or gross national product?

4. As measured by GNP per capita, which nation has the highest standard of living in the world? Are other countries catching up? Discuss.

5. Which is more significant as to a nation's competitiveness—employment cost per hour or unit labor cost? Discuss.

6. How does hierarchy affect unit labor costs? Consider the facts about executive pay compared to pay of the rank and file worker.

7. How would you summarize the relative competitiveness of the United States with other countries in the steel industry? Be specific.
8. Are the Pacific Rim countries an economic threat to the United States? Explain.
9. Do cultural differences in employee attitudes toward their employers have a bearing on competitiveness? Discuss.
10. Is our labor force well educated compared with those of our leading competitors? Discuss.
11. Does our national debt have any bearing on

the ability of the United States to compete effectively in international markets? Discuss.
12. What other factors affect our competitiveness in international markets?
13. What measures in terms of organization, employment, and pay practices can the United States use to increase our competitiveness in international markets?
14. How do you evaluate the effectiveness of measures taken by IBM, GE, and Hewlett-Packard to achieve greater international competitiveness?

Notes

1. Monroe W. Karmin, "Will the U.S. Stay Number One?" *U.S. News and World Report* (Feb. 2, 1987): 22.
2. Carla S. O'Dell, "Innovative Reward Systems—The Productivity Payoff," *ACA Conference Highlights* (1986): 6.
3. Ibid.
4. Reprinted by permission of the *Harvard Business Review*. Excerpt from "Competitiveness: 23 Leaders Speak Out" by Ralph Z. Sorenson (July/August 1987). Copyright © 1987 by the President and Fellows of Harvard College; all rights reserved.
5. O'Dell, *op. cit.*, p. 6.
6. For a comment on this issue, see "Will the U.S. Stay Number One?," *U.S. News and World Report* (Feb. 2, 1987): 122.
7. George Ruben, "Labor Management Scene in 1986 Reflects Continuing Difficulties," *Monthly Labor Review* 110, no. 1 (January 1987): 37, 45.
8. Walter Read, "Productivity, Motivation, and the Individual" (Address before the annual meeting of the American Compensation

Association, Toronto, Canada, Oct. 9, 1987).
9. Ibid.
10. Ibid.
11. John F. Welch, Jr., "Managing for the Nineties" (Presentation at the annual meeting of Share Owners, Waukesha, Wisconsin, April 27, 1988).
12. Ibid.
13. Mark Potts, "GE's Management Mission," *Washington Post* (May 22, 1988).
14. John F. Welch, "Competitiveness from Within—Beyond Incrementalism" (Presentation as the Hatfield Fellow Lecture, Cornell University, April 26, 1984).
15. Mark Potts, *op. cit.*
16. Welch, *op. cit.*
17. The foregoing observations have been summarized from material made available to the author by the Hewlett-Packard Company and used by them internally in an Executive Seminar Series in 1988.
18. Lloyd Brooks, "Oil Industry Survival Tactics," *ACA News* 29, no. 4 (June 1986): 5.
19. Such plans are discussed in Chapter 13.

References

Asian Productivity Organization (APO). *Comparative Information on Productivity Levels and Changes in APO Member Countries.* Tokyo, Japan, 1986.

Bohlander, George W. "Declining Productivity: Trends and Causes." *Arizona Business* 28 (February 1981): 3–13.

Brooks, Lloyd G. "Oil Industry Survival Tactics: Compensation Strategies in a Troubled Industry." *ACA News* (June 1986): 5.

Deming, W. Edwards. *Quality, Productivity, and Competitive Position.* Cambridge, MA: MIT Center for Advanced Engineering Study, 1982.

Gandel, Mattye. "Two-Tier Pay Scales—Innovative or Destructive?" *Employment Relations Today* 12, no. 3 (Summer 1985): 165–173.

Harris, C. Lowell, ed. "Control of Federal Spending." *Proceedings of the Academy of Political Science* 35, no. 4 (1985).

International Survey Research Limited. *Employee Attitudes towards Their Employers: An International Perspective.* Chicago, London, Tokyo, 1986.

Kahn, Herman. *The Next 200 Years, A Scenario for America and the World.* New York: William Morrow and Co., 1976.

Karmin, Monroe W. "Will the U.S. Stay Number One?" *U.S. News and World Report* (February 2, 1987): 18–22.

Lawrence, Robert Z. "Why Protectionism Doesn't Pay." *Harvard Business Review* 87, no. 3 (May–June 1987): 60–67.

Lord, Lewis J., and Horn, Miriam. "The Brain Battle." *U.S. News and World Report* (January 19, 1987): 58–64.

Morley, James W., ed. "The Pacific Basin: New Challenges for the United States." *Proceedings of the Academy of Political Science* 36, no. 1 (1986).

Neef, Arthur, and Thomas, James. "Trends in Manufacturing Productivity and Labor Costs in the U.S. and Abroad." *Monthly Labor Review* (December 1987): 25–30.

O'Dell, Carla S. "Innovative Reward Systems—The Productivity Payoff." *ACA Conference Highlights,* American Compensation Association (1986): 5–11.

Read, Walter. "Productivity, Motivation, and the Individual." Address before the annual meeting of the American Compensation Association, Toronto, Canada, October 9, 1987.

Ross, Irwin. "Employers Win Big in the Move to Two-Tier Contracts." *Fortune* 111, no. 9 (April 29, 1985): 82–93.

U.S. Department of Labor, Bureau of Labor Statistics. "Output Per Hour, Compensation, and Unit Labor Costs in Manufacturing, Twelve Countries, 1950–1986." December, 1987.

U.S. Department of State, Bureau of Intelligence and Research. *Economic Growth of OECD Countries,* 1975–85. Report No. 1254AR (Revised), 1986.

Ukawa, Ambassador Hidetoshi. "Facts and Figures, Japan–U.S. Relations." Remarks by Consul General of Japan to Downtown Economic Club Luncheon, New York, November 4, 1987.

Young, John. *Global Competition: The New Reality.* Report of the President's Commission on Industrial Competitiveness. Washington, DC: U.S. Government Printing Office, 1985.

Legislative and Legal Aspects of Pay and Benefits

3

Chapter Outline

- The Private Sector
- The Public Sector
- Summary
- Case Study—A New Labor Relations Law

From a look at pay and benefits in economic terms, we turn to a more specialized area—legislative and legal aspects of industrial relations in the United States. This system is comprised of different layers, including congressional legislation and presidential executive orders; administrative rulings of the National Labor Relations Board and decisions of the courts; collective bargaining agreements arrived at between unions and management; and within the scope of these agreements, the settlements reached through grievance procedures, arbitration, and the like. Legally, everything from a U.S. Supreme Court decision as to the constitutionality of an act of Congress to an informal agreement between a supervisor and a union representative in the shop with respect to handling a worker's complaint can have an impact on pay and benefits. There is a strong tendency on the part of the courts both to accept decisions made at lower levels, thus limiting legal intervention to points of law, and to encourage the peaceful resolution of disputes within the collective bargaining system.

In a sense, in the legal environment we have described labor has more power in the private sector than in the public sector. Because of this important difference between these sectors, I shall treat them separately.

The Private Sector

The following list of the more important laws and executive orders will serve as a convenient reference for our discussion.

Civil Rights Act of 1866
Civil Rights Act of 1870
Civil Rights Act of 1871
Railway Labor Act of 1926
Bacon-Davis Act of 1931
Norris-LaGuardia Act of 1932
Social Security Act of 1935
National Labor Relations Act of 1935
Walsh-Healey Act of 1936
Fair Labor Standards Act of 1938

Wage Stabilization Act of 1942
Portal-to-Portal Act of 1947
Labor-Management Relations Act of 1947
Defense Production Act of 1950
Welfare and Pensions Reporting and Disclosure Act of 1958
Labor-Management Reporting and Disclosure Act of 1959
Manpower Development and Training Act of 1962
Equal Pay Act of 1963
Civil Rights Act of 1964, Title VII
Service Contract Act of 1965
Executive Order 11246 (1965)
Age Discrimination in Employment Act of 1967 and Executive Order 11141
Executive Order 11375 (1967)
Federal-State Extended Unemployment Compensation Act of 1970
Economic Stabilization Act of 1970
Occupational Safety and Health Act of 1970
Equal Employment Opportunity Act of 1972
Self-Employment Individual Tax Retirement Act of 1972
Education Amendments Act of 1972
Rehabilitation Act of 1973
Comprehensive Employment and Training Act of 1973
Health Maintenance Organization Act of 1973
Employee Retirement Income Security Act of 1974
Emergency Unemployment Compensation Act of 1974
Tax Reform Act of 1975
Compensation Extension Act of 1977
Revenue Act of 1978
Age Discrimination in Employment Act Amendments of 1978
Pregnancy Discrimination Act of 1978
Multi-Employer Pension Plan Amendment Act of 1980
Executive Order 12190 President's Advisory Committee on Small & Minority Business Ownership (1980)
Economic Recovery Tax Act of 1981
Tax Equity and Fiscal Responsibility Act of 1982
Job Training Partnership Act of 1982
U.S. Commission on Civil Rights Act of 1983
Social Security Act Amendments of 1983
Executive Order 12426 President's Advisory Committee on Women's Business Ownership (1983)
Migrant & Seasonal Agricultural Worker Protection Act of 1983
Executive Order 12432 Minority Business Enterprise Development (1983)
Federal Supplemental Compensation Act of 1982 Amendment
Retirement Equity Act of 1984

Executive Order 12462 President's Advisory Committee on Mediation
and Conciliation (1984)
Age Discrimination in Employment Amendments of 1986
Job Training Partnership Act Amendments of 1986
Tax Reform Act of 1986
Sexual Abuse Act of 1986
Immigration Reform and Control Act of 1986
Higher Education Amendments Act of 1986
Older Americans Act Amendments of 1987
Medicare and Medicaid Patient and Program Protection Act of 1987
Civil Rights Restoration Act of 1987

Certain of these enactments, such as the Social Security Act, Welfare and
Pensions Reporting and Disclosure Act, Health Maintenance Organization Act,
and Employee Retirement Income Security Act, will be considered in Chapter 13
on employee benefits. Other aspects will be summarized in four categories:
(1) collective bargaining, (2) fair labor standards, (3) equal employment opportunity, and (4) occupational safety and health.

Collective Bargaining

Our discussion of collective bargaining will include the National Labor Relations
Board (NLRB), issues subject to collective bargaining, arbitration and conciliation, strikes that threaten national health and safety, and restraints on unions.

National Labor Relations Board

Both the Railway Labor Act of 1926 (limited to that one industry) and the Norris-
LaGuardia Act of 1932 encouraged the use of collective bargaining. The process
became an essential part of national labor policy with the passage of the National
Labor Relations Act of 1935. Section 7 of that act reads in part:

Employees shall have the right to self-organization, to form, join, or assist labor
organizations, to bargain collectively through representatives of their own
choosing, and to engage in other mutual aid or protection, and shall also have
the right to refrain from any or all such activities except to the extent that such
right may be affected by an agreement requiring membership in a labor organization as a condition of employment as authorized in section 8(a)(3).

Structure of the Board.   Carrying out the provisions of the National Labor Relations Act is placed in the hands of the National Labor Relations Board. Under the
act as amended by the Labor-Management Relations Act of 1947, the board consists of five members appointed by the president with the consent of the Senate.
A general counsel is also appointed by the president with the consent of the Senate. Members serve 5-year terms, while the counsel serves for 4 years. Continuity

and nonpartisanship are ensured by the requirement that board members' terms be staggered and a tradition that not more than three of the board members belong to the same political party.

Functions of the Board.   The board acts to

1. Prevent unfair labor practices on the part of employers or labor organizations.
2. Conduct secret ballot elections among employees in appropriate collective bargaining units to determine whether or not they desire to be represented by a labor organization.
3. Conduct secret ballot elections among employees covered by a union-shop agreement to determine whether or not they wish to revoke the union's authority to make such agreements.
4. Determine in cases involving jurisdictional disputes which of two competing groups of workers is to be the exclusive bargaining agent.
5. Conduct secret ballot elections among employees in national emergency situations.

Provisions of the act with regard to unfair labor practices are detailed and complex. Alvin Goldman, however, summarizes them in a useful way:

> Section 8 is divided into lettered subsections, the *first two of which are the source of most unfair labor practice charges* [italics added]. Section 8(a) prohibits employers from engaging in various forms of conduct that interfere with the protected right of workers to act or refrain from acting in concert. Section 8(b) prohibits labor organizations from engaging in various forms of conduct that interfere with the protected right of workers to act or refrain from acting in concert or that interfere with the protected right of employers not to be subjected to coercive pressures concerning labor disputes in which they are not directly involved.[1]

When a union wishes to be certified as the exclusive bargaining agent for a group of employees, it must submit a petition to the NLRB with evidence that at least 30 percent of the employees in the prospective bargaining unit wish to be represented by the union. Once a valid petition has been filed, a rival union can intervene if it can show that at least one employee in the bargaining unit favors it. But an employer can submit a petition if he can assert that a labor organization has demanded that it be recognized as the bargaining agent of the employees.[2] On the basis of the evidence, the NLRB decides both on the appropriateness of the bargaining unit and whether the board will conduct an election by secret ballot to determine the wishes of the majority. More than one union may be on the first ballot, but employees may also vote for no union. If there is no majority, a runoff election is held between the two top choices. Decertification elections involving revocation of a union's authority to represent an employee group follow a similar procedure.

Issues Subject to Collective Bargaining

Under provisions of the National Labor Relations Act as amended, "wages, hours, and other terms and conditions of employment" are mandatory subjects for collective bargaining; that is, neither the union nor the company can refuse to bargain about these issues. A 1971 Supreme Court decision held that there is no duty to bargain about subjects not falling within these categories.[3] However, not only base pay, but also employee benefits such as vacation pay, fall in the mandatory category. Other issues included in collective bargaining agreements have been union security, strikes and lockouts, and grievance procedures.

Union Security. Almost all union contracts include a provision to help the union keep its status as collective bargaining agent. Such provisions include the union shop, the agency shop, and maintenance of membership. The closed shop, which requires employees to be union members before they are hired, is illegal under the National Labor Relations Act as amended. A union shop typically requires the worker to join the union after 30 days of employment (7 days in the construction trades). Under an agency shop, the workers does not have to join a union but must pay a fee equal to the union dues. Some contracts merely state that during the term of the contract those who are already union members must retain their membership. This is a maintenance-of-membership clause and is less prevalent.

Strikes and Lockouts. Typically, the failure of the collective bargaining process involves a strike, and for union members the right to strike is taken seriously. The union, however, does not like the idea of the company using the opposite tactic—a lockout. Not surprisingly, most contracts limit both actions, especially during the period of the contract. A common limitation is one imposed on "wildcat strikes," or those that are not formally authorized by the union.

Grievance Procedures. Grievance procedures are included in most union contracts as a way of settling disputes arising during the term of a union contract. Such disputes usually involve disagreement about how to interpret or apply the contract. The typical procedure begins with a discussion between the worker and the immediate supervisor. If there is disagreement, a union committee member may next discuss the matter with the supervisor. If disagreement continues, a higher level union representative may discuss the matter with a higher level manager, and so on. As the procedure moves up the organizational levels, it becomes more formalized. At the highest level, if agreement still cannot be reached, the matter may go to arbitration for settlement.

Arbitration and Conciliation

Both arbitration and conciliation involve referring a matter to a third party for a solution. In both processes the third party may be a board of three or five members rather than an individual, although the use of one individual is more common. The important distinction between arbitration and conciliation (or mediation) is that the arbitrator makes decisions, which normally are accepted by the two conflicting parties. The conciliator, on the other hand, attempts to bring about agreement by consulting separately with each side and communicating back and forth between parties.

Most arbitration in U.S. labor-management relations involves a single arbitrator chosen on an *ad hoc* basis to resolve a specific dispute. Sources of arbitrators are the American Arbitration Association and the Federal Mediation and Conciliation Service. The choice of a particular arbitrator is typically a matter of agreement between the two contesting parties. Costs are usually split evenly between the parties. The procedures are informal but do involve the presentation of evidence and the testimony of witnesses and in this sense resemble a court procedure. In the arbitration process, a party's refusal to make information available to the other side where it is relevant to settling a grievance may be treated by the NLRB as an unfair labor practice.[4] In most cases the NLRB accepts the arbitrator's award as controlling, in this way lending support to arbitration as a means of settling certain disputes arising under union contracts.

In the conciliation (or mediation) process, the third party is not the decision maker, but nevertheless helps to settle disputes peacefully. The Federal Mediation and Conciliation Service makes its personnel available (but does not force them on the parties). In the private sector, conciliators facilitate settlements in the collective bargaining process, especially where both sides appear to be a long way from agreement, as well as settle disputes that threaten national health or safety.

Strikes That Threaten National Health or Safety

Under the Labor-Management Relations Act of 1947, there is a special procedure available for handling strikes that appear to threaten national health or safety. It involves the following steps:

1. The president appoints a board of inquiry to investigate the issues, gather testimony and evidence, and make a report.
2. The president can direct the attorney general to petition a federal district court to enjoin the strike.
3. On the issuance of the injunction, both parties are under a mandate to cooperate with the mediation efforts of the Federal Mediation and Conciliation Service.
4. The president reconvenes the board of inquiry. It audits the negotiations and reports on the progress of the parties at the end of 60 days.
5. Within 15 days after receipt of the report, the NLRB conducts a secret ballot election to determine whether the employees are willing to accept the employer's most recent settlement offer.
6. Within 5 days, the NLRB must certify the results of the election to the attorney general.

7. At this point the injunction is dissolved. The president reports to Congress about the results of the inquiry and the election and makes any appropriate recommendations.

Goldman notes that between 1947 and 1972 the procedure was used 30 times and involved 25 injunctions. In half of these cases the injunction lasted the full 80 days without a settlement, and in every case where it came to a vote, the employer's last offer was overwhelmingly rejected.[5]

Restraints on Unions

The National Labor Relations Act of 1935 was modified first by the Labor-Management Relations Act of 1947 and second by the Labor-Management Reporting and Disclosure Act of 1959. The latter act imposed a degree of federal regulation of internal union affairs and placed restraints on the use of union funds. These provisions arose out of Senate hearings which revealed that

> a number of unions were governed by dictatorial power brokers; on occasion national union leaders perpetuated themselves in office through the support of representatives from fictitious locals; some national unions exploited locals through the device of imposing trusteeships over locals whose leadership was independent and whose treasuries were fat; union members often were fearful of retribution if they voiced objections to union leadership; union finances often were poorly managed; and management sometimes received favorable treatment by bribing union officials.[6]

The new provisions relating to internal union affairs were designed to protect the individual union member with respect to (1) the right to vote, (2) freedom of expression, (3) freedom of assembly, (4) the right to sue the union, (5) the right to full and fair hearing, (6) the right to information, and (7) the right to local self-determination. Other provisions imposed restrictions on the use of union funds for union elections and for other political activities.[7]

Fair Labor Standards

The Fair Labor Standards Act of 1938 covers most wage earners in the private sector. Historically, it arose out of the need to curb child labor and to protect workers (in practice, usually women) against being paid substandard wage rates. The major thrust of the act is to provide a minimum hourly wage ($3.35 since January 1, 1981) and for pay at time-and-a-half (one and one-half times the regular wage rate) for working more than 40 hours per week. The computation of the regular wage rate includes

> wages; salaries; shift differentials; commissions, piecework earnings; non-cash wages; on-call pay; incentive, attendance or other non-discretionary bonuses.[8]

Subminimum Wages

The act allows for payment of subminimum wages if specifically approved by the wage-hour administrator for:

Learners in semi-skilled occupations

Apprentices in skilled occupations

Messengers in firms primarily engaged in delivering letters and messages

Handicapped persons, including those persons employed in a sheltered workshop

Students in retail or service establishments, in agriculture or in their own educational institutions

For employees who receive over $30 per month in tips, up to 40% of the minimum wage requirement may be covered by tips[9]

Depending on the particular group, rates for the subminimum wages are set at some fraction (75 to 80 percent) of the regular minimum wage rate that would otherwise apply.

Exclusions

Generally excluded from the wages and hours provisions of the act are

Retail and service establishment employees if sales mostly made within the state (except for laundries, dry cleaners, hospitals, nursing homes and schools)

Executives

Administrative employees

Professional workers

Outside salespeople

Employees of seasonal amusement or recreational establishments or camps

Independent contractors (who are not employees)

Casual babysitters and companions to the disabled

Volunteers (who work without pay)[10]

Exclusion from Overtime Requirements

The following groups (with qualifications for some groups) are excluded only from the overtime requirements of the act:

Employees subject to the Motor Carrier Act

Interstate railroad and airline employees

Employees primarily engaged in sales or service of automobiles, trucks, or farm implements; or in sales of trailers, boats or aircraft, where employed by non-manufacturing establishments

Agricultural employees

Taxicab drivers

Employees of amusement and recreational establishments holding national park or forest concessions

Commission employees in retail or service establishments

Domestic service employees[11]

Enforcement Provisions

Enforcement of the provisions of the Fair Labor Standards Act (FLSA) rests jointly with the U.S. Department of Labor and the individual worker. Either can act to enforce the provisions of the act.

While the minimum wage is mostly set by law, it is administratively set at the prevailing rate for the particular type of work involved at a particular locality in the cases covered by the Bacon-Davis Act, the Walsh-Healey Act, and the Service Contract Act. These acts cover firms working on federal construction projects or doing business with the federal government under contracts. In these instances, where the wage is not fixed by law, the process

> is very time consuming and costly and has been criticized for these and other reasons. Vigorous legislative efforts to amend the process have been attempted in recent years but to date have been unsuccessful.[12]

If a worker or a group of workers, but not a union, believe they have been underpaid under FLSA, they can sue in federal court to recover the back wages they believe to be due them. However, the Labor Department's Wage-Hour Division maintains offices in many cities, and workers can bring such matters to them to be worked out informally by negotiation between the division and the employer. If the matter cannot be resolved at that level, the secretary of labor can go into federal court.

Equal Employment Opportunity

More wide-ranging and influential in scope than the Fair Labor Standards Act are the early civil rights acts after the Civil War, Title VII of the Civil Rights Act of 1964, the Equal Pay Act of 1963, the Age Discrimination in Employment Act of 1967, as well as executive orders and laws relating to federally assisted programs. Here we shall discuss the legal and legislative framework, leaving to the next chapter a deeper exploration of the issues.

Early Civil Rights Acts

Following the Civil War, two amendments to the Constitution were passed—the Thirteenth Amendment, which abolished slavery, and the Fourteenth Amendment, which gave the right of citizenship and the right to vote to the former slaves and forbade any state to deny them equal protection of the laws. These amendments were supported by the Civil Rights Acts of 1866, 1870, and 1871. These acts, long neglected, have recently been used as a basis for discrimination actions in federal court.[13] Areas covered by the acts relate to "equal rights under the law," "property rights," state laws depriving a person of rights, and conspiracies to interfere with civil rights.

Title VII of the Civil Rights Act of 1964

This title of the 1964 act prohibits discrimination in employment because of race, color, religion, sex, or national origin. It affects employers, employment agencies, and labor unions, but not bona fide private membership organizations. It also prohibits specified unlawful employment practices. To assure that the provisions of Title VII are carried out, an Equal Employment Opportunity Commission was created.

The Employer.   It is unlawful for the employer to

1. Fail or refuse to hire.
2. Discharge.
3. Discriminate with respect to compensation or terms, conditions, or privileges of employment.
4. Limit, segregate, or classify employees or job applicants in a way to deprive the individual of employment opportunities or otherwise adversely affect the individual's status as an employee.
5. Discriminate in apprenticeship or on-the-job training programs.

The Employment Agency.   An employment agency may not

1. Fail or refuse to refer for employment.
2. Otherwise discriminate against.
3. Classify or refer for employment any individual on the basis of race, sex, color, religion, or national origin.

The Labor Union.   A labor union must not

1. Exclude or expel an individual from membership.
2. Otherwise discriminate against.
3. Limit, segregate, or classify its membership or applicants for membership.
4. Classify or fail or refuse to refer for employment any individual in a way that would deprive an individual of employment opportunities.
5. Cause an employer to discriminate against an individual.
6. Discriminate in apprenticeship or on-the-job training programs.[14]

Equal Employment Opportunity Commission.   The Equal Employment Opportunity Commission (EEOC) has five commissioners appointed by the president with approval by the Senate. The president designates two of the five as chair and vice chair and also appoints a general counsel. The commissioners serve 5-year terms and the counsel a 4-year term. The counsel is responsible for all litigation except that before the Supreme Court, which is handled by the attorney general.

A charge under the act can be filed by the aggrieved person or by someone else in his behalf. The latter condition allows for a class action suit (a suit in support of more than one individual). A charge can also be filed by one of the commissioners. If there is a state or local law also prohibiting the practice, the EEOC cannot process a charge until either (1) action has been completed under the state or local law or (2) 2 months have passed. However, charges can be filed simultaneously with EEOC and at the local or state level.

Following the initial filing of charges, the EEOC investigates the truth of the charge. If it finds "reasonable cause" to believe the charge is true, it tries to eliminate the unlawful employment practice by conference, conciliation, and/or persuasion.

If this effort is unsuccessful, the EEOC can take the case to a federal district court. The court can exercise broad powers under the act, including granting an injunction requiring the employer, employment agency, or union to take "such affirmative action as may be appropriate." In the situation where the charged party is a state or local government, a similar action can be initiated, but by the attorney general rather than the EEOC.

In situations involving widespread violations, as contrasted with relatively isolated violations, the EEOC may omit the normal procedure and go directly to a federal district court. In such a situation the attorney general is empowered to convene a special three-judge district court to hear the case. The decisions of such a court are appealable directly to the U.S. Supreme Court.[15]

Equal Pay Act of 1963

The Equal Pay Act requires of the employer equal pay for equal work within the same establishment regardless of sex. Equal work is specified as that which (1) requires equal skill, (2) requires equal effort, (3) requires equal responsibility, and (4) is performed under similar working conditions. But equal pay is not required if differences arise due to a seniority system, a merit system, or a system that measures earnings by quantity or quality of production.[16]

There is still a debatable issue that neither the Equal Pay Act nor Title VII of the Civil Rights Act appears to take into account—the issue of comparable worth. That is, should two very different positions in the same organization—one held mostly by males and the other held mostly by females—offer the same pay if they are of comparable worth? We shall explore this issue both in the next chapter and in later chapters on job evaluation and job pricing.

Age Discrimination in Employment Act of 1967

This act, now under the surveillance of the EEOC, prohibits employment discrimination based on age for individuals between ages 40 and 70. As in the case of Title VII of the Civil Rights Act, the employer, the employment agency, and the labor union are all affected.

The Employer.   The employer is forbidden to

1. Fail or refuse to hire.
2. Discharge.
3. Otherwise discriminate with respect to compensation, terms, conditions, or privileges of employment.
4. Limit, segregate, or classify employees so as to deprive the individual of employment opportunities or adversely affect the individual's status as an employee.
5. Reduce the wage rate in order to comply with the act.

The Employment Agency.   The employment agency must not

1. Fail or refuse to refer for employment.
2. Otherwise discriminate against any individual.

The Labor Union.   The labor union must not

1. Exclude or expel any individual from membership.
2. Otherwise discriminate against any individual.
3. Limit, segregate, or classify its membership or classify or fail or refuse to refer for employment any individual to deprive him of employment opportunities or adversely affect his status as an employee or applicant for employment.

Exceptions.   Some exceptions are permitted under the act, such as where age is a bona fide occupational qualification or where discharge of an individual for good cause is involved. Employers are allowed to observe the terms of a bona fide seniority or employee benefit plan (such as retirement plan), but the act still specifies that

> no such seniority system or employee benefit plan shall require or permit the involuntary retirement of any individual (between the ages of 40 and 70).[17]

Presidential Executive Orders

As indicated earlier, not all of the legal framework for equal employment opportunity arises from legislation. Some of it arises from executive orders issued by the president of the United States. Goldman reports on how these orders got started:

> In 1941, President Franklin Roosevelt, acting in his capacity as chief executive officer of the federal government, adopted the policy that, for reasons of efficiency and integrity, the United States will not do business with employers who

maintain discriminatory hiring or personnel practices. It took some twenty years, however, and additional Executive Orders issued by Presidents Truman, Eisenhower, and Kennedy, before the administrative techniques, staffing and determination for the enforcement of this policy was developed to the point where some measurable impact was being made upon the personnel practices of those who do business with the federal government.[18]

Under Executive Order 11246, federal government contractors are forbidden to discriminate on the basis of race, color, religion, sex, or national origin. Under Executive Order 11141, age is also included. While enforcement procedures stress conciliation, Title VII of the Civil Rights Act can be applied. The federal contract may also be canceled and the employer disqualified from other government contracts.

Discrimination Under Federally Assisted Programs

Several acts prohibit discrimination under programs where businesses or other organizations benefit from federal financial assistance. Title VI of the Civil Rights Act of 1964 prohibits discrimination on account of race, color, or national origin under any program or activity receiving federal financial assistance. Under Title IX of the Education Act of 1972, discrimination on the basis of sex is prohibited in any education program. Title I of the State and Local Fiscal Assistance Act of 1972 bars state or local governments from discriminating on account of race, color, national origin, sex, religion, or age, or against qualified handicapped workers.[19]

Occupational Safety and Health

The Occupational Safety and Health Act of 1970 (OSHA) was passed at a time when

> more American lives were being lost through workplace accidents than through U.S. participation in the then bloody Vietnamese Civil War.[20]

The Role of the Employer

The act requires employers to provide workers with an environment on the job that is free from hazards likely to cause death or serious physical harm. With the advice of an advisory panel known as the National Institute for Occupational Safety and Health, the secretary of labor develops the necessary safety and health standards. The employer is required to

1. Submit to government inspection of the workplace.
2. Keep records on safety and health experience.
3. Inform workers of their rights.
4. Supervise employees in a way to avoid unnecessary hazards.

The Role of Government

Following each plant inspection, the OSHA investigator informs management of violations found, opportunities for abatement that will be allowed, and proposed penalties for violations. Then the investigator, with the approval of the OSHA area director, typically sets a time during which the employer can take action to correct the violations. If deficiencies are not corrected, the three-member Occupational Safety and Health Review Commission created by the act can issue a complaint against the employer, who is then subjected to a hearing before an administrative law judge. The judge receives evidence, makes findings of fact, and reaches conclusions of law. The judge's decision becomes that of the commission. Appeals go to a U.S. Court of Appeals, which typically restricts itself to questions of law and normally upholds the commission's decision. These steps are the normal procedure. But if the OSHA investigation reveals a hazard expected to result in imminent death or serious injury, the secretary of labor can obtain an injunction from a U.S. District Court to have the hazard corrected.[21]

The Public Sector

There are important differences in the labor-relations climate between the private and the public sectors. These can be seen in part from the pieces of legislation and executive orders pertaining to the public sector:

Pendleton Act (Civil Service Commission) of 1883
Lloyd-LaFollette Act of 1912
Civil Service Retirement Act of 1920
Classification Act of 1923
Hatch Act of 1939
Veterans' Preference Act of 1944
Federal Employees Pay Act of 1945
Annual and Sick Leave Act of 1951
Government Employees Incentive Awards Act of 1954
Executive Order 11491 (1969)
Federal Pay Comparability Act of 1970
Civil Service Reform Act of 1978
Federal Employees Flexible and Compressed Work Schedule Act of 1982
Fair Labor Standards Amendments of 1985
Executive Order 12552 Productivity Improvement Program for the Federal Government (1986)
Federal Employees Retirement System Act of 1986

The Rights of Public Employees

The rights of employees in the public sector have been built into civil service laws designed to replace the old "spoils" system with a system based on merit. The historical changes in the federal civil service began with the Pendleton Act of 1883, under which a three-member Civil Service Commission was established, with no more than two members from the same political party. The act also established a list of federal jobs for which employment was to be based on the results of a competitive examination. Furthermore, a worker so hired could not be discharged for refusing to contribute to a political campaign.

In 1897 President William McKinley established by executive order that a worker hired into the federal civil service could not be removed except for just cause. Formal legal procedures to assure this policy were incorporated in the Lloyd-LaFollette Act of 1912. The Civil Service Retirement Act of 1920 established pensions for federal workers. The Classification Act of 1923 provided for a detailed system of testing, classifying, and paying federal workers.

The Federal Employees Pay Act of 1945 established a 40-hour week and overtime, and the Annual and Sick Leave Act of 1951 set up a schedule for vacations, holidays, and leaves of absence. The Federal Pay Comparability Act of 1970 attempts to establish greater equality of pay between workers in the federal government and workers in the private sector who perform comparable work. The Civil Service Reform Act of 1978 relates to performance evaluation of federal employees. Executive Order 11491 provides for a viable labor-management relations structure for federal employees.

Under the Fair Labor Standards Amendments of 1985, employees of states, political subdivisions of states, and interstate governmental agencies may be given compensatory time off in lieu of overtime. If given, the time is paid for at a rate not less than 1½ hours for each hour of employment for which overtime otherwise would be required.

The Federal Employees Flexible and Compressed Work Schedule Act of 1982 provides that federal employees under certain conditions can be authorized to participate in flexible work time or compressed workweek programs. Such arrangements are discussed further in Chapter 4.

Executive Order 12552 of 1986 was initiated to encourage productivity improvement in the federal government. The goal of the program is a 20 percent productivity increase in affected functions by 1992, with productivity referring to the efficiency with which resources are used to produce a government service or product at specified levels of quality and timeliness. The heads of executive departments and agencies are held responsible for reaching this goal. The Executive Order assigns a supporting role of formulating goals, policies, standards, and guidelines and identifying statutory barriers to the director of the Office of Management and Budget. In addition, it asks the director of the Office of Personnel Management to review existing incentive programs and practices and other relevant personnel practices, and to make or recommend changes to support productivity improvements as well as to develop programs to minimize negative impacts on employees and to implement training or retraining programs related to productivity improvements.

Two other acts affecting public employees, the Hatch Act of 1939 and the Veterans' Preference Act of 1944, appear to conflict with other social goals. The

Hatch Act, which restricts the political activity of federal employees, is viewed by many federal workers as too restrictive of their rights as citizens. The Veterans' Preference Act appears to conflict with the idea of a merit system and with equal rights for women.

The Classification Act, the Federal Pay Comparability Act, and the Civil Service Reform Act will be discussed in later chapters, while Executive Order 11491 will be considered later in this chapter.[22]

Collective Bargaining

For public employees, management is also a representative of government. This tends to make management stronger relative to the union than is the case in the private sector. Although public employees typically do not have the right to strike, collective bargaining is still employed. If the dispute cannot be settled, it results not in a strike but in an impasse. Mediation and arbitration tend to play a larger role in the process than they do in the private sector. We shall look at bargaining in the public sector for three different groups: federal employees (except postal workers), postal workers, and state and local workers. In addition, we shall examine the problem of union security.

Federal Employees (Excluding Postal Workers)

For most federal employees, the legislative framework for collective bargaining is provided by Executive Order 11491. Excluded from coverage are (1) the Postal Service; (2) the military services; (3) agencies concerned with internal security, foreign intelligence, or foreign affairs; and (4) the Tennessee Valley Authority.

Exclusive Recognition and National Consultation Rights. Under this executive order, a bargaining unit can be granted one of two different forms of recognition: exclusive recognition or national consultation rights. A bargaining unit that can gain the support of a majority of the employees in a secret ballot election will receive exclusive recognition, giving it the right to negotiate agreements covering all employees in the unit and to be present and participate in all formal employee-management discussions regarding personnel policies, practices, and grievances. Agreements can cover matters "affecting working conditions" but not wages or hours.[23]

If a bargaining unit cannot demonstrate majority support but can show that a "substantial number" of employees in the unit wish to be represented by it, it can gain national consultation rights. This recognition gives it the right to be notified of proposed changes in personnel policies and an opportunity to comment on them, to suggest changes, and to have its views fully considered.[24]

The Assistant Secretary and the Bargaining Unit. In conjunction with these representation elections, the assistant secretary of labor for labor-management relations must determine the appropriate bargaining unit. In general, units are certified on the basis of the plant, installation, craft, or any other likely basis. However, certain guidelines for certification must be followed:

1. Managers, supervisors, or personnel officers are excluded from the unit.
2. Security employees must be in separate units from other workers.
3. Professional and nonprofessional employees cannot be in the same unit unless a majority of the professional employees agree to be included.

The assistant secretary also handles questions arising from union or agency charges of violation of provisions of the executive order.

Federal Labor Relations Council. A three-member Federal Labor Relations Council—the secretary of labor, the director of the Office of Personnel Management, and the director of the Office of Management and Budget—reviews the decisions of the assistant secretary and adopts regulations interpreting the executive order. The council also articulates its activities with a Federal Services Impasses Panel (now seven members, appointed by the president). It reviews situations where an impasse has been reached and can take action to resolve the impasse.[25]

Grievances. Disagreements between a union and an agency under an existing collective bargaining agreement are resolved by advisory arbitration. Even though awards are advisory rather than binding, they have in practice been accepted. In some instances there is a question as to which procedure should apply—the grievance procedure under a contract with an exclusive bargaining representative or the usual appeals procedure under the Office of Personnel Management. Such decisions are made by the assistant secretary.

Postal Workers

Collective bargaining for postal workers is provided for under the National Labor Relations Act. The scope of bargaining thus is broader than for other federal workers and includes wages, hours, and other conditions of employment. However, postal workers, like other federal employees, are not allowed to strike. The Postal Reorganization Act of 1970 provides a special procedure for collective bargaining applicable to postal workers:

1. A period is allowed for collective bargaining without intervention.
2. During this period if an impasse is reached and/or the two sides cannot agree on a method of resolving it, a fact-finding panel investigates and reports back its findings (with or without recommendations) within a specific period.
3. If, during another specified period, no agreement is reached, an arbitration panel is selected.

4. Within 45 days after its appointment, the panel makes its award which is final and binding and becomes part of the collective bargaining agreement.[26]

State and Local Workers

State and local government labor organizations and government officials representing management have conflicting ideas about the nature of the collective bargaining unit. Management has usually favored broad-based bargaining units, while unions have sought more narrowly based units. In some states units have to correspond with state government departments. In other states it is a matter of a state law relating to public employee bargaining, or it is left up to a state employment relations commission or board. At the local government level, the bargaining unit is often handled by a state agency on a case-by-case basis.[27]

In a broad sense, the same format for collective bargaining for federal employees also prevails at the state and local level. Impasses are resolved by mediation, fact finding, arbitration, or some combination of these processes. The differences lie in the sequence of events following an impasse.

Mediation.   In most states either side can call for the services of a mediator, or mediation may be required. If mediation is involved, a single mediator or a panel may be chosen. If a panel is used, often each side will choose an even number of members, and then they in turn will select another member.

Fact Finding.   In many states an alternative to mediation is that either side can initiate a fact-finding procedure. In some states the fact finder's report is kept confidential to encourage further negotiations; in others, it is made public. Fact finding can be combined with mediation, but this is not usually the case.

Arbitration.   Most states encourage resolution of impasses by arbitration, and some require it. When arbitration is called for, it may involve the idea of the last offer; that is, the arbitrator must choose one or the other side's last bargaining offer and cannot make a compromise award.[28]

Union Security

In Abood v. Detroit Board of Education,[29] the U.S. Supreme Court held that the encroachment on freedom of association resulting from compelling a public employee to join a union or pay the equivalent of union dues (the check-off) was justified by the state's interest in minimizing employee conflicts and being able to negotiate a single contract. In close to half of the states, some union shop or agency shop provisions have been negotiated at either the state or local levels, and in most such cases a check-off of union dues or the equivalent was required.[30]

Federal employee unions, including those in the Postal Service, are barred by law or executive order from having a union shop. But, this time with the exception of the Postal Service, they are permitted to include a check-off provision. In the Postal Service the provision is generally mandatory.[31]

The Fair Labor Standards Act and Public Employees

Recent federal legislation has extended coverage of FLSA to state and local government employees. But in The National League of Cities v. Usery,[32] the Supreme Court held this to be an unconstitutional encroachment on state sovereignty in areas of traditional government functions. According to Goldman, it is still uncertain whether this ruling applies to workers who do not perform traditional services.[33]

Equal Employment Opportunity and Public Employees

Nondiscrimination in federal government employment is covered by Executive Order 11478.[34] Also, Section 717 of Title VII of the Civil Rights Act of 1964 protects federal workers (including those in the Postal Service) from discrimination based on race, color, religion, sex, and national origin. Cases involving discrimination on account of age are processed by the Office of Personnel Management.[35]

Public employees of state and local governments are generally protected by laws covering the same ground as federal laws. Sometimes these laws also cover smaller employers who are not involved in interstate commerce.[36]

The Occupational Safety and Health Act and Public Employees

By executive order, federal employees are also protected by OSHA. State and local government employees are not so protected except where a state has its own program similar to OSHA.

Summary

The industrial relations legislative and legal framework within which pay and benefits for employees are determined ranges from legislation passed by Congress and presidential executive orders to informal handling of a worker's complaint between the supervisor and a union representative in the shop. Apart from this similarity, the legislative and legal environments in the private and public sectors are significantly different.

In the private sector, the National Labor Relations Act ensures the right of collective bargaining and the right to strike. Mandatory subjects of collective bargaining include wages, hours, and other terms and conditions of employment. The National Labor Relations Board (NLRB) acts to prevent unfair labor practices on the part of employers or unions. The NLRB conducts secret ballot elections among employees to determine whether they wish to be represented by a union and also whether they wish to revoke such authority. Where competing unions are involved, the NLRB attempts to settle jurisdictional disputes.

In the private sector, the most prevalent form of union security is the union shop. Most union contracts include a grievance procedure as a means of settling disputes arising during the term of a union contract. Arbitration is usually the final step in this procedure.

There are numerous pieces of legislation governing the private sector. Special procedures under the Labor-Management Relations Act of 1947 are provided for strikes that threaten national health or safety. The Labor-Management Reporting and Disclosure Act imposes federal regulation of internal union affairs and places restrictions on the use of union funds. The Fair Labor Standards Act provides for a minimum wage and requires payment of time-and-a-half for work in excess of 40 hours a week. Most support for equal employment opportunity is provided by Title VII of the Civil Rights Act of 1964, the Equal Pay Act of 1963, the Age Discrimination Act of 1967, and Executive Order 11246. The Occupational Safety and Health Act of 1970 attempts to secure for workers a safer and healthier job environment.

In the public sector, civil service laws have been enacted to encourage hiring on merit instead of the old "spoils" system. For public employees, management also represents government, so management is stronger compared with the union than is the case in the private sector.

In public sector collective bargaining, employees typically do not have the right to strike. Bargaining is characterized by impasses, mediation, fact finding, and arbitration. Collective bargaining contracts in the public sector typically have weaker union security provisions. For federal employees, the union shop is prohibited by law or executive order.

Case Study

A New Labor Relations Law

Yolanda Mahdavi was the first person of Iranian extraction to be elected governor of this state in the deep South. Standing six feet four inches tall, she projected an image of enthusiasm and energy. At first there had been skepticism and even ridicule of her candidacy, but she was an effective speaker and the tide turned in her favor. She had won over her opponent, General Justus Tolliver, by a narrow margin.

Now she was governor and there was work to do. Leaning over her spacious desk toward the intercom, she said, "Pete, come in here a moment, will you?" "Coming!" was the answer. Shortly, Colonel Peder (Pete) Westerholm, the governor's new legislative assistant, appeared. The colonel, a retired National Guard officer, had majored in political science (and football) at Old State. He was also tall, with an ebullient, outgoing personality. During the campaign he had helped Mahdavi gain support among people living in the more rural parts of the state.

"Colonel," she said, "do you remember what we promised to that group of workers I talked to near the state capitol building? I want a new law governing labor relations for workers in state and local government jobs!"

"Governor," he replied, "we sure do need to do something. It's a hell of a mess the way it is. But whatever we do, we'll need to talk to the AFL-CIO leaders and some of the industry people, too. We'll need to get their ideas."

"I'm aware of that. But right now we have to get a specific proposal worked out," she urged.

"What do you think? Should we take the existing legislation, whatever is there, and rework it, or do you want a completely new proposal?"

"First of all," said the governor, "I want a new proposal which would cover public workers at state, county, and local levels. Second, you need to think of specific steps for the entire collective bargaining process. Third, you need to consider the requirements for different types of public workers. For example, you can't treat police officers the same as clerical employees."

"Governor, it looks like I have my work cut out for me."

"Well, your political science background will help. However, there are a lot of details to consider. To handle public labor relations statewide, should we have a state board? Should there be an administrator, too? Which employees would be eligible to be represented by a union and which would be excluded? How would representation elections work? And what about union security and the right to strike?—Oh, and this might help you, too."

The governor handed him a sheet listing different occupations:

Police and fire department workers
School teachers and college professors
Clerical workers
Professional workers, including nurses
Other hospital workers
Public transportation workers
Sanitation workers
Park and recreation workers
Welfare workers

The meeting concluded on a friendly note, and Colonel Westerholm left the room.

Role Assignment

You are Colonel Westerholm, the governor's new legislative assistant. Work out a proposal for a new labor relations law covering public employees in the state. Be prepared to discuss your proposal.

Questions for Discussion

1. Should the courts, the NLRB, or someone else make most of the decisions concerning industrial relations in the United States? Explain your answer.

2. What are the more important differences in collective bargaining between the private sector and the public sector?

3. Do you agree with the methods used by the NLRB in conducting representation elections? Why or why not?
4. Should all subjects be mandatory subjects for collective bargaining, or should collective bargaining be restricted to wages, hours, and terms and conditions of employment? Explain.
5. Should all forms of union security (including the closed shop) be allowed in the private sector? Why or why not?
6. What is the difference between mediation and arbitration?
7. What procedures are specified under the Labor-Management Relations Act of 1947 for settling strikes that threaten national health or safety? Can you think of any ways in which these procedures could be improved?
8. Should the federal government intervene in the internal management of a labor union? Why or why not?
9. What is the purpose of the Fair Labor Standards Act of 1938? Do you agree or disagree with the provision for subminimum wages in certain cases?
10. What are the obligations of the employer, the employment agency, and the union under Title VII of the Civil Rights Act of 1964?
11. What are the powers of the EEOC? If the commission thinks there has been a violation of Title VII of the Civil Rights Act, what can it do about it?
12. What is the significance of Executive Order 11246? Explain.
13. What is the purpose of the Occupational Safety and Health Act of 1970 (OSHA)?
14. For employees of the federal government (other than in the Postal Service), how does the collective bargaining process work?
15. What is the purpose of Executive Order 12552 (1986)?

Notes

1. Alvin L. Goldman, *Labor Law and Industrial Relations in the United States of America* (Deventer, The Netherlands: Kluver, 1979), 123.
2. Ibid., 276.
3. Allied Chemical and Alkali Workers v. Pittsburgh Plate Glass Co. For a detailed discussion of mandatory and nonmandatory subjects, see Goldman, *op. cit.*, 210–11.
4. Goldman, *op. cit.*, 309.
5. Ibid., 292.
6. Ibid., 187.
7. For a detailed analysis, see Goldman, *op. cit.*, 186–96.
8. Louis B. Livingston and John H. Leddy, "Fair Labor Standards Act: Substance," in *Labor and Employment Law* (Philadelphia: American Law Institute–American Bar Association Committee on Continuing Education, 1981), 575.
9. Ibid., 573.
10. Ibid.
11. For details of this and other substantive aspects of the act, see Livingston and Leddy, *op. cit.*, 578 and 567–80.
12. Goldman, *op. cit.*, 315.
13. Peter M. Panken, "Statutes and Orders Prohibiting Discrimination in Employment," in *Labor and Employment Law* (Philadelphia: American Law Institute–American Bar Association Committee on Continuing Education, 1981), 9 (42 U.S.C. Sections 1981–85).
14. For further details, see Panken, *op. cit.*, 3–6.
15. See Goldman, *op. cit.*, 328–30, for full details of what is discussed here in summary form.
16. Panken, *op. cit.*, 6.
17. Ibid., 8.
18. Goldman, *op. cit.*, 115.
19. See Panken, *op. cit.*, 12.
20. Goldman, *op. cit.*, 235.
21. For a detailed discussion, see Goldman, *op. cit.*, 318–26.
22. Goldman, *op. cit.*, 79–84.
23. Ibid., 221.
24. Ibid.
25. See Goldman, *op. cit.*, 312–13 for a more detailed discussion.
26. See Goldman, *op. cit.*, 220.

27. See Goldman, *op. cit.*, 227–28.
28. See Goldman, *op. cit.*, 219 for further details.
29. 431 U.S. 209 (1977).
30. Goldman, *op. cit.*, 235.
31. Ibid., 235.

32. 426 U.S. 833 (1976).
33. Goldman, *op. cit.*, 54.
34. Panken, *op. cit.*, 11.
35. Goldman, *op. cit.*, 331 and 336.
36. Panken, *op. cit.*, 11.

References

Goldman, Alvin L. *Labor Law and Industrial Relations in the United States of America.* Deventer, The Netherlands: Kluver, 1979.

Henderson, Richard I. "Contract Concessions: Is the Past Prologue?" *Compensation and Benefits Review* 18, no. 5 (September–October 1986): 17–30.

Kaplan, Rochelle K. "Human Resources Issues in the Courts." *ACA News* 30, nos. 2, 3, and 5 through 9 (February–March 1987 through January 1988).

Kohl, John P., and Stephens, David B. "Expanding the Legal Rights of Working Women." *Personnel* 64, no. 5 (May 1987): 46–51.

Murphy, Austin J., and Nickles, Don. "The Fair Labor Standards Act Amendments of 1985." *Labor Law Journal* 37, no. 2 (February 1986): 67–74.

Nelson, Richard R. "State Labor Laws: Changes During 1987. *Monthly Labor Review* 111, no. 1 (January 1988): 38–61.

Scalise, David J., and Smith, Daniel J. "Legal Update: When Are Job Requirements Discriminatory?" *Personnel* 63, no. 3 (March 1986): 41–48.

Scott, Clyde, and Bain, Trevor. "How Arbitrators Interpret Ambiguous Contract Language." *Personnel* 64, no. 8 (August 1987): 10–14.

Smith, Ralph E., and Vavrichek, Bruce. "The Minimum Wage: Its Relation to Incomes and Poverty." *Monthly Labor Review* 110, no. 6 (June 1987): 24–30.

Sullivan, Frederick L. "Immigration Legislation: An Update." *Personnel* 64, no. 12 (December 1987): 26–32.

Sullivan, Frederick L. "Sexual Harassment: The Supreme Court's Ruling." *Personnel* 63, no. 12 (December 1986): 37–44.

Summers, Lawrence H. "A Fair Tax Act That's Bad for Business." *Harvard Business Review* 87, no. 2 (March-April 1987): 53–59.

Thieblot, Armand J., Jr. *Prevailing Wage Legislation: The Davis-Bacon Act, State Little Davis-Bacon Acts, The Walsh-Healey Act, and the Service Contract Act.* Philadelphia: University of Pennsylvania, Wharton School Industrial Research Unit, 1986.

Tinsley, LaVerne C. "State Workers' Compensation: Legislation Enacted in 1987." *Monthly Labor Review* 111, no. 1 (January 1988): 63–68.

Unions and Inequities in Pay and Benefits

4

Chapter Outline

- Labor Unions in the United States
- Inequities in Pay and Benefits Relating to Race and Sex
- Summary
- Case Study—Frick Department Stores
- Case Study—A Matter of Professional Ethics

In earlier chapters we looked at national and international economic trends as well as legislative and legal aspects of pay. In the present chapter we turn to unions—their impact on inequities in pay and benefits—and also to some of the remaining unsolved problems of inequity, relating especially to race and sex.

Labor Unions in the United States

The history of unions in the United States is indissolubly linked with the struggle for freedom, and what has been achieved is more drenched in violence and blood than many people today would like to believe. In earlier years, with the law on the side of company management, companies usually came out ahead in battles with the unions.

Robert Ozanne has traced union history through a discussion of McCormick and International Harvester from 1860 to 1960.[1] This struggle involved not only wage cuts, riots, and bombings, but in 1886, the destruction of some unions representing workers at McCormick. These years also saw the Pullman strike of 1894, where President Grover Cleveland sent in federal troops to stop the strike. Even in recent years, labor relations at the Koehler Company (a Wisconsin manufacturer of plumbing equipment) and at the Farah Manufacturing Company (a Texas firm in the clothing business) have been characterized by violence. The struggle for the rights of farm workers under the leadership of César Chávez in Texas and California, too, has been long and bitter. The more recent instances illustrate that where the cause is just and other strategies fail, union militancy may still be the only way to a solution.

Up until the 1930s, wages tended to rise during times of prosperity (which might have happened without unions), and this was accompanied by union growth. Conversely, in the depression of the 1870s and other periods of depression or recession, wages tended to fall (which again might have happened in the absence of unions),[2] and unions became weaker, often disintegrating altogether. Fortunately for the United States, neither union progress through violence nor union death through economic decline is typical any longer of U.S. labor unions.

60

The Increased Role of Unions

In 1932 only slightly more than 5 percent of the total labor force was unionized, compared with roughly 25 percent in the mid-1950s. In an important sense, the 25 percent figure tends to understate the power of unions because many non-union firms must also offer close to the equivalent of or better than what union firms win in order to stay competitive in the labor market or to defend themselves against organizing efforts of unions. This applies especially in construction, public utilities, railroads, and much of the manufacturing sector where, despite the 25 percent figure for the labor force as a whole, well over 90 percent of production and production-related workers are unionized in the largest plants. And, of course, the actions of the largest companies exert great influence on what happens in their respective industries.

Although the overall percentage of the labor force that is unionized is tapering off, we cannot conclude that unionism is in a long-range decline. (We will return to this point in Chapter 15 when we discuss pay and benefits of professionals.) The single most important thing to bear in mind is this: The Great Depression of the 1930s and Franklin D. Roosevelt's New Deal combined with the activist roles played by union leaders within a completely new environmental framework created the tremendous advance in the role of unions in the United States.

The progress of the unions is due to leaders such as John L. Lewis of the United Mine Workers (UMW) and Walter Reuther of the United Automobile Workers (UAW) and many others in the union ranks who won the necessary broad base of support among the American public. As a result, U.S. unions have attained enormous political and economic power.

The increased role of the unions has meant that Americans in general have greater security in their jobs today than they had earlier and that battles which at one time had to be fought in the streets and often never could be won were instead resolved in new and more constructive ways. While strikes, picketing, and boycotts continue, legal frameworks permit a wider range of union actions. Injunctions, strikebreakers, and calling in federal troops are no longer the typical remedies sought by management.

Labor in the United States, while less politically oriented than in most European countries, still seeks political action on issues where it has not been able to reach its objectives through the collective bargaining process. Such action takes the form of supporting or opposing legislation at local, state, and national levels. Some of the resulting legislation was discussed in Chapter 3.

Labor's Magna Carta: The Wagner Act

The most important labor measure ever enacted in the United States, the Wagner Labor Act of 1935 (more formally known as the National Labor Relations Act), provided the mechanism for a peaceful method of settling labor disputes—collective bargaining. Not unlike the peace treaty signed between two nations following a war, collective bargaining should be thought of not as purely economic, but as political. The "treaty" or labor-management agreement is more commonly and less accurately called a union contract. The heart of this "treaty" is the wage-effort bargain, wherein it is agreed what labor will do on its part in exchange for what management will pay on its part. Thus, the National Labor Relations Act gave unions vastly increased power in determination of wages.

Collective bargaining has become a permanent part of our society and is likely to penetrate into other sectors where unions have had little strength. Minor shifts in the extent of union membership, or efforts favoring state right-to-work laws, seem unlikely to affect this outcome.

Craft versus Industrial Unions

Within this new framework, labor's effect on pay structures depends on whether it is organized on craft or industrial (plantwide) lines. Before 1935 most unions were craft, and such unions were nationally prominent. In 1935, when John L. Lewis and his colleagues broke away from the American Federation of Labor (AFL) and formed the Congress of Industrial Organizations (CIO), new strength was given to plantwide, companywide, and often industrywide organization of workers.[3] Under craft union contracts, pay for a given job varies from locality to locality. This is also true of industrial unions in those situations where a contract covers only a single plant. But for most industrial unions with contracts covering many plants, pay for the same job in the same company is typically uniform throughout the United States.

Workers in Industrial Unions

In the middle of the pay ladder are those in the protected sector—the blue-collar and nonsupervisory white-collar workers. Their pay is typically either covered under a union contract or influenced by union pay patterns. To illustrate, we shall look at two contrasting kinds of pay scales: the scale for production workers in the steel industry and that for construction workers. Steelworkers are members of an industrial union, and construction workers are members of craft unions. An industrial union typically represents all or most of the production, maintenance, and related workers in a plant, company, or industry. The craft union, on the other hand, typically includes in its membership workers in a particular craft or skill or in closely related trades. A significant difference between the two is that the focus of power in the industrial union tends to be at the national level, while in the craft union the power tends to rest more in the hands of the locals.

This difference is reflected in the resulting pay structures. For example, the union wage scale (for nonincentive jobs) agreed to by the United Steelworkers and USX Corporation can be seen in Table 4–1. Notice that the hourly rates range from $9.876 to $14.199. A laborer would be at the lower end of the pay scale, while a roller in an 80-inch hot strip rolling mill would be at or near the

TABLE 4–1
*Hourly rates for nonincentive jobs agreed to between USS Division of USX
Corporation and United Steelworkers of America (AFL-CIO).*

Job Class	Hourly Rate	Job Class	Hourly Rate
1–2	$ 9.876	19	$12.173
3	10.011	20	12.308
4	10.146	21	12.443
5	10.281	22	12.578
6	10.416	23	12.713
7	10.511	24	12.848
8	10.686	25	12.983
9	10.821	26	13.118
10	10.957	27	13.253
11	11.092	28	13.389
12	11.227	29	13.924
13	11.362	30	13.659
14	11.497	31	13.794
15	11.632	32	13.929
16	11.767	33	14.064
17	11.902	34	14.199
18	12.037		

Source: Agreement between USS Division of USX Corporation and the United Steelworkers of America, Production and Maintenance Employees, Feb. 1, 1987.

upper end of the scale. The important thing about an agreement of this kind is its broad national reach. This contract involved, on the union side, the presidents of 35 to 40 union locals, and it has an impact on about 25 different localities in about 7 different states.

Under this type of contract, the roller would be paid at exactly the same rate in any plant in any of these localities. In other words, under such industrial union contracts involving large companies with multiplant operations, there are interjob differentials but no area differentials.

Workers in Craft Unions
The pay structure in craft unions is significantly different from that in the industrial unions. Data on wage rates (but not employee benefits) used to be collected by the Bureau of Labor Statistics, but no longer. The new figures shown in Table 4–2 are those of the Construction Labor Research Council. They cover both pay and employee benefits per hour. The figures, gathered by states and summarized by geographic regions, are more inclusive than the former BLS data in that they take in both Alaska and Hawaii.

The table shows the hourly wages plus employee benefits for each of the trades reported on by the Council, including the highest and lowest pay and benefits packages for each trade and also the percentage differential. The trades are

TABLE 4–2
Union wages and supplements in construction labor on January 1, 1988.

Trade	Low	High	% Diff.
Laborers	$10.04	$21.25	112
Painter	13.81	25.82	87
Electricians	16.61	30.80	85
Elevator Constructor	18.39	34.04	85
Cement Masons	13.91	25.35	82
Teamsters	13.24	22.73	72
Bricklayers	15.78	27.08	72
Iron Workers	16.21	27.76	71
Crane Operator	15.81	26.70	69
Sheet Metal	17.79	29.66	67
Insulators	18.37	30.23	65
Carpenters	14.83	24.40	65
Pipe Fitters	19.23	30.26	57
Plasterers	16.06	24.82	55
Mill Wrights	15.48	22.13	43
Boilermakers	18.96	25.86	36
Plumber	23.73	29.65	25

Note: Teamsters shown in the table are only those specifically covered in building contracts.
Source: Construction Labor Research Council.

ranked in order of the percentage differential from the highest to the lowest. As an example, the highest-paid union laborers in construction got $21.25 an hour while the lowest-paid got $10.04 an hour. As can be seen, the high was more than double the low figure for a 112 percent differential. At the other end of the scale, the highest-paid plumbers covered by union contracts got $29.65 an hour while the lowest-paid received $23.73 an hour, for a 25 percent differential. In general, the highs were for the Southwest Pacific or the Middle Atlantic regions, while the lows were for the Southeast or South Central regions. One qualifier on all of these observations is that the figures involve regional averages. Considerably greater spreads were typically reflected in the former BLS data, which were for metropolitan areas rather than the broader geographic regions.

With the earlier BLS data, direct comparisons were more easily made with the steelworker data since both concerned base pay, excluding employee benefits. Even though that is not the case with the data in Table 4–2, useful comparisons can be made. Without straining data that are not completely suitable for this particular purpose, it is still clear that there are, as in the case of the steelworkers contract, interjob differentials. The construction laborer tends to be at the bottom of the ladder, the crafts like electrician and plumber to be at the top, and other jobs such as carpenter to lie somewhere in between. More importantly, craft union pay packages reflect not only interjob but quite marked interarea differentials—in sharp contrast to the pay differentials for an industrial union as illustrated by the steelworkers' contract.

Union Concerns and the General Public

Success of union efforts has almost always depended on getting a measure of support from the general public. For example, contrast the support given to Walter Reuther in 1946 in the strike against General Motors with the evident lack of support accorded to the National Football League in 1987. It is difficult for a union to generate much sympathy when the workers involved are already drawing pay in the hundreds of thousands of dollars. To a somewhat lesser degree, such an attitude has also affected the Airline Pilots Association. Even unions whose workers do indeed suffer from pay and benefits inequities, as in the case of César Chávez and his United Farm Workers Union, often find it difficult to secure the necessary support of the general public.

To a greater or lesser degree, concerns of union members are shared by the general public. Such matters of mutual interest, but not always of agreement, relate to unemployment, inflation, strikes (especially of public workers), and concerns about relative pay (or pay equity).

Unemployment

The typical citizen as a worker wants a job with an adequate income and some degree of security. Most people prefer regular full-time work to part-time or intermittent work. When there is widespread unemployment, or when workers in a particular plant are laid off, payrolls are reduced. When plants are completely shut down and entire communities are affected, unemployment becomes a serious problem.

In recent years, economists have tended to emphasize the trade-off between unemployment and price increases. The general public, however, has felt that if there has to be inflation, at least there should be full employment. If, of course, the only cure conceived for unemployment is increased aggregate demand, it poses a problem. If there is much slack in the economy in terms of idle capacity, it can be argued that the increase in aggregate demand will tend to restore full employment without price increases, or at least that the increases can be held to small increments. Otherwise, a substantial reduction in the percentage of unemployment could result in a more rapid increase in prices, other things being equal.

Structural Unemployment.   In some cases unemployment may not be caused by inadequate demand. Instead, unemployment may be structural; that is, it may be avoidable if the job vacancies and the job seekers were brought together. Little can be done if a person is unwilling to move to a new region or to change occupations. However, more information about job openings must be available to the unemployed. In some cases employers hide the information, thinking that they can fill their own vacancies. Despite some gains in the development of new opportunities for minorities under union apprenticeship programs, some unions restrict unduly the number of job openings.

Information about job openings and job seekers is vital if we are to permanently lower unemployment levels. Such information could and should be readily available on a national basis. If executives in industry can have similar types of information relating to stock prices available on consoles on their desks, officials in federal, state, and local offices throughout the country should be able to have the needed information in equally accessible form, perhaps on a giant display board where anyone entering the office can see it.

Inflation

If prices rise too rapidly, the public reacts quickly and sales may be affected. Rising prices often result from rising costs, and some of the costs are the result of increases in pay and fringe benefits. So long as incomes are climbing, most people (workers included) continue to complain about rising prices but keep on paying them. Expectations of even higher prices induce them to buy now. Also, people tend to spend what they earn rather than save it. This lack of saving contrasts with high saving rates in other nations such as Japan. Often the ordinary citizen will refuse to buy items regarded as overpriced.

In certain cases, such as the rising cost of medical care, the response may become more political. If prices of medical care rise three or four times faster than the general cost of living, there can be little doubt that federal legislation encouraging group medical practice and fixed fees as well as reasonable (as opposed to excessive) salary schedules for physicians will become a reality.

The typical person seeks an adequate standard of living, and this is reflected in cost-of-living or escalator clauses in union contracts designed to offset higher consumer prices. Many pension plans provide similar indexing of benefits to protect retired employees.

Collective bargaining agreements between large companies and large unions tend to add to the cost-push inflation in those instances where the added costs are not offset by increased productivity. As we saw in Chapter 2, such cost effects make us less competitive in international markets.

Strikes and Government Workers

Public opposition to strikes stems from inconvenience and/or the lack of availability of goods or services, especially vital services such as police and fire protection, medical care, or the safety of our airways. Thus, there is greater opposition to strikes among government employees. The general public, however, is coming to recognize the right of a decent standard of living for all workers—including those in government employment—and unions have fought hard to obtain such rights for government employees. The public has a right to expect that pay and benefits for government workers be at levels that appear to be in line with comparable jobs in the same area.

The public seldom complains about the incomes of athletes or entertainers, perhaps because they are paid on a user basis rather than by income taxes. That is, people feel they have less say as to how their taxes are spent, whereas they don't have to go to a movie or sports event if they don't want to.

Concerns about Relative Pay

Most workers have an interest in relative pay—how one person is paid compared to another. This can be viewed in a somewhat narrow theoretical sense in terms of equity theory, or it can be viewed in a much larger context.

Equity Theory. Equity theory, essentially a theory relating to the justice of interpersonal relationships, emerged from a central thesis of Aristotle's theory of ethics. Applied to a work environment, the theory postulates that a worker judges equity by looking at the ratio between his input (work) and his outcome (pay). The worker compares his ratio with that for another worker. If the ratio is the same, equity prevails; if not, there is inequity. If he sees inequity, he will somehow attempt to restore equity.[4]

There is evidence that this reaction to inequity operates for positive as well as negative perceptions of equity. Studies of the worker's inequity reactions in the workplace have dealt with four situations: (1) underpayment on an hourly basis of compensation, (2) overpayment on an hourly basis, (3) underpayment on a piece-rate basis of compensation, (4) overpayment on a piece-rate basis. As an illustration of the positive case, overpayment in situation (2) might well be expected to cause the worker to increase the quantity and/or quality of his production. In situation (4), the expectation would be a lower quantity of output but higher quality. Robert Vecchio has confirmed this last hypothesis.[5]

Other research suggests that equity theory holds only under certain conditions:

1. Work-related behavior outside the actual work setting is at a minimum.
2. Outcomes are fixed.
3. Work groups have high cohesion.
4. Persons and comparison workers perform identical tasks.
5. Workers have limited aspirations toward promotion.
6. Both the workers and the job demands are characterized by relatively short time perspectives.
7. There is little secrecy concerning outcomes.[6]

Yoram Neumann has tested equity theory in a general way among a group of 80 managers under working environments with three different levels of uncertainty: low, moderate, and high. He concluded that

> equity theory may not apply universally for all situations but is rather restricted to tasks with a high level of perceived certainty. In other situations, where information concerning the task and its characteristics is quite unpredictable and less certain, the assessment of the reward system as equitable or inequitable can be a very difficult task.[7]

A Broader View. In a larger sense, workers compare the pay or pay/performance ratio not only for individuals in similar jobs, but also for individuals in dissimilar jobs, or groups of people.

At the lowest pay levels, the public's views have been reflected in minimum wage legislation. Nevertheless, increases in the minimum wage are often called inflationary. They are inflationary, as is any other wage increase, if not accompanied by increased productivity. Many union people argue that the added productivity is typically forthcoming because the employer will make capital improvements (e.g., add new machinery).

Many people believe that the minimum wage should eventually be set at a fixed percentage relationship to prevailing hourly wages in an area or industry. What economic rationale can justify a minimum wage that varies from 30 percent of prevailing average wage rates at one time to 70 percent at another, based on the current political makeup of Congress?

In addition to the minimum wage issue, the public is concerned with pay inequities relating to race and sex. We will examine these issues after briefly looking at the role of unions in relieving pay inequities.

Union Accomplishments in Removing Inequities in Pay and Benefits

Unions have accomplished much that probably would not have been accomplished in their absence.

1. Improved the wages, hours, and working conditions of millions of workers through collective bargaining.
2. Obtained many important employee benefits for workers.
3. Worked unceasingly for the health and safety of their members.
4. Developed strong grievance procedures to protect the rights of employees under the terms of their union contracts.
5. Devised ways of combating technological unemployment.

Union Actions of More Debatable Value

Some actions by unions are of debatable value, such as

1. Work rules of a feather-bedding nature which protect the worker at the expense of the customer—domestic or foreign.
2. Seniority rules—especially narrow departmental seniority—having adverse effects on minorities or women in situations where they happen to be the last to be hired, often for discriminatory reasons.
3. Across-the-board dollar pay increases instead of percentage increases. I shall comment on this point in Chapter 15.

Inequities in Pay and Benefits Relating to Race and Sex

With these thoughts in mind, we can turn to newer areas in which issues are yet to be resolved. Here the dominant action groups are the Southern Christian Leadership Conference (SCLC), the League of United Latin-American Citizens (LULAC), and the National Organization for Women (NOW)—rather than the American Federation of Labor and Congress of Industrial Organizations (AFL-CIO). And, of course, there are also coalitions of organizations jointly striving to bring about change. The dimensions of the remaining problems are strongly suggested by the relevant pay and employment ratios.

Trends in Median Money Incomes

Low incomes of blacks and other minorities compared with those of whites do not result entirely from discrimination, at least in the direct sense. However, our history of segregated housing, inadequate transportation and segregated public facilities, segregated and inferior education, as well as biased juries and artificial restraints on the voting process has contributed to the inequities we see today. The influence of these factors has not suddenly become extinct. Likewise, we must deal with an equally pervasive problem—equal rights for women.

The trends with respect to pay inequities based on race and sex are shown in Figure 4–1. This diagram shows median money incomes. That is, for any particular point on a line, half that group made more than the amount of money shown and the other half earned less.

Three observations can be made about Figure 4–1. First, throughout the entire period the lines retain the same order; that is, the lines show that whites are paid more than blacks* and that women are paid less than men. The lines never cross or reverse their relative positions. Second, the gap between the lines for white and black men is gradually narrowing. However, it appears that many decades will pass before the gap disappears. In contrast, the two lines for white and black women are getting much closer; the gap could disappear at almost any time in the future. The third observation is that the line for black men has more fluctuations reflecting business cycle changes, but these appear to be lessening.

The relative income position of blacks can also be illustrated by using percentages. In Table 4–3, for example, the 1948 median money income figures from Figure 4–1 for black men ($1,363) is divided by the figure for white men ($2,510) to get a percentage of 54.3 for men. This percentage means that black men aged 14 and over in 1948 earned a little more than half as much as white men. The figures in the other two columns of Table 4–3, for families and for women, are computed in the same way. The income of black families remained at slightly over half of white family incomes from 1948 to 1963. The percentage rose until 1970, after which the pattern was irregular, fluctuating between 60 and 65 percent. Several factors explain this pattern. When businesses moved out to the suburbs and away from blacks in the city centers, more blacks moved back to the South in search of jobs. They found jobs, but they were paid less. At the same time, the executive

---

*The Census Bureau uses the single term *black* to represent blacks and other minority races in the United States. The designation *black* does not refer to Spanish-surnamed Americans who can be included under any race. The information given in Figure 4–1 and Table 4–3 reflects Census Bureau usage.

TABLE 4–3
Black median money incomes as a percentage of white median incomes.

Year	Families	Men	Women
1948	53.5%	54.3%	43.5%
1949	51.1	48.5	46.3
1950	54.3	54.4	44.8
1951	52.7	55.1	42.5
1952	56.9	54.9	38.7
1953	56.1	55.3	58.6
1954	55.7	49.8	54.3
1955	55.2	52.7	52.2
1956	52.7	52.5	57.5
1957	53.5	53.0	57.9
1958	51.3	49.9	58.7
1959	51.7	47.1	61.6
1960	55.4	52.7	62.0
1961	53.4	51.7	67.1
1962	53.4	49.3	67.2
1963	53.0	52.0	67.0
1964	56.0	56.7	70.2
1965	55.1	53.9	72.8
1966	60.0	55.4	76.1
1967	61.9	57.2	80.3
1968	62.6	60.7	81.2
1969	63.3	59.0	84.7
1970	63.7	60.2	92.0
1971	63.0	60.1	89.6
1972	61.6	61.6	95.7
1973	60.4	63.0	93.1
1974	64.0	64.3	91.7
1975	65.4	63.1	92.4
1976	63.3	62.6	94.9
1977	60.6	61.2	88.5
1978	64.0	63.8	92.4
1979	60.7	64.9	93.2
1980	63.2	62.7	95.7
1981	62.1	63.5	92.0
1982	61.9	64.4	89.6
1983	62.1	63.8	88.2
1984	61.8	63.2	91.5
1985	64.0	66.4	88.0
1986	64.4	63.8	87.5

Note: Data are for black and other minority races except for persons of Hispanic origin. Figures for men and women include persons 14 years of age and older.
Source: U.S. Bureau of the Census, *Consumer Population Reports,* Series P-60, Consumer Income.

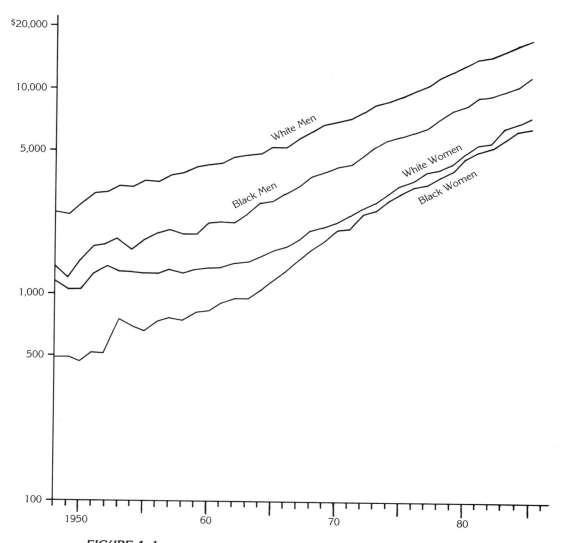

FIGURE 4–1
*Median money incomes for blacks and whites from the late 1940s to
1986. Data are for workers 14 years of age and older. Data for blacks
also include data for other minority races in the United States,
excluding Spanish-surnamed individuals. (From U.S. Bureau of the
Census,* Consumer Population Reports, *Series P-60,* Consumer
Income.*)*

71

branch of the federal government changed its attitude toward antipoverty measures such as the Community Action Programs and the OEO Job Corps Centers. At these centers, such as the one at San Marcos, Texas, blacks and others in need of work had been able to acquire training under conditions where the expectations of getting a job after completion of training were high.

Black men's incomes as a percentage of white men's incomes followed a similar path to that traced by the ratio for families, where more than one member may be in the labor force. The two series—black men and black families—both start at around 55 percent and end up somewhat over 60 percent through the 1970s. The path for men seems more uncertain, with recession-caused dips in several years.

The ratio of black women's income to white women's income has, as we would expect from the closing of the gap in the money values we saw earlier, been rising. While in 1948 the ratio was less than 45 percent, it reached almost 96 percent in 1972 and stayed above 90 percent during most of the 1970s. However, this rising ratio results as much from the rising relative income positions of women (as compared with men in general) as it does from the rising income of black women. This aspect will be explored later.

Changing Employment Shares of Four Minority Groups

One way in which pay and benefits improvements come about is through increased employment opportunities. To be able to define these opportunities, the Equal Employment Opportunity Commission (EEOC) accumulates data that show what share each ethnic minority has in various occupational groups. These data are derived from reports required to be made to the commission under the law. Because they strongly represent the largest companies in the private sector, the data tend to be biased. Only employers of 100 or more employees are required to file, excluding agricultural and private household workers, government employees, and most construction workers. Despite such limitations, the data are still useful.

With the aid of EEOC data, it is possible to explore some of the employment ratios for several different minorities and to compare minorities with one another. Employment ratios for four different ethnic groups are shown in Table 4–4.

The figures in Table 4–4 can be interpreted in two interesting ways. As an example, officials and managers in 1966 were 0.9 percent black, 0.6 percent Spanish-surnamed Americans, 0.3 percent Asian Americans, and 0.1 percent American Indians. From this comparison we can see that in 1966 blacks accounted for most of the minority employment in this group. Figures can also be compared over time. For Asian Americans, the employment share for officials and managers went from 0.3 percent in 1966 to 1.5 percent in 1986, quintupling their share. For black Americans, the corresponding change was from 0.9 percent to 4.7 percent, more than quintupling. So, for the period from 1966 to 1986, blacks gained more rapidly for this occupational group.

TABLE 4–4
Minority shares of employment in various occupational groups in 1966 and 1986.

Occupational Group	Blacks		Spanish-surnamed Americans*		Asian Americans*		American Indians	
	1966	1986	1966	1986	1966	1986	1966	1986
Officials & managers	0.9%	4.7%	0.6%	2.5	0.3%	1.5%	0.1%	0.3%
Professionals	1.3	4.7	0.8	2.2	1.3	4.3	0.1	0.2
Technicians	4.1	9.4	1.4	4.0	0.9	3.2	0.2	0.4
Sales workers	2.4	9.9	1.4	5.0	0.4	1.5	0.2	0.3
Office and clerical	3.5	13.3	1.6	5.4	0.6	2.2	0.1	0.4
Skilled craft	3.6	9.0	2.0	5.7	0.3	1.2	0.2	0.5
Operatives	10.8	17.1	3.1	7.8	0.3	2.0	0.2	0.5
Laborers	21.1	19.5	6.1	12.6	0.5	2.0	0.4	0.5
Service workers	23.0	24.3	4.0	9.7	0.8	2.6	0.3	0.5
All occupational groups	8.2	12.3	2.5	5.8	0.5	2.3	0.2	0.4

*For 1986, some persons formerly classified as Spanish-surnamed Americans were transferred to the Asian (or Pacific Islander) group. For national data, the effect would not invalidate trends described in the text.
Note: Small differences from published data reflect rounding.
Source: Equal Employment Opportunity Commission, EEO-1 Reports.

Using the first type of comparison for 1966, we find that blacks had larger shares of employment than any of the other three minorities in all occupations except one. They tied with Asian Americans in the share of professional employees. In 1986 blacks held onto their leads and regained the lead with respect to the professional group. Asian Americans, however, continued to have a large share of employment in this category (at least compared with other minorities).

Rates of increase from 1966 to 1986 in shares held by each minority in each occupational group varied. Blacks more than quintupled shares among officials and managers, a faster rate of advance than for other minorities. They also raced ahead faster than other minorities for professional and sales personnel. In skilled crafts blacks doubled their shares, but other groups increased their shares more rapidly. American Indians scored the fastest pace among office and clerical workers. Asian Americans quadrupled their shares of operatives, faring better in this respect than other minority groups. For laborers, blacks reduced their shares to their benefit, while other groups increased their shares, affecting them adversely. All groups increased their shares of service work, with a probable adverse effect.

Minority employees are often hurt by seniority clauses in union contracts. Because they have been excluded for so long from certain occupational groups, they have fewer years of seniority and thus are laid off first. Here affirmative action under the EEOC and union contract provisions come into conflict. Even when union contracts provide for seniority on a plantwide basis, the injustice of barring the employee from being hired in the first place is compounded when the clause forces the employee to be laid off first. A suggested cure would be to attach seniority to the individual rather than to the job. That is, seniority could be tied to the individual's total work experience, perhaps by means of the employee's social security records. Then, an older employee who leaves one job to join another company is not forced to start at the bottom of the ladder in the new firm. Although present seniority practices may please those now in the organization—both union and management—a strong case can be made that such practices are not in the public interest because of adverse effects on productivity. An alternative in the case of minorities and women would be to institute a system providing constructive seniority under federal law. Where the EEOC finds that any group has been excluded from a particular class of employment, any member of such a group joining the organization would be given automatic constructive seniority for the period of time when he or she normally might have otherwise joined the company within that employment class. Where it is difficult to determine the time period, a flat amount such as 1 to 3 years might be awarded.

Employment Shares of Black Men

Black men's employment shares for each occupational group, in the two years for which the EEOC tabulated the results, are given in Table 4–5. Between 1966 and 1986, black men increased their employment shares in every major occupational group except laborers and service workers. They also increased slightly their overall share of all occupational groups. The decrease in shares in the laborer

TABLE 4–5
Black men's employment shares in 1966 and 1986.

Occupational Group	1966	1986
Officials & managers	0.7%	2.8%
Professionals	0.7	1.9
Technicians	1.5	3.9
Sales workers	1.0	3.5
Office & clerical	0.9	2.4
Skilled craft	3.2	7.6
Operatives	8.3	10.3
Laborers	17.5	12.7
Service workers	13.2	11.0
All occupational groups	5.7	5.9

Note: Small differences from published data reflect rounding.
Source: Equal Employment Opportunity Commission, EEO-1 Reports.

and service worker groups probably benefited them economically because these are activities in which there are many blacks and they earn too little.

Employment Shares of Black and White Women

The EEOC data on employment shares in different occupational groups can also be used to explore the opportunities given to women. Employment shares for both white and black women have changed significantly between 1966 and 1986 (Table 4–6).

Among white women, the share of jobs in office and clerical work was still twice the share they had of all occupations in 1986. For black women, their share

TABLE 4–6
Women's employment shares in 1966 and 1986.

Occupational Group	White Women		Black Women	
	1966	1986	1966	1986
Officials & managers	9.1%	21.9%	0.2%	1.9%
Professionals	13.1	38.3	0.6	2.8
Technicians	27.7	34.8	2.6	5.5
Sales workers	36.4	46.6	1.4	6.4
Office & clerical	68.2	66.5	2.6	10.9
Skilled craft	5.6	7.3	0.4	1.4
Operatives	24.0	23.8	2.5	6.9
Laborers	18.7	22.7	3.6	6.8
Service workers	31.7	35.6	9.8	13.3
All occupational groups	27.9	34.6	2.5	6.3

Note: Small differences from published data reflect rounding.
Source: Equal Employment Opportunity Commission, EEO-1 Reports.

in clerical work was close to the share for all occupations in 1966 but almost 50 percent more than the all-occupation share in 1986. Over this period, the white proportion remained the same, while the black share quadrupled. While office jobs do not pay as well as managerial or professional jobs, they pay better (at least for full-time employees) than many other jobs.

For laborers, the white shares in both years were less than the white shares for all occupations, while the black shares in this group exceeded the all-occupation ratios. These figures help to explain in part lower incomes for black women. From 1966 to 1986, however, black women increased their share of all occupational groups 2½ times compared with a much slower advance for white women.

In the service worker group, shares for both black and white women—already in excess of all-occupation averages—increased from 1966 to 1986. This change hurt both groups economically.

In the operative group, blacks more than doubled their shares and whites showed little change. According to U.S. Bureau of the Census data, women operatives tend to earn less than laborers. Thus, while the ratio changes in this group probably did not affect the median income for white women, the median income for black women most likely decreased.

In both 1966 and 1986, white women had larger shares of sales occupations than they did for all occupational groups. Black women had a smaller share of this group than their overall share in 1966, but in 1986 sales and overall shares were about the same. Nevertheless, shares in this group increased for both whites and blacks over this period, with the increase for the latter being more than fourfold. It is important to keep in mind, however, that women tend to work as salesclerks rather than as traveling industrial salespersons, which are jobs typically held by men. Pay for women in these jobs is low compared with what they might earn in several other occupational groups. Thus, the increases in employment shares, especially for black women, would tend to lower their incomes.

Among the higher paying occupational groups (professionals, managers, technicians, and skilled craft workers), black women in each case increased their shares from 1966 to 1986. The increases ranged from more than doubling for technicians to nine times as large a share for officials and managers. For the skilled crafts, black shares more than tripled, and they more than quadrupled for professional occupations. In these occupational groups, white women advanced less rapidly in their shares than black women.

Comparable Worth and Income Trends by Sex

Much of the foregoing discussion tends to confirm in terms of occupational employment and earnings trends what we observed earlier in the chapter—a narrowing of the gap between the incomes of white women and black women. This naturally raises the question: What about the much larger gap between the income of men and women?

Figure 4–2 shows women's median money incomes as a percentage of men's for all women workers and for those who are year-round full-time workers.

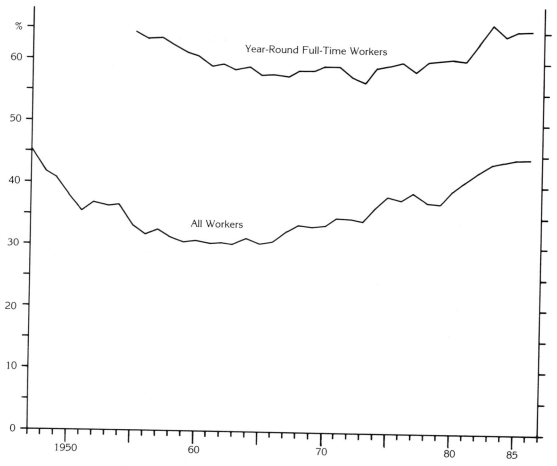

FIGURE 4–2
Women's median money incomes as a percentage of men's median incomes. Data for year-round, full-time workers are compared with all women workers. (From U.S. Bureau of the Census, Consumer Population Reports, Series P-60, Consumer Income.)

It is clear that women who work year-round on a full-time basis are relatively better off as to income than are women workers in general (which includes part-time workers). As to the *trends* shown in the diagram, a trough in the percentages for all women workers appears to have been reached in the early 1960s. After that, the percentage rises (even though it is still below 40 percent) until the 1980s. For year-round full-time working women the percentage also appears to be rising, but percentage levels remain low.

Comparable Worth: An Overview

The problem of comparable worth, while closely related to the field of job evaluation, has much wider ramifications. We shall consider it here in overview, in terms of the patterns of jobs in one particular industry, and with respect to recent developments in the United States and abroad. Finally, we shall examine a few alternative solutions.

We have already seen the overall trends in pay both for full-time year-round workers and for women workers in general and looked at employment shares for women. But how do women perceive the problem?

The Problem as Seen by Women. Laura Gasaway, a professor of law at the University of Oklahoma, describes the problem of comparable worth as follows:

> Working women . . . are subject to a vicious cycle. Occupational segregation creates crowding and controls the woman's initial job assignment. The initial job assignment in turn determines promotion opportunities and perpetuates occupational segregation. Crowding intensifies job segregation, reduces wages, and contributes to unemployment. All of these interrelated factors encourage wage discrimination and the undervaluation of women's work. This intricate maze of traditional employment practices consigns women to poor pay and dead-end jobs.[8]

The problem is seen as a nexus of unequal pay and unequal employment opportunities:

> Job segregation will continue, however, if large salary differentials remain. These wage differentials discourage men from entering female-dominated occupations. In addition, women who apply for male-intensive jobs meet with hostility that, in part, results from the perception that a female is displacing a male to whom the job rightfully belongs. If employers compensated both men's and women's jobs on the basis of comparable worth, there would be less impetus for males to seek traditional male jobs and less hostility toward women seeking the same jobs. Thus, a policy of comparable worth actually encourages job integration, and may in fact be more successful than a policy of equal employment opportunity standing alone.[9]

The Problem as Seen by Management. George T. Milkovich, who favors management's viewpoint on comparable worth, argues with the latter definition of the problem. He sees at least two basic policy options:

> One is to reduce the earnings gap between men and women by requiring employers and unions to raise the rates for relatively lower paid jobs (in which larger proportions of women have traditionally been employed) to match rates for higher paid, "male dominated" jobs. The other is to avoid tampering with the vast array of wage structures and wage determination systems found in the economy and, instead, rely upon the removal of discriminatory barriers that have historically hindered women's entry into the higher paid jobs, through vigorous enforcement of equal employment and affirmative action practices.[10]

The Problem as Seen by a Union Leader. In contrast to the preceding view, many union leaders are committed to the idea of equal pay for equal work in a broad philosophical way. For example, James Cary, testifying on behalf of the Industrial Union Department of the AFL-CIO, argues that the comparable worth approach would eliminate

1. Paying lower wages to women on the same job as men.
2. Changing a man's job by modifying it slightly with a much lower rate of pay for women, a rate not justified by the modification.
3. Paying women lower wages irrespective of the value of the work performed. This occurs in situations where men and women work in different types of jobs in the same plant.[11]

Segregation of Jobs by Sex: An Example

An industry wage survey of the men's and boys' suits and coats industry, conducted by the Bureau of Labor Statistics, illustrates the problem of comparable worth.[12]

The survey covered over 61,000 production workers in the industry, of whom roughly 48,000 were women and 13,000 were men. Although scattered over all regions of the United States, some 27,000 workers were in the Middle Atlantic states and another 13,000 in the southeastern states. The average hourly rate was $5.80 for the men and $4.70 for the women. In all but one of the 26 job classes paying less than $5.50 per hour, there were higher proportions of women; in all job classes paying $5.50 or more per hour there were higher percentages of men. Furthermore, of the 38 specific occupations for which pay information was given both for men and women, the women's rates were lower in every instance except one, the job of spreader. In this job there was a difference of $.10 per hour: $5.32 for the women and $5.22 for the men.

The Pecking Order. Some of these pay differences may be due to seniority, but it is hard to tell. At least as important as seniority, however, is what must be realistically termed the pecking order—that is, who gets what job.

Figure 4–3 shows the pecking order in terms of average hourly earnings. These are straight-time earnings and do not include overtime or shift differentials or similar complicating factors. The three spindles portray those jobs that are mostly handled by men, those that are mostly handled by women, and those that are shared. Shared jobs are those in which 40 to 60 percent of the workers on the job are women. Those jobs in which more than 60 percent of the workers are women are considered mostly women jobs, and those in which less than 40 percent of the workers are women are categorized as mostly men jobs.

From the diagram we can see that there are many different jobs in the category of sewing machine operator. Out of 23,600 operators who work on coats, over 22,200 are women. Another 4,000 operators work on trousers, and 3,900 of them are women. Both of these categories are subdivided into various jobs, such as basters and pocket setters and tackers. Instead of being shown individually

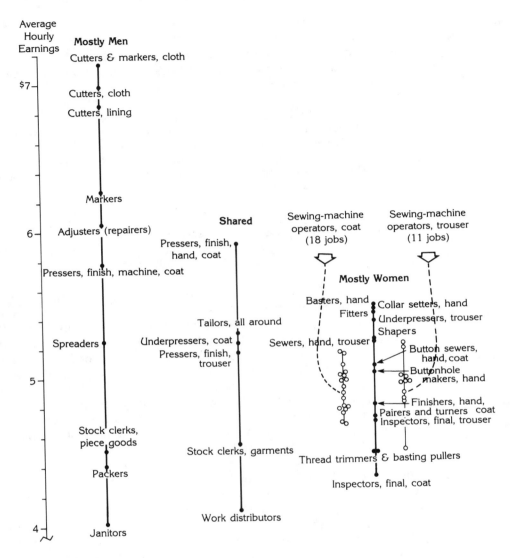

FIGURE 4–3
Average hourly earnings for various jobs in the men's and boys' suit and coat manufacturing industry. See text for explanation of the three categories of jobs shown. (From U.S. Bureau of Labor Statistics, Industry Wage Survey: Men's and Boys' Suits and Coats, April 1979, Bulletin 2073, October 1980, Table 4 and pp. 9 and 10.)

80

with labels in Figure 4–3, these jobs are grouped into two strings of open circles on either side of the spindle representing mostly women jobs. Sewing machine operators working on coats are subdivided into 18 jobs, and those sewing trousers are subdivided into 11 jobs.

The highly structured nature of these production jobs is evident in the diagram. For jobs in which there are mostly men, top pay exceeds $7.00 per hour. This rate is far above the top women's job, which pays about $5.50 per hour. While it is true that some of the mostly men jobs are the lowest paying, these jobs require practically no skills at all. One shared job—work distributor—is lower paying than any of the jobs in which there are mostly women. The individual in this job does not perform the work but just distributes it. Also relatively low on the pay scale are the mostly men jobs of stock clerk, piece goods, and the shared job of stock clerk, garments. An interesting puzzle concerns the position of the job of inspector final, coat. If the company wants its inspection done well, why is that job paid the most poorly of any of the jobs held mostly by women?

Legal and Political Action in the United States

For a number of years there was a legal struggle to determine how the Equal Pay Act of 1963 applied to Title VII of the Civil Rights Act of 1964 with regard to equality of pay for women. The Equal Pay Act (see Chapter 2) stressed equal pay for equal work (not comparable work or work of equal value), defining equal work as that which (1) requires equal skill, equal effort, and equal responsibility, and (2) is performed under similar working conditions. Under the Bennett Amendment, also passed in 1963, the equal work standard established in the Equal Pay Act was carried over into Title VII. Early court decisions tended not to favor a comparable worth approach but to confine remedies to situations involving equal pay for identical or nearly identical work.

The Gunther Decision. In 1981 the U.S. Supreme Court's decision in County of Washington v. Gunther[13] changed the situation. In this case four female guards in a county jail were being paid 70 percent of what the male guards were receiving. There were some differences in the duties, with the male guards handling more prisoners and the female guards devoting more time to clerical duties. However, the county had evaluated the female guards' work as being worth 95 percent rather than 70 percent of the work performed by the male guards. So the female guards brought suit, charging intentional sex discrimination under Title VII of the Civil Rights Act. They argued that the Bennett Amendment was not restricted to cases involving equal work, while the county argued the contrary. A U.S. district court ruled that the guards could not get equal pay status since the jobs were not identical. However, the court of appeals reversed the lower court's decision, and the U.S. Supreme Court supported the court of appeals. The Supreme Court held that claims of sex-based discrimination could be brought under Title VII, even where there was no equal but higher paying male job, so long as the suit is not based on "seniority, merit, quantity or quality of production, or any other factor than sex.[14]"

Action in Idaho and Washington.   Action on the idea of equal pay for jobs of comparable worth has occurred mostly in the public sector. For example, the state of Idaho installed a job evaluation plan, using the Hay guide chart–profile plan, for state employees. Wages for clerical workers increased 10 to 20 percent after the system was implemented, while wages for other job categories stayed about the same.[15] An in-depth comparable worth study of state civil service jobs in the state of Washington found salaries for "women's jobs" to be only 80 percent of those for "men's jobs" of similar worth. Because of a change in governors, no action was taken in this instance.[16]

Action in California and Other States.   Action on comparable worth in three states—California, Massachusetts, and Michigan—is worth noting.

California has enacted legislation to insure that state employees in "female-dominated" jobs are paid the same amount as employees in "male-dominated" jobs where the work is comparable in value. "Female-dominated" jobs are those in which at least 70 percent of the workers are women.[17]

The San Jose, California, city council used a comparability index to rate municipal jobs. Rating factors included accountability, problem solving, stress, environmental hazards, and general know-how. The study revealed that the work of city-employed nurses was comparable to that of fire-truck mechanics, even though nurses were paid $772 per month less. Other women were earning 2 to 10 percent less than the average for all city jobs. Shortly after the Gunther decision, city workers went out on strike. The city settled, agreeing to spend $1.5 million to correct pay disparities.[18]

Later in 1981 in San Jose, California, the California Nurses Association (CNA) went on strike against four hospitals. The CNA labor representative, Maxine Jenkins, defined the issue in this way:

> The average RN should be earning at a level that reflects the worth of her work in comparison with jobs involving comparable stress, skill, knowledge and responsibility.[19]

Significantly, the CNA rejected the traditional market approach to collective bargaining. Jenkins offered this explanation:

> The market approach ignores the fact that nurses' salaries are pegged too low in the first place because nursing is a predominantly women's profession. By focusing on salaries that other hospitals offer, most contract negotiations perpetuate inequities.[20]

Instead, the CNA espoused the equity method. This method, according to Jenkins, assumes that previous pay levels and policies are irrelevant. It sets salary goals by evaluating the content of the work and its comparability with other jobs.[21]

She also called attention to the wages of skilled workers on expansion programs under way at San Jose hospitals. Carpenters and mechanics were making $17 to $20 per hour, and construction workers were making $15 per hour, "nearly 50 percent more than most registered nurses."[22]

In addition to California, both Massachusetts and Michigan have instituted studies of civil service salaries. The Michigan study rates each job under a point system which includes the factors of education, experience, skill, supervision, and decision making. The study has revealed many jobs that are structured by sex.[23]

International Action

Internationally, the International Labour Organization's Convention No. 100 and the European Economic Community's Article 119 of the Treaty of Rome both deal with the subject of comparable worth. Of the two, Article 119 has had a broader application. The official position of the ILO is broader and more flexible than "equal pay for substantially similar work."[24] The commission (the secretariat) of the European Economic Community, however, in its 1979 report made clear that it interpreted Article 119 not in terms of the same work but rather work of equal value (or comparable worth).[25]

The commission describes favorably a law enacted in the Netherlands in 1975 that provides for equal pay for work of equal value. As Janice Bellace reports, the law

> does not require a woman complainant to compare herself to a man who is in the same firm working on substantially similar work. Instead, a female complainant may compare her wage to that commonly paid by the employer to a male employee performing work of equal value or broadly similar work. If no such comparable man is employed, the female claimant may attempt to find a comparable man in a similar company, although the wage scales of that company would be compared to those prevailing in her company. The Dutch statute . . . states that value is to be determined by reference to the work's value under a job evaluation system. If the particular job in question has not been evaluated under a system, the statute provides that the job's value will be determined "on an equitable basis" by the Equal Pay Commission of the Netherlands.[26]

A Way Out: Improved Job Evaluation

Recent events in the United States and abroad suggest that establishing an equitable system of job evaluation is an important step in measuring the comparable worth of different jobs.

Job Evaluation and Pricing. The purpose of job evaluation is to establish a system of internal equity among jobs in the organization. But methods of job evaluation are not without their weaknesses. The guideline method, for example, as we shall see in Chapter 6, tends to give too much emphasis to the market and not enough to internal equity.

It is also important to reconcile internal and external job worth in the process of job pricing. In a scatter diagram, as long as both points and pay rates range from a low to a high and both points and pay are going in the same *direction* (i.e., there is some degree of positive correlation between the two series), the precision of the fit is not too important. In fact, if external and internal job worths fit exactly, a probable destruction of the internal equity structure is implied. If substantial parts of the market (or markets) are artificially distorted to begin with, an exact fit merely perpetuates the distortion. As an example of distorted market rates, consider the typical pay rates in the nursing field.

Validation. In Chapter 5 we shall consider the problems of validation and reliability that affect job analysis and job evaluation. The process of validation can be mathematical, a matter of human consensus, or a combination of the two. Now a crucial question is: Does agreement of the points in a job evaluation point plan with market rates of pay constitute validation of the plan if the market itself is invalid?

In the validation process, Donald Schwab concentrates on what he describes as job evaluation practice (as proposed to theory). He distinguishes between key jobs (for which market rates can readily be determined) and nonkey jobs. He divides the validation process into development, which is performed only on key jobs, and implementation. In the latter step, the results of development are applied to nonkey jobs. In the development phase, factors are identified, *a priori* weights are assigned to each factor, and factors and weights are modified to obtain a correspondence between key job wages and job evaluation results. When the relationship does not appear suitable,

> several procedures are commonly employed to increase the correspondence. First, the sample may be changed through the addition, or more likely the deletion, of key jobs. Second, factors may be added or deleted. Third, jobs may be reevaluated and, finally, the *a priori* weighting system may be changed.[27]

In Schwab's method, the point pattern from the job evaluation plan is simply altered to suit market rates of pay.

Other mathematical approaches to validation work only with the elements of the job evaluation plan itself. For example, the Factor Evaluation System (FES) developed by the federal government (see Chapter 7) uses such a technique. Its stated objectives, which were accomplished, were to obtain

1. A reliable and valid hierarchical alignment of a representative sample of white-collar jobs that were interval scaled in terms of their "whole-job" classification value relative to each other.
2. A valid and weighted set of job factors.[28]

The undertaking involved 64 rating panels of five members each. Thirty-two panels rank-ordered 147 benchmark job descriptions, while another 32 panels rank-ordered the same jobs by factor. In essence, the whole-job rankings served as the criterion, but only after testing for (1) interrater reliability, (2) intrarater reliability, and (3) rank-rerank reliability. Validity of the job factors was established using multiple correlation with whole-job values as the dependent variable.[29]

The human element of consensus validation was not entirely absent in the development of the Factor Evaluation System. At one point only five tentative factors were being considered, and these proposed factors were reviewed by those employee unions and professional organizations with exclusive recognition.[30] On the other hand, little has been published about the composition of the 64 panels by race, nationality, or sex. In order to evaluate better the consensus validity of FES factors, this type of information is needed. David Thomsen stresses this point:

> It is my opinion that several of the factors can predict sex—for example, personal contacts—to a greater extent than other factors. And it is my understanding that the weights and point combinations should raise concerns for racial minority groups who have historically held "laborers" jobs.[31]

Because of the lack of information in this particular case, we can only conclude that purely mathematical validation is not enough if minority groups or women are inadequately represented in the groups doing the rating.

Avoiding Discrimination on Account of Race, Sex, or Age.   Thomsen suggests specific rules to eliminate discrimination in job evaluation plans:

1. Use a single plan where possible rather than multiple plans.
2. Select factors that reflect the working environment and the organization's objectives.
3. Free factors, scales, and weights of bias—for any one factor as well as the sum of the weightings.
4. Eliminate as much as possible subjective measurement error in connection with the data fed into the model.
5. Eliminate bias in the evaluation committee that reviews a job evaluation model's errors and predictions.
6. Sustain an updated system of job measurements to insure that bias has not indirectly entered into the system.[32]

To reinforce these efforts, special committees could be used to help weed out biases in the plan. For example, a committee made up entirely of women or entirely of one minority group would elect its own chair. This leader may even be an outsider. A group of blacks might be accompanied by one of their national or prominent local leaders, a group of women by a delegate from the National Organization for Women (NOW), or a group of older people by a delegate from the Gray Panthers.

Another suggestion would be to break out the data for women or a particular minority group in the organization and compare that group's pay structure with the structure for the entire organization.

Another problem with differences in pay arises from the fact that women tend to work in low-wage firms and men work in high-wage firms.[33] Perhaps high- and low-wage firms should be brought together in an area rather than an industry cooperative plan in order to minimize such pay differentials.

Another Solution: Collective Bargaining and Arbitration

Solving the problem of comparable worth through collective bargaining and arbitration is hindered by the small percentage of women in labor unions.[34] Where disputes over pay result in grievances, arbitration can certainly be used to handle them in a systematic way. There are, however, some disadvantages to the arbitration route, as cited by Herbert Northrup:

1. It is quite expensive.
2. The procedure can be quite lengthy, and settlements lag while unrest and dissatisfaction continue.
3. To the detriment of good relationships and industrial peace, excessive resort to arbitration clogs the machinery and prevents cases from being heard and expeditiously determined.
4. It means a third party establishes the job relationships and rates of pay.[35]

A Third Approach

Those who believe that not enough progress has been made in the area of equal pay and comparable worth want to push for new laws and executive orders and take legal action in the courts. For those who desire a society with less government intervention, a better solution would be for all organizations to strive for better, bias-free job evaluation plans.

Working Conditions for Women

Whether women are full-time or part-time workers depends on economic needs, marital status, and other factors. Fewer married women, especially those with young children, participate in the labor force (in the economic sense) than single women. But in 1981, 48 percent of married women with children under 6 years of age worked outside the home.[36] A higher percentage of black than white women work, and a larger proportion of black women work for economic reasons.

Family Aspects of Pay

A recent study of the economic well-being of men versus women contrasting two selected years—1959 and 1983—concludes that despite large structural changes in the economy and major antidiscrimination legislation, the economic well-being of women did not improve . . . The women to men ratio of money income almost doubled, but women had less leisure time while men had more, an increase in the proportion of adults not married made more women dependent on their own income, and women's share of financial responsibility for children rose.[37]

Victor R. Fuchs, a Stanford professor and research associate with the National Bureau of Economic Research, argues that sex differences in the labor market are likely to persist as long as parents are responsible for children and this responsibility is borne disproportionately by women.[38] For women with child-rearing responsibilities, the overcrowding earlier cited by Gassaway as tending to depress market rates of pay for certain women's jobs appears to be importantly linked to the number of children in the household. Fuchs finds that not only do women with children earn less per hour than those with no children, but that the average hourly wage drops with each additional child. Conversely, he finds that men with children have higher hourly earnings than those without children and that for men there is no systematic relation between number of children and earnings. Fuchs goes on to explain that

> even when mothers stay in the labor force, responsibility for children frequently constrains their choice of job; they accept lower wages in exchange for shorter or more flexible hours, location near home, limited travel, and the like.[39]

Some attempts to restructure the workweek could remedy the problems of working women with home responsibilities, but others would not. For example, many full-time workers who commute might prefer a 4-day workweek and a 10-hour day, but this arrangement might be unacceptable to a worker with young children. More apt solutions are either employee-chosen staggered hours or flexitime.

Flexitime

Flexitime, the more significant of the two arrangements for working women with home responsibilities, started in Germany in the mid-1960s, spread rapidly in Europe, and became popular in the United States in the 1970s.[40] Under flexitime the period during which an organization is open for business (for example, from 6 A.M. to 8 P.M.) is known as the bandtime or bandwidth. The plan works this way:

> A "core" time is established during which all employees must be on the job each day. They may arrive and depart, however, whenever they wish during flexible periods that lie beyond the core time and are still within the total bandtime or bandwidth. Furthermore, their choice of schedules within these limitations may vary daily. In some organizations, employees must work enough combined core and flexible time to complete a full workday each day. In others the length of the workday may vary, as long as a stipulated number of hours is completed each week, fortnight, or month. . . . Lunch hours may be fixed or flexible.[41]

Advantages of Flexitime.   Although flexitime benefits all workers in general, it is especially relevant to a better working environment for women. Its advantages, which apply both to the private and public sectors, include

1. Increased morale.
2. Increased control over work scheduling and processes.
3. Reduced commuting time.
4. Better fit to personal life style. (Example: suits early risers as well as late starters.)
5. Reduced absenteeism.
6. Reduced tardiness.
7. Reduced turnover.
8. Reduced overtime.
9. Reduced costs.
10. Increased productivity.

These advantages must be qualified, however. The flexitime idea is not suitable for certain work settings, as we shall see. Also, we must examine the quality of the research on which these conclusions are based and the reality of some of the alleged advantages.

Suitability in Certain Work Settings.   Experienced users of flexitime state that it is

> unfeasible under certain conditions—in the case of multiple shifts on assembly-line operations, in machine-paced work where continuous worker coverage was needed, in small organizations with only a few workers, and in operations requiring extensive communication and interfacing.[42]

Quality of Research.   Robert Golembiewski and Carl W. Proehl, Jr., summarized 32 studies of flexitime in the public sector and indicated that 23 of them included hard data (such as accounting records) as well as soft data (employee and supervisor opinions). However, they also pointed out that (1) only two studies used both an experimental and a control group; (2) only two studies incorporated statistical tests of the significance of the results; and (3) only two studies contained adequate longitudinal evidence.[43]

Questions as to Productivity and Other Factors.   Despite favorable published reports, doubts remain as to some alleged advantages of flexitime. These doubts relate mostly to claims of increased productivity, reduced turnover, and decreased costs. The results on productivity, for example, appear to be mixed.[44]

Part-Time Work
While less than 3 percent of men aged 25 to 64 work part-time voluntarily, one out of every five women does so.[45] But whether they work part-time voluntarily or

do so because full-time jobs are unavailable, they make an important contribution. Nancy Rotchford and Karlene Roberts found that

> managers who do employ part-time workers view part-time employment positively, reporting low absenteeism, approximately equal or lower turnover, and equal or in many cases higher productivity among part compared to full-time workers.[46]

One part-time working arrangement used by some employers is where two employees cover one particular job, each working half a day. As to the feasibility of this approach, Jo Hartley recommends conducting surveys and studies to determine

1. The percentage of employees who would voluntarily change from full- to part-time status if given the opportunity.
2. The number of new people who would enter the labor force if more or better part-time jobs were available.
3. Jobs particularly suitable for division.
4. The best ways to break down various types of jobs by time (part-day, part-week, or alternate week); by level of complexity; or by choice of the involved employees.
5. Management objections to part-time employment.
6. Present and potential management motives for utilizing part-time employment.[47]

Part-time workers usually receive fewer benefits than regular full-time employees. Many organizations that give employee benefits to part-timers reduce the amount of the benefit by proportioning it to hours worked. However, most organizations need to do more for the part-time worker.[48] Increased costs to management would be offset by improved employee morale, greater work force solidarity, and improved economic security for part-time workers. Another improvement, which would assure employees that the employer is giving equal pay for equal work, would be to provide proportionate seniority or merit pay increments to part-time as well as full-time workers.

Seniority
Unlike most men, women are often sporadic participants in the work force in the economic sense. That is, they may hold down a job for a few years, drop out to raise a family or for other reasons, and come back into the work force sometime later. Similar to the man-made conventional working day is the male-dominated union tradition of seniority. Unions and managements often struggle over seniority; management typically argues for departmental seniority, which tends to hold key employees in what are regarded as critical jobs, while unions more often argue for plantwide or areawide seniority. Either type of seniority still poses a serious obstacle to the woman who comes back into the job market and joins a dif-

ferent organization. She must build seniority all over again, losing any she might have gained from previous work experience. More thought needs to be given to individual career seniority, discussed earlier in this chapter. Present rigid seniority policies unfairly restrict the labor force reentrant who may often be more qualified in terms of experience than many of those already on the payroll.

Summary

Unions play an important role in the labor movement. The progress of unions in the United States has been marked by violence and bloodshed, and economic depressions have often destroyed unions. With the passage of the National Labor Relations Act in 1935 under Franklin D. Roosevelt and the rise of the industrial unions led by John L. Lewis, labor has played a new and more influential role. The percentage of unionized workers in the labor force rose from little more than 5 percent in 1932 to roughly 25 percent in the mid-1950s. In construction, public utilities, railroads, and much of the manufacturing sector, over 90 percent of the production and production-related workers are unionized in the largest plants. For this reason we cannot conclude that unions are necessarily in a long-range decline.

Mostly within the larger framework of the AFL-CIO, American unionism is characterized by a duality between industrial unions and craft unions. Industrial unions are organized plantwide, companywide, or industrywide—and pay scales for a particular job are often the same in any part of the United States. By contrast, craft unions such as those in the building trades are more often organized locally, and pay scales are characterized by pronounced interarea differentials.

To an important extent, unions depend on public support. At the same time, union members have concerns much in common with the general public. For example, they feel strongly about matters such as unemployment, inflation, strikes, and questions of relative pay.

Unemployment and its relation to job security is especially critical. Much unemployment is structural and cannot be remedied merely by the creation of more demand. Such unemployment can be avoided by a closer matching of job vacancies to job seekers. But actually doing this continues to be a major problem.

Inflation concerns union members, who often push for escalator clauses in union contracts. Collective bargaining contracts can result in pay increases leading to price increase, making the United States less competitive in international markets.

Strikes tend to be looked at askance by the general public where health and safety are involved—the strike by air traffic controllers and public response to it is a good example. There seems to be a feeling on the part of the public that government workers should not be allowed to strike at all, even though unions have pushed hard for this right. But the public is coming to realize the justice of a decent standard of living for all workers—even those in government.

Relative pay is a real concern for all workers. In situations where two workers are near each other in a plant, equity theory seeks to explain the reason for workers' attitudes. But pay equity in a broader sense does not lend itself to such a simple rationale. While differences in feelings between any two workers can be important, the more significant problems are between groups.

What have unions done to help resolve inequities in pay and benefits? The answer is, much: improvements in wages, hours, and working conditions through collective bargaining, substantial increases in employee benefits, improved health and safety measures, grievance procedures for the resolution of disputes while a union contract is in effect, and ways of combating technological unemployment.

Another vital question is whether the unions have done some things of debatable value. What about working rules that protect the worker at the expense of the customer, seniority rules having adverse effects on women and minorities, actions to curb foreign imports at the expense of the American consumer, and across-the-board dollar pay increases?

It is important to realize that new groups such as the Southern Christian Leadership Conference (SCLC), the League of United Latin-American Citizens (LULAC), and the National Organization for Women (NOW) are likely to play a more significant future role in resolving the large remaining inequities in pay and benefits which are tied in with problems of age, sex, race, and color.

Relative incomes of black families, black men, and black women, as well as those of other major minority groups, continue to lag behind the corresponding levels for whites.

Employment shares, a measure of employment opportunities, have increased for minority groups in almost every major occupational group since 1966. For the categories of laborers and service workers, however, the trends are conflicting. Employment shares for blacks in these groups have decreased, but the shares for other minority groups have increased. Black men's employment shares in the different occupation groups and changes in these shares help to explain in part the income changes for black men. Where seniority clauses in union contracts have the practical effect of excluding minorities from being retained or promoted, retroactive constructive seniority may be necessary to provide an equitable solution.

The shares of white and black women's employment in different occupation groups and changes in these shares help to explain income changes for women and the gap between the races. For women in general, their incomes as a percentage of men's incomes have risen slightly since the mid-1960s, but the trend for year-round, full-time workers is now in doubt.

The problem of comparable worth (equal pay for work of equal value) is evident in the gap between men's and women's median incomes. Industry studies by the Bureau of Labor Statistics show that job structuring in the men's and boys' suits and coats manufacturing industry (in the Middle Atlantic states as well as in the South) is heavily biased with regard to sex in a clear-cut pecking order. In general, women earn more in shared jobs (in which 40 to 60 percent of the workers are women) than in jobs dominated by women.

As the result of the struggle for comparable worth, market-based collective bargaining is being replaced by equity bargaining in an increasing number of situations. The California Nurses Association focused on this issue in their 1981 strike against San Jose hospitals.

Even though job evaluation typically involves subjective elements, it still is one of the best ways to achieve internal equity within the organization. Validation of job evaluation plans and the factors used should avoid reliance on market pricing, especially in situations where the effect is to reinforce discrimination. The problem of discrimination in pay on account of sex or race must be resolved along with problems relating to equal employment opportunity.

The Fuchs study strongly indicates that there are substantial differences in hourly earnings for women with child-care responsibilities depending on the number of children in the family and that this constrains women to accept lower pay for reasons such as shorter or more flexible hours, location nearer home, less travel, and so forth.

Flexitime, arranging the sharing of full-time jobs, and making part-time jobs more attractive are ways in which employers can improve working conditions for women. Women suffer unduly from conditions of part-time work. This can be ameliorated by offering proportionate seniority or merit pay increments and more employee benefits to part-timers, even if such benefits are reduced in proportion to hours worked. Present seniority clauses penalize labor force reentrants, who are more often women. Career seniority would provide a cure to this dilemma.

Case Study

Frick Department Stores

The Frick Department Stores corporation has four major stores. One is located in downtown Hammondville, a Southern city with a population of 500,000. The other three are in the outlying suburbs.

David Frick, Jr., chairman of the board and chief executive officer of Frick Department Stores, is the son of the founder, David Frick, Sr., who organized the original store 30 years earlier. David is philosophically allergic to unions—not an unusual sentiment in Hammond County.

Most of the top executives, including the store managers, have been with the company for many years and are well paid. For salesclerks and others in lower level jobs, it is a different story. The prevailing pay rates—salaries for the clerks and wages for the others—are below the rates for other stores or similar jobs in the community. Pay increases have been infrequent, and some employees have worked for the corporation for years without pay increases, despite the rising cost of living. A year or so ago the company reorganized, and the pay of some employees was cut. When pay increases do occur, they come at unpredictable times and appear to be calculated on a personal basis.

Except for a few of the higher ranking executives, most employees work a six-day week. During peak periods employees work overtime and get compensatory time off, but there is no premium pay for overtime. The company pays little in the way of employee benefits other than those which are required by law.

However, the company does provide a pension plan based on average pay and length of service.

While there have been few personnel changes in management, turnover at the lower levels has been above average for retail trading companies in the region.

Once in a while one or more of the employees receives a letter from a union representative explaining the benefits of joining a union and inviting him or her to visit with the representative. Frick and the store managers do their best to discourage any union activities, and once or twice there have been storewide meetings at which Frick or one of the store managers would tell the employees that they really had nothing to gain from joining a union.

Nonetheless, sentiment among the employees is slowly changing, and some employees have quietly signed up with the Service Employees International Union, which had sent out a letter inviting employees to join. A recent event has sparked further interest. About a year ago one of the salesclerks left to join the Marines. Ramón Martínez, who had worked in the stockroom, became the new salesclerk. Although he was encouraged to do the work, he was asked to continue to help out in the stockroom when needed. He waited for a pay increase as evidence of his new status as a salesclerk, but the increase never came through. When he asked the store manager about this, he got no satisfaction. Losing patience, he left the store, telephoned a union organizer for the SEIU, and arranged a meeting with him.

Role Assignment

You are Gustav Aronson, union organizer for the SEIU. You have just talked with Ramón Martínez and are now familiar with the facts as described here. What actions would you take next and why?

Case Study

A Matter of Professional Ethics

Ms. Stein is the new personnel assistant at Good Samaritan, a private general hospital in a southeastern coastal town of 50,000. She was hired upon graduation from State University with a degree in personnel administration, and her future seemed rosy indeed. The personnel department is made up of Stein, the personnel director, and the secretary-receptionist. Stein is responsible for all the interviewing, except for registered nurses (R.N.'s).

Among the materials given Stein on her first day on the job was a copy of a memo from Armstrong Snook, the administrator of Good Samaritan. From it she learned that no blacks were to be hired for nonunion positions within the hospital. The reason given for this policy was that it would prevent further unionization within nonunion positions. It seems that a few years ago a black switchboard operator organized other operators and brought in a union to represent them.

This memo shocked Stein. When she was hired, the personnel director hadn't told her of this policy. She confronted her boss, reminding him that it was in violation of the 1964 Civil Rights Act as well as contrary to her own beliefs. She even threatened to resign. The director reasoned that resigning would not solve the problem, saying that even if she resigned, someone else would be hired to carry out the policy. Although he didn't agree with the policy either, he believed that in time it might be changed. So Stein stayed on.

A year later, nothing had changed. In fact, things had gotten worse. An executive secretarial position was open, and Stein found that the applicants were being judged on appearance rather than work record or skills. One black, who had been turned down for this job, left abruptly, apparently angry.

Stein knew she couldn't go on this way. Either she had to resign or report the violations to the proper federal authority. Even so, she was afraid of being labeled in such a way that it could threaten her whole career. Just as she was leaving her desk to confront her boss, the same woman who had been turned down for the executive secretarial position walked in the door. She still looked angry.

Role Assignment

You are the personnel assistant. What action would you take and why?

Questions for Discussion

1. Why does a worker sometimes perceive relative pay as more important than the absolute level of pay?
2. Which issue is more important to the worker, unemployment or inflation?
3. According to equity theory, if hourly paid workers perceive themselves to be overpaid, how are they likely to react?
4. It is no longer appropriate for a union to be militant. Do you agree or disagree? Why?
5. Discuss the following statement: Since unionism is now on the decline, collective bargaining as a device for the peaceful settlement of disputes is now obsolete.
6. Explain why passage of the Wagner Act was important to labor.
7. How do craft and industrial unions differ in their approaches to area pay differentials?
8. What has happened over the years to the median money incomes of blacks as a percentage of the median money incomes of whites? Consider families, men, and women. How do you explain these trends?
9. Comment on the changes over the years in the employment shares held by blacks, Spanish-surnamed Americans, Asian Americans, and American Indians in the managerial and professional occupational groups.
10. What are the trends in median money incomes of women as a percentage of the median money incomes of men? For all workers? For year-round full-time workers?
11. How do you account for the relatively far lower money incomes of women compared with the money incomes of men, even for year-round full-time workers?
12. What effect do union seniority clauses have on the employment opportunities of women and minorities? Does the situation call for new contractual provisions or new legislation? Discuss.
13. What is meant by comparable worth? Is it the same thing as equal pay for equal work?
14. Some reference is made in this chapter to the matter of crowding in regard to employment. What is the significance of this factor?
15. Do you agree with the statement that many jobs tend to be segregated by sex (that is, that there are "men's jobs" and "women's jobs")? Have any examples of such segregation come to your personal attention?
16. What was the significance of the Supreme Court decision in County of Washington v. Gunther? Discuss.
17. What is equity bargaining? Do you think this type of approach to collective bargaining is

likely to be pursued more often in the future?

18. What do you think of the Fuchs findings with regard to the earnings of women with child-rearing responsibility? Are these findings significant? If so, why?

19. What are the pros and cons of changing traditional working hours to flexitime? Should all businesses adopt flexitime? Discuss.

20. What problems arise with respect to women and part-time work? What can be done to improve the situation?

21. What of future problems with respect to inequities in pay and benefits? Are these likely to be resolved mostly by unions or through the influence of other groups? Discuss.

Notes

1. Robert Ozanne, *Wages in Practice and Theory* (Madison: The University of Wisconsin Press, 1968).

2. For an analysis of the extent to which unionism has increased wages compared with what might have happened in the absence of unionism, see H. Gregg Lewis, *Unionism and Relative Wages in the United States* (Chicago: The University of Chicago Press, 1963). A more recent study suggests that the magnitude of the wage differential brought about by unions may be as large as 20 percent. See David Metcalf, "Unions, Incomes Policy and Relative Wages in Britain," *British Journal of Industrial Relations* 15, no. 2 (July 1977): 158–75.

3. The later formation of the AFL–CIO in 1955 did nothing to reverse this particular development.

4. For a more extensive discussion of the theory, see William Austin and Elaine Hatfield, "Equity Theory, Power, and Social Justice," in *Justice and Social Interaction,* ed. Gerold Mikula (Bern, Switzerland: Hans Huber Publishers, 1980).

5. Robert P. Vecchio, "An Individual-Differences Interpretation of the Conflicting Predictions Generated by Equity Theory and Expectancy Theory," *Journal of Applied Psychology* 66, no. 4 (August 1981): 470–81.

6. K. E. Weick, "The Concept of Equity in the Perception of Pay," *Administrative Science Quarterly* 11 (1966): 414–34.

7. Yoram Neumann, "A Contingency Approach for Understanding Equity Theory and Its Predictions," *Social Behavior and Personality* 8, no. 2 (1980): 157–58.

8. Laura N. Gasaway, "Comparable Worth: A Post-*Gunther* Overview," *The Georgetown Law Journal* 69, no. 5 (June 1981): 1131. Reprinted with the permission of the publisher, © 1981 The Georgetown Law Journal Association. For a research study on the initial placement aspect, see M. Susan Taylor and Daniel R. Ilgen, "Sex Discrimination Against Women in Initial Placement Decisions: A Laboratory Investigation," *Academy of Management Journal* 24, no. 4 (December 1981): 859–65.

9. Gasaway, *op. cit.,* 1168–69.

10. George T. Milkovich, "The Emerging Debate," in *Comparable Worth: Issues and Alternatives,* ed. E. Robert Livernash (Washington, D.C.: Equal Employment Advisory Council, 1980), 26.

11. Robert E. Williams and Douglas S. McDowell, "The Legal Framework," in *Comparable Worth: Issues and Alternatives,* ed. E. Robert Livernash (Washington, D.C.: Equal Employment Advisory Council, 1980), 214.

12. U.S. Bureau of Labor Statistics, *Industry Wage Survey: Men's and Boys' Suits and Coats, April 1979,* Bulletin 2073, October 1980.

13. *U.S. Law Week* (June 9, 1981), 4623.

14. See Gasaway, *op. cit.,* pp. 1134–45, for a full discussion of the Gunther decision and related cases.

15. Gasaway, *op. cit.,* pp. 1159–60.

16. Ibid., 1160.

17. See "California Decrees Comparable Worth of Women's Work," *American Journal of Nursing* 81, no. 11 (November 1981): 1967, 1984, 1987.

18. See "Women Underpaid, EEOC is Told: Report Backs 'Comparable Worth,' " *American Journal of Nursing* 81, no. 11 (November 1981): 2000.

19. See "San Jose RNs Seek Raise to $30,000 in Contract Talks," *The American Journal of Nursing* 81, no. 11 (November 1981): 1968. Copyright © American Journal of Nursing Company.

20. Ibid.

21. Ibid.

22. Ibid.

23. See "Women Underpaid, EEOC is Told: Report Backs 'Comparable Worth,' " *op. cit.,* p. 1987.

24. See Janice R. Bellace, "A Foreign Perspective," in *Comparable Worth: Issues and Alternatives,* ed. E. Robert Livernash (Washington, D.C.: Equal Employment Advisory Council, 1980), 137–72.

25. See Bellace, *op. cit.,* 145.

26. Bellace, *op. cit.,* 156.

27. Donald P. Schwab, "Job Evaluation and Pay Setting: Concepts and Practices," in *Comparable Worth: Issues and Alternatives,* ed. E. Robert Livernash (Washington, D.C.: Equal Employment Advisory Council, 1980), 49–77.

28. Charles H. Anderson and Daniel B. Corts, *Development of a Framework for a Factor-Ranking Benchmark System of Job Evaluation* (Washington, D.C.: Personnel Research and Development Center, U.S. Civil Service Commission, 1973), iii.

29. See Anderson and Corts, *op. cit.,* for full details.

30. Anderson and Corts, *op. cit.,* 7.

31. David J. Thomsen, "Compensation and Benefits: More on Comparable Worth," *Personnel Journal* 60, no. 5 (May 1981): 352–53.

32. Ibid., pp. 352–54.

33. "Women Underpaid, EEOC is Told: Report Backs 'Comparable Worth,' " *op. cit.,* 1994.

34. See Gasaway, *op. cit.,* 1167.

35. Herbert R. Northrup, "Wage Setting and Collective Bargaining," in *Comparable Worth: Issues and Alternatives,* ed. E. Robert Livernash (Washington, D.C.: Equal Employment Advisory Council, 1980), 124.

36. For further discussion, see Howard Hayghe, "Marital and Family Patterns of Workers: An Update," *Monthly Labor Review* 105, no. 5 (May 1982): 53–56.

37. Victor R. Fuchs, "Sex Differences in Economic Well-Being," *Science* 332 (April 25, 1986): 459.

38. Ibid., p. 464.

39. Ibid., pp. 462–463.

40. For a good historical analysis, see Pam Silverstein and Jozetta H. Srb, *Flexitime: Where, When, and How?* (Ithaca: New York State School of Industrial and Labor Relations, Cornell University, 1979).

41. See Jo Hartley, *Hours of Work When Workers Can Choose* (Washington, D.C.: Business and Professional Women's Foundation, 1975), 62.

42. Reprinted, by permission of the publisher, from Donald J. Peterson, "Flexitime in the United States: The Lesson of Experience," *Personnel,* January–February 1980. (New York: AMACOM, a division of American Management Associations, 1980) 22. Copyright © by AMACOM. All rights reserved.

43. Robert T. Golembiewski and Carl W. Proehl, Jr., "Public Sector Applications of Flexible Workhours: A Review of the Available Evidence," *Public Personnel Review* 40, no. 1 (January–February 1980): 75. For an example of a study using a control group and testing the statistical significance of the results, see Jay S. Kim and Anthony F. Campagna, "Effects of Flexitime on Employee Attendance and Performance: A Field Experiment," *Academy of Management Journal* 24, no. 4 (December 1981): 729–41.

44. See Petersen, *op. cit.,* pp. 27–28, and Golembiewski and Proehl, *op. cit.,* pp. 76–77 (column in the table relating to measured productivity). For a more optimistic view, see Stanley D. Nollen, "Does Flexitime Improve Productivity?" *Harvard Business Review* 57, no. 5 (September–October 1979): 12–22.

45. Nancy L. Rotchford and Karlene Roberts, "Part-Time Workers as Missing Persons in Organizational Research," *Academy of Management Review* 7, no. 2 (April 1982): 229.

46. Ibid.

47. Hartley, *op. cit.*, 24.
48. For a full discussion, see Rotchford and Roberts, *op. cit.*, 230.

References

"1987 AMS Flexible Work Survey." Willow Grove, PA: Administrative Management Society, 1987.

BNA Special Report. *The Comparable Worth Issue.* Washington, DC: Bureau of National Affairs, 1981.

Bailey, James E. "Personnel Scheduling with Flexshift: A Win-Win Scenario." *Personnel* 63, no. 9 (September 1986): 62–67.

Bellak, Alvin O. *Comparable Worth: A Practitioner's View.* Philadelphia, PA: Hay Management Consultants, 1984.

Burkhalter, Bettye B., et al. "Auditing the Compensation Function for Race- and Sex-Based Salary Differences: Further Needed Refinements." *Compensation and Benefits Review* 18, no. 4 (July–August 1986): 35–42.

"County OKs Comparable Worth." *The Times.* San Mateo, CA: March 19, 1986.

Fuchs, Victor R. "Sex Differences in Economic Well-Being." *Science* 232 (April 25, 1986): 459–464.

Gutek, Barbara. *Sex and the Workplace: The Impact of Sexual Behavior and Harassment on Women, Men, and Organizations.* San Francisco: Jossey-Bass Publishers, 1986.

Jacoby, Stanford M. *Employing Bureaucracy: Managers, Unions, and the Transformation of Work in American Industry, 1900–1945.* New York: Columbia University Press, 1985.

Jones, Edward W., Jr. "Black Managers: The Dream Deferred." *Harvard Business Review* 64, no. 3 (May–June 1986): 84–93.

Katz, Marsha; Lavan, Helen; and Malloy, Maura Sendelbach. "Comparable Worth: Analysis of Cases and Implications for HR Management." *Compensation and Benefits Review* 18, no. 3 (May–June 1986): 26–38.

Larwood, Laurie; Stromber, Ann H.; and Gutek, Barbara A. *Women and Work: An Annual Review, Vol. 1.* Beverly Hills, CA: Sage Publications, 1985.

Latack, Janina C., and Foster, Lawrence W. "Implementation of Compressed Work Schedules: Participation and Job Design as Critical Factors for Employee Acceptance." *Personnel Psychology* 38, no. 1 (Spring 1985): 75–92.

Mahoney, Thomas A. "Understanding Comparable Worth: A Societal and Political Perspective." *Research in Organizational Behavior* 9: 209–245.

McCoy, Ramelle, and Morand, Martin J., eds. *Short-Time Compensation: A Formula for Work Sharing.* New York: Pergamon Press, 1984.

Mitchell, Daniel J. B. "The 1982 Union-Wage Concessions: A Turning Point in Collective Bargaining?" *California Management Review* 25, No. 4 (Summer 1983): 78–92.

Moore, Lynda L. *Not as Far as You Think: The Realities of Working Women.* Lexington, MA: Lexington Books, 1986.

Nelson, Daniel. "Unions' Struggle to Survive Goes Beyond Modern Technology." *Monthly Labor Review* 110, no. 8 (August 1987): 41–45.

Olney, Peter B., Jr. "Meeting the Challenge of Comparable Worth: Part 2." *Compensation and Benefits Review* 19, no. 3, (May–June 1987): 45–53.

Shank, Susan E. "Women and the Labor Market: The Link Grows Stronger." *Monthly Labor Review* 111, no. 3 (March 1988): 3–8.

Shaw, Lois B., and Shapiro, David. "Women's Work Plans: Contrasting Expectations and Actual Work Experience." *Monthly Labor Review* 110, no. 11 (November 1987): 7–13.

Stromberg, Ann H.; Larwood, Laurie; and Gutek, Barbara A. *Women and Work: An Annual Review, Vol. 2.* Beverly Hills, CA: Sage Publications, 1986.

Tober, Pamela A. "The Emerging Flexible Workplace." *Compensation and Benefits Review* 20, no. 1 (January–February 1988): 70–74.

Job Analysis, Job Descriptions, and Computer Applications

5

Back in Chapter 1, I referred to organizational hierarchy and predominantly managerial rational devices such as job analysis, job evaluation, and performance evaluation. This chapter will tackle the first of these—job analysis. We will also look at job descriptions, including job specifications, and computer applications.

Preparation for and Conduct of Job Analysis

Job analysis is an attempt to identify the more significant features of a job. The facts developed by a job analyst are summarized in a written document, typically a job description. Job descriptions in turn provide information about the relative worth of different jobs within an organization. From management's point of view, job descriptions are part of job evaluation, which will be explored in later chapters. Of course, job descriptions are also useful for unions engaged in collective bargaining. Job analysis and job descriptions assist in resolving the problem of equity within the organization. They likewise serve other purposes with respect to personnel policy in hiring, promoting, setting performance standards, work force planning, and employee training and development.

To develop an effective system for analyzing jobs in an organization, the job analyst must follow some basic steps:

1. Gain the support of management at high and low levels and the support of union leaders and shop stewards.
2. Make sure that the purpose of the activity is communicated to the workers whose jobs are to be analyzed.
3. Do the necessary organizational and background research.
4. Gather the necessary specific information about the jobs as they are analyzed, and verify it.

Implementation of job analysis where none existed is obviously more of an undertaking than the analysis of new jobs or a new analysis of existing jobs.

Gaining Management and Union Support

Where job analysis is being implemented for the first time, the job analyst may encounter the human problem of resistance to change. It is therefore essential that the process have the support of management at all levels and of employees whose jobs are directly affected. Where a union is involved, its support will also be needed. As we shall see in Chapter 6 a joint union-management job evaluation committee will typically be the appropriate group to help in implementing the analysis and to settle any disagreements.

Orientation for the Workers

Because job analysis interferes with the everyday work activities at the job site (especially where it is to be done for many jobs) and may even be seen as a threat to the employees' job security, it is important that there be adequate orientation for the workers.

A formal announcement indicating the reasons for the job analysis is the first step. It is best if the source of the formal announcement is such that the support of both the top management and the union leadership is assured. Follow-up can be accomplished through other media of communication such as company news organs and through the cooperation of first-line supervisors and union stewards. The process can be explained at meetings where employees have their questions answered.

Organization Research and Planning

While top-level committees as well as supervisors and union stewards have important roles in orientation, the job analyst is directly accountable for conducting the analysis of jobs.

Technical tools of the job analyst are organization charts, work flow charts (such as Figure 5–1), and the *Dictionary of Occupational Titles.*

The formal organization chart, if reasonably current, helps the analyst to identify which jobs exist. One of its shortcomings is that it may stress the reporting and hierarchical relationships and underplay other equally important aspects of jobs. Some of these aspects will become evident from examination of the type of work flow chart shown in Figure 5–1. The flow of work can easily be as important as the flow of authority and/or responsibility and in any event provides additional useful information.

The *Dictionary of Occupational Titles* is a particularly useful planning tool. It contains titles (sometimes, but not always, including alternate titles) and generic job descriptions, which sometimes explain variations. An example is shown in Figure 5–2.

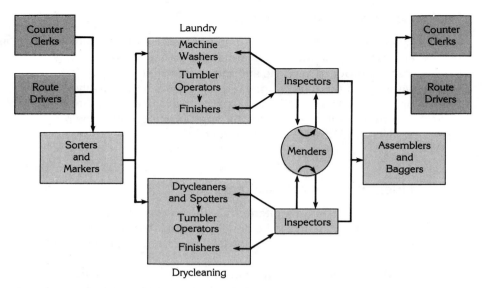

FIGURE 5–1
Work flow chart for a laundry and dry cleaning plant. (From U.S.
Bureau of Labor Statistics, Occupational Outlook Handbook,
1978–79 Edition.)

The detailed classification system in the *Dictionary of Occupational Titles* allows an analyst to obtain more information on particular jobs, especially alternate job titles and related types of jobs. For certain jobs, such as that of the job analyst, there is little additional information to be gleaned. However, many jobs fall into several related categories. Auto-body designer, for example, is a job for which much detail is provided (Figure 5–3).

Another useful tool for the analyst is a publication of the U.S. Employment Service, *Estimates of Worker Trait Requirements for 4,000 Jobs.* It provides information on such worker traits as general education, vocational training, specific aptitudes, temperaments, and interests as well as physical capacities needed and typical working conditions.

Gathering Information About Company Jobs

Having obtained this sort of organizational and general background information, the analyst gathers much more detailed information about each job in the organization using techniques such as:

1. Questionnaires
2. Interviews
3. Observation

JOB ANALYST (profess. and kin.) 166.088. occupational analyst. Collects, analyzes, and develops occupational data concerning jobs, job qualifications, and worker characteristics to facilitate personnel, administrative, or information functions in private, public, or governmental organizations: Consults with management to determine type, scope, and purpose of analysis, and compiles staffing schedules, flow charts, and other background information about company policies and facilities to expedite study. Studies jobs being performed and interviews workers and supervisory personnel to ascertain physical and mental requirements of jobs in relation to materials, products, procedures, subject matter, and services involved. Writes job descriptions, specifications, detailed analysis schedules, and narrative and statistical reports, reflecting such data as physical demands, working conditions, skills, knowledges, abilities, training, education, and related factors required to perform jobs. Conducts related occupational research, utilizing publications, professional and trade associations, and other media to verify or standardize data. Submits written reports pertaining to personnel policies, morale, absenteeism, turnover, job breakdown and dilution, organization, staffing, and related items. Utilizes data to evolve or improve wage evaluation systems, counseling and interviewing aids, training and testing programs, and other personnel practices. May write descriptions or monographs of jobs, processes, and industrial patterns or trends for publication. May be designated according to phase of analysis performed as PHYSICAL-DEMANDS ANALYST.

POSITION CLASSIFIER (gov. ser.) personnel technician; position analyst; wage-classification and position specialist. Analyzes and evalutes civil service positions to allocate them to established classifications: Studies duties, characteristics, and qualifications of positions to determine level of difficulty and responsibility, and recommends allocation of positions to specific classes. Writes standards governing allocation of positions. Drafts organizational and functional charts for use in position surveys and reorganizations. Develops and administers tests to determine qualifications of job applicants. Conducts wage surveys of similar positions in private industry to recommend equitable wage allocations. Writes recruitment announcements to obtain applicants. Consults with officials to keep informed of work program and to determine if classification program meets operating needs. Interprets classification policies and standards and assists in defining qualification requirements for classes of positions. May recruit job applicants.

FIGURE 5–2
Generic job description. (From U.S. Department of Labor.)

4. Diary or log
5. A combination of these

Job Analysis Questionnaires

An important method of gathering job information is the job analysis questionnaire. The questionnaire used by a Southern bank for its exempt personnel is shown in Figure 5–4.

AUTO-BODY DESIGNER (auto. mfg.)
      body designer, auto
      designer, auto body
AUTO-BODY LAY-OUT DRAFTSMAN (auto. mfg.)
      body draftsman, auto design
      draftsman, auto-body design
      lay-out man, auto-body design
CABLE-LAY-OUT MAN (tel. & tel.)
DESIGN DRAFTSMAN, ELECTROMECHANISMS (profess. & kin.)
DETAILER (profess. & kin.)
  AUTO-BODY-DESIGN DETAILER (auto. mfg.)
      body-design detailer, auto
      detailer, auto-body design
      panel detailer
  DETAIL MAN, FURNITURE (profess. & kin.)
  DRAFTSMAN, DETAIL (profess. & kin.)
      detail man
      mill detailer
  DRAFTSMAN, SHIP DETAIL (profess. & kin.)
DRAFTSMAN APPRENTICE (profess. & kin.)
DRAFTSMAN, BLACK AND WHITE (profess. & kin.)
      delineator
DRAFTSMAN, COMMERCIAL (profess. & kin.)
DRAFTSMAN, HEATING AND VENTILATING (profess. & kin.)
DRAFTSMAN, MAP (profess, & kin.)
      cartographer
      map maker
      mapper
  Draftsman, Records (profess. & kin.)
DRAFTSMAN, OIL AND GAS (petrol production; petrol refin.)
DRAFTSMAN, PLUMBING (profess. & kin.)
DRAFTSMAN, REFRIGERATION (profess. & kin.)
DRAFTSMAN, TOPOGRAPHICAL (profess. & kin.)
      photo-cartographer
MULTIPLEX-PROJECTION TOPOGRAPHER (profess. & kin.)
      multiplex operator
      stereo operator
      stereo-plotter operator
      stereoptic projection topographer
TECHNICAL ILLUSTRATOR (profess. & kin.)
      engineering illustrator
      production illustrator
TRACER (any ind.)
      draftsman, junior

FIGURE 5–3
Auto-body designer and similar jobs. (From U.S. Department of Labor.)

POSITION DESCRIPTION QUESTIONNAIRE
(Exempt Positions)

Position Title _____

Functional Title of Supervisor _____ Date _____

Company _____ Division _____ Office _____

Department _____ Section _____ Unit _____

Questionnaire Completed By _____

I. Basic Functions

Briefly describe the overall objectives, goals and purposes of the position. This statement should be a general summary of the responsibilities of the position.

II. Specific Duties and Responsibilities

In this section, describe each significant duty of the position as completely as necessary to impart a thorough understanding to someone who is not familiar with the job. Use concise and specific statements indicating **what** the duties are, but not how they are to be accomplished. Begin each statement with an action verb, such as "Supervises," "Plans," "Administers," "Approves," "Prepares," etc. **List duties in order of their importance (most important first).** Estimate the percentage of working time spent on each day. Continue on additional sheet, as necessary.

Per Cent of Time	Description

III. Complexity and Difficulty

1. Describe the most complex or difficult aspects of the position influenced by such elements as competitive conditions, legal or contractual requirements, and professional practices. What is the extent of analysis, planning and creative thinking required to resolve these situations?

2. What kind, and how much knowledge of a special field or special skills are required to perform the duties of the position? (For example: accounting, law, economics, financial analysis, programming, etc.)

3. What is the minimum education or equivalent experience that would be required to perform the duties of this position? **(optional)**

IV. Scope and Impact

1. What are the magnitudes of revenue volume, profits, costs, assets, or deposits affected by the position? (For example, total deposits of branch, total loans outstanding, total market value of investment portfolio.)

FIGURE 5—4
Position description questionnaire for exempt positions used by a bank.

4. Positions over which functional (staff) responsibility is exercised. That is, positions which do not report directly but receive functional guidance. For example, a Loan Administration Officer may have functional responsibility for the lending activities of branch personnel.

Position	Nature of Staff Supervision

5. Positions with which regular contact is maintained. Other than direct superior or subordinates, indicate the positions within or outside the Bank which require regular contacts with the position. Specify the purpose of such contacts.

Inside the Bank

Position	Purpose of Contact

Outside the Bank

Position	Purpose of Contact

6. The name, composition and purpose of any committee in the Bank of which this position serves as a member.

---

2. Describe the most important decisions and judgments required in the duties of this position. Indicate if they are (a) self made (b) shared (c) normally recommended to higher authority for approval.

3. How do the decisions in 2 above impact on the following:
   a. increasing revenues and costs
   b. controlling and reducing costs
   c. improving the quality of service
   d. broadening the range of the bank's business
   e. protecting, conserving or increasing the bank's assets

V. **Organizational Relationships**

1. Functional title of immediate supervisor over this position

2. Position title(s) of direct subordinate(s) (if two or more have the same title, indicate the number in each position).

POSITION TITLE	EXEMPT	NON-EXEMPT	TOTAL NUMBER OF INCUMBENTS

3. Total number of employees who report to this position, directly _____ ; through subordinates _____

FIGURE 5-4
(Continued)

The questionnaire is divided into five parts: (1) basic functions; (2) specific duties and responsibilities; (3) complexity and difficulty; (4) scope and impact; and (5) organizational relationships.

The first part contains a general summary of the position, while the other parts go into more detail. The section on duties and responsibilities stresses the use of verbs such as *supervises, plans, administers, approves,* and *prepares.* It also calls for duties to be listed in order of importance, asking for the percentage of time taken by each duty. The section on complexity and difficulty of the job examines the extent of analysis, planning, and creative thinking required as well as the extent to which specialized knowledge, education, and experience are needed. The section on scope and impact characterizes how performance of the job affects the success of the bank in carrying on its operations. The nature of the decision making and specific areas of the bank's activities are detailed in this section.

The last part of the questionnaire examines several dimensions of organizational relationships. It includes the title of the employee's immediate superior as well as the number and types of employees directly supervised or over whom functional (staff) responsibility is exercised. In order to check this information, the employee is asked about regular contacts both inside and outside the bank and the purpose of the contacts. Another question relates to the employee's participation on committees.

An interesting contrast to the bank questionnaire is one used by a large supermarket company (Figure 5–5).

While the bank questionnaire provides much space for answers to questions, the supermarket questionnaire provides little except for the last two questions relating to objectives and end results. Also, the bank questionnaire has fewer questions, and there is a perceivable logical structure to the questionnaire. This is less evident in the supermarket company's questionnaire, but the latter includes more questions and more details. From the viewpoint of the job analyst, these characteristics may be more beneficial in developing a larger volume of pertinent information about the job.

Sometimes a questionnaire asks the worker to draw the organization chart the way she sees it. Since this chart illustrates the relative worth of jobs within the organization, it is interesting for the job analyst to have access not only to the official organization chart but to the worker's perception of it.

Interviewing

Employees usually complete their own questionnaires. Where this is impractical, the analyst can use the questionnaire as the basis for interviewing—the second method of acquiring information in the job analysis process. It is essential that the analyst establish good rapport with the employee. First, the analyst should notify the employee's immediate superior before the visit. The latter will often introduce the analyst to the worker. While conducting the interview, the analyst should refrain from taking too many notes, since this may make the worker feel ill at ease.

POSITION ANALYSIS QUESTIONNAIRE

POSITION NO.

POSITION TITLE:

DATE:

WRITTEN BY:

REPORTS TO:

APPROVED BY:

1. Why does this position exist?

2. What results are expected?

3. Who does the position report to?

4. What other positions report to the same superior?

5. With whom are the most frequent contacts inside the company?

Give example:

6. With whom are the most frequent contacts outside the company?

Give example:

7. On what committees is the position represented?

8. Is much travel involved?

Where?

Why?

9. What positions report to this?

Outline briefly the scope of each subordinate position and the type of subordinate whether special qualifications or long experience are needed.

10. How is control over subordinates exercised?

11. What information for control is used?

12. With what subordinate position is the most direct contact?

Why?

13. Is it necessary for the person performing this job to have as much technical know how and specialist knowledge as his subordinates?

Why?

14. Is there any subordinate position from which the successor to this position is most likely to come?

Why?

15. What specific technical training or experience has the incumbent had?

16. What aspect of technical or specialized training or experience is most important?

17. How could training or experience have best been gained?

18. Is the job more administrative or more technical?

19. How is supervision of subordinates accomplished?

20. What do you feel is the greatest challenge in your job?

21. What is the most satisfying part of your job?

22. What is the least satisfying part of your job?

23. What part of your job gives you the most opportunity to tread new paths?

24. What part of the job gives you the most opportunity to be creative?

25. What types of problems do you deal with in your job on your own authority?

Give example of the most difficult decision that you can make without prior approval of your superior before action on the problem.

26. What types of problem do you refer to a higher authority before action?

Give example of the least important problem that you would take to your superior before taking action on it.

27. What types of problems do you consult with others before action?

Give example of such a problem.

28. What types of problems should be brought to the superior's attention?

29. What authority does the position have for:

a. Hire and fire?

b. Capital expenditure?

c. Current expenditure?

d. Setting prices?

FIGURE 5–5

Position analysis questionnaire used by a large supermarket company. The questionnaire is used to gain the incumbent's perspective on her position and organizational relationships. Information determined from the questionnaire is input into the quantified job evaluation system developed and implemented throughout industry by Albert Ramond and Associates of Chicago, Illinois, who supplied the questionnaire.

e. Changing production methods?

f. Changing marketing methods?

g. Changing design?

h. Changing quality standards?

i. Changing salaries?

30. What are the major rules, regulations, precedents or personal control within which this job operates?

31. What are the three most important characteristics you would look for in a replacement?

1.

2.

3.

32. When you get away from the work what facet of it, more than any other, is most worrying?

33. If you were your boss what criterion would you use to measure this position's performance?

34. What is the bulk of your time spent on?

35. What do you consider the most difficult types of problem that you have to solve?

Give example:

a. of problem

b. of how you solve them

36. What types of goals are set by this job?

Give example:

How far ahead?

37. Does the job establish costs or pricing limits?

Give example of limitations of this.

38. Does the job establish or determine specifications, designs or quality standards?

Give example:

39. What do you consider to be the goals or objectives that have been set for your job for which you are held accountable for achievement?

List them in order of importance as you see them.

1.

2.

3.

4.

5.

6.

7.

8.

9.

10.

40. What are the end results of the above goals or objectives as you understand them?

List the end results of each of the above goals or objectives in respective order.

1.

2.

3.

4.

5.

6.

7.

8.

9.

10.

FIGURE 5–5
(Continued)

109

Instead, most of the report can be written later from memory. At the conclusion of the interview, the analyst should thank the worker for her cooperation.

Observation of the individual working on the job is often required as a means of verifying the facts presented during the interview. Often interviewing and job observation will take place simultaneously at the job site except in cases where the nature of the job precludes it.

Use of a Diary or Log

A diary or log can be used in situations where the work cycle is long or where the time span of discretion, as described by Elliott Jaques,[1] (see Chapter 6) is great. Certain professional positions lend themselves to this method. Examples would be forest ranger, architect, or university professor.

Verification of Facts

After gathering information, the analyst must check out its accuracy. This can be done by revisiting the job site, where any inconsistencies about the job as reported by the supervisor and worker can be checked out. In some cases, where the results from talking with one worker on a job are unsatisfactory and a number of workers do the same job, the analyst may arrange for a job conference in which several of the workers can contribute facts about the job. This method has the particular advantage of resolving inconsistencies pertaining to the actual job content. The process of verification continues until the analyst feels that an accurate picture of the job as *it is now being performed* has been obtained.

Probably the best results are likely to accrue to the job analyst who combines these various techniques (questionnaires, interviews, observation, and use of diaries or logs) with appropriate follow-ups to be sure of the accuracy of the information.

Computer Applications in Job Analysis

As to computer applications to problems of job analysis, it is clear that a quite small company having at least a microcomputer, with the use of appropriate software, can handle job analysis and job descriptions more easily than without a computer. With a data base program, jobs can more easily be compared with each other. And with a word processing capability preparing and especially updating of job descriptions can be done far more efficiently. For larger corporations more advanced computerized techniques—such as an automated job description system—can be quite costly to develop. However, with the larger number of jobs the more advanced computerized techniques are nonetheless more cost effective as shown by a lower cost per job. Even so, computers do not give all the answers since some steps in job analysis still require human judgement.

1. The analysis process is often assigned to entry-level employees who do not know the organization well and are not well prepared to dispute line managers who exaggerate a position.
2. The process requires an investment of up to 10 hours to produce a job description (including time for interviews), drafting, typing, reviewing, editing, and retyping).
3. The time commitment makes it difficult to keep job descriptions current.
4. The process is dependent on the analyst's perception of each job and her ability to elicit all relevant information from incumbents and/or supervisors.
5. Different analysts can be expected to produce somewhat different descriptions for a given job.[2]

Computer applications of job analysis often combine job analysis, job evaluation, and job pricing. But it is not necessary that this be the case. It is still a management decision as to how far through this chain the process extends. At the far end of the chain a strong case can be made that one of the chief tasks, if not the most important of all, is to work out a balance between internal equity and external market pricing. If this be so, pricing should be a separate process. As to job evaluation, it is well to remember that digital computers generate numbers. They do not generate judgments. So if the human judgments of a representative job evaluation committee are important, then job evaluation should be separate from job analysis.

Regardless of how far through the chain a company carries the process, it faces a major basic decision with regard to job analysis and that is whether to develop its own approach or to have an outside consultant come in. In this chapter we shall discuss an example of each.

The Bank of America Example

The Bank of America stresses pay for performance in its salary program. Pay increases are all on merit. Job families—groups of jobs related by the functions performed and the skills required—were established by the bank for most jobs. Each job within a family has specific levels of required skills and responsibilities. Examples of job families include secretaries, accountants, systems professionals, and branch managers. Job families provide visible career paths for employees.

The bank's plan, in the new computerized version, evaluates all jobs using seven factors:

1. Problem solving and analysis
2. Autonomy or authority
3. Impact of decisions
4. Influence (inside and outside the bank)
5. Skills, knowledge, and abilities
6. Management responsibilities and type of work managed
7. Physical impact

Job Profile Questionnaire

The bank asks each employee or a representative employee in that job to fill out a highly detailed questionnaire called the Job Profile, which comprises 19 pages and 34 closed-end questions. The employee's immediate supervisor answers a few questions relating to the position's managerial responsibilities and skills requirements, and must concur with the employee's responses on other questions. An example from the profile relating to a job's influence involving contacts outside the bank is shown in Figure 5–6.

The profile defines contacts in three ways: the *type* of contact, the purpose or complexity of the contact, and the frequency of the contact. Take, for example, contacts with customers. The employee is asked about both the most common contact and the most complex contact (thereby measuring the range of the contact). Then, for each type of contact, the purpose of the contact must be matched with one of eight choices, and the frequency of the contact must be indicated with one of five choices allowed.

A somewhat simpler question from the profile relates to job independence (AUTONOMY in the computer printouts). This is shown in Figure 5–7.

This section of the profile involves multiple-choice answers to only three questions, there being three, five, and six possible answers for the questions in that order. In the computer printout or authorized profile for the job of product analyst, which is shown in Figure 5–8, we can see that the answers to questions in Section 3 of the profile were response 3 to question 5, 1 in response to question 6, and 3 for question 7. Answers to the other questions in the profile are also shown.

In a later page of the same computer printout, we see that the three replies to the job independence question are converted into a point score of 83 under AUTONOMY. The other numbers on the same line show the point values for the other factors and a point total of 343 for the job.

While the Bank of America did not reveal the exact way profile question replies were converted to points, the general basis of valuation would suggest a certain logic: If in Figure 5–7 the entire job independence (autonomy) factor was considered to be worth 100 points and if question 5 is less important than 6 or 7, it might have a total possible score of say, 30 points. Within the 30 points, it would be natural to value more highly the job where the employee determines her own daily work activities, while the employee whose manager assigns and schedules the activities would be given the least value. Under these assumptions the point values might well be 10 for answer 1, 20 for answer 2, and 30 for answer 3. Such considerations will be discussed more fully in a later chapter dealing with point job evaluation plans.

The Compare Function

Before any job is assigned to a pay grade, a process known as the compare function is used to meet the primary underlying purpose of the bank's computerized job analysis (and job evaluation) approach, which is to assure equity between dif-

```
                                    Scales

   Purpose                                           Frequency

   1. Furnish/obtain readily available information      1. Daily
   2. Clarify basic information and/or procedures       2. Weekly
   3. Explain detailed data, policies, and/or procedures 3. Twice a month
   4. Interpret or define complex, technical, and/or highly sensitive  4. Monthly
      data, policies, and/or procedures                 5. Quarterly
   5. Negotiate terms, agreements, deals, or contracts
   6. Develop new business relationships
   7. Resolve serious and critical business issues of major concern
      to the Corporation
   8. Serve as an official BAC spokesperson in a public or community
      relations context
```

CONTACTS OUTSIDE BAC . . .

CONTACT

a. Customers

A. Most Common	PURPOSE	① ② ③ ④ ⑤ ⑥ ⑦ ⑧
	FREQUENCY	① ② ③ ④ ⑤
B. Most Complex	PURPOSE	① ② ③ ④ ⑤ ⑥ ⑦ ⑧
	FREQUENCY	① ② ③ ④ ⑤

b. Vendors, Suppliers, Equipment Service Personnel

A. Most Common	PURPOSE	① ② ③ ④ ⑤ ⑥ ⑦ ⑧
	FREQUENCY	① ② ③ ④ ⑤
B. Most Complex	PURPOSE	① ② ③ ④ ⑤ ⑥ ⑦ ⑧
	FREQUENCY	① ② ③ ④ ⑤

c. Community Organizations/Government Agencies/ Regulators/Legislators

A. Most Common	PURPOSE	① ② ③ ④ ⑤ ⑥ ⑦ ⑧
	FREQUENCY	① ② ③ ④ ⑤
B. Most Complex	PURPOSE	① ② ③ ④ ⑤ ⑥ ⑦ ⑧
	FREQUENCY	① ② ③ ④ ⑤

d. Media

A. Most Common	PURPOSE	① ② ③ ④ ⑤ ⑥ ⑦ ⑧
	FREQUENCY	① ② ③ ④ ⑤
B. Most Complex	PURPOSE	① ② ③ ④ ⑤ ⑥ ⑦ ⑧
	FREQUENCY	① ② ③ ④ ⑤

e. Other Companies/Firms

A. Most Common	PURPOSE	① ② ③ ④ ⑤ ⑥ ⑦ ⑧
	FREQUENCY	① ② ③ ④ ⑤
B. Most Complex	PURPOSE	① ② ③ ④ ⑤ ⑥ ⑦ ⑧
	FREQUENCY	① ② ③ ④ ⑤

FIGURE 5–6
**Bank of America (BAC) profile question on contacts outside the
bank.**

SECTION 3: JOB INDEPENDENCE

This section measures the amount of independence your job requires you to have.

5. Who plans your daily work? (Mark one)

    ① My manager assigns and schedules my daily work activities.

    ② My manager assigns my daily work activities, I decide in what order they will be completed.

    ③ I determine and schedule my daily work activities.

6. What level of involvement/authority do you have in developing unit/departmental goals and business plans? (Mark one)

    ① I work with my manager in developing my _own_ objectives, but do not get involved in developing the unit's operating plans.

    ② I <u>assist</u> in developing the unit's operating plan.

    ③ I <u>develop</u> the unit's operating plan.

    ④ I <u>develop</u> operating and business plans for major organizational units.

    ⑤ I <u>develop</u> broad organizational policies and missions.

7. How often are your work activities reviewed and/or approved by your manager? (Does _not_ refer to timing of your PPC&E reviews.) (Mark one)

    ① Daily

    ② Weekly

    ③ Twice a month

    ④ Monthly

    ⑤ During a period of work which generally extends up to two months

    ⑥ At major milestones of a project or a period of work which extends up to three months.

FIGURE 5–7
Bank of America profile question on independence.

ferent jobs within the organization. With the creation of job families, some 9,000 jobs at the bank have been reduced to 2,000. This does not mean that 7,000 people lost their jobs but that the bank was able to consolidate multiple descriptions for a single job. Using the compare function, the bank tries to keep down the number of jobs by slotting into existing positions. Thus, the structure of jobs has been improved. Comparisons can help determine if the position being evaluated can be slotted into an existing position or simply validate the computer-calculated grade of the position being evaluated by looking at similar jobs and how they are

POSITION NUMBER: 6109
POSITION TITLE: PRODUCT ANALYST

*** SECTION 2: SOLVING JOB PROBLEMS ***

```
1    : 2      2A  : 2      2B  : 3      2C  : 2
3A  : 2      3B  : 2      3C  : 3      3D  : 1      3E  : 1      4   : 3
```

*** SECTION 3: JOB INDEPENDENCE ***

```
5   : 3      6   : 1      7   : 3
```

*** SECTION 4: DECISIONS MADE ON THE JOB***

```
 8   : 3      9   : 2     10   : 1     11   : 2
12A :        12B :        12C :        12D :        12E :        12F :        12G :
12H :        12I :        12J :        12K :
```

*** SECTION 5: JOB INFLUENCE ***

```
13      : 1
14A-AP: 2    14A-AF: 1    14A-BP: 3    14A-BF: 2
14B-AP: 2    14B-AF: 2    14B-BP: 3    14B-BF: 3
14C-AP: 1    14C-AF: 3    14C-BP: 2    14C-BF: 4
14D-AP: 1    14D-AF: 4    14D-BP: 2    14D-BF: 4
14E-AP:      14E-AF:      14E-BP:      14E-BF:
15      : 1
16A-AP: 2    16A-AF: 2    16A-BP: 2    16A-BF: 3
16B-AP:      16B-AF:      16B-BP:      16B-BF:
16C-AP:      16C-AF:      16C-BP:      16C-BF:
16D-AP:      16D-AF:      16D-BP:      16D-BF:
16E-AP:      16E-AF:      16E-BP:      16E-BF:
```

*** SECTION 6: TYPE OF WORK***

```
17A : 2      17B : 2      17C : 2      17D : 2      17E :        17F : 3      17G :
```

*** SECTION 7: MANAGEMENT RESPONSIBILITY ***

```
18 : 1      19 :        20 :
```

*** SECTION 8: COMPLETED BY MANAGER ***

```
21  : 2244 22  : 2      24  : 2      25  : 2      26  : 1
27A1: 2    27A2: 4      27B1: 1      27B2: 5      27C1:        27C2:
27D1: 2    27D2: 4      27E1: 2      27E2: 4      27F1: 1      27F2: 5
28A :      28B :        28C :        28D :        28E :        28F :
28G :      28H :        28I :        28J :        28K :        28L :
28M :      28N :        28O :        28P :        28Q :        28R :
28S :      28T :        28U :        OTH:                      28V :
29  :      30  : 2      31  : 2
32A :      32B :        32C :        32D:         32E :        32F :        34  :
```

FIGURE 5–8
Computer printout, authorized profile for position of product analyst.

115

```
AUTHORIZED PROFILE        04/27/88 10:00:28                    PAGE   4

POSITION NUMBER: 6109
POSITION TITLE: PRODUCT ANALYST

AUTH DATE:     12/15/86
OWNER UNIT:     5302    BAPS HUMAN RESOURCES
COMP ANALYST: DE RAAD KA

GRADE: 75                  JOB FAMILY: 1505              PAYLINE:  G
GAA:                       FLSA:      E                  OVERRIDE:
                           MGR CODE:  1
```

PROB- LEM SOLVG	AUTO- NOMY	DECSN MAKNG	INT INFLU RESP	EXT INFLU RESP	SKILL KNOWL ABLTY	MGMT RESP	TYPE OF WORK	PHYS IMPCT	TOTAL PTS
100	83	49	36	18	46	3	3	5	343

FIGURE 5–9
Computer printout, point summary by factors for product analyst.

graded. Jobs to be compared are chosen both from the job family of the job being evaluated and from job families chosen by the compensation analyst because they are in some way similar to the job family of the job being evaluated. The jobs chosen must also meet two special criteria: total points must fall within plus or minus 50 points of the position under evaluation *and* they must have the same point values for at least two of the four following factors: problem solving; autonomy; decision making; and skills, knowledge, and abilities. The four factors are considered to be the most important of the compensable factors and carry the most weight in the scoring process.

I shall illustrate how the compare procedure works using position 4969, that of auditor. Auditor actually shows up on two different lines in Figure 5–10. Points for the various factors for the auditor job are shown on the top ***COMPOSITE DATE*** line. This is the *newest* evaluation of the the auditor's job whereas the showing on the fifth line is an earlier evaluation. The position is listed in both places so that the two evaluations can be compared. Thus, one can see whether the more recent reevaluation differs, if at all. Do the changes that were perceived when the job was sent in for reevaluation show up as a change in the factors? The end result is either a reevaluation of the factors or leaving the factors and grade as is.

But let us go back to the details of the full analysis. The auditor job on the ***COMPOSITE DATA*** line is compared with other jobs in the same job family

RUN DATE : NOV 09 1987
USER-ID : USCOMP
UNIT NAME & NO. : US COMPENSATION RESEARCH 3604
BATCH NUMBER : 0740
EVALUATION INTENT : RV

POSITION NUMBER : 4969
POSITION TITLE : AUDITOR
JOBFAMILY & SUBFAMILY : 02 01
CURRENT SALARY GRADE : 78 01
TOTAL POINTS : 78
PROPOSED GRADE : 78 495

DETAIL COMPARE REPORT

MATCHING ON COMPENSABLE FACTORS AND TOTAL POINTS: 445 – 545

JOB FAMILY	POSITION NUMBER	POSITION TITLE	PROB-LEM SOLVG	AUTO-NOMY	DECSN MAKNG	INT INFLU RESP	EXT INFLU RESP	SKILL KNOWL ABLTY	MGMT RESP	TYPE OF WORK	PHYS IMPCT	GRADE	TOTAL PTS
02C1	4969	***COMPOSITE DATA***	150	83	75	74	10	92	3	3	5	78	495
01C4	3306	SR OPS MGR-COMM'L BN	125	83	75	47	67	75	20	16	5	70	515
	3735	MGR, OPNS LOCSC	125	83	97	61	27	92	20	16	5	79	526
	7894	ASST MGR NY OPERS	125	83	97	61	27	92	13	16	5	78	519
01.01	4969	AUDITOR	150	66	75	74	10	92	3	3	5	78	478
	6507	SR RISK INSUR OFF	150	83	75	74	52	92	3	3	5	79	537
	6730	ASST MGR EXPNS CONTR	125	83	75	49	10	110	3	3	5	79	478
	6736	TRAVEL MANAGER	100	83	75	36	39	92	13	16	5	79	463
0203	2016	SR CREDIT REPRT ANLY	175	93	75	61	18	75	3	3	5	77	459
	3661	ASSOC CREDIT EXAM OF	125	83	75	36	10	110	3	3	5	78	498
	3662	CREDIT EXAM OFFICER	125	83	75	61	10	110	3	3	5	77	450
	3663	SR CREDIT EXAM OFFCR	175	83	75	61	10	110	3	3	5	79	475
	4610	SR ADMIN OFFICER	150	83	97	74	13	110	3	3	5	79	538
02C4	6274	FCS C/I ACCT. ADMIN.	125	83	75	49	67	110	3	3	5	79	543
	0088	PROCDRS WRTNG ANALYS	150	83	49	49	39	110	3	3	5	78	520
	0302	SR ASSOC CMPLNC ANLS	125	83	75	61	10	110	3	3	5	78	491
	2735	COMPL ANALYST	125	83	75	61	52	92	3	3	5	77	457
	6246	SVC QUALITY ANALYST	125	83	75	74	18	92	3	3	5	78	499
	6293	MGR, FCS COMPL & Q4	150	83	75	49	27	92	3	3	5	78	478
0205	2513	LEGAL INVESTIGATOR	150	83	75	49	39	110	3	3	5	78	487
	7521	SR INVESTIGATOR	125	83	75	74	67	92	3	3	10	73	517
	2522	INVESTIGATOR	125	63	75	61	67	92	3	3	10	79	532
	4470	SAFETY LIAISON OFCR	125	83	75	74	52	92	3	3	5	78	512

FIGURE 5–10
Computer printout, detail compare report for auditor.

117

and also with jobs in four other families. And the point values are shown for each of nine columns across the sheet. (There are nine because the influence factor is broken down into internal and external, and management is broken into management responsibilities and type of work managed.) Let us look at position 6507 SR RISK INSUR OFF and compare it factor by factor against the composite. The point values all match except for EXT INFLU RESP, so looking at all factors we have eight matches. And on the earlier mentioned major factors we have four matches.

These same summary figures appear on the first line of Figure 5–11, the summary report, opposite position 6507 SR RISK INSUR OFF. There are eight in the category of # TOTAL CF (compensable factor) MATCHES and, to the left of this, four for the # MAJOR CF MATCHES. By contrast, at the bottom of the report for position 7894 ASST MGR NY OPERS, we have only three for # TOTAL MATCHES and only two in the # MAJOR MATCHES. Thus the jobs on the summary report nearest the top match the auditor's job the most closely and those at the bottom the least closely.

One further device used with the computerized compare function is a one-paragraph descriptor (job description) for all current positions, which can be called up on the screen or printed out as an additional tool for comparing jobs.

Using an Outside Consultant

For the hopeful potential user of outside consulting as a way of developing a computerized (or more computerized) job analysis approach, there is a plethora of consulting firms ready, willing, and able to furnish this service. While the cost may be considerable, so may be the advantages in terms of the broader view of a particular firm's problems to be gained from an outside consultant. Also, employee acceptance of the plan is often greater when it comes from someone outside the organization.

The Wyatt Plans

Discussing two different plans offered by the Wyatt Company, a compensation, benefits, and actuarial and consulting firm, will illustrate what a consulting firm can do. While both plans go beyond job analysis into job evaluation, and indeed into general salary administration, the emphasis in this chapter is on the job analysis aspects. One of these plans is a salary management process which uses factors and results in points. It is known as FACTORCOMP™. The other plan is a mathematically more sophisticated, more highly computer-driven system known as MULTICOMP™. Neither plan can be characterized as an "off-the-shelf" plan, such as the point plan used by the National Electrical Manufacturers Association

```
RUN DATE          : NOV 09 1987                                    POSITION NUMBER        : 4969
USER-ID           : USCOMP                                         POSITION TITLE         : AUDITOR
UNIT NAME & NO.   : US COMPENSATION RESEARCH   3604                JOBFAMILY & SUBFAMILY  : 02  01
BATCH NUMBER      : 0740                                           CURRENT SALARY GRADE   : 78
EVALUATION INTENT : RV                                             TOTAL POINTS           : 78
                                                                   PROPOSED GRADE         : 78      495
```

SUMMARY REPORT

POINTS: LOW - 445   HIGH - 545

JOB FAM	POSITION NUMBER	POSITION TITLE	OWNER	# MAJOR CF MATCHES	# TOTAL CF MATCHES	TOTAL POINTS	TOTAL POINTS DIFF	GRADE
0201	6507	SR RISK INSUR OFF	3229	4	8	537	42	79
0204	6223	MGR, FCS COMPL & QA	5302	4	7	487	8	73
0201	4969	AUDITOR	3604	3	8	478	17	78
0205	4470	SAFETY LIAISON OFCR	3604	3	7	512	17	78
0204	6246	SVC QUALITY ANALYST	3229	3	7	476	17	78
0204	0302	SR ASSOC CMPLNC ANLS	3606	3	7	457	38	77
0204	2735	COMPL ANALYST	3604	3	6	499	4	78
0205	2513	LEGAL INVESTIGATOR	3604	3	6	517	22	78
0205	2521	SR INVESTIGATOR	3604	3	6	532	37	77
0205	2522	INVESTIGATOR	3604	3	5	519	24	78
0201	6736	TRAVEL MANAGER	3229	3	5	459	36	77
0203	3663	SR CREDIT EXAM OFFCR	3604	3	4	539	43	79
0201	3662	CREDIT EXAM OFFICER	3604	2	6	475	20	78
0201	6730	ASST MGR EXPNS CONTR	3229	2	6	463	32	78
0203	3661	ASSOC CREDIT EXAM OF	3229	2	6	450	45	77
0203	4610	SR ADMIN OFFICER	3229	2	6	543	48	79
0203	2016	SR CREDIT REPRT ANLY	3606	2	5	498	3	78
0204	0038	PRCCDRS WRTNG ANALYS	5302	2	5	491	4	73
0203	6294	FCS C/I ACCT. ADMIN.	3209	2	5	520	25	78
0104	3306	SR OPS MGR-COMM'L BN	3604	2	3	515	20	78
0104	7894	ASST MGR RV OPERS	3209	2	3	519	24	76
0104	3735	MGR, OPNS LOCSC	3209	2	3	526	31	79

FIGURE 5–11
Computer printout, summary report for auditor.

119

(NEMA) to be discussed in Chapter 7. Wyatt tailors plans more closely to the needs of the client organization.

There are some differences between FACTORCOMP™ and MULTICOMP™. While the former normally uses 10 to 25 factors, the latter usually uses 25 to 40. Also, the MULTICOMP plans involve more sophisticated data analysis generating more accurate predictions of the dependent variable—either the market rate or other variable designated by the client.

While Wyatt's FACTORCOMP is like the point method of job evaluation, it does not start with a predetermined set of factors, points, and degrees. It is both more highly customized to the needs of each client and more computerized. Typical steps in developing and implementing an effective FACTORCOMP PROCESS include:

1. Plan the project.
2. Define compensation strategy.
3. Select benchmark jobs.
4. Analyze market salaries.
5. Revise your salary grade structure.
6. Define compensable factors.
7. Develop job description form or job questionnaire.
8. Collect job content information.
9. Review, revise, and confirm information on jobs.
10. Develop factor points and weights.
11. Develop cost implications.
12. Develop computer software.
13. (Optional) Develop computerized, narrative job descriptions.
14. Write final report, document process, and train staff.
15. Communicate to employees.[3]

For companies using FACTORCOMP, Wyatt points out the ease and effectiveness with which the process can be maintained if done on a personal computer and promises to their clients a custom computer system that will:

permit data entry of the questionnaire information;

calculate points and the recommended salary grade and graphically display these;

provide monitoring reports for summarizing the job evaluation process and results; and

provide basic salary administration monitoring reports to answer questions directed to human resources by management[4]

Broader Aspects of the Wyatt Approach

While we have examined some aspects of MULTICOMP, perhaps more interest attaches to Wyatt's general approach, which can be described in broad terms somewhat as follows:

1. Wyatt draws on the three distinct technologies of psychometrics, computers and computer software, and statistics.
2. Wyatt's customizing of plans for particular clients gives full recognition to the culture and value system of the client organization.
3. Wyatt relies on building a strong information base through the use of closed-end questionnnaires.
4. Wyatt makes a conscious attempt to eliminate factors and weights in any plan that might involve possible bias against women or minorities.
5. Wyatt starts out by first gathering information on a number of benchmark jobs—jobs for which the client organization can establish both an internal ranking and an external value.
6. Wyatt uses information gathered with respect to the benchmark jobs as a basis for computer and statistical methods to develop the job evaluation "model," or way of combining the job analysis information to determine the job grade.
7. Wyatt generates computerized rather than purely narrative job descriptions.
8. In the consulting process, the company encourages a high degree of employee and management participation in developing the new plans.

In connection with the computerized approach it advocates, Wyatt favors user-friendly computer programs so that the degree of computer sophistication required by the user is not overly demanding. Menu-driven programs such as the tableaux shown in Figure 5–12 are typical. The user starts with the main menu and proceeds from there depending on which option is selected, with an X option allowing return to the main menu or exiting the system.

The data fed into the computer are initially generated by using the results of closed-end questionnaires, similar to those we saw earlier in the case of the Bank of America. Note that the processing information question asks for rough figures (10 percent intervals) rather than extremely precise ones, as can be seen in Figure 5–13.

Statistical processes, mentioned above in point (1), are an important factor in the success of the computer operations of the Wyatt job analysis/evaluation/administration plans. Some MULTICOMP applications are:

Single regression analysis is used during the initial stages of design to test the strength and functional relationship of each compensable factor and the chosen proxy for job value to the organization, i.e., salary, grades.

Various multiple regression techniques simultaneously "weight" all of the final compensable factors to describe the organization's value system as it relates to job value.

```
ZDDDDDDDDDDDDDDDDDDDDDDDDDDDDDDDDDDDDDDDDDDDDDDDDDDDDDDDDDDDDDDDDDDDDDDDDDDDDD?
3                      THE FEIN SERVICE COMPANY                              3
3                       Salary Management System                            3
3                              Main Menu                                    3
CDDDDDDDDDDDDDDDDDDDDDDDDDDDDDDDDDDDDDDDDDDDDDDDDDDDDDDDDDDDDDDDDDDDDDDDDDDDDD4
3                                                                           3
3                  1 - Add New Job Data                                     3
3                  2 - Change Existing Job Data                             3
3                  3 - Delete Job Data                                      3
3                  4 - Report Menu                                          3
3                  5 - Salary Administration Menu                           3
3                  6 - Position Profile Comparison                          3
3                  7 - Display Grade & Salary Range For A Job               3
3                  8 - Job Description Menu                                  3
3                  9 - Salary Structure Functions Menu                      3
3                  I - Reindex All Databases                                3
3                  P - Reset Printer                                        3
3                  X - Exit System                                          3
3                                                                           3
3                                                                           3
3                                                                           3
CDDDDDDDDDDDDDDDDDDDDDDDDDDDDDDDDDDDDDDDDDDDDDDDDDDDDDDDDDDDDDDDDDDDDDDDDDDDDD4
3                       Choose an option : :                                3
@DDDDDDDDDDDDDDDDDDDDDDDDDDDDDDDDDDDDDDDDDDDDDDDDDDDDDDDDDDDDDDDDDDDDDDDDDDDDDY


ZDDDDDDDDDDDDDDDDDDDDDDDDDDDDDDDDDDDDDDDDDDDDDDDDDDDDDDDDDDDDDDDDDDDDDDDDDDDDD?
3                      THE FEIN SERVICE COMPANY                              3
3                       Salary Management System                            3
3                            Data Change Menu                               3
CDDDDDDDDDDDDDDDDDDDDDDDDDDDDDDDDDDDDDDDDDDDDDDDDDDDDDDDDDDDDDDDDDDDDDDDDDDDDD4
3                                                                           3
3                  1 - Position Information                                 3
3                  2 - Position Description                                 3
3                  3 - Knowledge & Skill, Planning & Scheduling             3
3                  4 - Supervision, Information Processing                  3
3                  5 - Problem Solving                                      3
3                  6 - Internal Contacts                                    3
3                  7 - External Contacts                                    3
3                  8 - External Contacts (continued)                        3
3                  9 - General Information - Scope Data                     3
3                 10 - All Sections of the Questionnaire                    3
3                 11 - Display Grade & Salary Range For A Job               3
3                  X - Return to Main Menu                                  3
3                                                                           3
3  Job Class Number:  011010     Questionnaire Number: 90                   3
3  Job Title:  Auditing Officer                                            3
CDDDDDDDDDDDDDDDDDDDDDDDDDDDDDDDDDDDDDDDDDDDDDDDDDDDDDDDDDDDDDDDDDDDDDDDDDDDDD4
3                       Choose an option :  :                               3
@DDDDDDDDDDDDDDDDDDDDDDDDDDDDDDDDDDDDDDDDDDDDDDDDDDDDDDDDDDDDDDDDDDDDDDDDDDDDDY
```

FIGURE 5–12
Typical user-friendly menus used by Wyatt.

IX Processing Information

The purpose of this section is to identify the level of processing information methods needed to successfully carry out the responsibilities of the job.

For the following questions, divide 100% among the categories listed below. Use multiples of 10% (e.g., 10%, 20%, 30%, etc.) for each applicable category. Use 0% to indicate "not applicable." Check to be certain the sum of the categories is 100%.

What percentage of time (over a long period, such as a year) does the position typically spend processing information in the following ways?

1. Fill out forms, record information, code information, copy information from one form to another, enter data into machines or computers. _____ %

2. Inspect forms, correspondence and other written information to determine whether required information is present and/or accurate. _____ %

3. Check/review accuracy of calculations, methods, procedures, and approach and/or determine if policy has been followed. _____ %

4. Compile information/data from multiple sources; investigate sources of information; gather and arrange and/or tally information. _____ %

5. Evaluate and examine information to make approval/disapproval decision; break down information to identify important aspects; combine information upon which to draw conclusions; conduct research to discover new approaches and applications. _____ %

6. Solve problems by reaching conclusions based on summaries of information; define solutions and take actions based on information processed by others. _____ %

100%

FIGURE 5–13
Example of a closed-end question used by Wyatt.

Several *sampling techniques,* including random, stratified random, and "matrix data base design" are used to insure that the correct number and type of benchmark jobs, and the appropriate balance, are obtained to adequately describe the entire organization and its value system.

Correlation analysis is applied to the development of MULTICOMP job evaluation to understand: (1) which compensable factors are independently stronger predictors of job value and (2) which factors are related to each other.[6]

The extent to which job descriptions can be written by computer can be argued either way. Wyatt says this about it:

> The process of describing jobs is less time-consuming and frustrating than in traditional approaches because the incumbent and/or supervisor checks boxes, fills in blanks from response scales, and assigns percentages to questions rather than writing a narrative description. Writing skill and knowing which words or phrases tend to be associated with higher grades are no longer important in determining the grade.[7]

Job Descriptions

We have looked at job analysis, including computerized versions, and we have seen that sometimes job analysis goes on to job evaluation and job pricing. At the start of the chapter, we also observed that job analysis usually resulted in a job description, but we have not said much about how the job description is produced. Up to a point it can be argued that even with computer assistance the very best job descriptions are likely to result where the analyst has a good command of the English language. However, newer automated job description systems can provide descriptions that are often indistinguishable from employee-written descriptions.

Job descriptions are important because they and the related job specifications are the building blocks of job evaluation. To illustrate the different parts of a job description, we shall look at some examples. Figure 5–14 shows a job description for an executive secretary. We shall comment on several parts of this description: the job title, the job summary, the nature of the work, and the job specifications.

Title

Typically, there are many more job titles in an organization than are really necessary. When two job titles do not really describe two different jobs, the former job title may have been changed to satisfy the ego of a worker who felt that the old title did not convey sufficient status. Such differences may also indicate duplication, empire building, or inefficiency. It is up to the job analyst to examine differences in job titles and eliminate those that are not really justifiable. On the other hand, a few jobs bearing the same title may actually be quite different. In such cases different titles should be used to match the differing job descriptions. John Patton, C. L. Littlefield, and Allen Self believe that a job title should be

```
                    JOB DESCRIPTION
              NATIONAL OFFICE SALARY PROGRAM

JOB TITLE:    Executive Secretary            GRADE:    6

JOB CODE:     06-N07-0                        DATE:    May, 1974
```

Job Summary

Performs varied secretarial and specialized office work generally for
General Managers or equivalent level executives. Takes and transcribes
shorthand dictation of letters, memos, minutes of divisional meetings and
reports. Compiles information and prepares various reports as assigned.
Frequently handles personal and confidential correspondence or materials.
Maintains confidential files of departmental or divisional personnel data,
cost information, planning data and other material of a similar nature.
Writes routine correspondence on own initiative. Performs other secretarial
tasks such as receiving visitors, answering and placing phone calls, and
making appointments. May give work direction to other clerical workers.
Performs miscellaneous duties as assigned.

Nature of Work

The job is performed under general supervision. The job holder decides
such things as the adequacy of travel arrangements, priorities in scheduling
appointments and the kinds of material to be provided for meetings. A
thorough knowledge of divisional and company administrative procedures is
required. Errors or omissions in work affect a large number of people and
often result in considerable confusion or loss of time. The job involves
frequent public contact. Because of the frequent absence of direct supervision, incumbents must take initiative in dealing with requests for
information.

Job Specifications

The position normally requires completion of high school or its equivalent.
The job holder must have at least five years of related experience, a
portion of which may be college or business school. The ability to type at
least 55 words per minute and to take dictation at 100 words per minute is
required. The job holder must possess human relations skills and maturity
of judgment.

APPROVED: _____*Schmidt*_____, Corporate Compensation

FIGURE 5–14
Job description for an executive secretary.

125

1. Functional, indicating as clearly as possible the nature of the work content.
2. Distinct, differentiating the job from all others in the group.
3. Familiar, following the general custom or practice of the firm or the industry.
4. Standard, facilitating wage and salary comparisons among firms or within the labor market.[8]

To achieve standardization, they suggest changing the title if the present job title is unique to the organization, but keeping the title if it is unique to the industry.

Job Summary

The job summary section of the job description should be written in narrative style. Notice also that the summary is concise and contains short sentences often starting with verbs (*performs, takes and transcribes, compiles, handles, maintains,* and *writes*). This part of the description typically does not go into many details, but neither is it vague.

Nature of the Work

This is the central part of the job description and its content varies. It may detail the conditions under which the job is performed—the nature of the supervision received, the effect of errors, and the need for initiative in dealing with requests for information. Another approach is to list the key functions of the job (in more detail than in the job summary) or the duties and responsibilities called for by the job.

Job Specifications

The last section describes job specifications. These range from certain factors within the job such as education and experience to specific skills such as speed of typing and dictation. A point to consider here is the difference between a job specification and a job requirement. If the job specification is completion of high school, is it a requirement for the occupant to be able successfully to do the work, or is it *only* a specification (that is, something the company would like to insist on)? Many persons are kept out of jobs because of job specifications. Where the indicated specification does not represent a bona fide job requirement, the job description may not comply with equal employment opportunity legislation. Job specifications are particularly important because they describe in a specific way the types of factors to be used in job evaluation, to be described in Chapters 6 through 8.

Figure 5–15 shows the job description for the junior position of compensation analyst in a large paper company. This position description serves a dual purpose as it also provides a basis for improved employee performance. Aside from the summary information at the top, the description has six parts: (1) purpose of the position; (2) responsibility for personnel supervised; (3) key working relationships; (4) responsibility for corporate resources; (5) education and experience requirements; and (6) principal duties. The last part accounts for almost half of the job description.

Job Specifications

Companies using job specifications may include them as part of a job description or move directly from job analysis to job specifications. Earlier, we looked at job specifications for an executive secretary. More detailed specifications are shown for a supervisor of data processing operations in Figure 5–16.

The first three columns show the job factors and subfactors with the approximate degree specified for each subfactor. The next column gives substantiating information from job analysis, and points are assigned in the last column. (Point systems will be described in Chapter 7.) This specific information can be used, as pointed out earlier, in connection with job evaluation.

Keeping Up to Date

Regardless of which practice is followed—including the job specification in the job description or using a job specification instead of a job description—it is important that the information be kept up to date. Otherwise technological change is likely to make the existing information meaningless. For this reason, every job or position description should include the date it became effective. Based on these dates, a review plan can be developed so that all job descriptions and specifications can, on a rotating basis, be reviewed at least annually. More frequent analyses should be made where needed, especially for those jobs known to be undergoing rapid technological change.

Subjectivity

Subjectivity characterizes the processes of job analysis, job evaluation, and performance evaluation. No matter how assiduously an organization strives for objectivity in these matters, the subjective aspect cannot be eliminated. One of the ways of minimizing subjectivity is to emphasize validity and reliability. To improve the validity and reliability of job analysis, the job analyst should ask several kinds of questions: (1) Does the analysis measure what it should be measuring? and (2) How consistent are the measures? Would the same analyst come

MAMMOTH PAPER CORPORATION

POSITION DESCRIPTION–PERFORMANCE IMPROVEMENT GUIDE Pos. No. 08766 08767

POS. TITLE _____ Compensation Analyst _____ EMPLOYEE: _____

DIV. OR DEPT. _____ Salary Administration _____ LOCATION _____ Headquarters _____

This position reports to (Title) _____ Manager, Salary Administration _____ Date September 1, 1977

A. BASIC PURPOSE OF POSITION: Give a brief statement of the main reason for the position's existence. This is roughly the equivalent of a one sentence answer to the question "Why does the company have the position?"

To assist in the administration of Corporate salary and position evaluation policies for the assigned Division and Functional areas.

B. RESPONSIBILITY FOR PERSONNEL SUPERVISED: List the number of employees who report to you directly and through subordinates.

Exempt ___ 0 ___ Non-Exempt ___ 0 ___ Hourly ___ 0 ___ Total ___ 0 ___

C. KEY WORKING RELATIONSHIPS:

1. Internal: Identify your most important working relationships with people inside the company other than your subordinates or your immediate superior. Indicate who they are and the nature, frequency, and reasons for the contacts.

Managers in assigned Divisions and Functional areas, daily, to discuss specific cases involving salary administration and position evaluation matters.

2. External: Identify your most important working relationships with people outside the company. Indicate who they are and the nature, frequency, and reasons for the contacts. Include customers, vendors, construction firms, associations and groups when a working relationship is involved, etc.

Compensation Analysts in other companies—weekly.
Representatives of various State and Federal agencies concerning comparative salary surveys—monthly.

D. RESPONSIBILITY FOR CORPORATE RESOURCES: (Complete for exempt positions only)

1. **CORPORATE ASSETS:** List the approximate values of the assets under your custody at any one time. $ _____ minimal _____

2. **EXPENDITURES:** List the estimated annual amounts of expenditures you normally approve or participate in recommending. (Include only those expenditures for materials, services, etc., purchased outside the Corporation.) $ _____ minimal _____

E. EDUCATION & EXPERIENCE REQUIREMENTS:

1. **EDUCATION:** Formal education or training normally required, e.g. "High School."
High School; some college or business school preferred.

2. **EXPERIENCE:** Minimum number of years of previous experience normally required, e.g.: "5 Years."
3 years' business experience. Must have ability to analyze data and reach logical conclusions. Must be able to relate well with higher management.

3. **ON THE JOB TRAINING:** (Non-Exempt only)

PREPARED BY T. E. Puckelbauer _____ APPROVED BY *James E. Smith*

FIGURE 5–15
Job description for the junior position of compensation analyst in a large paper company.

128

F. PRINCIPAL DUTIES: Describe the major tasks or duties you perform regularly. List them in order of importance to achieve the Basic Purpose. Do not include duties normally assigned all supervisors such as training subordinates, organizing work, etc. unless they are more than normal activities. (For nonexempt see note below)

20% **1** Evaluate exempt positions and recommend grades which reflect proper relativity internally and externally.

10% **2** Initiate salary surveys involving other companies in the paper industry and in other industries.

10% **3** Participate in salary surveys initiated by other companies for exempt positions.

15% **4** Analyze survey results to determine Company position. Make recommendations for changes, as appropriate.

15% **5** Prepare charts and graphs of survey results for review with higher management.

10% **6** Assist Compensation Administrator in conducting reviews of Divisional grading structures and recommending changes.

5% **7** Review and approve exempt salary increases which exceed guidelines where the new salary falls below the midpoint of exempt grade 11.

5% **8** Maintain current benchmark position records and position descriptions.

2% **9** Prepare and maintain production and sales scope data for assigned areas.

8% **10** Complete special projects as assigned.

11

12

13

14

15

FOR NONEXEMPT IN COLUMN F SHOW % OF TIME FOR EACH DUTY.

FIGURE 5–15
(Continued)

129

JOB SPECIFICATIONS

Factor	Subfactor	Degree	Substantiating Data	Points
Knowledge	Education	5+	Requires knowledge of theory and concepts related to hardware and software applications. A minimum of a four-year business administration program preferred, with technical school certificate or CDP certificate required.	98
Knowledge	Experience	6+	Must have at least five years of experience and training in data-processing operations, data preparation, and programming.	130
Knowledge	Skill	7−	Requires great skill in interpersonal contact as well as technological skill in methods, systems, and equipment used in data-processing operations.	95
Problem Solving	Interpretation	5+	Analyzes and evaluates broad amount of theoretical and technical knowledge on the efficient use of data-processing resources and their effective interface with human resources.	78
Problem Solving	Compliance	4	Develops from both specific and abstract sources directives and procedures that are understandable by the operating personnel responsible for output.	42
Problem Solving	Communication	6	Requires broad communication abilities. Must be able to communicate technical or sophisticated concepts in simple terminology/basic language. Must maintain liaison with other departments and hardware vendors.	123
Decision Making	Interpersonal	5−	Frequently exchanges routine and nonroutine information as well as "state of the art" knowledge; instructs, coaches, trains, and counsels subordinates and nonsubordinates performing similar assignments in their work areas; closely coordinates activities involving other managers.	73
Decision Making	Managerial	4	Receives general supervision with broad guidelines; directs small group of subordinates performing technical functions in operations of data-processing system within a multiprogramming environment.	53
Decision Making	Assets	4	Has some opportunity for influencing planning and control of rather narrow field involving capital assets valued at less than $500,000. Assists in establishing, implementing, and controlling budget for the operation and training of personnel and the purchase of material at less than $150,000.	48

Total Points: 740

FIGURE 5–16
The job specifications portion of a job description for a supervisor of data processing operations. (From Richard I. Henderson, **Compensation Management: Rewarding Performance in the Modern Organization,** *2nd ed. [Reston, Va.: Reston Publishing Co., 1976], p. 142. Used by permission.)*

130

up with a different result at another time? If several persons looked at the same job, would they come up with different results?

Validity

Validity can be looked at in terms of content validity, predictive validity, and construct validity. In testing for content validity, the analyst asks whether the sample of work performance analyzed is fairly representative of the job. Are some important aspects of the job not considered? A good way to assure content validity is to secure expert judgment as to what should be included in the job analysis. This usually requires a group evaluation by workers in the particular job, their supervisors, and others as appropriate. Predictive validity can be used where sample size permits. If employees are required to take a qualification test before being hired, do the test scores predict success or failure on the job? Are those who scored the highest on the test the most successful on the jobs? And are those who achieved a lower score (but still were hired) less successful on the job?

Reliability

Reliability refers to consistency of the same rater over time or the consistency of different raters in rating the same individual. Thus, if employees are rated by the same supervisor in a performance appraisal during one month and again six months later, one would expect an employee rated high the first time to rate high the second time; conversely, an employee rated low the first time would probably be rated low the second time. If in general this were true, we would have a high test-retest reliability. Where two different observers using an identical rating instrument rated the same group of workers, one might expect in general that an employee rated high by one observer would also rate high by the other observer; conversely, an employee given a low score by one observer would probably score low when rated by the other observer. If in general this were true, we would have a high interobserver reliability. With good reliability in either case, we would not expect perfect agreement (a correlation of 1.0) but perhaps a correlation of .70. If either reliability showed a correlation of .20, for example, we would say the rating device was unreliable.

Summary

Job analysis is one of a cluster of rational managerial devices that tend to support organizational hierarchy. Other devices in the cluster are job evaluation, job pricing, and performance evaluation.

Job analysis provides the basis for job descriptions and job specifications. Computers, through the use of data bases, can facilitate detailed cross comparisons in the job analysis process. And the use of word processing makes it easier to write better job descriptions and to keep descriptions up to date. But computers are typically costly and are not a substitute for human judgments. Such judgments are required not only of higher level personnel but also in carrying out the job analysis process.

The job analyst, an entry level job in the compensation and benefits unit, watches industry and area trends and uses other background information such as the generic job descriptions provided by the *Dictionary of Occupational Titles* to develop job descriptions. Internal company background information such as that available from organization charts and work flow charts is also used by the analyst.

More detailed specific information about jobs is obtained through observation, questionnaires, personal interviews, or some combination of these methods. First, the analyst must notify the worker's immediate superior of the intended job analysis if the analyst is to establish the necessary rapport with the worker. Information obtained from the worker is carefully rechecked with the worker, the immediate superior, and other employees who come in contact with the worker to develop accurate analyses, job descriptions, and job specifications.

When computers enter the picture, job analysis sometimes extends onward into the job evaluation process, but if human judgments are important, the two processes should remain separate.

However, as pointed out by the Wyatt Company, job analysis without the assistance of computers suffers from certain shortcomings:

1. When the process is done by entry-level employees, exaggerated position descriptions by managers are less likely to be contested.
2. Doing the analysis without computers may require 10 hours to produce a job description.
3. This time commitment makes it more difficult to keep descriptions current.
4. Reliability of the analysis depends on the analyst's perception of each job and her ability to get all relevant information from workers or their supervisors.
5. Different analysts can be expected to come up with differing job descriptions for the same job.

At the Bank of America, the primary purpose of the job analysis (and job evaluation) plan is to assure equity as to the worth of different jobs within the organization. A representative sample of employees completes a detailed questionnaire called the Job Profile, which includes many closed-end questions relating to eight major job factors. The computer converts the information into points. All jobs whose total point scores fall within the same range are assigned the same job grade. The computer's elaborate compare function allows comparisons with other jobs in the same job family and also with jobs in other job families. With the creation of job families, the Bank has reduced the number of job descriptions from 9,000 to 2,000. The Bank is also exploring the use of one-paragraph descriptors by which job descriptions can be more readily compared with each other on the screen.

Another approach to using computers in job analysis is to hire outside consultants. The use of such consultants may be costly to install but is more cost effective for the larger corporations. It may afford client companies the advantage of a broader view of its problems. Also, any job analysis/job evaluation plan may be better received if it comes from outside the organization. Two alternative plans offered by the Wyatt Company—FACTORCOMP® and MULTICOMP®—emphasize tailoring plans to meet the particular needs of the client organization. FACTORCOMP® is a system that does result in points but does not start out with a predetermined set of factors, points, and degrees. Rather, these elements evolve during the consultation process. MULTICOMP® involves a larger number of job factors as well as more detailed and accurate predictions of the market rate or other dependent variable designated by the client.

The Wyatt consulting approach

1. Draws on three technologies including psychometrics, computer science, and statistics.
2. Relates to the culture and value system of the client.
3. Gathers information using closed-end questionnaires.
4. Consciously attempts to eliminate factors or weights in any plan that might involve bias against women or minorities.
5. Starts with benchmark jobs.
6. Uses computer and statistical techniques to develop suitable job factors.
7. Relies more heavily on computerized rather than purely narrative job descriptions.
8. Encourages a high degree of employee and management participation in the process of developing and installing new plans.

Whether arrived at by traditional or new computerized methods, the typical job description includes a title, a narrative summary of the job, a section on duties, and a section on job specifications. Job titles should correspond with the job performed, and standardization of job titles within each industry is desirable. The remainder of the job description should employ concise sentences starting with verbs.

Job specifications should be distinguished from job requirements. Is a particular specification merely something management would like the worker to have, or is it necessary to do the job? Job specifications, because they tie in closely with job factors, are essential to the process of job evaluation.

To avoid job obsolescence, job descriptions should be dated and reviewed yearly on a rotating schedule. More frequent reviews may be required for jobs undergoing rapid technological change.

Subjectivity must be minimized in job analysis in order for it to be effective. Validity and reliability are important concepts for the job analyst to keep in mind when analyzing and describing jobs.

**Case
Study**

Marie Manseau

Marie Manseau is an attractive woman in her early thirties. She recently lost her husband in an airplane accident. She dresses attractively, has a pleasing personality, and gets along well with other employees of the White House news summary office. The main function of the office is to compile a daily news summary from newspaper and wire service reports. This summary is distributed to the president and other White House officials.

Under a new reorganization plan, the activities of the office are under the direct supervision of Tim Halligan, Assistant Press Secretary for Domestic Affairs. Short and fat, with a bushy red mustache, Halligan is easy to work with. He is part of the larger news team which functions under the general guidance of Arnold Segal, the president's press secretary.

Reporting to Halligan are four sections which handle international affairs, domestic politics, economics, and science and technology. Working under each section head are a number of writers. The distribution of writers by section is international affairs, 5; domestic politics, 4; economics, 2; and science and technology, 5. The section heads meet each morning to receive major writing assignments from Halligan. In addition, writers in each section routinely scan stories from the wire services and from a selected list of major newspapers and other periodicals for items of interest to their section. They then prepare news summaries of the assigned and routine items for the attention of their section head.

Section heads are Tom Douglas (international affairs), Richard Clarfield (domestic politics), Marie Manseau (economics), and Roosevelt Smith (science and technology). Manseau, the newest section head, is classified as a staff writer and the others are classified as editors. The editor's job pays about 25 percent more than that of staff writer.

Duties of the section heads are comparable. Each section head supervises the writers within the section, assigns writers to particular news items, edits copy prepared by the writers to conform with the specialized White House style and syntax rules, rewrites or requires the rewriting of articles submitted by the writers in the section, contributes to editorial comment in the daily summary, and together with Halligan participates in the layout of material to fill the available space.

All members of the section have to work hard. Although the official hours are 8 A.M. to 4 P.M., the day usually runs much longer; the work is often not finished until late at night. There is considerable pressure on the job because each daily summary has to be distributed promptly at 4 P.M. to the president and top White House officials.

As the head of the economics section, Manseau encounters certain international items she is supposed to coordinate with Douglas. However, she has discovered that he has a rather surly disposition. So, when such items come up, she goes instead to Mark Chao, the Assistant Press Secretary for Foreign Affairs, who usually can give her the answers she needs. That is not established procedure, since the entire news summary office is under Halligan's authority.

But that is the way she handles this problem, and she has never run into trouble doing her job in this way.

Role Assignment

As a compensation analyst, you have been asked by Halligan to prepare a job description of the new job being performed by Manseau. What would you include, and what is your reasoning? (Consider both the information in the case and relevant material in the Dictionary of Occupational Titles.)

Questions for Discussion

1. What is the difference between a job analysis and a job description?
2. What is the difference between a job description and a job specification?
3. Why do companies use job descriptions? What is the most important reason for using job descriptions?
4. Discuss this statement: "A job analysis should have as its ultimate objective the analysis of the most efficient way to perform the job rather than the way in which the job is now being done."
5. Of what value is the *Dictionary of Occupational Titles* in the work of the job analyst?
6. What techniques should the job analyst use to gather information? To what extent should techniques differ depending on the types of jobs and why?
7. Under what circumstances is a diary or log an appropriate method for gathering information about a job?
8. What things should be kept in mind when developing job titles?
9. What are some of the disadvantages of *not* computerizing the job analysis process?

Consider the Wyatt company criticism.

10. Is it desirable to combine the job analysis and job evaluation processes? Justify your answer.
11. Comment on the job analysis procedures, as described in the chapter, used by the Bank of America.
12. Describe some of the broader aspects of the Wyatt Company's approach to job analysis.
13. Can computers be used to write job descriptions? Be detailed and specific in your answer.
14. Compare job specifications with job descriptions. Of what special value are job specifications?
15. What needs to be done to be sure that job descriptions do not become obsolete?
16. When doing job analyses, job descriptions, and job specifications, what are the more important communications aspects a job analyst should consider? With respect to the worker? With respect to the worker's immediate supervisor? With respect to others?
17. What is meant by validity and reliability? What bearing do they have on job analysis?

Notes

1. Elliott Jaques, "Taking Time Seriously in Evaluating Jobs," *Harvard Business Review* 57, no. 5 (September–October 1979): 124–32.

2. The Wyatt Company, *Salary Management: The Wyatt Company's MULTICOMP® Process,* (San Francisco, CA), 3–6, 4.

3. The Wyatt Company, *Salary Management: The Wyatt Company's FACTORCOMP®️ Process* (San Francisco, CA) 3–6.
4. Ibid., 5.
5. The Wyatt Company, *Salary Management: The Wyatt Company's MULTICOMP®️ Process, op. cit.,* 19.
6. The Wyatt Company, *Salary Management:*

The Wyatt Company's MULTICOMP®️ Process, op. cit., 21.
7. Ibid., p. 7.
8. John A. Patton, C. Littlefield, and Stanley Allen Self, *Job Evaluation,* 3rd ed. (Homewood, IL: Richard D. Irwin, 1964), p. 82. Copyright © 1964 by Richard D. Irwin, Inc.

References

Arvey, Richard D., et al. "Potential Sources of Bias on Job Analytic Processes." *Academy of Management Journal* 25, no. 3 (Sept. 82): 618–629.

Carlisle, Kenneth E. *Analyzing Jobs and Tasks.* Englewood Cliffs, NJ: Educational Technology Publications, 1986.

Daniel, Christopher. "Tomorrow's Computer Skills—Today." *Personnel* 65, no. 4 (April 1988): 28–34.

Davis, John H. "Statistics, Computers, and the Big Picture." *ACA News* (July/August 1986): 3, 6.

Gael, Sidney. *Job Analysis: A Guide to Assessing Work Activities.* San Francisco: Jossey-Bass, 1983.

Hartman, Stephen W., and Siegel, Joel G. "Management Applications for Micro DBMS." *Personnel* 64, no. 2 (February 1987): 69–72.

Henderson, Richard I. "Job Descriptions: No Mystical Solutions." *ACA News* (September 1986): 5, 8.

Henderson, Richard I., and Clarke, K. L. *Job Pay for Job Worth: Designing and Managing an Equitable Job Classification and Pay System.* Research Monograph No. 86. Atlanta: Georgia State University College of Business Administration.

Jeanneret, P. R. "Equitable Job Evaluation and Classification with the Position Analysis Questionnaire. *Compensation Review* 12, no. 1 (1980): 32–42.

Kosidlak, Janet G. "DACUM: An Alternative Job Analysis Tool." *Personnel* 64, no. 3 (March 1987): 14–21.

Levine, Edward L., et al. "Evaluation of Job Analysis Methods by Experienced Job Analysts.

Academy of Management Journal 26, no. 2 (June 83): 339–347.

Lopez, Felix M., et al. "An Empirical Test of Trait-Oriented Job Analysis Techniques. *Personnel Psychology* 34, no. 3 (Autumn 1981): 479–502.

Olson, H. C.; Fine, S. A.; and Jennings, M. C. "The Use of Functional Job Analysis in Establishing Performance Standards for Heavy Equipment Operators." *Personnel Psychology* 34, no. 2 (1981): 351–64.

Pay, Rex G. "Computerized Pay Planning in a Competitive Market." *Personnel* 64, no. 8 (August 1987): 61–70.

Plachy, Roger J. "Writing Job Descriptions That Get Results." *Personnel* 64, no. 10 (October 1987): 56–63.

Silverman, Stanley B., et al. "The Effects of Age and Job Experience on Employee Responses to a Structured Job Analysis Questionnaire." *Public Personnel Management* 13, no. 3 (Fall 1984): 355–358.

The Wyatt Company. *Salary Management: The Wyatt Company's FACTORCOMP®️ Process.* San Francisco, CA.

The Wyatt Company. *Salary Management: The Wyatt Company's MULTICOMP®️ Process.* San Francisco, CA.

U.S. Department of Labor. *Dictionary of Occupational Titles,* 4th ed. Washington, DC: U.S. Government Printing Office, 1977, and 1986 Supplement.

U.S. Department of Labor. *Selected Characteristics of Occupations Defined in the Dictionary of Occupational Titles.* Washington, DC: U.S. Government Printing Office, 1981.

Overview: Job Evaluation

Chapter Outline

- Five Major Methods of Job Evaluation
- Other Methods of Job Evaluation
- Prevalence of Different Job Evaluation Plans
- Subjectivity and Quality of Job Evaluation Factors
- Implementation of Job Evaluation Plans
- Summary
- Case Study—Millozzo Chemical Company

As we have seen, management, especially the compensation manager, is continually faced with balancing the external markets for different jobs with internal equity—the relative worth (not necessarily in money terms) of one job compared to another.

External market factors, both national and international, have a substantial influence on both pay and employee benefits. If there were a single monolithic labor market and if all jobs turned over frequently so there was an active market for every job, then the problem of internal consistency within the organization would be less important. We saw, however, that labor markets for many jobs are disjointed or thin. For some jobs (such as tax collectors in government) there may be no market value, and, as with women clerical workers, for example, even market values may not provide a reliable basis for external pricing of jobs.

Americans have sought remedies through the political process for perceived abuses of human rights, such as the exploitation of children and women in factories. This effort resulted in the minimum wage laws, which not only affected external markets but also had an effect on equity among interjob relationships within the organization. More recently, the March on Washington led by civil rights leaders, the resulting Civil Rights Act of 1964, and especially the implementation of Title VII regarding equal employment opportunity focused attention on equity within organizations (including labor unions). Women led by groups such as the National Organization for Women (NOW), are equally concerned with matters of internal equity. We have not yet truly had a march of women on Washington, but the possibility of such a march in the future is not to be ignored.

American labor unions, first the craft unions and later also the industrial unions, have typically sought to improve the lot of the worker not just in the market but inside the organization or, in the case of the construction unions, at the workplace. Not only wages, but *hours and working conditions* have played an important role in the collective bargaining process. Under union contracts, or labor-management agreements as they are more correctly described, grievance procedures focus especially on matters of internal equity.

Historically, with some exceptions, management has tended to be on the defensive rather than to exert a leadership role in matters of internal equity. In past years, internal equity in many companies was determined even more than in recent years on an essentially subjective basis, with little rational justification.

However, in World War II it became difficult for firms to acquire the employees they needed to meet the demands of war production. Job evaluation provided a means to justify pay increases for key personnel. Since then, more and more companies have adopted job evaluation plans.

Five Major Methods of Job Evaluation

In Chapter 5 we discussed job analysis, job descriptions, and computer applications. Well-analyzed jobs translated into meaningful job descriptions provide a solid foundation for effective job evaluation. The five methods of job evaluation now in common use are (1) ranking, (2) predetermined grading, (3) point method, (4) factor comparison, and (5) guide chart–profile method. We will discuss each method briefly here, leaving detailed descriptions to later chapters.

Ranking

Ranking involves taking all the jobs in the organization and ranking them from highest to lowest. This is a simple method which is often useful where the organization is small or the number of people to be rated is small.

Predetermined Grading

Predetermined grading (or job classification) involves setting up a number of pay grades and then assigning each job to a particular pay grade. First, each pay grade is given a broad description. Once this has been done, each job description is compared with the different pay grade descriptions to see which grade best matches the job description.

Although this method is used by some small organizations, it has had its principal application among government employees, especially at the federal level. In this method and the ranking method, emphasis is on the job as a whole. In contrast, the next three methods emphasize factors within the job.

Point Method

The point method involves the selection and definition of job factors, the assignment of point values to each factor, and the evaluation of each job to determine the total points for the job. This method is widely used in private industry and is still the most popular method.

Factor Comparison

The factor comparison method[1] is similar to the ranking method, but jobs are ranked in a different way. Two separate types of ranking are developed. First, selected key jobs are ranked by factor: that is, the jobs are ranked using one factor at a time. Second, the factors are ranked within each key job; that is, for a particular job the different factors are ranked according to importance. Then, the two sets of rankings are mathematically reconciled to develop a point scale. The worth of other jobs is determined graphically by comparing new jobs against key jobs. Factor comparison is more widely used among exempt salaried employees than among nonexempt blue-collar and white-collar workers. Because its more complex mathematical base makes it harder for employees to understand, this method is not used as often as the point method.

Guide Chart–Profile Method

The guide chart–profile method is the most recent among the methods in common use. Like the point and factor comparison plans, it emphasizes job factors. Each job is evaluated using three guide charts. Each chart is a matrix from which an appropriate number is taken. The guide charts are for (1) know-how, (2) problem solving, and (3) accountability. The numbers from the guide charts are used to develop a point total for each job. Finally, point values derived from the guide charts are checked against standard profiles for all jobs as well as for the particular type of job—line, staff, or research. This plan, while somewhat complex, has increased in use, especially among professional and supervisory workers.

Universality of Major Job Evaluation Methods

While major methods of job evaluation (JE) differ, there is a certain universality to the different methods. Typically, all of the methods build upon some form of job analysis and use job descriptions as a basis for comparing different jobs. To a certain extent, the ranking process is involved in most of the techniques. Ranking is, of course, used both in the ranking method and the factor comparison method; these two methods differ mainly in whether the job as a whole or factors within jobs are considered. And under the point method, a device called the factor comparison check is used as a way of checking the accuracy of point evaluations. In allocating a job to a particular grade using the predetermined grading method, it helps to rank two jobs as to which requires the most knowledge. In the Hay guide chart–profile method, an analyst may have to ask which of two jobs should be ranked higher to determine the position of a job within a cell on a guide chart. Also, most of the methods, including the point, factor comparison (percentage), and guide chart–profile methods, all use points. More recently, the federal government's predetermined grading method has added the factor evaluation system, which applies points to the factors within jobs, to assist in deciding to what grade (envelope of jobs) each particular job should be assigned.

Other Methods of Job Evaluation

Other methods of job evaluation include (1) the time span of discretion approach; (2) maturity curves; and (3) the guideline method. Maturity curves will be covered in Chapter 15 when we discuss the pay of professionals.

Time Span of Discretion

The concept of the time span of discretion was developed by Elliott Jaques.[2] It is an appealing method of job evaluation because it does away completely with the need for detailed job descriptions and provides a single internal measure applicable to every job at every level of the organization. The time span of discretion, as used by Jaques, refers to

> the maximum period of time during which the use of discretion is authorized and expected, without a review of that discretion by a superior.[3]

Jaques looks at the period from the time a task is assigned to the time it is reviewed after completion, even if there is some delay in this review. Many measurements are taken, and the longest time is used as the measure of the importance of that particular job. His measurement scale extends from one-half day through weeks, months, and years to a maximum of ten years. The time span for a simple blue-collar or clerical task can be expected to be short, while that for a high-ranking executive would be long. Even though there is a problem of exact measurement of the time span, this method is seen as far more objective than the normal committee review and subjective judgments which come into play under the more conventional methods of job evaluation mentioned earlier. Jaques does not rely on judgments of personnel experts or on those of anyone except the worker's immediate superior and, as a check when necessary, the superior's boss.

Measurement of Successive Approximations

In attempting to measure the time span of discretion in hard-to-measure situations, Jaques advocates questioning the superior in a way to elicit successive approximations until a measure can be agreed upon.

> Thus, for example, if you ask a manager when he expects a subordinate to have completed the development of a design, he may reply that he could not give an exact date; he expects the subordinate to get on with it as quickly as he can and to get it done along with a number of other tasks that he has been allocated. If you then ask whether it would be all right if the subordinate completed it within the next ten years, the manager will probably laugh and say, "Oh, no! He doesn't have that much time." Does he expect it to be completed within the

next few hours? No, it would be quite impossible for him to do so; he would need at least some months to do it along with the rest of the work that he has to do. You might then ask him if he would allow the subordinate, say, a year to complete it, to which he might reply, "No, not that long—possibly something more like six months." You can then refine the questions and help the manager to converge upon the maximum number of months that would constitute the longest target completion time that he would allow the subordinate when he allocated the task.[4]

Multiple Tasks versus Single Tasks

Conceptually, Jaques looks at two kinds of situations: one involving a job where the worker has to carry out several different tasks more or less simultaneously, and the other where the worker performs single tasks but turns them out in succession.

For multiple tasks, the longest task is controlling. Jaques points out that the worker can put off the longest task in order to complete short-term tasks, but that the longest task cannot be pushed beyond its target completion date.

For single tasks, the problem of measurement is more complex. For example, in cases where the single task involves work being turned out in batches of similar work, it may be only necessary for the superior to check completion of a number of batches at periodic intervals. Another example is that of a copy typist:

> Sometimes she is given one task at a time; sometimes she is given a few tasks at once, but is told what order to do them in, finishing one task at a time so that she has no responsibility for deciding priorities. . . . Her manager directly reviews her work, sometimes immediately it is finished and sometimes delayed for hours or days.[5]

Figure 6–1 illustrates the time span of discretion approach. Tasks are shown from A through DD by horizontal bars. The vertical arrows indicate the review points; if an arrow follows a series of dashes, the review is delayed rather than immediate. The longest time spans are those for tasks B, K, and R, each involving almost three days.

What Critics Say

Jaques's time span of discretion concept is considered to be effective in measuring differentials of worth for scientific and engineering positions.[6] Edward Lawler agrees that the concept is interesting and potentially quite important but questions it on the grounds of practicality.[7] David Belcher has criticized the concept on the grounds that the plan limits job evaluation to a single compensable factor but qualifies this criticism by pointing out that some companies do use such single-factor plans.[8]

1 day

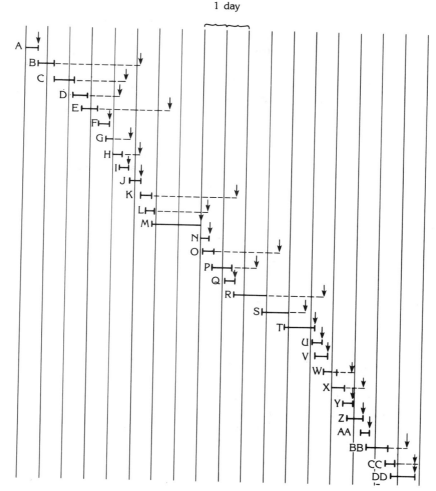

FIGURE 6–1
Time span of discretion for a copy typist. (From Elliott Jaques,
Equitable Payment, *2nd ed. [Carbondale and Edwardsville, Ill.:*
Southern Illinois University Press, 1970], p. 133. Copyright ©
Heinemann Educational Books Ltd.)

Guideline Method

Another of the less conventional methods is the guideline method (which has nothing to do with the Hay guide chart–profile method). This plan reverses the usual job evaluation sequence. First, an area wage survey is conducted to identify market rates for a large number of key jobs in the organization. In a separate process, a schedule is constructed of pay grades with midpoints about 5 percentage points apart. Then, particular jobs are tentatively assigned to one of these pay grades according to the closeness of the market rate to the grade midpoint. Next, the tentative assignments are reviewed to reconcile them with the requirements of internal equity. After this has been done, jobs other than the key jobs from the market survey are ranked in comparison with the key jobs and assigned to labor grades.[9] A serious question about the guideline method is whether it goes too far in the direction of pricing jobs while paying insufficient attention to internal organizational relationships or job content. As one writer for the American Management Association has commented,

> The issue of marketplace pay discrimination is important because the market value approach to setting pay levels, an approach in widespread use, is already acknowledged as being highly suspect.[10]

Prevalence of Different Job Evaluation Plans

In a 1988 survey done at the request of the President's Advisory Committee on Federal Pay, the American Compensation Association looked at the methods of job evaluation reported by 1,367 ACA members.[11] It analyzed pay practices of six different groups within the responding organizations including executives/managers, scientists/engineers, customer representatives, exempt staff, clerical employees, and hourly employees. Some of the results, taking all six groups collectively, are shown in Table 6–1.

Whether the above results are valid or whether, on the other hand, respondents may not be clear about the difference between job evaluation and job pricing—which are not the same—remains in doubt. Another survey conducted by Sibson & Company in 1986 does not support the ACA findings.[12] In their survey, covering a somewhat smaller but still meaningful sample, they looked at the job evaluation methods covering four groups—officer/executive, exempt, salaried nonexempt, and hourly nonexempt. The results are shown in summary form in Table 6–2.

TABLE 6–1
Methods used in job evaluation, ACA survey.

	Low Group	*High Group*
Market pricing	45.1%	65.0%
Point factor	36.4	56.2
Whole job ranking	14.0	22.6
Factor comparison	7.4	12.1
Other	3.8	9.9
None	1.0	7.1

Note: In the ACA Survey, percentages did not total 100% for the individual employee groups due to multiple responses.
Source: American Compensation Association, *ACA News,* Jan. 1988.

TABLE 6–2
Methods used in job evaluation, Sibson & Co., Inc.

	Low Group	High Group
Combination	31%	39%
Point factor	23	32
Market pricing	13	19
No formal method	4	10
Internal ranking or classification	6	9
Factor comparison	4	7
Other	2	3

Note: In the Sibson Survey percentages did total 100% for the individual groups.
Source: Sibson & Co., Inc. *1986 Salary Planning Survey.*

The same general method is used in this table as in Table 6–1. That is, the percentages are the ranges for all the groups taken collectively. The results of the two surveys are inconsistent. The Sibson & Company survey shows market pricing coming in about third—behind combination and point factor. It does not seem that the differences are due to the passage of time or the sample sizes. A more likely explanation may be in the way questions were worded in the two surveys. So a serious problem remains as to whether in fact market pricing really *is* the most prevalent method of job evaluation. On one point the two surveys agree: Where there is a combination of methods the most frequent pairs are ranking/market pricing and point factor/market pricing. Perhaps market pricing has gained ground compared to earlier surveys, but the extent of this change remains in doubt.

Subjectivity and Quality of Job Evaluation Factors

While job evaluation plans may seem to lend objectivity to the process of determining a job's relative worth in an organization, they are nonetheless essentially subjective rather than objective in character. Job evaluation plans typically suffer from all sorts of biases—both in the structure of the measurement devices themselves and in the ways in which they are used. As we saw in Chapter 4, validity and reliability enter into the problem of comparable worth. Validity and reliability apply especially to the choice of factors, point values, and so on in job evaluation.

Implementation of Job Evaluation Plans

There is a tendency for the higher level management to regard job evaluation as something desirable for employees below the vice-presidential level. This attitude needs to be weighed against the importance of setting an example; management's participation in job evaluation will convey the message that management is backing the plan and will add to its acceptability.

Single Plan versus Multiple Plans

Whether an organization uses a single plan for all employees or separate plans for different groups within the organization is an important decision. Many organizations, especially multiplant or multinational firms, have different plans for plant workers, clerical workers, sales personnel, technical and professional workers, and supervisors and executives. In the words of Herbert G. Zollitsch and Adolph Langsner,

> It is practically an impossible task to develop a single compensation structure that is applicable and satisfactory to all the different types of jobs and employees found in a company of 500 employees or more.[13]

This view may be overly pessimistic. Using an excessive number of plans could lead to coordination problems, and there is still something to be said for a single plan, even in the largest organizations. For example, the federal government's general schedule is a single job evaluation plan. It is significant that as of March 1987, this plan covered close to 1.5 million employees.[14]

Nevertheless, in a sizable number of larger companies, especially in unionized situations, there are often at least two plans: one covering nonexempt blue-collar and nonsupervisory white-collar workers, and the other covering exempt employees.

Administrative Aspects

Two aspects must be considered when implementing a job evaluation plan. One is administrative and requires individual leadership, and the other involves plan acceptance and calls for group participation.

As to the administrative aspect, it is up to one individual to take the lead in implementing a new job evaluation plan or in handling the later day-to-day administration of it, regardless of how the question of employee participation is resolved. This person must have the necessary technical expertise to provide any committees with information and technical guidance. An outside consultant may be needed more often for initiating a new plan than for administering the plan. This may be especially advisable for technical reasons (especially if one of the more complex methods is to be used) or in a situation where there is a certain amount of internal conflict within the organization and where the new plan may gain greater acceptance if introduced by an outsider.

Employee and/or Union Participation

A more critical problem is that of plan acceptance. A new job evaluation plan provides an important opportunity for allowing employee and/or union participation in a vital aspect of the organization's life. Lawler stresses just how important the role of the employee is in the implementation of a new plan:

It does not make much difference which of the better known methods is used; what makes a tremendous difference, however, is who uses the method and how. Without employee involvement, the results of the evaluation will look good and logical to the members of management, but they will be seen by the workers as a management decision that is arbitrary and at points irrational. On the other hand, if the workers are legitimately involved in the process, the results may not look as neat and logical to management, but the important point is that they will not need to be defended to the employees. The employees who were involved in setting the rates will take on this role.[15]

Zollitsch and Langsner recommend the formation of two groups to assist in implementing a new job evaluation plan: a permanent committee and an advisory committee. The first committee is composed of roughly half management and half employee (or union) representatives. Included among the management representatives is the administrator who installs the new plan. The second committee (also split between management and employee delegates) is formed for a particular department when jobs in that department are being studied by the permanent committee. The second committee ceases to function after it has served its purpose.[16]

Two other recommendations for installing a job evaluation plan merit some consideration. First, the permanent committee should have not just one plan but a full exposition of different types of plans presented to it. The advantages and disadvantages of each plan can then be fully explored and discussed before there is a commitment to one particular plan. Study of the plans at the department level may be desirable if a wider base of support is needed. Such full and free participation may not be easy for a management used to an autocratic style, but if the alternative is the rejection of the plan, management may be willing to make the extra effort.

Second, employees should be reassured that no present employee will have pay or benefits reduced as a result of the plan. Management must determine the costs of installation, including the probable savings that will develop later when new employees come in at lower pay rates for some jobs as well as the increases in pay for other jobs called for by the plan.

Summary

With respect to compensation, management tries to achieve a balance between internal equity and external markets. In the absence of collective bargaining, internal equity is usually obtained through some method of job evaluation.

The chief methods of job evaluation in current use include ranking, predetermined grading, the point method, factor comparison, and the guide chart–profile method. Ranking is most often used in smaller companies or where the number of employees is small. Predetermined grading (or job classification) finds its greatest use in government. Ranking and predetermined grading emphasize the job as a whole, while the other three methods work more with factors within the job. For larger organizations and rapidly growing organizations, these three methods are more likely to be appropriate. The point method is more widely used among blue-collar and nonsupervisory white-collar workers. In general, this plan is more easily accepted by employees than are other methods. The factor comparison and the Hay guide chart–profile methods are more complex and are less readily accepted by employees. However, the Hay guide chart–profile method is coming into increasing use, especially among professional and supervisory employees.

In less common use but of growing interest are other methods of job evaluation, such as maturity curves and the time span of discretion.

Unions tend to favor job evaluation, but do encounter difficulties with existing plans. Whether a single plan or several plans are installed is an important policy decision. Large organizational size does not necessarily preclude use of a single plan. Successful implementation and maintenance of a job evaluation (JE) plan requires a trained individual to administer details of the plan as well as acceptance of the plan by the employees directly affected. Job evaluation committees provide a natural vehicle to accomplish this. Often there is a permanent committee, assisted by one or more departmental committees which are active only when jobs in that particular department are being evaluated. The most important aspect of job evaluation committees is that there be joint participation by management and employee (or union) representatives in both installation and maintenance of the plan.

Case Study

Millozzo Chemical Company

The Millozzo Chemical Company is a manufacturer of inorganic chemicals used in heavy industry. Having started as a small partnership, the company expanded rapidly over the decades and now employs over 500 workers.

During the past year, the company's president attended a regional meeting of The Conference Board, at which the subject of job evaluation was discussed at length. Upon his return, he decided to install a job evaluation plan for the company's office employees and asked the personnel director to take charge.

The personnel director, after giving the matter some thought, developed a plan that he deemed suitable for the organization. He designated a committee consisting of himself, a job analyst, and a person from the department whose employees were to be evaluated. As the committee moved from department to department, its third member was replaced by a representative of the new department.

After all the jobs were evaluated, the new plan was put into effect. Reaction to the plan has been mixed, with some department managers favoring it and some opposed. In those departments where the managers are not in favor of the plan, job descriptions often are not kept up to date even when there are important changes in job content. When one of these managers seeks a pay increase for an employee, using as an argument increased job duties and responsibilities, the increase is often turned down by the personnel director with the comment that these duties are not shown in the job description. The personnel director uses this tactic as a way of assuring that job descriptions are kept up to date. Despite this fact, these particular managers have remained adamant about putting the plan into effect within their departments. On the other hand, those managers who first favored the plan still favor it.

The personnel department has also received a number of complaints from employees. Where two employees hired at about the same time are doing similar work, the complaint has been, "Why does the other employee get more than I do for the same work?" In other cases, the manager has not informed the employee about the rate range for his job or what is necessary for the employee to get an increase in pay.

Role Assignment

You have been hired as the new manager of compensation and benefits. You have learned about the situation as described above. The director of personnel has asked for your analysis and recommendations in connection with the job evaluation plan.

Questions for Discussion

1. Why worry about job evaluation? Why can't a company use market rates for each job instead?
2. What are the five methods of job evaluation in common use? What are the differences among these methods?
3. If you were a manager of compensation and benefits, what factors would you consider in deciding on a method of job evaluation for the employees in your company?
4. What is the time span of discretion, and how can it be used to evaluate jobs?
5. Are job evaluation plans objective or subjective? Discuss.
6. Discuss the prevalence of different JE plans.
7. Should job evaluation be used for all employees or only for those below a certain level in the organization?
8. Should an organization have a single plan for all employees to be covered, or should there be more than one plan?
9. Is it necessary to have a responsible executive who takes the lead with respect to installation of a job evaluation plan? Why not leave it all up to a committee?
10. To what extent is employee participation desirable in the installation and maintenance of a job evaluation plan? What effect will the presence or absence of a union have on the situation?
11. What assurances do employees need to be given concerning the implementation of a job evaluation plan, and how should they be communicated?
12. From a management point of view, what information about possible additional costs and possible additional savings is needed before a job evaluation plan is implemented? Consider both short-term and long-term aspects.

Notes

1. The method described here is the percentage method, which has in general superseded the original money method.
2. Elliott Jaques, *Equitable Payment,* 2nd ed. (Carbondale and Edwardsville, Ill.: Southern Illinois University Press, 1970). Copyright © Heinemann Educational Books Ltd.
3. Ibid., 21.
4. Ibid., 104.
5. Ibid., 132.
6. Thomas Atchison and Wendell French, "Pay Systems for Scientists and Engineers," *Industrial Relations* 7, no. 1 (October 1967): 48.
7. Edward E. Lawler, *Pay and Organizational Effectiveness* (New York: McGraw-Hill, 1971), 213. Reproduced with permission of the publisher.
8. David W. Belcher, *Compensation Administration* (Englewood Cliffs, N.J.: Prentice-Hall, 1974), 143.
9. For further discussion of this method, see J. D. Dunn and Frank M. Rachel, *Wage and Salary Administration: Total Compensation Systems* (New York: McGraw-Hill, 1971), 185–86.
10. Reprinted, by permission of the publisher, from Ernest C. Miller, "Equal Pay for Comparable Work," *Personnel* (September–October, 1979). (New York: AMACOM, a division of American Management Associations, 1979) 5. Copyright © by AMACOM. All rights reserved.
11. "Salary Management Practices Survey Completed," *ACA News* 30, no. 9 (January 1988): 1.
12. *1986 Annual Salary Planning Survey,* Chicago, IL: Sibson & Company, Inc., September 1985, 9.
13. Herbert G. Zollitsch and Adolph Langsner, *Wage and Salary Administration,* 2nd ed. (Cincinnati: South-Western Publishing Co., 1970), 105.
14. Letter to the author from Barbara L. Fiss, Assistant Director for Pay and Performance Management, U.S. Office of Personnel Management, Nov. 12, 1987.
15. Lawler, *op. cit.,* 260.
16. Zollitsch and Langsner, *op. cit.,* 207.

References

Bartley, Douglas L. *Job Evaluation: Wage and Salary Administration.* Reading, MA: Addison-Wesley, 1981.

Crandall, N. Frederic. "Microcomputer Use on the Rise in Job Evaluation." *ACA News* 29, no. 1 (February 1986): 6.

Designing and Developing Your Own Job Evaluation System, 2nd ed. Nashville, TN: Don Burris & Associates, 1987.

Doverspike, Dennis, and Barrett, Gerald V. "An Internal Bias Analysis of a Job Analysis Instrument." *Journal of Applied Psychology* 69, no. 4 (November 1984): 648–662.

Fried, N. Elizabeth. "Selecting a Secretarial Job-Evaluation System." *Compensation and Benefits Review* 18, no. 3 (May–June 1986): 64–69.

Greene, Robert J. "Valuing Occupations: An Empirical Study." *ACA News* 31, no. 1 (February 1988): 7.

Hoffman, Carl C. "Multiple-Pay Systems: Are They Worth the Risk?" *Compensation and Benefits Review* 19, no. 1 (January–February 1987): 36–46.

Janes, Harold D. "Union Views on Job Evaluation: 1971 vs. 1978." *Personnel Journal* 58, no. 2 (February 1979): 80–85.

Jaques, Elliott. *Equitable Payment,* 2nd ed. Carbondale, IL: Southern Illinois University Press, 1970.

Jaques, Elliott. "Taking Time Seriously in Evaluating Jobs," *Harvard Business Review* 57, no. 5 (September–October 1979): 124–132.

Madigan, Robert M., and Hoover, David J. "Effects of Alternative Job Evaluation Methods on Decisions Involving Pay Equity." *Academy of Management Journal* 29, no. 1 (March 1986): 84–100.

"Ontario Grapples with Pay Equity Legislation." *ACA News* 30, no. 6 (August 1987): 10.

Risher, Howard. "Job Evaluation: Problems and Prospects." *Personnel* 61, no. 1 (January–February 1984): 53–66.

Romanoff, Kent; Boehm, Ken; and Benson, Edward. "Pay Equity: Internal and External Considerations." *Compensation and Benefits Review* 18, no. 3 (May–June 1986): 17–25.

"Salary Management Practices Survey Completed." *ACA News* 30, no. 9 (January 1988): 1, 8.

Schuster, Jay R. "How to Control Job Evaluation Inflation." *Personnel Administrator* 30, no. 6 (June 1985): 176–173.

Thomason, George. *Job Evaluation: Objectives and Methods.* London: Institute of Personnel Management, 1980.

Treiman, Donald J. *Job Evaluation: An Analytic Review.* Washington, DC: National Academy of Sciences, 1979.

Ranking, Predetermined Grading, and Point Methods

7

Chapter Outline

- Ranking
- Predetermined Grading
- Point Method
- Summary
- Case Study—Seaford Summer Resort
- Case Study—Old Dime Box Savings and Loan Association

The three methods of job evaluation to be considered in this chapter are quite different from one another. The first two methods—ranking and predetermined grading—both treat the job as a whole as being the significant thing to examine, while the third method—the point method—involves looking at the factors within each job. Another significant difference between the ranking and the predetermined grading methods is that the former focuses more on the individual job while the latter is more concerned with matching the jobs with job classes.

Ranking

As is true of all of the methods of job evaluation in common use, the ranking method uses detailed and up-to-date job descriptions in the evaluation process. The first step in ranking is to put the job titles on 3-by-5 inch index cards, keeping the complete job descriptions available to resolve doubtful cases.

By using a table like 7–1, you can compare each job with every other job. After listing the job titles on cards, arrange the jobs in alphabetical order and number them both vertically and across the top to form a matrix. Only half the matrix needs to be used since there is no need to compare, for example, job 3 with job 2 and then later to compare job 2 with job 3. To see how the entries in the table work, take job 1. Using the cards, compare bookkeeping machine operator (job 1) with clerk, accounting (job 2). You decide that the two jobs should be ranked about equally. Because it is a draw, a dash is placed opposite job 2 and under job 1. Then you compare clerk, file (job 3) with bookkeeping machine operator (job 1). Because you decide that job 1 should rank higher, you enter 1 in the appropriate space. Continue down the column, comparing each of the other jobs against job 1 and recording the winner of each contest. When you get to job 7, you decide that the secretary should rank higher than bookkeeping machine operator, so you enter 7 as the winner. Against job 8 you enter another dash for a draw, and you enter 1s again for the last two contests. Now, you set aside the card for job 1. Next you take job 2 (clerk, accounting) and compare each of the other jobs with *it,* making the appropriate entries as you go. As can be seen in the table, you move across (with a draw in column 1) and then down column 2, indicating the

TABLE 7–1
A systematic way of ranking jobs.

	Job No.	1	2	3	4	5	6	7	8	9	Wins	Draws	Wins Plus Half of Draws	Member A Ranking
Bookkeeping machine operator	1										6	2	7	3
Clerk, accounting	2	—									6	1	6.5	4
Clerk, file	3	1	2								0	2	1	9
Clerk, order	4	1	2	4							4	1	4.5	5
Keypunch operator	5	1	2	—	4						1	1	1.5	8
Messenger	6	1	2	—	4	5					0	1	.5	10
Secretary	7	7	7	7	7	7	7				9	0	9	1
Stenographer, general	8	—	8	8	8	8	8	7			7	1	7.5	2
Switchboard operator-receptionist	9	1	2	9	4	9	9	7	8		3	1	3.5	7
Typist	10	1	2	10	—	10	10	7	8	—	3	2	4	6

winners of the contests as you go—four 2s, 7, 8, and finally two more 2s. Now, you set aside the card for job 2, take job 3, and go through the same procedure.

After the matrix is complete, you then record the number of wins and the number of draws opposite each job number. For example, for job 1 there are six wins and two draws. After the two columns for wins and draws, another column shows the total of wins plus half the number of draws for each job. The figures in this column in turn provide the basis for the final column—your ranking of the jobs. Notice, however, that the last two columns are in inverse order. The number 1 ranking goes to the job with the largest number of wins plus half of draws (secretary), while the number 10 ranking goes to the job with the smallest number of wins and half of draws (messenger).

The next phase in the ranking method is to obtain the pooled judgment of a group, in this case the members of a job evaluation committee. Table 7–2 shows how this is accomplished. The first column shows the rankings worked out by committee member A (the rankings we have followed above; see Table 7–1). Since committee members B and C view the jobs differently, their rankings differ somewhat from those provided by member A. All rankings are averaged to give the new ranking shown in the last column of the table. Notice that, in this final ranking, two jobs happen to rank the same. Such a result is to be expected from time to time. Equal rankings should be allowed where appropriate.

TABLE 7-2
Job ranking by a job evaluation committee.

Job	Committee Members			Avg.	New Ranking
	A	B	C		
Bookkeeping machine operator	3	3	4	3.3	3
Clerk, accounting	4	7	2	4.3	4
Clerk, file	9	9	10	9.3	8
Clerk, order	5	8	5	6	6
Keypunch operator	8	6	8	7.3	7
Messenger	10	10	9	9.7	9
Secretary	1	1	1	1	1
Stenographer	2	2	3	2.3	2
Switchboard operator-receptionist	7	4	6	5.7	5
Typist	6	5	7	6	6

Advantages and Disadvantages

Ranking as a method of job evaluation is clearly better than no job evaluation at all. For smaller companies and small numbers of employees it is probably more economical than the more complex methods of job evaluation. It is perhaps the simplest method of job evaluation, but this simplicity comes into doubt when large numbers of employees are to be ranked. Even more serious is the inherent qualitative defect of ranking. Such a crude method may determine that one job is inherently worth more than another within the organizational structure, but it does not answer the question of how much more. Managers need an answer to that question if they are to work out equitable pay differentials within the internal organizational structure.

Predetermined Grading

The second of the two less quantitative methods is the predetermined grading (or job classification) method. As indicated in Chapter 6, in this method you develop a system of job grades or classes and assign each job to a particular grade. To start such a plan,

1. Obtain job descriptions for key jobs at all levels throughout the range of the pay structure—at the bottom, at several points along the upward reaches of pay, and also at the top.
2. Review job descriptions to see what common job factors can be found at each level in the organization.
3. Use these common factors to develop written descriptions for the desired number of pay grades.

4. Using additional jobs, test the grade descriptions by trying to assign these jobs to them.
5. Rewrite the grade descriptions.

The federal government's general schedule is the predominant example of a predetermined grading method. Figure 7–1 illustrates pay grade descriptions used by the executive branch of the federal government. Notice that the description for the lower level GS-1 grade is concise, while that for the higher level GS-18 is more elaborate.[1]

Anatomy of GS Grade Descriptions

An easier way to understand how the anatomy of a grade description works is to look at an exploded view. Figure 7–2 shows such an analysis for the first four GS grades.

The analysis shows aspects of the rather complex sentences in the formal grade descriptions in columns so the variables can be examined. The first four

---

Grade GS–1 includes those classes of positions the duties of which are to perform, under immediate supervision, with little or no latitude for the exercise of independent judgement—(A) the simplest routine work in office, business, or fiscal operations; or (B) elementary work of a subordinate technical character in a professional, scientific, or technical field.

Grade GS–18 includes those classes of positions the duties of which are—(A) to serve as the head of a bureau where the position, considering the kind and extent of the authorities and responsibilities invested in it, and the scope, complexity, and degree of difficulty of the activities carried on, is exceptional and outstanding among the whole group of positions of heads of bureaus; (B) to plan and direct or to plan and execute frontier or unprecedented professional, scientific, technical, administrative, fiscal or other specialized programs of outstanding difficulty, responsibility, and national significance, requiring extended training and experience which has demonstrated outstanding leadership and attainments in professional, scientific, or technical research, practice, or administration, or in administrative, fiscal, or other specialized activities; or (C) to perform consulting or other professional, scientific, technical, administrative, fiscal, or other specialized work of equal importance, difficulty, and responsibility, and requiring comparable qualifications.

FIGURE 7–1
Examples of federal government grade descriptions. (From U.S. Office of Personnel Management, 1987.)

GS	Supervision	Latitude for Exercise of Independent Judgment	Training & Experience	Knowledge	Office, Business, or Fiscal Operations	Professional, Scientific, or Technical Field	Other
1	Immediate	Little or none	—	—	Simplest routine work	Elementary work of a subordinate, technical character	—
2	Immediate	Limited	Some training or experience	—	Routine work	Subordinate technical work of limited scope	Performance of other work of equal importance, difficulty, and responsibility, and requiring comparable qualifications
3	Immediate or general	Some in accordance with policies, procedures, and techniques	Some training or experience	Working knowledge of a special subject	Somewhat difficult and responsible work	Subordinate technical work of limited scope	Performance of other work of equal importance, difficulty, and responsibility, and requiring comparable qualifications
4	Immediate or general	Yes, in accordance with policies, procedures, and techniques	Moderate amount of training, and minor supervisory or other experience	Good working knowledge of a special subject or a limited field/office, laboratory, engineering, scientific, or other procedure and practice	Moderately difficult and responsible work	Subordinate technical work	Performance of other work of equal importance, difficulty, and responsibility, and requiring comparable qualifications

FIGURE 7–2
The anatomy of general schedule (GS) grade descriptions.

columns indicate the extent of the supervision, the latitude of judgment allowed for, training and experience needed, and the knowledge required. The next three columns are alternative columns allowing for variation in the nature of the work. For example, for grade GS-2, jobs include office, business, or fiscal operations involving routine work *or* professional, scientific, or technical jobs involving subordinate technical work of limited scope *or* performance of other work of equal importance, difficulty, and responsibility and requiring comparable qualifications. This last alternative allows for even more flexibility. Ascending shades of meaning pervade the table. For example, under office, business, or fiscal operations is simplest routine work, routine work, somewhat difficult and responsible work, and, finally, moderately difficult and responsible work.

Still another aspect of the federal plan is that additional factors are introduced with each grade. For example, training or experience does not enter until grade 2, knowledge does not come in until grade 3, and supervisory experience is not involved until grade 4. Conceptually, this approach encompasses but one of two alternative methods: to introduce additional factors at higher and higher job grades, or to retain the same factors throughout all grades but increase the degree of each factor as the employee moves up through the different levels. The greater the heterogeneity of the jobs covered by the plan, the greater is the need for introducing additional factors at the higher levels.

After the grade descriptions have been developed comes the difficult step of matching job descriptions against grade descriptions, or putting each job into the most appropriate grade. Even with good job descriptions, the task is difficult because there is an inherent problem with matching a precisely drawn job description against even a broadly drawn set of grade descriptions. As a practical matter, specific *factors* within the job description have to be compared against specific *factors* in the grade descriptions. This would not be true if all jobs followed a completely consistent gradual ascending gradation in each factor, as is typically the case for the grade descriptions. For example, suppose a particular job description evaluates a job as requiring working knowledge of a particular subject but involving little or no latitude for the exercise of independent judgment (see Figure 7–2). On the first factor, the evaluator would place the job in GS-3, but on the second factor, GS-1 or GS-2. To what GS grade should the job be assigned? Judgments will be affected by benchmark jobs in each grade. Whether considering benchmark jobs assists or hinders the grading process depends on the quality of the original decisions in placing these jobs in their existing grades. A further problem arises if an evaluator puts too much emphasis on the particular person now occupying a job rather than on the job itself. A way of offsetting personal considerations to some degree is to use committee review or evaluation rather than to rely solely on a job analyst or a classification specialist.

The Federal Pay Schedule

The federal government's general schedule covers most of the civilian employees of the executive branch, including, as noted earlier. over one million workers. The classification plan first went into effect in 1923 and was most recently changed in 1949. The schedule of rates as of February 1987 is shown in Table 7–3.

Within each pay grade there are 10 pay steps, with movement into higher steps based on seniority. The worker who puts in a year in each step can reach steps 2, 3, and 4; by putting 2 years in each step she can get to steps 5, 6, and 7; and, finally, by spending 3 years in each step the worker can reach steps 8, 9, and 10. To speed the rate of advance, an employee must typically be promoted to a higher grade. As can be seen from the starred data, the overlap at the upper levels with the executive schedule (political appointees) negates some of the rates for the higher grades. Also, there are irrational variable (rather than fixed) differences between steps in grades 1 and 2.

Advantages and Disadvantages

The predetermined grading (or job classification) method of job evaluation, like the ranking method, is less quantitative and is not used as often in industry as the other major methods (point, factor comparison, and the guide chart–profile methods). Where small companies or small numbers of employees are involved, it may be easy to administer, and it can be tied in to collective bargaining where unions are in agreement. The plan has long been used by the federal government. It is also used by most state governments and by many counties and municipalities.

An advantage of the method is its flexibility. Two disadvantages are (1) the work involved in developing adequate grade descriptions and (2) knowing how to classify a job that may belong to one class on the basis of a certain factor but to another class on the basis of a different factor.

Point Method

The ranking and predetermined grading methods of job evaluation already considered emphasize the whole job—it is either ranked or put into a grade. To make this kind of decision, it is sometimes necessary to look at the factors that make up the job. The point, factor comparison, and guide chart–profile methods all require more detailed attention to specific factors within the job. We turn now to the point method.

An organization that decides to install a point plan may use one that has already been developed or develop its own. Choosing to use an existing plan has the advantage of not having to call in outside professional help to develop a plan. On the other hand, an existing plan may not be the best one for the organization, and it may be less acceptable to employees than a plan tailored to the company's particular needs.

TABLE 7–3
The general schedule in use by the executive branch of the federal government.

	Pay Steps									
	1	2	3	4	5	6	7	8	9	10
GS-1	$ 9,619	$ 9,940	$10,260	$10,579	$10,899	$11,087	$11,403	$11,721	$11,735	$12,036
2	10,816	11,073	11,430	11,735	11,866	12,215	12,564	12,913	13,262	13,611
3	11,802	12,195	12,588	12,981	13,374	13,767	14,160	14,553	14,946	15,339
4	13,248	13,690	14,132	14,574	15,016	15,458	15,900	16,342	16,784	17,226
5	14,822	15,316	15,810	16,304	16,798	17,292	17,786	18,280	18,774	19,268
6	16,521	17,072	17,623	18,174	18,725	19,276	19,827	20,378	20,929	21,480
7	18,358	18,970	19,582	20,194	20,806	21,418	22,030	22,642	23,254	23,866
8	20,333	21,011	21,689	22,367	23,045	23,723	24,401	25,079	25,757	26,435
9	22,458	23,207	23,956	24,705	25,454	26,203	26,952	27,701	28,450	29,199
10	24,732	25,556	26,380	27,204	28,028	28,852	29,676	30,500	31,324	32,148
11	27,172	28,078	28,984	29,890	30,796	31,702	32,608	33,514	34,420	35,326
12	32,567	33,653	34,739	35,825	36,911	37,997	39,083	40,169	41,255	42,341
13	38,727	40,018	41,309	42,600	43,891	45,182	46,473	47,764	49,055	50,346
14	45,763	47,288	48,813	50,338	51,863	53,388	54,913	56,438	57,963	59,488
15	53,830	55,624	57,418	59,212	61,006	62,800	64,594	66,388	68,182	69,976
16	63,135	65,240	67,345	69,450	71,555	73,660*	75,765*	77,870*	79,975*	
17	73,958*	76,423*	78,888*	81,353*	83,818*					
18	86,682*									

*The rate of basic pay payable to employees at these rates is limited to the rate for level V of the Executive Schedule, which is currently $72,500.

Source: U.S. Office of Personnel Management, February, 1987.

Using an Existing Plan

The point plans used by the National Electrical Manufacturers Association (NEMA) and the American Association of Industrial Management (AAIM) are in wide use in the electrical and metal products manufacturing industries.[2] Except for minor definitional differences, the plans for production workers of the two organizations are substantially identical. However, their plans for clerical, technical, and supervisory workers differ as to the number and choice of factors.

Developing a New Plan

In a situation where an organization constructs a plan either for general use or for the use of certain employee groups, management must:

1. Choose suitable job factors.
2. Define each factor and each degree.
3. Assign point values to each degree of each factor.
4. Evaluate each job in terms of the assigned point values.

Choosing Job Factors

The choice of job factors depends on the employee group whose jobs are to be evaluated and the type of organization. The diversity in job factors for an eastern electric utility company of medium size (more than 1,000 but less than 5,000 workers) is shown in Figure 7–3.

Factors for Different Groups in the Same Company.   The company shown in Figure 7–3 reported that it used AAIM plans for its production as well as its clerical and technical workers but a different plan for its exempt workers. Two aspects of this approach are important: What are the common factors used for all three employee groups? and, What is the nature of the differences in factors used? Education and experience and working conditions are factors common to all three groups. So also, with some subtle differences, is the factor of contacts with others. For both production and clerical and technical workers the factor is listed under responsibility, while for exempt workers it appears as a separate factor. Initiative and ingenuity (production) and complexity of duties (clerical and technical) are likewise similar factors. Several factors are common to at least two of the groups: mental or visual demand, supervision given (supervisors only), and safety (listed as "hazards" for production workers).

However, *differences* among employee groups in the factors used appear to be at least as significant as the *similarities*. For example, production jobs have more factors concerned with physical demands and hazards than do clerical and technical jobs. Also, the scope and nature of responsibilities differ among the three groups. The one subfactor of contacts, or work with others, is common to all three groups, but other subfactors differ. For example, the clerical and tech-

Non-exempt Production	Non-exempt Clerical & Technical	Exempt
Education	Education	Education
Experience	Experience	Experience
Physical demand		
Mental or visual demand	Mental or visual demand	
Initiative and ingenuity	Complexity of duties	Resources Planning Problem solving
	Supervision received	Contacts
	Supervision (given)*	Supervision (given)

Responsibility
  Equipment or process
  Material or product
  Safety of others
  Work of others
	Responsibility
	  Errors
	  Contacts with others
	  Confidential data	

Working conditions	Working conditions	Work conditions
Hazards		Safety
*Applies to supervisors only.		

FIGURE 7–3
Factors used for three employee groups in an eastern medium-sized
electric utility company.

nical jobs involve the confidentiality of data. In both technical and clerical (at least for lower-level supervisors) and exempt groups, supervision appears. Supervision may, to a lesser degree, be covered for production workers under the two subfactors of safety of others and work of others. Finally, for exempt workers, there is less detailed emphasis on responsibility (almost as if such employees are responsible just to themselves) and more on long-range or thinking factors such as resources, planning, and problem solving.

Factors for Clerical Workers in Different Organizations.   As mentioned earlier, factors used in a particular plan will depend on the nature of the organization as well as the different employee groups within the organization. We can see some of these differences by comparing factors used in different organizations for the same type of employee group.

Figure 7–4 shows the factors used for clerical workers in several types of organizations. The factors listed have rough rather than precise comparability. As

Southern Bank (large, nonexempt)	Southern Bank (medium-sized, nonexempt)	Midwestern Electric Utility (medium-sized, salaried exempt managers)	Midwestern Manufacturing Company (large, clerical workers)	National Electrical Manufacturers Association (salaried workers*)
Knowledge	Knowledge and skill	Knowledge, skill, and judgment	Education	Education
Skills	Experience and on-the-job training		Experience	Experience
	Complexity of duties			Complexity of duties
	Contacts and supervision	Contacts outside company	Contacts with others	Contacts
		Supervision received and exercised	Task assignment control	
			Work direction-guidance-training	
Responsibility	Responsibility for loss	Impact on business results	Responsibility	Monetary responsibility
			Errors	
	Mental effort		Work flow attentiveness	
	Physical effort	Physical effort		
		Working conditions	Working conditions	Working conditions

*For supervisory jobs only, NEMA adds two other factors: type of supervision and extent of supervision.

FIGURE 7–4
Factors used for clerical workers in various organizations.

164

can be readily seen, the number of factors used does not appear to be a function of size. The large bank reported using fewer factors than the medium-sized one, and the large manufacturing company used three times the number that the large bank did. Unless supervisors are specifically considered, employee contacts with other people either inside or outside the organization seems to be more important as a factor than supervision. Factors such as knowledge, skills, and experience appear to be important for all the organizations. Responsibility likewise shows up in most cases. Curiously, one of the two banks attaches little importance to working conditions. The large manufacturing company uses three factors not present in the other organizations. Task assignment control relates to supervision received by the worker. Work direction–guidance–training measures the extent to which the employee may train or provide guidance as to work duties to others at the same or lower level; that is, it involves something less than supervision in the usual sense. Work flow attentiveness, which is similar to mental effort, relates to how much concentration and coordination of mind and eye is required depending on the flow of work. As such, it is evaluated as being closely tied in with working conditions.

Factors for Supervisory Workers.　Higher up the hierarchical ladder, notice the greater diversity in factors used in point plans. Figure 7–5 shows the factors reported by a large southern bank, a large supermarket company, and a medium-sized utility company for their supervisory workers. At this level, only the utility is concerned with working conditions and safety. There is some tendency to use fewer factors; the bank and the supermarket company use only three, but the supermarket company includes three subfactors under each. There is, across the board, some similarity of factors but it is not marked. The bank includes "difficulty and scope," while the supermarket company includes under results expected the phrase "scope of action." The bank reported complexity as a factor, while the supermarket uses the phrase "organization diversity and complexity." "Impact" appears to correspond to "results expected." In general, however, diversity predominates.

Objectivity in a Subjective Process.　Selecting factors to be used is a subjective process. The nature of the organization and the composition of the work force are important, but the organization must be attentive to the objectivity of the factors used.

In particular, factors chosen should apply to the job and not to the individual. Cooperation and attitude are not appropriate factors with which to evaluate a job. There is also a fine distinction to be made on a factor such as initiative and ingenuity. Although this factor normally applies to an individual, it is still true that a job may *require* that the job holder exercise initiative and use ingenuity. In general, such requirements can be recast in a more objective, more job-related, and less individual-related form by naming the specific tasks that must be mastered on the job, although it is not always possible to measure each factor quantitatively. Personal attitudes should be kept out of job evaluation wherever possible and

Southern Bank (large, exempt)	Supermarket Company (large, exempt, administrative & executive)	Eastern Electric Utility (medium-sized, exempt)

Difficulty and scope	Abilities required
	  Accumulated knowledge
	  Human relations
	  Managerial abilities
		Education
		Experience
		Contacts
		Supervision

Complexity	Performance demand
	  Application of abilities
	  Organization diversity &
	    complexity
	  Decision impact
		Resources
		
		Planning
		
		Problem solving

Impact	Results expected
	  Scope of action
	  Annual dollar flow
	  Mandate for action	

		Safety Work conditions

FIGURE 7–5
Factors used for supervisory workers in three different organizations.

used for performance evaluation, which will be treated later. Even in performance evaluation, as we shall see, greater objectivity can be achieved by using behavioral scales related closely to particular jobs.

Defining Factors and Degrees

After the factors have been selected, you must define each factor in writing. Then, you divide each factor into degrees, and describe each degree of each factor. An example, from the NEMA plan for salaried employees, is shown in Figure 7–6.

It is not necessary that each factor be subdivided into the same number of degrees. One factor may have more or fewer degrees than another. The NEMA plan for salaried jobs uses eight degrees for the experience factor, and the corresponding AAIM plan uses seven degrees for the same factor. However, experience is a readily quantifiable factor and thus is easy to divide into more degrees.

COMPLEXITY OF DUTIES

This factor evaluates the complexity of the duties in terms of the scope of independent action, the extent to which the duties are standardized, the judgment and planning required, the type of decisions made and the area within which the individual on the job is required to exercise discretion.

1ST DEGREE

Simple, repetitive duties where the employee is usually told what to do at frequent intervals. Little or no independent action or judgment required since the duties are done under immediate supervision or are so standardized and simple as to involve little choice as to how to do them.

2ND DEGREE

Routine duties where the employee works from detailed instructions. Standard procedure limits independent action and judgment to minor decisions not difficult to make since the choices are limited. Minor decisions involve items such as simple checking of work, obvious errors, when to ask for assistance.

3RD DEGREE

Plan and perform a sequence of semi-routine duties working from standard procedures or generally understood methods. Some discretion, independent action and judgment are required to decide what to do, determine permissible variations from standard procedures, review facts in situations, determine action to be taken, within limits prescribed.

4TH DEGREE

Plan and perform difficult work where only general methods are available. Discretion, independent action and judgment are required regularly to analyze facts, draw conclusions, plan work, make decisions, evaluate situations, take or recommend action.

5TH DEGREE

Plan and perform complex work which involves new or constantly changing problems where there is little accepted method of procedure. Considerable ingenuity and judgment are required to plan work, deal with factors not easily evaluated, interpret results, make decisions which carry with them a great deal of responsibility.

FIGURE 7–6
Description of factor and degrees in the NEMA salaried job rating plan. (From the National Electrical Manufacturers Association.)

For most factors, a small number of degrees will facilitate the work of the job evaluation committee. Neither NEMA nor AAIM uses less than five degrees for any factor, although some other plans do use as few as three degrees for some factors.

Assigning Point Values

When the descriptions of factors and degrees are completed, you develop and assign point values to each degree of each factor. Table 7–4 shows how this has been done for production workers in a large manufacturing company in the Midwest.

Notice in Table 7–4 that the number of degrees is not the same for each factor. Also, each factor shows an arithmetic progression. The increment between any two degree levels for education is 12, while for experience it is 15. An arithmetic progression is preferable to a geometric progression in constructing the point scale. (The reasons for this preference will be explained in Chapter 10 when we discuss pricing the job structure.) Some plans, including both the NEMA and AAIM plans for clerical and related workers, use something closer to a geometric progression for supervisory factors but arithmetic progressions for other factors. The logic of this decision is certainly debatable.

The weighting of factors in the point plan poses an interesting question. If all factors averaged out to a third-degree rating, we would get one set of relative weights. If we use the top degree for each factor, we would get a second set of

TABLE 7–4
Point plan for production workers in a large midwestern manufacturing company.

Factors	1st Degree	2nd Degree	3rd Degree	4th Degree	5th Degree
SKILL					
1. Education	12	24	36	48	—
2. Experience	15	30	45	60	75
3. Complexity of duties	15	30	45	60	—
EFFORT					
4. Physical demand	10	20	30	40	50
5. Mental and/or visual demand	10	20	30	40	50
RESPONSIBILITY					
6. Consequence of errors	12	24	36	48	60
7. Responsibility for safety of others	7	14	21	28	35
8. Responsibility for work of others	7	14	21	28	—
JOB CONDITIONS					
9. Working conditions	7	14	21	28	35
10. Hazards	5	10	15	20	25

relative weights. But since the actual averages may vary from factor to factor, the *effective* relative weights may well differ from either of these two sets of rates.

Evaluating Jobs

After the point system has been worked out and a summary table developed, the job evaluation committee compares each job with its job description to decide how many points each job should be given on each factor, based on the degree of the factor best applying to the job. The committee pools judgments of all its members to derive the final results. In-between point values are not allowed after the averaging. In other words, the final results reflect committee agreement as to the appropriate degree for each factor. Table 7–5 shows how points are distributed by factor for 10 clerical, supervisory, and technical positions based on the NEMA plan. The data in the table do not represent results for an actual company, but do show how the plan is applied to a particular set of jobs. Actual data would vary depending on the organization and upon the judgments of the job evaluation committee.

A useful device to have available for the job evaluation committee, especially in the early stages of the development of a point plan, is a matrix showing benchmark jobs for each degree of each factor. Designating benchmark jobs makes it easier for the committee to rate new jobs. Such a matrix for the plan used by a large midwestern manufacturing company for its clerical and technical workers is shown in Figure 7–7. Two qualifiers to using benchmarks are: (1) do not let the matrix become obsolete, and (2) beware of placing too much emphasis on the person presently holding the job to be evaluated.

One way of ascertaining how well the committee has rated the jobs is to use a factor-comparison check. A factor-comparison check ranks each job separately on each factor. For example, for the factor "experience" the rank order of the jobs might be (1) sales engineer; (2) interviewer, employment, and supervisor, cost section; (3) secretary, class B, and tabulating machine operator; (4) nurse, industrial, and keypunch operator, class A; (5) telephone operator–receptionist; and (6) typist and mail clerk. Since this ranking agrees with the point ratings, the choice affirms the point values. If there were a disagreement, it would be cause for reevaluating one or more jobs.

The Federal Government and the Point System

Earlier I mentioned some of the difficulties involved in assigning jobs to particular grades under the predetermined grading method, whose principal user is the U.S. federal government. In 1975, after intensive study and the use of outside consultants, the government finally adopted a point system called the factor evaluation system (FES), which is used within the broader framework of its predetermined grading system, the General Schedule. The FES, which covers grades GS-1 through GS-15, excluding supervisors, makes the task of assigning

Factors	Degrees 1	Degrees 2	Degrees 3	Degrees 4
Education	File Clerk Duplicating Mach. Oper. I	Sr. Secretary Clerk Typist II	Sr. Project Recorder	Sr. Purchasing Clerk
Experience	Mail Clerk	Secretary I	Sr. Secretary	Executive Secretary
Task Assignment Control	File Clerk Mail Clerk	Secretary II	Personnel Technician	Sr. Project Recorder
Errors	Secretary I	Accounting Clerk I	Sr. Purchasing Clerk	✕
Working Conditions	Sr. Secretary Clerk Typist	Tab. Oper. II	Duplicating Mach. Oper. I	✕
Work Flow Attentiveness	Secretary I	Accounting Clerk I	Manuscript Typist	✕
Responsibility	Mail Clerk File Clerk Clerk Typist	Sr. Secretary	Executive Secretary	Sr. Project Recorder
Contact with Others	File Clerk Keypunch Operator I	Clerk Typist I	Sr. Secretary	Receptionist Sr. PERT Analyst
Work Direction	File Clerk	Sr. Computer Operator	Lead Switchboard Oper. Sr. Inventory Analyst	✕

FIGURE 7–7
Factor/degree matrix for clerical and technical workers in a large midwestern manufacturing company.

170

TABLE 7–5
Summary of points by job and factor for ten selected jobs.

Job	Education	Experience	Complexity of Duties	Responsibility		Supervision		Working Conditions	Total Points
				Monetary	Contact with Others	Type	Extent		
Mail clerk	40	25	40	10	10	—	—	10	135
Typist	40	25	40	5	5	—	—	10	125
Keypunch operator, class A	40	75	40	10	5	—	—	15	185
Telephone operator-receptionist	40	50	40	5	20	—	—	10	165
Nurse, industrial	80	75	60	20	20	—	—	15	270
Tabulating machine operator	60	100	60	10	10	—	—	15	255
Secretary, class B	60	100	60	10	10	—	—	5	245
Interviewer, employment	80	125	60	20	20	—	—	10	315
Supervisor, cost section	80	125	60	40	20	20	5	10	360
Sales engineer	100	150	80	60	60	—	—	15	465

Source: National Electrical Manufacturers Association.

jobs to particular grades somewhat easier. It applies a primary standard to jobs within occupations or occupational groups and then to selected benchmark jobs.

Primary Standard

The primary standard describes nine factors (including levels of each factor), which are converted into points. A conversion scale allows jobs to be assigned to GS grades based on total points for each job.

Factors.   The factors and the range of points for each factor are shown in Table 7–6.

Conversion Scale.   The scale for converting total points for each job into the correct GS grade assignment is shown in Table 7–7.

Level of Factor under Primary Standard.   Just where within the point range a particular job falls depends on the appropriate level for each factor. For example, the factor "supervisory controls" has five different levels, each with a different point value (in-between point values are not allowed). Or read the primary standard description for Level 2–2.

> The supervisor provides continuing or individual assignments by indicating generally what is to be done, limitations, quality and quantity expected, deadlines, and priority of assignments. The supervisor provides additional, specific instructions for new, difficult, or unusual assignments including suggested work methods or advice on source material available.
>
> The employee uses initiative in carrying out recurring assignments independently without specific instruction, but refers deviations, problems, and unfamiliar situations not covered by instructions to the supervisor for decision or help.

TABLE 7–6
Factors and point ranges.

Factor	Point Range
1. Knowledge required by the position	50–1850
2. Supervisory controls	25–650
3. Guidelines	25–650
4. Complexity	25–450
5. Scope and effect	25–450
6. Personal contacts	10–110
7. Purpose of contacts	20–220
8. Physical demands	5–50
9. Work environment	5–50

TABLE 7–7
Factor evaluation system grade conversion table.

GS Grade	Range
1	190–250
2	255–450
3	455–650
4	655–850
5	855–1100
6	1105–1350
7	1355–1600
8	1605–1850
9	1855–2100
10	2105–2350
11	2355–2750
12	2755–3150
13	3155–3600
14	3605–4050
15	4055–up

The supervisor assures that finished work and methods used are technically accurate and in compliance with instructions or established procedures. Review of the work increases with more difficult assignments if the employee has not previously performed similar assignments.

Application of Standard to Occupations

The point system has still further refinements. The federal bureaucracy includes a great variety of different kinds of occupations or occupational groups in the GS-1 to GS-15 range of jobs. In ascending order in terms of total points, it ranks jobs such as clerk-typist, accounts maintenance clerk, purchasing agent, statistician (economic), and attorney-advisor (general). But each of these jobs happens to be in a different occupation or occupational group. Within any *one* such group the range of factors and factor levels is much smaller than the overall range. The system allows for ranking despite the variations by providing specific information within the context of the occupation or occupational group, including descriptions of factor levels and of benchmark positions. Specificity makes things easier in two ways. The less abstract level descriptions are easier for the first-line supervisor to interpret, while at the same time higher level supervisors can use the primary standard factor level descriptions to see that job evaluation practices do not become too uneven among different organizational units over which they have authority.

Level of Factor for the Specific Occupation or Group.   To illustrate the difference between the primary standard and the guidance at the occupational level, contrast the occupational description for supervisory controls, Level 2–2, against the primary standard description for Level 2–2.

GS-305

Level 2–2—125 points—The clerk receives instructions from the supervisor on non-recurring assignments and changes in procedures. Most assignments are performed independently according to established procedures and previous experience. The supervisor is consulted when problems arise for which there are no precedents. The work is reviewed for accuracy by spot-checking or selective sampling, and may be reviewed occasionally for compliance with regulations.

Benchmark Position Description.   As a further aid to the first-line supervisor, the system provides benchmark position descriptions against which other jobs in the unit can be compared. For example, for the GS-305 occupation, we can look at the benchmark job description for Mail Clerk GS-3, and in particular at the job specification for supervisory controls, Level 2–2.

MAIL CLERK GS-3

Factor 2, Supervisory Controls—Level 2–2—125 points
Works under general supervision of unit supervisor. A senior clerk is available to assist on unusual problems. Completed work is reviewed by statistical sampling for compliance with instructions.

Advantages and Disadvantages of Using the Point Method

There are several advantages to the point method. First, the wide choice of factors, degrees, and point values allows for flexibility. Second, the method is relatively easy for the employee to understand, and differences between jobs can be explained in terms of job content. Third, points can be used in connection with other aspects of job evaluation, such as the assignment of jobs to particular pay grades.

There are also disadvantages to the point method. First, because of the difficulty of working out the original point scale, outside professional help may be required to initiate a company-tailored plan. Second, it takes time to install.

Summary

The ranking method of job evaluation relates to the individual job while predetermined grading emphasizes job classes or grades. Both ranking and predetermined grading involve the whole job while the point method emphasizes factors within the job.

In the ranking method, each job must be systematically compared with every other job. Ranking is more suitable for smaller organizations and small numbers of employees. A serious disadvantage of the method is that, in deciding that one job is worth more than another, the question of *by how much* is left unanswered.

Predetermined grading requires that descriptions of job grades be developed. Individual job descriptions are then matched against grade descriptions. The vital elements of the grade descriptions are the factors used. Grades can be built using the same factors at all levels but requiring an increasing degree of each factor at each higher level in the grade structure. Alternatively, grades can be built using only a few factors at the lowest levels and adding factors at each higher level. The general schedule used by the federal government reflects both these concepts.

A dilemma arises when one factor in a job best matches a lower grade while another factor in the same job best matches a higher grade. To resolve this problem, the federal government installed the factor evaluation system (FES), essentially a point system, within its predetermined grading plan.

The point method of job evaluation focuses on the specifics of job content. An organization wanting to install a point plan can use existing plans such as those developed by NEMA or AAIM, or it can tailor a plan for its use.

Development of a new plan requires (1) choice of suitable job factors, (2) definition of each factor and degree, (3) assignment of point values to each degree of each factor, and (4) evaluation of each job in terms of the assigned point values. Within larger organizations, two to three plans covering different employee groups is typical. The most common distinction is between production and related workers, and the clerical, technical, and supervisory employees. Many companies either use another method of job evaluation for supervisors and executives or have a separate point plan.

Job factors used in a point plan should apply to the job, not the person. In some cases a factor may describe an attribute normally applied to a person, such as initiative or ingenuity. Wherever possible, such a factor should be recast in terms of the kinds of tasks required of the job holder.

The number of degrees for each factor can vary from three to eight and need not be the same for all factors. Point assignments to degrees are most workable using arithmetic rather than geometric progressions. Effectively weighing different factors under a point plan depends not just on the point plan itself but also on the degree levels actually assigned to particular jobs.

In evaluating jobs, job evaluation committees reach agreement in terms of point values for specific degrees of each factor. In-between point values are not allowed. One way of ascertaining how well the committee has rated the jobs is to use a factor-comparison check. In a factor-comparison check, each job is ranked separately on each factor. If such a ranking agrees with the point ratings, the point values are affirmed. If there were a disagreement, one or more jobs would have to be reevaluated. Advantages of the point method include flexibility, ease of understanding, and ease of allocation of jobs to pay grades. Disadvantages include the requirement of professional help to install the plan and the time it takes to install the procedure.

Case Study

Seaford Summer Resort

An entrepreneur with some money to invest has decided to set up a summer resort on the Florida coast. Land has been obtained, the cottages and other structures built, and the time has come to hire the necessary work force. It is to consist of 25 waiters, 5 lodging quarters cleaners, 2 desk clerks, 1 cashier, 5 bartenders, 4 dishwashers, 3 cooks, 1 chef, and 1 bookkeeper as well as a jazz trio and a calypso quartet.

Role Assignment

You are the new owner and manager of the Seaford Summer Resort. You expect to be able to get college students to fill the first two categories of jobs. You have to decide on a job evaluation plan for your personnel. Given the alternatives of either the ranking or the predetermined grading method, which plan would you use, and how would you evaluate these jobs?

Case Study

Old Dime Box Savings and Loan Association

The job evaluation committee of the Old Dime Box Savings and Loan Association gathered together around the long table in the conference room to hear what President Robert DeWitt had to say. The committee chairperson opened with some brief introductory remarks and then turned the meeting over to the president.

The president stated that he had been thinking seriously about the need for developing a job evaluation plan to cover the managerial employees in the association. After some discussion, it was generally agreed as to which personnel were to be included in this group.

Next, the president proposed that the following factors be used: (1) responsibility for planning; (2) study and research; (3) creative work; (4) contacts with other association employees; (5) contacts with persons not employed by the association; (6) responsibility for administration; and (7) influence on the progress of the organization. Some committee members suggested adding the factors of education, experience, initiative, physical demand, and job conditions. After further discussion, the meeting finally adjourned without the committee's having reached a decision.

Role Assignment

You are a member of the job evaluation committee and you have just come from the meeting. What factors would you include for evaluating the managerial positions in a savings and loan association under a point plan? Justify your answer.

Questions for Discussion

1. In what way do the ranking and predetermined grading methods of job evaluation differ?
2. Are job descriptions really necessary if the ranking method is used? Be prepared to justify your reasoning.
3. What are the advantages and disadvantages of using the ranking method?
4. How can your organization develop a plan using the predetermined grading method of job evaluation?
5. In what two ways is an ascending order of pay grades developed under a predetermined grading plan?
6. What are some of the advantages and disadvantages of using the predetermined grading method?
7. In installing a point plan, how would you decide whether to devise a new plan for your company or to use an existing industrywide plan?
8. Assuming you decide to install a new plan, how would you decide which factors to use? For factory workers on an assembly line? For clerical workers in an accounting department? For scientists in a research organization?
9. Is it necessary to use the same number of degrees for each factor? Discuss.
10. Can all factors be quantitatively measured? For which factors could this be a problem?
11. How many factors should be used in a point plan? Do you see any dangers in using a large number of factors? Explain.
12. Should factors relate to the job or to the individual who does the job? Does this pose any problems?
13. Suppose three raters end up giving three different figures for a particular degree of a factor for a given job. Should the average of the three figures be used to get the point value for the job? Why or why not?
14. What is meant by a factor-comparison check? How does it work?
15. What are some of the advantages and disadvantages of the point method?
16. How does the factor evaluation system work?

Projects

Ranking Method of Job Evaluation. Prepare a pay and benefits manual covering 25 clerical jobs in the San Juan Valley National Bank using the ranking method of job evaluation. The project will consist of the following four phases:

1. Prepare a written description of the organization's compensation policies, including employee benefits.
2. Rank jobs by inherent value (not dollars).
3. Construct a scatter diagram and line of regression, assuming equal spacing of jobs on the horizontal axis.
4. Set pay ranges and assign jobs to pay grades.

For benefit costs, see Chapter 13. For scatter diagram, line of regression, and the like, see Chapter 10. However, convert ranks to points for this phase (e.g., let the bottom rank be 1 and top rank be 25). For job descriptions, see Appendix A, jobs 101 to 125. Actual pay rates will be furnished by your instructor at the appropriate time.

Predetermined Grading Method. Prepare a pay and benefits manual covering 25 professional and technical jobs in a manufacturing company—the E. Z. Jones Corporation—using the predetermined grading method of job evaluation. The project will consist of the following five phases:

1. Prepare a written description of the organization's compensation policies, including benefits.
2. Define each labor grade (the U.S. government general schedule in Appendix E will be helpful in this phase).
3. Assign each job to a labor grade.
4. Construct a scatter diagram and line of regression, assuming equal spacing of labor grades on the horizontal axis.
5. Set pay ranges for each labor grade.

For benefit costs, see Chapter 13. For scatter diagram, line of regression, and the like, see Chapter 10. For job descriptions see Appendix A, jobs 201 to 225. Actual pay rates will be furnished by your instructor at the appropriate time.

Point Method of Job Evaluation. Prepare a pay and benefits manual covering 25 jobs in the Niemoeller Manufacturing Company using the point method of job evaluation. The project will consist of the following five phases:

1. Prepare a written description of the organization's compensation policies, including employee benefits.
2. Develop the point system.
3. Rate the jobs and prepare the summary table of job ratings.
4. Construct a scatter diagram and line of regression.
5. Construct pay boxes, including pay and point ranges.

For benefit costs, see Chapter 13. For scatter diagram, line of regression, and so forth, see Chapter 10. For job descriptions, see in Appendix A, jobs 006, 007, 009, 013, 019, 022, 107, 117, 119, 120, 122, 123, 124, 203, 208, 209, 212, 215, 216, 220, 222, 224, 304, 305, and 306. Actual pay rates will be furnished by your instructor at the appropriate time.

Notes

1. See Appendix E for all grade descriptions under the federal government's general schedule.
2. See Appendix B for definitions of factors for production jobs by the National Electrical Manufacturers Association (NEMA) and Appendix C for definitions of factors used in evaluating clerical, technical, and supervisory jobs (NEMA).

References

Candrilli, Alfred J., and Armagast, Ronald D. "The Case for Effective Point-Factor Job Evaluation, Viewpoint 2." *Personnel* 64, no. 4 (April 1987) 33–36.

Doverspike, Dennis, et al. "Generalizability Analysis of a Point-Method Job Evaluation Instrument." *Journal of Applied Psychology* 68, no. 3 (August 1983):476–483.

Finkelstein, James A., and Hatch, Christopher H. "Job Evaluation: New Technology, New Role for HR Managers." *Personnel* 64, no. 1 (January 1987):5–10.

Lawler, Edward E. III "What's Wrong with Point-Factor Job Evaluation." *Personnel* 64, no. 1 (January 1987):38–44.

Meritt-Haston, Ronni, and Wexley, Kenneth N. "Educational Requirements: Legality and Validity." *Personnel Psychology* 36, no. 4 (Winter 1983):743–754.

National Electrical Manufacturers Association. *Guide for the Use of NEMA Job Rating Plan (hourly rated jobs).* New York: National Electrical Manufacturers Association, 1959.

———. *Job Rating Plan (hourly rated jobs).* New

York: National Electrical Manufacturers Association, 1959.

———. *Manual of Procedure for Use of NEMA Salaried Job Rating Plan.* New York: National Electrical Manufacturers Association, 1964.

———. *NEMA Salaried Job Rating Plan.* New York: National Electrical Manufacturers Association, 1949.

Oliver, Philip M. *The Factor Ranking–Benchmark–Guide Chart Evaluation Plan.* 2 vols. Orrington, ME: P.M. Oliver, 1984.

Pasquale, A. M. *A New Dimension to Job Evaluation, AMA Management Bulletin 128.* New York: American Management Association, 1969.

Penner, Maurice. "How Job-Based Classification Systems Promote Organizational Ineffectiveness." *Public Personnel Management* 12, no. 3 (Fall 1983):268–276.

Plachy, Roger. "The Case for Effective Point-Factor Job Evaluation, Viewpoint 1." *Personnel* 64, no. 4 (April 1987): 30–32.

Plachy, Roger J. "The Point-Factor Job Evaluation System: A Step-by-Step Guide, Part 1." *Compensation and Benefits Review* 19, no. 4 (July–August 1987):12–27.

———. "The Point-Factor Job Evaluation System: A Step-by-Step Guide, Part 2." *Compensation and Benefits Review* 19, no. 5 (September–October 1987):9–24.

Slater, Terry. "Development of Job Classification Standards in the United Nations." *Public Personnel Management* 12, no. 3 (Fall 1983):299–313.

U.S. Office of Personnel Management. *Background Paper on Federal Employees' Compensation Reform.* Washington, DC: U.S. Government Printing Office, 1979.

Factor Comparison and Guide Chart–Profile Methods

8

Chapter Outline

- The Factor Comparison Method
- The Guide Chart–Profile Method
- Summary
- Case Study—State Legislative Branch
- Case Study—The Theophilos Company

Like the point method, the two methods of job evaluation we will consider in this chapter—the factor comparison method and the guide chart–profile method—emphasize the factors within a job rather than the job as a whole.

The Factor Comparison Method

The factor comparison method has one feature in common with the ranking method—it uses ranking. However, in the factor comparison method the ranking does not relate to the job as a whole, but to factors within the job. The factor comparison method uses two kinds of ranking: jobs are ranked separately on each factor and are then ranked on how important the various factors are within each job. Ranking is usually accomplished by either the money method[1] or the percentage method, with the percentage method being used more often. However, since the money method is easier to understand and also serves as a good way to introduce most of the basic concepts involved, it will be discussed first.

The Money Method

The money method of factor comparison requires that you:

1. Tentatively select jobs you believe to be key jobs.
2. Rank key jobs by factor.
3. Tentatively assign a money value to each factor within each job based on the actual pay rate for the job.
4. Reconcile the results of steps 2 and 3 so as to make final identification of the key jobs.
5. Plot the key jobs on the factor comparison scale.
6. Enter other jobs on the scale by visually comparing them with key jobs.

Selecting Key Jobs
Key jobs are jobs you believe have a fair rate of pay, both as to equity within the organizational structure and with respect to the outside market for employees in

these jobs. Key jobs should not be all in one part (such as the upper end) of the pay structure. Instead you should consider a few high-paying, a few low-paying, and a good scatter of in-between jobs. The jobs you initially select as key jobs will not always end up being used as such. During the course of developing a workable job evaluation plan, you are likely to reject some of the tentative key jobs, as we shall see later.

Ranking Jobs by Factor

The next step, ranking jobs by factor, is similar to what was described in Chapter 7 for ranking. However, in the money method jobs are not ranked as a whole; instead, they are ranked on each factor separately, as shown in Table 8–1.

Table 8–1 uses separate columns for each of the four factors of education, initiative and ingenuity, responsibility, and working conditions. While other factors might better serve the needs of a particular organization, these four factors illustrate how jobs are ranked by factor in money method plans. In any event, using only a small number of factors greatly facilitates the work of installing a new plan.

Note that the carpenter ranks the highest in three out of the four factors, while the janitor tends to fall at the bottom of the rankings. Not so, however, for working conditions. Poor working conditions are generally believed to rate extra compensation, so on this factor janitor ranks at the top.

Assigning Money Values to Factors Within Each Job

Following the ranking by factor, you examine the actual pay rates for each job to decide what portion of each job should be paid for each factor within the job. Details of this process are shown in Table 8–2.

In this table you allocate a portion of the actual wage rate to each factor on the basis of the importance of each factor compared to the total paid for the job. Thus, for machinist, responsibility accounts for $4.06 of total pay while working conditions only account for $2.66, with education and initiative and ingenuity

TABLE 8–1
Ranking of jobs by factor.

Job	Factor			
	Education	Initiative and Ingenuity	Responsibility	Working Conditions
Machinist, maintenance	1	2	2	2
Forklift operator	2	3	1	3
Janitor	2	4	3	1
Carpenter, maintenance	1	1	1	2

TABLE 8–2
Money value of factors within jobs (unadjusted).

Job	Factor				
	Education	Initiative and Ingenuity	Responsibility	Working Conditions	Actual Wage Rate
Machinist, maintenance	$3.64	$3.64	$4.06	$2.66	$14.00
Forklift operator	1.16	2.23	3.91	1.60	8.90
Janitor	0.45	0.90	1.13	1.27	3.75
Carpenter, maintenance	3.12	4.03	3.64	2.21	13.00

each accounting for $3.64. For janitor, all of the parts of the total are lower, but a relatively larger share is allocated to working conditions.

The next step is to change the money allocations to bring them more into line with the rankings in Table 8–1. For the factor of initiative and ingenuity, the money values follow the ranking in correct order. That is, carpenter gets the highest amount, janitor the lowest amount, and the other two fall in between in the correct order. At the other extreme, the dollar amounts for working conditions don't agree at all with the rankings. For responsibility, the machinist appears to get too much and the carpenter and forklift operator amounts are close but not quite in agreement. The trick is to lower some amounts and raise others while still keeping the actual totals at the actual wage rates. In other words, plus and minus changes have to balance out as much as possible, essentially a matrix problem.

In the end, while most of the money allocations can be made consistent with the rankings there is little flexibility in this case with the machinist. To meet the ranking requirements, the rate allocated to education for the machinist job was reduced by $.14, working conditions was reduced by $1.06, and responsibility by $.13. The small increase of $.31 in initiative and ingenuity was not enough to offset all the reductions. The computed wage rate worked out to only $12.98 compared to the actual rate of $14.00. So, you discard this job from the list of key jobs.

Table 8–3 reflects both discarding the machinist job and incorporating the changes in money value for those jobs that are retained. Having successfully

TABLE 8–3
Money value of factors within jobs (adjusted).

Job	Factor					
	Education	Initiative and Ingenuity	Responsibility	Working Conditions	Computed Wage Rate	Decisions
Machinist, maintenance	$3.50	$3.95	$3.93	$1.60	$12.98	Discard
Forklift operator	0.90	2.51	3.94	1.55	8.90	Keep
Janitor	0.90	0.30	0.88	1.67	3.75	Keep
Carpenter, maintenance	3.50	3.96	3.94	1.60	13.00	Keep

come through the two conflicting sets of judgments as to ranking and money allocation, these jobs become the new key jobs.

Constructing and Using the Factor Comparison Scale

Having identified the key jobs, you are now ready to construct the factor comparison scale, as shown in Figure 8–1.

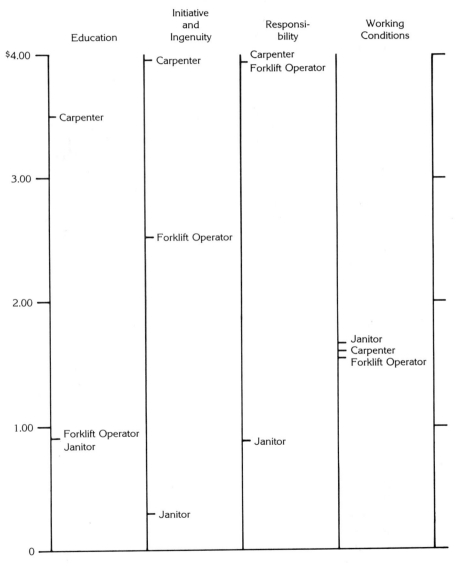

FIGURE 8–1
Factor comparison scale for three jobs under the money method.

Notice that the columns in the diagram correspond to the columns in Table 8–3. The height of the vertical scale is controlled by the largest single amount in the table for a specific factor—$3.96 for the carpenter for initiative and ingenuity. The final money values for each key job for each factor are plotted in the column for that particular factor. The education scale goes from a low of $.90 to a high of $3.50, initiative and ingenuity from $.30 to $3.96, responsibility from $.88 to $3.94, and working conditions from $1.55 to $1.67.

You can now fit all additional jobs into this network of key jobs simply by inspection. Moreover, as new jobs are added, it becomes progressively easier to add still more jobs because jobs can be matched against a wider array of similar jobs. The new pay rate for any of the added jobs is easily obtained by plotting the job and adding together the dollar values for each of the four factors.

Special Features of the Money Method

One feature of the money method of factor comparison is unique. Unlike the other more widely used methods of job evaluation, in the money method both the evaluation and pricing processes are accomplished together. This feature can be either a strength or a weakness, depending on how you look at it. Other methods of job evaluation first determine points, ranks, or grades through job evaluation, and pricing is a separate and distinct procedure. The money method of factor comparison links the two procedures directly, which has the advantage of simplicity. However, there is a disadvantage in tying the evaluation process *too* closely to money values. Because money values may be quickly outdated, the rank and money matrix quickly becomes obsolete. Perhaps the most pungent criticism of the original money method is that raised by Richard Henderson:

> It is very difficult to judge (even for experts) the relative value of different factors within the job, whereas judgment is much more valid and reliable when comparing one job to another by a particular factor.[2]

Another criticism of the money method relates to forcing dollar amounts into the matrix of money values. As we saw in Table 8–2, possible changes in any one factor, done solely to achieve a desired rank order, varied considerably.

The Percentage Method

Because of the difficulties encountered by users of the original money method, many firms now use a different approach known as the percentage method.[3] Unlike the money method, the percentage method does not combine job evaluation and pricing the pay structure. The two processes are separate and distinct, as is true in other major methods of job evaluation. Instead of money allocations, the percentage method uses ranking for factors within each job. This feature still does not avoid the Henderson criticism, but even this criticism loses force where decisions are by rank and do not require precise money allocations.

The percentage method of factor comparison involves the following phases:

1. Tentatively selecting jobs believed to be key jobs.
2. Ranking key jobs by factor (vertical judgment).
3. Ranking factors within each key job (horizontal judgment).
4. Combining vertical and horizontal judgments to generate point values for each factor within each job.
5. Plotting the key jobs on the factor comparison scale.
6. Entering other jobs on the scale by visual comparison with key jobs.

Selecting Key Jobs

The first phase in the percentage method is identical to the first phase of the money method, with one slight difference. Even though the same criteria as before apply to the selection of key jobs, the jobs selected tend to be final rather than tentative under the percentage method. This is so because there is nothing in the later phases that tends to reject a key job once it is selected.

The Various Computational Steps

Once the selection of key jobs is made, the remainder of the phases under the percentage method are all mechanically mathematical—so much so that I will leave the details all to a single table, Table 8–4, which illustrates, using four jobs and four factors, the nine steps that are the mathematical framework. I will not laboriously follow every computation (which is evident in the table), but I will provide a running commentary on the process.

The table refers to four job numbers, 901 (typist), 902 (telephone operator–receptionist), 903 (computer analyst), and 904 (employment interviewer).

In the first three steps, you rank the four jobs separately on each factor, one at a time. Note that in these three tables you read *down.* The computations lead to the factor percent values shown in step 3.

In the next three steps, you determine the ranking of each factor within each job, one job at a time. Note that in these tables you read *across.* The computations lead to the job percent values shown in step 6.

The data in step 7 come from step 3 and step 6. Also in this step, you compute reciprocals (1 divided by the number) and adjust as explained.

In step 8, you develop point values for F (factor) and J (job) for each numbered job, and in step 9 the pairs of point numbers in each cell (the intersection of job number and job factor) are combined to give the point values for the scale in step 9. In order to complete step 9, you need to find the nearest interval, using a table such as Table 8–5.

Constructing and Using a Factor Comparison Scale

The data in step 9 are used to construct a factor comparison scale as shown in Figure 8–2 on page 191. This is a ratio scale. That is, the vertical distance from

TABLE 8—4
Nine computational steps of the percentage method.

Job Number	Education and Experience	Complexity of Duties	Responsibility	Working Conditions	Total
STEP 1—RANK OF KEY JOBS BY FACTOR					
901	4	3	4	1	
902	3	3	2	1	
903	2	2	3	2	
904	1	1	1	3	
STEP 2—FACTOR PERCENT RATING (Read down.)					
901	25	50	25	100	
902	50	50	75	100	
903	75	75	50	75	
904	100	100	100	50	
	250	275	250	325	

(To get % intervals, divide 100% by number of jobs. Thus: 100/4 = 25.)

Job Number	Education and Experience	Complexity of Duties	Responsibility	Working Conditions	Total
STEP 3—FACTOR % VALUES (Read down.)					
901	10	18	10	31	
902	20	18	30	31	
903	30	27	20	23	
904	40	37	40	15	
	100	100	100	100	
STEP 4—RANK OF FACTORS WITHIN JOBS					
901	1	2	4	3	
902	1	2	3	4	
903	1	2	3	4	
904	1	2	2	3	
STEP 5—JOBS % RATING (Read across.)					
901	100	75	25	50	250
902	100	75	50	25	250
903	100	75	50	25	250
904	100	75	75	50	300

(Note: To get % intervals, divide 100% by number of factors. Thus: 100/4 = 25.)

Job Number	Education and Experience	Complexity of Duties	Responsibility	Working Conditions	Total
STEP 6—JOB % VALUES (Read across.)					
901	40	30	10	20	100
902	40	30	20	10	100
903	40	30	20	10	100
904	33	24	24	19	100

TABLE 8-4
Continued.

Job Number	Education and Experience	Complexity of Duties	Responsibility	Working Conditions	Total
STEP 7—FACTOR/JOB RATIOS					
901	0.25	0.60	1.00	1.55	3.40
902	0.50	0.60	1.50	3.10	5.70
903	0.75	0.90	1.00	2.30	4.95
904	1.12	1.54	1.67	0.79	5.12
	2.62	3.64	5.17	7.74	19.17
Reciprocals	0.382	0.275	0.193	0.129	0.979
R,Adjusted	7.48	5.38	3.78	2.53	19.17

(Note: Adjustment Factor 19.17/.979 = 19.581 [Factor].)

STEP 8—POINT TOTALS DISTRIBUTED FROM STEPS 3 AND 6
(i.e., 748 × 10% = 75.)

Job Number	Education and Experience F	J	Complexity of Duties F	J	Responsibility F	J	Working Conditions F	J	Totals
901	75		97		38		78		
		136		102		34		68	340
902	149		97		113		78		
		228		171		114		57	570
903	224		145		76		59		
		198		148		99		50	495
904	300		199		151		38		
		169		123		123		97	512
	748		538		378		253		1917

(Note: Point totals [vertical and horizontal] in Step 8 are taken from Step 7 with decimal points moved two places to the right.)

STEP 9—POINT VALUES FOR SCALE

Job Number	Education and Experience	Complexity of Duties	Responsibility	Working Conditions
901	100	100	38	76
902	200	132	115	66
903	200	152	87	57
904	230	152	132	66

(Note: From each cell in Step 8 average the F & J values and find nearest value on 15% interval scale.)

Source: Edward N. Hay, "Creating Factor Comparison Key Scales by the Per Cent Method." *Journal of Applied Psychology* 32, no. 5 (October 1948):456–64.

TABLE 8–5
15% intervals based on 100.

230	66	19
200	57	16
174	50	14
152	43	12
132	38	10
115	33	9
100	29	8
87	25	7
76	22	

50 to 100 is the same as from 100 to 200, as one would expect for a geometric progression. The ticks on the vertical axis on this scale represent point values at 15 percent intervals. Jobs can only be plotted at these points, not at any in-between values. Once you plot the key jobs, you can fit other jobs in by inspection.

Advantages and Disadvantages of the Factor Comparison Method

An overview of both advantages and disadvantages of the factor comparison method is given by Alan Nash and Stephen J. Carroll, Jr.:

> This method is conceptually the most sophisticated, and when it is properly applied probably results in reliability that is equal to or better than that of any other methods. Furthermore, it has the added advantage of increasing the probability that the evaluated wage structure will be maximally congruent with the existing structure, because it is anchored via the use of key jobs to that structure. This occurs because the existing compensation for such key jobs is assumed to be correct, and they are used as benchmarks or guides in determining the worth of all other jobs being evaluated. Of course, the extent to which this is an advantage is a function of how widely agreed it is that the anchor jobs selected are presently being compensated correctly. In spite of these strong advantages, factor comparison is not recommended except in installations where the work force is concerned with and capable of understanding it. It is probably the most costly to install and maintain and is so complex that it is virtually impossible to explain to an ordinary aggrieved employee who wants to know why his job is not being paid more.[4]

The arguments put forth by Nash and Carroll apply with somewhat less force if the percentage method is used. We shall discuss these arguments as they relate to key jobs, complexity, and employee acceptance.

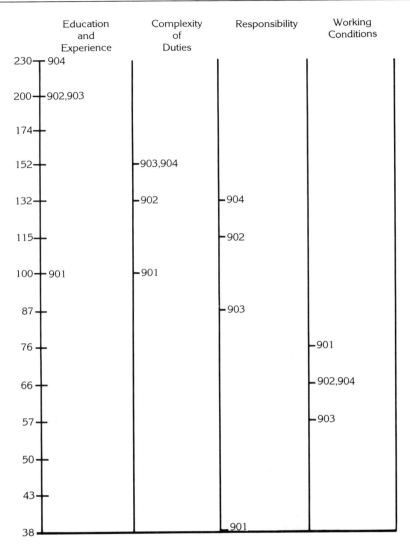

FIGURE 8–2
Factor Comparison scale for four jobs under the percentage method.

Key Jobs
Under both the money and percentage methods, key jobs are the basis upon which all other jobs are evaluated. Clearly, use of key jobs allows the plan to be finely tailored to the existing organization and pay structure. As pointed out earlier, the screening process for key jobs is tighter under the money method, while under the percentage method the jobs selected first are more likely to remain key

jobs. On the other hand, the selectivity is far more critical under the money method, where the volatility of the economy can make rates and therefore the evaluation of a job quickly obsolete. Such economic influences are not as critical with the percentage method.

Complexity

There can be little argument that the factor comparison method is more complex—at least to install—than other factor-oriented methods of job evaluation. However, most factor comparison plans use only four or five job factors. This is fewer than the number commonly used in other factor-based methods of job evaluation. Also, it can be argued that it is cheaper to maintain a factor comparison plan than other factor-oriented methods. Because new jobs can be evaluated purely by inspection on a visual scale, such a plan ought not to be expensive, especially with the newer percentage plans. A more complex plan ought not to be rejected solely on account of complexity or even its installation cost, provided the plan best suits the organization's particular need.

Employee Acceptance

Factor comparison plans are in use, according to Nash and Carroll, in only 10 to 20 percent of organizations using job evaluation.[5] The complexity, especially in installation, of such plans is clearly a disadvantage both for the percentage and the money method.

Even with such difficulties, the factor comparison method can be introduced with effective employee orientation and participation. Zollitsch and Langsner observe that such installations are more successful if union-management relations are harmonious and when agreement can be reached as to the selection of key jobs.[6]

The Guide Chart—Profile Method

The guide chart—profile method or Hay method, one of the three methods of job evaluation that emphasize factors within a job, was developed by Hay Associates, a management consulting firm. While this method is sometimes considered a factor comparison method, it differs sufficiently from both the money method and the percentage method to earn a place for itself among the principal methods of job evaluation.

The guide chart—profile method is used by many large multiplant firms and also by numerous smaller firms. Despite its complexity, it has come into increasing use in the white-collar sector among clerical workers, professionals, and supervisors at all levels. Plans typically cover exempt salaried employees, but often include nonexempt salaried and blue-collar workers, too.

Installation of the Plan

A management consultant team of trained and skilled practitioners install and maintain a typical guide chart–profile plan. Steps in the installation typically include

1. Studying the organization and selecting and adjusting guide charts.
2. Selecting a sample of benchmark jobs covering all levels and functions.
3. Analyzing jobs and writing job descriptions in terms of the three universal factors.
4. Selecting a job evaluation committee consisting of line and staff managers, a personnel department representative, often employees, and a Hay consultant.
5. Evaluating benchmark jobs and then all other jobs.[7]

The Guide Charts

The most important documents available to the committee are the guide charts themselves. Companies typically use three guide charts—for know-how, problem solving, and accountability—although companies employing large numbers of blue-collar workers normally add a fourth chart relating to working conditions. With the exception of the problem-solving chart, the organization may expand the scales to reflect its size and complexity and modify definitions of factors to meet its own needs (and values).[8]

The guide charts described in this chapter are based on more detailed charts in use by one particular company, which we shall refer to here as the E. Z. Jones Company. The charts have been simplified both to encourage a "hands-on" learning experience through the pay and benefits project at the end of this chapter and to restrict the disclosure of information on the original guide charts, which are copyrighted by Hay Associates.

Know-how

Know-how is defined for the E. Z. Jones Company as "the sum total of every kind of skill, however acquired, required for acceptable job performance." Figure 8–3 shows the simplified guide chart for know-how. Know-how is measured along both a vertical axis from top to bottom and a horizontal axis from left to right. The smallest point value is in the upper left and the largest is in the lower right-hand corner. From top to bottom on the vertical axis, the increasing numbers of points represent higher levels of education and/or greater experience. The horizontal axis represents, from left to right, increasing managerial know-how. The problem, then, is to identify where a particular job should be located on this vast field of numbered cells. It is a little like locating a place on a map. Within the guide chart,

E. Z. JONES CORPORATION
HAY GUIDE CHART
KNOW-HOW
(Points)

MANAGERIAL KNOW-HOW

Procedures, Techniques and Disciplines	III. Hetero-geneous			IV. Broad			V. Comprehen-sive			VI. Major Corporate Management			VII. Overall Corporate Management		
	1*	2	3	1	2	3	1	2	3	1	2	3	1	2	3
C. Vocational	152	175	200	200	230	264	264	304	350	350	400	460	460	528	608
	175	200	230	230	264	304	304	350	400	400	460	528	528	608	700
	200	230	264	264	304	350	350	400	460	460	528	608	608	700	800
D. Advanced vocational	200	230	264	264	304	350	350	400	460	460	528	608	608	700	800
	230	264	304	304	350	400	400	460	528	528	608	700	700	800	920
	264	304	350	350	400	460	460	528	608	608	700	800	800	920	1056
E. Basic technical specialized	264	304	350	350	400	460	460	528	608	608	700	800	800	920	1056
	304	350	400	400	460	528	528	608	700	700	800	920	920	1056	1216
	350	400	460	460	528	608	608	700	800	800	920	1056	1056	1216	1400
F. Seasoned technical specialized	350	400	460	460	528	608	608	700	800	800	920	1056	1056	1216	1400
	400	460	528	528	608	700	700	800	920	920	1056	1216	1216	1400	1600
	460	528	608	608	700	800	800	920	1056	1056	1216	1400	1400	1600	1840
G. Technical special-ized mastery	460	528	608	608	700	800	800	920	1056	1056	1216	1400	1400	1600	1840
	528	608	700	700	800	920	920	1056	1216	1216	1400	1600	1600	1840	2112
	608	700	800	800	920	1056	1056	1216	1400	1400	1600	1840	1840	2112	2432
H. Professional mastery	608	700	800	800	920	1056	1056	1216	1400	1400	1600	1840	1840	2112	2432
	700	800	920	920	1056	1216	1216	1400	1600	1600	1840	2112	2112	2432	2800
	800	920	1056	1056	1216	1400	1400	1600	1840	1840	2112	2432	2432	2800	3200

*1, 2, and 3 indicate extent of human relations skills required.

FIGURE 8–3

Guide chart for know-how. (Copyright © 1981 by Hay Associates. Used by permission.)

column heads, captions, and definitions help narrow the search for an appropriate point value.

Education and Experience.   The vertical scale in Figure 8–3, which roughly measures education and experience, refers to procedures, techniques, and disciplines. Among these three there is a certain amount of overlap. Each of the descriptive terms below this heading (*vocational, advanced vocational, basic technical specialized, seasoned technical specialized, technical specialized mastery,* and *professional mastery*) is defined, as the degrees are under the point method. For instance, the E. Z. Jones Company defines *vocational* as "procedural or systematic proficiency, which may involve a facility in the use of specialized equipment." Professional mastery is considered to be "exceptional competence and unique mastery in scientific or other learned disciplines." For the E. Z. Jones Company, this is taken to mean national or international expertise in the field.

Managerial Know-How.   The levels of managerial know-how shown on the horizontal axis in Figure 8–3 are heterogeneous, broad, comprehensive, major corporate management, and overall corporate management. The heterogeneous level is described as "operational integration of diverse management activities in an organizational unit; or administration of a function on a corporate-wide basis." Near the top, the major corporate management level involves "administration of functional areas and/or assigned operating complexes and their integration into the corporate whole." The different levels of managerial know-how appear to follow the layers of hierarchy typical of larger multiplant corporations in the United States.

Human Relations Skills.   There is yet another detail to the know-how guide chart shown in Figure 8–3. Horizontally, within each nine-cell managerial know-how block, there are smaller cells representing human relations skills. The three categories of skills are numbered in rising order of importance: (1) basic, (2) important, and (3) critical. The basic level calls for "ordinary courtesy and effectiveness in dealing with others." For the important level, "understanding, influencing, and/or serving people are important considerations." In the critical classification, "alternative or combined skills in understanding, selecting, developing, and motivating people are important in the highest degree." Thus we see that the factor of know-how involves three different variables—education and experience, managerial know-how, and human relations skills. When these variables are analyzed, a single number is chosen to represent the point value of know-how for a particular job.

Problem Solving
Problem solving is defined, in the E. Z. Jones Company, "as the amount of original, self-starting thinking required by the job for analyzing, evaluating, creating, reasoning, and arriving at conclusions."

The guide chart for problem solving (Figure 8–4) is arranged in the same general way as the one for know-how, with the numbers increasing from top to bottom and from left to right. The vertical dimension refers to freedom to think (thinking environment); the horizontal axis portrays the thinking challenge. The data in the guide chart are percentages rather than points. The percentage chosen for a particular job is multiplied by the points obtained in the know-how chart to give a single point value for problem solving. The indicated rationale for this procedure is that "you can think only with what you know."

The guide chart in Figure 8–4 includes the same kinds of captions, column heads, and definitions as appeared on the guide chart for know-how. This information makes it possible to identify just where within the guide chart a particular job can be placed.

Thinking Environment.   On the vertical axis the detailed levels of thinking environment are strict routine, routine, semiroutine, standardized, clearly defined, broadly defined, generally defined, and abstractly defined. Strict routine specifies "simple rules and detailed instructions," whereas an abstractly defined thinking environment involves "general laws of nature or science, business philosophy, and cultural standards."

Thinking Challenge.   The horizontal axis portrays the levels of thinking challenge present in the jobs. The levels range from repetitive, which involves "iden-

E. Z. JONES CORPORATION
HAY GUIDE CHART
PROBLEM-SOLVING
(Percentages)

Thinking Environment	THINKING CHALLENGE				
	1. Repetitive	2. Patterned	3. Interpolative	4. Adaptive	5. Creative
A. Strict routine	10	14	19	25	33
B. Routine	12	16	22	29	38
C. Semiroutine	14	19	25	33	43
D. Standardized	16	22	29	38	50
E. Clearly defined	19	25	33	43	57
F. Broadly defined	22	29	38	50	66
G. Generally defined	25	33	43	57	76
H. Abstractly defined	29	38	50	66	87

FIGURE 8–4

Guide chart for problem solving. (Copyright © 1981 by Hay Associates. Used by permission.)

tical situations requiring solution by simple choice of learned things," to creative, where "novel or nonrecurring pathfinding situations" require "the development of new concepts and imaginative approaches."

Accountability

For the E. Z. Jones Company, accountability is defined in its salary administrative policy manual as follows:

> Accountability means being held answerable for what happens to something; that something being an identifiable, measured end result, and is therefore, effect, not cause. This concept identifies accountability as the achievement or "pay-off" factor. It is the basis upon which achievement is measured. Know-how and problem-solving produce nothing until they are put to work, and accountability measures the effect they can produce.

How accountability comes into play is indicated in the guide chart for accountability (Figure 8–5). Like the other two charts, this one has the smallest point value in the upper left-hand corner and the largest in the lower right-hand corner. The vertical dimension refers to the freedom to act, while the horizontal one involves dollar magnitudes.

Freedom to Act. The freedom to act differs from the freedom to think, a dimension seen in the guide chart for problem solving. Thus, for a particular job, broad freedom in the thinking environment may be accompanied by little freedom to act in the sense of putting ideas into effect. The real questions to be answered are, What is the power of the individual to act independently, and what restraints are placed on such action?

Again, specific categories are provided to describe the freedom to act: prescribed, controlled, standardized, generally regulated, directed, oriented direction, guided, and strategic guidance. Jobs with prescribed freedom to act are subject to direct and detailed instructions and require close supervision. In contrast, jobs operating under strategic guidance, "by reason of their size, independent complexity, and high degree of effect on company results, are subject only to guidance from top management as represented by the president."

Magnitude. On the horizontal axis of Figure 8–5, the broad categories of small, medium, large, and very large relate to the magnitude of accountability. They are described in terms of dollar values. These values may reflect objectives in terms of goals (market quotas), extent of control (operating budgets), or sphere of influence (total revenues for a plant or region). In general, the measures represent the dollars entrusted to or affected by the individual holding the job.

Impact on Results. Each dollar category on the horizontal axis is subdivided according to the impact of the job on end results. This impact is described in an

E. Z. JONES CORPORATION, HAY GUIDE CHART, ACCOUNTABILITY (Points)

M A G N I T U D E

Freedom to Act	(2) Small $180M–$1.8MM				(3) Medium $1.8MM–$18MM				(4) Large $18MM–$180MM				(5) Very large $180MM–$1.8MMM			
	R*	C	S	P	R	C	S	P	R	C	S	P	R	C	S	P
A. Prescribed	14	19	25	33	19	25	33	43	25	33	43	57	33	43	57	76
	16	22	29	38	22	29	38	50	29	38	50	66	38	50	66	87
	19	25	33	43	25	33	43	57	33	43	57	75	43	57	76	100
B. Controlled	22	29	38	50	29	38	50	66	38	50	66	87	50	66	87	115
	25	33	43	57	33	43	57	76	43	57	76	100	57	76	100	132
	29	38	50	66	38	50	66	87	50	66	87	115	66	87	115	152
C. Standardized	33	43	57	76	43	57	76	100	57	76	100	132	76	100	132	175
	38	50	66	87	50	66	87	115	66	87	115	152	87	115	152	200
	43	57	76	100	57	76	100	132	76	100	132	175	100	132	175	230
D. Generally regulated	50	66	87	115	66	87	115	152	87	115	152	200	115	152	200	264
	57	76	100	132	76	100	132	175	100	132	175	230	132	175	230	304
	66	87	115	152	87	115	152	200	115	152	200	264	152	200	264	350
E. Directed	76	100	132	175	100	132	175	230	132	175	230	304	175	230	304	400
	87	115	152	200	115	152	200	264	152	200	264	350	200	264	350	460
	100	132	175	230	132	175	230	304	175	230	304	400	230	304	400	528
F. Oriented direction	115	152	200	264	152	200	264	350	200	264	350	460	264	350	460	608
	132	175	230	304	175	230	304	400	230	304	400	528	304	400	528	700
	152	200	264	350	200	264	350	460	264	350	460	608	350	460	608	800
G. Guided	175	230	304	400	230	304	400	528	304	400	528	700	400	528	700	920
	200	264	350	460	264	350	460	608	350	460	608	800	460	608	800	1056
	230	304	400	528	304	400	528	700	400	528	700	920	528	700	920	1216
H. Strategic guidance	264	350	460	608	350	460	608	800	460	608	800	1056	608	800	1056	1400
	304	400	528	700	400	528	700	920	528	700	920	1216	700	920	1216	1600
	350	460	608	800	460	608	800	1056	608	800	1056	1400	800	1056	1400	1840

*Indicates impact (Remote, Contributory, Shared, Primary).

FIGURE 8–5
Guide chart for accountability. (Copyright © 1981 by Hay Associates. Used by permission.)

ascending scale: remote (R), contributory (C), shared (S), and primary (P). Where the impact is remote, few points are allotted; for primary impact, more points are given.

For the E. Z. Jones Company, remote impact refers to the routine recording of information for use by others. Contributory impact refers to offering advice to others who take important action. Shared impact means that the individual occupying the job has equal impact with others, either inside or outside the organization, on company results. Primary, the highest category, indicates a controlling impact. In practice, most positions have more than a remote impact.

Accountability, then, actually consists of three variables—freedom to act, magnitude, and impact. These variables are used to locate a job on the accountability guide chart and thus determine the total points for accountability.

Summarizing Guide Chart Results

The next step is to summarize the results derived from the individual guide charts. Table 8–6 shows how the total points are computed for a line job, a division head in charge of a manufacturing facility. The points for each of the three major factors shown in the guide charts are added together to get the point value for the job. For problem solving, the percentage on the guide chart is multiplied by the points for know-how to get the points for problem solving.

Profiling

Finally, the guide chart–profile method calls for checking the results obtained from the guide charts by profiling. For example, the point values in Table 8–7 for know-how, problem solving, and accountability give the "profile" of the job of division head. Hay Associates has discovered from working with the many companies that have installed their plan that they can check each guide chart profile against standard profiles for (1) all jobs, (2) line jobs, (3) staff jobs, and (4) research jobs.

Such comparisons are facilitated by a technical characteristic of the guide charts. The figures in the body of each chart represent a geometric progression in which steps are 15 percent apart. Such a scale is shown in Figure 8–6. The scale is similar to that used in the percentage method of factor comparison described earlier.

TABLE 8–6
Total value (points) for a division head.

Know-how	460
Problem solving (50% × 460)	230
Accountability	400
	1090

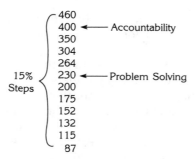

FIGURE 8–6
Profiling as done for a division head of a manufacturing facility (line job).

For profiling of jobs, Hay Associates recommends the following rules:

1. For any job, points for accountability and points for problem solving should be no more than four steps apart.
2. For line jobs, accountability should be two, three, or four steps higher than problem solving.
3. For staff jobs, accountability and problem solving should be equal or not more than one step apart either way.
4. For research jobs, problem solving should be two, three, or four steps higher than accountability.

For the job of division head of a manufacturing facility, for example, Figure 8–6 shows that accountability at 400 points is four steps higher than problem solving at 230 points. Since these values meet the criterion, the profile checks out with the conclusions reached by the committee using the three guide charts. The process is now complete.

Job Descriptions

For firms using the Hay guide chart–profile method, job descriptions do not follow exactly the same pattern as those in general use for other job evaluation plans. Instead, they are tailored to fit this type of plan.

A typical job description under the Hay plan is shown in Figure 8–7. This job description includes two features especially designed to tie in with the use of the guide chart–profile method of job evaluation. It includes dimensions and lists accountabilities.

For the position shown, dimensions include the revenues for the division, the annual operating budget, and the number of employees. Dimensions used will, of course, vary with the nature of the job. Any significant measure, such as sales, purchasing volume, traffic volume, payroll, budget, capital expenditures, or number of employees, can be used. Also, the dimension may refer directly to the position or to a higher level of unit or of the company. For example, dimensions for an advertising manager might include the department's budget as well as the sales for the company as a whole.

Pages 3 and 4 of the position description list seven different accountabilities. In general, the emphasis is on what the occupant of the position is accountable for rather than on the specific duties of the job.

Advantages and Disadvantages of the Hay Method

Some companies use the Hay guide chart—profile method not only for executive and professional jobs but also for office clerical and blue-collar jobs. A few other firms have abandoned the system because they thought it was too cumbersome and costly, and still others have used the system only for higher-ranking executive positions.

Users of the Hay guide chart—profile method cite many advantages:

1. The system is considered to be well thought through and to be of excellent quality.
2. Resolution of problems of internal equity is a strong aspect of the system.
3. It is especially suitable for higher-level executive jobs.
4. It works well for highly structured jobs and situations.

And in addition to actually installing guide chart—profile plans for individual companies, Hay Associates also provides users with summary data so that a company may compare itself to other users of the method in terms of pay and point values.

The guide chart—profile system does have some disadvantages:

1. The system depends heavily on the consultant both for installation and for maintenance, which is costly.
2. The point structure may be unduly inflexible.
3. Some critics think that the system is not as suitable as other methods for evaluating creative jobs, such as certain positions in the sales area.
4. Relating the evaluated job structure to the market is not always well handled.
5. Some companies question the value of the profiling aspect of the plan. (Occasional bootleggers of the plan often abandon this feature of it.)

GARRETT CORPORATION - MINOT MINING DIVISION

POSITION DESCRIPTION

Position Title: Vice President - Finance   Reports to: President

Incumbent: G. G. Garrotto   Prepared by: K. Korunich

                                 Date: September 22, 1981

Approvals: _____
                  Incumbent   Date

           _____
                  Supervisor   Date

POSITION PURPOSE:

This position is accountable for integrating and managing the accounting, financial analysis and planning, data processing and purchasing and warehousing functions to meet identified service levels within approved operating budgets; as well as providing a variety of financial and nonfinancial business advice to the President and key management staff.

DIMENSIONS:

1981 Division Revenues: $ 65 MM

Department Operating Budget: $ 700 M

Employees: 19

NATURE AND SCOPE:

The position reports to the President, Minot Mining Division, as do the positions of General Mill Manager, Mine Manager, District Exploration Manager, Administrative Manager, and Regulatory Affairs Manager. The incumbent is a key member of the organization's executive staff.

This position is new (May 1981) and in the process of evolving. Recent additions include the strengthening of the financial analysis and planning functions and the reassigment of the purchasing and warehousing functions

---

POSITION DESCRIPTION
Vice President - Finance
Page Two

from the mill and mine operations. The latter two functions were reassigned to improve internal controls, provide additional staff management support to line operations, and consolidate the functions in one organization.

The position received financial direction from the Corporate Treasurer in the areas of consolidations, federal taxes, cash management, credit and banking relations.

Reporting to the position are the following:

Controller who, with a staff of 10, is accountable for accounting activities and controlling the assets of the Company. This includes such activities as general ledger; accounts payable/receivable; payroll; cost reporting; joint venture accounting; and tax preparation for federal (forwarded to Corporate for consolidation) and state (filed directly) returns.

The Controller is also responsible for the administration of contract bidding procedures and for providing controls in all areas to ensure adherence to Corporate policy. This position is also involved in the development of improved management operating and financial reports; inventory control systems; assisting managers in the identification and analysis of financial problems.

Manager of Data Processing who, acting as an individual contributor, is accountable for providing the Company with required data processing services. This requires the incumbent to act as analyst, programmer and minicomputer operator as well as to analyze the short and long-term hardware needs of the Company.

Financial and Planning Analysts (3), who are assigned on a project basis and accountable for the completion of such projects as plant capital investment analyses, gathering data for long-range planning, and short and long-term market analyses and projections, and the coordination of the budgeting process and the monitoring of variances.

Purchasing and Warehousing Organization (consisting of a Chief Purchasing Agent, Mine Purchasing Agent, Mill Purchasing Agent and warehouse employees), which is accountable for the purchase of capital equipment, operating materials and supplies at competitive prices - considering quality, service and delivery. The warehousing function is responsible for ensuring receipt of goods, maintenance of inventory and issuance of materials as authorized. These two functions are in the process of being reorganized and assimilated into the Finance Department.

FIGURE 8–7
Typical job description used under the guide chart–profile method.

POSITION DESCRIPTION
Vice President - Finance
Page Three

Records Administrator, who is accountable for the development of a central file system consolidating records and files throughout the Division.

The incumbent personally maintains relations with the outside auditors; manages and structures the Finance organization; develops reporting techniques for the internal staff; performs a variety of special projects at the President's direction; and provides the President with advice regarding general Company management and accomplishment of Company objectives.

Internal contacts include the President (daily) to discuss general business matters and other key executives (weekly) to provide advice regarding those activities in the Finance organization's purview. External contacts include outside auditors (quarterly) to discuss and resolve audit comments; legal counsel (quarterly) to provide information needed in lawsuits; consultants (monthly) to discuss information needs and findings; and state tax officials (yearly) to discuss production taxes.

The incumbent may approve hires and terminations within the Finance Department's budget, recommend the viability of projects with long-term impact on the Company, and restructure the Department to meet identified operating needs. Items referred to the President for approval include the final budget; transfers from Home Office banking; nonroutine contracts; significant legal issues; and joint venture agreements.

Significant challenges include the building of a professional organization which exhibits a high level of initiative in solving and/or preventing problems.

PRINCIPAL ACCOUNTABILITIES:

1. Provide responsive and cost effective financial and accounting services to assure reporting and financial commitments are met and controls and records are maintained consistent with Division and Corporate policy and professional standards.

2. Direct the Purchasing and Warehousing functions in such a manner as to ensure cost effective and responsive services with an appropriate level of controls established and maintained.

POSITION DESCRIPTION
Vice President - Finance
Page Four

3. Provide timely financial analyses and planning to help ensure that operating and investment decisions are thoroughly analyzed and considered.

4. Provide for accurate, timely, and relevant reports to senior management to ensure that business information needs are met and trends are readily identified.

5. Select, train, develop and motivate employees to ensure the attainment of departmental and divisional goals.

6. Contribute to the development and implementation of overall strategy so that appropriate options are considered in the decision-making process.

7. Provide timely, accurate and cost effective data processing services to meet current Division needs, and plan necessary system upgrades to assure effective future service.

FIGURE 8–7
(continued)

203

Summary

The factor comparison method of job evaluation uses a graphic rating scale on which key jobs are plotted and against which other jobs can be compared visually on specific job factors.

The money method of factor comparison requires (1) tentatively selecting key jobs; (2) ranking jobs by factor; (3) tentatively assigning a money value to each factor based on actual pay rates; (4) reconciling the last two steps to identify true key jobs; (5) plotting key jobs on the factor comparison scale; and (6) entering other jobs by comparing them to key jobs by visual inspection.

The money method of factor comparison is the only job evaluation method in which job evaluation and pricing are accomplished at the same time. This does make for simplicity. However, tying job evaluation so closely to a volatile economy where changing markets can make for quick obsolescence of the pay structure is a serious disadvantage. For this reason, many companies have shifted from the money method to the percentage method. The latter method differentiates job evaluation from pricing.

The percentage method of factor comparison requires (1) selecting key jobs; (2) ranking jobs by factor; (3) ranking factors within each job; (4) combining the two preceding judgments to get point values for each factor within each job; (5) plotting key jobs on a factor comparison scale; and (6) placing other jobs by visual comparison with key jobs.

The key job concept helps to tailor a plan to a particular organization. Under both methods of factor comparison, complexity (except for the use of a smaller number of factors) tends to be a problem. Complexity hinders employee acceptance of factor comparison plans. However, these difficulties do not preclude the use of such a plan where it best serves the organization's needs. Successful installation of a factor comparison plan is more likely where harmonious union-management relations already prevail. In either a union or a nonunion situation, effective employee orientation and participation are essential. And even though such plans may be more difficult to install, their maintenance is probably less expensive than for other factor-based methods of job evaluation.

The Hay guide chart—profile technique has come into increasing use as a major quantitative method of job evaluation, especially for clerical, professional, and supervisory jobs. Installation of the plan must be done by a management consultant team of trained and skilled practitioners from the Hay organization.

The method involves two processes—using guide charts and profiling. The three guide charts discussed in this chapter relate to know-how, problem solving, and accountability. Each guide chart is a two-dimensional matrix. The guide chart for know-how has education and experience on its vertical axis and managerial know-how on its horizontal axis. The latter tends to follow the levels of hierarchy in the organization. Within each nine-cell block on the horizontal axis, the third variable of human relations skills is measured.

The guide chart for problem solving describes the thinking environment on its vertical axis and the thinking challenge on the horizontal axis. In this guide chart, the numbers represent percentages. The percentage chosen for a particular job is multiplied by know-how points to get problem solving points. The stated rationale for this procedure is that "you can think only with what you know."

On the accountability guide chart, the vertical axis represents the freedom to act. The horizontal axis portrays the magnitude of accountability in terms of the dollar values related to the job. The dollar values measured vary with the nature of the work. Horizontal 12-cell blocks are subdivided to allow for the impact on end results.

Point values derived from these three guide charts are added together to get a single point value for each job. In a process called profiling, each *actual* profile is compared against four *standards* (profiles for all jobs, line jobs, staff jobs, and research jobs) with respect to two variables—problem solving and accountability. Know-how, the third variable, is included within problem solving. In profiling, a geometric progression with a 15 percent difference between steps is used. The Hay method specifies the following rules for profiling: (1) In the profile for any job, accountability points and problem solving points should not be more than four steps apart; (2) For line jobs, accountability should be two, three, or four steps higher than problem solving; (3) For staff jobs, accountability and problem solving should be equal, or not more than one step apart either way; and (4) For research jobs, problem solving should be two, three, or four steps higher than accountability.

A major advantage of the Hay method is the extent to which it provides for internal equity. A major disadvantage is the extent to which a company must rely on an outside consultant for both installation and maintenance of the system.

Case Study

State Legislative Branch

In a prominent western state, an advisory commission was appointed by the governor to review the salaries paid to the different positions in the legislative branch of the state government. After lengthy hearings and discussion of alternative job evaluation methods, the commission decided to use the factor comparison method to evaluate these jobs.

As of now, the lowest paying jobs include legislator; majority leader, senate; majority leader, general assembly; minority leader, senate; minority leader, general assembly; chair, appropriations committee, senate; and chair, appropriations committee, general assembly. Paying somewhat more than these jobs but less than all the other legislative jobs are president of the senate and speaker of the general assembly. The remaining jobs all pay more. They are, ranging from lowest to highest paying, state auditor; deputy legislative budget and finance director; revisor of statutes; assistant state auditor; legislative budget and finance director; research director, law revision and legislative services committee; legislative counsel; and chief counsel, law revision and legislative services committee.

Role Assignment
You are called in by the commission as a pay and benefits consultant. Assuming that a factor comparison plan is adopted, what factors would you recommend to be used and why?

Case Study

The Theophilos Company

The Theophilos Company is a large multiplant manufacturing company with operations in 16 midwestern states. After having had unsatisfactory results with another method of job evaluation, the company decided to try the Hay guide chart–profile method. It now uses the method for all of its exempt professional and executive jobs. In the process of installing the system, the director of compensation and benefits, with the assistance of a companywide job evaluation committee and a Hay consultant, evaluated each job using the guide charts and then moved into the profiling phase. The readings from the guide charts for two jobs are shown in the following table:

Job Number	Type of Job	Know-how	Problem Solving	Accountability
14327	Staff	1216	50%	800
39244	Research	1400	87%	700

Role Assignment
You are the director of compensation and benefits for the Theophilos Company. Check to see whether the two profiles appear to be reasonable. Be prepared to discuss your conclusions.

Questions for Discussion

1. What is the essence of the factor comparison method? Describe it in general terms.
2. What steps are necessary to develop a factor comparison plan using the percentage approach?
3. Is the evaluation of new jobs easier or more difficult under the factor comparison method than it would be under another method of job evaluation?
4. Why is a ratio scale used in the percentage method of factor comparison?
5. Should more or fewer factors be used with the factor comparison method compared with the point method? Why?
6. What are the advantages and disadvantages of the factor comparison method?
7. In what ways is the guide chart–profile method similar to the other major methods of job evaluation?
8. Can the guide chart–profile method be used with all types of employee groups? Discuss.
9. What are the important differences between the guide charts for know-how and for problem solving?

10. How does freedom to think in the problem solving guide chart differ from freedom to act in the accountability guide chart?
11. Is the guide chart–profile method applicable to companies of all sizes?
12. What is meant by profiling? How is it done?
13. Can the same type of job description as that used with point or factor comparison plans also be used with the guide chart–profile method? Justify your answer.
14. What appear to be the advantages and disadvantages of the guide chart–profile method? Discuss.

Projects

Percentage Method of Factor Comparison. Prepare a pay and benefits manual covering 25 supervisory and executive jobs in Cosmopolitan University using the percentage method of factor comparison. The project will consist of the following five phases:

1. Prepare a written description of the organization's compensation policies, including benefits.
2. Select key jobs and factors, and rank factors and jobs.
3. Do computations to develop the point scale.
4. Prepare a graphic factor comparison scale on which you enter key jobs and rate the remaining jobs. Use a color scheme to indicate key jobs.
5. Construct a scatter diagram and a line of regression, and determine new pay rates.

For benefit costs, see Chapter 13. For scatter diagram and line of regression, see Chapter 10. For job descriptions, see Appendix A, jobs 301 to 325. Actual pay rates will be furnished by your instructor at the appropriate time.

Guide Chart–Profile Method. Prepare a pay and benefits manual covering 25 professional, technical, and executive jobs for Cypress Consolidated, Inc., a conglomerate manufacturing company. Use the guide chart–profile method of job evaluation. The project will consist of the following five phases:

1. Prepare a written description of the organization's compensation policies, including benefits.
2. Determine point values for each job using the guide charts.
3. Check the resulting profiles for acceptability and reexamine where indicated.
4. Construct a scatter diagram and a line of regression.
5. Construct pay boxes, including pay and point ranges.

For benefit costs, see Chapter 13. See Figures 8–2, 8–3, and 8–4 for guide charts. For scatter diagram and line of regression, see Chapter 10. For job descriptions, see Appendix A, jobs 401 to 425.

Notes

1. For further discussion, see Edward N. Hay, "Creating Factor Comparison Key Scales by the Per Cent Method." *Journal of Applied Psychology* 32, no. 5 (October 1948): 456–64.
2. Richard L. Henderson, *Compensation Management* (Reston, Va.: Reston Publishing Co., 1976), 121–22, and his reference to Hay's article, "The Application of Weber's Law to Job Evaluation Estimates." *Journal of Applied Psychology* 34, no. 2 (1950): 102–4.
3. See Eugene J. Benge, Samuel L. H. Burk, and Edward N. Hay, *Manual of Job Evaluation* (New York: Harper & Brothers, 1941).

4. Allan N. Nash and Stephen J. Carroll, Jr., *The Management of Compensation* (Monterey, CA: Brooks/Cole Publishing Co., 1975), 131–32.
5. Ibid., 132.
6. Herbert G. Zollitsch and Adolph Langsner, *Wage and Salary Administration,* 2nd ed. (Cincinnati: South-Western Publishing Co., 1970), 184.
7. David W. Belcher and Thomas J. Atchison, *Compensation Administration,* 2nd ed. (Englewood Cliffs, NJ: Prentice-Hall, Inc., 1987), 196.
8. Ibid.

References

Belcher, David W. and Atchison, Thomas J. *Compensation Administration,* 2nd ed. Englewood Cliffs, NJ: Prentice-Hall, Inc., 1987, 187–195 on factor comparison method and 195–196 on the Hay guide chart–profile method.

Bellak, A. D. "The Hay Guide Chart–Profile Method of Job Evaluation." *Handbook of Wage and Salary Administration,* 2nd ed. Edited by Milton Rock. New York: McGraw-Hill, 1983, 384–412.

Hay, Edward N. "The Application of Weber's Law to Job Evaluation Estimates." *Journal of Applied Psychology,* 34, no.2 (1950): 102–104.

———. "Creating New Factor Comparison Key Scales by the Per Cent Method." *Journal of Applied Psychology,* 32, no. 5 (1948): 456–464.

Hay, Edward N., and Purves, Dale. "The Profile Method of Job Evaluation." *Personnel* (September 1951): 162–170.

———. "A New Method of Job Evaluation: The Guide Chart–Profile Method." *Personnel* (July 1954): 72–80.

Hay Group Environmental Scan Report. Reprint IR3–MA. Philadelphia, PA: Hay Reprint Department, 1987.

Henderson, Richard I. *Compensation Management: Rewarding Performance,* 4th ed. Reston, VA: Reston Publishing Co., Inc., 1985, 306–308 on the factor comparison method and 311–320 on the Hay guide chart–profile method.

Milkovich, George T., and Newman, Jerry M. *Compensation,* 2nd ed. Plano, TX: Business Publications, Inc., 1987, 117–125 on the factor comparison method and 142–147 on the Hay guide chart–profile method.

Pay and Benefits Surveys

Chapter Outline

- Why Conduct a Survey?
- Sampling Techniques in Government and Private Industry
- Government Surveys
- Nonprofit Association Surveys
- Private Industry Surveys
- Summary
- Case Study—Borgerson National Bank

Earlier, we saw that one of the primary functions of the wage and salary administrator is to reconcile the internal worth of different jobs with external market values. We have also noted the impact on pay structures of craft and industrial unionism. We must also consider that under collective bargaining unions still have to pay attention to what is happening to market rates for particular jobs. In this chapter, we shall examine some of the more detailed reasons for conducting surveys to determine market rates, as well as the techniques employed.

Why Conduct a Survey?

Aside from the obvious need to reconcile internal with external job worth, there are many other reasons for an organization to conduct a survey of pay and benefits. Among these are

1. To gain more information about one or more particular jobs for which there is a great demand.
2. To test whether the company's entire pay structure may be too low.
3. To find out more about starting rates for entry-level jobs.
4. To look at pay differentials for selected jobs.
5. To get more information about employee benefits.
6. To get more facts about related matters, such as hours of work, frequency of pay reviews, automatic and merit pay increases, and trends in pay and benefits.

Sampling Techniques in Government and Private Industry

Unlike sampling the weight of the contents of tomato cans in a food cannery, sampling in industry does not typically involve a random selection of data to get a representative sample. This is especially true of pay and benefit surveys. Usually, the sample is stratified; that is, all companies are included in the largest category, 50 percent in the next category, 20 percent in the next, and perhaps 5 percent in the last category. Where the universe is small, the sample desired may be 100 percent—the entire universe. There is, nonetheless, a tendency for government samples to be based on much more reliable sampling techniques than those used by private industry. David Belcher states this point well:

> Although BLS [Bureau of Labor Statistics] surveys include all the organizations (above a certain size calculated so as not to affect results) in the area of industry by carefully selecting a sample that represents the total, few private surveys do so. Most private surveys select participant organizations without a census of the organizations in the universe and with little regard for sampling principles. Often, the primary criterion for inclusion in the survey is willingness to participate. Organizations conducting their own surveys can, of course, select for participation the organizations that they consider to be their labor market competitors. Participant organizations can be selected by area, industry, size, or some combination of these variables. If all organizations selected provide information, no sample is involved—the entire universe has been surveyed. But if some organizations decline to participate or if participants are selected from the universe, a sampling problem emerges that may well attenuate the value of the data.[1]

Government Surveys

Government surveys include area and industry wage surveys and the national survey of professional, administrative, technical, and clerical pay—all conducted by the Bureau of Labor Statistics.

Area Wage Surveys

Among the most useful of the government surveys at the federal level are the area wage surveys conducted by the Bureau of Labor Statistics. Under a new 90-area program initiated in January 1987, the Bureau of Labor Statistics surveys 32 areas annually and the remaining areas in alternate years. Surveys include the following sectors: manufacturing; transportation, communications, and other public utilities; wholesale trade; retail trade; finance, insurance, and real estate; and services. Data are obtained by personal visits, mail questionnaires, and telephone interviews.

Table 9–1 shows part of a typical area wage survey. Weekly earnings for office clerical and professional and technical workers as well as hourly earnings for maintenance, toolroom, powerplant, material movement, and custodial workers are included in the full report, although a portion of the report reproduced here shows only the hourly earnings of material movement and custodial workers. To see how the data are arranged, look at the line for truckdrivers in manufacturing. The 1,330 workers sampled had hourly earnings of from $4.00 to $4.50 at the low end, ranging upward as far as $13.00 to $14.00. The detailed frequency distribution is summarized by three measures—the mean, the median, and the interquartile range. For each job the mean is computed by totaling the earnings of all

TABLE 9–1

Hourly earnings of material movement and custodial workers in Phoenix, Arizona. The jobs shown are common to more than one industry.

Occupation and Industry Division	Number of Workers	Hourly Earnings (In Dollars)[2] Mean	Median	Middle Range	3.35 and Under 3.50	3.50 – 4.00	4.00 – 4.50	4.50 – 5.00	5.00 – 5.50	5.50 – 6.00	6.00 – 6.50
Truckdrivers	5,062	10.82	11.35	9.31–11.99	–	–	21	64	136	83	92
Manufacturing	1,330	10.63	10.90	9.85–11.98	–	–	3	–	25	5	12
Nonmanufacturing	3,732	10.88	11.35	9.09–12.98	–	–	18	64	111	78	80
Transportation and utilities	1,005	13.37	14.70	11.58–14.87	–	–	–	10	–	4	–
Truckdrivers, light truck	559	6.75	6.40	5.25– 7.75	–	–	21	64	104	53	47
Manufacturing	136	8.37	8.50	7.47–10.15	–	–	3	–	14	—	2
Nonmanufacturing	423	6.23	5.75	5.00– 7.50	–	–	18	64	90	53	45
Truckdrivers, medium truck	645	10.89	10.40	7.15–14.87	–	–	–	–	21	25	38
Manufacturing	98	9.77	10.26	9.55–10.55	–	–	–	–	–	–	10
Nonmanufacturing	547	11.09	14.87	7.00–14.87	–	–	–	–	21	25	28
Truckdrivers, heavy truck	1,228	10.62	10.75	9.85–11.98	–	–	–	–	–	–	7
Manufacturing	813	11.12	11.21	10.70–11.98	–	–	–	–	–	–	–
Nonmanufacturing	415	9.64	10.31	8.15–10.41	–	–	–	–	–	–	7
Truckdrivers, tractor-trailer	2,268	11.68	11.35	11.35–12.98	–	–	–	–	–	–	–
Nonmanufacturing	2,115	11.65	11.35	11.35–12.98	–	–	–	–	–	–	–
Transportation and utilities	448	12.61	11.58	11.58–14.70	–	–	–	–	–	–	–
Shippers	267	6.73	5.50	4.50– 7.25	–	–	66	55	11	44	–
Manufacturing	62	7.01	7.25	5.50– 7.25	–	–	–	11	–	11	–
Receivers	268	7.50	7.85	4.65– 9.27	–	29	29	15	20	12	5
Nonmanufacturing	195	7.32	6.45	4.10–10.39	–	29	29	15	20	1	5
Shippers and receivers	122	7.80	8.50	7.33– 8.51	–	–	1	9	17	–	–
Manufacturing	92	7.60	8.30	5.45– 8.90	–	–	–	9	17	–	–
Warehouseman	3,022	9.08	10.31	5.35–12.08	–	33	549	138	54	53	33
Manufacturing	515	10.60	10.48	8.50–12.24	–	–	–	–	–	–	4
Nonmanufacturing	2,507	8.77	10.04	4.50–12.08	–	33	549	138	54	53	29
Order fillers	288	8.62	8.69	7.48–10.04	–	–	1	1	1	1	–
Material handling laborers	276	7.12	7.50	5.69– 8.10	–	–	–	–	50	48	1
Nonmanufacturing	212	6.80	6.53	5.69– 7.50	–	–	–	–	50	48	1
Forklift operators	605	8.66	8.87	7.38–10.00	–	–	6	3	9	87	3
Manufacturing	328	7.44	7.85	5.66– 8.67	–	–	6	3	9	66	3
Nonmanufacturing	277	10.10	10.00	8.88–12.20	–	–	–	–	–	21	–
Guards	3,211	5.35	4.75	4.25– 6.00	66	157	1171	312	367	124	403
Manufacturing	360	8.09	7.98	7.20– 9.28	–	–	3	–	18	22	5
Nonmanufacturing	2,851	5.00	4.50	4.25– 5.60	66	157	1168	312	349	102	398
Guards I	3,030	5.16	4.52	4.25– 6.00	66	157	1171	312	367	123	403
Manufacturing	183	7.62	7.85	6.24– 9.04	–	–	3	–	18	22	5
Nonmanufacturing	2,847	5.00	4.50	4.25– 5.50	66	157	1168	312	349	101	398
Guards II	179	8.57	8.15	7.53– 9.68	–	–	–	–	–	1	–
Manufacturing	175	8.61	8.25	7.55– 9.68	–	–	–	–	–	–	–
Janitors, porters, and cleaners	3,337	4.56	3.75	3.50– 5.00	693	1250	418	102	163	161	85
Manufacturing	376	7.66	8.00	6.50– 9.07	–	3	15	25	19	20	8
Nonmanufacturing	3,001	4.17	3.65	3.50– 4.25	693	1247	403	77	144	141	77

Source: U.S. Bureau of Labor Statistics, Bulletin 3040–22, June 1987.

212

TABLE 9–1
Continued

Number of Workers Receiving Straight-Time Hourly Earnings (In Dollars) of—

6.50 – 7.00	7.00 – 7.50	7.50 – 8.00	8.00 – 8.50	8.50 – 9.00	9.00 – 9.50	9.50 – 10.00	10.00 – 10.50	10.50 – 11.00	11.00 – 11.50	11.50 – 12.00	12.00 – 12.50	12.50 – 13.00	13.00 – 14.00	14.00 – 15.00	15.00 and Over
87	120	280	36	162	254	171	445	360	776	710	139	246	195	649	36
19	31	36	6	67	38	153	99	210	74	419	128	3	2	–	–
68	89	244	30	95	216	18	346	150	702	291	11	243	193	649	36
–	6	22	4	12	50	–	27	–	–	183	3	–	–	648	36
24	24	121	2	23	10	–	56	1	4	1	4	–	–	–	–
8	7	25	2	23	10	–	35	1	4	1	1	–	–	–	–
16	17	96	–	–	–	–	21	–	–	–	3	–	–	–	–
52	46	39	18	23	12	21	45	12	3	4	6	–	–	280	–
–	2	–	4	–	8	21	28	12	3	4	6	–	–	–	–
52	44	39	14	23	4	–	17	–	–	–	–	–	–	280	–
–	21	75	7	54	20	150	242	186	28	438	–	–	–	–	–
–	–	–	–	33	20	132	12	186	28	402	–	–	–	–	–
–	21	75	7	21	–	18	230	–	–	36	–	–	–	–	–
–	7	15	9	51	212	–	82	161	702	267	129	246	195	156	36
–	7	15	9	51	212	–	78	150	702	255	8	243	193	156	36
–	–	–	–	–	50	–	24	–	–	183	–	–	–	155	36
–	26	–	4	–	–	9	1	18	–	–	–	–	33	–	–
–	26	–	4	–	–	9	1	–	–	–	–	–	–	–	–
7	12	29	3	26	25	1	21	18	–	–	–	–	–	–	16
7	4	6	2	22	–	–	21	18	–	–	–	–	–	–	16
3	2	12	7	51	4	14	1	–	1	–	–	–	–	–	–
2	1	12	7	27	4	12	–	–	1	–	–	–	–	–	–
67	49	67	78	97	141	36	569	99	12	56	389	1	437	4	60
3	30	23	50	38	15	24	120	20	11	3	114	–	–	–	*60
64	19	44	28	59	126	12	449	79	1	53	275	1	437	4	–
50	36	11	7	70	11	11	77	11	–	–	–	–	–	–	–
20	6	68	49	10	1	2	18	1	1	1	–	–	–	–	–
16	2	55	18	4	–	–	18	–	–	–	–	–	–	–	–
4	78	22	57	131	34	18	54	4	18	1	22	18	36	–	–
4	71	15	57	75	16	—	—	3	—	—	–	–	–	–	–
–	7	7	–	56	18	18	54	1	18	1	22	18	36	–	–
52	63	59	297	18	43	29	33	17	–	–	–	–	–	–	–
26	52	55	39	18	43	29	33	17	–	–	–	–	–	–	–
26	11	4	258	–	–	–	–	–	–	–	–	–	–	–	–
51	20	15	281	8	30	6	19	1	–	–	–	–	–	–	–
26	11	11	23	8	30	6	19	1	–	–	–	–	–	–	–
25	9	4	258	–	–	–	–	–	–	–	–	–	–	–	–
1	41	44	16	10	13	23	14	16	–	–	–	–	–	–	–
–	39	44	16	10	13	23	14	16	–	–	–	–	–	–	–
124	91	48	51	17	140	9	3	–	22	–	–	–	–	–	–
28	13	48	51	17	104	–	3	–	22	–	–	–	–	–	–
96	78	–	–	–	36	9	–	–	–	–	–	–	–	–	–

the workers and dividing by the number of workers. The median represents the pay point at which half the workers earned more than the rate shown and half earned less. The interquartile, or middle, range refers to the middle 50 percent of the workers.

Each job shown in the area wage survey is covered by a matching job description, which serves two purposes. First, it helps to assure greater uniformity of reporting by respondents during data collection. Second, it allows any company to match one of its jobs against a survey job.

Once a company is able to match a job shown in the survey, it must decide which measure to use for comparing its wage rates to those in the survey. Of the measures shown, the mean, while the most commonly referred to, is least useful as a policy guide. It is subject to distortion from workers who are paid extremely low or extremely high rates. The mean also does not tell much because it is not necessarily the most typical figure. On the other hand, the median is not subject to distortion from workers paid at extreme rates. Also, the median has meaning because it indicates exactly the middle of the distribution. By looking at the median, a company can tell whether or not it is paying more or less than the wage received by the typical worker. The measure of the middle range allows for a more refined policy. For example, if a manufacturing company wished to pay an hourly rate for truckdriver that is in the top quarter of the employees surveyed, it could do so by paying such a worker more than $11.98.

The full frequency distribution in the right-hand columns of Table 9–1 makes possible a still more precise policy. A company could, by using relatively simple calculations, find the 90th percentile and thus pay workers in this occupation a rate in the top 10 percent of the distribution.

Industry Wage Surveys

The advantages of the area wage surveys are that they are timely and based on scientific sampling techniques. A disadvantage is that the jobs surveyed are limited to those common to many industries and exclude government, construction, and extractive industries. This disadvantage can be offset in part by using the industry wage surveys by the Bureau of Labor Statistics. An industry wage survey for textile mills is shown in Table 9–2.

Table 9–2 does not show the entire textile mills industry; it covers only cotton and man-made fiber textile mills. The table summarizes data both by geographic regions and occupations. For each occupation in each region of the United States and for the United States as a whole, two pieces of information are shown: the number of workers and the average hourly earnings.

The particular occupations shown by groupings in Table 9–2—carding and drawing; spinning; spooling, winding, and twisting; slashing and warping; and weaving—are peculiar to this industry.

The industry wage survey summarized in Table 9–2 was conducted in June 1985, but the report was not available until February 1987. It is divided into two parts—one dealing with the cotton and man-made fiber textile mills, and the other with wool yarn and broadwoven fabric mills. The report shows average hourly earnings by type of mill, type of area, size of mill, and method of wage payment (time or incentive).

Occupational earnings are also shown by detailed class intervals for the industry and by major geographic regions within the industry. Other tables show by region the method of wage payment (broken down by percentage for different types of time payment and individual and group incentive arrangements), scheduled weekly hours, shift differentials, paid holidays, years of service required for specified weeks of paid vacations, and details about different types of health, insurance, and retirement plans. An appendix at the back of the report gives job descriptions for the occupations summarized in the report.

The chief advantage of industry wage surveys is the detail they provide about industry-related jobs. However, because they are conducted infrequently, the surveys often reflect outdated wage figures.

National Survey of Professional, Administrative, Technical, and Clerical Pay

Another federal government survey that fills an important need is the national survey of professional, administrative, technical, and clerical pay. The data in this report are arranged as in other Bureau of Labor Statistics reports. In addition to the measures of mean, median, and interquartile range (middle 50 percent), this survey includes detailed percent distributions of employees by salary bracket. While it has other uses, this report serves the special purpose of providing a basis for setting federal government white-collar salaries under the Federal Pay Comparability Act of 1970. The survey is weak in its coverage of those middle management jobs that in industry tend to parallel and often exceed professional pay scales.

Pay data for clerical, technical, administrative, and professional workers are expressed in terms of monthly and annual salaries. Pay ranges for some of these jobs can be seen in Figure 9–1 on page 218.

For each of these jobs (except for messenger, which has a single classification), more than one level is represented. For example, there are five levels of secretaries with carefully differentiated job descriptions depending on duties and organization levels. Similarly, there are eight levels of engineers. The diagram shows the range of the medians for all the levels in each of the jobs.

It is evident that the range of the medians is much greater for those jobs at the upper end of the pay scale compared with those at the lower end. For example, the range for attorneys extends from roughly $30,000 to more than $101,000, while the range for secretaries is only from about $16,000 to around $27,000.

While other factors such as sex and race also enter in, many of the differences in levels of pay between jobs can be explained by differences in skill, experience, education, and training.

TABLE 9–2
An industry wage survey for textile mills, June 1985.

Department and Occupation	United States		New England		Middle Atlantic		Southeast		Southwest	
	Number of Workers	Average Hourly Earnings	Number of Workers	Average Hourly Earnings	Number of Workers	Average Hourly Earnings	Number of Workers	Average Hourly Earnings	Number of Workers	Average Hourly Earnings
Carding and drawing										
Card grinders	661	$7.23	—	—	—	—	639	$7.25	7	$7.91
Card strippers	72	6.21	19	$5.81	—	—	51	6.40	—	—
Card tenders (finishers)	3,132	5.78	108	5.95	—	—	2,886	5.78	48	5.75
Comber tenders (cotton)	690	6.06	—	—	—	—	682	6.04	—	—
Drawing-frame tenders	3,753	6.07	20	5.94	—	—	3,559	6.07	68	6.42
Opener tenders	1,161	5.53	—	—	—	—	1,105	5.51	—	—
Picker tenders	403	5.75	—	—	—	—	375	5.74	—	—
Slubber tenders	3,661	6.49	—	—	—	—	3,604	6.49	—	—
Texturing-machine operators	3,492	6.32	—	—	96	$5.23	3,386	6.35	—	—
Spinning										
Doffers, spinning frame	7,832	6.45	26	5.58	—	—	7,716	6.45	—	—
Section fixers	3,427	7.37	79	6.95	18	6.03	3,255	7.39	52	7.36
Spinners, ring frame	14,057	5.92	228	6.05	131	5.87	13,342	5.92	146	6.14
Spinners, frame, other than ring	277	6.36	104	6.42	—	—	—	—	—	—
Dyeing-machine tenders, yarn	277	6.61	55	6.15	—	—	162	6.58	—	—
Spooling, winding, and twisting										
Twister tenders, ring frame	5,862	5.95	211	5.58	225	5.45	5,107	6.00	—	—
Uptwisters (man-made fibers)	1,306	5.54	71	5.84	83	5.20	1,142	5.54	—	—
Winders, yarn	14,084	5.89	414	5.80	351	5.30	13,028	5.90	74	6.03

Slashing and warping										
Slasher tenders	2,865	6.44	31	6.79	74	6.27	2,711	6.44	49	6.51
Warper tenders	2,304	6.32	31	6.46	116	6.94	2,096	6.26	55	6.82
Slow speed	288	6.26	—	—	24	7.87	255	6.07	—	—
High speed	2,016	6.32	28	6.49	92	6.69	1,841	6.29	55	6.82
Weaving										
Battery hands	2,336	5.59	98	5.94	35	5.69	2,155	5.56	—	—
Doffers, cloth	1,516	5.71	67	5.93	51	5.86	1,380	5.70	18	5.72
Drawing-in machine tenders	630	6.60	60	6.43	15	6.01	546	6.59	—	—
Loom fixers	7,578	8.27	257	8.02	281	8.38	6,917	8.27	—	—
Box shuttle looms	1,062	8.04	31	8.16	24	8.65	999	8.03	—	—
Jacquard shuttle looms	261	8.64	—	—	73	8.56	180	8.66	—	—
Plain and dobby shuttle looms	2,957	8.27	136	7.70	99	8.51	2,647	8.28	—	—
Shuttleless looms	3,052	8.34	74	8.53	—	—	2,918	8.32	—	—
Loom-winder tenders	255	5.74	19	7.39	—	—	199	5.61	—	—
Tying-in machine operators	1,677	7.01	39	7.75	68	7.70	1,533	6.97	29	7.00

Source: U.S. Bureau of Labor Statistics, Bulletin 2265, February 1987.

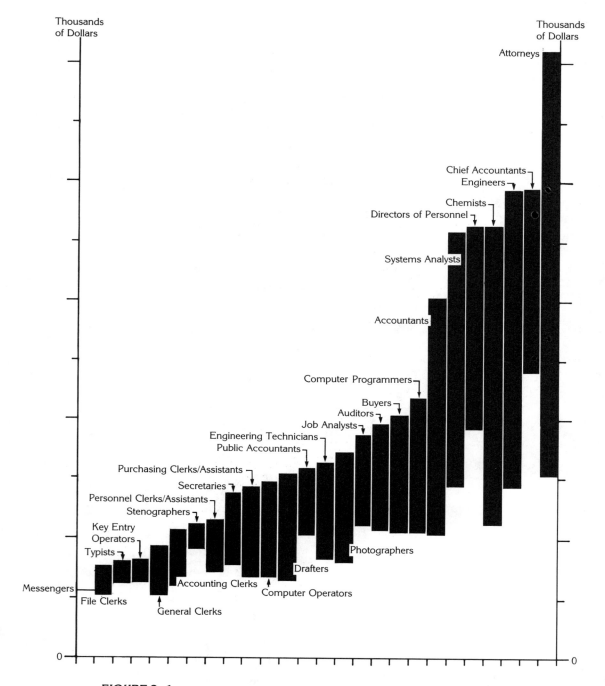

FIGURE 9–1
Median annual salaries for clerical, technical, administrative, and
professional workers. Data are for March 1986. Source: U.S.
Bureau of Labor Statistics.

218

Nonprofit Association Surveys

Some surveys are conducted by nonprofit associations. For example, the International City Management Association (ICMA) conducts annual salary surveys on municipal and county administrators and department heads. In 1986 ICMA conducted personnel practices surveys covering police and fire departments. The response rate for the fire questionnaire was 41 percent and for the police questionnaire about 35 percent. Table 9–3 shows the annual salaries for fire department and police department personnel in Riverside, California.

In addition to the salaries shown in the table, the two surveys included other aspects of personnel policies, such as selection criteria, training, and departmental budgets.

TABLE 9–3
Annual salaries for police and fire personnel in Riverside, California, in 1986.

Police Department

Position	Minimum	Maximum
Chief	71,605	71,605
Deputy Chief	45,600	55,428
Captain	45,600	55,428
Lieutenant	39,396	47,880
Sergeant	35,736	41,364
Corporal	29,400	35,736
Detective	29,400	35,736
Motor Officer	24,780	33,012
Private	24,180	32,412

Fire Department

Position	Minimum	Maximum
Chief	66,840	66,840
Deputy Chief	46,272	57,948
Asst. Chief	40,620	47,028
Captain	36,264	39,972
Engineer	31,320	34,536
Arson Investigator	24,180	32,412
Code Inspector	24,180	32,412
Emergency Med. Technician	23,376	31,320
Firefighter	23,376	31,320

Note: Only a single rate is shown for Police Chief and Fire Chief.
Source: Victor S. DeSantis, *Police and Fire Salaries* (Washington, DC: International City Management Association, 1987).

Private Industry Surveys

Because government surveys fail to meet some needs, surveys by private organizations, even though sometimes not as well done scientifically, fill the gap. Industry associations, chambers of commerce, research organizations, banks, unions, and consulting firms conduct private surveys. A meeting of compensation specialists in competing organizations is another method used by industry.

The American Compensation Association

The American Compensation Association (ACA) is an association of compensation and benefits professionals. Among its many activities is conducting an annual salary budget survey. The survey asks for information about different types of salary increases (see Figure 9–2). These are (1) general increase, which is any across-the-board adjustment; (2) cost of living allowance (COLA); (3) merit budget; (4) promotional increases; and (5) lump sum increases (which exclude Christmas bonus, suggestion awards, profit-sharing bonus, or executive bonus). Since the survey is on two sides of a single sheet of paper, better survey response is more likely.

The Conference Board

The Conference Board, a business research organization, conducts surveys of top executive compensation and compensation of overseas personnel. Figure 9–3 shows three pages of the form used by the Conference Board to gather information on the pay and benefits of top executives.

U.S. Chamber of Commerce

The United States Chamber of Commerce, among its many activities, conducts a yearly survey of employee benefits. The results of the survey are discussed in more detail in Chapter 13 on employee benefits. Figure 9–4 shows the part of the survey form used by the Chamber to get the vital information on benefits.

The American Management Association and the Administrative Management Society

The American Management Association (AMA) conducts compensation surveys of top management, middle management, supervisors, sales personnel, and engineers and scientists. The Administrative Management Society (AMS) conducts surveys of office personnel and middle management.

The AMS office salary survey includes national data for the United States and Canada, regional data for the United States, and data for particular localities, many not covered by the Bureau of Labor Statistics. The AMS survey also covers some jobs not included by the federal agency.

1987/1988 SALARY BUDGET SURVEY

Please return questionnaire no later than July 10, 1987.

1. Check the industry which best fits your operation. Check only one. (Multi-industry companies should submit a form for each industry.)

☐ Aerospace
☐ Airlines
☐ Apparel Manufacturing
☐ Automotive & Farm Equipment
☐ Building Materials
☐ Chemical
☐ Communications
☐ Computer Service & Software
☐ Construction/Engineering
☐ Consultants
☐ Cosmetics
☐ Diversified
☐ Education
☐ Electrical & Electronic

☐ Finance/Banks
☐ Food & Beverage
☐ Forest & Paper Products
☐ Gas Transmission Lines
☐ Government
☐ Hospitals & Health Care
☐ Hotel/Motel
☐ Instrument Manufacturing
☐ Insurance
☐ Manufacturing
☐ Mining
☐ Nonprofit, Miscellaneous
☐ Ofc. Computer & Business Equip.
☐ Petroleum

☐ Petroleum Services
☐ Pharmaceutical
☐ Printing & Publishing
☐ Reasearch & Development
☐ Restaurant
☐ Retail
☐ Rubber
☐ Steel, Aluminum, Copper, Nickel
☐ Textiles
☐ Tobacco
☐ Transportation
☐ Utilities
☐ Other (list below)
_____

2. What region covers the majority of your employees reported below?

☐ Eastern ☐ Central ☐ Southern ☐ Western ☐ Canada

3. What is your salary increase program for 1987?

	Number of Covered Employees	General Increase	COLA	Merit Increase	Total Increase
Nonexempt Salary		%	%	%	%
Exempt Salary		%	%	%	%
Officer/Executive		%	%	%	%
Total					

4. What are your salary increase plans or estimates for 1988?

	General Increase	COLA	Merit Increase	Total Increase
Nonexempt Salary	%	%	%	%
Exempt Salary	%	%	%	%
Officer/Executive	%	%	%	%

5. (a.) If you use a salary range structure, by what percentage did you increase the ranges in 1987?

Nonexempt ____ % Exempt ____ % Officer/Executive ____ %

(b.) By what percentage do you plan to increase the salary range structure for 1988?

Nonexempt ____ % Exempt ____ % Officer/Executive ____ %

Continued on reverse side ▶

Return to: American Compensation Association, 6619 N. Scottsdale Road, Scottsdale, Arizona 85253-7802.

Please make mailing label corrections below (please print):

Name _____
Title _____
Firm Name _____
Address _____
City _____ State _____ Zip _____

6. What is the percentage spread between salary range minimums and maximums? Check one for each group of positions.

% SPREAD BETWEEN RANGE MINIMUM & MAXIMUM

	Under 30%	30-39%	40-49%	50-59%	60-99%	100% and over	No formal range
Nonexempt Positions	☐	☐	☐	☐	☐	☐	☐
Exempt Positions	☐	☐	☐	☐	☐	☐	☐
Officer/Executive Positions	☐	☐	☐	☐	☐	☐	☐

7. What is the average time interval between salary increases? Check one for each group of positions.

TYPICAL FREQUENCY OF SALARY INCREASES

	10 mos. or less	11 mos.	12 mos.	13-14 mos.	15-17 mos.	18-21 mos.	22-24 mos.
Nonexempt Positions	☐	☐	☐	☐	☐	☐	☐
Exempt Positions	☐	☐	☐	☐	☐	☐	☐
Officer/Executive Positions	☐	☐	☐	☐	☐	☐	☐

8. (a.) What are your salary increase plans for other items such as bona fide promotions, reclassifications, equity adjustments, step increases, etc., in 1987?

Nonexempt ____ % Exempt ____ % Officer/Executive ____ %
☐ We do not budget these items.

(b.) What are your salary increase plans or estimates for other items such as bona fide promotions, equity adjustments, step increases, etc., in 1988?

Nonexempt ____ % Exempt ____ % Officer/Executive ____ %
☐ We do not budget these items.

9. (a.) Did you grant lump sum increases in the following years: *(Refer to definition under General Instructions.)*

	Yes	No			Yes	No
1986: Nonexempt	☐	☐	1987: Nonexempt		☐	☐
Exempt	☐	☐	Exempt		☐	☐
Officer/Executive	☐	☐	Officer/Executive		☐	☐

(b.) If yes, did you add the increase to the base salary?

	Yes	No			Yes	No
1986: Nonexempt	☐	☐	1987: Nonexempt		☐	☐
Exempt	☐	☐	Exempt		☐	☐
Officer/Executive	☐	☐	Officer/Executive		☐	☐

(c.) What was the average percent of base pay granted by lump sum increases?

1986: Nonexempt ____ % Exempt ____ % Officer/Executive ____ %
1987: Nonexempt ____ % Exempt ____ % Officer/Executive ____ %

10. What percentage of employees who were eligible for a merit increase received a merit increase in 1987?

Nonexempt ____ % Exempt ____ % Officer/Executive ____ %

FIGURE 9–2
American Compensation Association salary budget survey form. *Source:* American Compensation Association. Used by permission, 1987.

Part II: Compensation Information

Note: Please rank executives according to *total compensation* (salary and bonus) earned for 1986.
Please report the full amount of each executive's 1986 salary and bonus including any deferred portion. Do not report 1986 long-term compensation in this section.
In addition, please indicate each executive's title and area of responsibility. For example, you might report:

Title	Responsibility
Senior Vice President	Finance
Vice President	International Operations
President	Company A (our largest subsidiary)

Please define "responsibility" as specifically as possible.

1. HIGHEST PAID EXECUTIVE

Title: _____ Responsibility: _____
Salary earned in 1986 $ _____
1986 Annual Bonus $ _____
1986 Salary Range Minimum $ _____ Maximum $ _____
Was the executive in this position at the beginning of 1986? ☐ Yes ☐ No

2. SECOND HIGHEST PAID EXECUTIVE

Title: _____ Responsibility: _____
Salary earned in 1986 $ _____
1986 Annual Bonus $ _____
1986 Salary Range Minimum $ _____ Maximum $ _____
Was the executive in this position at the beginning of 1986? ☐ Yes ☐ No

3. THIRD HIGHEST PAID EXECUTIVE

Title: _____ Responsibility: _____
Salary earned in 1986 $ _____
1986 Annual Bonus $ _____
1986 Salary Range Minimum $ _____ Maximum $ _____
Was the executive in this position at the beginning of 1986? ☐ Yes ☐ No

4. FOURTH HIGHEST PAID EXECUTIVE

Title: _____ Responsibility: _____
Salary earned in 1986 $ _____
1986 Annual Bonus $ _____
1986 Salary Range Minimum $ _____ Maximum $ _____
Was the executive in this position at the beginning of 1986? ☐ Yes ☐ No

5. FIFTH HIGHEST PAID EXECUTIVE

Title: _____ Responsibility: _____
Salary earned in 1986 $ _____
1986 Annual Bonus $ _____
1986 Salary Range Minimum $ _____ Maximum $ _____
Was the executive in this position at the beginning of 1986? ☐ Yes ☐ No

6. Do you have an "annual" executive bonus or incentive plan (that is, a bonus based solely on one year's performance and paid soon after the close of the year)? ☐ Yes ☐ No
If "yes," did you pay a bonus for 1986 performance? ☐ Yes ☐ No
1985 performance? ☐ Yes ☐ No

7. Please indicate your average 1986 salary increase for the following employee groups:
Nonexempt Salaried _____ %
Exempt Salaried _____
Executive _____

8. Please indicate the 1987 salary increase budget for the following employee groups:
Nonexempt Salaried _____ %
Exempt Salaried _____
Executive _____

9. Please indicate the projected 1988 salary increase budget for the following employee groups:
Nonexempt Salaried _____
Exempt Salaried _____
Executive _____

10. Does your company have a stock option plan (or plans) for key employees? ☐ Yes ☐ No
If "yes,"
a. Does the plan allow you to grant:
(1) only "incentive stock options" (ISO's)? ☐ Yes ☐ No
(2) only "nonqualified stock options" (NQO's)? ☐ Yes ☐ No
(3) both ISO's and NQO's? ☐ Yes ☐ No

b. If you have a stock option plan:
(1) do you provide for stock-for-stock exercise ("stock swaps")? ☐ Yes ☐ No
(2) do you attach "stock appreciation rights" (SAR's)? ☐ Yes ☐ No.

c. Did you make a regular grant of stock options during 1986? ☐ Yes ☐ No.
If "yes,"
(1) for the five highest-paid executives, what was the dollar size of the grants; that is, the number of shares times market value at the time of grant?

Highest Paid $ _____ Fourth $ _____
Second $ _____ Fifth $ _____
Third $ _____

(2) what types of options were granted during 1986?
only ISO's? ☐ Yes ☐ No
only NQO's? ☐ Yes ☐ No
both ISO's and NQO's? ☐ Yes ☐ No

d. For each of the five highest-paid executives who exercised a stock option or SAR during 1986, what was the net value realized in shares (market value less exercise price) or cash?

Highest Paid $ _____ Fourth $ _____
Second $ _____ Fifth $ _____
Third $ _____

11. Do you have a plan for "restricted stock" awards to executives—that is, grants of stock subject to restrictions and forfeiture until "earned out" by continued employment over a specified period of time? ☐ Yes ☐ No
Note: Under restricted stock awards, the executive pays nothing for the stock; therefore, do not include stock options.
If "yes," what was the value of the awards granted during 1986 for each of the five highest-paid executives? (The value of the award is the number of shares times market value at the time of grant.)

Highest Paid $ _____ Fourth $ _____
Second $ _____ Fifth $ _____
Third $ _____

12. Do you have an executive incentive plan based on the attainment of long-term (usually three to five years) performance goals, usually called a "performance share or unit" plan? ☐ Share Plan ☐ Yes ☐ No
☐ Unit Plan ☐ Yes ☐ No

a. If "yes," what was the total value of "shares" or "units" *granted* in 1986 contingent on the attainment of future performance goals?

Highest Paid $ _____ Fourth $ _____
Second $ _____ Fifth $ _____
Third $ _____

b. How much was paid out in 1986 from this plan to each of the five highest paid executives based on the attainment of performance goals?

Highest Paid $ _____ Fourth $ _____
Second $ _____ Fifth $ _____
Third $ _____

Your name and title (please print) _____

Company name and address _____

Your telephone number _____

Your organization is a (check one):
☐ Parent company
☐ Subsidiary
 Please indicate parent company _____
☐ Other operating entity
 Please indicate _____

THANK YOU

FIGURE 9–3

Compensation pages of Conference Board survey form for top executive pay and benefits, 1987.
Source: The Conference Board. Used by permission, 1987.

Show *actual data or best estimate for employees covered in survey.*

A. GROSS PAYROLL FOR EMPLOYEES IN SURVEY:
- For this item, report *actual wages (not* take-home pay after deductions have been made). Report on line A-1 the straight-time wages for all hours, including pay for time not worked, plus payments in lieu of vacations and holidays.
- Report premium and bonus payments on lines other than line A-1. Thus, if the rate is $10.00 an hour for straight time and $5.00 additional for overtime after 40 hours, for each hour of overtime worked after 40 hours, $10.00 would be entered on line A-1, and $5.00 on line A-2.

[Include BONUS AND PREMIUM PAY ONLY on lines 2-6. Report straight-time pay on line 1.]

		Total amount for 1985
1. Straight time for employees in survey	$	33
2. Overtime premium pay	$	45
3. Holiday premium pay	$	57
4. Shift differential	$	69
5. Earned incentive or production bonus	$	81
6. Other (Specify)	$	93
7. TOTAL GROSS PAYROLL		105

B. LEGALLY REQUIRED PAYMENTS (employer's share only):

1. Old-Age, Survivors, Disability, and Health Insurance (employer FICA taxes)	$	120
2. Unemployment Compensation (federal and state taxes)	$	132
3. Workers' Compensation (estimate cost if self-insured)	$	144
4. Railroad Retirement Tax		156
5. Railroad Unemployment and Cash Sickness Insurance		168
6. State sickness benefits insurance		180
7. Other (Specify)		192
8. TOTAL		204

C. VOLUNTARY OR AGREED-UPON PAYMENTS (employer's share only):

ITEMS C-1, C-4 AND C-6—PENSION AND INSURANCE PREMIUMS. For pension and insurance premiums, report net payments after deducting any dividends or credits returned to employer by insurer. In *pension programs,* the company's long-term commitment is fixed, not tied to profits. Profit-sharing payments are reported as item F-1.

ITEM C-4—LIFE INSURANCE. Exclude premiums for life insurance purchased under a pension plan. Such premiums should be reported under item C-1.

ITEM C-6—MEDICAL CARE INSURANCE. Include premiums which supplement Medicare coverage of retired employees.

1. Pension plan premiums under insurance and annuity contracts (net)	$	219
2. Payments to uninsured trusteed pension plans	$	231
3. Pension payments under unfunded pension programs	$	243
4. Life insurance premiums (net)	$	255
5. Death benefits not covered by insurance	$	267
6. Hospital, surgical, medical, and major medical insurance premiums (net)	$	279
7. Hospital, surgical, medical and major medical payments self-insured		291

ITEM C-8—LIFE AND HEALTH INSURANCE COMBINED. *If unable to separate life and health insurance premiums above, report combined premiums as item C-8. If reported separately above, do NOT fill in item C-8.* If short-term disability, dental, or other insurance premiums are included, report this inclusion on questionnaire.

8. Life and health insurance combined	$	303
9. Short-term disability, sickness or accident insurance (company plan or insured plan)	$	315
10. Salary or wage continuation or long-term disability insured, self-administered, or trust)		327
11. Dental insurance premiums		339
12. Discounts on goods and services purchased from company by employees		351
13. Employee meals furnished by company		363
14. Child care		375
15. Parking		387
16. Physical and mental fitness programs		399
17. Other (vision care, prescription drugs, etc. Specify:)		411
18. TOTAL		423

D. PAID REST PERIODS, COFFEE BREAKS, LUNCH PERIODS, WASH-UP TIME, TRAVEL TIME, CLOTHES-CHANGE TIME, GET-READY TIME, ETC. [*]
- This should be reported *if* time is paid for, whether or not there is a formal work rule providing for such time off. A simple rule of thumb is that if employees typically take two 10-minute rest periods per day, this would amount to approximately 4% of gross payroll; if two 15-minute breaks are taken, the figure would come to 6% of gross payroll (Item A-7).

		Total amount for 1985
	$	438

E. OTHER PAYMENTS FOR TIME NOT WORKED:
- If you lack exact data for these items, please give your best estimate.

1. Payments for or in lieu of vacations	$	450
2. Payments for or in lieu of holidays not worked	$	462
3. Sick leave pay	$	474
4. Payments required under guaranteed workweeks or work year	$	486
5. Jury, witness, and voting pay allowances		498
6. National Defense, State or National Guard duty		510
7. Payment for time lost due to death in family or other personal reasons		522
8. Maternity leave pay		534
9. Other (Specify)	$	546
10. TOTAL		558

F. OTHER ITEMS:
1. Profit-sharing payments (Company contributions are based on current profits of the business, fluctuating with current profit levels).

(a) Current cash payments	$	573
(b) Payments to deferred profit-sharing trusts		585
2. Contributions to employee thrift or stock purchase plans (Company contributions are *not* tied to current profit levels, but are a fixed proportion of amount contributed by employees).	$	597
3. Christmas or other special bonuses (not tied to profits), service awards, suggestion awards, etc.		609
4. Employee education expenditures (tuition refunds, seminar attendance, etc.)		621
5. Payments to union stewards or officials for time spent in settling grievances or in negotiating agreements		633
6. Special wage payments ordered by courts, wage adjustment boards, etc.		645
7. Other (Specify)	$	657
8. TOTAL		669

G. EMPLOYEE PAYROLL DEDUCTIONS: (employees' share only):
- For this question, report deductions from *employer* pay. Employer contributions are reported in questions B and C.

1. Old-Age, Survivors, Disability, and Health Insurance (employee FICA taxes)	$	684
2. Railroad Retirement Tax		696
3. State sickness benefits insurance tax		708
4. Pension plan premiums or contributions		720
5. Life insurance premiums	$	732
6. Hospital, surgical, medical, and major medical insurance premiums or contributions	$	744
7. Other (Specify) Do not include deductions for income tax.	$	756
8. TOTAL		768

Questions continue on the next page.

CONFIDENTIAL

FIGURE 9–4

Portion of U.S. Chamber of Commerce survey form for employee benefits, 1986. Source: U.S. Chamber of Commerce. Used by permission, 1986.

223

Included in the AMS middle management salary survey are such jobs as plant manager; marketing manager; sales manager; personnel manager; auditing manager; accounting manager; purchasing manager; building services manager; general foreman; employment manager; administrative/office services manager; credit and collection manager; customer service manager; warehouse manager; payroll manager; foreman; accounts receivable supervisor; accounts payable supervisor; shipping/receiving supervisor; and mailroom supervisor. Average salaries for these jobs in the United States are shown in Table 9–4.

As is also true of BLS surveys, each job is described. In addition to the average salaries shown here, the AMS survey provides data on the number of workers in each job, the median, and the middle range (the first and third quartiles). Also included is the number of companies, typically *not* shown in BLS area surveys. Additional information is provided on employee benefits.

Planned Meetings of Compensation Specialists

Thomas H. Patten, Jr., reports that a planned meeting is sometimes used to obtain adequate survey information. He describes the process as follows:

TABLE 9–4
Average salaries for middle management.

Job	Salary
Plant manager	50,400
Marketing manager	48,600
Sales manager	47,800
Personnel director	43,100
Auditing manager	42,600
Accounting manager	40,200
Purchasing manager	37,800
Building services manager	37,700
General foreman	36,500
Employment manager	35,300
Admin/office services manager	34,400
Credit & collection manager	34,300
Customer service manager	33,700
Warehouse manager	32,900
Payroll manager	31,200
Foreman	30,000
Accounts receivable supervisor	27,400
Accounts payable supervisor	27,300
Shipping/receiving supervisor	27,100
Mailroom supervisor	23,000

Source: Administrative Management Society, 4622 Street Road, Trevose, PA 19047. Data are for 1988.

The compensation specialist, bringing with him the information he has on jobs in his organization, meets for a day or one-half day with pay specialists representing competition in the local market. The group exchanging information sits down at a table and divulges the information it has. Group members ask one another about rates and clarify understandings they have about position titles and job content. . . . The participants can determine the number of employees in a category or classification, discuss fringe benefits, and end up with a survey and perspective in which each has much confidence.[2]

Summary

In order to balance internal job worth with external market values, the wage and salary administrator may use a pay and benefits survey. A company may conduct surveys to (1) gain information about jobs for which demand is great; (2) determine whether the entire pay structure of the organization is too low; (3) learn more about starting rates; (4) examine interjob differentials; (5) learn more about employee benefits; or (6) obtain more information on related matters such as hours worked or frequency of pay reviews.

Survey techniques used by government tend to be more scientific than those used in private surveys. Stratified rather than random samples are more often used, but where the universe is small, the entire universe may be analyzed. Surveys can be conducted by telephone, by written questionnaires, or by personal visits. Where written questionnaires are used, they should be kept to as few pages as possible and restricted to information really needed.

Useful summary measures of pay developed by surveys include the mean, the median, and the range of the middle 50 percent of workers (interquartile range) in a particular job in a certain industry or locality. Many surveys include frequency distributions from which more refined measures can be computed. Job descriptions for each job title covered in the survey assure greater uniformity in survey replies and more accurate interpretation of results by users.

Area wage surveys conducted by the U.S. Bureau of Labor Statistics provide timely information based on a scientific sample. However, such surveys cover only those jobs common to many industries and exclude government, construction, and extractive industry workers. Industry wage surveys can be used to offset the first of these disadvantages, but they are conducted less frequently than the area surveys. Information on municipal government workers is available from BLS, and the U.S. Office of Personnel Management conducts surveys on state employees.

For salaried workers in the private sector, the annual BLS survey of pay for professional, administrative, technical, and clerical employees is useful.

Organizations such as the American Management Association (AMA) and the Administrative Management Society (AMS), as well as industry associations, chambers of commerce, research organizations, banks, unions, individual companies, and consulting firms, conduct surveys of pay for jobs not adequately covered by government surveys. Less elaborate surveys are conducted by consulting firms to meet the needs of particular clients, but they often use inadequate sampling techniques. This disadvantage can be offset by the use of field representatives, agents, or personal contacts to verify the quality of information received.

Another approach sometimes used is a planned meeting of compensation specialists to obtain relevant and accurate information for a competitive industry or regional group of companies.

Case Study

Borgersen National Bank

Horace Tamaki, the new personnel officer of the Borgerson National Bank, one of the largest but newer banks in the Phoenix, Arizona metropolitan area, was surprised. On the previous day he had had a conversation with the president of the bank, Andrew Hanedanian. During the conversation, the president had asked about the high rate of turnover among some of the word processors at the head office. Tamaki's duties included handling compensation and employee benefits for both exempt and nonexempt employees. He, too, had wondered about the turnover among the word processors, and the president's question spurred him to analyze the problem further. It appeared to be confined largely to one classification of word processors. He looked at a Phoenix area wage survey and tried to match the survey data against those for the bank, as shown in the table at the top of page 227.

While Tamaki had known that the bank had not participated in the survey, he had had no idea the bank's own pay figures were so far out of line. He checked out the Bureau of Labor Statistics description of the Word Processor II for nonmanufacturing and compared it with the bank's own job descriptions. The differences appeared to be minor. He also checked out the bank's job description with one of his staff assistants and determined to his satisfaction that the description was accurate and up to date.

Role Assignment
You are Horace Tamaki. What action would you take and why?

Questions for Discussion

1. Why is it important to conduct surveys on pay and employee benefits?
2. Can random sampling be used in such surveys? Explain.
3. Which type of survey is typically more scientific in approach—a private industry survey or a government survey?
4. Which measure is most useful in evaluating survey results—the mean or the median?
5. Why consider the middle 50 percent of workers doing a particular job rather than looking at the entire frequency distribution? Explain.
6. What are the advantages and disadvantages of area wage surveys compared with industry wage surveys?
7. What kinds of government surveys cover public workers in state and local governments?
8. Why should private surveys be conducted, and who conducts them?
9. What techniques must be used to obtain the most accurate survey results?

Weekly earnings for word processor II (nonmanufacturing).

Weekly Earnings*	Number of Workers	
	Phoenix	Borgersen
$120–140	—	01
140–160	—	03
160–180	—	02
180–200	—	04
200–220	—	07
220–240	13	05
240–260	02	03
260–280	08	01
280–300	43	—
300–320	89	—
320–340	53	—
340–360	22	—
360–380	32	—
380–400	01	—
400–420	01	—
420–440	01	—
440–460	09	—
Median	$315	$209

*Earnings brackets include pay from $120 and under $140 and so forth.
Source: U.S. Bureau of Labor Statistics and Borgersen National Bank.

Notes

1. David W. Belcher, *Compensation Administration* (Englewood Cliffs, N.J.: Prentice-Hall, 1974), 465. Reprinted by permission of Prentice-Hall, Inc., Englewood Cliffs, N.J.

2. Thomas H. Patten, Jr., *Pay: Employee Compensation and Incentive Plans* (New York: The Free Press, 1977), 172. Copyright © 1977 by The Free Press, a Division of Macmillan Publishing Co., Inc.

References

Administrative Management Society. *AMS Salary Survey of Middle-Level Management Personnel.* Willow Grove, PA: Administrative Management Society, 1986.

Alexander Group, Inc. *Current Practices in Sales Incentives.* Scottsdale, AZ: The Alexander Group, Inc., 1988.

American Electronics Association. *1987 Professional Engineers Salary Survey.* Santa Clara, CA: American Electronics Association, 1987.

Belcher, David W.; Ferris, N. Bruce; and O'Neill, John. "How Wage Surveys Are Being Used." *Compensation and Benefits Review* 17, no. 4 (September–October 1985): 34–51.

Construction Labor Research Council. *Construction Labor Rate Trends and Outlook.* Washington, DC: Construction Labor Research Council, February 1988.

Executive Compensation Service. *1986–87 Professional and Scientific Industry Report.* Ft.

Lee, NJ: Executive Compensation Service, 1987.

General Mills, Inc. *Industrial Flight Survey*. Minneapolis, MN: General Mills, 1987.

Hewitt Associates. *Salary Survey for Smaller Manufacturing Companies*. Lincolnshire, IL: Hewitt Associates, 1987.

International City Management Association. *Police and Fire Salaries in 1986*. Washington, DC: International City Management Association, 1986.

Mercer-Meidinger-Hansen. *Finance, Accounting, and Legal Compensation Survey*. Deerfield, IL: Mercer-Meidinger-Hansen, Inc. 1987.

———. *6th Annual Materials Management Compensation Survey*. Deerfield, IL: Mercer-Meidinger-Hansen, Inc., 1987.

O'Brien, Joan C., and Zawacki, Robert A. "Salary Surveys: Are They Worth the Effort?" *Personnel* 62, no. 10 (October 1985): 70–74.

Reggio and Associates. *Data Processing Salaries*. Chicago, IL: Reggio and Associates, Inc., 1986.

Syer, Gregory A. "The Exempt Salary Survey, Part 1: Collecting Information." *Personnel* 63, no. 6 (June 1986): 45–49.

———. "The Exempt Salary Survey, Part 2: Analyzing and Reporting Data." *Personnel* 63, no. 7 (July 1986): 24–31.

U.S. Bureau of Labor Statistics. *Area Wage Survey: Phoenix, Arizona, Metropolitan Area, June 1987*. Bulletin 3040–22. Washington, DC: U.S. Government Printing Office, 1987.

———. *Industry Wage Survey: Hospitals, August 1985*. Bulletin 2273, Washington, DC: U.S. Government Printing Office, 1987.

———. *Industry Wage Survey: Textile Mills, June 1985*. Bulletin 2265. Washington, DC: U.S. Government Printing Office, 1985.

———. *National Survey of Professional, Administrative, Technical, and Clerical Pay in the Service Industries, March 1987*. Bulletin 2290. Washington, DC: 1987.

———. *National Survey of Professional, Administrative, Technical, and Clerical Pay, March 1986*. Bulletin 2271. Washington, DC: U.S. Government Printing Office, 1986.

Walker, C. Terrence. "Salary Analysis: Using Quantitative Analysis and Descriptive Modeling." *Compensation and Benefits Review* 17, no. 4 (September–October 1985): 52–59.

Job Pricing

Chapter Outline

- The Typical Pay Structure
- Alternative Lines of Relationship: Percentage Differentials
- Implementation of a New Pay Structure
- Pay Adjustments Within Rate Ranges
- Summary
- Case Study—Law and Public Safety Department
- Case Study—Pong Machinery Company

Whatever method of job evaluation is used, the relative worth of jobs within the organization, or internal equity, must be related to the market value of jobs that surveys have helped determine.[1] This is precisely what a pay structure does, even under collective bargaining. In this chapter, we shall explore development of the typical pay structure, assuming a straight-line relationship; alternative pay structures, which involve fixed or rising percentage relationships; the implementation of the pay structure; and pay adjustments within rate ranges.

The Typical Pay Structure

The steps in developing a pay structure are (1) constructing a scatter diagram; (2) determining rate ranges and constructing pay boxes; and (3) considering the problem of overlap.

Scatter Diagram and Line of Relationship

The first step in the development of the typical pay structure is drawing a scatter diagram. Figure 10–1 illustrates how this is done under a point system. Job points are on the horizontal axis, and monthly salaries are shown on the vertical axis. Dots are plotted on the diagram, with each dot representing one job. For example, find 500 job points on the horizontal scale. Locate a dot directly above this value and then look at the vertical scale. This job pays a monthly salary of about $410. The path of the dots shows about what we might reasonably expect—jobs carrying higher point values tend to be paid at a higher rate. The diagonal line expresses the relationship between the two variables, points and salaries. It was drawn using the equation shown in Figure 10–1, which was computed by the method of least squares.[2] This method results in the only straight line that can be drawn minimizing the sum of the squares of the vertical distances of the dots from the line. Thus, given the same information, any two observers would arrive at the same result.

Alternatively, a line of relationship can be drawn by the "eye-squares" method. Simply draw a straight line through the scatter of dots. This is often done

230

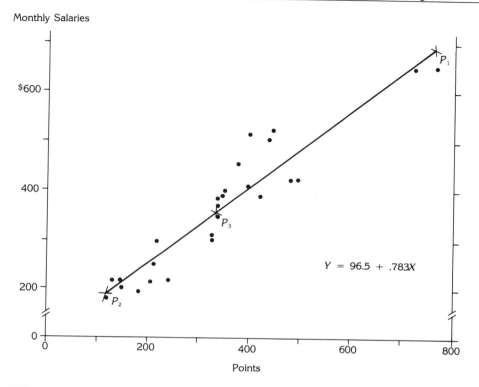

FIGURE 10–1
Scatter diagram used under the point system.

so that there is an approximately equal number of dots above and below the line. But the number of lines that meet this requirement is almost limitless. Furthermore, the line can be drawn without meeting this requirement; for example, a line can be drawn from the center of a cluster of low-paying jobs to the center of a cluster of high-paying jobs. In actual practice, such a line may serve as well as the mathematical line provided agreement can be reached, for example, in a collective bargaining situation, as to how the line is to be drawn.

No matter how the line of relationship is drawn, if single rates are used rather than rate ranges (to be discussed shortly), the rate for any job can be found by identifying the point value on the horizontal scale, reading upward to the diagonal line, and then reading across to the pay scale. For example, in Figure 10–1, a point value of 700 for a job would call for a monthly salary of about $630.

The dots on the scatter diagram can be plotted using either the actual rates now being paid, area rates from a survey, or adjusted actual rates. The latter situation may arise where a survey shows company rates are lagging behind. The method of adjustment is important because of its effects on costs of pay (and employee benefits) and pay differentials. The type of adjustment often agreed to is an across-the-board increase (Figure 10–2).

As an example, assume an hourly rate increase of $.40. For the sweeper this would be a 10 percent hike, but for the millwright it would be only 5 percent. Thus, the flat cents-per-hour increase narrows pay differentials. At least in the short run, this method may be less costly to management. In the longer run, however, any cost savings may prove illusory if craft workers later push for a restoration of their previous differentials.

The scatter diagram can be used for the point, factor comparison (percentage), and the guide chart–profile methods. It also can be used in the ranking or predetermined grading methods if, instead of points, rankings or grades are spaced at equal intervals along the horizontal axis. The usual lines of relationship can be drawn in.

Rate Ranges and Pay Boxes

While single rates are common, as in the steel industry example cited in Chapter 4, rate ranges are often used instead, usually in conjunction with point ranges. This method is shown in Figure 10–3.

Employees in the highest pay grade with jobs evaluated at more than 1,097 points make from $520 to $675 per month. Although single rates make administration easier from the standpoint of predictability of labor costs, they provide less flexibility. When rate ranges are used, it is easier to provide lower starting rates, there is more flexible adjustment to outside labor markets, and upward movement is allowed within a pay grade.

Consistent with industry practice, the rate range boxes shown in Figure 10–3 are taller at the higher salary levels than at the lower levels. Given the diag-

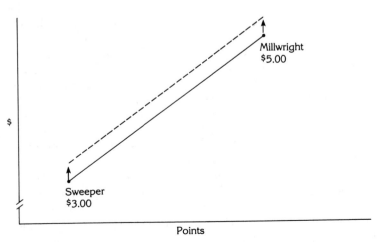

FIGURE 10–2
Effects of an across-the-board increase in pay on the pay structure.

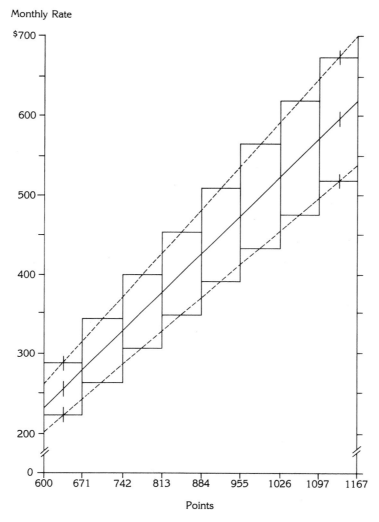

FIGURE 10–3
Graphic method of assembling a pay structure using rate ranges and points.

onal line of relationship between pay and points, assembling the pay structure involves the following steps:

1. Determine the width of boxes.
2. Determine the height of boxes.
3. Mark the midpoints of tops and bottoms of the highest and lowest boxes.
4. Draw limit lines.
5. Complete pay boxes.

The width of the boxes, assuming they are of equal width, can be determined using the formula

$$i = \frac{H - L - (N - 1)}{N}$$

where i is the width of the box, H is the high and L the low for points, and N is the desired number of pay grades. When this formula is used, point ranges do not overlap. For example, in Figure 10–3, the high and low for points are respectively 1,167 and 600, and the desired number of boxes is 8. This works out to a width (i) of 70 points. Thus, the intervals are 600–670, 671–741, and so on.

Where H and L are small numbers, the preceding width formula should not be used. For example, in assigning ranks to pay grades in the predetermined grading method, an entirely different procedure should be followed. Suppose the rankings run from 1 to 25. Then take the following steps:

1. Experimentally, try 3 to 6 rankings per box. See what seems to work.
2. Try for an equal number of jobs in each box, except that the top box can have fewer.
3. Construct the pay boxes so the edges always fall between rankings.

Having determined the widths, calculate the heights of the boxes next. The procedure for this is illustrated in Figure 10–4.

In this case, assume 20 percent limits are desired; that is, the tops of the boxes are to be set 20 percent above the bottoms. With this 20 percent rate range and a midpoint of the rate range (which can be read off our line of relationship) of $4.00 per hour,

$$
\begin{aligned}
X + 10\%X &= \$4.00 \\
1.1X &= \$4.00 \\
X &= \$4.00/1.1 = \$3.636 \text{ (bottom of pay rate range)} \\
\$3.636 \times 120\% \text{ (or 1.2)} &= \$4.363 \text{ (top of pay rate range)}
\end{aligned}
$$

The pay structure with its eight pay boxes, shown earlier in Figure 10–3, is, of course, the result. Another way to derive this pay structure is to start with the line derived from the scatter diagram, with the widths all marked off. Then, just for the highest and lowest pay grades, find the middle and mark it with a tick. On the vertical axis, identify the corresponding pay rate. After deciding what percentage limits to use, apply them to this figure to get the top and bottom of the highest pay grade. Draw in the top and bottom of the box using this information, and mark a tick at the middle of both the top and the bottom. Next, do the same thing for the lowest pay grade. Then, connect the two sets of ticks, as shown by the dashed diagonal limit lines. The tops and bottoms of the remaining boxes are drawn in as illustrated.

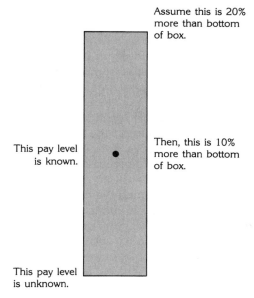

Assume this is 20% more than bottom of box.

This pay level is known.

Then, this is 10% more than bottom of box.

This pay level is unknown.

Let unknown pay level be *X*.

Then, $X + 10\%X$ = known midpoint of box.

FIGURE 10—4
Computing the tops and bottoms of pay boxes, assuming a 20 percent pay rate range.

Motivation and Overlap

An acid test of the effectiveness of a base pay structure is the degree of overlap between adjacent boxes. If there is little or no overlap, an employee may feel that promotion to a higher-paying job is so remote that it is no longer a realistic goal. On the other hand, if overlap is excessive, the employee may see the next pay grade as no challenge.

Overlap exists whenever the bottom of a pay box is below the top of the pay box to the left. To measure overlap, take a pair of adjacent pay boxes. Using a ruler, measure the part of the division line between the two boxes common to both of them. Divide this distance by the height of the right-hand box to obtain the percentage of overlap. The pay structure in Figure 10–3 reveals an overlap for the two highest boxes of about 65 percent and around 30 percent for the two lowest boxes. There is some agreement about how much overlap is desirable. John Patton, C. L. Littlefield, and Allen Self cite favorably a structure with overlap ranging from 65 percent at the low end to 60 percent at the high end. Overlap of 50 percent is considered acceptable by David Belcher and J. D. Dunn and Frank Rachel.[3]

A systematic approach to establishing the desired degree of overlap involves using zero-overlap boxes, illustrated in Figures 10–5 and 10–6. The diagonal line in Figure 10–5 shows the usual relationship between pay on the vertical axis and points on the horizontal axis. The line extends from 0 to 800 points. Use a compass or pair of dividers to mark off the desired number of boxes—eight in this case. Next, construct the zero-overlap boxes for the two boxes at the low end and the two boxes at the high end of the structure. In general, boxes are drawn so that the diagonal line runs through their centers. To get zero-overlap boxes, let the top of the lower (left) box be at the same pay level as the bottom of the upper (right) box. (There is one qualifier about these boxes: If the bottom of the lowest box is below the equivalent of the minimum wage, zero-overlap boxes may not be possible.)

The next series of steps relates to obtaining the desired overlap at the upper end of the pay structure, as shown in Figure 10–6. At the left end of the structure, keep the same dimensions for the lower (left) box as appeared in Figure 10–5. However, at the right end of the structure, construct a much taller box—just how tall is a matter of judgment. First, find the center of the old zero-overlap box at the right end of the structure (see Figure 10–5). From this center point move upward

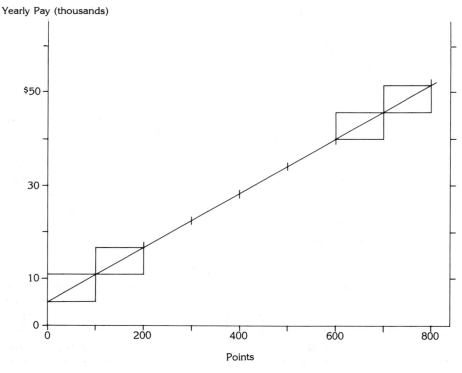

FIGURE 10–5
Drawing in zero-overlap boxes.

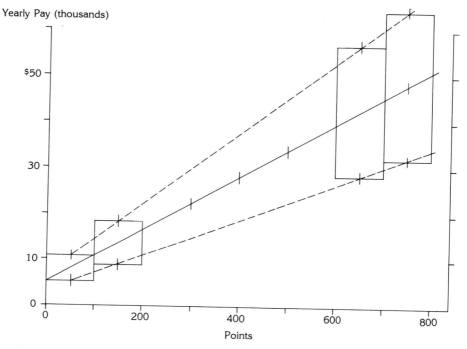

FIGURE 10–6
Obtaining the desired overlap at the upper end of the pay structure.

an arbitrary distance and make a dot. Move downward the same distance and make another dot. Next, draw in a dashed diagonal line connecting the upper dot with the middle of the top of the lowest pay box, as shown in Figure 10–6.

Draw in a second diagonal connecting the lower dot to the middle of the bottom of the lowest pay box. Working from the two diagonal lines, draw in the highest box and the next-to-the-highest box in the usual way. Then, test the two highest boxes for the percentage of overlap. If the overlap is too much, shorten the highest box and repeat the procedure. You don't have to worry about the two lower boxes because the overlap at the lower end of the structure will always be less.

Other ways of reducing overlap are to increase the slope of the line (which may require reworking of points, grades, or rankings), reduce the number of boxes, or use wider and wider boxes.

Alternative Lines of Relationship: Percentage Differentials

In all of the discussion so far, we have assumed that a diagonal straight line best expresses the relationship between points, ranks, or pay grades on the horizontal axis and pay on the vertical axis. Actually, the straight line is sometimes used even where it is not a good expression of the relationship that exists. Where single rates are used, the straight line may show a particular rate to be higher than it would be if a curve were used, thus increasing labor costs. Where pay rate ranges are used, the effects may be camouflaged but they are still present. In any event, such increases in costs may well be passed on to the consumer, adding to cost-push inflation. Longer range effects may also emerge in the form of craft union demands for restoration of pay differentials, as discussed earlier in this chapter.

Whether for these or other reasons, many companies recognize a line of relationship between pay and points other than a straight line.[4] A government study revealed that firms use both constant and rising percentage differentials between midpoints of pay grades. The intergrade spread was defined as the "percent by which the minimum salary of a grade was exceeded by the minimum salary of the next higher grade." To determine whether a company uses constant or rising percentage differentials, the scatter must be examined. If the dots of the scatter appear to form a curve instead of a straight line, the data should be replotted on semilog graph paper, which has the usual horizontal scale but a ratio scale on the vertical axis. (Such a scale is familiar to business students who have looked at a stock market report where a rising straight line shows what a 20 percent per year rise in the price of a stock would look like. This, of course, is just a geometric progression with a multiplier of 1.2.) On such a grid the scatter will tend to form a straight line if there is a constant percentage increase between midpoints of pay grades. An upward curving line results if there are rising percentage increases between pay grades. These two possibilities are shown in Figure 10–7.

Pay Structure Using Constant Percentage Differentials

Where the scatter of dots suggests a constant percentage differential between the midpoints of pay grades, a suitable pay structure can be built using graphic methods. To do so,

1. Decide on midpoints for the lowest and highest pay grades.
2. Use a sheet of semilog paper with enough cycles to include both the highest and the lowest midpoints.
3. Decide on the number of pay grades.
4. Using equal spacing, mark off on the horizontal axis the desired number of pay grades.
5. Plot the two midpoints.
6. Using a sharp pencil, draw a straight line connecting these two points.
7. Read off the midpoints for the other pay grades.[5]

Percentage limits for the grade structure can be computed using the technique described earlier in this chapter, except that this must be done separately

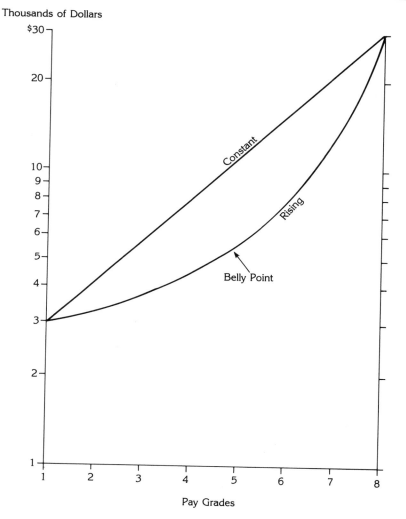

FIGURE 10–7
Constant percentage differentials in relation to rising percentage differentials.

for each pay grade. The resulting structure appears in Figure 10–8. This new pay structure has some interesting properties. One is that the percentage overlap is the same for all pairs of boxes at the lowest as well as the highest levels of pay. A second is that the degree of overlap is just under 50 percent. Third, it takes quite wide limits to achieve this result, 120 percent in this particular case.

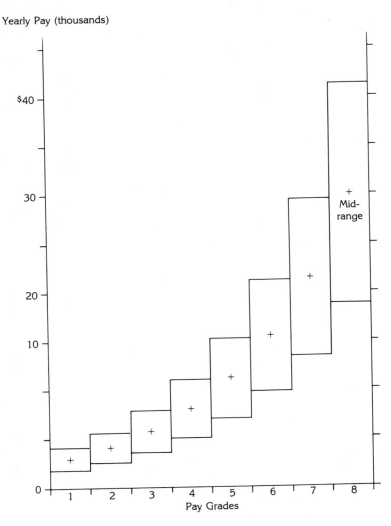

FIGURE 10–8
Pay structure using constant percentage differentials and 120 percent limits.

Pay Structure Using Rising Percentage Differentials

The rising curved line in Figure 10–7 illustrates rising percentage differentials between the midpoints of pay grades. The line is only one of many that might be drawn, the critical values being the lowest and highest midpoints of pay grades and an arbitrary belly point. The belly point should be near the middle of the pay grades and not too far below the straight line. The graphic approach to constructing a pay structure when rising percentage differentials are involved includes the following steps:

1. On a sheet of semilog graph paper, identify the midranges of the lowest and highest pay grades and a belly point.
2. Draw two straight lines, connecting each of the two midranges with the belly point.
3. On each of the two lines, construct a perpendicular bisector.
4. Extend the bisectors until they meet. The meeting point will be equidistant from all three original points.
5. Using the meeting point as the center, with the aid of a compass, make a circle that passes through all three original points.
6. Where the circle passes through the vertical pay grade lines, identify from the dollar scale the midranges for the in-between pay grades.[6]

The belly point shown in Figure 10–7 represents rapidly rising percentage differentials—an unlikely situation. If the belly point in this figure were $7.728 thousand, it would lie close to the straight line. In this case the percentage differentials between pay grade midpoints would be slowly rising from 25 percent to 53.5 percent. The resulting structure using this belly point is illustrated in Figure 10–9 on page 242. The limits were computed and drawn in the same manner as for the constant percentage differentials in Figure 10–8.

A pay structure using rising percentage differentials is different from one using constant percentage differentials. Near the lower end of the pay structure in Figure 10–9, the degree of overlap is roughly 67 percent, but near the top of the structure the overlap is less than 30 percent. In contrast, the pay structure in Figure 10–8 has a uniform overlap throughout of slightly under 50 percent.

Implementation of a New Pay Structure

Whatever pay structure is worked out—whether based on a straight line relationship, constant percentage differentials, or rising percentage differentials—immediate human problems emerge when a new plan is installed. What happens to the employee who falls below the bottom of the pay box? And what about the worker whose job is above the top of the pay box? In answer to the first question, for the new structure to be meaningful, the employee should be raised to a position within the box. The second situation is harder to resolve. Such cases, known as "red-ringed" rates, call for special consideration. Fairness suggests that the overpayment is management's mistake and that the employee ought not to be penalized by a pay reduction. One solution is to keep the worker now in the job at the present rate of pay and pay a new employee in the same job at a lower figure within the newly established rate range. Another possibility would be to promote the employee to a job where the present pay rate would fall within the rate range required by the new pay structure. This might well call for additional on-the-job training.

A special situation arises when an across-the-board pay increase takes place. If the worker is kept in the same job, does the already overpaid employee share in such gains? Presumably not, if the "red-ringed" rate is eventually to be brought

Yearly Pay (thousands)

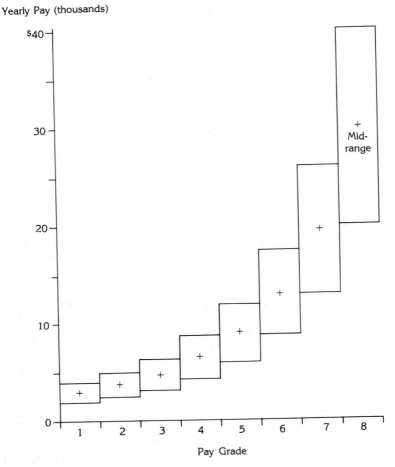

FIGURE 10–9
Pay structure using slowly rising percentage differentials and 100 percent limits.

into line with the rest of the pay structure. However, since the original overpayment came about through management's action, it is only fair for them to explain the situation to the employee.

Pay Adjustments Within Rate Ranges

Pay progression within pay grade ranges varies from company to company. Some provide for merit increments only, some for seniority increments only, and others for some combination of the two. A typical progression based on seniority incre-ments is that provided for under the job classification plan used by Western Union and the United Telegraph Workers (AFL-CIO), which is shown in Table 10–1.

Many companies do not divide the range into fixed increments but give pay hikes on an individual basis, an arrangement which gives more flexibility to the manager but poses more uncertainty for the employee.

Today many companies, and many more government agencies, tend to emphasize merit rather than seniority in adjusting pay within pay grades. For example, the salary administration program in a major division of a large U. S. manufacturing company (which we shall refer to as the E. Z. Jones Company) closely articulates pay changes within each pay grade through the mechanism of the *compa-ratio*. This is the percentage of an individual's salary compared to the midpoint of his pay grade. For the E. Z. Jones Company, the salary for any partic-ular job ranges from 80 percent to 120 percent of the midrange. For example, an individual making $16,000 in a job with a midrange of $20,000 would have a compa-ratio of 80 percent.

The compa-ratio is also used as a guide to division allocation of salaries to particular departments. Thus, a department where the average compa-ratio is rel-atively low—for example, around 95 percent—would get a larger allocation for salaries compared with another department with a higher average compa-ratio.

Merit aspects of pay increases are considered further in Chapter 12, which considers individual and group incentives.

Summary

Pricing of the job structure is a way to relate internal and external job worth. The first step in developing a pay structure is the construction of a scatter diagram, in which jobs are plotted with pay on the vertical axis and points, rankings, or pay grades on the horizontal axis. A mathematical line of relationship (assuming a straight line) can be drawn by using the method of least squares, or a line can be

TABLE 10–1
Pay progression within rate range for a multilith operator based on length of service.

Months of Service	Monthly Salary
0	$1,355
6	1,387
12	1,421
24	1,456
36	1,503
48	1,539
60	1,626

Source: Western Union Telegraph Co. in contract with United Telegraph Workers (AFL-CIO). Rates as of August 7, 1986.

drawn in by the "eye-squares" method. In a collective bargaining situation, either method is satisfactory, provided the parties agree as to how the line is to be drawn.

Once the line of relationship is established, it must be decided whether to use a single rate or a rate range for each job. Single rates allow predictability of labor costs, while rate ranges give management greater flexibility. If rate ranges are used, there is the problem of overlap. If there is too little overlap, employees may be discouraged about the prospects of advancement. On the other hand, too much overlap may eliminate any challenge to the employee. For pay structures built on a straight-line assumption and having greater pay rate ranges at higher levels, the degree of overlap is greater for the higher pay grades and less for the lower pay grades.

Companies with pay structures not based on a straight-line assumption often use constant or rising percentage differentials between pay grades. When a constant percentage differential between pay grades and fixed percentage limits are used, there is the same percentage of overlap for both high and low pay grades. Structures based on rising percentage differentials do not have this advantage.

When a new pay structure comes into effect, workers who are underpaid are normally moved up into the appropriate pay boxes. Those who are overpaid are identified as having "red-ringed" rates and require special attention.

Within rate ranges, pay increases are typically based on merit, seniority, or a combination of both. Some companies favor rate ranges comprised of fixed increments, while others believe such increments are inflexible. A useful device for allocating merit pay increases is the compa-ratio—the ratio of an employee's pay to the midrange pay. The compa-ratio can be used for departmental salary allocations and for individual merit pay increases. The ratio can be tied in with pay increases based on performance evaluation, with specific provisions for both minimum review periods and maximum percentage limits to merit increases. Further flexibility to the compensation framework is provided when starting salaries, and procedures for promotions, transfers, and demotions are specified.

Case Study

Law and Public Safety Department

A committee of the state legislature in a mid-Atlantic state developed a point plan to replace an existing job classification plan for the employees in the law and public safety department. The following table shows the salary rates currently being paid for each job and the points as developed by the job evaluation committee.

Role Assignment

As a specialist in wage and salary matters, you have been called in by the committee as a consultant. Using the information given, construct a scatter diagram and draw in the line of relationship by eye. After deciding on a desirable number of pay grades, draw in the pay boxes, paying attention to the degree of overlap. Use the techniques illustrated in Figure 11–6. Be prepared to discuss your solution with the committee.

Job	Salary	Points
Attorney general	$95,000	340
First assistant deputy attorney general	90,000	289
Colonel and superintendent, state police	85,000	262
Director, division of motor vehicles	77,500	262
State medical examiner	85,000	250
Director, division of alcoholic beverage control	77,500	215
Director of criminal investigation	62,600	231
Director, division of civil rights	61,200	220
State superintendent of weights and measures	56,400	169

Case Study

Pong Machinery Company

Pong Machinery Company is a large manufacturer of electrical machinery. As the result of a new job evaluation plan, pay rate ranges have been worked out for each of 20 different labor grades covering hourly paid production and maintenance employees. For the highest labor grade, the midpoint is $8.00 and the rate range is from $7.20 to $8.80. In the lowest labor grade, the midpoint is $3.20 and the rate range is from $3.00 to $3.40. However, the wage and salary administrator has not yet decided what to do about pay rate increments within rate ranges. For example, how many increments should there be for the highest labor grade? Should there be the same number for the lowest labor grade? Should the increments be based on seniority, merit, or some combination of the two? If the latter, how would this work? Would the frequency of review for possible increases be the same or different for all increments?

Role Assignment

You are the wage and salary administrator. The vice president of personnel has asked you to continue work on this phase of the new job evaluation plan. Be prepared to discuss your results with her.

Questions for Discussion

1. What is the purpose of using a scatter diagram in connection with pricing the job structure?

2. Compare the effect of a flat cents-per-hour pay increase for all jobs with the effect of a fixed percentage increase.

3. What are the pros and cons of using rate ranges rather than single rates for each job?

4. What is meant by overlap, and how is it measured? Why is it important?

5. What is the advantage of starting with zero overlap boxes at the lower end of the pay structure? Couldn't any other degree of overlap be used?

6. In plotting pay and points for different jobs in a company, does a straight line always best express the relationship? What are some of the other possibilities?

7. For a given pay structure, is there any advantage in using constant percentage differentials between pay grades?

8. What are the pros and cons of using slowly rising versus constant percentage differentials?

9. What are some of the human problems that arise in implementing a new pay structure? How should workers whose pay falls above or below a pay box be handled? Why?

10. In general terms, what considerations should govern pay adjustments within pay rate ranges?

11. What is the compa-ratio, and how is it used?

Notes

1. Market inequities and the issue of comparable worth were explored in Chapter 4.

2. This method requires solution of the equation $Y = a + bX$, where Y values are salaries and X values are points. The Ayres method for solving this equation is as follows: (1) Set up columns for X, Y, XY, X^2, and Y^2; (2) total each column to get ΣX, ΣY, etc.; (3) divide ΣX by N, the number of dots, to get the average value of X; (4) divide ΣY by N to get the average value of Y; (5) find b by substitution in the formula below:

$$b = \frac{\Sigma XY - \frac{(\Sigma X)(\Sigma Y)}{N}}{\Sigma X^2 - \frac{(\Sigma X)^2}{N}}$$

(6) substitute in the formula $Y = a + bX$ the values obtained in the preceding steps, and solve for a; (7) in the new formula, enter three arbitrary values of X and find the corresponding Y values; (8) draw a line through the new points, as shown in Figure 11–1. The solution to the equation can be obtained more quickly by using an electronic pocket calculator with a curve fitting program.

3. John A. Patton, C. L. Littlefield, and Stanley Allen Self, *Job Evaluation*, 3rd ed. (Homewood, Ill.: Richard D. Irwin, 1964), 270–71; David W. Belcher, *Compensation Administration* (Englewood Cliffs, NJ: Prentice-Hall, 1974), 285; and J. D. Dunn and Frank M. Rachel, *Wage and Salary Administration* (New York: McGraw-Hill, 1971), 225.

4. U.S. Bureau of Labor Statistics, *Salary Characteristics in Large Firms, 1963*, Bulletin 1417 (Washington, DC: U.S. Government Printing Office, 1964), Table 11, p. 17.

5. The same results can be obtained by using the following formula:

$$r = \sqrt[n]{\frac{Y_H}{Y_L}} - 1$$

where r is the desired constant percentage stated as a decimal, n is desired number of pay grades minus 1, Y_H is the highest midrange, and Y_L is lowest midrange. In Figure 10–8, r works out to .3895 (or roughly a 39 percent differential between the midranges of pay grades). Thus, the midranges are a geometric progression using a multiplier of 1.3895. The equation can be solved easily with an electronic pocket calculator.

6. Midranges in this case can also be derived by a formula using a Gompertz curve

$$Y = ka^{b^x}$$

in the particular case where log a is positive and b is greater than 1. For further discussion, see Leonard R. Burgess, *Wage and Salary Administration in a Dynamic Economy* (New York: Harcourt, Brace and World, 1968), 50–51.

References

Beggs, Steven D. "The 'Lead-Lag' Problem: Adjustments Needed for Salary Comparisons." *Compensation and Benefits Review* 18, no. 6 (November–December 1986): 44–54.

Bergmann, Thomas J. et al. "Pay Compression: Causes, Results, and Possible Solutions." *Compensation and Benefits Review* 15, no. 2 (Second Quarter 1983): 17–26.

Brennan, E. James. "Everything You Need to Know About Salary Ranges." *Personnel Journal* 63, no. 3 (March 1984): 10–17.

Burroughs, Julio D. "Pay Secrecy and Performance: TDhe Psychological Research." *Compensation and Benefits Review* 14, no. 3 (Third Quarter 1982): 44–54.

Ellig, Bruce R. "Pay Policies While Downsizing the Organization: A Systematic Approach." *Personnel* 60, no. 3 (May–June 1983): 26–35.

Gomez-Mejia, Juis R., and Balkin, David B. "Pay Compression in Business Schools: Causes and Consequences." *Compensation and Benefits Review* 19, no. 5 (September–October 1987): 43–55.

Greene, Robert J. "Issues in Salary Structure Design." *Compensation and Benefits Review* 14, no. 2 (Second Quarter 1982): 28–33.

Moran, Patrick F. "Equitable Salary Administration in High-Tech Companies." *Compensation and Benefits Review* 18, no. 5 (September–October 1986): 31–40.

Naughton, Hugh V. "Integrated Support for Salary Administration." *Personnel* 63, no. 8 (August 1986): 8–12.

Porter, Felice, and Keller, Richard L. "Public and Private Pay Levels in Large Labor Markets." *Monthly Labor Review* 104, no. 7 (July 1981): 22–26.

Reggio and Associates. *Area Salary Differentials.* Chicago, IL: Reggio and Associates, 1988.

Weinberger, Theodore E. "Auditing Graded Job Structures for Classification Consistency." *Compensation and Benefits Review* 17, no. 4 (September–October 1985): 14–21.

Performance Evaluation

11

Chapter Outline

- Who Does the Performance Evaluation?
- Systems of Performance Evaluation
- Politics of Performance Evaluation
- Rating Errors and Rater Training
- Keeping the System Up To Date
- Performance Evaluation and Motivation
- Summary
- Case Study—Ashizawa Food Company

Performance evaluation (or appraisal) is another one of the cluster of processes described in earlier chapters that tend to reinforce the managerial tendency to think in hierarchical terms. Performance evaluation not only tends to reinforce hierarchy but is subject to political manipulation of a most destructive sort.

Performance evaluation stresses the individual in the job rather than the job itself. In jobs where workers are on incentive pay, a topic to be explored in Chapter 12, performance evaluation will still be important because base pay is affected. But many, if not most, jobs are not on an incentive basis. Jobs usually involve outputs that are hard to measure quantitatively, or there are many measures and their relative value is not always clear. These situations increase the importance of performance evaluation and the likelihood of its being a highly subjective, personalized process.

Performance evaluation can be used to increase pay and to promote an individual as well as to improve employee performance. An effective performance evaluation will also improve employee motivation. An overview of the performance evaluation (appraisal) process can be seen in Figure 11–1.

Who Does the Performance Evaluation?

Performance evaluation can be conducted by any of the following evaluators:

1. The employee's superior.
2. Subordinates.
3. Peers.
4. The employee.
5. Other individuals.
6. Combinations of the above.
7. Groups.
8. Assessment centers.

Evaluation by Superior

In most organizations, due to their hierarchical nature, the employee's immediate superior is the evaluator. It is the immediate supervisor who hands out the

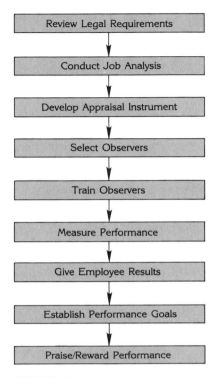

FIGURE 11–1
The performance appraisal process [From Gary P. Latham and Kenneth N. Wexley, **Increasing Productivity Through Performance Appraisal** *(Reading, Mass.: Addison-Wesley, 1981), Fig. 1–1. Reprinted with permission.]*

rewards and punishments and who is in a position to observe an employee's behavior in relation to job objectives and organizational goals.[1] On the other hand, the supervisor's attitude can profoundly influence the evaluation. Since the evaluation process is highly subjective, the evaluation by the superior is often biased. Ratings by the worker's immediate superior are neither as valid nor as reliable as peer ratings.[2]

Evaluation by Subordinates

Exxon, Weyerhauser, and Texas Instruments are examples of companies that have chosen a different approach: evaluation by subordinates. Such ratings, with anonymity of the raters assured, can serve as a check against bias in a superior's rating of a manager. The process can work in two ways, by bolstering the position of an effective manager who is underrated by a superior or by discovering an ineffective manager who is overrated by a superior. The second situation can be handled in a constructive way through the use of team building, which we shall discuss later in this chapter. The use of subordinate evaluation must be qualified, however. It is difficult to keep an employee's views confidential where the number of subordinates is small. Gary Latham and Kenneth Wexley recommend that subordinate rating not be used where there are less than four subordinates.[3]

Evaluation by Peers

Peer ratings involve individuals at the same level in the organization. They rate one another, typically using standardized rating scales, and these ratings are summarized and used to evaluate the individual. This method is often used to evaluate faculty members in one department within a university. Ratings are usually kept confidential in the sense that the individual rated does not know how she was rated by any one rater. Among the advantages to rating by peers is that

> they not only see how an employee interacts with them, but also see how that employee interacts with subordinates as well as the boss.[4]

By computing an average or median from the peer ratings, management obtains a more reliable rating than it can get from a single rating. In general, peer ratings are more reliable and more valid than ratings by supervisors. However, there are disadvantages to peer rating, one having to do with validity in particular situations:

> The major drawback of peer evaluations is that in order for them to be valid, group members must have close contact with one another. . . . For example, it is not enough for salesmen who work in different geographical areas to meet once a month for a staff meeting; they must frequently observe one another on the job if the ratings are to be reliable and valid.[5]

Another criticism relates to competitive aspects, as described by L. L. Cummings and Donald Schwab:

> A win-lose game among peers tends to inhibit honesty in evaluating perceived rivals. In addition, a highly competitive organizational reward system should suggest a caution of a different nature in the use of peers for appraisal. Such systems place an employee, when requested to evaluate his peers, into one or more of several possible psychological conflicts. For example, conflicts may arise between evaluating one's peer highly and maximizing one's own chances of a large salary increase or between evaluating him poorly and maintaining his friendship. It is for such reasons that peer appraisals have been found invalid, or even disruptive, in some organizations.[6]

Self-Evaluation

Self-evaluation is the second most widely used type of performance evaluation in industry. General Electric tried having the employee fill out a self-evaluation form and later discussing it with his or her supervisor. This process produced the following results:

1. The self-appraisals were rated as more satisfying and constructive by the managers than the traditional supervisory-prepared appraisals.
2. There was less defensiveness on the part of subordinates regarding the appraisal.
3. Discussions based on self-ratings more often resulted in superior on-the-job performance than did the traditional appraisal.
4. Low-rated employees were especially likely to show an improvement in performance, as rated by managers, after a self-review discussion.[7]

Self-evaluation is particularly valuable for individuals who work in isolation, where they are the only persons who observe their performance. Examples are forest rangers and those university professors who spend most of their time doing research.

On the negative side, there is some evidence that self-ratings are less reliable than ratings by supervisors or peers. Curiously, studies are split as to whether self-ratings are usually higher than ratings by superiors; some found this to be so, and some found the opposite to be true.[8]

Evaluation by Other Individuals

Employees may also be evaluated by other individuals. Latham and Wexley tend to look upon evaluation by outsiders unfavorably, at least in part, because of the lack of normal on-the-job interaction between the person rated and the outsider.[9] However, certain individuals other than supervisors, peers, or subordinates do interact meaningfully with the employee and can be important evaluators. For example, a statistician in an accounting department to a paper company is also a section head, and, at least by the formal organization chart, her peers are the other section heads in the department. But on a professional level, the statistician may have more meaningful interaction with personnel performing statistical functions in other departments—wood and traffic, personnel, treasury, purchasing, and engineering.

Another example is the independent advisor. In Japan, each new employee has a senior executive not in the direct chain of command act as her advisor. The U.S. Army uses a similar approach. A sponsoring officer is appointed as an unofficial adviser for each reserve officer who goes on a tour of summer duty in the Pentagon. Such individuals can make a positive contribution to the performance evaluation process.

Combination Evaluations

Combinations of different evaluations may provide a better base for making decisions about career growth patterns, motivation toward improved performance, and appropriate monetary awards.

A method that extends the General Electric procedure mentioned earlier combines evaluation by a superior and self-appraisal. In this approach, both fill out the evaluation form separately well in advance of the interview.

> At the appraisal interview, the manager and the subordinate compare their evaluations. Differences of one point in the ratings are recorded on the official appraisal form at the higher rating, regardless of who assigned the higher rating. For those areas on which ratings differ by two or more points, the manager and the employee have an in-depth discussion to identify and clarify the reasons for differences.[10]

Just as subordinate ratings can be a manager's defense against an unfair rating by a superior, combining a superior's rating with peer ratings provides a defense for the rank-and-file employee against an unfair rating by a supervisor.

Latham and Wexley advocate a combination of self-, subordinate, peer, and superior evaluations because it maximizes the total information available on direct first-hand observation of the employee's job.[11]

Group Evaluation

So far we have mostly talked about ratings that one or more individuals perform independently. A group such as a committee can also review performance. The U.S. Army, for example, has boards of officers select the enlisted men for officer candidate schools. An advantage of this approach is that it avoids the bias that a soldier's company commander may have.

Assessment Centers

Assessment centers may also evaluate performance. Such a center was set up by the American Telephone and Telegraph Company.[12] The company assessed the potential of 355 young managers and compared the forecast against later measures of actual performance such as salary increases and changes in rank in a longitudinal study. The methods used to assess the managers included (1) situational tests, such as group exercises and in-basket exercises (including both a manufacturing problem and a group discussion); (2) paper and pencil ability tests; and (3) personality questionnaires. The first two methods were better predictors of success than the third. Results of the personality questionnaires indicated that a complex of characteristics was more predictive than any single trait.

In this assessment process self-ratings, peer ratings, and observer ratings were all used as additional means of developing information. A group brought together specifically for the purpose of assessing these managers spent at least 15 hours per manager after evidence from all sources had been made available. The results were astounding! Of those individuals judged to have middle management potential, 80 percent have reached this goal. Moreover, 95 percent of those judged lacking in management potential have not advanced beyond the first managerial level. Because the assessment data were held in confidence, they had no influence on the careers of the managers being studied.

The main advantage of the typical assessment center is that many evaluation techniques can be used on a group of employees at the same time. Such centers are sometimes criticized because parts of the evaluation process involve simulated rather than on-the-job performances. This characteristic, however, does not seem to have seriously detracted from their success, particularly in identifying possible candidates for promotion in the organization.

In more recent years this approach has become popular for employees in the public sector.[13]

Systems of Performance Evaluation

Systems of performance evaluation include the use of standardized rating scales, management by objectives, and behaviorally based systems.

Standardized Rating Scales and Measurements of Traits

Standardized rating scales may take the form of a checklist, or they may go into more detail to include definitions of factors and degrees of each factor.

The form shown in Figure 11–2 covers nonexempt personnel (those not excluded from the wage and hours limitations of the Fair Labor Standards Act) of Batton, Barton, Durstine & Osborn (BBDO), an advertising company with more than 1,000 employees. The form assesses six levels of evaluation, ranging from no basis and unsatisfactory at the low end to outstanding at the high end against only five factors: knowledge, quantity and quality of work, cooperation, and dependability. Where supervision is part of the job, the form includes the factors of supervisory ability, judgment, and personality, describing each of the factors briefly. It also records two other factors, attendance and punctuality (in the lower left-hand corner of the form), but these are not considered as important as the other factors. Ample space is available for remarks. The evaluation must be discussed by the supervisor with the employee, and the employee has an opportunity to comment on the evaluation. Any comments must be initialed by the employee.

The form shown in Figure 11–3 is used by a paper company with over 5,000 employees for its nonexempt workers. Notice on this form that even though only six factors are used, each is defined. In addition, each of the five levels of performance is described to enable the rater to make an accurate judgment. There is also plenty of room for comments.

The rater is required to review the results with the employee, and the employee indicates at the bottom of the second page of the form that she has

BBDO
NON-EXEMPT PERSONNEL
PERFORMANCE EVALUATION

_____   _____
(First Name)   (Last Name)   (Date Prepared)

_____   Six-Month Evaluation _____
(Position/Title)

_____   Annual Evaluation _____
(Dept/Account Group/Office)

FACTORS	EXPLANATION	NO BASIS	UNSAT	MIN ACCEPT	GOOD	SUPER-IOR	OUT-STAND-ING
Knowledge	Extent of knowledge in present position.						
Quantity	Volume of work produced.						
Quality	Accuracy & thoroughness.						
Cooperation	Attitude & ability to work with others.						
Dependability	Extent of supervision required.						
/////////	Rate only if needed on job.	/////////////////////////////////					
Supervisory Ability	Leadership qualities.						
Judgment	Ability to be discreet and make sound decisions.						
Personality	Disposition and impression made on others.						

Remarks: Furnish any information which, in addition to that shown above, would be helpful in appraising this employee.

_____

_____

_____

_____

This evaluation was discussed with employee on _____
                                                         (Date)

Employee's comments were: _____

_____

_____
                                              (Initials of employee)

Attendance Record: Poor ____ Fair ____ Good ____

Punctuality Record: Poor ____ Fair ____ Good ____

Does this employee have potential to accept more
    responsibility?   No ____ Yes ____
a supervisory position?   No ____ Yes ____

(Evaluator's name) _____

(Position) _____

Time with Employee: Less than 6 months _____
                     6 months to 1 year _____
                     More than 1 year _____

SALARY RECOMMENDATION ON REVERSE SIDE

GEN 1301 (11/1/74)

FIGURE 11–2
Example of a nonexempt performance evaluation form. (From
Batton, Barton, Durstine & Osborn, Inc. Reprinted with permission.)

256

NON-EXEMPT PERFORMANCE REVIEW

EMPLOYEE _____ POSITION TITLE _____ ORGANIZATION _____ DATE _____

Select the rating which best describes the level of performance of the employee under each of the following performance factors. Note the reason why you selected the particular rating under "Comments".

VOLUME OF WORK
Consider work output and general job capacity; productivity

Inefficient output. Slow. Usually behind with work.	Productivity acceptable. Some improvement desirable in areas outlined below.	Consistently performs all duties promptly.	Superior output. Often expends extra effort to produce more than expected.	Exceptional producer. Anticipates future requirements. Well prepared for increased duties.
☐	☐	☐	☐	☐

COMMENTS: _____

KNOWLEDGE OF JOB
Consider the clear understanding of the facts or factors pertinent to job

Inadequate knowledge	Adequate grasp of essentials. Some assistance periodically required.	Thorough detail knowledge. Follow-up seldom required.	Superior job knowledge. Well informed.	Exceptional grasp of responsibilities. Consistently adding new capabilities.
☐	☐	☐	☐	☐

COMMENTS: _____

QUALITY OF WORK
Consider neatness, accuracy and dependability of results regardless of volume

Erratic. Inclined towards carelessness. Occasionally work doesn't meet standards.	Some rework required. Inconsistent accuracy.	Produces accurate dependable work. Reliable contributor.	Consistently produces quality work. Complete attention to detail.	Does work of the highest level. Produces results showing skillful grasp of project objectives.
☐	☐	☐	☐	☐

COMMENTS: _____

ATTITUDE
Consider personality and temperament; cooperation with supervisor and co-workers; loyalty to the company

Indifferent. Unduly sensitive. Source of friction. Questionable loyalty.	Somewhat uncooperative, inclined to argue. Fair attitude.	Interested. Works well with others, assists associates willingly.	Displays positive attitude. Takes pride in work. Seeks improvement.	Enthusiastic. Fosters good will at all levels. Eager to increase contributions.
☐	☐	☐	☐	☐

COMMENTS: _____

Form 852 309 (Rev. 6/76)

INITIATIVE
Consider the ability to contribute, suggest, plan and carry out new ideas. Creativity and imagination

Shows no desire to learn new tasks or to plan work. No creative aptitude displayed.	Shows some desire to learn new tasks. Needs close supervision. Slight creative ability displayed.	Displays ability to learn new tasks without difficulty. Periodically offers new ideas.	Learns new tasks quickly. Work often complete ahead of schedule. Frequently has new ideas.	Regularly seeks new tasks & generates new concepts. Informed, creative attitude regularly displayed.
☐	☐	☐	☐	☐

COMMENTS: _____

GROWTH POTENTIAL
Consider ability to handle job of increased scope and responsibility, self-improvement efforts and record of past accomplishments

Unknown.	Limited without further efforts to improve.	Capabilities used well in present job. More experience required to establish growth potential	Demonstrates promise for further growth in near future.	Promotable now. Present job may limit contribution.
☐	☐	☐	☐	☐

COMMENTS: _____

GENERAL COMMENTS

State any other comments which are appropriate in describing this employee's performance _____

HI	LO	HI	LO	HI	LO	HI	LO	HI	LO
DISTINGUISHED Outstanding, exceptional, far above others. Excellent potential for advancement. (5-10%)		**COMMENDABLE** Superior, clearly substantially above required performance. (15-20%)		**GOOD TO VERY GOOD** Highly regarded performer, valuable contributor, fully competent. (50-55%)		**ADEQUATE** Acceptable performance. Does work well but needs improvement in some areas. (15-20%)		**UNSATISFACTORY**	

RATED BY: _____ DATE: _____

REVIEWED BY: _____ DATE: _____

EMPLOYEE (Has Reviewed) _____ DATE: _____

COMMENTS BY EMPLOYEE: _____

NOTE: IF SALARY ACTION IS RECOMMENDED WITH THIS REVIEW, ATTACH PROPER FORM.
DISTRIBUTION: WHITE – Corporate Personnel; PINK – Supervisor; YELLOW – Employee.
Form 852-309-2 (Rev. 6/76)

FIGURE 11–3
Example of a nonexempt performance evaluation form used by a large paper company.

257

seen it. The employee may comment on the evaluation in writing. Corporate policy requires that before the rated employee sees the review, it must be discussed by the rater and *her* superior.

The frequency of performance reviews depends on where the employee stands within the salary rate range. According to the company's policy statement, there should be performance reviews for all personnel at least annually. But the policy requires that nonexempt employees be reviewed every 6 months until the employee's salary reaches the midpoint of the salary grade. The review is annual thereafter.

The advantage of using performance evaluation forms of the type shown in Figures 11–2 and 11–3 is that they are standardized and call for traits that appear to be desirable for the typical worker. Who will doubt the desirability of having workers who are cooperative and have fine personalities? Assessing the volume of work conveys the idea that a worker should be efficient, and rating the quality of work reflects the importance of a worker's being accurate and neat. Disadvantages of using the standardized instrument with traits (and even some more readily measurable items such as volume and quality of work) are that (1) the factors do not apply with equal validity to all workers and (2) they do not tell an employee *how* to improve performance.

Management by Objectives (MBO)

A method often used to evaluate exempt employees is management by objectives, or MBO. The first page of an employee evaluation form for a large paper company using this method is shown in Figure 11–4.

The form lists the objectives on the left side in order of importance, and the rater describes the employee's progress during the year on each item on the right side. Affirmative action objectives are also listed, and a statement of goals for the following year appears on a later page.

The essence of the process is that the employee and supervisor sit down together and discuss what the employee's goals are until they reach agreement. Then, at the end of the period under review, they come to an agreement as to how well the employee has accomplished these goals. One weakness of the method is that the employee may get off the track in a relatively long period of time (often a year) between setting the goals and the later review. This shortcoming of the MBO approach can be offset either by more frequent meetings between the supervisor and the employee to be rated or by day-to-day coaching of the employee by the immediate supervisor. Studies done at General Electric suggest that day-to-day coaching even *without* the more formal MBO approach is more likely than MBO to bring employee goals into some measure of agreement with company goals. However, MBO does have the advantage of stating specific objectives so employees and supervisors can see what they are and think about them.[14]

The MBO approach is free from the weaknesses of the standardized rating scales already discussed because it can be tailored to fit each worker's particular job and it states specific objectives for worker action. However, the objectives are

EXEMPT PERFORMANCE REVIEW

Name _____ Date _____

C. Is there a comprehensive and continuing safety program functioning within the incumbent's area of responsibility?
Yes ____ No ____

D. In what way has the safety program under the incumbent's control been improved since the last appraisal? Include your evaluation of the quality, organization, and effectiveness of those safety meetings for which the employee is directly responsible.

E. How many accidents have occurred to employees within the incumbent's area of responsibility during 24 months prior to appraisal?

Prior Calendar Year ____   Prior Two Calendar Years ____

1. Lost Time ____
2. Doctor Cases ____

F. Summary Appraisal

HI	LO	HI	LO	HI	LO	HI	LO	
DISTINGUISHED		COMMENDABLE		GOOD TO VERY GOOD		ADEQUATE		UNSATISFACTORY
Outstanding, exceptional, far above others. Excellent potential for advancement (5-10%)		Superior, clearly substantially above required performance (15-20%)		Highly regarded performer, valuable contributor, fully competent (50-55%)		Acceptable performance. Does work well but needs improvement in some areas (15-20%)		

G. Goals for the following year (Be specific identify).

H. Rated By _____ Date _____

Reviewed By _____ Date _____

Employee (has reviewed) _____ Date _____

Comments by employee (include personal goals) _____

NOTE: SEE SALARY ADMINISTRATION POLICY (#4.31) FOR INSTRUCTIONS IN THE PROCEDURE FOR SALARY CHANGE ACTION.

Form 852-143-2 (Rev. 6/76)   DISTRIBUTION   White - Corporate Personnel.   Pink - Supervisor.   Yellow - Employee

EXEMPT PERFORMANCE REVIEW

Name of Person Rated _____   Date of Review _____

Position _____   Date on Present Position _____

Last ____ First ____ Middle Initial ____   Date Hired _____

Division ____ Department ____   District or Plant _____

Rated by _____   Position _____

I have written employee rated: ____ Years
I have supervised employee rated: ____ Years

A. Activities
State the performance objectives established during the past year in order of importance.

1.

B. Appraisal
Give, in some specific detail, your opinion of how well the employee accomplished the objectives.

1.

Affirmative Action objectives

Form 852-143 (Rev. 6/76)

FIGURE 11—4
Example of a management by objectives (MBO) performance appraisal form.

259

strongly oriented in the direction of cutting costs and improving productivity and are based on specific quantitative measurements. Because not all jobs readily lend themselves to quantitative measurements of this type, the MBO approach may not be effective in all cases. In addition, actual gains or losses compared with planned quantitative goals may be attributed to the individual when the causes (such as a material shortage) are outside the control of the individual being rated. As Latham and Wexley put it:

> If the employee is well liked or highly disliked by the supervisor, biases in the causal attribution of behavior will benefit the liked employee and harm the disliked person. There is no question as to how many products were produced or sold. But, one person will receive undeserved credit for good outcomes; the other person will receive undeserved blame for poor outcomes.[15]

Behaviorally Based Systems

Because of the shortcomings of standardized rating scales, there have been recent efforts to develop rating scales more closely related to observed behavior on the job. Two such systems are now being used. Behaviorally anchored rating scales and behavioral observation scales are both derived from job analysis of critical incidents. The supervisor notes—at the time they occur—incidents that illustrate particularly effective or ineffective behavior on the part of the employee. Analysis of these incidents over a period of time provides an objective, factual basis for evaluating an employee's on-the-job performance. This behavioral approach avoids the vagueness of standardized rating scales and the overemphasis on quantitative measures typical of management by objectives.

Civil Service Reform Act of 1978

The Civil Service Reform Act of 1978 strongly supports the behavioral approach. This act covers all federal employees, except those in the Central Intelligence Agency, the foreign service, and the General Accounting Office as well as judges, physicians, dentists, nurses, and individuals appointed by the president. Under this act, agencies are required to develop evaluation systems that

1. Encourage employee participation in setting performance standards.
2. Base standards on critical elements of the job.
3. Indicate in writing the method of job analysis used.
4. Inform the employee about the critical requirements of the job before any performance evaluation takes place.
5. Provide an evaluation based on the critical requirements of the job.[16]

Federal employees had had mixed feelings about the former methods of performance evaluation, despite the fact they had confidence and trust in their coworkers and felt that their supervisor dealt well with subordinates, and they prefer the new appraisal methods.[17]

Behavioral Job Analysis

Both behaviorally anchored rating scales and behavioral observation scales involve a different type of job analysis from the one discussed in Chapter 5. Rather than stressing development of a precise job description, this type of job analysis emphasizes the behaviors called for by the job, mainly through the analysis of critical incidents.

Both systems require an inventory of critical incidents, which are gathered in the following steps:

1. The job analyst interviews approximately 30 people, including supervisors, peers, subordinates, and clients, who are aware of the objectives of the job and who see people perform it daily.
2. The job analyst explains to the person interviewed the purpose of the interview.
3. The analyst attempts to get the person's opinion as to the five key things an employee *must* be good at to do the job effectively.
4. The analyst asks the person to cite 10 critical incidents—5 of effective and 5 of ineffective behavior—that took place in the last 6 to 12 months.[18]

Behavioral job analysis emphasizes direct first-hand observation. The analyst asks three detailed questions about each incident:

1. What were the circumstances surrounding this incident? In other words, what was the background? What was the situation?
2. What exactly did the individual *do* that was either effective or ineffective?
3. How is the incident you described an example of effective or ineffective behavior? In other words, how did this affect the task(s) the individual was performing?[19]

Behaviorally Anchored Rating Scales

The first of the two systems is behaviorally anchored rating scales. An application of the technique is shown in Figure 11–5.

To develop a behaviorally anchored rating scale,

1. A group is formed consisting of people who are thoroughly familiar with the job to be rated. Inclusion in the group of not only managers but also workers who perform the job will facilitate later acceptance of the rating scales.
2. The group agrees on the performance dimensions of the job. [In Figure 11–5, the one dimension shown is "organization of checkstand."]

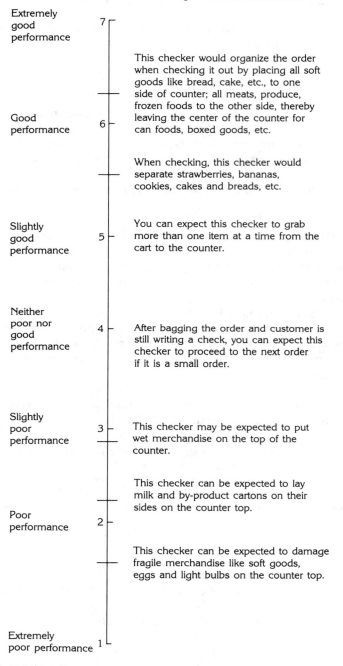

Performance Dimension: Organization of Checkstand

Extremely good performance — 7

This checker would organize the order when checking it out by placing all soft goods like bread, cake, etc., to one side of counter; all meats, produce, frozen foods to the other side, thereby leaving the center of the counter for can foods, boxed goods, etc.

Good performance — 6

When checking, this checker would separate strawberries, bananas, cookies, cakes and breads, etc.

Slightly good performance — 5

You can expect this checker to grab more than one item at a time from the cart to the counter.

Neither poor nor good performance — 4

After bagging the order and customer is still writing a check, you can expect this checker to proceed to the next order if it is a small order.

Slightly poor performance — 3

This checker may be expected to put wet merchandise on the top of the counter.

This checker can be expected to lay milk and by-product cartons on their sides on the counter top.

Poor performance — 2

This checker can be expected to damage fragile merchandise like soft goods, eggs and light bulbs on the counter top.

Extremely poor performance — 1

FIGURE 11–5

Behaviorally anchored rating scale for one dimension used to evaluate the performance of checkout clerks in a supermarket. [From Lawrence Fogli; Charles L. Hulin; and Milton R. Blood, "Development of First-Level Job Criteria," Journal of Applied Psychology 55 *(February 1971): 3–8. Copyright © 1971 by the American Psychological Association. Reprinted by permission.]*

3. Incidents which indicate effective, ineffective (or even mediocre) job behavior are identified by the group.
4. Incidents are converted to expectational statements. For example, where a critical incident might involve putting a large wet bag of frozen fish on the counter, the appropriate expectational statement might read, "This checker may be expected to put wet merchandise on the top of the counter."
5. Next, each statement is assigned by the group to a particular dimension. For such assignment the vote of a large majority (often 75%) is required. Statements which are vague, duplicate each other, or are not considered truly job related are discarded.
6. Finally, each statement is rated by the group on a 1 to 7 (or 9) scale where 1 is extremely poor and 7 or 9 extremely good performance. Again, where substantial agreement as to the location on the scale of a particular statement is lacking, the statement is eliminated.[20]

Behaviorally anchored rating scales have been developed for various groups, including nurses, police personnel, grocery store check-out personnel, engineers, department store managers, university faculty members, systems and programming analysts, and dieticians.[21] In fact, one of the advantages of using behaviorally anchored scales is that scales are specifically job related compared with the generality of standard rating scales. If the supervisor has recorded examples of critical incidents for the person rated during the period covered by the evaluation, the system can be useful both for counseling and for motivation.[22]

There are also some disadvantages to this system. For example, if 300 incidents are accumulated in developing the rating scales, and if only 7 dimensions are determined (with 7 expectational points per scale), then in effect only 49 incidents are put to use. Also, raters may be hard put to decide on the dimension to which a particular incident should be assigned. Even if the dimension is evident, it may be difficult to match the incident against the few points provided on each scale.[23]

Behavioral Observation Scales
The second of the two behavioral systems to be considered is behavioral observation scales. An example is shown in Figure 11–6. To develop behavioral observation scales:

1. Group critical incidents to form each behavioral item.
2. Group behavioral items to form criteria.[24]
3. Test the validity of criteria assignments.
4. Attach a five-point scale to each behavioral item. (Notice in Figure 11–6 that negative items are handled by reversing the "almost never" and "almost always" labels as in items 2 and 3.)
5. Have observers (peers and supervisors) use the scale and test to eliminate items that do not differentiate between effective and ineffective performance. For example, an item on which almost everyone is rated the same is eliminated.[25]

VI PROGRAM DIRECTOR/LANE INSPECTOR

1. Provides input to the General Manager regarding effectiveness of all personnel on all of the above behaviors, thus serving as a Lane inspector/consultant to the General Manager.

   Almost never 1 2 3 4 5 Almost always

2. Thinks of ideas for increasing business

   Almost never 1 2 3 4 5 Almost always

3. Is repeatedly asked to do the same thing

   Almost always 1 2 3 4 5 Almost never

4. Works long hours when necessary (for example over 40 hours)

   Almost never 1 2 3 4 5 Almost always

5. Spot checks the lanes during weekends (for example drops in unexpectedly at a lane for 10 minutes)

   Almost never 1 2 3 4 5 Almost always

6. Fair and consistent in dealing with employees (does not show favoritism to any one employee)

   Almost never 1 2 3 4 5 Almost always

7. On special occasions such as customer birthday parties, stays with the party showing the people how to bowl and helps them to have a good time

   Almost never 1 2 3 4 5 Almost always

8. Takes charge of at least one shift per week

   Almost never 1 2 3 4 5 Almost always

9. Keeps storage room in Pine Street spotless

   Almost never 1 2 3 4 5 Almost always

10. Comments positively on the scores of customers

    Almost never 1 2 3 4 5 Almost always

11. Praises people for a good shot

    Almost never 1 2 3 4 5 Almost always

12. Sends out invitations for a bowling tournament in a timely manner

    Almost never 1 2 3 4 5 Almost always

13. Helps individuals to form teams to bowl in a tournament

    Almost never 1 2 3 4 5 Almost always

14. Gets trophies to customers on schedule

    Almost never 1 2 3 4 5 Almost always

15. Actively promotes the selling of shoes

    Almost never 1 2 3 4 5 Almost always

16. Actively promotes the selling of bowling balls

    Almost never 1 2 3 4 5 Almost always

17. Asks for and listens openly to concerns of league captains

    Almost never 1 2 3 4 5 Almost always

18. Offers help in solving league problems

    Almost never 1 2 3 4 5 Almost always

19. Comes to agreement with the league on steps to be taken to resolve a problem

    Almost never 1 2 3 4 5 Almost always

20. Gets involved in too many things at the same time

    Almost always 1 2 3 4 5 Always never

21. Staff knows where to get hold of program director at all times

    Almost never 1 2 3 4 5 Always always

22. Forgets little things has been asked to do

    Almost always 1 2 3 4 5 Almost never

23. Is able to set priorities on a daily basis. Sets up a check list of key things is going to accomplish each day

    Almost never 1 2 3 4 5 Almost always

24. Is upset by what employees think of him, for example is overly worried what people will think if reports to the General Manager an employee who did not do something properly

    Almost always 1 2 3 4 5 Almost never

25. Asks people to do things rather than ordering

    Almost never 1 2 3 4 5 Almost always

26. Asks fellow employees for their ideas for promoting business

    Almost never 1 2 3 4 5 Almost always

27. Asks customers for their ideas for promoting business

    Almost never 1 2 3 4 5 Almost always

28. Makes customers comfortable through casual conversation about their background and interests

    Almost never 1 2 3 4 5 Almost always

29. Expresses a desire to help customers improve their bowling scores

    Almost never 1 2 3 4 5 Almost always

30. Makes it clear that has confidence that the customers can improve their bowling

    Almost never 1 2 3 4 5 Almost always

31. Asks customers if there is anything can do to help them

    Almost never 1 2 3 4 5 Almost always

32. Avoids responding with hostility or defensiveness when receiving a complaint

    Almost never 1 2 3 4 5 Almost always

33. Recognizes and acknowledges the other person's viewpoint

    Almost never 1 2 3 4 5 Almost always

34. States the company's position nondefensively

    Almost never 1 2 3 4 5 Almost always

35. Delegates work that should do by self

    Almost always 1 2 3 4 5 Almost never

36. Completes assigned jobs

    Almost never 1 2 3 4 5 Almost always

37. Meets deadlines

    Almost never 1 2 3 4 5 Almost always

38. Keeps customers informed of changes, for example, tells them about new prices and why they are going into effect, informs them of tournaments, tells them about improvements in the lanes

    Almost never 1 2 3 4 5 Almost always

    38–122 123–141 142–160 161–179 180–190
    very poor unsatisfactory satisfactory excellent superior

    Total:____

FIGURE 11–6

A behavioral observation scale used in a bowling alley company. [From Gary P. Latham and Kenneth N. Wexley, Increasing Productivity Through Performance Appraisal (Reading, Mass.; Addison-Wesley, 1981). Reprinted with permission.]

264

The scale shown in Figure 11–6 includes a range of numbers for different score totals. These are determined by management and differ for each job.

Compared with behaviorally anchored rating scales, behavioral observation scales

1. Have many more items, which tend to improve validity.
2. Provide better coverage of critical behavioral aspects of each job.
3. Provide such good coverage of almost all behavioral aspects required by the job that they can be used to provide a job preview for job applicants.
4. Are easier for the rater to interpret.
5. Can be defended without building up a supporting file of critical incidents for each employee who is to be rated.[26]

Politics of Performance Evaluation

It is sometimes said that ability, like the cream in a bottle of milk, naturally rises to the top. But this may not always be the case, and even where it is, it may be difficult to stay on top. Political assassinations in recent years in the United States have made this latter point too clearly to be denied. In the business world and especially in the evaluation of individual performance, similar political factors are also at work. For example, where employees at one level are competing for a limited number of openings at the next higher level, it is hard to believe that peer ratings will be really objective. A natural tendency would be to avoid rating the other candidates too high lest you in effect end up being rated relatively too low. Self-preservation is the first law of nature.

A recent study involving in-depth structured interviews with 60 executives from 7 large companies who had performance evaluation experience in 197 organizations is most revealing.[27] The authors conclude that

> accuracy is *not* the primary concern of the practicing executive in appraising subordinates. The main concern is how best to use the appraisal process to motivate and reward subordinates.[28]

The authors of the study, Clinton O. Longenecker, Henry P. Sims, Jr., and Dennis A. Gioia, think that internal company politics greatly influences the individual performance evaluation process. However, they feel honest ratings can result from the proper organizational climate (characterized by qualities such as openness and trust between managers and subordinates) and management viewing the rating process as important. Top management should explain *why* performance evaluations are done and openly discuss the *political* (and legal) aspects of the evaluation process. Management should also minimize the number of people who have access to the written appraisal.[29] If, on the other hand, top managers do ratings poorly, their behavior will tend to move down through the organization.

Rating Errors and Rater Training

As is also true of job analysis and job evaluation, the process of individual or group performance evaluation is open to rating errors. In those unusual organizations where internal political factors have been kept under tight rein by top-flight managers who think that rating *accuracy* really matters, we can examine some of the rating errors and the type of training that can help raters avoid or at least minimize them.

Rating Errors

Among the kinds of rating errors are (1) contrast effects; (2) first impression; (3) halo (and horns); (4) similar-to-me; (5) central tendency; and (6) negative and positive leniency.

Contrast Effects

The error of contrast effects involves rating the individual by comparing her against another individual instead of against the standard by which the individual is supposed to be rated. For example, in hiring, a candidate who meets the requirements for the job may be rejected only for looking bad compared with two previous candidates.

First Impression

In rating at periodic intervals, as is typically done in performance rating, a person who performs well at first and receives a good rating often continues to get a good rating when in fact she has not continued to perform well. The first impression makes its mark.

Halo and Horns

The halo effect takes place when a person is rated on a number of things at the same time. The rater observes that the individual does well at one thing and proceeds to assume that she does well on all the items. The horns effect is the opposite of this. The rater perceives an individual to do poorly on one item and assumes she should be rated poorly on all the items.

Similar-to-me

The similar-to-me effect is the tendency of the rater to rate more favorably someone who is like herself.

Central Tendency

Some raters may tend to rate all individuals close to the middle of the rating scale—a "playing it safe" strategy.

Negative and Positive Leniency

Some raters, particularly supervisors, are inclined to be hard on the employee to avoid unwarranted expectations of raises, promotions, or challenging assignments. Others tend to rate employees too highly.[30]

Rater Training

Latham and Wexley conduct a 6- to 8-hour workshop using videotapes to improve the performance of raters on the job. This program highlights specific skills of the job rater:

> The workshop consisted of videotapes of job candidates being evaluated. The trainees gave a rating on a 9-point scale according to how they thought the manager in the videotape rated the candidate; they also rated the candidate. Group discussions concerning the reasons for each trainee's rating of the job candidate followed. In this way, the trainees had an opportunity to *observe* other managers making errors, to *actively participate* in discovering the degree to which they were or were not prone to making the error, to receive *knowledge of results* regarding their own rating behavior, and to *practice* job-related tasks to reduce the errors they were making.[31]

Keeping the System Up To Date

In Chapter 5 we discussed the need to keep job descriptions up to date. This is also true of performance evaluation instruments, no matter what system is used. However, the case for review is even more important for the behaviorally based systems because they are more oriented to the particular job. New evaluation instruments may be called for whenever there is a substantial change in the organization's (1) goals, (2) technology, (3) procedures, or (4) work flow.[32]

Performance Evaluation and Motivation

The process of performance evaluation and employee motivation are related. In all too many cases the relation is negative; that is, the supervisor who does the rating may attach little importance to the process and may even resent having to carry it out. When this attitude rubs off on the employee, there is a negative overall motivational effect. Under behaviorally based systems, more positive results can be achieved. For example, when behavioral observation scales are used, motivation can be achieved when the employee

1. Participates in the development of, or changes in, the evaluation instrument.
2. Receives feedback from the supervisor and/or other raters.
3. Agrees with the supervisor on specific goals related to the feedback.
4. Participates with others in team building.
5. Has good performance rewarded by monetary incentives.
6. Has the benefit of reinforcement of effective behavior from contacts with the supervisor outside of the formal evaluation sessions.[33]

Participation in the Development of the Rating System

When employees participate to some degree in planning the processes by which pay is determined, motivation is enhanced, as Lawler has pointed out. In the case of behavioral observation scales, the instrument

> is not based on the opinions, no matter how expert, of outsiders. This alone facilitates commitment to, and understanding of, these performance measures by the people who use them.[34]

The Evaluation Meeting: Feedback and Goal Setting

In our discussion of management by objectives, we mentioned the importance of the frequency of performance evaluation meetings. This point is applicable to behaviorally based systems as well. According to Kenneth Keleman and Kathleen Glover, the frequency of review should not be based on a fixed period but should vary with the need. As they see it,

> Frequent, non-redundant information should be given when an individual is inexperienced or the task complex, and frequency reduced to maintain performance levels when the task is learned.[35]

A broader basis for mutual problem solving in the performance evaluation interview will be provided if the supervisor, in addition to her own evaluation, can have available the results of peer and perhaps other evaluations. In this way, the feedback can be more effective. When behavioral observation scales are used, the supervisor can follow this model as a guide for conducting the interview:

1. Explain the purpose of the meeting . . . to provide recognition for areas in which the employee is doing well and to discuss any problems the employee may be experiencing on the job.

2. At the beginning of the meeting . . . describe to the employee what was done that deserves recognition and why it deserves recognition. Be specific so the employee knows exactly what needs to be done to maintain this appreciation. If blanket praise is given, the employee may be inadvertently reinforced for mediocre as well as excellent behavior.
3. Ask the employee if there are areas on the job where you can provide assistance.
4. If the employee fails to mention areas that you feel are important, discuss no more than two where you feel improvement is needed. Focusing on more than two broad criteria . . . can overwhelm the employee and increase defensiveness.
5. Ask for and listen openly to the employee's concerns. It may well be the case that your initial concerns are not justified.
6. Come to agreement on steps to be taken by each of you.
7. Mutually agree upon a specific score that the employee will strive to attain on the subsequent appraisal.
8. Finally, agree on a follow-up date, to determine the extent to which the employee's and supervisor's concerns have been eliminated and progress has been made on the goals that have been set.[36]

Team Building

Team building is an organization development (OD) technique that can be used when performance evaluations are done anonymously by the employee's peers and/or subordinates. Where there are many peers or subordinates, a delegation of perhaps five representatives from the larger group will meet with the employee. The employee takes the available feedback from the performance evaluation and breaks it into three areas:

1. Things that I can change immediately.
2. Things that I can't change . . . even if my life depended upon it. Let me explain why.
3. Things I think we as a group can change with your help.[37]

The group then agrees on issues to be resolved, for example, over a 3-month period, and specific actions are taken by those in the group to resolve these issues. Meetings often last 1 to 3 hours and are held twice a month.[38]

Monetary Incentives

Pay increases and promotions as well as counseling are all relevant parts of motivation, and all can be tied in to performance evaluation. Latham and Wexley qualify how money can motivate:

1. Money must be valued . . . by the worker.
2. Money must be tied to all important facets of the job.

3. The employee must perceive that money is tied to performance.
4. The amount of money must be seen by the workers as worthy of their efforts.
5. The money must be given soon after the desired behavior and/or outcome has taken place.
6. The employee must trust management to dispense the rewards equitably.[39]

Reinforcing Effective Behavior

As mentioned in our discussion of management by objectives, formal performance evaluation meetings between the employee and the supervisor are not enough. Effective behavior needs reinforcement outside these formal meetings. Reinforcement can be accomplished on a day-to-day basis either on the supervisor's initiative or when the employee asks for help. Latham and Wexley stress both positive and negative reinforcers. An example of a positive reinforcer is praise by the supervisor when a report is turned in on time. An example of a negative reinforcer is when the sales manager ceases to complain about one salesperson's expense account, which has almost always been way over budget, when the amount for the latest month is way below budget.[40]

There is evidence that a variable schedule of reinforcement better motivates an employee than does the repetition of the same reinforcement every time the behavior takes place. This occurs in part because a person tends to resent being praised for behavior that has become routine and is already well learned and internalized. At that point, praise is a better motivator when the performance is more than the usual, such as a desk editor complimenting a newspaper reporter on a particularly well-written story.

Summary

Performance evaluation is another among the cluster of rational managerial processes that tend to reinforce hierarchical thinking. Performance evaluation emphasizes the individual in the job rather than the job itself. It can be used to motivate and to improve the performance of the employee in her job. Performance evaluation can also serve as a basis for pay increases, promotions, and other forms of recognition.

Most organizations rely on rating by the employee's immediate superior, who is in a position to observe the employee but who also may be biased. Peer rating and subordinate rating can be used to broaden the evaluation base and offset possible bias in the rating of the worker's immediate superior. Self-evaluation, despite some limitations, is a useful supplement to other forms of evaluation. It is also the second most widely used form of evaluation.

Individuals inside the organization, other than the worker's superior, peers, or subordinates, can also contribute to the evaluation process. The Japanese "uncle" approach—the appointment of an older advisor (a person not in the direct chain of command) to advise each new employee—is an example. Group evaluation, sometimes used in academic hiring, is regularly used to select officer candidates in the military services.

Assessment centers are used to evaluate candidates for promotion to higher managerial positions. Candidates are put through in-basket exercises, business games, interviews, and tests. Quantitative measurements and observations are then pooled and evaluated by a team of specialists.

Standardized rating scales are sometimes used to evaluate performance, but the factors employed often do not relate closely to what a worker actually does on the job. Such scales typically tell a worker little about areas for improvement.

The management by objectives (MBO) system brings the employee and supervisor together to set goals for the upcoming year. On a specified date, they compare accomplishments with the objectives jointly agreed to. This system emphasizes quantitative goals. But users sometimes misdirect blame or credit for particular outcomes.

Behaviorally based rating scales contain specific examples of expected or actual behavior based on critical incidents, which are tied closely to the particular job. These incidents are used to describe effective, ineffective, or in-between behavior on the job. Behavioral observation scales, as compared with behaviorally anchored rating scales, use a larger number of critical incidents, are easier for the rater to interpret, and can be defended without building a supporting file of critical incidents.

In the past there has been a strong tendency to concentrate on improved accuracy in the rating process and to pay much less attention to the environment in which the rating takes place. However, recent research has suggested that internal political aspects tend to greatly influence the evaluation process to the extent that rating accuracy is typically *not* the rater's primary concern. An example is where peers are competing for a limited number of jobs at the next higher level. Self-preservation being at stake, it is doubtful that their ratings are likely to be objective!

Among top-flight managers who think that rating *accuracy* really matters, subjectivity is still a problem in rating. Specialized training for raters can be used to reduce the extent of errors in rating.

When either peer or subordinate ratings are used to supplement supervisor ratings, and where the quality of the ratings is not seriously at issue, team building can be used to solve mutual problems and to increase motivation.

Case Study

Ashizawa Food Company

Ed Zamora, chief statistician for a large food processing company, sat in the office of his immediate supervisor, Don Ziegler, the company controller. The subject of discussion was the management by objectives (MBO) program which Ed had learned about for the first time at this meeting.

Don, with a yellow pad in front of him, asked Ed to come over and sit beside him so he could show him how the system worked. He drew a line down the middle of the sheet. On the left side he wrote the heading "Routine duties"; on the right side he jotted down "Key Objectives." The routine duties, Don explained to Ed, would include having Ed's section get out the statistical reports on time to company executives and mill managers, the association reports to industry associations, and the government reports to the governmental agencies. He asked Ed to name other routine duties and then jotted them down in no particular order. After some discussion, they agreed to specific performance standards for each routine duty. For example, each report going to the executives and mill managers was to be under a tight time standard. Report No. 1 was supposed to be out the first working day of the month, while Report No. 10 did not have to go out until the fifteenth working day. They agreed for the forthcoming year that if these reports were produced on time or earlier 85 percent of the time, Ed's performance would be judged average; if 75 percent of the time, poor; and if 95 percent of the time, excellent.

The key objectives in the right-hand column, Don explained, were goals just for this coming year. Don had in mind several goals, such as developing an improved system of sales reports, improving the quality of industry reports through the industry statistical committee of which Ed was a member, and so on.

They discussed these goals for a while and Don entered them, adding, "Oh, by the way, we'd better put down eliminating any reports which aren't needed." He then added that goal to the list. Don closed the session by saying, "OK, that's it. I'll have this typed up and a year from now we'll review your progress! OK?"

About a year later, Don left a note for Ed to come in and see him. Don greeted Ed in friendly fashion but got to the point rather quickly, reminding Ed of their discussion a year earlier about the MBO program. He sat across from Ed with the MBO form in front of him and a pad on which he took a few notes as they talked. At first Don just asked a few specific questions about progress on some of the routine responsibilities and key objectives. Then he looked up and said, "Ed, the way it looks to me, you've done well on the routine responsibilities. But frankly, I'm not as satisfied as I'd like to be about what you've done on the key objectives. The president really feels strongly on this business of cutting down on unnecessary reports, and now it looks as if we have more reports than ever!"

Ed was taken aback. He simply had no idea the president attached that much importance to reducing the number of reports, and he resented Don's hitting him on that one objective when he had worked so hard on the others. He had improved the system of sales reports and completely revamped the industry reports—something for which he had been praised by other members of the industry statistical committee. He was about to speak up when Don raised his hand and said, "Look, don't get me wrong, Ed. You'll get your raise this year, but all I can do for you is about 5 percent. You need to do some more thinking about the key objectives for next year." Don paused and stood up, saying, "Ed, you'll have to excuse me. I have a meeting coming up in a few minutes."

Role Assignment

You are a consultant to the vice-president for human resources and have become familiar with Ed's experience as reported here. What changes would you recommend in the company's MBO program? Explain your reasoning.

Questions for Discussion

1. What purposes are served by evaluating employee performance?
2. What are the advantages of using peer evaluation rather than evaluation by the worker's immediate superior? Are there any disadvantages?
3. Compare self-evaluation to peer rating. Under what circumstances should self-evaluation be used?
4. What are the advantages and disadvantages of using group rather than individual performance evaluation?
5. What is an assessment center? How does it work? What are its advantages and disadvantages?
6. How does management by objectives (MBO) work? What are the pros and cons of using this system?
7. What is the significance of the Civil Service Reform Act of 1978? What effect is it likely to have?
8. What is meant by a behaviorally anchored rating scale? How can one be developed?
9. How does the behavioral observation scale work? How does it differ from the behaviorally anchored rating scale?
10. Is keeping the performance evaluation system up to date using behavioral observation scales more or less of a problem than it would be using standardized rating scales? Discuss.
11. How do monetary incentives tie in with performance evaluation?
12. What role does reinforcement play in the evaluation process? What is the difference between positive and negative reinforcement? What can be said about the timing of reinforcement?

Notes

1. Gary P. Latham and Kenneth N. Wexley, *Increasing Productivity Through Performance Appraisal* (Reading, MA: Addison-Wesley, 1981), 80.
2. Ibid.
3. Ibid., 92.
4. Ibid., 85.
5. Ibid., 87.
6. L. L. Cummings and Donald P. Schwab, *Performance in Organizations* (Glenview, IL: Scott, Foresman, 1973), 105.
7. Latham and Wexley, *op. cit.*, 82. Based on G. A. Bassett and H. H. Meyer, "Performance Appraisal Based on Self-Review," *Personnel Psychology* 21 (1968): 421–30.
8. Latham and Wexley, *op. cit.*, 83.
9. Ibid., 92–96.
10. See Latham and Wexley, *op. cit.*, 83, about research reported in K. S. Teel, "Self-Appraisal Revisited," *Personnel Journal* 57 (1978): 364–67.
11. Latham and Wexley, *op. cit.*, 96.
12. See Douglas W. Bray and D. L. Grant, "The Assessment Center in the Measurement of Potential for Business Management," *Psychological Monographs* 80, no. 17 (1966). This monograph was edited by Gregory A. Kimble.
13. For example, see Joyce D. Ross, "A Current Review of Public Assessment Centers: A Cause for Concern," *Public Personnel Management* 8, no. 1 (1979): 41–46.
14. For an extended discussion of the MBO approach, see Anthony P. Raia, *Managing by Objectives* (Glenview, IL: Scott, Foresman, 1974).
15. Latham and Wexley, *op. cit.*, 128.
16. Ibid., 29.
17. Lloyd G. Nigro, "Attitudes of Federal Employees Toward Performance Appraisal and Merit Pay: Implications for CSRA Implementation," *Public Administration Review* 41, no. 1 (1981): 84–86.
18. Latham and Wexley, *op. cit.*, 49.
19. Ibid., 50.
20. For discussion, see William J. Kearney,

"Behaviorally Anchored Rating Scales—MBO's Missing Ingredient," *Personnel Journal* 58, no. 1 (1979): 20–25.
21. For example, see Marjorie F. Fruin and John P. Campbell, "Developing Behaviorally Anchored Scales for Rating Dietician's Performance," *Journal of the American Dietetic Association* 71, no. 2 (1977): 111–15.
22. Latham and Wexley, *op. cit.*, 53–54.
23. Ibid.
24. Not shown in Figure 11–6. However, for managers in the strategic planning group in one company, 20 behavioral items were grouped under three criteria—team playing, planning/forecasting, and interactions with subordinates.
25. Latham and Wexley, *op. cit.*, 56–60.
26. Ibid., 61–63.
27. Clinton O. Longenecker, Henry P. Sims, Jr., and Dennis A. Gioia, "Behind the Mask: The Politics of Employee Appraisal," *The Academy of Management Executive* 1, no. 3,

(1987): 183–93.
28. Ibid., 199.
29. Ibid., 190–91.
30. See Latham and Wexley, *op. cit.*, 100–104, for a detailed discussion of these errors.
31. Latham and Wexley, *op. cit.*, 107.
32. Ibid., 74.
33. See Latham and Wexley, *op. cit.*, for an extensive treatment of this subject.
34. Latham and Wexley, *op. cit.*, 179.
35. Kenneth S. Keleman and Kathleen W. Glover, "An Overview and Analysis of Feedback-Performance Relationships in Goal Oriented Systems," paper delivered at the spring 1977 meetings of the Western Division, Academy of Management, at Sun Valley, Idaho, 12.
36. Latham and Wexley, *op. cit.*, 153–54.
37. Ibid., 143.
38. Ibid.
39. Ibid., 141–42.
40. For a more detailed treatment, see Latham and Wexley, *op. cit.*, 129–33.

References

Adams, H. Lon, and Embley, Kenneth. "Performance Management Systems: From Strategic Planning to Employee Productivity." *Personnel* 65, no. 4 (April 1988): 55–60.

Albert, William F. "It's Time for Your Organization's Performance Review." *Personnel Journal* 64, no. 12 (December 1985): 51–55.

Banks, Cristina G., and Murphy, Kevin R. "Toward Narrowing the Research-Practice Gap in Performance Appraisal." *Personnel Psychology* 38, no. 2 (Summer 1985): 335–346.

Banks, Cristina G., and Roberson, Loriann. "Performance Appraisers as Test Developers." *Academy of Management Review* 10, no. 1 (January 1985): 128–142.

Bernardin, H. John, and Klatt, Lawrence A. "Managerial Appraisal Systems: Has Practice Caught Up to the State of the Art?" *Personnel Administrator* 30, no. 11 (November 1985): 79–86.

Cabris, Gerald, T., et al. "Rewarding Individual and Team Productivity: The Biloxi Merit Bonus Plan." *Public Personnel Management* 14, no. 3

(Fall 1985): 231–244.

Cascio, Wayne F., and Ramos, Robert A. "Development and Application of a New Method for Assessing Job Performance in Behavioral/Economic Terms." *Journal of Applied Psychology* 7, no. 1 (February 1986): 20–28.

Deets, Norman R., and Tyler, D. Timothy. "How Xerox Improved its Performance Appraisals." *Personnel Journal* 65, no. 4 (April 1986): 50–52.

Dipboye, Robert L. "Some Neglected Variables in Research on Discrimination in Appraisals." *Academy of Management Review* 10, no. 1 (January 1985): 116–127.

Eaton, Newell K., et al. "Alternate Methods of Estimating the Dollar Value of Performance." *Personnel Psychology* 38, no. 1 (Spring 1985): 27–40.

Edwards, Mark R., and Sproull, J. Ruth. "Making Performance Appraisals Perform: The Use of Team Evaluation." *Personnel* 62, no. 3 (March 1985): 28–32.

Edwards, Mark R., et al. "Solving the Double Bind in Performance Appraisal: A Saga of Wolves, Sloths, and Eagles." *Business Horizons* 28, no. 3 (May–June 1985): 59–68.

Ferris, Gerald R. "The Influence of Subordinate Age on Performance Ratings and Causal Attributions." *Personnel Psychology* 38, no. 3 (Autumn 1985): 545–558.

Freedman, Stuart. "Performance-Based Pay: A Convenience Store Case Study." *Personnel Journal* 64, no. 7 (July 1985): 30–34.

Gibb, Peter. "Appraisal Goals and Controls." *Personnel Journal* 64, no. 8 (August 1985): 89–95.

Gomez-Mejia, Luis R., et al. "Improving the Effectiveness of Performance Appraisal." *Personnel Administrator* 30, no. 1 (January 1985): 74–83.

Henderson, Richard I. *Performance Appraisal.* 2nd ed. Reston, VA: Reston Publishing Company, 1984.

Ilgen, Daniel R., and Favero, Janet L. "Limits in Generalization from Psychological Research to Performance Appraisal Processes." *Academy of Management Review* 10, no. 2 (April 1985): 311–321.

Kreitner, Robert. "PM—A New Method of Behavior Change." *Business Horizons* 18, no. 6 (December 1985): 79–86.

Lanza, Peggy. "Team Appraisals." *Personnel Journal* 64, no. 3 (March 1985): 46–53.

Latham, Gary P., et al. "The Development of Behavioral Observation Scales for Appraising the Performance of Foremen." *Personnel Psychology* 32, no. 2 (1979): 299–311.

———— and Steele, Timothy P. "The Motivational Effects of Participation vs. Goal Setting on Performance." *Academy of Management Journal* 26, no. 3 (September 1983): 406–417.

———— and Wexley, K. N. *Increasing Productivity Through Performance Appraisal.* Reading, MA: Addison-Wesley, 1981.

Lee, Cynthia. "Increasing Performance Appraisal Effectiveness: Matching Task Types, Appraisal Process, and Rater Training." *Academy of Management Review* 10, no. 2 (April 1985): 322–331.

Lefton, Robert E. "Performance Appraisals: Why They Go Wrong and How to Do Them Right." *National Productivity Review* 5, no. 1 (Winter 1985–86): 54–63.

Levine, Hermine Zagat. "Performance Appraisals at Work." *Personnel* 63, no. 6 (June 1986): 63–71.

Licker, Paul S. "The Automated Office and Performance Appraisal." *Personnel* 64, no. 7 (July 1987): 14–20.

Longenecker, Clinton O., et al. "Behind the Mask: The Politics of Employee Appraisal." *The Academy of Management Executive* 1, no. 3 (August 1987): 183–193.

Lowe, Terry R. "8 Ways to Ruin a Performance Review." *Personnel Journal* 65, no. 1 (January 1986): 60–63.

Martin, David C. "Performance Appraisal, 2: Improving the Rater's Effectiveness." *Personnel* 63, no. 8 (August 1986): 28–33.

Naffziger, Douglas W. "BARS, RJPs, and Recruiting." *Personnel Administrator* 32, no. 2 (August 1985): 85–96.

Nathan, Barry R., and Alexander, Ralph A. "The Role of Inferential Accuracy in Performance Rating." *Academy of Management Review* 10, no. 1 (January 1985): 109–115.

Oliver, John E. "Performance Appraisals that Fit." *Personnel Journal* 64, no. 6 (June 1985): 66–71.

Read, Paul R., and Kroll, Mark J. "A Two-Perspective Approach to Performance Appraisal." *Personnel* 62, no. 10 (October 1985): 51–57.

Romberg, Roberta V. "Performance Appraisal, 1: Risks and Rewards." *Personnel* 63, no. 8 (August 1986): 20–41.

Shapiro, Gloria L., and Dessies, Gary. "Are Self-Appraisals More Realistic Among Professionals or Nonprofessionals in Health Care?" *Public Personnel Management* 14, no. 3 (Fall 1985): 285–292.

Shore, Lynn McFarlane, and Bloom, Arvid J. "Developing Employees through Coaching and Career Development." *Personnel* 63, no. 8 (August 1986): 34–41.

Slattery, Paul D. "Performance Appraisal Without Stress." *Personnel Journal* 64, no. 2 (February 1985): 49–52.

Slusher, E. Allen, and Sims, Henry P. "The Practice of Business Commitment through MBO Interviews." *Business Horizons* 18, no. 2 (April 1985): 5–12.

Smith, David E. "Training Programs for Performance Appraisal: A Review." *Academy of Management Review* 11, no. 1 (January 1986): 22–40.

Steel, Brent S. "Participative Performance Appraisal in Washington: An Assessment of Post-Implementation Receptivity." *Public Personnel Management* 14, no. 2 (Summer 1985): 153–171.

Waldman, David A., and Avolio, Bruce J. "A Meta-Analysis of Age Differences in Job Performance." *Journal of Applied Psychology* 71, no. 1 (February 1986): 33–38.

Weitzel, William. "How to Improve Performance through Successful Appraisals." *Personnel* 64, no. 10 (October 1987): 18–23.

Woods, James G., and Dillion, Theresa. "The Performance Review Approach to Improving Productivity." *Personnel* 62, no. 3 (March 1985): 20–27.

Young, Stanley. "Politicking: the Unsung Managerial Skill." *Personnel* 64, no. 6 (June 1987): 62–68.

Individual and Group Incentives

12

An incentive is supposed to be something that incites or stimulates a person toward action, and so-called incentive plans have been initiated to bring about such a result. But the label is no guarantee that the plan will provide a real incentive. And many other pay elements without the label may in fact have an incentive effect. Such an effect can arise from almost any kind of job improvement—an increase in base pay, a promotion, the receipt of a fringe benefit such as a suggestion award, or even changes without money value, such as a new supervisor or more interesting work to do.

The term *incentive* is often overworked when applied to such programs as stock option plans, which will be described separately in Chapter 14. But there are two kinds of pay arrangements where the term *incentive* is certainly more meaningful, even if the plans do not bring forth the desired result. The first, a form of base pay, is most frequently referred to as incentive pay. The second is extra pay *in addition* to base pay and is often called a bonus. Both types of pay arrangements will be simply referred to here as incentive plans.

Incentive pay is distinguished from other forms of compensation in that it is an extra reward for extra effort. This typically means payment is based wholly or partly on output rather than on time. Incentive plans can be based on individual or group output.

In this chapter we shall first consider the overall motivation models developed according to expectancy theory. Then, we shall explore individual incentives in private industry, individual incentives in the federal government, and group incentives. We shall conclude with a few general observations on incentive plans.

Expectancy Theory

Expectancy theory attempts to explain motivation of an individual in a work environment. The theory approaches this problem in two ways: relating levels of effort to levels of output, and relating levels of output to specific rewards. Highly individualistic, expectancy theory relies greatly on people's perceptions.[1]

Victor Vroom's early version of the theory was comprised of two models: the behavioral choice model and the valence model. A hypothetical example of the valence model is illustrated in Figure 12–1.

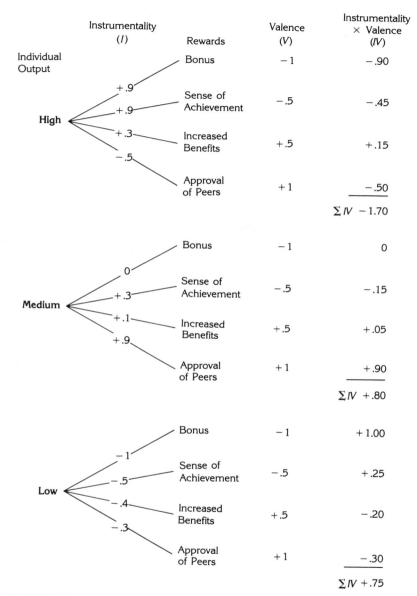

FIGURE 12–1
A hypothetical illustration of expectancy theory.

To understand the valence model, we must understand two new concepts: instrumentality and valence. I shall define these concepts using Figure 12–1 as an illustration. It shows, for example, that for a high level of individual output a reward in the form of a bonus has a perceived instrumentality of +.9, while approval of peers in this situation shows an instrumentality of $-.5$. Instrumentality

> is defined conceptually by Vroom as the degree to which the person sees the outcome in question as leading to the attainment of other outcomes. Instrumentality varies from minus one (meaning that the outcome in question is perceived as always *not* leading to the attainment of the second outcome) to plus one (meaning that the outcome is perceived as *always* leading to the attainment of the second outcome).[2]

Thus, in Figure 12–1 we see that a high level of output (a first level of outcome) is perceived by the worker as having a high instrumentality toward getting a reward (a second level of outcome) in the form of a bonus. On the other hand, the same high output level is perceived as having a negative instrumentality toward gaining peer approval. In contrast, a medium level of output is viewed as highly instrumental in obtaining the approval of peers, but as having no instrumentality (neither plus nor minus) in obtaining a bonus. And, of course, a low level of output is viewed as having negative instrumentality in achievement of a bonus or other rewards.

The desirability of a particular level of output depends not only on instrumentalities but on valence. Valence, as conceived by Vroom, is the anticipated satisfaction from an outcome,[3] to be measured, once more, on a scale running from -1 to $+1$. Thus, the hypothetical worker in Figure 12–1 anticipates much satisfaction from approval of peers, strong dissatisfaction with getting a bonus and some degree of dissatisfaction toward having a sense of achievement.

To obtain the figures on the right side of Figure 12–1, multiply the instrumentality by the valence. For example, for high output, the instrumentality of $+.9$ for bonus multiplied by the bonus valence of -1 results in a figure (*IV*) of $-.90$. The $+1$ result for bonus at a low output is justifiable; to the worker, a bonus has a negative valence and a negative instrumentality. Thus, the contribution of a bonus to the value of the option of low output should be positive, which it is. For each output level, total the *IV*s. It is apparent that for this particular worker a medium level of output has the greatest (weighted) valence and therefore would be the most desirable level. However, for a *different* worker both valences and instrumentalities would probably differ. This might well change the decision as to the most desirable output level.

The processing of variables in Vroom's other model—the behavioral choice model—is analogous to that in the valence model, but the components are different. The behavioral choice model relates levels of effort to individual output levels in terms of expectancies rather than instrumentalities, and it applies valences to individual output levels rather than rewards. Expectancy is defined by Vroom as an individual's belief concerning the probability that the behavior in question will be followed by the outcome of interest. An expectancy is a perceived probability and therefore ranges from 0 to $+1$.[4]

As in the valence model, cross-multiply the data and sum the products for each level of effort. The effort level with the highest sum is the one with the greatest motivational force.

The advantages of expectancy theory include its great allowance for individual differences, its decision-making approach, and its detailed structuring of the motivation process.[5]

There are also some weaknesses in the two theoretical structures:

1. They may be too mathematically complex. For example, their multiplicative features may make these models less predictive than additive models.[6]
2. There is some question as to whether the two models are logically interrelated.
3. The models may be too static, with not enough consideration given to longitudinal studies.
4. They may also be too rigid when first level outcomes are considered. Production levels cannot always be controlled by the employee; that is, the models may apply better to incentive pay than to workers on hourly pay.

Both types of work situations—incentive pay and hourly pay—have been examined using expectancy theory. For example, Dale Jorgenson, Marvin Dunnette, and Robert Pritchard

manipulated performance-outcome instrumentality by paying employees in a temporary situation created for purposes of the experiment on either an hourly basis (low instrumentality) or a type of piece rate (high instrumentality). After individuals had worked for three four-hour days under their respective pay systems, each group switched to the other system and worked for three more days. The data indicated that people under the high instrumentality pay system performed higher than those under the low instrumentality system for the first three days. Furthermore, immediately following the shift in pay systems, and for all three subsequent days, the performance of subjects who were shifted to the high instrumentality system was higher than their performance under the low instrumentality system and higher than the performance of those subjects who were shifted to the low instrumentality system.[7]

Individual Incentives in Private Industry

Individual incentives in private industry will be discussed in terms of (1) merit pay increases, (2) piece rates and related systems, (3) the Lincoln Electric Company plan, (4) IBM and incentive pay, and (5) incentive plans for sales personnel.

Merit Pay Increases

According to expectancy theory, the employee has to believe both that extra effort will result in extra accomplishment and that extra accomplishment (performance) will be highly instrumental in getting extra pay, promotions, and other rewards. David Belcher sees management as communicating a rather ambiguous message:

> Most organizational rewards (both pay and others) are tied to remaining with the organization and exhibiting certain task behaviors required by the job; such rewards are often called system rewards. Only part of the rewards is tied to results or accomplishments. As system rewards become a larger proportion of the total, the less difference . . . extra effort can make. . . . Almost all organizations add pay increases to the wage or salary (thus adding to the proportion of system rewards) instead of paying separately for accomplishment when it is earned.[8]

In the past, pay increases have generated much confusion. For most companies, changes in pay levels (excluding those related to promotions) have involved one or more of the following: across-the-board or general increases, escalator or COLA (cost-of-living allowance) adjustments, seniority or time-in-grade increases, and merit increases. Managements often have not been honest with employees about the nature of the increase. Especially during periods of inflation an employee may think he is getting a merit increase, but if the only increase is less than the change in the cost-of-living index, serious doubts arise as to the role of merit. Some consultants are pessimistic indeed about the value of merit pay if considered as the conventional pay increase. For example, Michael Nash states

> I would like to see us drop the hypocrisy of saying that merit pay motivates. I don't think that merit pay motivates at all. Except for hard-number kinds of measures, such as return on investment, etc. it is difficult to evaluate performance. Think of all the "mechanistics" that you go through to distinguish between an average employee and a distinguishable, commendable and competent performer—when the end result is that someone gets an eight percent as opposed to a six percent salary increase. Forget merit pay. It's more trouble that it's worth.[9]

More recently, with lessened inflation and increased foreign competition, the matter of merit has taken a different turn. There is more talk about lump sum bonuses or merit increases. The American Compensation Association salary budget survey for 1987 indicated that only 8 percent of respondents granted lump sum increases. But of those granting such increases, only one out of eight companies added the increase to the base salary; seven out of eight firms did *not!*[10] In a survey conducted by the Conference Board covering 330 companies, the corresponding ratio was about 7 out of 10 companies. Again, companies are cutting back on fixed forms of compensation while increasing the flexible portion. Another of the findings in the Conference Board survey is less encouraging. Of their respondents, 99 percent say they have a traditional merit increase program, either alone or with a lump sum arrangement.[11] It looks as though most managers are still wedded to the traditional merit increases, few being willing to try a lump sum arrangement.

Some of the confusion could result from different use of terminology. The Conference Board study uses the term *lump sum option* to describe only lump sum merit increases that later are added to base pay, while ACA includes under *lump sum* both those that are added and those that are not. Both types are paid immediately (not paid out at regular pay period intervals), based on the idea that the closer a bonus payout is to the time during which it is earned the greater the motivational force.

Piece-Rate and Related Systems

Pay dependent on individual output takes the form of piece rates and related devices. In the piece-rate system the stress is directly on output, whereas the emphasis is on time in the standard hour plan, which is described by Pinhas Schwinger:

> An estimate is made of the time needed for the average skilled worker, working at a normal pace, to complete one unit of output. . . . This time is set as the "standard" time for a unit of output. If the work is finished within the standard time, the worker's wage is standard time × the hourly wage. If the work takes longer than the standard time, the worker's salary is: the actual time × the hourly wage. . . . For example, if the allowed time is 6 hours and the worker finished his task in 4.5 hours, his salary will be: 6 × the hourly wage (even though the actual time is only 4.5 hours).[12]

Even though it is stated in terms of time saved rather than in terms of units turned out, this plan is identical in its *results* to a piece-rate plan using a fixed piece rate (to be described later in this chapter).

In still other plans the emphasis is on cooperation. An example is the Lincoln Electric Company plan, which we will discuss later, even though a piece rate is still an important feature of the plan.

Most piece-rate and related plans involve (1) the setting of a normal or standard level of performance, (2) a guaranteed minimum level of pay, and (3) some way of relating the piece rate to the level of output. The normal or standard level of performance typically is determined by engineers using techniques such as time and motion study. After engineers scientifically break a job down into its elements, they use stopwatches to find the length of time it takes to perform the different elements. After allowances are made for rest periods, personal time off, and so on, engineers try to set a normal or standard time for the job, assuming an average worker producing at normal speed. The guaranteed rate is typically paid at a level of output below or at that level. Above it, the higher piece rates come into effect. We shall consider falling, fixed, and rising piece rates as well as union views about piece-rate and related plans.

Falling Piece Rates

Some of the early plans, including the Halsey 50–50 plan and the Rowan plan, involved falling piece rates. Table 12–1 illustrates the effect of falling rates. The rate drops from $.025 per piece at an output of 100 pieces to $.020 per piece at the 200-piece level. The worker's earnings nevertheless increase from $2.50 to $4.00 per hour—an increase of 60 percent for doubling production.

Notice that in this case the decrease in piece rates is slight. There are two reasons why it can hardly be otherwise. One is the actual arithmetic of the plan; for example, if the interval between rates were 2 mills (tenths of a cent) rather than 1 mill, the earnings of the 200-piece level would actually be dropping from the two previous levels of output. The other reason is that even a 60 percent hike in wages in return for a 100 percent increase in output may be weak in motivating the worker, and the desired higher levels of output simply may not be forthcoming.

If the system does motivate the worker, not only does the worker get increased earnings, but with a declining piece rate management is assured of a declining unit labor cost. This is only part of management's gain, however. It is assumed here and in Tables 12–2 and 12–3 that there is an overhead (O.H.) cost of $100 per worker. As shown in the fourth column of Table 12–1, this amounts to $1.00 per piece at the 100-piece level, but only $.50 per piece at the 200-piece level of output. When the piece rate in the second column, which is the unit labor cost, and the overhead cost per piece are added together, the total cost per piece is found (ignoring the material cost, which is assumed to be constant throughout). Under this system, the total cost per piece declines from $1.025 to $.520. This figure is important because it can mean increased sales and profits for management, with perhaps some of the gain being passed on to the consumer through lower prices.

TABLE 12–1
Falling piece rate system.

No. of Pieces	Piece Rate	Worker's Earnings	Per Piece	
			O.H. Cost	Total Cost
100	$.025	$2.50	$1.000	$1.025
120	.024	2.88	.833	.857
140	.023	3.22	.714	.737
160	.022	3.52	.625	.647
180	.021	3.78	.556	.577
200	.020	4.00	.500	.520

TABLE 12–2
Fixed piece rate system.

No. of Pieces	Piece Rate	Worker's Earnings	Per Piece O.H. Cost	Per Piece Total Cost
100	$.025	$2.50	$1.000	$1.025
120	.025	3.00	.833	.858
140	.025	3.50	.714	.739
160	.025	4.00	.625	.650
180	.025	4.50	.556	.581
200	.025	5.00	.500	.525

Fixed Piece Rates

Next, let us assume that the piece rate is fixed, a characteristic of straight piece work, standard hour, and Bedaux systems. This approach eliminates one advantage to management—a reduced unit labor cost. The worker, however, will benefit by doubling earnings from $2.50 to $5.00 per hour at the same time that production increases from 100 to 200 pieces (Table 12–2).

Under this system the worker has more motivation, which means that there is at least greater probability of achieving the desired output. The $100 of overhead per worker is still spread over the same number of pieces produced, so management retains that advantage. Total cost per piece also declines as output increases from the 100- to the 200-piece level. Because it is simple and easy to understand and appears to be a fairer plan, fixed piece-rate plans are more often successfully installed and less often opposed by unions than falling piece-rate plans. Furthermore, management still benefits from reduced unit costs.

Rising Piece Rates

A rising piece rate system is illustrated in Table 12–3. Earnings at the 200-piece level are 4 times as large as those at the starting level. As with fixed piece rates,

TABLE 12–3
Rising piece rate system.

No. of Pieces	Piece Rate	Worker's Earnings	Per Piece O.H. Cost	Per Piece Total Cost
100	$.025	$ 2.50	$1.000	$1.025
120	.030	3.60	.833	.863
140	.035	4.90	.714	.749
160	.040	6.40	.625	.665
180	.045	8.10	.556	.601
200	.050	10.00	.500	.550

management lacks the advantage of a declining unit labor cost, but keeps the advantage of spreading overhead cost over more units of production. The overall result is that total cost per piece drops from $1.025 to $.55. Moreover, this increase in production is far more likely to be realized because the system gives a greater incentive to the worker. Notice that management gains even with a *rising* piece rate. In other words, the fall in overhead cost per unit is more than enough to offset the rising unit labor cost or piece rate.

Union Views

Many, if not most, unions oppose piece-rate plans. Lloyd Reynolds points out some drawbacks of these plans—specifically, the tendency of management to retime a job and reduce the piece rate, and the resulting tendency of workers to hold back on output by exerting social pressure against the more efficient workers for the maintenance of artificially low group norms. As he sees it, the critical aspects of the plan are who controls setting the piece rate and how changes in the rates are handled.[13]

Reynolds describes group social pressure, the other factor, in this way:

> There is a tendency of incentive workers to hold down production at all times, and for different workers on a job to maintain about the same rate of output. Workers who rise much above the accepted rate are called "speed artists," "company men," and other uncomplimentary names. Unless they desist from their high rate of production, they are likely to find that things happen to their machines, that wrenches fall accidentally on their heads, and that they are ostracized by their fellows. The result is that incentive systems usually fail to obtain maximum effort from the faster workers.[14]

One survey of opinion among labor union leaders reveals sharply contrasting union attitudes about incentive pay systems.[15] At one extreme, six of the thirteen responding unions indicated strong opposition to incentive pay plans. This viewpoint was voiced by an officer in the Bakery and Confectionery Workers' Union:

> Incentive plans, whether group or individual, are devices designed by companies trying to keep costs of production down. Group plans have as their basis the idea of pitting worker against worker for the benefit of the employer. Until such a time arrives that will see incentive plans designed solely for the benefit of employees, which we don't anticipate, we will be opposed to the introduction of new incentive plans.

At the other extreme, a few very large unions appear to favor incentive plans, even to the point of pushing for increased coverage. For example, the United Steelworkers Union reported that in the basic steel industry the union was instrumental in extending coverage from 55 percent to 87 percent of the employees as the result of a labor arbitration decison. Its latest contract with USX includes definitions of direct incentive, indirect incentive, and no-incentive jobs. It specifies that a job does not qualify for incentive only

> (1) if there is no realistic opportunity to make an appreciable contribution to production or to efficiency by performance above non-incentive performance, or, (2) if the costs to the Company of installation and adequate administration of an incentive are excessive in relation to the cost benefits that should be achieved by an incentive.

The United Steelworkers contracts provide that incentive standards are expressed in standard hours. As I pointed out earlier, *standard hours* refers to hours to be paid for at the standard hourly wage rate. For example, if 1.0 hour per piece is the standard, and 12 pieces were produced in an 8-hour turn (shift), 12 hours would be earned. The extra 4 hours paid would mean 50 percent incentive earnings for the turn.

In the International Ladies' Garment Workers' Union (ILGWU) over 80 percent of the employees are paid on a piecework basis, which has been traditional in the needle trades. Under the union contract covering workers in the New York area, not only does the union share jointly with management the control over incentive pay installation and administration, but the workers are protected in several other significant ways:

1. Minimum hourly rates for each craft (such as operators and pressers, skirt operators and skirt pressers, finishers, machine pressers, and skirt finishers) provide an income floor.
2. Such minimum rates are required to be at least 15 percent higher than the federal minimum wage and must change with any change in the minimum wage law.
3. A second set of minimum hourly rates applies to a worker of average skill.
4. Under rules determined jointly by labor and management, eligible workers are also paid a semiannual bonus.

Despite the differences among unions about incentives, there seems to be a common union philosophy. Many unions oppose incentive pay plans, but where plans already exist they attempt either to participate jointly with management, at least in the administration of the plan, or alternatively to protect their members from the plan's adverse effects through collective bargaining. Protection is sought through specific contract provisions, existing grievance procedures, or arbitration. A leader in the Boilermakers Union states that

> philosophically the union is opposed to wage incentive programs as set forth in the Constitution. Where they exist we try to negotiate and administer effective protective language.[16]

While generally opposed to incentive plans, the Graphic Arts Union, in its latest contract with Mead Products, omits disputes over incentive pay standards from the grievance procedure and provides instead that a joint standing committee of three union and three management representatives shall work out such disputes on request. Under another provision of the contract, either party can submit an unresolved dispute about standards to arbitration.

The president of the International Brotherhood of Electrical Workers (IBEW) explains at length the union's philosophy:

> The IBEW is opposed to the use of wage incentive systems and has made an extensive effort to make our local unions aware of the many problems that result in the use and misuse of such systems. One of the major problems with wage incentive systems is the establishment of production standards using work measurement techniques, such as stop-watch time studies, standard data, and predetermined work measurement systems. I am sure you realize the great amount of subjective judgment that is involved in the development and application of the work measurement systems. . . . The IBEW has organized many manufacturing plants that have had wage incentive plans in existence at the time the plants were organized. For this reason the IBEW maintains an Industrial Engineering Section within our Research and Education Department which provides training and field assistance to our local unions and field staff representatives in an attempt to minimize the harmful effects of the systems.[17]

The president of the Amalgamated Meat Cutters Union cites two other restraints built into union policies and practices regarding incentive pay plans:

1. We have always insisted that incentive pay be in direct proportion to increased output. In other words, a one percent increase in output above a guaranteed daywork base should always be rewarded by a one percent increase in basic pay.
2. In our contracts we have sought always to maintain established levels of earning opportunity when jobs are changed by changed equipment, methods, materials, or other conditions. This has meant that our collective bargaining agreements specify that where a job has been changed, only the changed elements of the job may be retimed.[18]

The Lincoln Electric Company Plan

For many years, the Lincoln Electric Company, a nonunion firm, has had an individual incentive plan which has brought the company so much success that it now manufactures over 40 percent of the arc welding equipment and supplies in the United States in the face of unsuccessful competition by such giants as Westinghouse and General Electric.

Just how effective the company has been as a whole can be gleaned from several facts. Since 1935 some of the company's product prices have increased only 30 percent, while wholesale commodity prices in the United States have gone up around 300 percent. Output per worker in the same period at Lincoln has climbed roughly 600 percent compared with a rise of only 200 percent for U.S. durable goods industries. Labor turnover rates at Lincoln since 1958 have stayed well below 1 percent, while in the electrical machinery industry the rate has ranged from 3 percent to around 4 percent.

The company's unique philosophy, as expressed by its chief executive officer, William Irrgang (in much the same words as his predecessor, James Finney Lincoln, who started the company's incentive plan), explains its success:

> The success of the Lincoln Electric Company has been built on two basic ideas. One is producing more and more of a progressively better product at a lower and lower price for a larger and larger group of customers. The other is that an employee's earnings and promotion are in direct proportion to his individual contribution toward the company's success.[19]

The Lincoln incentive system includes (1) piece rates for most factory jobs, (2) a year-end bonus, (3) high cash awards for suggestions made by workers, (4) a guarantee of employment for 75 percent of the standard 40-hour week, and (5) an advisory board for top management consisting of elected employees.

Employee's Right to Challenge Rate

An employee has the right to challenge any piece rate. To handle a challenge, the company takes the worker off the piece rate and puts him on a time rate. A committee including the worker, the immediate supervisor, the director of personnel, and a time study specialist takes over. The supervisor checks the job for any changes in method since the original standard was established. If this does not resolve the problem, a more detailed analysis is undertaken; later, if necessary, the specialist demonstrates the correct method for doing the job. If, after discussion, the grievance is still not worked out, the *specialist* performs the job for a day or more. The resulting time he takes to do the job is then accepted as the new standard.[20]

While the year-end bonus is determined for the company as a whole, each worker's share is determined by merit ratings of individuals in each department or work group using the factors of dependability, quality, output, and ideas and cooperation.

IBM and Incentive Pay

Earlier, in the chapter on economic aspects of pay, I related some of the methods used by IBM to reduce excessive supervisory layers, to achieve greater productivity through work force rescheduling, and to encourage redeployment of employees towards their most useful roles within the organization. While these and individual incentive bonuses are all part of a wider effort to compete more effectively internationally, we shall discuss here only IBM's merit and bonus policies.

Despite the weaknesses of merit pay and doubts about its effectiveness in the way it is usually handled, some of the largest American companies, of which IBM is a significant example, have been able to administer merit pay and/or individual bonuses with successful results. While IBM does use performance appraisal, it also stresses constant communication between the manager and the employee. The company strives to administer merit pay so as to allow the employee to influence his earnings while the company maintains cost flexibility. Compared to other merit pay systems, IBM reports that

1. We have variable timing rather than an annual increase.
2. The increase is related directly to performance and, therefore, is earned rather than an entitlement caused by range movement or calendar change.
3. We try to focus on the rate of pay rather than size of the increase.
4. Finally, we use structure limits and maximums to ensure that merit differentials match the individual's contribution.[21]

The size of the awards available is indicated in Table 12–4.

Everyone in the company is eligible for these awards, and in any one year approximately one out of every four employees actually earns an award.[22]

Employee Stock Ownership Plans

Another incentive device that has been increasing in popularity is the Employee Stock Ownership Plan (ESOP). It has been possible for years for company employees (especially of publicly held corporations) to obtain shares of stock in their own companies, whether management liked it or not. And many companies have had stock purchase plans to encourage employee stock ownership by selling stock at a slight discount.

The more recent Employee Stock Ownership plans have had the advantage of more favorable tax treatment. In the 1970s, Congress created the tax-credit ESOP (then called a TRASOP), which benefited only firms undertaking eligible investment projects. In 1983, the Tax Credit Stock Ownership Plan (PAYSOP) superceded tax-credit ESOPs. Under the PAYSOP, the employer received a tax credit for stock contributions and the employee was exempt from current taxes on the company contribution. The effective tax subsidy was thus more than 100 percent. In 1986, Congress allowed the PAYSOP to expire. However, in 1984, a

TABLE 12–4
Individual merit awards at IBM, maximum limit.

Suggestion	$150,000	Outstanding Tech. Achievements	25,000
Informal	1,500	Outstanding Innovation	25,000
Division	25,000	Invention Achievement	3,600
Corporate	No limit		

new provision passed by Congress allowed banks and other institutions lending to an ESOP to deduct half their interest income on such loans from their taxes, and this provision still applies.[23]

Information from the National Center for Employee Ownership indicates the tax incentives provided to ESOPs have been effective. The number of ESOPs has been steadily increasing every year since 1975, as has the cumulative number of employees participating in such plans. The number of plans has increased from 1,600 to well over 8,000 and the number of employees from over 245,000 to close to 8,000,000.[24]

To establish an ESOP a company sets up a trust. For a nonleveraged ESOP here is the mechanics for it:

1. Each year the company gives stock to the ESOP, or gives cash to the ESOP to buy stock. Employees pay nothing.
2. ESOP holds the stock for employees and periodically notifies them how much they own and how much it is worth.
3. Employees collect stock or cash when they retire or otherwise leave the company, according to a vesting schedule.[25]

An alternative type of ESOP, the leveraged ESOP, works in much the same way except that ESOP borrows the money to purchase the company stock. The borrowing works this way:

1. A bank, or other financial institution, lends money to the ESOP with a company guarantee.
2. The ESOP buys stock from the company or from existing shareholders.
3. The company makes annual tax deductible contributions to the ESOP, which in turn repays the bank.
4. Employees collect stock or cash when they retire or leave the company.[26]

Because of tax advantages cited earlier, a leveraged ESOP can be used by a company primarily to raise money at a lower cost.

In other cases ESOPs have been used to thwart unfriendly takeover bids. With enough stock in the hands of the ESOP an unwanted raider can be rebuffed.[27]

Whatever other advantages to ESOPs, Congressional intent in establishing them was to encourage employee stock ownership on the theory that when workers obtain company stock and thus become part owners of the company, they will be motivated to do a better job. The central issue is whether ESOPs do act as incentives. A survey conducted by the ESOP Association in 1987 reported that only 16 percent of responding companies said productivity was strongly improved, although 59 percent said it was somewhat improved.[28] Whether ESOPs are effective in boosting morale and productivity appears to depend on the attitude of company management. Is there an ESOP committee on which rank-and-file employee ESOP participants can air their views? Stated more broadly, does management allow the idea of ownership, even partial ownership, of the company by employees to have real meaning?

Pay Plans for Sales Personnel

The individual incentive plans considered so far have been concerned with productive efficiency. However, other activities, such as marketing, also make use of incentive pay schemes.

William Lazer found that well over four out of five companies use some kind of incentive pay along with salary to compensate salespersons. The form of compensation should be related to the specific sales job to be done; that is, where service or nonsales tasks are important, the fixed element of salary should be supplemented, but where sales depend on personal selling effort, either a commission or a bonus should be used. He adds, however, that most compensation plans combine salary and some form of incentive pay. He attaches little importance to whether the incentive pay should take the form of a commission or a bonus but stresses how a company can tailor the incentive pay to its needs:

> The commission rate may be set as a fixed percentage or a sliding scale. Commissions may vary by product, customer, or level of sales realized. The commission base may also vary. It can be based on gross sales, gross margins, or net profits.[29]

Individual Incentives in the Federal Government

There are two types of incentive systems available to federal employees: merit pay and bonuses under the Civil Service Reform Act of 1978 for managers and senior executives, and awards under the Federal Incentive Awards Program passed by Congress in 1954 and signed by President Eisenhower.

The Civil Service Reform Act of 1978 not only included provisions relating to performance appraisal (see Chapter 11) but included other provisions affecting the pay of two groups: (1) top executives in the Senior Executive Service and (2) federal middle managers (GS-13 through GS-15). Other new provisions covering middle managers became effective in 1984.

Bonuses for Federal Executives

A career executive in the first group can receive a lump sum performance award annually, ranging between 5 and 20 percent of base salary (an opportunity open to approximately half the executives in the group although actual awards have typically fallen short of this goal). The award is based on a supervisor appraisal and must be approved by an agency performance review board composed of senior executives and by the agency head.

A career executive can also receive rank awards following nomination by the agency head and selection by the President. The executive may win a lump sum payment of $10,000 and a designation as a meritorious executive (an opportunity open to 5 percent of the executives); or win a lump sum payment of $20,000 and a designation as a distinguished executive (an opportunity open to only 1 percent of the executives, again with the actual number of awards varying). An executive may receive the same rank award only once every 5 years.

Merit Increases and Performance Awards for Middle Managers

Under the Performance Management and Recognition System, which became effective in October 1984, middle managers in the GS-13 through GS-15 grades can get merit increases and performance awards, in addition to customary general increases, provided they achieve a performance appraisal of "fully successful" or higher. At the lowest rating (two levels below "fully successful") they are not eligible even for a general increase, and at the next lowest rating (one level below "fully successful") they can get only one half of a full general increase.

A merit increase is defined as one ninth of the rate range—the dollar value of one step increase. The middle manager rated "outstanding" (two levels above "fully successful") gets one merit increase regardless of present step within the pay grade. The manager rated "exceeds fully successful" (one level above "fully successful") gets one merit increase if occupying one of the first three steps, but only one-half merit increase if on one of the higher steps. The "fully successful" manager gets one merit increase if on one of the first three steps, but only one-third merit increase if occupying a higher step.

A middle manager will be paid a performance award of not more than 10 percent nor less than 2 percent of base pay if rated "outstanding." An agency head may decide to make the award as much as 20 percent of base pay for "unusually outstanding performance." If rated "exceeds fully successful" or "fully successful" the manager may be paid a performance award, but not more than 10 percent of base pay. Middle managers are also eligible for cash rewards, described under *Productivity Incentive Awards.*

The rest of the professionals, who occupy grades GS-5 through GS-17, receive step increases depending on time in grade if their most recent rating of record is "fully successful" or better. There are extra quality step (nonautomatic) increases, but they are rare.

Productivity Incentive Awards

Under the federal government's incentive awards program, started in 1954 under President Dwight Eisenhower, awards are made to encourage civilian employees to increase productivity and improve the efficiency and economy of government operations. The program provides for both individual and group bonuses, but certain features of the program, which are linked directly with performance appraisal, emphasize individual bonuses. An agency can grant a maximum award of $25,000, whether to an individual or a group. Thus, a group award of $25,000 to five people would mean an award of $5,000 to each individual. But there is little doubt that some group motivation is also achieved by the program through the annual publicity comparing the number and size of awards given to each participating department or agency.

Employee recognition includes nonmonetary awards (such as medals, certificates, and plaques) and monetary recognition through performance awards, quality step increases, special acts or service awards, and awards for suggestions and inventions. The quality step increase involves a step increase in the normal pay intervals for general schedule (GS) employees in addition to the usual step increase. A performance award is a lump sum cash award representing a percentage of the employee's base pay.

Awards for Suggestions, Inventions, and Special Acts or Services

These awards are based on benefits to the government. The amount of the award is calculated on an estimate of the dollar benefits for the first year of use of the contribution, as can be seen in Table 12–5.

This arrangement would seem to encourage small rather than large innovations. Where tangible benefits for the first year are only $1,000, the award is 10 percent, but where the benefits are as great as $1,000,000, the award is less than 1 percent. Awards over $10,000 require the approval of the Office of Personnel Management, which can approve awards up to $25,000. However, the President may approve an additional amount for an even greater award.

Awards for Suggestions Resulting in Intangible Benefits

An award can also be made for suggestions resulting in intangible benefits (Table 12–6). The award is based on both the value of the benefit and the extent of application. Awards vary from a low of $25 to a high of $10,000, which is the highest that can be awarded at the department or agency level. Higher awards up to a maximum of $25,000 can be made but have to be approved by the Office of Personnel Management.

TABLE 12–5
Incentive awards for suggestions resulting in tangible benefits to the U.S. federal government.

Estimated Benefit	Award	Percentage of Estimated Benefit
$1,000	$ 100	10.0%
10,000	1,000	10.0
50,000	2,200	4.4
100,000	3,700	3.7
500,000	5,700	1.1
1,000,000	8,200	0.8
1,400,000	10,200*	0.7
4,360,000	25,000**	0.6

*Awards over $10,000 require the approval of the Office of Personnel Management.
**Maximum award authorized by the Office of Personnel Management. A presidential award may be paid in addition to the $25,000.
Source: U.S. Office of Personnel Management, *Federal Personnel Manual*, August 14, 1981, p. 451-C-1.

TABLE 12–6
Incentive awards for suggestions resulting in intangible benefits to the U.S. federal government.

Value of Benefit	Extent of Application			
	Limited	Extended	Broad	General
Moderate	$ 25–100	$ 100–250	$ 250–500	$ 500–1,000
Substantial	100–250	250–500	500–1,000	1,000–2,500
High	250–500	500–1,000	1,000–2,500	2,500–5,000
Exceptional	500–1,000	1,000–2,500	2,500–5,000	5,000–10,000

Source: U.S. Office of Personnel Management, *Federal Personnel Manual,* August 14, 1981, p. 451-C-3.

The categories of limited, extended, broad, or general application are carefully specified. For example, a limited application affects the functions, mission, or personnel of one office facility, installation, or organizational element of a headquarters, or it affects a small area of science or technology. At the other extreme, a general benefit affects the functions, mission, or personnel of several regional areas or commands or an entire department or large independent agency, or it is in the public interest throughout the nation or beyond.

The value of the benefit to the government is also carefully specified. Moderate value involves change or modification of an operating principle or procedure which has moderate value sufficient to meet the minimum standards for a cash award, or an improvement of rather limited value of a product, activity, program, or service to the public. A suggestion of exceptional value is the initiation of a new principle or major procedure or a superior improvement to the quality of a critical product, activity, program, or service to the public.

Combination Awards

In certain situations a contribution may have both tangible and intangible benefits to the government. In this case the amount of the award is based on the total value of the contribution to the government—a combination of the award amount based on tangible and the award amount based on intangible benefits. Further details for the federal incentive award system are described in the *Federal Personnel Manual.*

Group Incentives

While international competitive conditions appear to have encouraged a new look at the value of individual incentive plans, group incentive plans also have a role to play. Before exploring the wider based plans, we shall consider small group plans based on the skills approach.

Pay for Skills and the Small Group

In a longer range historical view, the idea of pay for increased skills is not new at all. It came about largely in the old craft unions. For example, a carpenter's apprentice was paid less than the journeyman carpenter, but through considerable training both in classes and on the job, over a period of time the apprentice could also become a journeyman at the same higher level of pay. The more recent approach to pay for skill involves small work groups and a type of decentralization of authority that tends to lessen the need for middle managers. Rosabeth Moss Kanter describes how one "pay for skill" plan works in a leading consumer goods company:

> Teams have responsibility for all aspects of production: operating the machinery, working with suppliers, inspecting the product for conformance to quality standards, and keeping records . . . Pay grows as the newcomer moves from entry to full team member . . . The real increases occur as the new team member progresses through as many as several dozen "skill blocks." The skill blocks move from general orientation (learning plant, operating hand tools, doing the simplest jobs, etc.) to on-the-job and classroom training to learn all aspects of one production process. Advanced operating skills involve the knowledge of more than one process. The multiskills requirement adds such skills as machine maintenance, quality control . . . and problem solving and leadership skills . . . All of this may occur within five years.[30]

Kanter reports that the results are a 30 to 50 percent reduction in unit costs, and in addition,

> Considerable savings are realized by eliminating a large number of supervisory jobs as the teams take on more and more functions (inspection, purchasing, record keeping) that would otherwise be performed by supervisors and specialized staffs at higher pay.[31]

At least one observer questions how far pay for knowledge systems will go. O'Dell says they are being used for craft production employees but not for engineers or scientists, for example.[32]

Companywide and Plantwide Group Plans

There are many differences among group incentive plans. Germany and the Scandinavian countries use codetermination (or *mitbestimmungsrecht*). Akin to this plan, but in certain respects markedly different, are the workers' councils in Yugoslavia and even the communes in the People's Republic of China. The particular features that encourage group performance in Japanese industrial firms are similar to those in what are considered to be group incentive plans in the United States.

Most U.S. group plans can be understood in terms of two broad aspects:

1. The economic arrangement, or how the bonus is determined and how it is distributed.
2. The political arrangement, or the extent of employee participation.

Prominent among U.S. firms' plans are the Scanlon, Rucker, and the National Steel–Steelworker plans.

The Scanlon Plan

One of the most widely used group plans is the Scanlon plan. Joseph Scanlon, an official of the United Steelworkers, developed the plan, which was first put to work at the LaPointe Machine Tool Company, a well-known manufacturer of broaching machines.

Economic Aspects. As can be seen in Figure 12–2, the bonus earned by the group depends on improved efficiency over time. Let us say that for some base period considered to be representative the total payroll was 40 percent of the sales value of production. Once this standard is agreed to, it is easy to determine on a month-to-month basis what the standard payroll figure would be. In the month illustrated in Figure 12–2, this figure turns out to be $80,000. After the actual payroll is computed, a small amount is added to it for a vacation reserve; this gives $60,900 for the adjusted payroll. The adjusted payroll figure is subtracted from the $80,000 standard figure to get an earned bonus of $19,100. However, there will not be a saving every month, so 20 percent is set aside as a reserve

	Latest Month	
Sales value of production		$200,000
Ratio		40%
Payroll at the ratio		$80,000
Actual payroll	$60,000	
Vacation reserve	900	
Adjusted payroll		60,900
Bonus earned		$19,100
Reserve for contingency (20%)		3,820
Bonus		$15,280

FIGURE 12–2
Hypothetical Scanlon plan computations.

for contingencies. The reserve of $3,820 is subtracted from the bonus, leaving $15,280 for immediate distribution. Of this, 25 percent goes back to the company and 75 percent, or $11,460, is the bonus paid out to the workers individually in proportion to their base pay.

Participative Aspects. As can be seen at the bottom of Figure 12–3, the Scanlon plan is designed to let union members and managers share equally in important operating decisions. Each department elects a union member, and management designates a management representative to sit on a 40-member production committee. This committee, composed of 20 management and 20 union representatives, meets twice a month and considers any suggestions about improving production methods, materials, machines, scrap control, and so on. Up to a certain amount of money, the committee can make decisions to put the cost-savings idea into effect. For changes involving larger amounts of money, the ideas are screened by a smaller committee. The screening committee in this example has six members, with the president, vice president of operations, and controller representing management and the president of the union local and two other union representatives speaking for the union.

In any given situation, the structure of committees will vary. For example, each department and each shift within a department can have its own committee. In any case, the idea behind the structure is to avoid the slow and often cumbersome conventional suggestion systems and to favor a direct confrontation of workers and managers under conditions where rational discussion can take place on an equal basis.[33]

Some of the positive things that have been done under Scanlon plans are described by a plant manager in the Parker Pen Company:

> We have generated this give-and-take between the two sides. If you want to tie it down to whether James produced 100 rather than 150 parts, well, it's not going to be that, because it's a group plan—all the way from the vice president down into our plant. Everyone participates. So we feel we can get increased productivity through generating the atmosphere for talking to people and giving them the opportunity to come forward with their ideas.[34]

A union leader at the same company reported that under the former individual incentive plan workers resisted the introduction of new equipment and new methods. But now, he adds,

> We welcome new equipment, because first of all we have an idea of what the company's problems are, and we know what is happening to us. Exactly the same thing was happening to us back in 1954, in terms of holding our place in the pen industry, as has happened in the steel industry, with both foreign and domestic competition getting the best of us. Now we have been able to meet that. We have been able to take home more money. In fact, people love the changes, because we see that jobs don't dry up and disappear.[35]

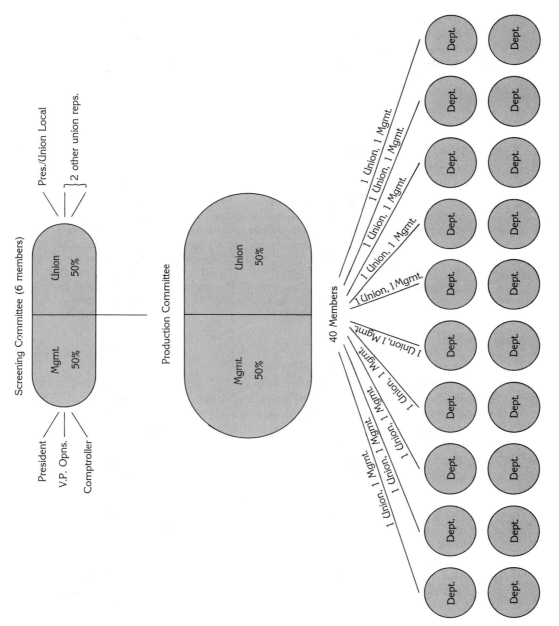

FIGURE 12–3
Organization of Scanlon plan committees.

The ratio of payroll to sales value of production does not necessarily remain fixed indefinitely. As Frances Torbert points out, it is essential to change the ratio if there are (1) price or wage changes, (2) major purchases of labor- or time-saving machinery, or (3) other events of a similar importance. If a change is to be made in the ratio, it is typically agreed upon in a memorandum of understanding.[36]

Use of the Plan in a New Organization. Edward Lawler urges that a Scanlon-type plan not be considered by a newly formed organization until the organization has some degree of predictability and regularity. He cautions that

> this kind of plan undoubtedly will not be applicable to all organizations. Factors that should be considered are organization size, the interdependence of the different operating parts of the organization, and of course the degree to which employees believe it is a desirable compensation system to have. . . . Usually these plans are meaningful only if they can be based on some significant history of operating results. In addition, they can perhaps best be understood and developed by employees after they have had some experience with how the organization operates, what cost data mean, and what they can contribute to greater organizational effectiveness.[37]

Gainsharing at National Steel

Under conditions of severe international competition, as discussed in the earlier chapter on the economic aspects of compensation, many managements have felt the necessity both to cut back employment and increase productivity. A collective bargaining agreement reached between the United Steelworkers of America and National Steel Corporation in 1986 incorporates these features. Under the plan, all full-time active employees can participate in quarterly gainsharing bonuses and an annual cash profit sharing payment.

Quarterly Gainsharing Bonus. Taking first the gainsharing bonuses, a percentage gainsharing score is derived from two factors—productivity improvement and work force improvement. Productivity improvement is measured by the tons of prime product shipped per employee at each location. *Work force* means the total number of actual employees at a location, including overtime equivalents (straight-time overtime hours worked each week, divided by 40 hours). *Productivity* equals the number of prime tons shipped divided by the work force:

$$\text{Productivity} = \frac{\text{Prime Tons Shipped}}{\text{Work Force}}$$

Work force improvement is determined by comparing the average number of employees during the preceding six months with the base number of employees:

Work force improvement =

$$\frac{\text{Base Number of Employees} - \text{Average Number of Employees}}{\text{Base Number of Employees}}$$

Work force improvement is measured both companywide (weighted 50 percent) and at the division level (weighted 20 percent). The remaining 30 percent of the gainsharing score is accounted for by productivity improvement measured only at the division level.

How the quarterly gainsharing bonus is derived is shown in Table 12–7 below.

The table shows that if a division achieves gainsharing of 17 percent, then each employee would earn a quarterly bonus of 5 percent of base pay for the previous three months.

Annual Cash Profitsharing. Turning now to the other half of the plan—the annual cash profit-sharing payment—we can see that union members fare better than their nonunion counterparts. Union members get a bonus of $.50 per hour (even if there is a loss), as can be seen in Table 12–8.[38]

General Considerations

Regardless of whether an organization decides on an individual plan or a group plan, it must consider the financial, operational, and participative aspects of its particular situation.

TABLE 12–7
Gainsharing score and quarterly bonus.

Gainsharing Score	Quarterly Bonus
0–1%	0%
2–5	1
6–8	2
9–12	3
13–15	4
16–19	5
20–22	6
23–26	7
27–29	8
30–33	9
34–36	10
Continuing to a maximum	
58–60	17

TABLE 12–8
Annual cash profit sharing payment.

	Bonus Amounts Per Compensated Hour	
Company Net Income	Hourly	Salaried
Loss	$ .50	$ .00
Break-even to $100 million	.75	.25
$100 million to $200 million	1.00	.50
$200 million to $300 million	1.25	.75
$300 million and up	1.75	1.25

Financial Considerations

The plan chosen must allow for business cycle changes that may result in irregular earnings or output. Thus, the organization should set aside a certain percentage of profits to allow for growth before profit sharing takes place. Also, it is advantageous to devise a method of funding to maintain payments to the employees even if employer contributions to the fund are irregular.

Operational Considerations

An operational limitation exists when a company's production flow or inventory storage capacity prevents it from achieving maximum outputs. This situation limits or perhaps even precludes the use of incentive pay.

Participative Considerations

Finally, both individual incentive plans and the various group plans require employee participation. Where both management *and* workers can jointly determine the structure of the incentive plan and participate in its administration, the plan is more likely to succeed.

Summary

The incentive label is no guarantee of motivation and many another factor, lacking the label, may nevertheless provide a meaningful incentive. Where incentive bonuses are based primarily on salary or rank, they can be said to be hierarchical. But in general, incentives plans are intended to relate pay to performance.

Expectancy theory attempts to explain motivation in terms of valences, expectancies, and instrumentalities. The valence model and the behavioral choice model rely greatly on people's perceptions of how levels of effort relate to levels of output and how levels of output relate to specific rewards. Whether such mechanistic explanations of complex human motivation are operational in the real world is open to question.

Incentive pay as pay for production is the alternative to pay for time (hourly or other). Or incentive pay can take the form of a merit increase in base pay or an addition to base pay in the form of a bonus.

Unfortunately, there is some tendency for the worker to look at any pay increase as being a merit increase when it actually may be for seniority, for increased cost of living, or simply a general increase—and management often does not make this matter clear.

The recent tendency has been toward use of lump sum merit increases, which may or may not result in an increase in base pay. The argument against increasing base pay due to merit is to keep tighter control over the fixed part of pay. The increase can be considered a one-time payment, and another such payment requires renewed performance by the employee.

Immediate payment of the lump sum amount tends to add motivational force by more closely relating pay to time of performance.

Individual plans in industry typically involve (1) setting a standard level of performance, (2) guaranteeing a minimum level of pay, and (3) relating the piece rate to the level of output. Slightly declining piece rates allow management to control costs better but do not motivate workers well. Fixed or rising piece rates still allow management to benefit from lower overhead costs per unit and yet provide increased motivation for the worker.

Unions, though often opposed to the installation of individual (and even group) plans, are more pragmatic about plans already in effect. They protect their members against adverse effects of such plans through collective bargaining, grievance procedures, or arbitration.

There are many other types of individual incentive plans. One of the most successful individual plans is the Lincoln incentive system. A special feature of the Lincoln Plan is the employee's right to challenge any piece rate.

Among the larger companies, IBM relies heavily both on pay for performance and a wide variety of individual incentives. It attempts to administer pay so as to allow the employee to determine his earnings while the company maintains cost flexibility.

Since the mid-1970s, Employee Stock Ownership Plans have become more important both among larger and smaller companies. In some instances companies have used such plans primarily as a way of raising money or as a way of repelling raiders in a leveraged takeover bid. If either of these is the situation, the plan is less likely to motivate employees. However, where management sets up an ESOP committee and treats employee shareowners, even if they are not in the majority, as important participants in running the company, then morale, productivity, and company profitability often are substantially increased.

Individual plans for sales personnel usually include a combination of salary and a commission or bonus.

In the federal government, career executives are eligible for bonuses and other awards. Middle managers can compete for merit increases and performance awards and can also participate in the productivity incentive award program.

Group incentive plans can be used for both smaller and larger groups. Small group plans based on pay for skills have been used to provide a combination of individual with group motivation, a means of obtaining a high degree of personal commitment, and significant reductions in operating costs.

Group incentives plans for larger groups are characterized by their economic and political aspects. The Scanlon plan, one of the most widely used group plans, bases the workers' earned bonus on improved efficiency over time. The bonus is computed using a ratio of payroll to sales value of production. Its political structure is such that management and union members share in decision making and administration of the plan.

Recently, gainsharing plans have generated new interest. Under the plan negotiated between National Steel and the United Steelworkers of America, full-time active employees can participate in quarterly gainsharing bonuses as well as annual cash profit sharing. Gainsharing is based on productivity improvement and work force reduction. The plan measures work force improvement both companywide and at the division level, while productivity improvement is measured only at the division level.

Companies that are deciding on an incentive plan need to consider certain financial, operational, and participative aspects of their particular situation. Financial aspects to consider are the degree of regularity of profits over the years in the industry as well as the best method of funding the plan. It is also desirable to examine how the plan will affect the production process so that production imbalances or excessive inventories are not created. There must be sufficient production capability to achieve the maximum outputs provided for by the plan so that the workers are not discouraged. Plans providing for participation of both management and workers (through the union or otherwise) tend to be more successful.

Case Study

Pinkney Metal Products

Pinkney Metal Products, located in a suburban industrial park outside the large metropolitan area of Pinkney, New York, is a job shop employing 50 machinists who are paid an hourly wage rate. Despite the large variety of jobs done, the shop keeps busy, thanks to two salespersons and the company's president, who are out on the road much of the time. The shop superintendent, Anton Wenschek, is a former machinist from a rival firm. He is in his early 70s and has been on the job for the last 6 months.

The machinists are highly skilled workers ranging from 40 to 60 years of age and whose average length of service with the company is 10 years or more.

For the shop as a whole, company President Juan Raimundo believes productivity is about average for the industry. However, the average hourly earnings of the machinists are slightly higher than the going rates in the Pinkney area.

With these thoughts in mind, the president decided to have a time-study expert check out some of the machinists on certain of the production runs. He planned to have the study begin on March 13, a day when it so happened that he was to be out of town attending a sales convention. Also, Anton Wenschek reported in sick that morning, leaving one of the foremen in charge.

Shortly after most of the machinists had started work, a young man in his 20s wearing a dark business suit came in and looked around at the production layout. He stopped near one of the machinists who was working on a turret lathe and introduced himself, adding that he had been asked to do some time studies. When the worker appeared skeptical, the young man said, "That's all right, you don't have to do a thing differently. Just keep on doing what you're doing now and I'll jot down the information I need." The machinist shrugged his shoulders and went back to work. The young man pulled out a stop watch. At this point one of the other machinists came over to the turret-lathe operator and whispered in his ear, "This character looks like a troublemaker. Better slow it down." The turret-lathe operator winked knowingly as the other machinist went back to his own machine. Meanwhile the young man, observing the end of the production run and the operator reaching for a new piece of stock to position on the lathe, clicked his stop watch and began to observe the new run.

The next day in his office, President Juan Raimundo discussed with the young man the results of the time study on the three jobs he had observed the previous day. After he had left, the president again glanced at the worksheet. He was puzzled. The time estimates seemed excessive, and he didn't know what to make of it.

Role Assignment

You are Anton Wenschek, the shop superintendent. You have learned about what happened, as discussed in the case. The president has asked for your analysis and recommendations.

Case Study

Rubtzoff Apparel, Inc.

Rubtzoff Apparel, Inc., manufactures women's dresses, skirts, and blouses. The company has 20 plants located in small cities in three states.

In one particular locality, labor is scarce and most of the workers are older women. They are paid hourly according to seniority: up to 6 months, $3.35 (the legal minimum); 6 months but less than 2 years, $3.55; and 2 years and over, $3.75.

The company also evaluates the work of each worker using a point system. Points are based on a standard output determined by a time and motion study. Company management considers a worker who achieves a daily average of 350 points to be producing at 100 percent efficiency. The following table shows the results from a recent week.

Workers	Points Earned
20	100–199
55	200–299
120	300–399
40	400–499
5	500 & over

At the end of each week the daily average for each worker is posted on a bulletin board. The workers are interested in seeing who made the most points and who was 100 percent efficient. Supervisors make a point of congratulating workers who reach 100 percent efficiency.

Several times since 1950, when the plant was organized, the workers have tried to form a union. In each case management, with help from the head office, made a concerted effort to talk with each worker and was able to persuade a large number to vote against the union. However, in the last election 2 years ago the vote was exceedingly close. The workers tend to favor an incentive plan, but management contends that the company cannot afford such a plan.

Role Assignment

You have been called in as a consultant to the company management. What actions would you recommend with regard to this plant and why?

Questions for Discussion

1. How does expectancy theory explain motivation?
2. Do incentive plans always motivate a worker toward improved performance? Explain your answer.
3. Is incentive pay a form of base pay or is it an addition to base pay?
4. Why might a worker be skeptical about the significance of a merit pay increase?
5. What features are common to most individual piece-rate plans?
6. Compare the effects of falling, fixed, and rising piece rates from the worker's point of view and from management's point of view.
7. What do union leaders think of individual incentive plans? How do you account for the substantial differences in their views?
8. How do you account for the success of the incentive plan used by the Lincoln Electric Company? If this same plan were adopted by another company, would it be equally successful? Why or why not?
9. How are salespersons usually compensated? What factors are considered in formulating the pay plan?
10. Describe the merit pay and bonus arrangements available to federal executives.
11. What are the productivity incentive awards used by the executive branch of the federal government?
12. How does the Scanlon plan work?
13. What general considerations should an organization consider when it decides to install an individual or group incentive plan?

Notes

1. For the full rationale of the theory as originally conceived, see Victor H. Vroom, *Work and Motivation* (New York: John Wiley and Sons, 1964).

2. See Terence R. Mitchell, "Expectancy Models of Job Satisfaction, Occupational Preference and Effort: A Theoretical, Methodological, and Empirical Appraisal," *Psychological Bulletin* 81, no. 12 (December 1974): 1094.

3. Ibid., 1071.

4. Ibid., 1054.

5. For an interesting application, see Richard L. Oliver, "Alternative Conceptions of the Motivation Components in Expectancy Theory," in *Sales Management: New Developments from Behavioral and Decision Model Research*, ed. Richard P. Bagozzi (Cambridge, MA: Marketing Science Institute, 1979), 40–63.

6. See Michael J. Stahl and Adrian M. Harrell, "Modeling Effort Decisions with Behavioral Decision Theory: Toward an Individual Differences Model of Expectancy Theory," *Organizational Behavior and Human Performance* 27, no. 3 (June 1981): 321.

7. Richard M. Steers and Lyman W. Porter, *Motivation and Work Behavior*, 2nd ed. (New York: McGraw-Hill, 1979), 233. Reproduced with permission of the publisher. For the original study, see Dale O. Jorgenson, Marvin Dunnette, and Robert D. Pritchard, "Effects of the Manipulation of a Performance-Reward Contingency on Behavior in a Simulated Work Setting," *Journal of Applied Psychology* 57, no. 3 (June 1973): 271–80.

8. Reprinted, by permission of the publisher, from David W. Belcher, "Pay and Performance," *Compensation Review*, 3rd Quarter 1980. (New York: AMACOM, a division of American Management Associations, 1980), 17. Copyright © by AMACOM. All rights reserved.

9. Michael M. Nash, "Design Issues in Executive Compensation," *ACA Conference Highlights, 1986 Edition:* 66.

10. *American Compensation Association News* (September–October 1987): 8.

11. Charles A. Peck, "Non-Traditional Merit Pay Results," The Conference Board, 845 Third Avenue, New York, NY 10022, June 1987.

12. Pinhas Schwinger, *Wage Incentive Systems* (Jerusalem: Keter Publishing House, 1975), 5.

13. Lloyd R. Reynolds, *Labor Economics and Labor Relations* (Englewood Cliffs, NJ: Prentice-Hall, 1949), 391–93.

14. Ibid., 392.

15. Leonard R. Burgess, 1977 Survey of Union Views on Incentive or Bonus Plans, unpublished survey. The sample included 73 national and international unions with memberships in industries having 25 percent or more of production and related workers paid on an incentive basis, as reported in *Monthly Labor Review* 87, no. 3 (March 1964), 272 and reproduced in Zollitsch and Langsner, *op cit.*, 530–31. Unions with less than 1,000 members, as reported in the 1964 *Directory of National Unions and Employee Associations*, were excluded. The 13 unions responding provided a qualitatively useful feedback.

16. Ibid.

17. Ibid.

18. Ibid.

19. From Employee's Handbook, The Lincoln Electric Company, 1974, as cited in Norman Fast and Norman Berg, The Lincoln Electric Company (Harvard Business School, 9–376–028). Copyright © 1975 by the President and Fellows of Harvard College.

20. Charles W. Brennan, *Wage Administration* (Homewood, Ill.: Richard D. Irwin, 1963). 293.

21. Walter H. Read, Director of Compensation, IBM Corporation, Address before the Annual Meeting of the American Compensation Association, in Toronto, Canada, Oct. 9, 1987.

22. Ibid.

23. Daniel J. B. Mitchell and Renae F. Broderick, "Flexible Pay Systems in the American Context: History, Policy, Research, and Implications." *Advances in Industrial and Labor Relations*, Vol. 5, edited by David Lewin, Donna Sockell, and David B. Lipsky. Greenwich, CT: JAI Press, 1989, forthcoming.

24. National Center for Employee Ownership.

25. *Employee Stock Ownership Plan, The Concept.* The ESOP Association, Washington, DC.

26. Ibid.

27. Mitchell and Broderick, *op. cit.,* 27–28.

28. *ESOP Survey 1987*, Washington, DC: The ESOP Association, May 1987.

29. William Lazer, *Marketing Management, A Systems Perspective* (New York: John Wiley and Sons, 1971), 390–95.

30. Rosabeth Moss Kantor, "From Status to Contribution: Some Organizational Implications of the Changing Basis for Pay," *Personnel* 64, no. 1 (January 1987): 34.

31. Ibid., 35.

32. Carla S. O'Dell, "Innovative Reward Systems—The Productivity Payoff," *ACA Conference Highlights, 1986 Edition,* 9.

33. For an interesting discussion of the plan, see Frances Torbert, "Making Incentives Work," *Harvard Business Review* 37, no. 5 (September–October 1959): 86–88.

34. National Center for Productivity and Quality of Working Life, *Recent Initiatives in Labor-Management Cooperation* (Washington, DC: National Center for Productivity and Quality of Working Life, 1976), 48.

35. Ibid.

36. Torbert, *op cit.,* 86.

37. Edward E. Lawler and Raymond N. Olsen, "Designing Reward Systems for New Organizations," *Personnel* 54, no. 5 (September–October 1977): 57–58. Published in New York by AMACOM, a division of American Management Associations.

38. This and other details of the plan taken from "Spencer Reports on Employee Benefits" published by Charles D. Spencer & Associations, Inc. as reported in *ACA News,* February–March 1987, 8.

References

The Alexander Group. *Current Practices in Sales Incentives.* Scottsdale, AZ: The Alexander Group, 1987.

Balkin, David B., and Groeneman, Sid. "The Effect of Incentive Compensation on Recruitment: The Case of the Military." *Personnel Administrator* 30, no. 1 (January 1985): 29–34.

Bond, Robert L., and Stein, Larry I. "KSOPs: A Marriage of Convenience." *Compensation and Benefits Review* 20, no. 2 (March–April 1988): 65–74.

Bradley, Keith, and Gelb, Alan. *Worker Capitalism.* Cambridge, MA: MIT Press, 1983.

Broderick, Renae, and Mitchell, Daniel J. B. "Who Has Flexible Wage Plans and Why Aren't There More of Them?" *Proceedings of the Thirty-Ninth Annual Meeting,* Industrial Relations Research Association, December 28–30, 1986, 159–166.

———. "Flexible Pay Systems in the American Context: History, Policy Research, and Implications." Paper Prepared for Pacific Rim Comparative Labour Policy Conference, Vancouver, Canada, June 1987. (Revised June 1987.)

Brown, Martin, and Philips, Peter. "The Decline of Piece Rates in California Commerce: 1890–1960." *Industrial Relations* 25, no. 1 (Winter 1986): 81–91.

Case, John. "Owner's Manual: Are ESOPs Dead or Alive?" *Inc.* 10, no. 6 (June 1988): 94–100.

Driscoll, James W. "Working Creatively with a Union: Lessons from the Scanlon Plan." *Organizational Dynamics* 8, no. 1 (Summer 1979): 61–80.

ESOP Survey 1987. Washington, DC: The ESOP Association, May 1987.

Executive Compensation Service. *Sales and Marketing Personnel Report.* Fort Lee, NJ: Executive Compensation Service, 1987–88.

Freedman, Robert J. "How to Develop a Sales Compensation Plan." *Compensation and Benefits Review* 18, no. 2 (March–April 1986):

41–48.

Geis, A. Arthur. "Making Merit Pay Work." *Personnel* 64, no. 1 (January 1987): 52–60.

Hatcher, Larry L., and Ross, Timothy L. "Organization Development Through Productivity Gainsharing." *Personnel* 62, no. 10 (October 1985): 42–50.

Hathaway, James W. "How Do Merit Bonuses Fare?" *Compensation and Benefits Review* 18, no. 5 (September–October 1986): 50–55.

Hauck, Warren C., and Ross, Timothy L. "Sweden's Experiments in Productivity Gainsharing: A Second Look." *Personnel* 64, no. 1 (January 1987): 61–67.

Heilman, M. E., et al. "Reactions to Prescribed Leader Behavior as a Function of Role Perspective: The Case of the Vroom-Yetton Model." *Journal of Applied Psychology* 69 (1984): 50–60.

Hewitt Associates. 1987 Profit Sharing Survey. Chicago, IL: Hewitt Associates and Profit Sharing Council of America, 1987.

Kanter, Rosabeth Moss. "From Status to Contribution: Some Organizational Implications of the Changing Basis for Pay." *Personnel* 64, no. 1 (January 1987): 12–37.

———. "The Attack on Pay." *Harvard Business Review* 65, no. 2 (March–April 1987): 60–67.

Lawler, Edward E. III, and Ledford, Gerald E., Jr. "Skill-Based Pay: A Concept That's Catching On." *Compensation and Benefits Review* 18, no. 1 (January–February 1986): 54–61.

Lincoln, James F. *A New Approach to Industrial Economics.* New York: Devin-Adair, 1961.

Mercer-Medinger-Hansen Survey of Hospitals. New York: Mercer-Medinger-Hansen, 1987.

Maese, Judy E. "Employee Stock Ownership Plans: The Benefits and the Potential Pitfalls." *Compensation and Benefits Review* 18, no. 1 (January–February 1986): 61–64.

Marcaccio, Tonia M. "Incentives to Sell Your Sales Team." *Personnel Journal* 64, no. 1 (January 1985): 44–47.

Martin, Anthony F., and Jackson, William R., Jr. "ESOP—Time to Reconsider." *Compensation and Benefits Review* 19, no. 3 (May–June 1987): 60–62.

McAdams, Jerry. "Rewarding Sales and Marketing Performance." *Personnel* 64, no. 10 (October 1987): 8–16.

Melbinger, Michael S. "Negotiating a Profit-Sharing Plan: A Survey of the Options." *Employee Relations Law Journal* 10, no. 4 (Spring 1985): 684–701.

Miller, Lynn E., and Grush, Joseph E. "Improving Predictions in Expectancy Theory Research: Effects of Personality, Expectancies, and Norms." *Academy of Management Journal* 31, no. 1 (March 1988): 107–122.

Mohr, Deborah A., et al. "A Group Wage Incentive System Can Boost Performance and Cut Costs." *Defense Management Journal.* (2nd Quarter 1986).

"National Steel's Gainsharing Plan Encourages Productivity, Work Force Reduction." *ACA News* 30, no. 2 (February–March 1987): 8.

Peck, Charles A. *Non-Traditional Merit Pay Survey Results.* New York: National Industrial Conference Board, June 1987.

Public Law 98–615 of Nov. 8, 1984, Title II—Performance Management and Recognition System (PMRS), and *Federal Register* August 30, 1985 and March 11, 1986.

Read, Walter. "Productivity, Motivation, and the Individual." Address before the Annual Meeting of the American Compensation Association, Toronto, Canada, October 9, 1987.

Ross, Timothy, et al. "How Unions View Gainsharing." *Business Horizons* 28, no. 4 (July–August 1985): 15–22.

Ryckman, W. G. *Compensating Your Sales Force.* Probus Publishing Company, 1986.

Schulhof, Robert J. "Five Years with a Scanlon Plan." *Personnel Administrator* 24, no. 6 (June 1979): 55–62.

Schwinger, Pinhas. *Wage Incentive Systems.* New York: John Wiley and Sons, 1975.

Smith, Blanchard B. "Lessons Learned from 11 Years of Training Managers in the Vroom-Yetton Model," a presentation to the Academy of Management, Boston, MA, August 1984.

Smyth, Richard. *How to Motivate and Compensate a Field Sales Force.* New Harbor, ME: Smyth and Murphy Associates, 1986.

Stahl, Michael J., and Harrell, Adrian M. "Modelling Effort Decisions with Behavioral Decision Theory: Toward an Individual Differences Model of Expectancy Theory." *Organizational Behavior and Human Performance* 27, no. 3 (June 1981): 303–25.

The Sullivan Group. 1986 National Survey of the Compensation of Hospital Executives and Managers. Detroit, MI: The Sullivan Group, 1986.

Sullivan, Jeremiah J. "Three Roles of Language in Motivation Theory." *Academy of Management Review* 13, no. 1 (January 1988): 104–115.

Tharp, Glen Charles. "Linking Annual Incentive Awards to Individual Performance." *Compensation and Benefits Review* 17, no. 5 (November–December 1985): 38–43.

Vroom, Victor H. "Reflections on Leadership and Decision-Making." *Journal of General Management, 1984* 9, no. 3: 18–36.

———. *Work and Motivation.* New York: John Wiley & Sons, 1964.

Wagel, William H. "A Software Link between Per-formance Appaisals and Merit Increases." *Personnel* 65, no. 3 (March 1988): 10–14.

Walker, Deborah, and Elinsky, Peter I. "ESOP's Fables." *Management Focus* 31, no. 6 (November–December 1984): 14–16.

Walton, Matt S. "How to Draft a Sales Compensation Plan." *Personnel* 62, no. 6 (June 1985): 71–74.

Weyher, Harry P., and Knott, Hiram. *ESOP: The Stock Ownership Plan.* 2nd ed. Chicago, IL: Commerce Clearing House, 1985.

Yetton, P. "Leadership and Supervision." In *Social Psychology and Organizational Behavior,* edited by M. Gruneberg and T. Wall. New York: John Wiley & Sons, 1984, 9–35.

Ziskin, Ian V. "Knowledge-Based Pay." *Compensation and Benefits Review* 19, no. 2 (March–April 1987): 56–66.

Employee Benefits

Chapter Outline

- Employee Benefit Trends
- Cross-Sectional Views
- Do Employee Benefits Motivate?
- Union Strategy: Liberalization of Employee Benefits
- Major Categories of Employee Benefits
- The Cafeteria Plan
- Summary
- Case Study—Briones Machinery, Inc.

Employee benefits are any benefits received by an employee in addition to base pay. While this chapter will emphasize economic benefits, the role of psychological benefits—pleasant working conditions, reasonable hours of work, a sympathetic supervisor, friendly coworkers, and the challenge of the work itself—deserves recognition. David Belcher divides these nonfinancial benefits into three groups, those associated with (1) the job, (2) the worker's performance, and (3) organization membership.[1]

The boundary between base pay and economic benefits is not well defined. Both the U.S. Chamber of Commerce and the U.S. Department of Commerce compile information on employee benefits, but they include different items. The Chamber of Commerce uses the term *employee benefits*, while the government refers to *supplements to wages and salaries*. The difference is more than a matter of semantics. From the viewpoint of the chamber, paid time off, such as rest periods, paid vacations, and holidays, is treated as part of employee benefits even though it is normally included in the paycheck. Extra pay for time worked on the job—shift differentials, production bonuses, premium pay for overtime (the increment beyond the straight-time rate), or premium holiday pay (pay for working on a holiday beyond the straight-time rate)—is not included as a benefit by the chamber, however. The U.S. Department of Commerce treats these two items in exactly the opposite manner. As a result, the government data show a smaller package of benefits than do the figures published by the Chamber of Commerce.

Employee Benefit Trends

The trends in major employee benefits over the years can be seen in Figure 13–1. For purposes of analysis, the data are shown on a ratio scale, which means that lines with greater slope show faster growth. We can see that some of the major benefits (in terms of the amounts set aside by the employer) have increased at dramatic rates. In fact, some benefits, which in rough order of magnitude in 1929 could be reckoned in the hundreds of millions of dollars, now must be thought of in tens of billions of dollars. For example, employer contributions to private pension and welfare funds are now close to the $200 billion level while before 1929, pension plans were mostly restricted to higher-paid executives. Individual states

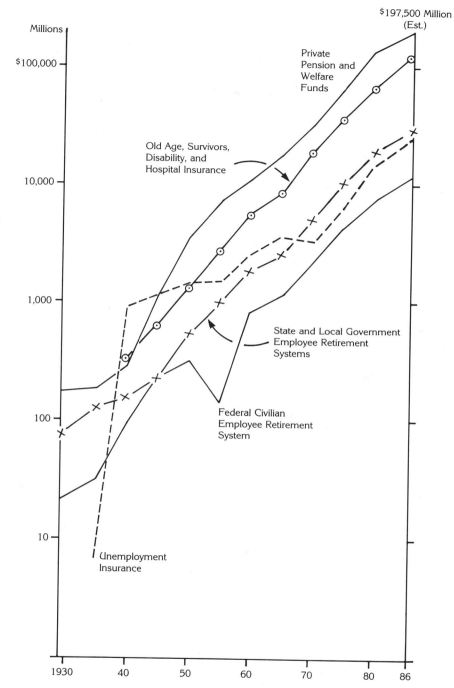

FIGURE 13–1
Trends in major employee benefits. Rapid growth was sparked by
passage of the Social Security Act in 1935. From U.S. Department of
Commerce, **National Income and Product Accounts of the United**
States, 1929–82: Statistical Tables, *and July 1987 issue of the*
Survey of Current Business.

had taken some initiative in developing benefit programs, evident in the passage of workers' compensation laws. With the passage of the Social Security Act under President Franklin D. Roosevelt in 1935, the federal government increased its role. First, two new benefits—unemployment insurance and old age and survivors benefits—were enacted into law. Second, a considerable stimulus was given to private pension and welfare plans, resulting from the federal government's new legislation encouraging labor-management collective bargaining agreements.

More recent developments include the emergence of hospital insurance as part of Old-Age, Survivors, Disability, and Health Insurance (OASDHI) and the rapid increase in retirement systems for federal civilian employees as well as for state and local government employees.

At least as significant as the absolute growth in dollars over the years is what has happened to employee benefits compared with payrolls. The Department of Commerce reports that supplements to wages and salaries have increased from about 1 percent in 1929 to almost 20 percent in 1986. For this same period, employee benefits as reported by the Chamber of Commerce increased from 3 percent to over 35 percent.

Cross-Sectional Views

Benefits as Percentage of Payroll by Industry

Based on its own survey of 833 reporting companies, the Chamber of Commerce came up with a slightly higher ratio of employee benefits to payroll of 39 percent for 1986. Some variation in the costs of benefits results from factors such as the industry, geographic region, and the size of the company. The variation due to industry group can be seen in Table 13–1.

We can draw a number of generalizations from the data. The highest industry ratio was in rubber, leather, and plastics, while the lowest ratio was in textiles and apparel.

Percentage of Companies Paying Specified Benefits

Another important point is the extent to which companies in different industries pay particular benefits (Table 13–2, pp. 316–317).

Notice that some fringes, such as three out of the four legal requirements, life insurance and medical insurance, and paid vacations and holidays, are almost universal. Some others are used much less frequently. For example, in 1986 only 9 percent of reporting hospitals made a payment towards a defined contribution plan (Item 2b) for their employees compared to 75 percent in the petroleum industry. (In both this and the later table regarding cost as a percent of payroll, Item 2b includes company contributions to profit sharing—both current cash payments and payments to deferred profit-sharing trusts—as well as stock

TABLE 13–1

Employee benefits as a percentage of payroll by industry groups.

Industry group	Total, all regions
Total, all industries	39.3
Total, all manufacturing	42.0
Manufacture of:	
Food, beverages, and tobacco	34.2
Textile products and apparel	28.8
Pulp, paper, lumber, and furniture	36.0
Printing and publishing	29.0
Chemicals and allied products	33.3
Petroleum industry	31.7
Rubber, leather, and plastic products	56.9
Stone, clay, and glass products	33.2
Primary metal industries	51.1
Fabricated metal products (excluding machinery and transportation equipment)	34.8
Machinery (excluding electrical)	34.5
Electrical machinery, equipment, and supplies	33.9
Transportation equipment	50.5
Instruments and miscellaneous manufacturing industries	36.0
Total, all nonmanufacturing	36.8
Public utilities (electric, gas, water, telephone, etc.)	38.7
Department stores	33.5
Trade (wholesale and other retail)	35.7
Banks, finance companies, and trust companies	30.4
Insurance companies	34.2
Hospitals	34.2
Miscellaneous nonmanufacturing industries*	38.3
Number of companies	833

*Includes research, engineering, education, government agencies, construction, etc.
Source: Reprinted with the permission of the Chamber of Commerce of the United States of America from *Employee Benefits 1986*, Table 9.

bonuses and contributions to Employee Stock Ownership Plans [ESOPs] discussed earlier in the chapter on incentive plans.) The petroleum figure reflects heavy contributions to thrift plans.

Benefit Costs as Percent of Payroll

Benefit costs as a percentage of payroll for companies paying the indicated benefits is shown in Table 13–3 on pp. 318–319. Such costs for all industries ranged from 0.2 percent for education to 6.2 percent for hospital, surgical, medical, and major medical coverage. Benefit costs for any particular benefit, however, often varied widely.

TABLE 13–2
The percentage of companies paying specified employee benefits.

Type of benefit	Total, all industries	Total, all manufacturing	Textile products and apparel	Petroleum industry	Rubber, leather, and plastic products	Primary metal industries	Electrical machinery, equipment, and supplies	Total, all nonmanufacturing	Public utilities (electric, gas, water, telephone, etc.)	Department stores	Trade (wholesale and other retail)	Banks, finance companies, and trust companies	Insurance companies	Hospitals
		Manufacturing industries						Nonmanufacturing industries						
1. Legally required payments (employer's share only):														
a. Old-Age, Survivors, Disability, and Health Insurance (employer FICA taxes) and Railroad Retirement Tax	99	100	100	100	100	100	100	99	99	100	100	100	100	100
b. Unemployment Compensation	97	100	100	100	100	100	100	96	97	100	100	97	99	95
c. Workers' Compensation (including estimated cost of self-insured)	94	95	100	81	100	100	100	94	99	86	100	89	96	96
d. State sickness benefits insurance	17	16	5	0	10	14	23	17	11	29	19	24	25	9
2. Retirement and Savings Plan Payments (employer's share only)														
a. Defined benefit pension plan contributions	58	58	47	44	50	86	53	59	70	57	44	55	65	65
b. Defined contribution plan payments	43	47	47	75	20	50	45	40	51	71	41	65	39	9
c. Money purchase plans	4	4	0	6	0	5	2	4	2	0	4	6	5	8
d. Pension plan premiums (net) under insurance and annuity contracts (insured and trusteed)	16	13	11	25	0	14	17	18	17	0	7	12	19	19
e. Costs of plan administration	46	41	63	63	40	36	32	49	51	57	33	61	56	45
f. Other	24	21	26	25	20	9	21	26	37	14	26	23	35	15
3. Life Insurance and Death Benefits (employer's share only)	93	92	95	94	100	100	91	94	96	86	89	95	98	96
4. Medical and Medically-Related Benefit Payments (employer's share only)														
a. Hospital, surgical, medical, and major medical insurance premiums (net)	98	97	100	94	100	95	94	99	98	100	100	100	100	100
b. Retiree (payments for retired employees) hospital, surgical, medical, and major medical insurance premiums (net)	34	32	26	19	20	36	28	35	44	43	26	47	48	15

TABLE 13–2

The percentage of companies paying specified employee benefits.

Type of benefit	Total, all industries	Total, all manufacturing	Textile products and apparel	Petroleum industry	Rubber, leather, and plastic products	Primary metal industries	Electrical machinery, equipment, and supplies	Total, all nonmanufacturing	Public utilities (electric, gas, water, telephone, etc.)	Department stores	Trade (wholesale and other retail)	Banks, finance companies, and trust companies	Insurance companies	Hospitals
		Manufacturing industries						Nonmanufacturing industries						
c. Short-term disability, sickness or accident insurance (company plan or insured plan)	41	52	42	25	60	50	66	33	26	43	44	24	44	37
d. Long-term disability or wage continuation (insured, self-administered, or trust)	61	48	32	44	40	64	47	71	72	71	37	88	82	77
e. Dental insurance premiums	56	53	21	50	40	59	68	58	66	43	44	52	51	67
f. Other (vision care, physical and mental fitness, benefits for former employees)	35	34	11	19	40	45	45	36	39	0	26	29	51	29
5. Paid Rest Periods, Coffee Breaks, Lunch Periods, Wash-Up Time, Travel Time, Clothes-Change Time, Get-Ready Time, Etc.	76	81	84	63	80	68	85	72	80	86	70	74	61	93
6. Payments For Time Not Worked														
a. Payments for or in lieu of vacations	86	85	84	88	80	86	91	87	95	86	78	67	93	97
b. Payments for or in lieu of holidays	83	82	74	75	80	86	89	84	96	71	56	68	93	83
c. Sick leave pay	76	65	58	63	50	55	68	85	95	86	74	76	85	89
d. Parental leave (maternity and paternity leave payments)	61	64	68	44	50	77	55	58	82	43	33	32	61	63
e. Other	42	39	42	50	30	55	43	44	66	14	30	26	47	39
7. Miscellaneous Benefit Payments														
a. Discounts on goods and services purchased from company by employees	18	12	21	19	20	0	6	21	24	71	37	15	24	33
b. Employee meals furnished by company	25	17	5	19	20	18	21	31	33	0	22	36	51	32
c. Employee education expenditures	76	70	47	69	60	73	81	79	84	29	63	86	91	85

Two lines at bottom omitted because of inaccuracies. Other data are not affected.

Source: Reprinted with the permission of the Chamber of Commerce of the United States of American from *Employee Benefits 1986*, Table 13.

TABLE 13–3
Average benefit costs as a percentage of payroll for companies paying these benefits.

Type of benefit	Total, all industries	Total, all manufacturing	Textile products and apparel	Petroleum industry	Rubber, leather, and plastic products	Primary metal industries	Electrical machinery, equipment, and supplies	Total, all nonmanufacturing	Public utilities (electric, gas, water, telephone, etc.)	Department stores	Trade (wholesale and other retail)	Banks, finance companies, and trust companies	Insurance companies	Hospitals
			Manufacturing industries							Nonmanufacturing industries				
1. Legally required payments (employer's share only):														
a. Old-Age, Survivors, Disability, and Health Insurance (employer FICA taxes) and Railroad Retirement Tax	6.1	6.6	6.8	6.4	7.1	7.1	6.5	5.6	6.7	6.9	7.0	6.2	6.8	6.9
b. Unemployment Compensation	1.1	1.3	2.5	2.0	1.6	2.4	0.8	0.9	0.6	1.5	1.3	0.8	0.9	0.4
c. Workers' Compensation (including estimated cost of self-insured)	1.1	0.9	1.1	3.2	3.3	2.1	0.5	1.3	0.9	1.6	2.2	0.4	0.3	0.7
d. State sickness benefits insurance	0.1	0.0	0.0	0.0	0.7	0.0	0.0	0.2	0.1	0.1	0.1	0.5	0.0	0.7
2. Retirement and Savings Plan Payments (employer's share only)														
a. Defined benefit pension plan contributions	5.0	4.8	2.2	0.5	3.6	9.4	0.9	5.3	6.5	1.6	2.6	3.0	4.1	3.0
b. Defined contribution plan payments	2.8	3.0	0.5	2.8	16.1	2.0	1.7	2.4	2.1	1.7	1.3	5.2	2.0	4.8
c. Money purchase plans	2.1	2.2	0.0	3.6	0.0	0.6	3.0	1.2	3.6	0.0	0.2	4.0	1.3	2.7
d. Pension plan premiums (net) under insurance and annuity contracts (insured and trusteed)	4.1	1.4	0.7	1.6	0.0	1.0	1.9	5.4	6.0	0.0	3.5	0.4	2.3	2.5
e. Costs of plan administration	0.3	0.2	0.1	0.1	0.2	0.3	0.1	0.3	0.4	0.4	0.0	0.4	0.3	0.4
f. Other	1.5	1.5	1.1	0.8	0.1	1.2	1.6	1.6	1.3	0.8	1.2	2.1	1.8	5.5
3. Life Insurance and Death Benefits (employer's share only)	0.5	0.5	0.8	0.6	1.6	0.6	0.4	0.5	0.6	0.2	0.3	0.5	0.6	0.2
4. Medical and Medically Related Benefit Payments (employer's share only)														
a. Hospital, surgical, medical, and major medical insurance premiums (net)	6.2	6.9	5.3	4.8	13.8	10.0	5.5	5.5	6.5	3.5	7.9	5.2	5.4	4.9
b. Retiree (payments for retired employees) hospital, surgical, medical, and major medical insurance premiums (net)	1.6	1.9	0.7	0.9	3.2	8.1	1.5	1.0	1.2	0.6	0.2	0.5	0.8	0.5

318

TABLE 13–3
Average benefit costs as a percentage of payroll for companies paying these benefits.

Type of benefit	Total, all industries	Manufacturing industries						Total, all nonmanufacturing	Nonmanufacturing industries					
		Total, all manufacturing	Textile products and apparel	Petroleum industry	Rubber, leather, and plastic products	Primary metal industries	Electrical machinery, equipment, and supplies		Public utilities (electric, gas, water, telephone, etc.)	Department stores	Trade (wholesale and other retail)	Banks, finance companies, and trust companies	Insurance companies	Hospitals
c. Short-term disability, sickness or accident insurance (company plan or insured plan)	0.9	1.1	0.1	0.3	1.1	0.8	1.2	0.6	1.0	0.3	0.5	0.4	0.5	0.7
d. Long-term disability or wage continuation (insured, self-administered, or trust)	0.3	0.3	0.2	0.2	1.1	0.3	0.1	0.3	0.4	0.1	0.1	0.2	0.8	0.2
e. Dental insurance premiums	0.8	1.0	0.6	0.6	1.7	1.2	0.8	0.7	0.8	0.4	0.5	0.5	0.7	0.6
f. Other (vision care, physical and mental fitness, benefits for former employees)	0.5	0.6	0.3	0.0	4.3	0.4	0.5	0.5	0.6	0.9	0.2	0.2	0.3	0.2
5. Paid Rest Periods, Coffee Breaks, Lunch Periods, Wash-Up Time, Travel Time, Clothes-Change Time, Get-Ready Time, Etc.	4.3	4.2	3.6	2.2	3.7	2.3	1.5	4.5	3.5	5.7	5.9	3.9	3.9	4.6
6. Payments For Time Not Worked														
a. Payments for or in lieu of vacations	5.6	5.5	4.0	5.3	8.2	6.4	6.1	5.8	6.0	4.6	5.1	4.3	5.1	6.2
b. Payments for or in lieu of holidays	3.4	3.7	2.7	3.1	3.6	2.0	3.9	3.1	3.3	3.0	0.7	3.5	3.6	3.3
c. Sick leave pay	1.8	1.4	0.1	1.3	1.0	0.5	1.6	2.0	1.9	1.4	1.0	1.1	1.9	2.4
d. Parental leave (maternity and paternity leave payments)	0.3	0.2	0.4	0.2	0.3	0.1	0.3	0.3	0.4	0.4	0.3	0.5	0.2	0.4
e. Other	0.6	0.6	0.1	0.7	0.9	0.9	0.7	0.5	0.5	0.1	0.1	0.6	0.9	0.8
7. Miscellaneous Benefit Payments														
a. Discounts on goods and services purchased from company by employees	0.8	0.6	0.3	0.1	0.3	0.0	0.1	0.9	0.3	2.2	1.2	0.4	0.3	0.2
b. Employee meals furnished by company	0.5	0.5	0.0	0.2	0.1	0.1	0.6	0.4	0.3	0.0	0.1	0.6	0.8	0.7
c. Employee education expenditures	0.2	0.2	0.0	0.1	0.1	0.0	0.2	0.2	0.2	0.0	0.1	0.4	0.3	0.5

Two lines at bottom omitted because of inaccuracies. Other data are not affected.

Source: Reprinted with the permission of the Chamber of Commerce of the United States of American from *Employee Benefits 1986*, Table 14.

Contributions towards life insurance and death benefits ranged from a low of 0.2 percent for department stores and hospitals to a high of 1.6 percent for rubber, leather, and plastics products.

In the selection of employee benefits, a corporation must also consider the extent to which the cost is shared by the employee. According to the Chamber of Commerce, total payroll deductions for employee benefits in 1986 averaged more than 10 percent of payroll. Deductions for specific benefits ranged from as low as 0.7 percent for medically related benefits to a high of 5.9 percent for OASDHI.

Do Employee Benefits Motivate?

The growth in employee benefits and the costs of such benefits have been well established, but there is another important aspect to consider. What do benefits accomplish? Do most companies install them (the ones not required by law) just to keep up with the competition, or do they provide positive motivation? Most studies have concluded that benefits have a negative effect or at best are neutral as motivators. They do have some tendency to hold an employee with a firm, and perhaps some benefits have to be offered to persuade an employee to join an organization. Some benefits, such as stock options, may strongly motivate employees under some circumstances. But, in general, do benefits motivate?

M. Scott Myers, in working with employees at Texas Instruments and following earlier leads from Frederick Herzberg, believes that employee benefits fall into the class of "dissatisfiers" rather than "motivators." He describes dissatisfiers in this way:

> Dissatisfiers are made up, essentially, of such matters as pay, supplemental benefits, company policy and administration, behavior of supervision, working conditions, and several other factors somewhat peripheral to the task. Though traditionally perceived by management as motivators of people, these factors were found to be more potent as dissatisfiers. High motivation does not result from their improvement, but dissatisfaction does result from their deterioration.[2]

Thomas H. Patten, Jr. has made the same point:

> In general we believe that fringe benefits have little or no incentive value because they do not motivate an employee to perform at work but rather to retain his name on the payroll for the purpose of protection from the contingencies of life; in other words, they "motivate" him to be a "member" for security purposes.[3]

Union Strategy: Liberalization of Employee Benefits

Unions discovered shortly after World War II that in a time of recession, when employers were especially reluctant to give general pay increases, the unions could push for increased employee benefits instead. Since then they have given much thought to what strategy to pursue with regard to benefits. In general, that strategy has been to get the employer to agree to a very small benefit in a particular field, which serves as a bridgehead that can be expanded later. When the original benefit is expanded and made more generous, the union says the benefit has been *liberalized.*

An example of how this strategy results in contract improvements for union members can be seen in Figure 13–2. In 1961 the United Automobile Workers won the right to strike over unresolved health and safety grievances—the bridgehead. In successive agreements in 1973, 1976, and 1979, the health and security provisions were liberalized to include specific new gains.

Major Categories of Employee Benefits

We have looked at employee benefits as trends, in cross section, as motivators, and as subject to liberalization by unions. Next we shall explore some of the major benefits in more depth: benefits relating to job security and technology, paid and unpaid leave, retirement benefits, and insurance and health benefits.

Job Security and Technology

Employee benefits can protect the worker against the uncertainty of technological change. In Japan the guarantee of lifetime employment, at least for male graduates of the leading universities in the largest corporations, has helped remove the need for benefits. In Germany *mitbestimmungsrecht* or codetermination for all companies with more than 500 employees has given German workers a share in decision making equal to that of management—a measure that serves as a protection against adverse effects of technological change. George McIsaac sees similar measures forthcoming in the United States. He says that the United Steelworkers decided

> that a demand for some form of guaranteed career employment security should be the cornerstone of their future annual negotiations. This year the union settled for increased protection against layoffs and plant closedowns for employees with more than 20 years service, who comprise about 40% of the industry's labor force.[4]

Job Security Provisions

The concern of U.S. unions is evident in the proliferation of union contracts containing various types of job security provisions. Table 13–4 lists the types of provisions included in more than 1,550 such agreements.

Unions use several devices to limit management's ability to introduce technological change without adequate consideration of the human relations impact.

AGREEMENT DATED SEPTEMBER 20, 1961—AUGUST 31, 1964

<u>Right to strike over unresolved health and safety grievances.</u> (1964 letter indicates it was provided by 1961 language)

AGREEMENT DATED DECEMBER 10, 1973—SEPTEMBER 14, 1976

<u>Full time local union health and safety</u> representatives provision (in some small plants the chairman of the shop committee has this function).

<u>Both National & Local Joint Committees</u> established with the right to:

<u>Inspect the plant; investigate major accidents; review lost time (and other) workplace accidents and then make recommendations or exercise rights under new complaint procedure.</u>

AGREEMENT DATED DECEMBER 13, 1976—SEPTEMBER 14, 1979

A full time local union health and safety representatives provision. (In some small plants the chairman of the shop committee has this function.)

Both National & Local Joint Committees established the right to:

Inspect the plant; investigate major accidents; review lost time (and other) workplace accidents and then make recommendations or exercise rights under new complaint procedure.

<u>Noise Abatement</u>	<u>Union notified of accidents and unsafe conditions</u>
<u>Additional testing and monitoring equipment.</u>	<u>Improved "No hands in die" policy</u>
<u>Greater local union participation in health and safety program</u>	<u>Joint annual training programs for plant health and safety representatives</u>
<u>Result of tests and exams for exposure to toxic agents given to employee in writing on request.</u>	<u>Precautionary measures taken for workers in a confined or isolated space.</u>

<u>Joint agreement after investigation that "imminent danger" exists is cause for machine or operation to be taken out of service and require corrective action.</u>

AGREEMENT DATED SEPTEMBER 14, 1979—SEPTEMBER 14, 1982

<u>Full time health & safety representatives for parts plants</u> with 600 employees. Parts plants between 500-599 will have a designated health & safety representative with a reservoir of 8 hours per week for representation.

FIGURE 13–2
The liberalization of employee benefits in health and safety provisions worked out in collective bargaining between the United Automobile Workers and General Motors. Underlining indicates a new provision or an improved provision. (From UAW Research Department, Collective Bargaining Gains by Date of Settlement, UAW–General Motors, 1937–1982, *pp. 14, 30, 34, and 39.)*

TABLE 13-4
Major job security provisions in union contracts.

Type of Provision	Number of Contracts
Limitation or prohibition of subcontracting	894
Advance notice of layoff	682
Severance pay	523
Interplant transfer	470
Reduction in hours during slack periods	282
Supplemental unemployment benefit	216
Relocation allowance	214
Preferential hiring, interplant	175
Wage-employment guarantees	173
Advance notice of technological change	162
Advance notice of plant shutdown or relocation	150
Division of work during slack periods	87
Regulation of overtime	58

Work rule and apprenticeship provisions are omitted.
Source: U.S. Bureau of Labor Statistics. *Characteristics of Major Collective Bargaining Agreements,* Bulletin 2095, January 1, 1980. Data are for 1980.

The most common job security provision is limitation or prohibition of subcontracting, as shown in Table 13-4. Other provisions pertain to advance notice of layoffs, severance pay, interplant transfers, reduction in hours during slack periods, and supplementary unemployment benefits.

An interesting observation is that unions include regulation of overtime in only a few contracts. Apparently, many workers do not really want to regulate overtime in their bargaining unless they cannot achieve their purpose through other union contract provisions. Also interesting is that the division of work during slack periods is among the least frequently mentioned contract provisions.

Supplemental Unemployment Benefits

Supplemental unemployment benefits (SUB) equalize interstate differences in the amount and duration of individual state unemployment benefits. SUB started out as the much more ambitious union demand for a guaranteed annual wage. Its leading proponent was Walter Reuther, then president of the United Automobile Workers.

Unlike state unemployment benefits, SUB benefits are paid for entirely by the employer. When first secured by the union in early contracts, SUB covered a period of less than a year. Now in many contracts SUB has come close to the original concept of a guaranteed annual wage. Although the idea originated in the auto industry, it has spread to other industries—especially into durable goods industries, where employment tends to be highly cyclical. This benefit, however, is not typically provided for in collective bargaining agreements.

SUB plans include more than just benefits on a weekly basis. For example, steel industry plans also include short week benefits for weeks when the employee works less than a specified number of hours and relocation allowances to encourage transfers to new company locations. Thus, such plans protect the worker against underemployment as well as unemployment.

Unions have attacked the problem of unemployment by pressing for SUB plans in collective bargaining as well as by promoting state and federal legislation that would correct the inequities in legally required unemployment benefits. Unions hope to standardize the duration of benefits and to set the level of benefit at a fixed percentage of the worker's wage. Given the tendency of industrial union contracts to establish uniform rates of pay for any particular job classification, this approach could eventually mean uniform maximum unemployment benefits in every state within the covered sector.

Severance Pay

Many union contracts provide severance pay for employees who are laid off permanently. Although it may be known as termination pay, dismissal allowance, or separation benefit, the purpose of the benefit is the same. Severance pay provides the worker with timely financial assistance to seek a new job. Usually a lump sum payment is given, with the amount determined by level of pay and length of service. As in the case of SUB, what is permitted, what the state requires to be offset against state unemployment compensation benefits, and other aspects of severance pay vary greatly among different states.

Paid and Unpaid Leave

Vacations

Table 13–5 shows the relation between length of service with the firm and average number of days of vacation for medium and large firms in 1986. The range is considerable—from a little over 5 days at 6 months of service to more than 22 days after 30 years of service, on the average.

The table is useful in deciding on a company's vacation policy. Even a closer fit might be achieved by gathering data for the firms in the company's particular industry.

Holidays

Another form of paid leave is paid holidays. Paid holidays for medium and large firms for 1986 are shown in Table 13–6. A few firms offer a set number of paid holidays plus half days, but this is not typical. The range was from no paid holidays to as many as 14 days.

TABLE 13–5
Length of service and average days of vacation for full-time workers, medium and large firms, 1986.

Length of Service	Average Number of Days of Vacation
6 months	5.5
1 year	8.8
3 years	10.5
5 years	12.7
10 years	15.7
15 years	18.5
20 years	20.6
25 years	22.2
30 years and over	22.7

Source: U.S. Bureau of Labor Statistics. *Employee Benefits in Medium and Large Firms, 1986.* Bulletin 2281, June 1987.

TABLE 13–6
Percent of full-time employees having each number of paid holidays, in medium and large firms, 1986.

Paid Holidays	% of Employees
No paid holidays	1
Under 5 days	2
5 days	1
6 days	4
7 days	6
7 + 1, 2, or 3 half days	1
8 days	7
8 + 1 or 2 half days	1
9 days	11
9 + 1 or 2 half days	1
10 days	24
10 + 1 or 2 half days	1
11 days	17
11 + 1 or 2 half days	1
12 days	10
13 days	4
14 days	5

Source: U.S. Bureau of Labor Statistics. *Employee Benefits in Medium and Large Firms, 1986.* Bulletin 2281, June 1987.

Leaves of Absence

Most firms make provision for leaves of absence—sometimes paid and sometimes not—along with other common types of paid leave such as lunch time and rest breaks. Information on the average length of leave for selected types of paid leaves is summarized in Table 13–7.

Lunch periods and rest breaks are typical types of paid leave, while the other three benefits shown in the table take up a much smaller part of the work year. One of the newer leave benefits is the personal leave. Most firms still do not provide (at least officially) for paid personal leaves, as can be seen in Table 13–8.

Retirement Benefits

Retirement benefits are another important segment of employee benefits. These include social security, now called old age, survivors, disability, and health insurance (OASDHI); private pension plans; thrift plans; and the retirement plans for state and local as well as federal government employees.

Retirement arrangements, whether specified in union-management agreements or otherwise developed within the private sector, typically include pension plans[5] and thrift and savings plans. Pensions are usually paid out in installments over a period of years, whereas the thrift or savings plans involve lump sum payouts.

Thrift Plans

Under most thrift plans, the employee sets aside a certain percentage of pay and the company makes a specific matching contribution. All payments are placed in a trust fund, with contributions to the fund being nontaxable. The typical lump sum payout is then taxed upon receipt at capital gains rates. Probably the first thrift plan was Shell Oil's, which was started in 1912. Under General Electric's savings and security program, the employee contributes from 1 to 6 percent of pay and the company matches half that contribution. Often the matching formula is dollar for dollar. In another approach, the company contribution increases with

TABLE 13–7
Average length of selected paid leave benefits in medium and large firms, 1986.

Benefit	Length of Leave
Lunch time—minutes per day	27
Rest time—minutes per day	26
Personal leave—days per year	3.7
Funeral leave—days per occurrence	3.2
Military leave—days per year	11.5

Source: U.S. Bureau of Labor Statistics. *Employee Benefits in Medium and Large Firms, 1986,* Bulletin 2281, June 1987.

TABLE 13—8
Percent of full-time employees in medium and large firms given indicated number of days of paid personal leave, 1986.

Days of Leave	% of Employees
None	75
1	2
2	5
3	3
4	4
5	4
More than 5	2
No maximum specified	3
Length of service	2

Source: U.S. Bureau of Labor Statistics *Employee Benfits in Medium and Large Firms, 1986.* Bulletin 2281, June 1987.

length of service. For example, in the Sears Roebuck program the company matches dollar for dollar the contribution of an employee with less than 5 years of service. The ratio of company contribution to employee contribution for an employee with 15 or more years of service and aged 50 or more is 4 to 1.

Pension Plans and Social Security

Private pension plans and federal social security differ in the way they relate benefits to preretirement income. Under social security, benefits are related to average earnings each year over a specified period of time. Private pension benefits are often based on earnings for the 5 highest years out of the last 10.

Under social security, the benefit for the lower paid worker is a higher percentage of preretirement earnings than is the case for the somewhat higher paid worker. In actual dollars, however, the higher paid worker gets a larger benefit. Under typical private plans, the higher paid worker gets not only more in dollars but also a higher percentage of preretirement income. These plans use a fixed ratio, such as 2 percent, which is multiplied by the number of years of service. This percentage figure is then applied to the pay base to arrive at the pension benefit. For example, an employee with 20 years of service at 2 percent would retire with an income of 40 percent of the pay base. As already described, the pay base uses an average for recent years. Under some plans, where the preretirement income is relatively low compared with other occupations, the fixed percentage ratio may be set higher. This is true for some pension plans covering teachers.

In many early pension plans, the amounts payable under social security were first deducted before an employee started to receive benefits under the private plan. This was known as the social security offset. Recent plans tend to pay the full pension benefit in addition to social security, discarding the offset feature.

This is one of the changes wrought by union-management negotiations in collective bargaining. Another change has been the development of bridge provisions. If an employee retires early under a private plan and does not receive social security benefits until later, the bridge fills in the income gap, thus assuring a smooth, continuing level of retirement income.

Under some contracts, retirement can be hastened for certain employees by the creation of "mutually satisfactory" conditions. That is, the company gives the employee a monetary inducement to retire early, benefits that are higher than the usual early retirement benefits. Sometimes these benefits are even more than those the employee would have received if she had waited until the normal retirement age.

As to retirement age, unions have pushed for both earlier and later retirement. That is, unions want the employee to be able to choose to retire before age 65 or after age 65. Where unions cannot achieve this, they push for a later mandatory retirement age.

Longer life expectancy and government policy have also contributed to the push for later mandatory retirement. California law has now forbidden mandatory retirement before age 70, and federal law has followed this lead. It might be more equitable to have retirement age determined by medical boards which would judge the employee's physical fitness to do the work rather than to rely on an arbitrary mandatory contractual retirement age.

Employee Retirement Income Security Act

The Employee Retirement Income Security Act of 1974 (ERISA) came about because of abuses of private pension plans. The Congressional hearings before passage of the act revealed that many employees either were given lesser benefits than they were promised or received no benefits at all because of inadequate vesting, death before retirement, or discontinuance of a plan because of inadequate financial planning or company reorganizations or mergers. Among the provisions of the act as amended are:

1. Tighter funding and reporting standards.
2. Creation of the Pension Benefit Guarantee Corporation, financed by employer contributions, to assure the employee a pension even if the company plan becomes insolvent.
3. Assurance of benefits to a surviving spouse where the employee dies before retirement.
4. Greater assurance of vesting benefits for the employee and restoration of previous service credits under certain conditions if a worker has a break in service and returns to the company.
5. Increased availability of Individual Retirement Accounts (IRAs) to workers who have no company plan or do not choose to join the company plan. IRAs are tax sheltered and are limited to 15 percent

of an employee's earnings up to a yearly maximum of $1,500. (Beginning in 1982, this amount was increased to a maximum of $2,000.)
6. A maximum allowable yearly benefit, initially set at $75,000, for the annual pension of an individual under a qualified plan.[6]

Vesting refers to the employee's right, after a specified age and length of service, to the company's contributions made on her behalf in case she leaves the company before retirement. Both the vesting provisions of the act and the availability of the IRAs are expected to lead to greater portability of pension plans between organizations.

Insurance and Health Benefits

Data from the Chamber of Commerce indicate life insurance premiums, other forms of insurance, and health benefits constitute an important part of the employee benefit package in both manufacturing and nonmanufacturing industries. This type of package is often the subject of collective bargaining agreements.

Many company plans include life, accidental death and dismemberment, paid sick leave, and accident and sickness insurance. Some plans feature long-term disability insurance. Health benefits often cover hospital care, convalescent care in an extended care facility, home health care, surgical and medical services (excluding major medical), maternity care, and ambulance charges. The company typically pays for all benefits.

Under many plans major medical coverage includes outpatient treatment for mental and nervous conditions (mental health care) and the full cost of prescription drugs. Certain plans cover dental or vision care or care in connection with alcoholism and drug addiction.

Health Maintenance Organizations

From the employee's point of view, the passage of the Health Maintenance Organization (HMO) Act of 1973 and the recent drive at the federal level for a national health care act are favorable developments in the area of employee benefits. Richard Henderson has this to say about HMOs:

> The HMO focuses its attention on providing medical care with emphasis on preventive medicine at a fixed, monthly fee. Because it concentrates on maintaining the health of the enrollee, it is able to minimize the high hospital costs that have forced rapid increases in medical insurance premiums. The typical HMO is a private, nonprofit concern that provides services through an affiliation of hospitals, clinics, doctors, nurses, and technicians. Its board of directors normally consists of physicians, hospital administrators, civic leaders, insurance executives, and personnel specialists from private companies.[7]

The Cafeteria Plan

The wide variety of economic benefits made available to employees of many companies poses problems relating to costs (especially in the case of duplicated or unwanted benefits) and motivation. In most companies management decides who gets which benefits, often with unsatisfactory results. At the other extreme, complete freedom for the employee to choose his or her benefit package may not be acceptable to management because of increased costs to cover smaller numbers of employees by a particular benefit. Such freedom may even create resentment when an employee who made an unwise decision early along the career path later comes to realize it was not really in his best interest. A natural compromise is the cafeteria method.

In the cafeteria method, management usually provides a basic minimum layer of protection for the employee. Beyond this the employee is free to choose further benefits, provided that a designated budgetary amount is not exceeded. TRW Systems, a young, nonunion aerospace firm with over 12,000 employees and a matrix-style organization, successfully implemented such a plan. Implementation was treated as a project and assigned to a manager who had managed other projects but was not a compensation person. First, a survey asked employees which of a number of benefits they would choose. Eighty percent indicated a choice. Survey results served both to reassure employees and to assist management in dealing with the insurance companies. As Jeffrey Wilkens explains,

> Under the program, each employee has the option of switching the mix of his insurance benefits to suit his personal needs. The current choices offered include four levels of hospital/medical insurance, eight employee life insurance plans, a dependent life insurance option and eighteen levels of Supplemental Accidental Death and Dismemberment insurance. By reducing the coverage in an insurance area where they think they are adequately covered, employees acquire dollar "credits" that can be applied to premiums in another area where they want more coverage. We require employees to maintain a minimum "core" coverage so that they will be assured some group insurance protection.[8]

Summary

Employee benefits can be monetary or psychological. Examples of psychological benefits are pleasant working conditions, reasonable hours, a friendly supervisor, friendly coworkers, and the nature of the work itself.

Economic benefits, however measured, have increased from a relatively small percentage of payroll in 1929 to a quite large percentage in recent years. This growth was spurred by the passage of the Social Security Act in 1935 which stimulated the development of private pension and welfare plans, mostly worked out through collective bargaining. In spite of this dramatic growth, the effect of employee benefits on motivation is an unresolved question.

Unions often improve benefits through collective bargaining from one contract to another, first obtaining a benefit in principle and then getting an increased benefit over a period of successive contracts. This is known as the liberalization of employee benefits.

Chamber of Commerce data show the prevalence of specific employee benefits in each industry as well as the cost of each benefit as a percentage of payroll for companies providing that particular benefit. Such data provide useful benchmarks for setting individual company policies.

Job security and protection against adverse technological change have been of less concern in Japan and Germany than in the United States. Among devices used in this country to meet the problem have been the SUB (supplemental unemployment benefits), severance pay, and limits on subcontracting.

Another group of benefits includes paid and unpaid leave. Examples are vacations, holidays, paid time off, and unpaid leaves of absence.

Retirement benefits include social security (OASDHI), private pension plans, thrift plans, and the like. While private pension plans provide installment payments after retirement, thrift plans typically offer a lump-sum payment. Employees in thrift plans typically contribute a certain percentage of pay, with the employer providing a matching amount—but not necessarily dollar for dollar. Under the Sears Roebuck plan, the matching amount increases with age and length of service. Pension plans, on the other hand, relate benefits to recent pre-retirement income. Federal social security benefits are related to the average pay of an employee over a specified time period. Private pension plans, however, set a certain percentage to be multiplied by years of service. The resulting percentage is then applied to the pay base chosen by the company to get the amount of pension benefit.

Unions have pushed for the right of an employee to choose retirement either before or after the age of 65. Recent legislation prohibiting mandatory retirement earlier than age 70 has strengthened the unions' position. In some instances a company can hasten retirement by providing special monetary inducements.

The Employee Retirement Income Security Act (ERISA) has tightened controls on the management of pension plans, especially with regard to vesting. This is expected to lead to greater portability of pensions between organizations.

Insurance protection for the employee—another benefit—typically includes life insurance, accidental death and dismemberment insurance, and the like. Most employees receive such health benefits as hospital care, convalescent care, home health care, surgical and medical services, and so on. Some plans include extras such as dental care, vision care, mental health care, and care for alcoholism and drug addiction.

Under the Health Maintenance Organization Act of 1973, HMOs have been formed to provide preventive medicine on a prepaid basis. Other far-reaching national health care legislation appears likely in the future.

Differing employee perceptions of the need for particular benefits as well as the costly duplication of benefits have led to the popularity of the cafeteria plan. Under this plan the company provides certain basic benefits, but the employee can choose among other benefits up to a designated budgetary amount.

Questions for Discussion

1. What are some of the more important trends in the growth of employee benefits?
2. Taking employee benefits as a percentage of payroll, are there important differences by industry?
3. How do you account for the differences in the number of companies paying each particular type of benefit?
4. How do you account for the wide variation among different industries in defined contribution payments as a percentage of payroll?
5. Do employee benefits motivate? If so, in what ways? Can the motivational aspect of benefits be improved? How?
6. What is meant by the liberalization of employee benefits? Give an illustration.
7. Discuss the relationship between employee job security and technological innovation.
8. What is the supplemental unemployment benefit (SUB), and what is its purpose?
9. What sort of policy does the typical company have with respect to vacation time and years of service?
10. What is the difference between a pension plan and a thrift or savings plan?
11. How are benefits computed under social security and under a private plan?
12. What are some of the more important provisions of the Employee Retirement Income Security Act (ERISA)?
13. What is a Health Maintenance Organization (HMO)?
14. What is meant by a cafeteria plan? What are its advantages and disadvantages?

Case Study

Briones Machinery, Inc.

Briones Machinery, Inc., manufactures a large variety of electrical machines. Last year the company had annual net sales of $50 million and a payroll (excluding benefits) of $15 million. Management is concerned with the company's competitive position in the industry and has recently become interested in the cafeteria approach to employee benefits. Their concern is not so much with top executive personnel, where turnover is not a serious problem, but with doing something for the employees generally. After discussion with the treasurer and comptroller, the president suggested that a cafeteria plan be explored but that the cost of all employee benefits should be held to not more than 30 percent of payroll.

The president wants to be able to look at a dollar budget for the first year that shows each major category of benefit. She wants the benefits to be listed and divided into two groups—mandatory and optional. The budget should indicate what proportion of the employees would be likely to subscribe for each optional item.

Role Assignment

You are the director of compensation and benefits. The president has asked you to come up with the proposed budget. Use the relevant industry data in Tables 13–1, 13–2 and 13–3. Be prepared to defend your choice of benefits.

Notes

1. For an extensive list of such items, see David W. Belcher, *Compensation Administration* (Englewood Cliffs, NJ: Prentice-Hall, 1974), 386–91.
2. Reprinted by permission of the *Harvard Business Review*. Excerpt from "Who Are Your Motivated Workers?" by M. Scott Myers (January/February 1964). Copyright © 1964 by the President and Fellows of Harvard College; all rights reserved.
3. Thomas H. Patten, Jr., *Pay: Employee Compensation and Incentive Plans* (New York: The Free Press, 1977), 524. Copyright © 1977 by The Free Press, a Division of Macmillan Publishing Co., Inc. Cited from Belcher, *op. cit.*, 347–48.
4. Reprinted by permission of the *Harvard Business Review*. Excerpt from "Thinking Ahead" by George S. McIsaac (September/October 1977). Copyright © 1977 by the President and Fellows of Harvard College; all rights reserved.
5. A substitute arrangement most frequently applying to executives who would otherwise be entitled to only limited pension benefits is deferred cash under contract. Under this arrangement, the employee gets a fixed number of installments of specified amount, or installments after retirement for life, without any past service requirement. See Leonard R. Burgess, *Top Executive Pay Package* (New York: Free Press and Graduate School of Business, Columbia University, 1963), Chapter III, for further discussion.
6. For an interesting discussion of the act, see Eugene B. Keough, "Why Does the Corporation Need to Know About Private Retirement Plans?" *1977 Regional Conference Proceedings of the American Compensation Association*, 17–21.
7. Richard I. Henderson, *Compensation Management: Rewarding Performance in the Modern Organization*, 2nd ed. (Reston, Va.: Reston Publishing Co., 1979), 288.
8. Jeffrey P. Wilkens, "Flexible Benefits Implementation," *1975 National Conference Proceedings of the American Compensation Association*, 85–88.

References

Aaron, Henry J., and Galper, Harvey. *Assessing Tax Reform*. Washington, DC: Brookings Institution, 1985.

Album, Michael J. "Weaving the Web: Administration of Pension and Welfare Plans." *Employment Relations Today* 12, no. 3 (Autumn 1985): 229–240.

Allen, Everett T., Jr. "Permanent Life Insurance: Look Before You Buy." *Compensation and Benefits Review* 18, no. 1 (January–February 1986): 26–33.

Appleton, John. "Managing 401(k) Plan Investment: The Compensation Manager's Role." *Compensation Review* 17, no. 1 (First Quarter 1985): 22–33.

Baderian, Steven D., and Stempel, Ivy B. "Coping with COBRA." *Compensation and Benefits Review* 19, no. 3 (May–June 1987): 28–36.

Bergmann, Thomas J., and Bergmann, Marylin A. "How Important Are Fringe Benefits to Employees?" *Personnel* 64, no. 12 (December 1987): 59–64.

Burkholder, John E. "Cafeteria-Style Benefits: No Free Lunch." *Personnel* 64, no. 11 (November 1987): 13–16.

Cavies, Deborah L. "How to Bridge the Benefits Communications Gap." *Personnel Journal* 65, no. 1 (January 1986): 83–85.

Chapman, Larry S., and Gertz, Nancy E. "A Prescription for Lower Healthcare Costs." *Personnel Journal* 64, no. 1 (January 1985): 48–55.

Cogger, Susan. "Billions Wasted on Misunderstood Benefits." *ACA News* 31, no. 2 (March–April 1988): 8–9.

Coleman, Barbara. *Primer on ERISA*. Washington, DC: Bureau of National Affairs, 1985.

Employee Benefits Research Institute. *Fundamentals of Employee Benefit Programs.* Waldorf, MD: EBRI-ERF Publications, 1987.

Gable, Myron, and Holoviak, Stephen. "Determining the Cost of Supplemental Benefits." *Compensation and Benefits Review* 17, no. 4 (September–October 1985): 22–33.

Grossman, Morton E., and Magnus, Margaret. "Benefits: Cost and Coverage." *Personnel Journal* 65, no. 5 (May 1986): 74–79.

Gustman, Alan L., and Steinmeier, Thomas L. "The Effect of Partial Retirement on Wage Profiles of Older Workers." *Industrial Relations* 24, no. 2 (Spring 1985): 257–265.

Hay Group. *The 1986 Hay/Huggins Benefits Comparison.* Philadelphia, PA: The Hay Group, 1987.

Herzlinger, Regina. "Can We Control Health Care Costs?" *Harvard Business Review* 56, no. 3 (March–April 1986): 102–110.

Hewitt Associates. *Salaried Employee Benefits Provided by Major U.S. Employers: A Comparison Study, 1981 Through 1986.* Lincolnshire, IL: Hewitt Associates, 1987.

Hewitt Associates. *Survey of Benefits for Part-Time Employees.* Lincolnshire, IL: Hewitt Associates, 1986.

International Foundation of Employee Benefit Plans. *Health Care Cost Management—1986.* Brookfield, WI: International Foundation of Employee Benefit Plans, 1987.

Johnson, Richard E. *Flexible Benefits—A How-To Guide.* Brookfield, WI: International Foundation of Employee Benefit Plans, 1986.

Klein, Daniel L. "COBRA: 20 Questions on Health Care Continuation." *Personnel* 63, no. 11 (November 1986): 10–15.

Kozlowski, Joseph G., and Olesky, Walter. *Complete Guide to Cost-Effective Employee Benefit Programs.* Englewood Cliffs, NJ: Prentice-Hall, Inc., 1987.

Lee, Rick. "Business-Health Coalitions." *Compensation and Benefits Review* 18, no. 1 (January–February 1986): 18–25.

Letzkus, William C. "Estimating Future Social Security Benefits." *Compensation and Benefits Review* 19, no. 1 (January–February 1987): 47–57.

Mainiero, Lisa A., and DeMichiell, Robert L. "Min-imizing Employee Resistance to Technological Change." *Personnel* 63, no. 7, 32–37.

O'Donnell, John B. "Employee Benefits in the Year 2000," *Compensation and Benefits Review* 19, no. 5 (September–October 1987): 25–35.

Parkington, John J. "The 'Trade-Off' Approach to Benefits Cost Containment: A Strategy to Increase Employee Satisfaction." *Compensation and Benefits Review* 19, no. 1 (January–February 1987): 26–35.

Phelan, Kevin. "Do HMOs Mean Lower Health Care Costs?" *Personnel Journal* 64, no. 3 (March 1985): 66–72.

Rabkin, Peggy A. "Recent Developments in Retiree Health Benefits." *Labor Law Journal* 36, no. 9 (September 1985): 675–687.

Reisler, Mark. "Game Plan for Business Coalitions on Health Care." *Harvard Business Review* 64, no. 6 (November–December 1986): 56–60.

Rizzuto, Paul A. "Pension Dilemmas: 2. Restructuring Pensions in a Volatile Environment." *Compensation and Benefits Review* 17, no. 5 (November–December 1985): 23–37.

Schechter, Jack H. "The Retirement Equity Act: Meeting Women's Pension Needs." *Compensation Review* 17, no. 1 (First Quarter 1985): 13–21.

Segal, Martin E., and Co., Inc. "Working Women and Employee Benefits." *Personnel Journal* 64 (September 1985): 73–81.

Smith, L. Murphy, and Putnam, Karl B. "Pension Dilemmas: 1. Inflation and Government Rules." *Compensation and Benefits Review* 17, no. 5 (November–December 1985): 16–22.

Soule, James C. "Child Care: The Off-Site Option." *Personnel Journal* 65, no. 4 (April 1986): 79–82.

Stoneberger, Peter W. "Flexible and Incentive Benefits: A Guide to Program Development." *Compensation and Benefit Review* 17, no. 2 (2nd Quarter 1985): 12–19.

"Supplements to Wages and Salaries by Type," *National Income and Product Accounts of the United States, 1929–82* and *Survey of Current Business*, July 1987. Washington, DC: Bureau of Economic Analysis, U.S. Department of Commerce, 1987.

Sutcliffe, Jon, and Schuster, Jay. "Benefits Revisited, Benefits Predicted." *Personnel Journal* 64, no. 9 (September 1985): 62–72.

Tane, Lance D. "Guidelines to Successful Flex Plans: Four Companies' Experiences." *Compensation and Benefits Review* 17, no. 3 (July–August 1985): 38–43.

Task Force of Consultants. "The Omnibus Budget Reconciliation Act of 1987: What it Means to Pensions and Employee Benefits." *Compensation and Benefits Review* 20, no. 2 (March–April 1988): 14–32.

Tokerud, Douglas. "New on the Pension Scene: the Cash-Balance Plan." *Compensation and Benefits Review* 18, no. 1 (January–February 1986): 33–42.

U.S. Bureau of Labor Statistics. *Employee Benefits in Medium and Large Firms*, 1985. Washington, DC: Superintendent of Documents, 1986.

U.S. Chamber of Commerce. *Employee Benefits 1986*. Washington, DC: U.S. Chamber of Commerce, 1987.

White, James F. "Preparing Benefit Statements." *Personnel* 63, no. 5 (May 1986): 13–18.

Wilson, Marie. "The Perceived Value of Fringe Benefits." *Personnel Psychology* 38, no. 2 (Summer 1985): 309–321.

Wyatt Company. *Top 50 Survey*. Washington, DC: Wyatt Company, 1986.

Pay and Benefits: Executives

14

Chapter Outline

In Chapter 1 we looked at the hierarchical aspects of top executive pay. We saw that it has a bearing on the entire pay structure in the largest organizations, that top pay as a multiple of average pay levels shows a much higher ratio for the United States than for Canada, Australia, and Japan. We inferred that this meant a much higher pay (and benefits) cost than would be the case with less hierarchy. And in Chapter 2 we looked at a few international comparisons and saw the competitive implications—one important step being for large corporations to reduce the number of layers in the organization.

There are, of course, other aspects to executive pay and these we shall explore in the present chapter.

The largest manufacturing companies have a tremendous impact on what happens in the U.S. economy. They also set a pattern with respect to pay and benefit practices for smaller companies within the private sector. Although this ripple effect permeates into the government sector as well, it is mostly confined to the lower levels of the executive branch. Congress has not been willing to allow private sector pay trends to affect the pay for Cabinet or sub-Cabinet level jobs. This substantial pay and benefits differential has an adverse effect on attracting, holding, and motivating federal executives. The bonuses for senior federal executives and merit pay provisions for middle managers under the Civil Service Reform Act of 1978 are a constructive improvement. Whether they are enough to offset the remaining substantial differences as to both base pay and benefits is not yet clear.

Executive Pay and Sales Volume

The pay of the chief executive appears to be correlated with the volume of a company's activity—sales for manufacturing or trading companies, operating revenues for utilities, total deposits for commercial banks, and net premium income for insurance companies—as illustrated in Figure 14–1.[1]

Figure 14–1 relates the pay of the chief executive officer (typically the highest paid) to sales for each company. For example, one company with sales of over $4 billion had a chief executive officer who was paid close to $850,000 in 1985. The data are plotted on a log-log scale—a ratio scale on each axis. Such a scale makes it possible to compare percentage increases in sales with percentage

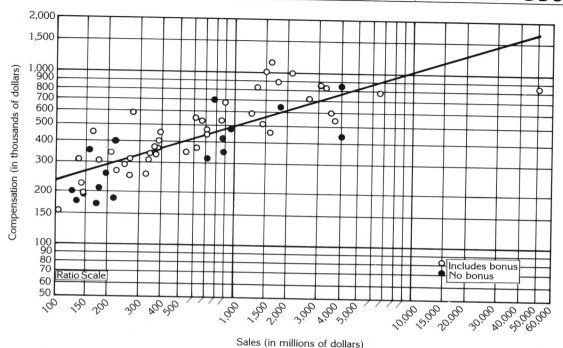

FIGURE 14–1
The positive correlation between a company's sales and the compensation of its chief executive officer for the nonelectrical machinery industry. Compensation includes salary or salary plus bonus. Source: Charles A. Peck, **Top Executive Compensation,** *1987 Edition, Report 889 (New York: The Conference Board, 1987): 7.*

increases in total compensation. If we read off the line of relationship, we see that an almost tenfold increase in sales from $200 million to $2,000 million is accompanied by a doubling in pay for the chief executive officer.[2]

Although sales and related volume measures are in common use as predictors of executive compensation, there is some evidence that a prediction equation using a combination of variables (but still including sales) can predict executive pay data more accurately.[3]

Taxes and Executive Pay

The pay package for an executive, especially at the higher levels, is affected by certain tax considerations. These considerations all tie in with tax avoidance. Avoidance does not mean tax evasion, which is illegal, but the careful analysis of tax legislation to develop forms of compensation beneficial to the individual executive and also to the corporation. This, of course, involves not only legal but ethical matters. Two of the more important aspects of pay for the individual are the tax treatment of business and personal deductions and the tax rate curve on fully taxable income.

Business expenses allowable under executive expense accounts reduce adjusted gross income. In addition, other allowable deductions can be taken against adjusted gross income. Figure 14–2 compares itemized deductions as a percentage of adjusted gross income for two years, 1976 and 1985 (the latest year

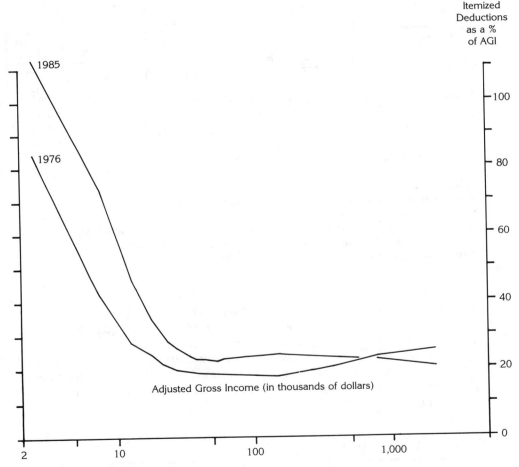

FIGURE 14–2
Itemized deductions as a percentage of adjusted gross income for two selected years. Data computed from Internal Revenue Service Statistics of Income—Individual Income Tax Returns.

available). The percentage appears to decline over the income brackets until somewhere around $50,000 of adjusted gross income. Then the behavior of the two curves differs slightly. The 1976 curve appears to rise slightly after about the $150,000 level, a trend that continues to the highest levels of income. By contrast, the 1985 curve reaches a minor peak around $150,000 and then curves downward slightly. Each year has its own particular pattern, but this two-year comparison suggests that the level of itemized deductions tends to level off at the higher income levels at around 20 percent to 25 percent of adjusted gross income.

Effective tax rate curves—that is, the individual income tax as a percentage of taxable income after deductions but before exemptions—have undergone pronounced historical change. Figure 14–3 illustrates the change by comparing 1955, the year after the significant Eisenhower tax reduction, with 1987, following President Reagan's tax reduction. At the top level, the tax rate has gone from a maximum of 87 percent to only slightly over 37 percent. At least as significant is that the entire tax rate curve is generally lower. The figures will differ slightly depending on the assumptions made, for example, about the number of exemptions. But the use of the effective tax rate curves is still the generally accepted measurement technique used by tax specialists in studying the personal income tax structure over the years.

Tax specialists also use this tax rate curve to design compensation packages that will defer income to a later period when the effective tax rate against the executive's income may be lower. Another way taxes on the individual can be minimized is to provide benefits subject to the capital gains rates rather than to the full individual income tax rate. The greater the disparity between the two rates, the greater the tendency to devise benefits of this kind. Recently both the decrease of the individual income tax rate and the increase in the maximum marginal long-term capital gains rate from 25 percent to 35 percent have reduced the differential between the two rates and therefore the need to devise benefits taxable as capital gains. In light of these considerations, it is interesting to see what has actually happened to the pay package for top executives.[4]

The Top Executive Pay Package

What top executives get, in terms of a total pay package, is typically never revealed in SEC figures or elsewhere. For a detailed discussion of exactly what such a total should include, see my *Top Executive Pay Package*.[5]

In Chapter 1, I used information about cash compensation (primarily salary and bonuses) for the top executives in the 100 largest industrials as a basis for comparison with the pay of top union leaders. I also used information about cash compensation in a larger number of U.S. companies to make some international comparisons.

Towers, Perrin, Forster, & Crosby also includes another set of numbers in its annual report on top executive pay that show something at least *approaching* total pay. For example, the data include 1-year annualized gain upon option exer-

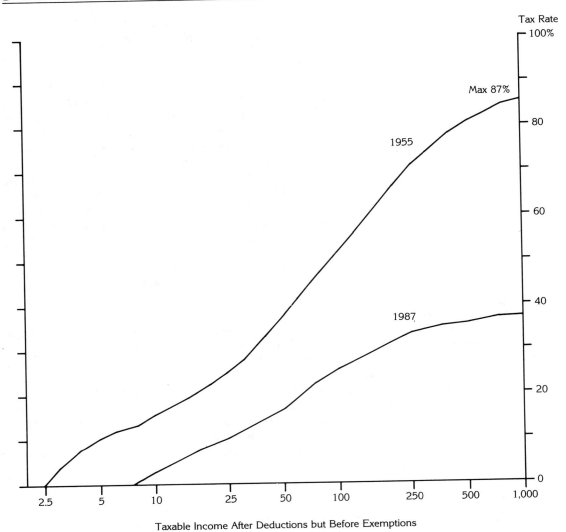

Taxable Income After Deductions but Before Exemptions
(in thousands of dollars)

FIGURE 14–3
Effective individual income tax rates for two selected years, for a married couple with two dependents. Data were computed from Internal Revenue Service **1040 Federal Income Tax Instructions,** *1987 Tax Rate Schedules, and matching information for 1955.*

cise and other long-term award payments (not just salaries and bonuses). Table 14–1 shows some of the totals.

The data are revealing. Among the top 100 companies, no one through the level of the fifth highest paid gets less than $200,000 in total direct compensation, and the median for all these levels is more than $.5 million. The highs at all

TABLE 14–1
Total direct compensation of top officers in thousands of dollars.

	Low	Median	High
Chief executive officer	$412	$1,380	$11,262
Second highest paid	254	962	3,563
Third highest paid	245	706	3,277
Fourth highest paid	231	622	4,260
Fifth highest paid	213	538	2,274

Source: Towers, Perrin, Forster, & Crosby, *1987 Top 100 Industrial Executive Compensation Study.*

these five levels are all in excess of $2 million. Finally, even the lowest-paid CEO gets over $400,000, with the typical CEO getting close to $1.4 million and the highest paid CEO being paid close to $11.3 million.

These data reinforce the conclusions reached earlier about the spread of compensation between top executives and the average worker in different nations as well as the implications of the spread for higher total labor costs and higher unit labor costs.

Salaries

Salary data have already been covered both in Chapter 1 and in the chapters relating to job evaluation. For executives, the Hay guide chart–profile method is probably the most widely used method of job evaluation. An alternative method, at least for executives, is the use of multiple correlation using regression equations.

In addition to job evaluation, some method of performance evaluation for executives is essential. It has become customary in many companies to think of performance for managers as best measured in terms of objectives, as under the management by objectives (MBO) system. Nonetheless, other methods such as behavioral observation scales (see Chapter 11) deserve consideration. An example of a behavioral observation scale for a managerial job is shown in Figure 14–4.

Bonuses

Bonuses were mentioned briefly in Chapter 12 with reference to incentive plans. Here I will describe the relation of bonuses to executive pay.

Bonuses for executives include payments both in cash and in stock, and the time of payment varies. For example, the bonus can be current, short-term deferred, or postretirement deferred. Current awards are typically paid to the executive shortly after the year for which the award is made. Short-term deferred awards, typical of the automobile manufacturers, are paid over a period of 4 or 5 years following the date of the award. Postretirement deferment is used by Texaco,

1. Overcoming Resistance to Change*
   (1) Describes the details of the change to subordinates.
       Almost Never   1   2   3   4   5   Almost Always
   (2) Explains why the change is necessary.
       Almost Never   1   2   3   4   5   Almost Always
   (3) Discusses how the change will affect the employee.
       Almost Never   1   2   3   4   5   Almost Always
   (4) Listens to the employee's concerns.
       Almost Never   1   2   3   4   5   Almost Always
   (5) Asks the employee for help in making the change work.
       Almost Never   1   2   3   4   5   Almost Always
   (6) If necessary, specifies the date for a follow-up meeting to respond to the employee's concerns.
       Almost Never   1   2   3   4   5   Almost Always

Total = _____

Below Adequate	Adequate	Full	Excellent	Superior*
6-10	11-15	16-20	21-25	26-30

*Scores are set by management.

FIGURE 14—4
Example of a performance dimension used in a behavioral observation scale for evaluating managers. (From Gary P. Latham and Kenneth N. Wexley, Increasing Productivity Through Performance Appraisal *[Reading, Mass.: Addison-Wesley, 1981]. Reprinted with permission.)*

General Electric, and many other companies with the intent of postponing the award to the retirement period when the executive's income will presumably be subject to a lower tax rate. Repeated awards, however, may so swell the level of retirement income as to deprive the executive of much of this advantage.

Only 28 of the 100 largest industrial corporations report bonus figures separately. The data for these 28 companies (see Table 14–2) show that the median bonus for the five highest-paid officers ranged from 78 percent of base salary for the Chief Executive Officer to 56 percent of base salary for the fifth highest-paid officer. However, one company paid its CEO a high of 197 percent of base salary, and another company paid its CEO a low of 23 percent of base salary. For the fifth highest-paid officer, the high and low percentages were, respectively, 257 percent and 23 percent.

TABLE 14–2

Bonuses as a percentage of base salary for the five highest-paid officers of the 100 largest industrial corporations.

	Low	*Median*	*High*
Chief Executive Officer	23%	78%	197%
Second highest-paid officer	23	69	207
Third highest paid	20	70	233
Fourth highest paid	23	61	243
Fifth highest paid	23	56	257

Source: Towers, Perrin, Forster, & Crosby, *1987 Top Industrial Executive Compensation Study.* Data are for 1986.

Bonuses for Division Managers

In developing an appropriate method of incentive compensation for executives who are plant managers or division managers in larger corporations, the questions of motivation comes up.

Should the executives in a given division be paid incentive compensation if the corporation as a whole didn't earn it?[6]

Robert Pursell answers this question with a strong yes and recommends four specific guidelines for top management regarding incentives for managers at the plant or division level:

1. Emphasize divisional results rather than corporate results.
2. Integrate the incentive program with planning and budgeting.
3. Focus on opportunity and improvement.
4. Consider the impact of planning assumptions on divisional targets and the potential consequences of change in the market or economic climate in which a division operates.[7]

Pursell shuns an overly mechanical use of ROI (return on investment) in comparing divisions, preferring instead a residual income approach. He defines residual income as net profit less a capital charge (e.g., 20 percent of a division's net assets). He also advocates inclusion of nonfinancial measurements because they represent the major things that must be done to ensure the future of a division's business.[8]

In his fourth recommendation to top management, Pursell stresses that performance targets be adjusted "retrospectively":

All performance targets are based on economic assumptions—and since such assumptions can obviously turn out to be incorrect, so can the targets on which they are based. Retrospective adjustment of targets in the face of fluctuations is most palatable when economic and market assumptions are made explicit from the outset and when everyone involved accepts that such adjustments may go either up or down—along with the actual fluctuations.[9]

Dividend Equivalents and Dividend Units

Before the Revenue Act of 1954 went into effect in 1955, dividend equivalents related to both bonuses and stock options where the executive received dividends on stock not yet possessed. Dividend units, authorized under the Revenue Act of 1954, were popular after 1955 because they involved a 4 percent dividend tax credit, which was discontinued in 1964. Even so, dividend units are still used by some companies today. Bethlehem Steel Corporation, a company strong on direct currently paid bonuses rather than deferred compensation, describes its plan as follows:

> Under the provisions of the plan the number of dividend units is determined by dividing an amount equal to 1 ½ % of the consolidated net income for the year by the market value of a share of Bethlehem Steel Common Stock at the beginning of the year. . . . Each dividend unit entitles the holder to receive cash payments equal to the cash dividends paid on a share of Bethlehem common stock after the crediting of the unit during his life. . . .[10]

Stock Options

The gist of the stock option is that the executive is given the right to buy the company's stock at the option price (usually the current market price at the time of grant) at a later time (up to 5 to 10 years later) when the market price is often much higher. Thus, if the option price is $20 a share, the executive can wait up to 5 years and buy the stock for $20 when the market price has risen to $50, with an unrealized capital gain of $30 a share. If the stock continues to rise during the required holding period, he can realize this amount, plus a further gain, upon sale of the stock (disregarding tax aspects). In theory, over the 5 years the stock price could drop *below* the option price and the executive would lose. It is a fact, however, particularly for the larger companies, that over time the tendency is for the price of the company's stock to rise, perhaps as much as 25 percent per year.

The models in Figure 14–5 show in simplifed form the key operational characteristics of various stock options. The apex at the left in each model represents the time the option to buy shares of stock is granted, and the gap between the two lines illustrates the opportunity for gain, assuming that the market price of the stock increases over the years. The longer the period during which the executive has a right to exercise an option to buy the stock and the shorter the required holding period before the stock can be sold, the greater is the opportunity for gain.

In 1950 Congress encouraged stock options by creating the restricted stock option. Under the restricted stock option, the executive could exercise his right to buy the stock over a period as long as 10 years and could sell it only 6 months after purchase. In 1955, the capital gain between the market price on sale and the option price was subject to a maximum tax of 25 percent, compared with individual effective tax rates that could be as high as 85.7 percent at the $1 million income level. Because of criticism from those who believed that special tax treatment of stock options was not in the public interest,[11] Congress in 1964 eliminated the restricted stock option and provided for the qualified stock option (see Figure 14–5).

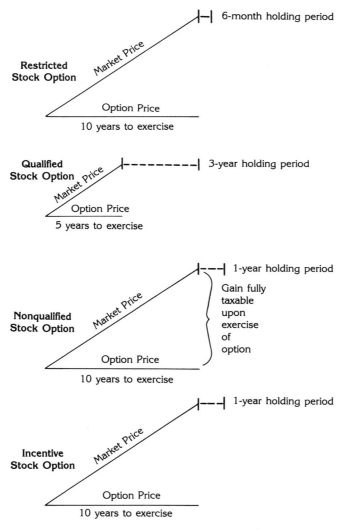

FIGURE 14–5
Stock option models.

The more important operational differences between the qualified stock option and the restricted stock option were the shortening of the period of possible exercise of the option from 10 to 5 years and the lengthening of the holding period from 6 months to 3 years. The difference between the market price and the option price at the time of sale was still treated as a capital gain. Since gain is recognized only upon sale, there was no tax if the executive did not sell.

Under the law, the qualified stock option required that if several options were granted over a period of years and the price of the stock dropped, the earlier, higher-priced options had to be purchased before the later, lower-priced options. Some companies sought to offset this feature by swapping options, as explained by Graef Crystal:

> If an executive has 10,000 shares at $50, and the stock drops to $30, the company gives him another 10,000 shares at $30. If those drop to $10, then he can have 10,000 shares at $10. The old grants are just cancelled. If the stock ever turns up the executive will make a lot of money.[12]

But Crystal doesn't think the practice is very beneficial:

> I don't have much sympathy for companies in the share-for-share option swapping business. I think they give a bad name to everything they are trying to accomplish. Ultimately, they will bring the wrath of their shareholders down on them. If there is enough abuse, they'll bring the wrath of the government down on all of us.[13]

Recent tax law changes, as explained earlier, have reduced the effective maximum personal income tax rate from 87 percent in 1955 to slightly over 37.5 percent in 1987 (as shown in Figure 14–3). The effect of the new legislation has been to reduce the tax advantage to the executive of any capital gains such as those formerly achieved under stock options. Not only have the tax rates on ordinary income dropped, but in 1969 the maximum marginal capital gains tax was increased to 35 percent, being phased in over several years. In 1976 Congress ended the special tax treatment for qualified stock options. It also extended from 6 months to 1 year (for 1978 and later) the required holding period for long-term capital gains. One effect of this change is to lengthen the holding period before an executive can sell stock acquired under a nonqualified stock option.

The model of the nonqualified stock option (see Figure 14–5) is roughly the same as that for the restricted stock option except for the tax treatment and the longer holding period. Under current regulations, the executive must pay a tax of up to 50 percent on the difference between the market price and the option price at the time he exercises his option. If he later sells the stock, any future gain is taxed as a capital gain.

The model at the bottom of Figure 14–7 illustrates another type of stock option—the incentive stock option—which was authorized under the Economic Recovery Tax Act of 1981. As in the case of the restricted stock option, the option to buy the shares can be exercised for a period up to 10 years following the grant of the option. The incentive stock option differs from the restricted stock option in that the required holding period is 1 year rather than 6 months. The gain is taxed in the same way as under the restricted stock option: No gain is recognized until the stock is sold, at which time the difference between the sales price and the option price is taxable at capital gains rates.

Some of the actual gains under recent stock options can be seen from the Atlantic-Richfield report for 1980 (Table 14–3). The options or tandem rights exercised or realized by the chairman of the board had a value of $896,000. In addition, he had potential but unrealized capital gains of $587,000.

Phantom Stock and Appreciation Rights

Some executives find it difficult to raise the necessary money to purchase stock under stock options. In this situation, they can use the device of phantom stock. Phantom stock involves paying the executive, after a certain period of deferment, the appreciation in value of the stock since the date the shares were awarded, without the executive having to pay money to buy the stock. Such stock bonuses have typically also involved the payment of dividend equivalents in cash. Stock appreciation rights involve similar benefits limited to the stock portion and often related just to a stock option.

Restricted Stock

Another way to reward executives is with a bonus in the form of restricted stock. The Phillips Petroleum incentive compensation plan, adopted in 1965, uses this method:

> The board may grant allotments in the form of cash, shares or restricted shares of the company's common stock. . . . Where all or part of a deferred settlement is in shares of stock, the participant's account will be credited with an amount equal to the dividends which would have been payable had the stock been

TABLE 14–3
Stock options and tandem rights for Atlantic-Richfield's highest paid executives (in thousands of dollars).

Executive	Exercised or Realized in 1980*	End-of-year Unrealized Value**
Chairman of the board	$ 896	$ 587
President	903	1,003
Executive vice president	331	627
All directors and officers	5,466	13,168

*Net value realized (market value less exercise price) or cash.
**Market value less exercise or base price.
Source: Atlantic-Richfield Company, proxy statement, March 16, 1981.

issued and outstanding. Where all or part of an allotment is in restricted shares of stock, such restricted shares shall be registered in the name of the participant, but may not be sold, assigned, transferred, pledged or otherwise disposed of without prior written consent of the board during the period specified by the board. A participant must agree to remain with the company for at least two years from the allotment date. When a participant's employment is terminated (except for death, disability or normal retirement) before an allotment is fully paid, the unpaid amounts are subject to forfeiture. The company intends to continue the plan indefinitely.[14]

Performance Shares or Units and Performance Stock Options

Another approach to executive compensation is to relate incentive rewards more closely to company performance through the use of performance shares, performance units, or performance stock options. For example, Atlantic-Richfield reports that along with other emoluments in its long-term incentive plan,

> participants may additionally be awarded performance units or performance stock options. Performance units result in a contingent cash payment payable five years after the date of grant. Performance stock options, with conditions identical to the non-qualified options, are exercisable after five years by participants who are not officers at date of grant. Performance units will become earned and performance stock options will become exercisable only to the extent certain conditions regarding return on shareholders' equity and cash dividends are met.[15]

Sun Company's goals in its management performance share plan illustrate the conditions involved in such plans:

> For the 1976 awards, the award committee fixed the program target for distribution in 1982 as an 8% increase in return on shareholder's equity for a 100% distribution, scaled down to a 50% distribution for a 4% increase.[16]

An important aspect of these plans is that, except where the stock option is included, there is no necessity for the price of the stock to rise so long as the desired corporate objective for return on investment is met.

Another category of plans attempts to avoid at least the day-to-day variation in the price of the company's common stock. One approach is the book value plan. Under this plan, an executive can purchase company stock at its book value and then at a later time sell the stock back to the company at its newer and often higher book value. Thus, if a company's net worth rises, so will the book value per share. This approach gets away from the more speculative market price per share and focuses the executive's attention more on company earnings than on manipulation of the price of the stock.[17]

Postretirement Benefits

Thrift and savings plans, pensions, and deferred compensation under contract have already been explored in Chapter 13. There we learned that the deferred compensation contract is typically a substitute for a pension for a new executive whose pension is low because of a short length of service. The deferred pay is usually either for a set number of years after retirement or for life. It is normally contingent on not working for a competing company, remaining available for consultation, and other stipulations. These have typically been individual arrangements, outside the company's pension plan.

Supplemental Executive Retirement Plan

Underlying the Employee Retirement Income Security Act (ERISA) of 1974 (see Chapter 13) was the desire of Congress to correct abuses in corporate handling of pension plans. The act set a yearly maximum of $75,000 (increased under the law to $124,000 in 1981) on what an executive could get from a qualified pension plan. Instead of accepting this implied ethical judgment, corporate lawyers exploited the weakness of the act. They liberalized pension benefits for top executives rather than reducing them. Two more layers of benefits have been added to get around the maximum set by ERISA. Excess (but unfunded) plans, allowable under the act, pay the difference between the prescribed maximum and the benefit payable under the qualified plan formula. Another layer, the Supplemental Executive Retirement Plan (SERP), boosts benefits even beyond the retirement formula benefit. These plans are also unfunded, with company contributions being made as benefit payments are due. Furthermore, there is no vesting of benefits; if the employee leaves the company other than through retirement, the benefit is lost.[18]

By having a SERP, an organization can

1. Provide retirement income in excess of that permitted from qualified plans under ERISA.
2. Recruit an executive in mid- or late-career whose normal pension would be inadequate because of short service.
3. Provide a distinct and additional element of compensation that will motivate qualified top level executives.
4. Encourage executives to remain with the company, at least until they qualify for early retirement benefits.
5. Encourage the early retirement of executives.
6. Provide where desirable, comparable total benefits for executives worldwide.[19]

In many cases the major purpose of having the SERP is to encourage earlier retirement of executives. As Jerry Rosenbloom and G. Victor Hallman suggest,

If the primary interest is in encouraging early retirement on a selective basis, it might be appropriate to provide full unreduced benefits only in company-initiated retirements.[20]

Trends in Executive Benefits

The annual studies by the consulting firm of Towers, Perrin, Forster & Crosby reveal some interesting trends.[21] The data for long-term incentive rewards for selected years 1971 to 1987 are shown in Table 14–4.

Over these years stock options have remained without any question the predominant form of long-range incentive compensation for corporate executives, being present throughout the period in more than 84 percent of the companies and in 97 of the 100 companies in 1987. A related form of compensation, stock appreciation rights, has shown the most pronounced rate of growth, initially offered by a single company but reported by 81 companies in 1987. Restricted stock/stock grants, reported by few companies in 1971, have also shown growth though not as pronounced. In 1987, they were reported by 44 companies. The use of performance units and performance shares have also shown considerable growth. Since these kinds of plans really demand more in the way of executive performance, the growth of these particular forms of incentive reward can be viewed as desirable. By contrast, neither phantom stock nor dividend units appear to have gained in popularity.

Pay and Benefits for International Executives

International executives fall into three special groups: expatriates, local nationals, and third country nationals. Expatriates are U.S. citizens working overseas for a U.S. company. Local nationals are employees who are citizens of the country

TABLE 14–4
Long-term incentive awards for top executives in the 100 largest U.S. corporations

	1971	75	79	83	87
Stock options	89	87	84	95	97
Appreciation rights	1	27	65	73	81
Performance units	1	6	26	42	52
Performance shares	0	5	12	17	33
Stock grants/restricted stock	N/A	5	8	29	44
Phantom stock	4	5	2	3	3
Dividend units	?	5	3	3	2

Source: Towers, Perrin, Forster, & Crosby, *1987 Top 100 Industrial Executive Compensation Study* and corresponding reports for earlier years.

where the overseas operation is being conducted. Third country nationals are citizens of a country other than the United States or the country in which they are working.[22]

Salaries and Bonuses for Executives Abroad

Base salaries for expatriates should be the same as those paid to comparable employees in the United States and should be tied in with some kind of job evaluation, according to J. D. Dunn and Frank Rachel.[23] Thomas H. Patten, Jr., disagrees:

> There is no reason to assume that the position of plant manager in an automobile assembly plant in a developing country is the same as that in a plant in the United States, West Germany, or Japan. Differences in volume, degree of automation, work force training and recruitment, and external political and plant-community relations make for corresponding differences in the position requirements of a plant manager.[24]

Job differences between countries do not constitute sufficient reason to exclude jobs in foreign countries from the reach of the company's job evaluation plan. Also, if a plant manager might later be moved back to a job in the United States, the same base pay system should be used, despite differences in some benefits. This argument would apply to other direct cash or stock benefits, too. David Belcher reports evidence that profit-based executive bonuses do not exclude international executives in U.S. multinational companies.[25]

Executive Benefits for International Service

Several employee benefits have been developed for company executives who are sent overseas. Among them are

1. Foreign service premium.
2. Hardship differential.
3. Intercity cost-of-living allowance.
4. Housing allowance.
5. Education allowance.
6. Moving and travel expenses.

Foreign Service Premium

In a survey of 28 companies with overseas operations, Graef Crystal found that three quarters of them pay a premium for foreign service. The premium is usually a percentage of base salary, ranging from 5 percent to 20 percent. At the higher percentage a cap is usually involved, such as a 15 percent premium with a $6,000 maximum.[26] Two thirds of the companies paying premiums made them virtually tax-free by reimbursing the executive for the amount of any tax.[27]

Compensation executives as well as executives living abroad question whether a foreign service premium should be paid. The concept used by some companies of a decreasing premium (20 percent for the first year, 15 percent for the second year, with a minimum of 5 percent) is based on the belief that the greatest adjustment for the overseas executive is likely to be in the early years of the assignment.[28]

Hardship Differential

Many companies not only pay a premium for overseas duty but also pay a hardship differential. In a study of 157 firms, Dunn and Rachel found 55 companies that paid such a differential, varying from 10 to 25 percent of base pay. The differential is paid to executives in certain locations involving "difficult or unhealthful living conditions or physical hardship."[29]

Intercity Cost-of-Living Allowance

Executives on overseas assignments are typically given a cost-of-living allowance which depends on the executive's spendable income and an intercity price index. Spendable income is estimated from the executive's base salary using a curve that relates the two. For example, at $30,000 an executive's spendable income might be 60 percent of salary, while at $60,000 it might be 50 percent. In dollars the change is from $18,000 to $30,000. Now suppose the executive's cost of living in Paris is 40 percent more than the cost of living in a U.S. city. The cost-of-living allowance would be 40 percent of spendable income: for the higher-paid executive, 40 percent of $30,000 or $12,000.[30]

The cost-of-living index used to compute the allowance is different from the usual Bureau of Labor Statistics index. While the BLS index compares prices now against 1967 (a comparison between two time periods), the index used in computing the cost-of-living allowance compares prices in Paris against Washington (a comparison between two cities). The usual standard is an intercity price index published by the U.S. State Department. If this index, which is based on the cost of living in Washington, D.C., is used, then an executive from a U.S. city with a lower cost of living would tend to be less well treated abroad, while one from a city with a higher cost of living would fare better. Another problem, unique to international comparisons, is that currency devaluations or revaluations affect the validity of the index. This problem is corrected by doing new pricing surveys after any such change.[31]

In light of the intricacies of the intercity cost-of-living index, Crystal stresses the importance of adequate communication:

> One company issues a . . . brochure and invites wives of expatriates to accompany the outside consultants on pricing trips to local retail outlets. Should the

expatriate question his cost-of-living allowance, the company furnishes him with detailed computer runs showing the assumed quantities of each index item, together with the U.S. and local prices. He can verify the number himself, and if he desires he can challenge specific assumptions or prices. In this company, there are no complaints regarding the cost-of-living allowance.[32]

Housing Allowance

Most of the companies in Crystal's study reported using a U.S. deductible, which the executive pays, with the company paying all or most of the amount in excess of the deductible as a housing allowance. When a fixed percentage of salary was used for the deductible, the range was from 10 percent to 20 percent. Other companies used a custom curve approach; that is, the percentage for the deductible increased with an increase in base salary.[33]

One company set a maximum monthly allowance by computing the difference between the average housing costs, among expatriates of all companies, in the particular city abroad (based on a survey) and the executive's U.S. housing cost (based on salary level). The company paid actual costs in excess of the U.S. housing cost up to the amount of the allowance, but warned that if the executive spent *less* than the U.S. housing cost, the difference would be deducted from his salary. Crystal describes how well this system works:

> First, an effective cap has been developed, and the pitfalls of the all-in-excess approach have been minimized. Second, the company has insured that its expatriates will live in at least a comfortable style. In this way, the expatriates' wives may feel somewhat more kindly toward the company.[34]

Other Allowances

Education allowances are typically provided to expatriates to cover expenses that are normally greater than would be incurred in the United States. Companies also usually pay for moving personal and household goods and for travel expenses.[35]

Tax Aspects

A problem of equity arises with respect to tax rates paid by the executive abroad. Compared with a U.S. citizen working in the United States who receives comparable pay, how can a company insure that the expatriate neither gains nor loses with respect to taxes? Two-way tax equalization is often used:

> We will deduct from your compensation package an amount approximating what you would have paid in income taxes had you been residing in the United States. Then we will reimburse you for all the income taxes, both United States and foreign, that you actually pay.[36]

Third Country Nationals and Local Nationals

The typical policy for local nationals (e.g., a French worker in a U.S. plant in France) is decentralization—let policy be determined locally. The reason for such a policy is that

> labor laws of various countries differ widely, and in general the supplemental benefit package is determined more by law than by custom. This is in sharp contrast to the United States. In foreign countries the cost of legally prescribed holidays, year-end bonuses, and other supplemental benefits may reach 50 percent or even more of total payroll costs.[37]

The problem of the third country national (e.g., a Spanish executive working in France for a U.S. company) is more difficult to resolve. Some logical approaches are suggested by Crystal:

1. Treat him as a local national of his host country and pay him a competitive amount of compensation by that country's standards.
2. Treat him as an expatriate of his own country and devise a package similar in concept to the U.S. package.
3. Treat him as an American expatriate.[38]

Summary

High levels of executive pay attract, hold, and motivate employees in the larger corporations. The differential in executive pay levels between industry and the federal government, however, has an adverse effect on federal government employees.

Sales volume and similar measures of activity help to explain the levels of executive pay in organizations of varying size, but more accurate measures are needed.

Tax aspects also have a bearing on the pay of the top executive. The differential between the individual income tax rate and the capital gains rate, which has decreased over time, has been an important consideration in designing executive pay packages.

Base salary is only one part of the executive pay package. It is typically the smallest part, as a percent of the total pay package. Increases in base salary are determined on the basis of performance evaluation, which for managers typically follows a management by objectives approach. Behavioral observation scales are also relevant, however.

Incentive pay—another component of executive compensation—for division managers should emphasize divisional rather than overall corporate results. Bonuses for the five highest paid officers in the 100 largest companies vary widely as a percentage of base salary. Postretirement benefits can include Supplemental Executive Retirement Plans (SERP), which increase pension benefits for executives.

From 1955 to 1981 the pay package of the top executive has shifted toward nonqualified stock options, option substitutes, and performance shares and units. Performance shares and units tend to focus the attention of executives more on long-run growth in return on investment and similar objectives and away from watching the market price of the stock. For the period from 1977 to 1981, more of the largest companies reported short-term benefits for executives.

International executives pose special compensation problems for multinational firms. Cost-of-living allowances and housing allowances are only two examples of the employee benefits covering such individuals. Companies giving a housing allowance provide for a U.S. deductible either as a fixed percentage of salary or with a decreasing percentage with increasing base salary. Compensation policy as to third country nationals is a difficult compensation problem to resolve.

Case Study

The McGinty Corporation

The McGinty Corporation is a conglomerate employing over 1,000 workers, and its plants are located in 15 states in the South and on the West Coast. Reporting to the president are two group vice presidents whose responsibilities include consumer products and industrial products. Reporting to the two group vice presidents are 10 product division managers. Although certain accounting, capital budgeting, research and development, and public relations functions are carried out in the company headquarters, most operations are decentralized to the product divisions. Each division manager is responsible for the overall profitability of his division. Once each year the group vice president meets with each division manager, receives a progress report on accomplishments in the past year, and hears the division manager's report on plans for the following year.

Following a meeting with his two group vice presidents, President Thomas McGinty, now in his second year as the company's chief executive officer, became concerned about the bonuses of his division managers. He felt that the existing bonus plan, which had been in effect for the past 5 years, was not achieving the desired degree of motivation. Under the present plan the amount available for bonuses for the next year is set arbitrarily by the board of directors. Half of this amount is awarded to the division managers, with each award based on the division's return on investment (ROI) for the previous year as reported by the company controller. The net income after-tax figure used in computing the return on investment reflects not only costs directly incurred by each division but also certain headquarters overhead amounts allocated according to divisional sales totals. The other half of the bonus money is allocated equally to the two group vice presidents, who make an additional bonus award to each division manager based on a merit review and performance evaluation. Thus, the bonus received by each division manager depends partly on the performance of the division and partly on merit rating. (The two group vice presidents are not eligible for bonuses but receive stock options instead.)

A number of problems had arisen under the current bonus plan. Some division managers were critical of the part of the bonus resulting from merit rating. One felt the ratings were quite arbitrary and depended too much on the personal evaluation of the group vice president, while another pointed out that merit ratings sometimes resulted in excessive bonuses—as much as 150 percent of base salary in one instance. The president was concerned when he found out that in some years a division manager whose division did well got a sizable bonus even though the company as a whole did poorly that year.

One of the group vice presidents was critical of the ROI formula used for the bonus. She pointed out that the net income figure used to determine the ROI reflected some costs over which the division manager had no control. She added that one or another division by its very nature had a lower ROI, which made it difficult for anyone assigned to that division to make a respectable bonus. For example, in the consumer products group the pharmaceutical division typically fared much better than the textile division. But this difference in profit levels reflected such recent industry averages as a 20.3 percent return on net worth for drugs and medicines compared to 3.7 percent for textile products.

For the McGinty Corporation as a whole, the average net income after taxes over the previous 5-year period was 15.3 percent of net worth.

Role Assignment

You have been called in as a consultant to the president. He wants your recommendations about a bonus plan for division managers. What changes would you recommend and why?

Questions for Discussion

1. Are pay levels of high-level executives in the federal government comparable to pay levels of higher-paid executives in industry? Explain.

2. What is the general relationship between the compensation of the chief executives in the larger companies and the size of the companies? Is this a reliable basis for forecasting levels of executive pay?

3. How do personal deductions and individual income tax rates affect the pay of top executives?

4. You are one of three former presidents of a corporation who now serve the corporation as the salary and bonus committee of the board. What type of performance evaluation will you use for evaluating the current chairman of the board and chief executive officer?

5. For the manager of a major operating division of a corporation whose performance is being measured using management by objectives, should performance goals decided upon for a particular year ever be altered retroactively? Why or why not?

6. Do you agree with the use of a Supplemental Employee Retirement Plan in order to retire early an executive whose services the corporation no longer wishes to retain? Justify your answer.

7. How do stock options work? What is the difference between a qualified and a nonqualified stock option?

8. What is the advantage of using performance shares or units, or a performance stock option, rather than a nonqualified stock option?

9. What are the pros and cons of using short-term and long-term incentives for top executives?
10. What can be said about trends among the newer employee benefits for top executives?
11. What benefits are typically made available to U.S. executives serving in corporate positions abroad?
12. Explain the difference between the Bureau of Labor Statistics cost-of-living index and an intercity cost-of-living index.
13. If you were vice president in charge of human resources for a multinational firm, what policy would you advocate as to pay and benefits for third country nationals in your firm?

Notes

1. Charles A. Peck, *Top Executive Compensation, 1987 Edition*, Report 889 (New York: The Conference Board, 1987), 7.
2. The formula for the line of relationship (or regression line) is log $Y = 1.7024 + .3289$ log X, where Y is compensation in thousands of dollars and X is company sales in millions of dollars. Preparing a table for plotting such a line is not difficult, once the equation is obtained, with a pocket computer having both power and log functions.
3. See for example Kenneth E. Foster, James Garro, and Linda Rosario, "Determinants of CEO Pay," *1975 National Conference Proceedings of the American Compensation Association*, 99–112.
4. For an analysis of taxes and the total pay package, see Leonard R. Burgess, *Top Executive Pay Package* (New York: Free Press and Columbia University Graduate School of Business, 1963), Chapter 7.
5. Leonard R. Burgess, *Top Executive Pay Package* (New York: Free Press of Glencoe and Columbia University, 1961).
6. Reprinted, by permission of the publisher, from Robert B. Pursell, "Administering Divisional Incentive Compensation," *Compensation Review*, 1st Quarter 1980. (New York: AMACOM, a division of American Management Associations, 1980) 19–20. Copyright © by AMACOM. All rights reserved.
7. Ibid., 19–20.
8. Ibid., 17.
9. Ibid., 19.
10. Bethlehem Steel Corporation, proxy statement, 1977, p. 9.
11. Burgess, *op. cit.* 198–205.
12. Graef S. Crystal, "Trends in Executive Compensation," *1975 National Conference Proceedings of the American Compensation Association*, 4.
13. Ibid., 5.
14. Phillips Petroleum Company, proxy statement, 1977, pp. 8–9.
15. Atlantic-Richfield Company, proxy statement, April 1, 1977, p. 9.
16. Sun Company, Inc., annual proxy statement, March 23, 1977, p. 9.
17. For a further discussion of such plans, see Frederic W. Cook, "Book-Value Stock as an Employee Stock Ownership and Incentive Device." *Compensation Review* 9, no. 3 (1977): 11–19.
18. Jerry S. Rosenbloom and G. Victor Hallman, *Employee Benefit Planning* (Englewood Cliffs, N.J.: Prentice-Hall, 1981), 361–64. Copyright © 1981. Reprinted by permission of Prentice-Hall, Inc., Englewood Cliffs, N.J.
19. Ibid., 362.
20. Ibid., 363.
21. Towers, Perrin, Forster & Crosby, *1987 Top 100 Industrial Executive Compensation Study*, p. 13, and similar earlier reports.
22. J. D. Dunn and Frank M. Rachel, *Wage and Salary Administration: Total Compensation Systems* (New York: McGraw-Hill, 1971), 340. Reproduced with permission of the publisher.
23. Ibid., 341.
24. Thomas H. Patten, Jr., *Pay Employee Compensation and Incentive Plans* (New York: The Free Press, 1977), 291. Copyright ©

1977 by The Free Press, a Division of Macmillan Publishing Co., Inc.

25. David W. Belcher, *Compensation Administration* (Englewood Cliffs, N.J.: Prentice-Hall, 1974), 566.

26. Reprinted, with permission of the publisher, from Graef S. Crystal, *Compensating U.S. Executives Abroad,* an AMA Management Briefing, (New York: AMACOM, a division of American Management Associations, 1972) 7. Copyright © by AMACOM. All rights reserved.

27. Ibid., 8.

28. Ibid., 10.

29. Dunn and Rachel, *op. cit.*, 343–44.

30. Crystal, *Compensating U.S. Executives*, p. 14.

31. For a full discussion of problems relating to the index, see Crystal, *Compensating U.S. Executives*, especially pp. 15–19.

32. Ibid., 21.

33. Ibid., 24–25.

34. Ibid., 27.

35. See Dunn and Rachel, *op. cit.*, 347.

36. See Crystal, *Compensating U.S. Executives*, pp. 29–30 for this and other details.

37. Dunn and Rachel, *op. cit.*, 348–49.

38. See Crystal, *Compensating U.S. Executives*, 43–45 for a full discussion of these options and related problems.

References

Amend, Patricia. "*Inc*'s Annual Compensation Survey," *Inc* (September 1986).

Benson, James M., and Suzaki, Barbara Walk. "After Tax Reform, Part 3: Planning Executive Benefits." *Compensation and Benefits Review* 20, no. 2 (March–April 1988): 45–46.

Bopren, Gary, et al. *Qualified Deferred Compensation Plans.* New York: Callaghan, 1985.

Brennan, E. James. "The IRS and Shareholder Employees." *Personnel Journal* 64, no. 9 (September 1985): 88–91.

Brooks, Brian J. "Long-Term Incentives for the Foreign-Based Executive." *Compensation and Benefits Review* 17, no. 3 (July–August 1985): 46–53.

Burgess, Leonard R. *Top Executive Pay Package.* New York: Free Press and Graduate School of Business, Columbia University, 1963.

Cochran, Philip L., et al. "The Composition of Boards of Directors and Incidence of Golden Parachutes." *Academy of Management Journal,* 28, no. 3 (September 1985): 664–671.

Crino, Michael D. "Tax Implications of Lump-Sum Distributions." *Personnel* 62, no. 4 (April 1985): 20–23.

Crystal, Graef. "Handling Underwater Stock Option Grants." *Personnel* 65, no. 2 (February 1988): 12–15.

Crystal, Graef S. *Questions and Answers on Executive Compensation: How to Get What You're Worth.* Englewood Cliffs, NJ: Prentice-Hall, 1984.

Crystal, Graef, and Silberman, Samuel J. "Not for Profit Organizations Need Incentive Compensation." *Personnel* 63, no. 4 (April 1986): 7–12.

"Currents in Compensation and Benefits (U.S. Executives Risk More Than Executives in Other Countries)." *Compensation and Benefits Review* 19, no. 6 (November–December 1987): 2.

"Currents in Compensation and Benefits (Poor Correlation between Pay and Performance of Chief Executive Officers)." *Pay and Benefits Review* 20, no. 2 (March–April 1988): 2.

Hornstein, Harvey A. "Managerial Courage: Individual Initiative and Organizational Innovation." *Personnel* 63, no. 7 (July 1986): 16–23.

Jackson, Lester B. "Executive Compensation: Where We Are and Where Are We Going?" *Personnel Administrator* 30, no. 6 (June 1985), 51–59.

Jones, Edward W. "Black Managers: The Dream Deferred." *Harvard Business Review* 64, no. 3 (May–June 1986): 84–93.

Kerr, Jeffrey L. "Diversification Strategies and Managerial Rewards: An Empirical Study."

Academy of Management Journal 28, no. 1 (March 1985): 155–179.

Kessler, Felix. "Executive Perks Under Fire." *Fortune* 112, no. 2 (July 22, 1985): 26–31.

Kovach, Kenneth A., and Render, Barry. "NASA Managers and Challenger: A Profile and Possible Explanation." *Personnel* 64, no. 4 (April 1987): 40–44.

Krupp, Neil B. "Reining in Runaway Expatriate Compensation." *Personnel* 62, no. 11 (November 1985): 73–76.

Kuhne, Robert J., and Toyne, Brian. "Who Manages the International Compensation and Benefits Function?" *Compensation Review* 17, no. 1 (1st Quarter 1985): 34–41.

Linney, Reid C., and Marshall, Charles T. "ISOs versus NQSOs: The Choice Still Exists." *Compensation and Benefits Review* 19, no. 1 (January–February 1987): 13–25.

Murdock, Burt A., and Ramamurthy, Babloo. "Section 404A Legislation: A Practical Look." *Compensation and Benefits Review* 18, no. 3 (May–June 1986): 49–58.

Murphy, Kevin J. "Top Executives Are Worth Every Nickel They Get." *Harvard Business Review* 64, no. 2 (March–April 1986): 125–132.

Patton, Arch. "Those Million-Dollar-A-Year Executives." *Harvard Business Review* 63, no. 1 (January–February 1985): 56–62.

Paul, Robert D., and Lawrence, Stewart D. "To Defer or Not to Defer: Risks and Considerations." *Compensation and Benefits Review* 18, no. 4 (July–August 1986): 15–20.

Peck, Charles A. *Top Executive Compensation.* 1987 ed. New York: National Industrial Conference Board, 1986.

Platt, Harlan D., and McCarthy, Daniel J. "Executive Compensation: Performance and Patience." *Business Horizons* 28, no. 1 (January–February 1985): 48–53.

Poster, Claudia Zeitz. "Executive Compensation: Taking Long-Term Incentives Out of the Corporate Ivory Tower." *Compensation and Benefits Review* 17, no. 2 (2nd Quarter 1985): 32–39.

Schechter, Jack H. "The Tax Reform Act of 1986: Its Impact on Compensation and Benefits." *Compensation and Benefits Review* 18, no. 6 (November–December 1986): 11–24.

Schuster, Jay R., and Zingheim, Patricia K. "In Hostile Takeovers: Protecting Key Personnel Compensation." *Compensation and Benefits Review* 19, no. 4 (July–August 1987): 44–53.

Smith, A. W., Jr. "Will Perquisites Survive?" *Compensation and Benefits Review* 17, no. 5 (November–December 1985): 44–52.

Spalding, Albert D. *Deferred Compensation: Accounting, Taxation, and Funding for Nonqualified Plans.* Englewood Cliffs, NJ: Prentice-Hall, 1985.

Speck, Raymond W., Jr. "Management Compensation Planning in Diversified Companies." *Compensation and Benefits Review* 19, no. 2 (March–April 1987) 26–33.

Stone, Raymond J. "Pay and Perks for Overseas Executives." *Personnel Journal* 65, no. 1 (January 1986): 64–69.

Sullivan, Donald E. "The Case for Nonqualified Stock Options: History Repeats Itself." *Compensation and Benefits Review* 18, no. 5 (September–October 1986): 48–49.

Swinford, David. " 'Unbundling' Divisional Management Incentives." *Compensation and Benefits Review* no. 6 (November–December 1987): 57–61.

Tarant, John. *Perks and Parachutes: Negotiating Your Executive Employment Contract.* New York: Linden Press/Simon and Schuster, 1985.

Tauber, Yale D. "Trends in Compensation for Outside Directors." *Compensation and Benefits Review* 18, no. 1 (January–February 1986): 43–52.

Tharp, Charles Glen. "Linking Annual Incentives and Individual Performance." *Personnel Administrator* 31, no. 1 (January 1986): 85–90.

Thayer, Paul W. "Seven Reasons to Choose Index Options." *Pension World* 21, no. 10 (October 1985): 34–37 and 50.

Towers, Perrin, Forster, and Crosby. *1987 Top 100 Industrial Executive Compensation Study.* New York: TPF & C, 1987.

Wagel, William H. "Working (and Managing) Without Supervisors." *Personnel* 64, no. 9 (September 1987): 8–11.

Williams, Monci Jo. "Why Chief Executives' Pay Keeps Rising." *Fortune* 111, no. 7 (April 1, 1985): 66–76.

Pay and Benefits: Professionals

Chapter Outline

- The Nature of a Profession
- Motivation of Professionals
- Professional Incomes and Base Pay
- Employee Benefits and Expense Accounts
- Individual versus Organizational Obsolescence
- The Role of Unions
- Summary
- Case Study—Seidenfeld Pharmaceutical Company

In the middle ranks of the hierarchical structure typical of the larger business organization—above the blue-collar and nonsupervisory white-collar workers often viewed by unions as their primary target but below the higher and distinctly nonunion executive levels at the top—are both middle managers and professional workers.

In Chapter 8, we saw that the guide chart–profile method uses separate profiles for professional staff and research jobs. In Chapter 9, we discussed pay levels for professional jobs such as auditors, accountants, engineers, chemists, directors of personnel, and attorneys. In Chapter 11, we distinguished between performance evaluation for nonexempt and exempt employees, with professionals as well as executives included in the latter group. In Chapter 14, we learned that executives received some benefits not typical of other exempt employees, but little was said about particular benefits for professionals. Thus, we shall focus on the professional employee in this chapter.

The Nature of a Profession

Who are the professionals? Perhaps the broadest and most authoritative guide is the U.S. Department of Labor's *Dictionary of Occupational Titles.* Using this source, we can obtain a representative list, shown in Table 15–1. No claim is made as to the inclusiveness of this list, but it covers a sufficient number of occupations for the purpose of discussion.

A profession has three chief characteristics:

1. A specialized field of knowledge.
2. Service orientation.
3. Autonomy.

As Table 15–1 shows, the specialized field of knowledge varies greatly from one profession to another. For example, a drafter typically requires only a 2-year course at a technical high school or junior college or a 3- or 4-year apprenticeship. At the other extreme, an osteopathic physician must have 3 years of preosteopathic college work and 4 years of study in an osteopathic college. She must

364

TABLE 15-1
Examples of professional occupations.

Accountants	Librarians
Actors & actresses	Mathematicians
Anthropologists	Meteorologists
Architects	Musicians
Artists	Nurses
Astronomers	Osteopaths
Biologists	Pharmacists
Chemists	Physicians & surgeons
Clergy	Physicists
Dancers	Political scientists
Dentists	Psychologists
Designers	Sculptors
Dieticians	Sociologists
Drafters	Statisticians
Economists	Surveyors
Engineers	Teachers
Geologists	Veterinarians
Historians	Writers & editors
Lawyers	

also serve a 12-month internship in an approved osteopathic hospital and pass a state board examination.[1]

A second characteristic of a profession is its service orientation. In some professions, such as the law or other professions involving independent practice, the service is to the individual client or, in medicine, the patient. In professions such as accounting and engineering the service is more often to an organization. In still others, such as the armed forces, the service is to the nation.

The third characteristic relates to the autonomy of the group. A professional group has certain guildlike aspects: It acts to control its membership and in this respect resembles some trade unions, especially the craft unions; and it sets its own ethical standards. The degree to which such standards are enforced depends on self-regulation, often through some kind of peer review, rather than regulation externally imposed by the government. In the long run, the extent to which government may feel it necessary to impose standards on a profession is strongly influenced by the quality of professional leadership exercised in the process of self-regulation.

Motivation of Professionals

Professionals who are part of a business organization rather than in private practice reach a point at which they can shift over to management if they feel they cannot advance financially as professionals. In many high-tech, matrix-type companies, the project manager job is a virtual gateway for technical staff to enter the managerial ranks.[2]

Some professionals take advantage of such opportunities. Many more do not. Earlier we cited the advantages of flattening the organizational structure in making American firms more competitive internationally. Flattening the organizational hierarchy is also one way of improving the status and motivation of the professional.

> In a flattened organization, there are fewer managers at middle levels to report to. Professionals can rely on themselves and their own standards to control their work. They can achieve greater autonomy over their own projects and operations even to the point of becoming in-house entrepreneurs.[3]

A dual ladder program is another way to improve motivation for professionals. As Joseph A. Raelin describes it,

> The dual ladder gives the professional the option of nonmanagerial advancement with comparable salary and status and often, autonomy and responsibility. Conflicts between management and professional employees are reduced, and communication channels are improved, since professionals may no longer feel the need to hold back information to create power for themselves.[4]

Professional Incomes and Base Pay

The ability of many professionals to either operate within an organization, or have an independent practice, or combine these two activities demonstrates the autonomy of professions. Those with an independent practice charge fees for services rendered, while other professionals typically are paid by salary. Milton Friedman and Simon Kuznets found that the incomes received by independent practitioners tended to be higher than those received by salaried professionals.[5]

Pay of Doctors

In general, the pay of medical doctors merits special attention because it influences the entire system of health care.[6] Duane Stroman cites three methods by which providers of health care are compensated:

1. Payment to providers (doctors) for each item of service rendered.
2. Payment of salaries or hourly wages.
3. Capitation payment, which involves paying providers (doctors) a stated amount for each patient on their subscriber list in return for a prescribed list of services.[7]

The fee method, used most often in the United States outside of the government sector, has been criticized on various counts. One is the subsidy-tax aspect.

The fee system, as Jethro Lieberman points out, is structured so that the rich pay more and charity patients pay less. He says that

> if the rich are to subsidize the poor, it is difficult to see that the redistribution of wealth by doctors is to be preferred to that carried on by the federal government.[8]

Another criticism of the fee system is that fees differ from one geographical area to another. In asking for federal action on a uniform national fee schedule, Ralph Nader's health research group cited a gallbladder operation fee of $1,000 in New York City but only $290 in Findlay, Ohio.[9]

Stroman cites another criticism of the fee-for-services approach:

> Organized medicine has generally argued that fee-for-service creates incentives for doctors to get their patients well and to render services as they are needed. But these incentives can be interpreted as working in the reverse way: they may create incentives to provide a wide range of unnecessary services, more expensive services, and hurried care because the patient is not in a position to know if the services rendered were either necessary or of high quality.[10]

The second method cited by Stroman, payment by salary, is already in wide use in government installations. Stroman cites benefits to the salary method:

> Salaries would appear to enhance medical services rather than leading to any deterioration of them. They appear to offer the best means of eliminating those unnecessary services fostered by fees, while their use would significantly reduce the mountain of paperwork required by fee billing.[11]

Capitation payment, while not usual in the United States, has a long and successful history in Great Britain, where it remains the principal method of payment for physicians.[12] As reported by Almont Lindsey, the practice started before the beginning of this century with the Friendly Societies, became well established under the Health Insurance Act of 1911, and remained in effect with the passage of the Health Service Law of 1946, which actually went into effect in 1948. The capitation method was supplemented by other payments to cover mileage for rural doctors, initial practice allowance for new doctors, and inducements to encourage medical practice in areas less well served by doctors.[13]

Pay of Scientists and Engineers

The periodic surveys conducted by the National Science Foundation provide much information about the salaries of doctoral scientists and engineers.[14] Table 15–2 shows the median salaries for different fields, with the top salary of $46,600 being paid to engineers and the lowest salary of $32,100 paid to sociologists/anthropologists.

TABLE 15–2
Median salaries of doctoral scientists and engineers.

Profession	Annual Salary
Engineers	$46,600
Physicists/astronomers	42,900
Chemists	41,900
Atmospheric scientists	41,600
Earth scientists	41,500
Economists	41,400
Medical scientists	41,200
Computer/information specialists	40,400
All fields	40,100
Agricultural scientists	37,900
Statisticians	37,400
Oceanographers	36,700
Mathematicians	36,400
Biological scientists	36,200
Psychologists	35,800
Other social scientists	35,000
Sociologists/anthropologists	32,100

Source: National Science Foundation, Characteristics of Doctoral Scientists and Engineers in the U.S., 1983. *Surveys of Science Resources Series,* NSF 85–303, Table B-16. Data are for 1983.

Job Evaluation for Professionals

Any consideration of job evaluation for professional employees must take into account essential differences between the professional employee and other types of employees. The professional employee's job is broader than that of the white-collar office worker engaged in clerical work or the blue-collar production worker in the plant. The professional shares this breadth of job with many of the exempt white-collar supervisory and executive employees. Having jobs with breadth does not exclude either the professional or the executive from being included in the job evaluation process or from being individually evaluated on performance. There is, however, a major difference between the job of the professional and that of the executive. The professional has a dual loyalty—to the profession and to the organization. In contrast, the executive has a single loyalty—to the organization. The major methods of job evaluation emphasize job content, some more than others. These methods, then, apply to a lesser extent to professionals than to other employees.

Major Methods of Job Evaluation

For some years now there has been skepticism about the relevance for professional employees of some of the more widely used and well-established methods of job evaluation. Of the five major methods—ranking, predetermined grading, point, factor comparison, and guide chart–profile—most place too much emphasis on job content and not enough on the individual and her career. The factor comparison and guide chart–profile methods are somewhat more flexible than the other methods, but they still tend to stress the professional's position in the organization. The guide chart–profile method tends to put excessive emphasis on organizational hierarchy.

Thomas Atchison and Wendell French compared the perceptions of equity of professionals paid under three methods of establishing pay differentials: job classification (predetermined grading), time span of discretion (see Chapters 6 and 7), and maturity curves. They concluded, among other things, that

> all three methods appear to produce results which are highly associated with what subjects felt was fair payment for their jobs. In terms of equity or fairness, the time span of discretion and the classification method resulted in significantly higher correlations with perceived ''fair'' payment than the maturity curve method.[15]

Since both the predetermined grading (job classification) and the time span of discretion methods have been discussed in earlier chapters, we will discuss only their specific applicability to professional employees here.

In the federal government, the predetermined grading method combined with generalized job descriptions permits a career planning approach relevant to the professional. Furthermore, the periodic government surveys of clerical, technical, administrative, and professional pay serve a useful and related purpose of allowing professionals with similar jobs in the private sector to compare their pay with government employees.

The single-factor nature of the time span of discretion method may be, with respect to professionals, both its strength and its weakness. The question can legitimately be raised as to whether the time span is truly an adequate measure for the work of the professional. On the other hand, the use of this *particular* single factor offsets in an important way the hierarchical tendencies of other methods to elevate the supervisor (even if his performance might actually be worth less to the organization). For example, professional staff persons assigned to do long-range planning and given a high degree of autonomy would presumably be well paid under the time span of discretion approach.

Maturity Curves

We have not explored maturity curves in previous chapters and thus we will discuss them in detail here. It is sometimes argued that the maturity curve approach is more a method of pricing than a method of job evaluation, since so little emphasis is placed on the job content. Despite this shortcoming, the maturity curve approach is so widely used, especially for certain groups such as engineers, that—job evaluation method or not—it merits attention. Furthermore, you may recall that one of the advantages of the money method of factor comparison is that job evaluation and pricing are not separate functions. The same might be said of maturity curves.

Maturity curves take various forms. Some involve years of experience on the job or in the work force.[16] Others are based on years since the receipt of a particular degree. Figure 15–1 shows some nationwide career salary curves for selected professional fields based on years of professional experience.[17] For example, it can be seen that a scientist with a doctoral degree in physics and 2 to 4 years of professional experience received a median salary of less than $32,000

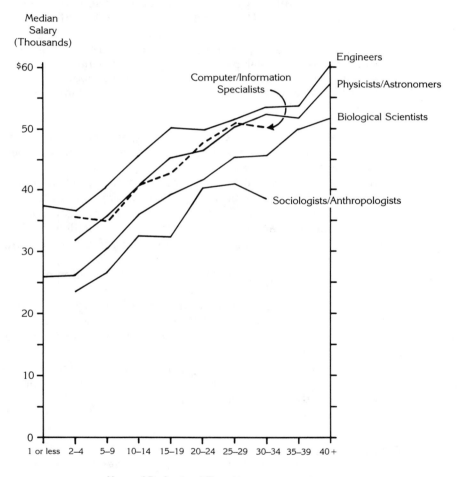

Years of Professional Experience

FIGURE 15–1
Maturity curves for doctoral scientists and engineers. Data are for 1983. (From National Science Foundation, "Characteristics of Doctoral Scientists and Engineers in the U.S., 1983," Surveys of Science Resources Series, NSF 85–303, 1985, Table B–16.)

in 1983, while a similarly educated physicist with 35 to 39 years of professional experience received close to $52,000.

A striking result seen in Figure 15–1 is the relatively strong financial showing of computer/information specialists compared to physicists/astronomers. Also, for three of the five curves there appears to be little evidence of leveling off in the later career years. However for both the computer/information specialists and the sociologists/anthropologists there are *dips* from the 25–29 year group to the 30–34 year group. However, other dips or slower increases occur in other experience groups. Such dips may be easily accounted for by the ebb and flow of people going into and out of the professions, often to take higher paying work in managerial or consulting jobs. So the two *ending* dips probably do *not* indicate employee obsolescence. They doubtless reflect the mix of persons included in the category.

The curves in Figure 15–1 represent artificial cohorts; that is, the individuals in the 10- to 14-year group are an entirely different group than those in the 20- to 24-year or the 40 years and over group. It might be inferred from these curves that sociologists/anthropologists who have been around a long time since their graduation are going to have their pay cut after 25 to 29 years of experience. This may not be so, however. A true cohort curve, which shows what actually happened to the *same* group of people, might not show this at all. It is often difficult to get the longitudinal data needed for such a curve, and to be useful in setting pay levels the curve would have to be adjusted for the changing cost of living over time. For operational purposes, the portion of the curves for the first 20 years may have more real value than the other end of the curves, where the samples are usually smaller.

For a professional, whose work and problems can vary greatly over time, the maturity curve supports the idea that greater experience brings with it an increased degree of performance. From the pricing point of view, the median for each degree of professional experience for a specified field in a given year provides a norm as to the going rate for that type of professional work.

Maturity Curves and Performance. A maturity curve does not, if used as the sole guide, recognize differences in performance within each cohort at a particular experience level. This shortcoming can largely be overcome where the volume of available data permits the use of maturity curves for different percentile levels. This approach is demonstrated in Table 15–3.[18]

Table 15–3 shows hypothetical salary data for industry for the first 10 years of professional engineering experience since the baccalaureate degree. In contrast to Figure 15–1, this table presents data for three successive surveys instead of a single year. For example, an engineer with 8 years of experience had a median salary of $25,572 in 1978, but by 1982 an engineer with the same number of years of experience would earn $29,357. In addition, Table 15–3 shows salary figures for the top and bottom deciles for engineers. At the top decile, for an engineer with 8 years of experience who made a salary of $37,995 in 1982, only 10 percent of the engineers made more and 90 percent made less. Conversely, at the bottom decile, an engineer with 8 years of experience who was paid $23,707 in 1982

TABLE 15–3
Hypothetical salaries for engineers in industry based on years of experience since the baccalaureate degree.

				Years Since B.S. Degree			
		0	2	4	6	8	10
Top	1978	$19,829	$22,769	$25,914	$29,333	$32,683	$35,555
Decile	1980	22,290	24,478	28,581	32,136	35,418	38,427
	1982	22,504	26,283	29,623	34,382	37,995	41,435
Median	1978	17,367	19,760	21,538	23,384	25,572	27,282
	1980	18,940	20,649	23,248	25,230	27,282	29,059
	1982	20,304	22,353	24,596	27,334	29,357	31,406
Bottom	1978	15,795	17,094	18,325	19,419	20,786	21,812
Decile	1980	17,094	18,188	19,624	20,854	22,290	23,589
	1982	18,480	19,643	21,073	22,539	23,707	24,919

Note: Data are hypothetical and are used for illustration only.
Source: "Salary Comparison Method for Experienced Technical Personnel," by James Tait Elder, copyright July 1968. Reprinted with the permission of *Personnel Journal,* Costa Mesa, California; all rights reserved.

earned more than 10 percent of the engineers in that category but less than the other 90 percent.

James Elder uses such data to construct diagrams for particular individuals relating actual pay to the industry data, as shown in Figure 15–2. The diagram compares the hypothetical actual salary of an engineer with a 1972 baccalaureate degree with the industry data taken from the maturity curves. To illustrate how the diagram is constructed, we will look at three points plotted for the lower decile. In 1978 the engineer would have been out of school 6 years, so we find the salary for 6 years of experience on the 1978 line for the bottom decile in Table 15–3. That salary is $19,419, which we plot for 1978. In 1980 the engineer would have 8 years of experience, so we find the appropriate salary in the 1980 survey, which is $22,290. In the same way, we get $24,919 for 1982. The remaining lines are plotted in the same way using the other two sections of Table 15–3.

The three lines in Figure 15–2 are extended to make it easier to relate actual salary to delayed survey data. As Elder points out, the extension of the line reflects (1) the movement of the employee into a later experience cohort, and (2) the probable increase which would be revealed by more recent survey data for each experience category. Framing the salary curve in this fashion defines a flexible salary range where not only experience and inflation can be taken into account but also performance on the job.

Employee Benefits and Expense Accounts

In Chapter 14 we learned that some employee benefits are designed especially for top executives. Now we shall go into more detail on four aspects of employee ben-

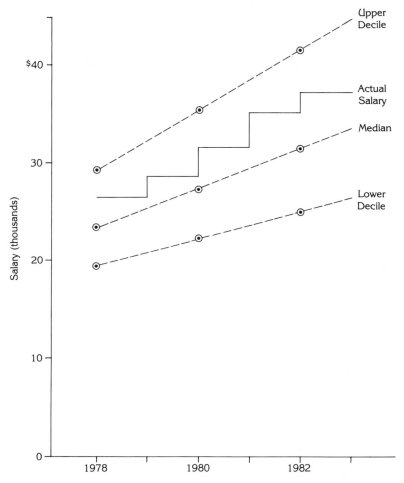

FIGURE 15–2
Comparison of maturity curve salary data with actual salary for an engineer with a 1972 baccalaureate degree. Data are hypothetical. (From "Salary Comparison Method for Experienced Technical Personnel," by James Tait Elder, copyright July 1968. Reprinted with the permission of **Personnel Journal,** *Costa Mesa, California; all rights reserved.)*

efits for professionals: (1) choice of benefits, (2) incentive plans, (3) retirement plans, and (4) expense accounts.

Cafeteria Plan for Professionals

The individual nature of the professional's work makes the cafeteria plan, as discussed in Chapter 13, a highly desirable option. Particular attention should be given to the varying needs of professionals in different fields.

Incentive Plans

Another form of incentive pay to develop besides those described earlier in this chapter might be bonuses for innovations resulting in measurable cost savings, such as the federal government's productivity incentive plan. DuPont's Class A Bonus plan provides similar but more generous benefits. The company has described the bonus as follows:

> Class A awards concerning a specific money-saving device or invention are made over a 5-year period in 3 parts roughly after the end of the first, third, and fifth years. However the first award may be in as short a period as 6 months, the period depending on the time needed to demonstrate the practicality of the scheme. If after the third year it looks as if the savings were strictly limited, the executive committee may treat the award as a two-part award and make the final award.[19]

Retirement Plans

Professionals who run their own businesses (even if they also work for a firm with its own pension plan) can set up their own plans under the Self-Employed Individuals Tax Retirement Act of 1962, also known as the Keogh Act or HR-10. Under this act, a professional can contribute to a plan 15 percent of self-employment income up to $7,500 a year. Most Keogh plans

> operate on a money purchase or defined contribution basis. These plans establish the contribution as a percentage of income, and the benefit is the amount that results from the contributions.[20]

The amount of this contribution is deductible for federal income tax purposes. The owner/employee may contribute an additional amount of 10 percent of income, but not more than $2,500 per year. However,

> tax deductions are not permitted on additional voluntary contributions, but there still may be a tax advantage because the contributions accumulate on a tax deferred basis until they are distributed.[21]

A Keogh plan may be funded with trusts, custodial accounts, government bonds, face amount certificates, annuities, or certain combinations of instruments. When the owner/employee retires or reaches age 70½, whichever occurs earlier, benefits must begin.

> Distributions received as annuity income are taxed according to the usual tax rules pertaining to annuities. When a distribution . . . is made in a lump sum, it is subject to the 10-year federal income tax averaging rules.[22]

Master or prototype plans approved by the Internal Revenue Service can be arranged through insurance companies, banks, or savings and loan institutions. A master plan is administered by the financial institution, while the prototype plan is administered by the self-employed individual.[23]

Expense Accounts

We have already seen the latitude allowed executives in handling their expense accounts. This freedom supposedly preserves the status of executives, but it can be argued that not enough freedom in this regard is given to professional employees.

Individual versus Organizational Obsolescence

Paul Thompson and Gene Dalton, who interviewed 200 professionals in five large research and development (R & D) organizations, discuss the obsolescence of older employees:

> Many R&D managers . . . are expressing grave doubts about the ability of older engineers to adapt to rapidly changing technology. Many are even asserting that the unwillingness or inability of individuals to change is the major cause of R & D problems. However, our research leads us to question that conclusion. In fact, we now believe that *organizational* obsolescence, not *individual* obsolescence, is the main culprit.[24]

The authors identify four career stages in the lives of the professional employees interviewed. They describe the stages roughly as follows:

1. An apprenticeship stage where the work is never entirely his or her own, the assignment is a portion of a larger project or activity, and he is expected to do most of the detailed and routine work on his part of the project.
2. The professional assumes responsibility for a definable portion of a project or process, works with relative independence and produces significant results that are recognized as his, begins to develop credibility and a reputation for competent work, and manages more of his own time and accepts more responsibility for outcomes.
3. A mentor stage where the professional develops a greater breadth of technical skills and applies them in several areas, begins to deal with the external environment for the benefit of others in the organization, and becomes involved in the development of people and the stimulation of others through ideas and information.
4. The professional exercises a significant influence over the future direction of a major part of the organization, tends to be engaged in

wide and varied interactions both inside and outside the organization, and is involved in the sponsoring and development of promising people who might fill future roles in the organization.[25]

Thompson and Dalton checked the progress of individual professionals in the R & D organizations and learned that performance ratings were related to their progress through the four career stages. If they failed to move up through the stages, their performance ratings tended to deteriorate. They discovered, however, that some organizations made this happen through such obstacles as (1) reward systems that moved the brightest persons out of technical work into management as rapidly as possible, thus devaluing technical contribution; (2) product planning structures that trap an engineer in a successful project, thus barring new assignments where the newer technologies could be learned; (3) cost systems that discriminated against older and typically higher paid workers by arbitrary requirements that overhead be allocated as a direct proportion of salary; and (4) thoughtless work force planning, involving layoffs at the beginning of the year and hiring new people at the end of the same year.

As a result of this study, the authors recommend three courses of action to organizations with professional employees: reward technical contributions, reduce barriers to movement, and focus on careers. Rewards for technical work can take many forms: a pay system flexible enough to allow managers to pay for movement of professionals through all four stages; more professional inputs in decision making; and increased visibility and status for nonmanagerial professional contributors. To reduce barriers to movement, they urge a 5-year limit on tenure in supervisory positions, accounting systems that do not bar seniors from working on new projects, and greater use of lateral transfers. Matrix organizations tend to focus better on careers by giving the professional a better chance at new projects, providing semiannual work force reviews, and monitoring each professional's career so that a major new project is assigned at regular intervals.[26]

The Role of Unions

Unions are aware of the possibilities offered by management's oversights in meeting the needs of the professional employee. Dennis Chamot, assistant to the executive secretary of the Council of AFL-CIO Unions for Professional Employees, points to their rapid recent growth compared with other unions.[27] More recent data (Figure 15–3) generally confirm what he said then about the trends.

Chamot shows considerable insight into the attitudes of the professional worker:

> One of the big differences between professional employees and all other non-management workers is that the professional employee expects that he will have a major role to play in deciding how to perform his job. Unlike a production worker or a secretary, the professional expects to help determine the problems

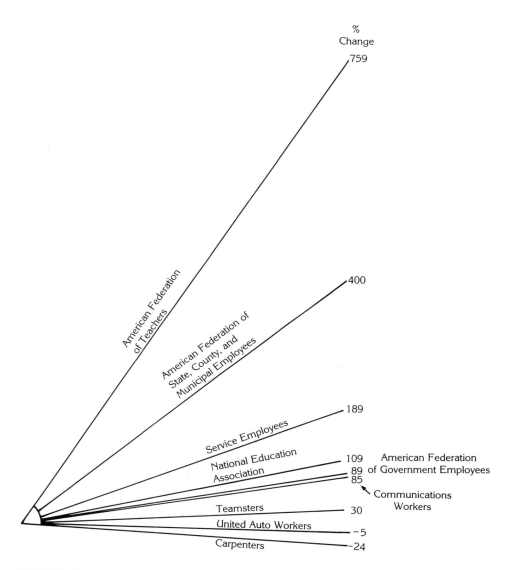

FIGURE 15–3
Percentage changes in membership from 1962 to 1985 for some professional unions and some of the older unions. Latest data from Bureau of National Affairs. Data for earlier years from Bureau of Labor Statistics and National Education Association.

377

he will work on and the approaches toward their solution. All too often, his expectations fall far short of reality. Dissatisfaction may result from inadequate technical support, insufficient opportunity to pursue interesting ideas, excessive interference by superiors, lack of sufficient input to project assignment decisions, and what not. Whether or not there are overriding economic considerations behind these decisions, the professional employee frequently feels that he is not treated with the respect he deserves.[28]

While the professional employee may be more philosophically inclined toward individual bargaining than collective, Chamot points out that this is no longer realistic for employees of large organizations. For example, he cites the changing situation in higher education:

Colleges and universities are moving away from the old system of collegiality and are increasingly employing full-time administrators who exercise considerable authority. Attempts to impose business practices (e.g., measurement of faculty "productivity") by people who are perceived, at least, as having insufficient teaching experience, threaten established notions of professional responsibilities, duties, and prerogatives. Unionization is looked on as a way for a faculty to improve its bargaining position with an administration that has grown too powerful in areas that have been traditionally the domain of the educators.[29]

Labor unions and professional groups have a growing community of interest. Neither can survive without the other. For unions to grow they must be able to tap new sources of membership, and they are finding that professional employees account for the most rapid rates of growth in union membership. In professional groups, employees who value their own autonomy find themselves under bosses who are often comparatively ignorant of professional educational qualifications. Collegiality has been replaced by coercion. Economic necessity—real or supposed—is invoked against professionals, eroding or sometimes destroying job security. They must also face management opposition to make adequate provision for the redress of often legitimate grievances.

Philosophically, both groups have to adjust. The unions have to alter their organizing approach to take into account the more individualistic and at least quasi-autonomous nature of the professional employee. Unions have to entice professionals into collective bargaining and away from individual bargaining, but in the process unions may have to fashion more individual bargaining devices, such as term employment contracts. Across-the-board, flat dollar pay increases will not satisfy professional workers who place greater emphasis on interjob percentage pay differentials. Professional groups, too, will have to change their approach. Coercion, stress on often artificially structured and sometimes meaningless measures of productivity, and loss of some freedom as well as job security have detracted from the importance of collegiality and individual bargaining.

Professionals need to ask themselves more seriously whether the professional association can resolve these problems or whether unionization might provide better solutions. The grievance procedure at the heart of most union contracts is especially effective in this regard but has little relation to individual bargaining. Collective bargaining, tailored to the special needs of the professional employee, seems to be a better answer. The gradual, chameleonlike change in the professional association, which increasingly takes on the coloration of a union, indicates a future trend in this direction.

Summary

A profession has a specialized field of knowledge, is service oriented, and is autonomous. A profession is considered autonomous because it controls the size of its membership and sets ethical standards enforced through self-regulation.

Professionals, we have observed, are motivated somewhat differently from other employees: Given opportunities to move over into management to secure higher pay, many did not do so. Flattened organization structures as well as dual career ladders improve motivation of professionals.

Professionals may be independent practitioners or salaried employees. Where they do similar work, the former receive higher incomes. Some critics believe that physicians should be either paid by capitation or given salaries rather than fees for services. Weaknesses in the fee system are its motivational impact, the subsidy-tax aspect, and inequities in fee schedules.

Because professional jobs tend to be more personalized than executive jobs, the more widely used methods of job evaluation may be inappropriate for professionals. Research has identified three methods perceived as equitable by scientists and engineers: predetermined grading, time span of discretion, and maturity curves. The typical maturity curve relates level of pay to age, years of service, or years since the receipt of a specified degree.

Maturity curves need to be interpreted with care. Often downturns in the curves are attributed to employee obsolescence on account of age, but the downward (and also upward) swings are usually the result of the mix of employees in a given age or years-of-service category.

For some professions, periodic surveys involve such large numbers of employees that maturity curves can be drawn not only to show median salary levels, but also the quartile and decile levels. Such data can be used to compare an individual's salary against industry data and to do so in a way to take into account the individual's job performance in making pay increase determinations.

Employee benefits for professionals should relate to the special needs of this group. The cafeteria plan approach to employee benefits, with benefits tailored to the professional's needs, is highly desirable. Certain types of incentive plans, such as DuPont's Class A Bonus or the productivity incentives used in the federal government, might also be used for professionals. Keogh plans have special retirement plan provisions covering those professionals who are owner-employees. Finally, professionals should be given more freedom in managing their expense accounts.

At least one study of individual versus organizational obsolescence suggests that organizations may be responsible for the failure of older employees to adapt to new technology. For professionals in R & D organizations, it was found that performance ratings were tied directly to how well an individual moved through the four successive stages of professional career development. Some organizations, however, blocked this progress by certain obstacles: outdated reward systems, product planning, and cost systems, and thoughtless work force planning. Such organizations can change by offering greater rewards for technical contributions, reducing the barriers to movement, and focusing more on career planning.

Unions for professional employees have experienced recent rapid growth. Although philosophically inclined to individual bargaining, the professional is finding that collective bargaining may be more realistic. In higher education, the movement away from collegiality toward full-time administrators has led faculty members to seek unionization as a means of improving their position when administrative power becomes excessive.

Case Study

Seidenfeld Pharmaceutical Company

The R & D laboratories of Seidenfeld Pharmaceutical Company employ only the most highly qualified scientists. More than 90 percent of its biologists and chemists have doctoral degrees. The administrative persons on the staff are on the average somewhat younger, and a few of them do not have degrees in scientific areas. The personnel manager, for example, has an MBA from a prominent business school in Ohio. The research staff is organized by project groups. Project leaders are pretty much the same over time, but the numbers and types of employees in each group change depending on work force needs as determined by the demands of the research and the decisions of the lab director and project leaders.

The compensation plan, excluding employee benefits, consists of three major elements: (1) the use of maturity curves, (2) a merit rating system, and (3) an annual pay increase budget. The maturity curve used for the biologists, developed from industry association data, groups individuals according to the number of years elapsed since the receipt of the doctoral degree and shows the median pay in a recent year for each group. This curve is adjusted upward using a trend factor so that the curve reflects current (not forecast) pay levels. Percentile curves cannot be used as there are not enough industry data to provide this detail. Thus, this adjusted maturity curve is taken as the guide for the pay level of the average professional biologist.

The merit rating system ties in with the maturity curve. The performance of each biologist is reviewed annually, but newly hired biologists are rated at 6-month intervals for the first 18 months. Pay increase percentages based on these reviews are related to the annual pay increase budget. That is, if the budgeted amount increased by 5 percent, a highly rated biologist would get a larger increase, while a lowly rated biologist would get a smaller increase or none at all. For the current year the rating scale is as follows: superior, 10 percent; above average, 7.5 percent; average, 5 percent; below average, 3 percent; and unsatisfactory, 0 percent. Pay increases for the biologists on a particular project are recommended by the project leader, but the final decisions are worked out between the project leader and the personnel manager because of the many biologists in each of the nine different project groups.

Dr. Wendy Michaelis, leader of Project Group 8 (Reptile and Related Venoms), emerged from a pay increase meeting with the personnel manager and came back to her office highly disturbed. She reflected on the personnel manager's enthusiasm for giving large pay increases to the newly hired biologists, while often agreeing to more modest increases for the more experienced biologists in the group. Michaelis was aware how difficult it is to attract, hold, and motivate new biologists of the quality they desired and that this influenced the personnel manager. The personnel manager had also compared the tremendous future potential of the younger workers to the more limited future potential of the older and more experienced employees. Michaelis, however, saw that in Group 8 the big raises went to the younger employees, leaving little money for the others who are more experienced and whose current performance is better than that of their less experienced colleagues. In the past 2 years, at least three of the more experienced professionals in the group had fallen considerably below where they ought to be in terms of the maturity curve. Michaels hated the prospect of having to discuss the pay decisions with these three colleagues and feared the adverse effect on the morale of the group.

Role Assignment

You have been called in as a wage and salary consultant by the director of the laboratory to review the existing compensation arrangements for professional employees. What changes would you make and why?

Questions for Discussion

1. How does the work of the professional differ from that of other workers?
2. In what ways do incentives for professional employees differ from those for other employees?
3. For a large business organization, what are the pros and cons of having a separate pay and benefits plan for professional employees?
4. For a professional, what are the relative advantages of working as an employee of a large organization versus being an independent practitioner?
5. How should doctors be paid? Consider alternative pay arrangements from the doctor's point of view as well as from the patient's point of view.
6. Which methods of job evaluation appear to you to be best suited for professionals? Justify your answer.
7. What are maturity curves? How do they work? What value do they have in determining the pay of professional workers?
8. Should the performance of professionals be evaluated using generally the same criteria as are used for supervisors and executives? Why or why not?
9. What type of incentive pay should be used for scientists?
10. What are the advantages of using a Keogh

plan for a management consultant?

11. Which is the greater problem, individual or organizational obsolescence? Defend your point of view.

12. What role do unions play among professional workers? Is this role likely to change in the future? Discuss.

Notes

1. For requirements for specific professions, see the latest *Occupational Outlook Handbook* published by the U.S. Department of Labor.
2. Joseph A. Raelin et al., "Why Professionals Turn Sour and What to Do," *Personnel* 62, no. 10 (October 1985): 29.
3. Ibid., 38.
4. Ibid., 39.
5. Milton Friedman and Simon Kuznets, *Income from Independent Professional Practice* (New York: National Bureau of Economic Research, 1945), 392–93.
6. For a discussion of these interrelationships, see Duane F. Stroman, *The Medical Establishment and Social Responsibility* (Port Washington, N.Y.: Kennikat Press, 1976).
7. Ibid., 11.
8. Jethro K. Lieberman, *The Tyranny of the Experts, How Professionals Are Closing the Open Society* (New York: Walker and Company, 1970), 273.
9. See *The National Underwriter*, February 26, 1977, 1.
10. Stroman, *op. cit.*, 21.
11. Ibid., 157.
12. For a full discussion, see Almont Lindsey, *Socialized Medicine in England and Wales* (Chapel Hill: University of North Carolina Press, 1962).
13. Ibid., Chapter VI.
14. National Science Foundation, *Characteristics of Doctoral Scientists and Engineers in the United States, 1983*, Surveys of Science Resources Series, NSF 85–303, Table B–16.
15. Thomas Atchison and Wendell French, "Pay Systems for Scientists and Engineers," *Industrial Relations* 7, no. 1 (October 1967): 44–56.
16. Leonard R. Burgess, *Top Executive Pay Package* (New York: Free Press and Columbia University Graduate School of Business, 1963), 13–24 (relating to the top executive's career salary curve).
17. National Science Foundation, *op. cit.*, Table B–16.
18. James T. Elder, "Salary Comparison Method for Experienced Technical Personnel," *Personnel Journal* 47, no. 7 (July 1968): 467–74.
19. For further discussion, see Burgess, *op. cit.*, 48.
20. Jerry S. Rosenbloom and G. Victor Hallman, *Employee Benefit Planning* (Englewood Cliffs, N.J.: Prentice-Hall, 1981), 342. Reprinted by permission of Prentice-Hall, Inc., Englewood Cliffs, N.J.
21. Ibid., 343.
22. Ibid., 345.
23. See Rosenbloom and Hallman, *op. cit.*, for full details.
24. Reprinted by permission of the *Harvard Business Review*. Excerpt from "Are R & D Organizations Obsolete?" by Paul H. Thompson and Gene W. Dalton (November/December 1976). Copyright © by the President and Fellows of Harvard College; all rights reserved.
25. Ibid., 107–9.
26. Ibid., 112–16.
27. Reprinted by permission of the *Harvard Business Review*. Excerpt from "Professional Employees Turn to Unions" by Dennis Chamot (May/June 1976). Copyright © 1976 by the President and Fellows of Harvard College; all rights reserved.
28. Ibid., 121.
29. Ibid., 122.

References

Armstrong, D. G. "Researchers' Incentives and the Dearth of Research Results." *Peabody Journal of Education* 58, no. 1 (1980): 55–60.

Carey, John L. *Professional Ethics of Public Accounting.* New York: Arno Press, 1980.

Chamot, Dennis. "Unions Need to Confront the Needs of New Technology." *Monthly Labor Review* 110, no. 8 (August 1987): 45.

Desmond, Glenn M. *How to Value Professional Practices.* Marina del Rey, CA: Valuation Press, 1980.

"Employees Satisfied with HMOs." *ACA News* 30, no. 5 (July 1987): 19.

Franklin, Jerry. "For Technical Professionals: Pay for Skills AND Pay for Performance." *Personnel* 65, no. 5 (May 1988): 20–28.

Kilgour, John G. "White-Collar Organizing: A Reappraisal." *Personnel* 63, no. 8 (August 1986): 14–19.

Lea, Dixie, and Brostrom, Richard. "Managing the High-Tech Professional." *Personnel* 65, no. 6 (June 1988): 12–22.

Lightfoot, Donald G. "Preferred Provider Organization Concepts and Arrangements." *Risk Management* (November 1985).

Mossholder, Kevin W., and Dewhirst, H. Dudley. "The Appropriateness of Management-by-Objectives for Development and Research Personnel." *Journal of Management* 6 (Fall 1980): 145–46.

National Science Foundation. *Characteristics of Doctoral Scientists and Engineers in the U.S., 1983.* Surveys of Science Resources Series, NSF 85–303, 1985.

Pollock, Michael A., and Tasini, Jonathan. "The Public Sector Is Labor's Success Story." *Business Week*, September 22, 1986.

Raelin, Joseph A. "Job Security for Professionals." *Personnel* 64, no. 7 (July 1987): 40–47.

Raelin, Joseph A., et al. "Why Professionals Turn Sour and What to Do." *Personnel* 62, no. 10 (October 1985): 28–41.

Rosenbaum, Bernard L. "Critical Skills for Successful Technical Professionals." *Personnel* 63, no. 10 (October 1986) 56–60.

Smith, Russell L., and Hopkins, Anne H. "Employee Attitudes towards Unions." *Industrial and Labor Relations Review* 32, no. 4 (1979): 484–95.

Spratt, Michael, and Steele, Bernadette. "Rewarding Key Contributors." *Compensation and Benefits Review* 17, no. 3 (July–August 1985): 24–37.

Overview: Compensation Management

16

Chapter Outline

- Hierarchy
- International Competitiveness
- Job Pricing and Unit Labor Costs
- Pay Cuts and Incentives
- Legal and Legislative Aspects
- Unions Versus Women and Minorities
- Job Analysis, Job Evaluation, and Performance Evaluation
- Pay Surveys
- Changes in Employee Benefits
- Organizational Layers and Professional Employees
- Executive Pay
- Summary

Hierarchy

Many of the things a compensation manager now has to do are essentially those he has always had to do, but the environment—especially the international environment—within which these actions have to be carried out has changed.

In early chapters we saw how the compensation manager is boxed in by internal and external hierarchical forces. I stressed the effect of layers of authority on how people are paid, and pointed out that other structures such as job analysis, job evaluation, and performance evaluation—as well as the process of job pricing—all tend to reinforce hierarchy. However, I also suggested that the hierarchical tendency may have sown the seeds of its own destruction. The tendency of the CEO's pay to be a greater multiple of the average worker's pay in the United States than is true of other nations is proving counterproductive.

International Competitiveness

High CEO pay is just one indicator of factors that have hurt the competitiveness of the United States versus other nations. Such practices have tended to result in higher total labor costs which are not sufficiently offset by increased productivity. We saw that among major steel producing countries, the United States now has lower unit labor costs than West Germany and Japan, but France, the United Kingdom, and especially South Korea all had lower unit labor costs than the United States. We also observed that not only Japan but also such Pacific Rim countries as South Korea, Taiwan, Singapore, and Hong Kong have been rapidly increasing their productivity. Other forces besides productivity—such as the quality of goods produced and the quality of the labor force (largely dependent on education), savings rates in different countries, and the availability of capital—also affect our competitiveness.

Job Pricing and Unit Labor Costs

We turn now to the linkage between job pricing and hierarchy. A weakness of job pricing using percentage differentials—and especially *rising* percentage differentials—is that if pay structures are built from the bottom up there is an obvious tendency towards pushing up the pay of the chief executive officer relative to the pay of the rank and file employee. This tendency leads to the very discrepancy I cited in the first chapter: the pay of the CEO becoming a high multiple of that of the average worker. And, of course, with so many employee benefits stated as a percent of pay, the result is a greater total labor cost and often greater unit labor costs. This can have serious international consequences. The *constant* percentage differential between pay grades with equal overlap from grade to grade, however, may have important motivational advantages. Of course, differentials can be preserved and total compensation costs kept reasonably low if the number of layers of authority is reduced, assuming that the size of the differentials is not increased to offset the reduction in number of layers.

Pay Cuts and Incentives

Managements in many companies, faced by union and employee objections to cuts in base pay have offered profit sharing or gainsharing, especially the latter. While many profit-sharing plans give large rewards as a percent of salary to higher ranking executives, the rank and file tend to be better motivated by gainsharing. The National Steel plan illustrates recent developments. ESOPs (employee stock ownership plans) appear to be especially effective in situations where the employees obtain a substantial share of control of the management of the company. Partly because of international competitive threats, not only group but also individual incentive plans have aroused new interest. Of these the best is still probably the Lincoln Electric Company. An interesting aspect of this plan is the special arrangement to allow an employee to challenge the piece rate if he wants to. Such arrangements promote employee confidence, which appears to have much to do with the acceptance of individual piece-rate plans.

Legal and Legislative Aspects

Legal and legislative aspects of pay, in one sense, limit the freedom of action of the compensation manager. And yet laws and legislation can act as a liberating force to encourage social change and both more effective utilization and improved motivation of employees. We saw that unions have achieved much for workers by pushing employers for more liberalized provisions in collective bargaining agreements as well as by grievance procedures to protect the rights of employees. But some of what they have pushed for—especially with regard to seniority provisions—may have had a negative effect on the progress of workers because of the adverse results for women and minorities.

Unions Versus Women and Minorities

The power of unions has had a pervading influence in manufacturing and in some nonmanufacturing areas such as construction, but the extent of the union influence has generally declined. Also, the direction of union growth has changed. Instead of pushing for pay *increases*, unions have increasingly had to contend with *decreases*. Unions, of course, have certainly not liked cuts in pay or unemployment for their members. But managements have resorted to two-tier pay plans, lump sum merit increases and the like through sheer necessity to cut costs so as to compete internationally.

Taking place side by side with shrinking union strength has been the achievement of greater roles in the economy by women and minorities. Comparable worth is a struggle that will continue until women achieve their full political, economic, and social rights. Much the same can be said for minorities, whose shares in different occupational groups are continuing to grow. However, substantial pay improvements may yet be many years away, despite the encouragement provided by Title VII of the Civil Rights Act. In the future, leaders among women and minorities can be expected to displace union leaders as the more dynamic forces in the human resources and compensation environment.

Where union members have been threatened with loss of employment or severe pay cuts, intransigent union attitudes have had to change so U.S. business can survive in international competition. Within work forces flexibility has increased, as illustrated in part by IBM's international approach to reducing the workweek while still gaining increased productivity.

Job Analysis, Job Evaluation, and Performance Evaluation

In job analysis there is an increasing tendency to rely on computers, and in many cases the software applies also to job evaluation. Computers are useful in automating such processes as keeping job descriptions updated and in reducing the number of duplicate jobs (thus reducing the numbers of layers of authority). These are desirable results in terms of our international competitive situation. On the other hand, questions can be raised as to whether we are trying to substitute mathematics for human judgment in areas where human judgments still must be made. If computerization provides a better basis for these judgments, fine. If, however, rationalization via the computer is designed to exclude active role participation of women or minorities, it is open to criticism. A strong political argument can be made that in setting up an equitable job evaluation plan management should invite a representative of the National Organization for Women (NOW) to sit in on the evaluation of jobs held by women, or have a representative of the League of United Latin American Citizens (LULAC) take part in discussion of jobs filled by Hispanics, or have a delegate from the National Association for the Advancement of Colored People (NAACP) or the Urban League take part in the evaluation of jobs held by blacks.[1]

Processes such as job analysis, job evaluation, and performance evaluation may need broader, not narrower or more mathematical, participation to achieve the best results. Part of the broader participation, especially in the formative stages where new plans are being put into effect, needs to come from outside the organization. Performance evaluation can go wrong in some situations. Where professionals at the same level are competing for a limited number of higher-ranking openings within an organization, it is hard to believe that peer ratings are really objective. If you vote the other person up, you in effect vote yourself down! In many situations in industry as well as in other walks of life, all it takes is to have an individual with real ability rise above the crowd and his head is shot off!

On the other hand, criticism of the rigidities of job analysis, job evaluation, performance evaluation, and job pricing overlook the fact that there are really few alternatives available. All that can reasonably be undertaken is to try to preserve individual rights and equity and yet have rational ways of performing these functions. While we have stated that the Hay Guide Chart–Proflie Method of job evaluation seems to be the most hierarchical, leaders among women have argued that it seems to be the fairest to women. Probably the best that can be done is to allow employees some freedom of choice as to the plan. There is also a need for employee participation in job evaluation plans. Employee participation in the early stages is more meaningful than at later stages. As to how many workers are covered by a plan or how many plans there are, the fact that there are bound to be rough edges at the intersections of multiple plans argues for a single plan, such as the General Schedule that covers 1.5 million federal employees.

Pay Surveys

The best pay surveys, scientifically speaking, are usually the government surveys. However, this does not argue against a company using a private survey or conducting its own survey to get information not otherwise available. A point for compensation managers to watch closely is women's complaints about depressed pay for jobs in occupations predominantly occupied by women. Such depressed market data ought *not* to be accepted as being representative of what people in that occupation are worth! That is one of the reasons nurses in San Jose went on strike using equity bargaining and not competitive market bargaining.

Changes in Employee Benefits

We have also looked at cultural differences—including the far greater satisfaction of United States employees with their employee benefits—with Japan. But, such benefits cannot just be taken for granted. We saw, for example, how the oil industry has tried to be more competitive by cutting back on employee benefits and with moves toward cafeteria plans to avoid unwanted benefits. In many companies, greater employee contributions towards benefits have been required. Greater emphasis has been placed on cost containment in medical plans, and there has been a movement towards health maintenance organizations (HMOs). In many firms there have been benefit reductions and the elimination of some benefits, together with less emphasis on executive perks.

Organizational Layers and Professional Employees

Along with cutting back on benefits as a means of competing more effectively, companies have been reducing the layers of authority in the organization; an IBM plan, for example, made retirement attractive to middle managers. An obvious implication of the move to reduce layers of authority is that many professionals are being encouraged to retire early or move into positions where they will be more valuable to the organization (the flexibility about internal job shifts practiced by Japanese firms). Alternatively, they may be caught in a reduction in force or forced to take a pay cut. To some extent, this trend has been countered by the greater unionization of professionals. We saw evidence that in this particular occupational group unions have shown rapid growth despite their decreasing membership in general.

Executive Pay

While executive pay is a much higher multiple of the average worker's pay in the United States than in other nations, in at least one area executive pay may be too low. In the senior executive ranks in the federal government, it is still all too typical that any business executive agreeing to take a cabinet or subcabinet post has to sacrifice a very substantial portion of his pay. The effect of this pay differential is to keep many able people in the private sector out of government service.

Absolute levels of executive pay as high as they are in the United States seem unnecessary to achieve the desired level of performance. The contrast of executive pay with the pay of rank and file workers, the resultant increase in total cost, and the often higher unit labor costs for American firms in international competition must be considered. Moreover, with the new tax legislation, the upper bracket income tax rates no longer justify the all-out efforts typical of recent years to avoid taxes via stock options and the like. The argument grows stronger for types of executive compensation that stress current or short-term deferred benefits as opposed to postretirement deferred benefits. Such an approach moves away from rewards primarily based on the price of the stock and toward rewards more closely related to company performance or to individual and/or group performance within relevant operating units of the organization. Again, for motivational reasons gainsharing or other plans stressing employee participation would appear to be important since such devices can reduce unit labor costs and foster improved U.S. competitiveness in international trade.

Notes

1. Reference here to women's, Hispanic, or black jobs does not imply jobs exclusively occupied by any group, or even for which the majority come from one group. Instead the reference is to jobs where one of these groups is significantly represented among present job occupants.

References

Periodicals of interest to the compensation administrator include:

ACA News, American Compensation Association

Academy of Management Review

Administrative Science Quarterly

AFL-CIO News, American Federation of Labor and Congress of Industrial Organizations

California Management Review

Compensation and Benefits Review, American Management Association

Fortune

Harvard Business Review

Human Resources Management, Ideas and Trends

Industrial and Labor Relations Review

Journal of Applied Psychology

Labor Law Journal

Monthly Labor Review

Personnel Psychology

Personnel, American Management Association

Public Personnel Management

The Personnel Administrator, American Society for Personnel Administration

U.S. News and World Report

Among general sources of information are:

American Compensation Association, et al. *National Survey of Non-Traditional Reward and Human Resource Practices.* Houston, TX: American Productivity Center, 1987.

Bookbinder, Stephen M., and Seraphin, Robert M. "Making Pay for Performance Work." *Personnel* 64, no. 9 (September 1987): 66–69.

Cissell, Michael J. "Designing Effective Reward Systems." *Compensation and Benefits Review* 19, no. 6 (November–December 1987): 49–55.

Cook, Frederic W. "Contaminants of Pay for Performance." *Personnel* 63, no. 7 (July 1986): 8–10.

Cumming, Charles M. "New Directions in Salary Administration." *Personnel* 64, no. 1 (January 1987): 68–69.

Ellig, Bruce R. "Strategic Pay Planning." *Compensation and Benefits Review* 19, no. 4 (July–August 1987): 28–43.

England, John D. "Developing a Total Compensation Policy Statement." *Personnel* 65, no. 5 (May 1988): 71–73.

Gmelch, Walter H., and Miskin, Val D. "The Lost

Art of High Productivity." *Personnel* 63, no. 4 (April 1986): 34–38.

Grant, Dale B. "Total Compensation Management." *Compensation and Benefits Review* 18, no. 5 (September–October 1986): 62–67.

Greenberg, Eric Rolfe. "Downsizing: Results of a Survey by the American Management Association." *Personnel* 64, no. 10 (October 1987): 35–37.

Levine, Hermine Zagat (ed.). "Compensation and Benefits Today: Board Members Speak Out, Part 1." *Compensation and Benefits Review* 19, no. 6 (November–December 1987): 23–40.

Lissy, William E. "Outlook on Compensation and Benefits." *Personnel* 63, no. 5 (May 1986): 68–73.

Mischkind, Louis A. "Seven Steps to Productivity Improvement." *Personnel* 64, no. 7 (July 1987): 22–30.

Naughton, Hugh V. "Integrated Support for Salary Administration." *Personnel* 63, no. 8 (August 1986): 8–12.

Smith, Michael L., et al. "Pay for Performance—One Company's Experience." *Compensation and Benefits Review* 19, no. 3 (May–June 1987): 19–27.

Whitney, James L. "Pay Concepts for the 1990s, Part 1." *Compensation and Benefits Review* 20, no. 2 (March–April 1988): 33–44.

Whitney, James L. "Pay Concepts for the 1990s, Part 2." *Compensation and Benefits Review* 20, no. 3 (May–June 1988): 45–50.

APPENDICES

Appendix Outline

Appendix A Job Descriptions

The job descriptions in this section cover (1) 25 blue-collar jobs in an engineering construction firm; (2) 25 clerical jobs in a bank; (3) 25 professional and technical jobs in a manufacturing company; (4) 25 supervisory and executive jobs in a university; and (5) 25 professional, technical, and executive jobs in a conglomerate manufacturing company.*

JOB DESCRIPTIONS FOR 25 BLUE-COLLAR JOBS IN AN ENGINEERING CONSTRUCTION FIRM

Job Title: Blacksmith A   **Job No. 001**

Organization Level: Reports to section supervisor. May work alone, but generally provides training guidance for 2–5 apprentices or learning workers.

Job Performance: (1) Makes all types of small tools from blueprints, sketches, or prototypes. (2) Forge welds metal and shapes heated metals using power machinery and hand tools. (3) Makes dies, jigs, molds, and forms. (4) Tempers and anneals metals. (5) Can identify and handle both ferrous and nonferrous metals with equal ability and does own layout work. (6) Supervises and provides on-the-job training and instruction to apprentice blacksmiths and helpers.

Educational Requirements: High school education and trade school training in blacksmithing, welding, metal working, or equivalents.

Experience or Training: Minimum of 2 years experience as an apprentice, and 3 months on-the-job training.

---

*The author would like to express his indebtedness to James E. Brewster, Ronald English, Dru Ertz-Berger, Henry T. Porter, Bruce G. Shulter, and William J. Singleton—all graduate students at Texas A & M University—who wrote the job descriptions in the first four groups.

Working Conditions: Work area is hot, noisy, and dirty. Requires 80–90% standing and squatting and 10–20% sitting. Lighting varies from good to fair. Possible eye and burn injuries.

Special Requirements: None

Job Title: Blacksmith B (learner)   **Job No. 002**

Organization Level: Works under technical supervision of Blacksmith A in groups of 2–5. Reports to section supervisor for all administrative actions.

Job Performance: (1) Makes and dresses small hand and machine tools. (2) Shapes heated metals with power machines and hand tools. (3) Forms plates and pipes and shapes by heating and using jigs. (4) Can handle both ferrous and nonferrous metals and lays out simple work.

Educational Requirements: Some high school education and ability to do simple mathematics.

Experience or Training: General aptitude for metal working. Job is used as a training classification.

Working Conditions: Work area is hot, noisy, and dirty. Requires 80–90% standing and squatting and 10–20% sitting. Lighting varies from good to fair. Possible eye and burn injuries.

Special Requirements: None

Job Title: Bricklayer A   **Job No. 003**

Organization Level: Reports to section supervisor. Supervises 2–3 apprentices and helpers.

Job Performance: (1) Lays brick, tile, concrete, cinder, glass, gypsum, and terra cotta block (except stone) to construct or repair walls, partitions, arches, sewers, or other structures. (2) Measures from pre-set reference points and marks guidelines for work layout. (3) Applies mortar to block end and sets in mortar bed, tapping with trowel to embed it in mortar, allowing for a specified uniform thickness of joints. (4) Removes excess mortar from block face and finishes mortar between bricks with trowel. (5) Breaks bricks for spaces using trowel edge. (6) Determines vertical and horizontal alignment of courses using plumb bob, gaugeline, and level. (7) Fastens brick and terra cotta veneers to existing structures with tie wires embedded in mortar between bricks. (8) Supervises and provides on-the-job training for apprentice bricklayers.

Educational Requirements: Must be able to read and understand basic measuring tools.

Experience or Training: 2–4 years experience as Bricklayer B.

Working Conditions: Works both indoors and outdoors during all types of weather. Requires 95% standing and stooping and 5% sitting.

Special Requirements: None

Job Title: Carpenter A   **Job No. 004**

Organization Level: Reports to section supervisor. Supervises and provides on-the-job guidance and training for 3–5 apprentice carpenters.

Job Performance: (1) Constructs, erects, installs, and repairs wood, plywood, and wallboard structures and items using hand and power carpenter tools in accordance with plans, sketches, blueprints, and governing building codes. (2) Prepares layouts utilizing the most economical use of materials; marks cutting and assembly lines; and shapes materials to the prescribed measurements using saws, chisels, and planes. (3) Assembles and fastens cut materials and verifies the structure trueness with plumb bob and level. (4) Erects structure framework and flooring, and installs related materials such as barrier paper, shock-absorbing, sound-deadening, and decorative panels for ceilings, floors, and walls. (5) Fits and installs prefabricated window frames, doors, trim, and hardware. (6) Constructs concrete pouring chutes and forms. (7) Erects scaffolding and ladders for assembling structures above ground level. (8) Supervises 3–5 apprentice carpenters.

Educational Requirements: High school and carpenter trade school or equivalent.

Experience or Training: 2–4 years experience as Carpenter B.

Working Conditions: Works both indoors and outdoors under varying weather conditions. Requires 90% standing and stooping and 10% sitting. Possible hazard of injury to eyes and extremities.

Special Requirements: None

Job Title: Crane Operator A   **Job No. 005**

Organization Level: Reports to section supervisor. May work directly under operational control of construction engineer.

Job Performance: (1) Operates either locomotive or tractor crawler crane and manipulates all controls on guy derrick. (2) Moves cranes on tracks, road, or uneven terrain. (3) Supervises other workers and helpers in placing blocking and out-riggers to prevent crane from overturning when lifting loads. (4) Must handle loads requiring expert skill and careful handling. (5) Is responsible for maintenance before, during, and after operation and for inspection for worn or frayed parts which constitute safety hazards.

Educational Requirements: High school reading and writing ability.

Experience or Training: Minimum of 5 years experience as Crane Operator B.

Working Conditions: Conditions vary with existing weather. Requires 90% sitting and 10% climbing and standing.

Special Requirements: Vision must be correctable for 20/20 with normal depth perception. Must have normal hearing.

Job Title: Electrician A   **Job No. 006**

Organization Level: Reports to section supervisor. Supervises and provides on-the-job guidance and training for 3–5 apprentice electricians.

Job Performance: (1) Plans, installs, and repairs wiring, electrical fixtures, and control equipment. (2) Prepares sketches showing location of all wiring and equipment from blueprints and insures that all hidden wiring is installed before completion of new walls, ceilings, and floors. (3) Lays out, bends, and installs electrical conduit using hand tools. (4) Pulls wire through conduit with aid of electrician's helper. (5) Splices wires and connects them to lighting fixtures and power equipment. (6) Installs control or distribution apparatus such as switches, relays, and circuit breaker panels. (7) Connects power cables to equipment and tests continuity of circuits to ensure electrical compatability and safety using standard instruments such as oscilloscope and ohmmeter. (8) Supervises 3–5 apprentice electricians.

Educational Requirements: High school and electrician's trade school or equivalent.

Experience or Training: 2–4 years experience as Electrician B.

Working Conditions: Normally indoors, with sometimes dusty or confining work areas. Requires 80–90% standing, squatting, and crawling, with 10–20% sitting.

Special Requirements: Must have normal color perception.

Job Title: Forklift Operator   **Job No. 007**

Organization Level: Reports to section supervisor. Generally works alone with minimal supervision.

Job Performance: (1) Drives gasoline- or electric-powered industrial truck equipped with forklift to lift, stack, move, or tier merchandise, equipment, or material in warehouse storage yard or factory. (2) Moves levers and depresses pedals to drive truck and control movement of forks. (3) Positions forks under loaded pallets, skids, or boxes and transports them to designated area. (4) Unloads and stacks materials. May inventory materials in work area and supply workers with materials as needed. (5) Performs maintenance on truck before, during, and after operation.

Educational Requirements: High school education.

Experience or Training: 6 months on the job.

Working Conditions: Generally good, but may work outside in adverse weather. Requires 95% sitting and 5% standing.

Special Requirements: Vision must be correctable to 20/20 with normal color and depth perception. Must have good coordination and normal hearing.

Job Title: Helper A   **Job No. 008**

Organization Level: Reports to section supervisor, but works under supervision of a skilled crafts worker.

Job Performance: Is a semiskilled worker performing tasks under direct guidance of a skilled crafts worker or under general supervision in jobs such as materials handling and simple machine tending. May learn a trade or occupation in this status.

Educational Requirements: High school reading and writing ability.

Experience or Training: None

Working Conditions: Work area is dirty, oily, and noisy. Requires 70% standing and 30% sitting, with some hazard of injury to extremities.

Special Requirements: None

Job Title: Laborer   **Job No. 009**

Organization Level: Reports to supervisor for daily assignments and generally works under supervision of A or B level crafts worker.

Job Performance: Performs general unskilled manual labor about the plant or job site such as cleaning, sweeping, hand trucking, material moving, digging, and general roustabout work.

Educational Requirements: Should understand some English.

Experience or Training: None

Working Conditions: Conditions are variable depending on the task assigned, but are generally dirty. Requires 90% or more standing, squatting, and kneeling.

Special Requirements: None

Job Title: Layout Person A   **Job No. 010**

Organization Level: Reports to supervisor of fabrication department, but generally works without supervision. May supervise and advise Layout Person B or C when required.

Job Performance: (1) Lays out all materials with dimensions and directions for fabrication of highly diversified products. (2) Works from sketches, drawings, and blueprints. (3) Knows all phases of shop operations and can visualize fabrication and assembly procedures. (4) Computes allowances for stretch-out and take-up materials and employs the most economical use of materials. (5) Can handle the most complicated work and solves any mathematical design problems. (6) Designs, details, or checks drawings against current American Society of Mechanical Engineers (ASME) codes to obtain specific results. (7) Makes up materials requirements. (8) Works without any direct supervision.

Educational Requirements: 2 years of college or equivalent and completion of industrial trade school.

Experience or Training: Minimum of 5 years experience as Layout Person B and 1 year on-the-job training. Considered equivalent to supervisor except in seniority and supervisory responsibility.

Working Conditions: Has desk and good lighting for computations. Spends 60% of time on the line and in actual layout with proportionate sitting and standing. Is subject to some plant noise.

Special Requirements: None

Job Title: Machine Operator A   **Job No. 011**

Organization Level: Reports to section supervisor, but works without direct supervision. Supervises 5–10 Machine Operators B and C.

Job Performance: (1) Sets up and operates any general metal working machines such as millers, borers, shears, punches, presses, and rollers. (2) Must complete widely varied jobs of fabrication in a superior manner with no direct supervision. (3) Sets up any of the machines for others to operate. (4) Performs maintenance on machines before, during, and after operation and is capable of diagnosing machine troubles. (5) Supervises and provides on-the-job training and instructions to Machine Operators B and C.

Educational Requirements: High school education or equivalent.

Experience or Training: Minimum of 2 years experience as Machine Operator B or exceptional demonstrated performance.

Working Conditions: Work area is oily, dirty, and noisy. Requires 90% standing and 10% sitting. Lighting is generally good. Possible hazard of injury to extremities.

Special Requirements: None

Job Title: Machinist A   **Job No. 012**

Organization Level: Reports to section supervisor. May work alone, but generally provides training guidance to 2–5 apprentices or learning workers.

Job Performance: (1) Sets up and operates all types of cutting, grinding, and shaping machines for cold metal. (2) Selects speed, feeds, and tools for the most economical production rate of these machines. (3) Knows tolerance and fits required on precision metal work and is capable of doing bench work. (4) Works from blueprints, drawings, and sketches involving the use of shop mathematics and measuring instruments. (5) Performs maintenance on machines before, during and after operation and is capable of diagnosing machine troubles. (6) Supervises and provides on-the-job training and instruction to apprentice machinists and helpers.

Educational Requirements: High school education and machinist trade school training or equivalent.

Experience or Training: Minimum of 2 years experience as a machinist and 6 months on-the-job training required.

Working Conditions: Work area is oily, dirty, and noisy. Requires 70% standing and 30% sitting. Lighting is good. Possible hazard of injury to extremities.

Special Requirements: Vision must be correctable to 20/20 in at least one eye.

Job Title: Electrical Maintenance Person A   **Job No. 013**

Organization Level: Reports to Chief Engineer, Plant and Equipment Maintenance. Supervises 5–10 Maintenance Persons B and C.

Job Performance: (1) Plans, installs, and maintains a wide variety of complex electrical equipment, such as involved timers and automatic controls, generators, and large switching circuits. (2) Prepares secondary electrical distribution centers; balances loads in large wire circuits. (3) Can diagnose and correct any electrical problems. (4) Must work extensively from wiring diagrams and schematics. (5) Supervises and provides on-the-job training to Maintenance Persons B and C.

Educational Requirements: High school education and electrical trade school completion or equivalent.

Experience or Training: Requires journeyman electrician training, 2 years experience as Maintenance Person B, and 6 months on-the-job demonstrated performance.

Working Conditions: Has desk and good lighting conditions. Spends 80% of time in maintenance supervision and troubleshooting with proportionate standing. Is subject to shop noise.

Special Requirements: Vision must be correctable to 20/20 with normal color perception.

Job Title: Electrical Maintenance Person B   **Job No. 014**

Organization Level: Reports to Maintenance Person A and usually works as senior of a 2-person team.

Job Performance: (1) Installs and maintains a variety of ordinary electrical equipment such as motors, lighting circuits, and starters. (2) Wires fairly complicated circuits. (3) Diagnoses and corrects trouble on general electrical equipment. (4) Works from drawings.

Educational Requirements: High school education.

Experience or Training: Must have worked as Maintenance Person C for 1 year.

Working Conditions: Spends 90% standing, squatting, or kneeling, and 10% sitting. Lighting and noise vary, but are generally good.

Special Requirements: Vision must be correctable to 20/20, and color perception must be normal.

Job Title: Brush or Spray Painter A   **Job No. 015**

Organization Level: Reports to section supervisor. Provides general supervison for 2–3 apprentices or learning workers.

Job Performance: (1) Mixes paints, lacquer, enamel, and other liquid coating materials. (2) Prepares surfaces and subsequently applies coatings in accordance with specifications using brush, dip, or spray equipment. (3) Erects scaffolding and ladders. (4) Assembles, maintains, and cleans all related working equipment.

Educational Requirements: High school reading and writing ability.

Experience or Training: 1 year experience as Painter B.

Working Conditions: Involves extensive standing, climbing, and stretching. Skin and eyes are subject to drying and irritating fumes, vapors, and solutions. Must work at heights 50% of the time.

Special Requirements: Must have good sense of balance. Needs normal color perception. Must not be allergic to paints and associated materials.

Job Title: Brush or Spray Painter B   **Job No. 016**

Organization Level: Reports to section supervisor. Works under general supervision of Painter A.

Job Performance: (1) Applies paints, lacquers, enamel, and other liquid coating materials using brush, dip, or spray equipment. (2) Prepares surfaces. (3) Erects scaffolds and ladders. (4) Cleans equipment.

Educational Requirements: None

Experience or Training: None

Working Conditions: Involves extensive standing, climbing, and stretching. Skin and eyes are subject to drying and irritating fumes, vapors, and solutions. Must work at heights 50% of the time.

Special Requirements: Must have good sense of balance. Needs normal color perception. Must not be allergic to paints and associated materials.

Job Title: Plasterer   **Job No. 017**

Organization Level: Reports to section supervisor. Supervises 1–2 helpers.

Job Performance: (1) Applies goals of plaster to interior walls and ceilings to produce finished surfaces as per blueprints, drawings, or oral instructions. (2) Directs helpers in mixing plaster and erecting scaffolding. (3) Spreads plaster over lath or masonry bases and smooths to attain uniform thickness. (4) Creates decorative textures in finish coat by marking with brush, trowel, roller, or other similar techniques. (5) May install precast ornamental plaster pieces by applying mortar to back and pressing in place. (6) Provides direct supervision over 1–2 helpers.

Educational Requirements: Must be able to read simple blueprint specifications.

Experience or Training: 2–4 years training as an apprentice plasterer.

Working Conditions: Works inside under humid conditions. Possible hazard of fall injury. Requires 95% standing and squatting and 5% sitting.

Special Requirements: Must have good sense of balance.

Job Title: Plumber A   **Job No. 018**

Organization Level: Reports to section supervisor. Supervises and provides on-the-job guidance and training for 3–5 apprentice plumbers.

Job Performance: (1) Assembles, installs, and repairs pipes, fittings, and fixtures of heating, water drainage, and sewage systems. (2) From plans and drawings, determines work aids required, sequence of installation, and most economical and feasible route for pipe. (3) Cuts holes in walls and floors for pipe passage and cuts; threads, bends, and joins pipe to obtain the desired system using power and hand tools. (4) Assembles and installs valves, pipe fittings, and pipes composed of metals as well as nonmetals such as glass and vitrified china. (5) Fills pipe systems with water or air and pressure checks for leaks. (6) Installs and repairs plumbing fixtures such as commodes, sinks, and water heaters; mends burst pipes and clogged drains. (7) Supervises 3–5 apprentice plumbers.

Educational Requirements: High school education and plumbers trade school or equivalent.

Experience or Training: 2–4 years experience as Plumber B.

Working Conditions: Dirty, wet, hot, and humid conditions. Requires 90% standing, squatting, and crawling, and 10% sitting.

Special Requirements: None

Job Title: Porter (Janitor)   **Job No. 019**

Organization Level: Reports to head custodian and works under general supervision.

Job Performance: (1) Keeps offices or working areas and general premises clean and orderly. (2) Performs any combination of sweeping, mopping, scrubbing, and buffing with both hand and power rotary brushes. (3) Cleans dust and dirt from all fixtures, office machines, walls, ceilings, and trash receptacles using brushes and vacuum cleaner. (4) Washes windows and other glass fixtures. (5) Cleans washrooms and restocks with paper and soap. (6) Replaces light bulbs. (7) Handtrucks some materials and bulk office supplies as required.

Educational Requirements: None

Experience or Training: None

Working Conditions: Generally pleasant surroundings with adequate lighting. Requires 90% standing and 10% sitting.

Special Requirements: None

Job Title: Tool Room Person A   **Job No. 020**

Organization Level: Reports to section supervisor. Supervises Tool Room Persons B and C.

Job Performance: (1) Has charge of storing tools, parts, and equipment. (2) Issues tools, parts, and equipment to and receives from workers. (3) Keeps records of receipts and issues and makes minor equipment repairs as necessary. (4) Requisitions new equipment and repair parts. (5) Repairs hand tools, cutting and gas welding torches, hoses, and gauges. (6) Supervises and trains Tool Room Persons B and C.

Educational Requirements: High school education.

Experience or Training: Minimum experience of 1 year as Tool Room Person B.

Working Conditions: Lighting is good and shop noise is minimal. Requires 50% standing and 50% sitting.

Special Requirements: None

Job Title: Tool Room Person B   **Job No. 021**

Organization Level: Reports to Tool Room Person A.

Job Performance: (1) Issues tools, parts, and equipment to and receives them from workers. (2) Keeps record of receipt and issuance of tools, parts, and equipment.

Educational Requirements: High school education.

Experience or Training: Minimum of 1 year experience as Tool Room Person C.

Working Conditions: Lighting is good and shop noise is minimal. Requires 70% standing and 30% sitting.

Special Requirements: None

Job Title: Light Truck Driver   **Job No. 022**

Organization Level: Reports to section supervisor. Generally works alone with minimal supervision.

Job Performance: (1) Drives truck with 3-ton or less capacity to transport materials and/or personnel to and from specific destinations. (2) Verifies loads against shipping documents, and prepares receipts for loads picked up. (3) May load and unload truck. (4) Performs maintenance and inspection of truck before, during, and after operation, and records usage information on daily trip ticket. (5) Performs emergency roadside repairs such as tire changes, bulb replacements, and tire chain installation.

Educational Requirements: High school education.

Experience or Training: 6 months as Assistant Truck Driver or equivalent.

Working Conditions: Work is both in and out of doors in all types of weather. Requires 80% sitting and 20% standing.

Special Requirements: Must have valid commercial driver's license. Vision correctable to 20/20 and normal color perception.

Job Title: Acetylene Welder (hand) A   **Job No. 023**

Organization Level: Reports to section supervisor. Provides general guidance and instruction to 2–5 apprentices or learners.

Job Performance: (1) Adjusts, assembles, and uses gas-fired welding equipment. (2) Is qualified under American Society of Mechanical Engineers (ASME) or other codes and tests. (3) Produces neat welds in horizontal, flat, vertical, and overhead positions in both ferrous and nonferrous metals. (4) Does limited gas-fired hand cutting on both straight and curved lines. (5) Provides on-the-job training to apprentices and learners.

Educational Requirements: None

Experience or Training: Minimum of 1 year experience as Acetylene Welder (hand) B or demonstrated superior job performance. Must pass certification tests.

Working Conditions: Work area is hot, noisy, and dirty. Requires 80–90% standing and squatting and 10–20% sitting. Lighting varies from good to fair. Possible eye and burn injuries.

Special Requirements: Must have normal hearing.

Job Title: Electric Welder A   **Job No. 024**

Organization Level: Reports to section supervisor. Provides general guidance and instructions to 2–5 apprentices or learners.

Job Performance: (1) Consistently produces welds requiring the highest degree of skill in any position. (2) Qualifies under X-ray, American Society of

Mechanical Engineers (ASME), and any other codes and tests. (3) Welds any type of metal or alloy with equal skill. (4) Provides on-the-job instruction and training to apprentices and learners.

Educational Requirements: None

Experience or Training: Minimum of 1 year experience as Electric Welder B or demonstrated superior job performance. Must pass all certification tests.

Working Conditions: Work area is hot, noisy, and dirty. Requires 80–90% standing and squatting and 10–20% sitting. Lighting varies from good to fair. Possible eye and burn injuries.

Special Requirements: Must have normal hearing.

Job Title: Electric Welder B   **Job No. 025**

Organization Level: Reports to section supervisor.

Job Performance: (1) Produces welds in horizontal, flat, and vertical positions. (2) Qualifies under the American Society of Mechanical Engineers (ASME) code. (3) Makes neat welds on alloys as well as carbon steel.

Educational Requirements: None

Experience or Training: Minimum of 2 years experience or on-the-job training. Must pass certification tests.

Working Conditions: Work area is hot, noisy, and dirty. Requires 80–90% standing and squatting and 10–20% sitting. Lighting varies from good to fair. Possible eye and burn injuries.

Special Requirements: Must have normal hearing.

JOB DESCRIPTIONS FOR 25 CLERICAL JOBS IN A BANK

Job Title: Safe Deposit Attendant   **Job No. 101**

Organization Level: Reports to Head Teller.

Job Performance: (1) Rents safe deposit boxes to bank customers. (2) Assists a renter in removing safe deposit box from vault and replacing it when finished. (3) Determines that the person who presents a key is authorized to have access to that box.

Educational Requirements: High school education.

Experience or Training: Minimum of 3 weeks on the job before fully qualified.

Working Conditions: 40% of time spent sitting at a desk while typing forms and renting boxes. 60% of time spent walking to and from the vault while assisting customers in removing and replacing their boxes.

Special Requirements: Must be bonded.

Job Title: Savings Teller   **Job No. 102**

Organization Level: Reports to Head Teller.

Job Performance: (1) Accepts currency or checks for credit to a customer's savings account, issues a receipt, and makes entry in customer's passbook. (2) Pays out currency to a depositor upon receipt of a properly filled out and signed savings withdrawal slip and upon presentation of a passbook.

Educational Requirements: High school education.

Experience or Training: Minimum of 8 weeks on the job before fully qualified.

Working Conditions: 90% of time spent standing or sitting on a stool while accepting or paying out savings deposits. The back and legs are often fatigued. 10% of time spent sitting at a counter while counting cash and balancing books.

Special Requirements: Must be bonded.

Job Title: Receiving and Paying Teller   **Job No. 103**

Organization Level: Reports to Head Teller.

Job Performance: (1) Accepts checks, currency, and silver from customers who maintain checking accounts for credit to their accounts, and issues a receipt for funds received. (2) Pays out currency upon presentation of properly signed checks which are drawn against funds on deposit in the bank and are payable to persons who have endorsed the checks. (3) Pays out currency on checks drawn on other banks, presented by customers or others, upon proper identification and approval by a bank officer.

Educational Requirements: High school education.

Experience or Training: Minimum of 8 weeks on the job before fully qualified.

Working Conditions: 90% of time spent sitting on a stool or standing while receiving or paying. The back and legs are often fatigued. 10% of time spent sitting while counting currency and balancing books.

Special Requirements: Must be bonded.

Job Title: Head Teller   **Job No. 104**

Organization Level: Reports to Cashier. Oversees 4 clerks.

Job Performance: (1) Controls the cash surplus of the bank. (2) Is reponsible for seeing that all tellers have enough cash for their day's business. (3) Is responsible for opening and closing the vault. (4) Must see that all tellers balance their accounts after the bank closes. (5) Oversees rental and opening of safe deposit boxes.

Educational Requirements: High school education.

Experience or Training: Minimum of 5 years as a teller or college education.

Working Conditions: 90% of time spent walking around helping and overseeing other clerks. 10% of time spent sitting at a desk checking figures.

Special Requirements: Must be bonded.

Job Title: Collateral Teller   **Job No. 105**

Organization Level: Reports to the Credit Investigator and Analyst. Is assisted by 1 clerk.

Job Performance: (1) Accepts stocks, bonds, and other securities pledged as collateral for a loan. (2) Examines securities to be sure they are in negotiable order and issues a receipt to the customer. (3) Upon final payment of the loan, the teller delivers the securities to the customer by mail.

Educational Requirements: High school education.

Experience or Training: Minimum of 6 months on the job before fully qualified.

Working Conditions: There are some distractions due to others working in the same area and some customer traffic. 85% of time spent sitting at a desk doing paperwork. 15% of time spent walking around gathering information and materials.

Special Requirements: Must be bonded.

Job Title: Audit Clerk   **Job No. 106**

Organization Level: Reports to Auditor.

Job Performance: (1) Checks daily balance sheet for accuracy. (2) Types reports for Auditor. (3) Periodically visits each department in the bank to check figures for accuracy. (4) Turns in to Auditor a report of errors found.

Educational Requirements: High school education.

Working Conditions: 80% of time spent sitting at a desk working adding machine or calculator. Often tedious with some eye strain. 20% of time spent sitting at desk checking figures.

Special Requirements: Necessary to have good finger dexterity due to long periods working with adding machine or calculator.

Job Title: Secretary   **Job No. 107**

Organization Level: Reports to President. Has informal control over all other clerks.

Job Performance: (1) Takes shorthand and types letters. (2) Gathers and delivers materials and information on request. (3) Receives visitors. (4) Makes appointments and phone calls on request. (5) Acts as assistant to the President in handling minor or routine affairs. (6) Acts as de facto supervisor and liaison between management and clerks.

Educational Requirements: High school education.

Working Conditions: Desk situated in an area exposed to the public. 30% of time spent walking when gathering or distributing information materials. 30% of time spent talking to customers on the telephone or in person. 30% of time spent sitting at a desk while typing. 10% of time spent overseeing clerks.

Special Requirements: Should have a good working knowledge of the business environment. Must have initiative and be able to accept business and social responsibilities. Work requires effective interpersonal relationships with all types of people.

Job Title: Collateral Clerk   **Job No. 108**

Organization Level: Reports to Collateral Teller.

Job Performance: (1) Writes up in the collateral register the description of stocks, bonds, and securities pledged with the bank as collateral for a loan. (2) Works as assistant to the Collateral Teller.

Educational Requirements: High school education.

Experience or Training: Minimum of 6 weeks on the job before fully qualified.

Working Conditions: 85% of time is spent at a desk writing or typing in the collateral register. Work is often tedious. 15% is spent standing or sitting while helping Collateral Teller.

Job Title: Credit Investigator   **Job No. 109**

Organization Level: Reports to Credit Analyst.

Job Performance: (1) Checks through business or trade channels on credit extended and records of payment for customers who have applied for a loan. (2) Attempts to check on the character and reputation of new customers who apply for a loan.

Educational Requirements: High school education.

Experience or Training: Minimum of 8 weeks on the job before fully qualified.

Working Conditions: 45% of time spent on telephone. 55% of time spent walking to different departments checking records.

Job Title: Credit Analyst   **Job No. 110**

Organization Level: Reports to Loan Officer. Is assisted by 3 clerks.

Job Performance: (1) Analyzes financial information supplied to the bank, either by the person who has applied for a loan or by Credit Investigator, to determine the applicant's financial responsibility. (2) Prepares financial information for the loan officer to use in a decision to extend credit. (3) Analyzes financial statements. (4) Makes report of financial condition of the businesses or customers who have applied to the loan officer for loans.

Educational Requirements: College education.

Experience or Training: Some previous experience as a credit investigator or loan clerk is desirable. If no experience, a minimum of 6–8 months on the job before fully qualified.

Working Conditions: 60% of time spent working at a desk. 40% of time spent in other departments collecting information.

Special Requirements: Some accounting training is desirable.

Job Title: Collector   **Job No. 111**

Organization Level: Reports to Junior Loan Officer.

Job Performance: (1) Is responsible for contacting, personally or by phone, customers who are behind in their loan payments. (2) Does some secretarial work for loan officers.

Educational Requirements: High school education.

Experience or Training: None.

Working Conditions: 95% of time spent on telephone, 5% of time spent walking to various departments collecting information on delinquent borrowers.

Special Requirements: Must be tactful and have a pleasant voice.

Job Title: Installment Loan Clerk   **Job No. 112**

Organization Level: Reports to Installment Loan Interviewer.

Job Performance: (1) Prepares all papers in connection with the installment loan, such as liability card, coupon book, and addressograph plates. (2) Mails coupon book to the borrower after the funds have been loaned. (3) Performs teller's job when teller is absent.

Educational Requirements: High school education.

Experience or Training: 8 weeks on the job before fully qualified.

Working Conditions: 60% of time spent walking to gather papers and having them certified by officers. 40% of time spent in a relatively private area working at a desk.

Job Title: Installment Loan Teller   **Job No. 113**

Organization Level: Reports to Installment Loan Interviewer.

Job Performance: (1) Reviews the note to determine that it is correctly signed and in order. (2) Disburses proceeds in accordance with instructions of the loan officer. (3) Accepts payments from the customer. (4) Works with Installment Loan Clerk when clerk falls behind.

Educational Requirements: High school education.

Experience or Training: 8 weeks on the job before fully qualified.

Working Conditions: Requires standing 50% of the time. Other 50% of time spent working at a desk.

Special Requirements: Must be bonded.

Job Title: Installment Loan Interviewer   **Job No. 114**

Organization Level: Responsible to Junior or Senior Loan Officer. Is assisted by 2 clerks.

Job Performance: (1) Reviews applications for loans from prospective borrowers. (2) Discusses the reason loan is to be made. (3) Obtains all necessary information. (4) Turns the file over to a loan officer.

Educational Requirements: High school education.

Experience or Training: Some training as an Installment Loan Clerk or Teller is desired. If no previous training, then a minimum of 8 weeks on the job is required before fully qualified.

Working Conditions: Work is done at a desk in an open area exposed to the public. 10% of time spent sitting at a desk while overseeing other clerks. 90% of time spent sitting at a desk while obtaining information from customers and making up files.

Job Title: Mortgage Loan Bookkeeper   **Job No. 115**

Organization Level: Reports to General Ledger Bookkeeper. Is assisted by 1 clerk.

Job Performance: (1) Posts new loans and payments to the mortgage loan liability ledger on bookkeeping machine. (2) Helps Installment Loan Bookkeeper when necessary. (3) Reviews books periodically for errors.

Educational Requirements: High school education.

Experience or Training: Minimum of 8 weeks on the job before fully qualified.

Working Conditions: 85% of time spent sitting while working a bookkeeping machine. 15% of time spent standing while reviewing figures in a ledger. Work is often tedious.

Special Requirements: Should be able to type in order to operate a bookkeeping machine.

Job Title: Installment Loan Bookkeeper   **Job No. 116**

Organization Level: Reports to General Ledger Bookkeeper. Overseas 1 clerk.

Job Performance: (1) Posts new loans to the installment liability ledger on bookkeeping machine. (2) Posts new payments to the installment liability ledger. (3) Helps other bookkeepers when necessary. (4) Oversees File Clerk.

Educational Requirements: High school education.

Experience or Training: Minimum of 8 weeks on the job before fully qualified.

Working Conditions: 80% of time spent sitting while working a bookkeeping machine. Some noise from bookkeeping machines. 15% of time spent reviewing figures. 5% of time spent overseeing File Clerk.

Special Requirements: Must be able to type in order to operate a bookkeeping machine.

Job Title: General Ledger Bookkeeper **Job No. 117**

Organization Level: Reports to Comptroller. Is assisted by 3 clerks.

Job Performance: (1) Posts all debits and credits of business transactions of the bank to the general ledger and subsidiary ledgers on bookkeeping machine. (2) Oversees Mortgage Loan Bookkeeper and Installment Loan Bookkeeper. (3) Helps Mortgage Loan Bookkeeper and Installment Loan Bookkeeper when necessary.

Educational Requirements: High school education.

Experience or Training: 2 years training as a bookkeeper.

Working Conditions: 60% of time spent sitting while working at bookkeeping machine. 35% of time spent reviewing figures. 5% of time spent overseeing and helping other bookkeepers.

Special Requirements: Must have general knowledge of work flow in a bank.

Job Title: Mortgage Loan Teller **Job No. 118**

Organization Level: Reports to Junior Loan Officer. Is assisted by 1 clerk.

Job Performance: (1) Insures that mortgage notes are properly signed and accompanied by proper supporting papers. (2) Disburses the proceeds in accordance with instructions of the loaning officer. (3) Accepts payments from the borrower and issues a receipt for the payment.

Educational Requirements: High school education.

Experience or Training: Minimum of 8 weeks on the job before fully qualified.

Working Conditions: 70% of time spent sitting at a desk taking payments by mail or from customers. 30% of time spent standing or sitting while helping and overseeing clerks.

Special Requirements: Must be bonded.

Job Title: Mail Clerk **Job No. 119**

Organization Level: Reports to Head Teller.

Job Performance: (1) Opens, sorts, and distributes all incoming mail. (2) Picks up and insures that all outgoing mail is properly sealed and has the proper postage. (3) Delivers outgoing mail to the post office.

Educational Requirements: High school education.

Experience or Training: Minimum of 2 weeks on the job before fully qualified.

Working Conditions: 60% of time spent sitting at a desk opening and sorting mail. 40% of time spent walking or standing while picking up and delivering mail or running it through a postage machine.

Special Requirements: Must be bonded.

Job Title: Receptionist   **Job No. 120**

Organization Level: Reports to Administrative Vice President.

Job Performance: (1) Greets all customers who wish to see the President, Executive Vice President, and Administrative Vice President. Checks to see if the officer the customer wants to see is busy. If not, the customer is ushered in. If the officer is busy, the receptionist makes the customer as comfortable as possible or makes an appointment if the customer doesn't want to wait. (2) The receptionist doubles as a secretary for the Administrative and Executive Vice Presidents. This includes taking dictation and typing only.

Educational Requirements: High school education.

Experience or Training: Minimum of 2 weeks on the job before fully qualified.

Working Conditions: There are some distractions due to flow of people by the desk and customers asking for information. 70% of time spent sitting or standing while dealing with customers. 30% of time sitting at a desk doing secretarial work.

Special Requirements: Work requires effective interpersonal relationships with all types of people.

Job Title: Check Filer and Sorter   **Job No. 121**

Organization Level: Reports to General Ledger Bookkeeper.

Job Performance: (1) Alphabetizes checks for the bookkeepers to run through their bookkeeping machines. (2) Files alphabetically the checks of checking account customers which have been paid and posted by the bookkeeping department pending return to the customer.

Educational Requirements: High school education.

Experience or Training: Minimum of 2 weeks on the job before fully qualified.

Working Conditions: 40% of time spent sitting at a desk sorting checks. 40% of time spent standing while filing checks. 20% of time spent walking around gathering and delivering checks.

Job Title: Switchboard Operator   **Job No. 122**

Organization Level: Reports to Cashier.

Job Performance: Answers telephone at main switchboard and connects caller with requested person or department.

Educational Requirements: High school education.

Experience or Training: Minimum of 2 weeks on the job before fully qualified.

Working Conditions: 100% of time spent sitting at a switchboard talking into a phone. Work is often monotonous.

Special Requirements: Must have a pleasant voice.

Job Title: Addressograph Operator   **Job No. 123**

Organization Level: Works under the Comptroller. Has no helpers.

Job Performance: (1) Prepares addressograph plates, which carry the name, address, and other pertinent information on an individual or firm. (2) Operates an addressograph machine, which transcribes the information from the plates onto envelopes or other blank forms. (3) Does some work as file clerk.

Educational Requirements: High school education.

Experience or Training: About 4 days are required to familiarize a new operator with the procedures and operation of machines.

Working Conditions: Work area is somewhat noisy because addressograph machine is located in the bookkeeping department next to bookkeeping machines. 85% of time spent sitting or standing while typing plates or running envelopes through the machine. 15% of time spent walking or standing while filing.

Special Requirements: Must be able to type.

Job Title: File Clerk   **Job No. 124**

Organization Level: Reports to General Ledger Bookkeeper.

Job Performance: Performs all functions in connection with filing of letters, checks, and documents. This includes feeding data into microfilm machine.

Educational Requirements: High school education.

Experience or Training: Minimum of 2 weeks on the job before fully qualified.

Working Conditions: 90% of time spent standing while filing. 10% of time spent sitting while committing letters, checks, and documents to microfilm.

Job Title: Mortgage Loan Clerk   **Job No. 125**

Organization Level: Reports to Mortgage Loan Teller.

Job Performance: (1) Handles all details in connection with a mortgage loan, such as preparing notices of principle and interest that are due and checking on payment of tax bills and insurance premiums. (2) Maintains mortgage loan files. (3) Does some typing for loan officer. (4) Helps Mortgage Loan Teller when necessary.

Educational Requirements: High school education.

Experience or Training: Minimum of 6 weeks on the job before fully qualified.

Working Conditions: 50% of time spent sitting at a desk preparing paperwork, checking paperwork, and typing. 50% of time spent standing while filing.

JOB DESCRIPTIONS FOR 25 PROFESSIONAL AND TECHNICAL JOBS IN A MANUFACTURING COMPANY

Job Title: Assistant to the Chief Accountant   **Job No. 201**

Organization Level: Reports to the Chief Accountant.

Job Performance: (1) Assists the Chief Accountant in the performance of major duties and responsibilities. (2) Represents Chief Accountant on plant visits. (3) Assists plant in the installation and maintenance of accounting procedures and records. (4) Reviews plant expense budgets and cost records for accuracy and compliance with procedures. (5) Reviews internal audits of plant operations. (6) Assists Chief Accountant in negotiations with local tax assessors as to plant property valuations. (7) Assists Chief Accountant in selecting and training personnel and administrating company personnel policies relating to division and plant accounting employees. (8) Accomplishes special surveys and analyses as directed.

Educational Requirements: Bachelor's degree in accounting.

Experience or Training: Minimum of 3 years of plant accounting.

Working Conditions: Has secretary and an office with adequate lighting. Requires 50% sitting and 50% standing or walking.

Job Title: Plant Accountant   **Job No. 202**

Organization Level: Responsible to Chief Accountant. Supervises two staff accountants and coordinates the activities of the accounting department with those of other line and staff functions.

Job Performance: (1) Directs the maintenance of Plant Accountant record cards of equipment and machinery and the preparation of required reports. (2) Reviews and approves the accounting of transfers relative to equipment and machinery. (3) Directs the implementation of company procedures in the taking of annual and special inventories, and works with supervisor and other staff department heads in developing and applying corrective measures to prevent inventory distortion. (4) Directs the accumulation and reporting of cost data within established time limits and in accordance with company instructions. (5) Directs the implementation of company procedures for timekeeping and production reporting and the accumulation and recording of data as a basis for preparing payrolls, budgetary control statements, and charges to inventory. (6) Works with supervisor in the preparation and revision, as necessary, of budgets of income based on projected sales and production data so that comprehensive plant budgets may be submitted for consideration and approval of division and head office personnel. (7) Directs the maintenance of payroll records and the preparation and distribution of payrolls and reports in accordance with company instructions consistent with terms and interpretations of any existing union agreements and government regulations with respect to overtime, holiday pay, and other items affecting payroll procedures.

Educational Requirements: Bachelor's degree in accounting and a C.P.A. certificate.

Experience or Training: Minimum of 5 years with a C.P.A. firm or 5–7 years working in a company's accounting department.

Working Conditions: Pleasant office and surroundings with adequate lighting.

Job Title: Staff Accountant   **Job No. 203**

Organization Level: Responsible to Plant Accountant.

Job Performance: (1) Maintains records for departments. (2) Assists in preparation of department budgets. (3) Compares operating statements with budgets and investigates areas of deviation. (4) Prepares plant operating performance and profits reports.

Educational Requirements: Bachelor's degree in accounting.

Experience or Training: No previous experience required.

Working Conditions: 75% of time spent in office, and 25% of time spent in other departments.

Special Requirements: Must be able to work effectively with other people.

Job Title: Plant Engineer I   **Job No. 204**

Organization Level: Responsible directly to Plant Manager. Supervises 50 employees.

Job Performance: (1) Plans, supervises, and coordinates all plant engineering activities performed by the engineering office and the maintenance and power sections. (2) Coordinates department activities with plant operating requirements. (3) Directs employee training. (4) Checks and approves department reports. (5) Enforces safety and housekeeping regulations. (6) Maintains department discipline. (7) Recommends discharge for cause. (8) Handles second-stage grievances. (9) Keeps abreast of engineering and related technical developments. (10) Is responsible for property and equipment valued at over $12 million.

Educational Requirements: Bachelor's degree in mechanical or industrial engineering.

Experience or Training: Minimum of 7–10 years working as a Plant Engineer II, III, or IV.

Working Conditions: 50% of time spent in office, and 50% of time spent at job sites.

Job Title: Plant Engineer II   **Job No. 205**

Organization Level: Responsible to Plant Engineer I. Supervises 26–50 employees.

Job Performance: (1) Prepares designs, cost estimates, and drafts of proposals. (2) Analyzes competitive bids. (3) Conducts engineering surveys. (4) Trains employees. (5) Enforces safety and housekeeping regulations. (6) Is responsible for equipment and property valued at $5–12 million.

Educational Requirements: Bachelor's degree in mechanical or industrial engineering.

Experience or Training: Minimum of 5–7 years working as a Plant Engineer III and IV.

Working Conditions: 70% of time spent at job site, and 30% of time spent in office.

Job Title: Plant Engineer III   **Job No. 206**

Organization Level: Responsible to Plant Engineer I. Supervises 10–25 employees.

Job Performance: (1) Prepares designs, cost estimates, and drafts of proposals, (2) Analyzes competitive bids. (3) Conducts engineering surveys. (4) Trains employees. (5) Enforces safety and housekeeping regulations. (6) Checks and approves time cards and work records. (7) Handles first-stage grievances. (8) Is responsible for property and equipment valued at $5 million.

Educational Requirements: Bachelor's degree in mechanical or industrial engineering.

Experience or Training: Minimum of 3–5 years working as Plant Engineer IV.

Working Conditions: 80% of time spent on job site, and 20% of time spent in office.

Job Title: Plant Engineer IV   **Job No. 207**

Organization Level: Responsible to Plant Engineer I. Supervises 5–10 employees.

Job Performance: (1) Trains employees. (2) Maintains discipline. (3) Approves new employees. (4) Recommends discharge for cause. (5) Requisitions supplies, materials, and services.

Educational Requirements: Bachelor's degree in mechanical or industrial engineering.

Experience or Training: Minimum of 1–3 years working as a Drafter in the engineering department.

Working Conditions: 90% of time spent on job site, and 10% of time spent in office.

Job Title: Power Engineer   **Job No. 208**

Organization Level: Responsible to Manager of Industrial Engineering. Supervises 1 assistant and 5 boiler room workers.

Job Performance: (1) Directs the operation and maintenance of a high pressure steam-electric power plant, to meet the plant's requirements of steam, electricity, water, and air. (2) Trains employees. (3) Maintains discipline.

Educational Requirements: Bachelor's degree in engineering or its equivalent.

Experience or Training: Minimum of 3–5 years experience in a power plant.

Working Conditions: Hot and sometimes dirty work. 50% of time spent in office, and 50% of time spent in boiler room.

Job Title: Drafter   **Job No. 209**

Organization Level: Reports directly to Manager, Industrial Engineering.

Job Performance: Prepares detailed drawings of parts, machinery, and structures, including isometric projections and sectional views as needed. May prepare working drawings of subassemblies or architectural drawings of new buildings. Occasionally works on design of improved machinery or on new company products, in close working relationship with engineers in the department.

Educational Requirements: High school education or equivalent. Knowledge of mechanical drawing desirable but not required.

Experience or Training: 6 months on-the-job training, or 1 year's experience in a job requiring extensive use of drafting equipment.

Working Conditions: 90% of time spent sitting or standing at a drafting table, and 10% of time spent conferring with engineers and in other activities. Involves some eye strain.

Job Title: Manager, Operations Engineering   **Job No. 210**

Organization Level: Responsible to Plant Manager. Supervises a staff consisting of a Civil Engineer, a Senior Standards Engineer, and a Project Engineer.

Job Performance: (1) Is responsible for developing and directing plans and programs for the installation, maintenance, and repair of all production equipment. (2) Makes recommendations for the purchase of new equipment. (3) Is familiar with new technical developments of production equipment. (4) Maintains a complete file of detailed blueprints and drawings of installations and equipment maintained. (5) Keeps historical records of cost data on equipment and machinery.

Educational Requirements: Bachelor's degree in mechanical engineering.

Experience or Training: Minimum of 7–10 years experience in a manufacturing plant.

Working Conditions: 85% of time spent in office, and 15% of time spent on job sites.

Job Title: Project Engineer   **Job No. 211**

Organization Level: Responsible to Manager, Operations Engineering.

Job Performance: (1) Directs and coordinates the activities of engineers and skilled crafts workers in the preparation of cost estimates. (2) Directs and coordinates the layout, design, and selection of equipment and systems. (3) Directs and coordinates the preparation of engineering drawings and sketches. (4) Directs and coordinates the requisition of materials on projects which may be assigned. (5) Trains new employees.

Educational Requirements: Bachelor's degree in mechanical engineering.

Experience or Training: Minimum of 3–5 years as an engineering drafter.

Working Conditions: 80% of time spent on job site, and 20% of time spent in office.

Job Title: Chief Chemist   **Job No. 212**

Organization Level: Reports to Plant Manager. Supervises 3 Shift Chemists. Works with other line and staff personnel to achieve plant objectives.

Job Performance: (1) Directs the operation and maintenance of the laboratory. (2) Coordinates activities with other departments. (3) Trains employees. (4) Prepares technical reports. (5) Requisitions laboratory and chemical supplies. (6) Enforces safety and housekeeping regulations. (7) Maintains discipline. (8) Approves new employees, and recommends discharge for cause. (9) Represents company at technical meetings. (10) Keeps abreast of pertinent new developments.

Educational Requirements: Bachelor's degree in chemical engineering or chemistry.

Experience or Training: Minimum of 5–7 years experience as a Shift Chemist.

Working Conditions: 80% of time spent in office, 10% of time spent in laboratory, and 10% of time spent in other departments.

Special Requirements: Ability to supervise others effectively and deal with people outside the department.

Job Title: Shift Chemist   **Job No. 213**

Organization Level: Reponsible to Chief Chemist. Supervises 8 Laboratory Technicians. Works with line and staff personnel in achieving plant objectives.

Job Performance: (1) Assists Chief Chemist in the operation of laboratory. (2) Conducts semicomplex to relatively complex standard quantitative and qualitative analyses to determine chemical and physical properties and composition of materials such as representative samples of raw material, work in process, finished goods, competitors' products, and new products as submitted. (3) Evaluates performance and adaptability of proposed purchases and makes recommendations thereon to supervisor. (4) Assists in investigation and solution of various technical problems; may investigate certain complaints and make recommendations. (5) Trains employees. (6) Prepares technical reports and keeps abreast of pertinent new developments. (Does not perform research functions, which are done by the Research & Technical Service Department.)

Educational Requirements: Bachelor's degree in chemical engineering or chemistry.

Experience or Training: No previous experience required.

Working Conditions: 90% of time spent in laboratory, 10% of time spent in other departments.

Job Title: Personnel Supervisor   **Job No. 214**

Organization Level: Reports directly to Plant Manager and functionally to Division Manager, Industrial Relations. Supervises 2 assistants and an office staff of 1 secretary and 2 clerical workers.

Job Performance: (1) Administers company industrial relations policies and programs within assigned operations, and provides effective guidance and assistance to line and staff department heads so as to achieve effective development and utilization of personnel throughout the plant. (2) Exercises direct control over assigned functions and personnel. (3) Coordinates the activities of the Industrial Relations Department with those of other line and staff departments. (4) Maintains relations with appropriate local groups to develop sound community relations. (5) Maintains communications with union representatives so as to contribute to development of good union-management relationships. (6) Maintains relations with designated colleges, universities, and other sources to facilitate procurement of qualified personnel.

Educational Requirements: Bachelor's degree in industrial engineering or personnel management.

Experience or Training: Minimum of 3 years experience in industrial engineering personnel management.

Working Conditions: Pleasant office and surroundings.

Job Title: Chief Accountant   **Job No. 215**

Organization Level: Reports to Division Vice President. Supervises 1 assistant, 1 Plant Accountant, and 2 Staff Accountants.

Job Performance: Is responsible for the administration of company accounting policies and procedures within the division in a manner which provides management with accurate and current performance data necessary to exercise fiscal control of operations and safeguard company assets.

Educational Requirements: Bachelor's degree in accounting and a C.P.A. certificate.

Experience or Training: Minimum of 5 years with a C.P.A. firm or 7–10 years working in a company's accounting department.

Working Conditions: Pleasant office and surroundings with adequate lighting. Requires 95% sitting and 5% standing. Extensive use of phone.

Job Title: Manager, Industrial Engineering   **Job No. 216**

Organization Level: Reports directly to General Manager, Industrial Engineering. Supervises 1 assistant, the Plant Industrial Engineer, and the Division Office Industrial Engineering unit.

Job Performance: (1) Administers company policies and procedures in the division in a manner which will provide management with information and guidance necessary for sound planning and decisions in maintaining effective and economical control of manufacturing operations, reducing costs, and increasing profits. (2) Exercises direct control over the Division Office Industrial Engineering unit and functional control over Plant Industrial Engineering units. (3) Coordinates the activities of the Industrial Engineering Department with those of other line and staff departments. (4) Participates in Division Management Committee activities as assigned by Division Vice President.

Educational Requirements: Bachelor's degree in industrial engineering.

Experience or Training: Minimum of 7–10 years experience in industrial engineering with a manufacturing firm.

Working Conditions: Pleasant office and surroundings.

Job Title: Plant Industrial Engineer   **Job No. 217**

Organization Level: Reports directly to Plant Manager and functionally to Division Manager, Industrial Engineering.

Job Performance: Develops and maintains or supervises the development and maintenance of a plant cost control structure to measure and control manufacturing performance, and assists management in attaining economical performance, reducing costs, and eliminating waste.

Educational Requirements: Bachelor's degree in industrial engineering or industrial technology.

Experience or Training: Specialized training in cost accounting. Minimum of 6 years working in industrial engineering department of a manufacturing firm.

Working Conditions: Pleasant office and surroundings. Requires 90% office work and 10% on-the-job evaluation.

Job Title: Quality Control Engineer   **Job No. 218**

Organization Level: Reports directly to General Manager, Industrial Engineering. Supervises 2 assistants and small office staff.

Job Performance: (1) Sets up and maintains a quality control system based on routine and special statistical reports covering process variables and quality of product. (2) Analyzes trends of variations which occur, working with quality control supervisors who act in liaison with product heads in applying corrective measures.

Educational Requirements: Bachelor's degree in mechanical engineering preferred.

Experience or Training: Minimum of 5 years experience in mechanical engineering with degree or 8–10 years experience without degree.

Working Conditions: Pleasant office and surroundings.

Job Title: Quality Control Supervisor   **Job No. 219**

Organization Level: Reports directly to Plant Manager and functionally to Quality Control Engineer. Supervises 1 assistant and 1 or 2 clerical assistants.

Job Performance: (1) Supervises the application of the quality control program and plant inspection procedures. (2) Works with other line and staff personnel in developing special programs, techniques, and data so that product quality is effectively measured.

Educational Requirements: Bachelor's degree in mechanical engineering preferred, or equivalent of 4 years of college.

Experience or Training: Minimum of 3 years experience with degree or 5 years experience without degree.

Working Conditions: Pleasant office and surroundings. Requires 85% office work and 15% on-site evaluation in the plant.

Job Title: Manager, Quality Control   **Job No. 220**

Organization Level: Reports directly to Division Manager, Industrial Engineering. Supervises 1 or 2 clerical assistants.

Job Performance: (1) Develops and directs the application of quality control procedures and techniques. (2) Works with other line and staff heads in the development of programs, procedures, techniques, facilities, and data which will assist the division in improving product quality.

Educational Requirements: Bachelor's degree in mechanical engineering or equivalent experience.

Experience or Training: Minimum of 2 years experience with degree or 4 years without degree.

Working Conditions: Requires 75% office work in pleasant office surroundings and 25% on-site inspection and evaluation work in the plant.

Job Title: Safety Director   **Job No. 221**

Organization Level: Reports directly to Plant Manager. Supervises 1 assistant and 1 secretary.

Job Performance: Formulates and administers an accident prevention program which encompasses the following: (1) Routine plant inspections to eliminate physical safety hazards. (2) Continuous job performance evaluations to substitute safe practices for unsafe employee activities. (3) Coordination with the training supervisor for continuous employee safety training.

Educational Requirements: Bachelor's degree in engineering technology preferred, or 5–7 years experience in industrial engineering safety.

Experience or Training: 1–2 years experience with degree or 5–7 years without degree.

Working Conditions: 30–40% of time spent working in pleasant office surroundings and 60–70% of time spent inspecting plant.

Special Requirements: Must have taken engineering safety courses in college or completed an engineering safety short course.

Job Title: Senior Standards Engineer   **Job No. 223**

Organization Level: Reports directly to General Manager, Industrial Engineering, and functionally to the Chief Standards Engineer. Supervises 1 or 2 assistants.

Job Performance: Assists Chief Standards Engineer to organize, plan, and study the installation of time study, incentive application, material studies, and related programs to increase production, reduce labor hours, and reduce costs.

Educational Requirements: Bachelor's degree in industrial engineering or industrial technology preferred.

Experience or Training: Minimum of 4 years experience in industrial engineering with degree or 8–10 years without degree.

Working Conditions: Pleasant office and surroundings with frequent trips to plant shops for program studies and analysis.

Job Title: Manager, Industrial Relations   **Job No. 224**

Organization Level: Reports directly to Division Manager, Industrial Relations. Supervises 1 assistant and 1 or 2 clerical workers.

Job Performance: Is responsible for the formulation, administration, review, and evaluation of company industrial relations policies and procedures covering the following areas: (1) Employee relations policies. (2) Union relations. (3) Organization development programs. (4) Training programs. (5) Wage and salary policies installation. (6) Employee benefit and activity programs. (7) Public relations activities.

Educational Requirements: Bachelor's degree in industrial relations.

Experience or Training: Minimum of 8 years experience in industrial relations.

Working Conditions: Pleasant office and surroundings.

Job Title: Civil Engineer **Job No. 225**

Organization Level: Reports directly to Chief Civil Engineer. Frequently supervises construction crews of 15–40 workers. Occasionally supervises 2–3 drafters.

Job Performance: (1) Supervises medium-sized construction projects. (2) Prepares working drawings for construction projects. (3) Conducts inspections to assure compliance with building codes.

Educational Requirements: Bachelor's degree in civil engineering.

Experience or Training: Minimum of 2 years experience in civil engineering.

Working Conditions: Works primarily outside on construction projects and occasionally at a drafting table in on-site construction office.

JOB DESCRIPTIONS FOR 25 SUPERVISORY AND EXECUTIVE JOBS IN A UNIVERSITY

Job Title: Athletic Director **Job No. 301**

Organization Level: Reports to Academic Council, which is chaired by Academic Vice President. Is assisted by a staff of 44, with 1 administrative assistant.

Job Performance: (1) Is responsible for the university's entire athletic program, including intramural, varsity, and freshman sports, the athletic physical plant and equipment, and the coordination of the physical education program with the available facilities. (2) Allocates budget funds within the scope of the athletic program. (3) Plans the athletic program with the consent of the Academic Council. (4) Hires the head coach, although the position may be coincidental with the Director's position. (5) Represents the university with respect to the athletic program. (6) Allocates monies available for athletic scholarships to students and seeks to induce prospective students to enter the athletic program.

Educational Requirements: Bachelor's degree in physical education or the equivalent, to be determined by the Academic Council.

Experience or Training: None specifically required; to be determined by the Academic Council in individual cases.

Working Conditions: Pleasant office with adequate lighting. Requires much walking around the athletic physical plant, however. Little actual time spent in office. Much travel by automobile and airline required. Many weekends spent working during the fall.

Special Requirements: Must have good understanding of psychology and the ability to deal with all sorts of people.

Job Title: Custodial Supervisor   **Job No. 302**

Organization Level: Reports to Manager, Physical Plant. Has a staff of 198, with 2 assistants.

Job Performance: (1) Is responsible for the acquisition of custodial personnel. (2) Allocates the staff among the various university buildings and sees to the equipping of each team. (3) Is responsible for the maintenance of the cleaning equipment and its replacement. (4) Prepares budget recommendations to submit to Manager, Physical Plant. (5) Coordinates custodial department's function with the department of maintenance to insure that each building is kept in the best possible condition.

Educational Requirements: Either a high school diploma with 10 years experience in a custodial supervisory capacity, or a bachelor's degree in management.

Experience or Training: See Educational Requirements.

Working Conditions: Ordinary office and plain surroundings. Extensive walking required in "inspection tours" and some time spent in workshop supervision.

Special Requirements: Must have ability to work with and supervise people and some limited knowledge of custodial equipment and its maintenance.

Job Title: Manager, Physical Plant   **Job No. 303**

Organization Level: Reports to the Director of Business Affairs. Has a staff of 1 assistant.

Job Performance: (1) Is responsible for the campus as a whole, including the custodial service, building maintenance, grounds maintenance, and utilities. (2) Coordinates all these activities and makes recommendations for improvements to the Director of Business Affairs. (3) Makes budget recommendations and long-range plans for the continued improvement of the overall appearance of the campus. (4) Works closely with the Planning Office and the Landscape Architect. (5) Scrutinizes all bids for building and grounds improvement to insure the optimum value, and makes recommendations to the Board of Directors. (6) Makes long-range plans for the expansion of the university utility service.

Educational Requirements: Bachelor's degree in engineering or related field including industrial technology, industrial engineering, and industrial management.

Experience or Training: Minimum of 5 years experience in industry in a capacity commensurate with the job description.

Working Conditions: Pleasant office and surroundings with considerable walking around the campus required. Work involves extensive use of the telephone, meetings, and conferences.

Special Requirements: Must have planning and coordinating ability.

Job Title: Director of Purchasing   **Job No. 304**

Organization Level: Reports to an officer at the vice-presidential level. Has a staff of 10, with 1 assistant.

Job Performance: (1) Is responsible for the purchase of all supplies and operation of the purchasing office. (2) Supervises the handling of all purchase requisitions. (3) Maintains records of all items kept in stock, as to both quantities on hand and usage rates, to assure that adequate quantities are kept on hand. (4) Acts in an advisory capacity concerning major equipment purchases.

Educational Requirements: Bachelor's degree in business administration.

Experience or Training: Minimum of 5 years experience either in a managerial capacity in retailing or as a supervisor in supply procurement in the armed services, or an industrial plant.

Working Conditions: Pleasant office and surroundings, with extensive use of the telephone.

Special Requirements: Extensive knowledge of the functioning of the university and its role in the community, as well as the ability to work with people.

Job Title: President   **Job No. 305**

Organization Level: Reports to the Board of Directors. Has a staff of 6, with 2 personal assistants.

Job Performance: (1) Administers the policies of the Board of Directors as chief executive officer. (2) Serves as chair of the Executive Committee. (3) Functions with and through the officers of the university. (4) Passes on the hiring, promotion, and termination of administrative and professional personnel.

Educational Requirements: Bachelor's degree is required, but graduate degree is preferred.

Experience or Training: Minimum of 15 years in a high-level administrative position in a university, industry, or military operation.

Working Conditions: Pleasant office and surroundings, with extensive use of the telephone. Attendance at numerous meetings and conferences required. Much travel by automobile and airline.

Special Requirements: Extensive knowledge of the functioning of the university and its role in the community, as well as the ability to work with people.

Job Title: Research Vice President   **Job No. 306**

Organization Level: Reports to the President. Has a staff of 5, with 1 assistant.

Job Performance: (1) Serves as chair of the Research Council and member of the Executive Committee. (2) Administers the allocation of research funds among various projects. (3) Formulates long-range plans for the use of existing facilities and acquisition of new research facilities. (4) Coordinates the use of research funds within the university. (5) Attends frequent meetings to discuss present and future research projects.

Educational Requirements: Doctor of philosophy degree in a scientific field.

Experience or Training: Minimum of 10 years experience in performance of research and 5 years in an administrative position in government, at a university, or in industry.

Working Conditions: Pleasant office and surroundings, with extensive use of the telephone. Requires much letter writing and extensive travel by airline and automobile.

Job Title: Academic Vice President   **Job No. 307**

Organization Level: Reports to the President. Has a staff of 9, with 1 assistant.

Job Performance: (1) Is responsible for all university academic matters, including recommendations of the various deans on undergraduate and graduate matters. (2) Supervises the functioning of the Director of Admissions; the Registrar; Head, Counseling and Testing Center; and the Office of Space Assignments and Utilization. (3) Screens the recommendations of the various deans and executives concerning employment, promotion, and termination of all academic and research personnel and passes them on to the President for final action. (4) Chairs the Academic Budget Review Committee.

Education Requirements: Terminal degree in any field.

Experience or Training: Minimum of 15 years in high-level administrative position in a college or university.

Special Requirements: Must have thorough knowledge of the functioning of an academic community. Ability to organize and administer.

Job Title: Director of Business Affairs   **Job No. 308**

Organization Level: Reports to the President. Supervises 1 assistant and the Business Manager.

Job Performance: (1) Coordinates the functions of purchasing, personnel, physical plant, retail services, and all departments concerned with operation of the university exclusive of the academic function. (2) Makes long-range plans and budget recommendations for the efficient operation of the university and for the improvement of services. (3) Is a member of the Executive Committee. (4) Acts as business advisor to the Board of Directors when requested.

Educational Requirements: Master of business administration degree.

Experience or Training: Minimum of 10 years in an administrative position in industry, business, or a college or university.

Working Conditions: Pleasant office and surroundings, with extensive use of the telephone. Attendance at numerous meetings and conferences and some travel by automobile and airline required. Much use of budget and operating statements.

Special Requirements: Must be familiar with cost allocation and cost saving techniques, as well as be knowledgeable about efficient business practices.

Job Title: Dean of the Graduate College   **Job No. 309**

Organization Level: Reports to the President. Has a department of 15, with 2 assistants.

Job Performance: (1) Works closely with the Registrar, through department assistants, in accepting students for admission to the various graduate programs. (2) Secures funds from available sources (e.g., the National Science Foundation, private grants, and fellowships) and allocates them to graduate students and graduate faculty members. (3) Is responsible for recordkeeping concerning graduate students and approval of petitions and degree plans. (4) Keeps the graduate faculty notified of the curriculum and changes, and works with department heads on curriculum planning. (5) Nominates, subject to approval of the President, faculty members to serve on the graduate faculty. (6) Serves on the Academic Council and Executive Committee.

Educational Requirements: Doctor of philosophy degree in any field.

Experience or Training: Minimum of 10 years teaching experience in a college or university, and 5 years experience in an administrative position in a college or university.

Working Conditions: Pleasant office and surroundings with adequate lighting. Requires extensive interaction with other university executives and meetings in several buildings on campus. Some travel by automobile and airline. Extensive use of the telephone.

Special Requirements: Must have ability to manage organizations and groups, with some experience in public relations techniques.

Job Title: Business Manager   **Job No. 310**

Organization Level: Reports to the Director of Business Affairs. Has a staff of 5 persons, with 2 assistants.

Job Performance: (1) Is responsible for overseeing the functioning and for maintaining the efficiency of the various retail operations of the university, including the bookstore, food service, laundry, gift shop, and public athletic facilities. (2) Operates through the several managers and represents them at budget meetings. (3) Allocates budget funds among them. (4) Sets policies concerning the retail operations in conjunction with the Director of Business Affairs.

Educational Requirements: Bachelor's degree in business administration.

Experience or Training: Minimum of 10 years in the field of retail management.

Working Conditions: Pleasant office and surroundings, with extensive use of the telephone. Must attend numerous staff meetings and often make presentations to the Executive Council.

Special Requirements: Must have ability to work with cost allocation and cost saving techniques, and ability to work with people.

Job Title: Director of Admissions   **Job No. 311**

Organization Level: Reports to the Academic Vice President. Has a staff of 36, with 2 assistants.

Job Performance: (1) Coordinates, with the Executive Committee and Academic Council, the requirements for entrance into the university. (2) Scrutinizes the records of entering students and passes on them. (3) Publishes catalogs concerning requirements for entrance and graduation, course information, and other pertinent details of attending the university. (4) Disseminates information to secondary schools to aid in recruiting students. (5) Coordinates, with the Counseling and Testing Center, the orientation programs for new students and the administering of scholastic achievement tests and graduate record examinations.

Educational Requirements: Bachelor's degree in any field.

Experience or Training: 2 years as Assistant Director of Admissions or 5 years as Registrar.

Working Conditions: Pleasant office and surroundings. Requires extensive use of the telephone and some travel by automobile and airline.

Special Requirements: Must have ability to organize and work with people.

Job Title: Registrar   **Job No. 312**

Organization Level: Reports to the Director of Admissions. Has a staff of 30, with 4 assistants.

Job Performance: (1) Organizes the registration procedure and coordinates the use of the data processing equipment for it. (2) Maintains records on student performance. (3) Coordinates the requirements of granting of degrees by each college with those of the university. (4) Gathers information from each academic department concerning semester courses and the times they are offered, and publishes registration schedules. (5) Coordinates the use of classroom facilities.

Educational Requirements: Bachelor's degree in any field.

Experience or Training: 2 years as Assistant Registrar or 3 years in an administrative position in a college or university.

Working Conditions: Ordinary office with noisy surroundings. Most of time spent sitting and conferring with students. Extensive use of telephone.

Special Requirements: Must have empathy for and understanding of people and their motivations.

Job Title: Head, Circulation Department   **Job No. 313**

Organization Level: Reports to the Library Director. Has a staff of 10, with 1 assistant.

Job Performance: (1) Formulates policy with the Library Director concerning the Circulation Department. (2) Hires personnel to staff the department. (3) Delegates to the assistant the hiring and supervision of part-time student workers and doorkeepers. (4) Coordinates with the representative of the Data Processing Center the application of the computer to the check-out procedure. (5) Is responsible for the maintenance of the bookshelf areas. (6) Administers stack checks to find missing books. (7) Coordinates the department's operation with those of the departments of cataloguing and reserve books.

Educational Requirements: Master's degree in library science.

Experience or Training: Minimum of 5 years experience in a college, university, or public library in an administrative position.

Working Conditions: Pleasant office and surroundings. Must deal with all types of persons, including students, faculty, and the general public.

Special Requirements: Ability to organize and administer. Must have empathy for and ability to work with people.

Job Title: Head, Counseling and Testing   **Job No. 314**

Organization Level: Reports to the Director of Admissions. Has a department of 8, with no assistants.

Job Performance: (1) Supervises the counselors in the performance of their functions of personal, educational, and vocational guidance. (2) Is responsible for the organizational structure and policy of the department, and allocates budget funds between prepared guidance tests and special equipment. (3) Supervises the administration of psychological tests to the university community, including facility, staff, and students. (4) Conducts research into student characteristics and makes long-range predictions of needs. (5) Maintains records on student entrance examinations, graduate record exams, and psychological tests. (6) Conducts guidance conferences at high schools to aid in college attendance decisions and operates orientation programs for entering freshmen.

Educational Requirements: Master's degree in educational psychology or related field.

Experience or Training: Minimum of 8 years in an administrative position concerned with personnel.

Working Conditions: Pleasant office and surroundings, with extensive use of the telephone. Much paperwork involved in grading tests and making studies.

Special Requirements: Must have empathy for and understanding of people and their motivations.

Job Title: Assistant Director of Information   **Job No. 315**

Organization Level: Reports to the Director of Information. Has a staff of 8, 3 of whom are newswriters.

Job Performance: (1) Directs the efforts of the newswriters in their acquisition and treatment of information. (2) Coordinates, with the Director, the dissemination of the information. (3) Administers the printing of house organs, serves as copy reader, and checks the validity of the information leaving the office. (4) Oversees the use of the printing equipment and that it is kept in good repair.

Educational Requirements: Bachelor's degree in journalism, public relations, or some related field.

Experience or Training: Minimum of 2 years as a member of the working press, or 1 year as a newswriter with a college or university information service, or 2 years on the job in industrial public relations.

Working Conditions: Pleasant office with adequate lighting and pleasing surroundings. Must deal with news editors and university employees and executives. Requires much travel by automobile and some by airline. Extensive use of the telephone and considerable use of the typewriter.

Special Requirements: Must have ability to work with and understand people and their motivation. Must have a working knowledge of printing and information dissemination techniques.

Job Title: Director of Information   **Job No. 316**

Organization Level: Reports directly to the President. Has a staff of 9, with 1 assistant.

Job Performance: (1) Administers the dissemination of information about the university to the public. (2) Works with newspapers, radio and television stations, and other media. (3) Oversees the publication of the several internal organs of the university. (4) Develops any of these organs within budget limitations.

Educational Requirements: Bachelor's degree in journalism, public relations, or some related field.

Experience or Training: Minimum of 2 years in an editorial position with some form of commercial media, or 1 year as assistant information director with a college or university, or 3 years on the job in industrial public relations.

Working Conditions: Pleasant office with adequate lighting and pleasing surroundings. Must deal with news editors and university employees and executives. Requires much travel by automobile and some by airline. Extensive use of the telephone and some limited use of the typewriter.

Special Requirements: Must have ability to work with and understand people and their motivation. Must have a working knowledge of printing and information dissemination techniques.

Job Title: Library Director   **Job No. 317**

Organization Level: Reports to the Executive Council, which is chaired by the President. Has a staff of 113, with 5 assistants.

Job Performance: (1) Delegates the operation of the library to each department head and oversees their operations. (2) Is concerned with the efficient utilization of facilities and makes policies to insure it. (3) Delegates the hiring of staff members to each department head, but interviews prospective department heads and assistants. (4) With and through assistants, determines the division and utilization of the library budget funds. (5) Plans long-range objectives and growth of the library with assistants. (6) Sits on the Academic Council. (7) Acts in liaison with the rest of the university community.

Educational Requirements: Doctor of philosophy degree in library science.

Experience or Training: Minimum of 5 years as assistant library director in a college or university, or 5 years as assistant library director in a public lending library, or 2 years as library director in either a public lending library or a college or university library.

Working Conditions: Pleasant office and surroundings with adequate lighting. May use executive-style meeting room. Quiet environment. Extensive use of telephone.

Special Requirements: Must have empathy for and ability to work with people. Must have working knowledge of current and past publications.

Job Title: Director of the Data Processing Center   **Job No. 318**

Organization Level: Reports to the Dean of the College of Engineering. Has a staff of 73, with 5 assistants.

Job Performance: (1) Is responsible for the operation of the Data Processing Center, including the array of computer equipment. Coordinates the use of the equipment among the administrative functions, academic functions, and research functions of the university. (2) Allocates time among these functions and charges each with time used according to the set rate. (3) Plans the addition, deletion, and rearrangement of the units comprising the computer installation, and makes budget recommendations to the Dean of Engineering for operation of the center. (4) Is directly responsible for hiring personnel to staff the center, but delegates their recruitment to one of the assistants. (5) Works closely with computer personnel.

Educational Requirements: Master's degree in computer programming or computer science.

Experience or Training: Minimum of 5 years experience in the field of computers, in either programming or designing systems.

Working Conditions: Pleasant office and surroundings with adequate lighting and a temperature-controlled atmosphere.

Special Requirements: Must have ability to organize and manage operations and personnel. Must have knowledge of the limits of computers.

Job Title: Assistant Dean of the College of Liberal Arts   **Job No. 319**

Organization Level: Reports to the Dean of the College of Liberal Arts. Has a staff of 4, with 1 administrative assistant.

Job Performance: (1) Is primarily responsible for the well-being of the students within the College of Liberal Arts concerning their academic work and extra-curricular activities related to academic pursuits. (2) Sits on the Academic Council. (3) Coordinates the actions and interactions of the several department heads within the college and intercollege. (4) Acts as advisor to the department heads in the organizing of their departments. (5) Assists the dean in representing the college to groups from other universities, high schools, and businesses. (6) Teaches one graduate course in educational counseling every other semester.

Educational Requirements: Doctor of philosophy degree in a discipline connected with those within the college.

Experience or Training: Minimum of 10 years classroom teaching experience in a college or university and 2 years in an administrative position in a college or university.

Working Conditions: Pleasant office and surroundings with adequate lighting. Requires extensive interaction with other university executives and meetings in the several buildings on the campus. Some travel by automobile and airline to meet with people on other campuses and businesses. Extensive use of the telephone.

Special Requirements: Must have ability to manage organizations and groups, with some experience in his or her field outside the university.

Job Title: Dean of the College of Liberal Arts   **Job No. 320**

Organization Level: Reports to the President. Has a staff of 11, consisting of 1 assistant dean and 10 department heads.

Job Performance: (1) Represents the College of Liberal Arts both outside and within the university in order to coordinate the programs with other disciplines and to tailor the educational program to contemporary society. (2) Sits on the Academic Council. (3) Allocates the budget within the college and solicits funds from outside the university for use within the college. (4) Interviews prospective department heads and other potential faculty members, but delegates the actual functioning of the individual departments to their respective heads. (5) Operates directly through the assistant dean. (6) Teaches one seminar per semester which varies from semester to semester.

Educational Requirements: Doctor of philosophy degree in a discipline connected with those within the college.

Experience or Training: Minimum of 10 years classroom teaching experience in a college or university and 4 years in an administrative position in a college or university.

Working Conditions: Pleasant office and surroundings with adequate lighting. Requires extensive interaction with other university executives and meetings in the several buildings on the campus. Some travel by automobile and airline to meet with people on other campuses and businesses. Extensive use of the telephone.

Special Requirements: Must have ability to manage organizations and groups, with some experience in his or her field outside the university.

Job Title: Head, Department of Journalism   **Job No. 321**

Organization Level: Reports to the Assistant Dean of Liberal Arts. Has a staff of 6 professors and 1 secretary.

Job Performance: (1) Organizes, oversees, and coordinates the department. (2) Hires professors with the approval of the Dean of Liberal Arts. (3) Sits on the Academic Council. (4) Determines the curriculum within the department, with the approval of the Academic Council. (5) Is responsible for the well-being of the students within the department. (6) With the aid of professors, dispenses available departmental scholarship funds to students within the department and recommends students for scholarship assistance from the College of Liberal Arts and the university. (7) Solicits funds for scholarships and special projects in the department from outside sources. (8) Teaches one course per semester. (9) Delegates the maintenance of the Journalism Library to one of the professors.

Educational Requirements: Doctor of philosophy degree in a discipline commensurate with curriculum of the Journalism Department. (This is subject to alteration at the discretion of the Academic Council in individual cases, applying the criterion of a terminal degree in the field in combination with professional experience.)

Experience or Training: Minimum of 5 years classroom teaching experience in a college or university. (See Educational Requirements.)

Working Conditions: Pleasant office and surroundings with adequate lighting. Requires extensive interaction with members of the College of Liberal Arts. Limited travel by automobile and airline. Extensive use of the telephone.

Special Requirements: Must have ability to manage organizations and groups. Some experience in dealing with the university community valuable, but not an absolute necessity.

Job Title: Personnel Director   **Job No. 322**

Organization Level: Reports to the Director of Business Affairs. Has a staff of 9, with 1 assistant.

Job Performance: (1) Screens applicants and coordinates the hiring, firing, and recruiting of university employees. (2) Develops long-range plans for the acquisition of new professors. (3) Delegates the job of training to each department head, keeping overall control. (4) Coordinates the application of basic university policy within each department. (5) Allocates the use of budget funds assigned to the department.

Educational Requirements: Bachelor's degree in business administration, personnel administration, psychology, or related field.

Experience or Training: Minimum of 2 years as assistant personnel manager in a college, a university, or industry; or 1 year as personnel manager in a college, a university, or industry.

Working Conditions: Pleasant office and surroundings with adequate lighting. Extensive use of the telephone. Much time spent meeting with and interviewing persons.

Special Requirements: Must have high degree of empathy for and ability to deal with people.

Job Title: Director of Food Services   **Job No. 323**

Organization Level: Reports to the Business Manager. Has a staff of 202, with 6 assistants.

Job Performance: (1) Is responsible for student dining halls, cafeterias, and all fountains and snack bars operated by the university. (2) Sees to the acquisition of top-quality food, determining the quantity necessary to buy at low prices. (3) Plans, with assistants, the menus for the year. (4) Introduces methods into the operation which will maintain quality while reducing costs. (5) Scrutinizes all bids to see if they meet the standards of the university. (6) Meets regularly with members of faculty, staff, administration, and students to continue the improvement of the food service. (7) Determines the prices to be charged for the various items offered.

Educational Requirements: Bachelor's degree in hotel, restaurant, and institutional operations; agricultural science; business administration; food nutrition; or related field.

Experience or Training: Minimum of 5 years experience in the field of food service operation.

Working Conditions: Pleasant office and surroundings, but much time spent in kitchens and dining facilities and in storage and cooling areas. Some travel is necessary to inspect suppliers' facilities.

Special Requirements: Must have thorough knowledge of foods and nutrition and ability to deal with people.

Job Title: Director of Bookstore   **Job No. 324**

Organization Level: Reports to the Business Manager. Has a staff of 37, with 3 assistants.

Job Performance: (1) Is responsible for the operation of the university bookstore and all affiliated operations. (2) Hires personnel to staff the store. (3) Gathers information from each academic department concerning textbook needs and approximations of number needed, and purchases an adequate supply. (4) Sets policy for buying used textbooks and prices offered for them. (5) Purchases other supplies needed by students and prices them. (6) Keeps costs at a minimum in order to keep prices as low as possible.

Educational Requirements: Bachelor's degree in business administration.

Experience or Training: Minimum of 3 years experience in managing a retail business.

Working Conditions: Ordinary office and surroundings with minimum lighting. Much time spent on the floor of the store and with sales clerks.

Special Requirements: Must have ability to operate retail selling establishment with knowledge of display techniques and ability to deal with people.

Job Title: Laundry Director   **Job No. 325**

Organization Level: Reports to the Business Manager. Has a staff of 58, with 2 assistants.

Job Performance: (1) Is responsible for both the operation of the laundry and dry cleaning facility and the planning of substation drop facilities and pickup and delivery schedules. (2) Hires personnel to staff the operation. (3) Is responsible for maintaining equipment and making budget recommendations and long-range plans for expansion and replacement of equipment. (4) Purchases supplies for use in the operation. (5) Prices the cleaning and laundering services on a per unit and per semester basis.

Educational Requirements: Either a bachelor's degree in dry cleaning and laundry management, or 10 years experience as a laundry manager.

Experience or Training: See Educational Requirements.

Working Conditions: Subject to extremely hot and humid surroundings, strong odors, and relatively dirty environment.

Special Requirements: Must have some mechanical inclination and a thorough knowledge of dry cleaning and laundry equipment. Must be able to allocate costs within the overall operation and have empathy for and ability to work with people.

JOB DESCRIPTIONS FOR 25 PROFESSIONAL, TECHNICAL, AND EXECUTIVE JOBS IN A CONGLOMERATE MANUFACTURING COMPANY

Job Title: Vice President, Research and Engineering   **Job No. 401**

Job Purpose: Occupant of job is accountable for managing the research and engineering functions of the company.

Dimensions: Department payroll is $5 million. Research and Engineering Department budget of $50 million.

Nature and Scope: Reports to the President. Supervises a department of 500 employees, including 100 doctoral scientists and 50 engineers.
Educational Requirements: Doctor of philosophy degree in a scientific field.
Experience and Training: Minimum of 10 years experience in performance of research and 5 years in an administrative position in government, at a university, or in industry.
Working Conditions: Pleasant office and surroundings, with extensive use of the telephone. Much letter writing and extensive travel by airline and automobile.

Principal Accountabilities: (1) Serves as chair of the Research Committee and member of the Executive Committee. (2) Administers the allocation of research funds among various projects. (3) Formulates long-range plans for the use of existing facilities and acquisition of new research facilities. (4) Coordinates the use of research funds within the organization. (5) Attends frequent meetings to discuss present and future research projects. (6) Runs the Research and Engineering Department.

Job Title: Vice President, Industrial Relations   **Job No. 402**

Job Purpose: Occupant of job is accountable for conducting the industrial relations activities of the corporation.

Dimensions: Company payroll of $500 million. Department payroll of $500 thousand.

Nature and Scope: Reports directly to the President. Supervises a staff of 50, with 5 assistants.

Educational Requirements: Master's degree in industrial relations or psychology.

Experience and Training: Minimum of 8 years experience in industrial relations.

Working Conditions: Pleasant office and surroundings.

Principal Accountabilities: (1) Manages employee relations policies. (2) Participates as management's representative in union-management relations. (3) Initiates and maintains organization development programs. (4) Conducts training programs. (5) Administers wage and salary policies. (6) Develops and maintains a system of employee benefits and fosters employee activity programs.

Job Title: Director of Data Processing Center   **Job No. 403**

Job Purpose: Occupant of job is accountable for managing the data processing center and conducting the data processing function.

Dimensions: Center payroll of $500 thousand.

Nature and Scope: Reports to the Controller. Has a staff of 50, with 5 assistants.

Educational Requirements: Master's degree in computer programming or computer science.

Experience and Training: Minimum of 5 years experience in the field of computers in either programming or designing systems.

Working Conditions: Pleasant office and surroundings with adequate lighting and a temperature-controlled atmosphere.

Special Requirements: Must have ability to organize and manage operations and personnel. Must have knowledge of the limits of computers.

Principal Accountabilities: (1) Is responsible for the operation of the Data Processing Center, including the array of computer equipment. Coordinates the use of the equipment. (2) Allocates time and charges each group or department with time used according to the set rate. (3) Plans the addition, deletion, and rearrangement of the units comprising the computer installation, and makes budget recommendations for operation of the center.

Job Title: Assistant Controller   **Job No. 404**

Job Purpose: Occupant of job is accountable for assisting the controller in the exercise of the control function.

Dimensions: Company assets of $1,200 million. Sales of $1,000 million.

Nature and Scope: Reports to the Controller.

Educational Requirements: Bachelor's degree in accounting.

Experience and Training: Minimum of 5 years of plant accounting experience.

Working Conditions: Personal secretary and an office with adequate lighting. Work requires 50% sitting and 50% standing or walking.

Principal Accountabilities: (1) Assists the Controller in the performance of major duties and responsibilities. (2) Represents the Controller on plant visits. (3) Assists plants in the installation and maintenance of accounting procedures and records. (4) Reviews plant expense budgets and cost records for accuracy and compliance with procedures. (5) Reviews internal audits of plant operations. (6) Assists the Controller in negotiations with local tax assessors as to plant property valuations. (7) Assists the Controller in selecting and training personnel and in the administration of company personnel policies relating to group and division accounting employees. (8) Accomplishes special surveys and analyses as directed.

Job Title: Controller   **Job No. 405**

Job Purpose: Occupant of job is accountable for managing the control function for the company.

Dimensions: Company assets of $1,200 million. Sales of $1,000 million.

Nature and Scope: Reports to the Administrative Vice President. Supervises 1 assistant and 5 section heads.
  Educational Requirements: Bachelor's degree in accounting with a C.P.A. certificate.
  Experience and Training: Minimum of 5 years with a C.P.A. firm or 7–10 years working in a company's accounting department.
  Working Conditions: Pleasant office and surroundings with adequate lighting. Work requires 95% sitting and 5% standing. Extensive use of the telephone is also required.

Principal Accountabilities: (1) Administers company accounting policies and procedures. (2) Provides management with accurate and current performance data to control operations and safeguard company assets. (3) Runs the Controller's department.

Job Title: Vice President, Public Relations   **Job No. 406**

Job Purpose: Occupant of job is accountable for handling the public relations activities of the company.

Dimensions: Department payroll of $200 thousand.

Nature and Scope: Reports directly to the President. Has a staff of 20, with 3 assistants.
  Educational Requirements: Bachelor's degree in journalism, public relations, or some related field.
  Experience and Training: Minimum of 2 years in an editorial position with one or more commercial media or 3 years on the job in an industrial public relations office.
  Working Conditions: Office with adequate lighting and pleasing surroundings. Will deal with news editors, employees, and executives. Extensive travel by automobile and some by airline and extensive use of the telephone required.

Special Requirements: Must have ability to work with and understand people and their motivation. Must have a working knowledge of printing and information dissemination techniques.

Principal Accountabilities: (1) Administers the public relations program of the company. (2) Works with newspapers, radio and television stations, and all other forms of media. (3) Oversees the internal publications of the company. (4) Guides the activities of the Vice President, the Washington office, the General Counsel, and the General Patent Counsel.

Job Title: Manager of Quality Control   **Job No. 407**

Job Purpose: Occupant of job is accountable for assuring quality control standards for all goods and services produced by the Metals Group.

Dimensions: Control Control budget of $250 thousand. Metals Group sales of $450 million.

Nature and Scope: Reports directly to the Metals Group Manager of Industrial Engineering. Supervises 1 assistant and 1 or 2 clerical assistants. Has functional authority over Division Quality Control Supervisors.
Educational Requirements: Bachelor's degree in mechanical engineering preferred, or equivalent of 4 years of college.
Experience and Training: Minimum of 3 years experience with a degree or 5 years experience without a degree.
Working Conditions: Pleasant office and surroundings. Position requires 25% office work and 75% on-site evaluation in the plants of the three divisions of the Metals Group.

Principal Accountabilities: (1) Supervises the application of the quality control program and plant inspection procedures. (2) Works with other line and staff personnel in developing special programs, techniques, and data so that product quality is effectively measured.

Job Title: Division Quality Control Supervisor   **Job No. 408**

Job Purpose: Occupant of job is accountable for assuring quality control standards within the division, consistent with company-wide quality control standards.

Dimensions: Department payroll of $30 thousand. Sales of Industrial Machinery Division of $170 million.

Nature and Scope: Reports directly to Plant Industrial Engineer, Industrial Machinery Division. Supervises 1 or 2 clerical assistants.
Educational Requirements: Bachelor's degree in mechanical engineering or equivalent experience.
Experience and Training: Minimum of 2 years experience with a degree or 4 years experience without a degree.
Working Conditions: Requires 75% office work in pleasant office surroundings, and 25% on-site inspection and evaluation work in the plant.

Principal Accountabilities: (1) Develops and directs the application of quality control procedures and techniques. (2) Works with other line and staff heads in the development of programs, procedures, techniques, facilities, and data which will assist the division in improving product quality.

Job Title: President and Chief Executive Officer   **Job No. 409**

Job Purpose: Occupant of job is accountable for the overall performance of the company.

Dimensions: Payroll of $500 million; total assets of $1,200 million; sales of $1,000 million.

Nature and Scope: Reports to the Board of Directors. Has a staff of 6, with 2 personal assistants in addition.

Educational Requirements: Bachelor's degree, but a master's degree in business administration is preferred.

Experience and Training: Minimum of 15 years in a high-level administrative position in an industrial, military, or other large organization.

Working Conditions: Pleasant office and surroundings, with extensive use of the telephone. Numerous meetings and conferences to attend and extensive travel by automobile and airline.

Special Requirements: Extensive knowledge of the functioning of the organization and its role in the community, as well as the ability to work with people.

Principal Accountabilities: (1) Is responsible for all company operations. (2) Serves as chair of the Executive Committee. (3) Functions with and through the officers of the corporation, which include 3 Executive Vice Presidents in charge of 3 operating groups—Forest Products, Chemicals, and Metals. (4) Guides the operations of 5 Vice Presidents who head Research and Engineering, Public Relations, Industrial Relations, Administration, and Planning.

Job Title: Division Staff Accountant   **Job No. 410**

Job Purpose: Occupant of job is accountable for assisting the plant accountant in carrying out accounting functions within the division.

Dimensions: Sales for Timber Division of $90 million.

Nature and Scope: Responsible to Plant Accountant, Timber Division

Educational Requirements: Bachelor's degree in accounting.

Experience and Training: No previous experience required.

Working Conditions: 75% of time spent in office, 25% of time spent in other departments.

Special Requirements: Must be able to work effectively with other people.

Principal Accountabilities: (1) Maintains records for departments, (2) Assists in preparation of department budgets. (3) Compares operating statements with budgets and investigates areas of deviation. (4) Prepares plant operating performance and profits reports.

Job Title: Plant Accountant   **Job No. 411**

Job Purpose: Occupant of job is accountable for managing the control function within the plant.

Dimensions: Department payroll of $30 thousand. Sales for Timber Division of $90 million.

Nature and Scope: Responsible to Vice President and Plant Manager, Timber Division (Forest Products Group). Supervises 2 staff accountants and coordinates the activities of the accounting department with those of other line and staff functions.

Educational Requirements: Bachelor's degree in accounting and a C.P.A. certificate.

Experience and Training: Minimum of 5 years with a C.P.A. firm or 5–7 years working in a company's accounting department.

Working Conditions: Pleasant office and surroundings with adequate lighting.

Principal Accountabilities: (1) Directs the maintenance of record cards for equipment and machinery and the preparation of required reports. (2) Reviews and approves the accounting of transfers relative to equipment and machinery. (3) Directs the implementation of procedures in the taking of annual and special inventories, and works with supervisors and other staff department heads in developing and applying corrective measures to prevent inventory distortion. (4) Directs the accumulation and reporting of cost data within established time limits and in accordance with company instructions. (5) Directs the implementation of procedures for timekeeping and production reporting, and directs the accumulation and recording of data as a basis for preparing payrolls, budgetary control statements, and charges to inventory. (6) Works with supervisors in the preparation and revision, as necessary, of budgets of income based on projected sales and production data. (7) Directs the maintenance of payroll records and the preparation and distribution of payrolls and reports in accordance with company instructions consistent with terms and interpretations of any existing union agreements and government regulations with respect to overtime, holiday pay, and other items affecting payroll procedures.

Job Title: Safety Director   **Job No. 412**

Job Purpose: Occupant of job is accountable for managing the safety program within the Group.

Dimensions: Safety budget of $150 thousand. Metals Group sales of $450 million.

Nature and Scope: Reports directly to the Manager of Industrial Engineering, Metals Group. Supervises 1 assistant and 1 secretary. Exercises functional authority over Division Safety Supervisors.

Educational Requirements: Bachelor's degree in engineering technology preferred, or 5–7 years experience in industrial engineering safety.

Experience and Training: 1–2 years experience with degree or 5–7 years without degree.

Working Conditions: 30–40% of time spent working in pleasant office surroundings and 60–70% of time spent inspecting plant.

Special Requirements: Must have taken engineering safety courses in college or completed an engineering safety short course.

Principal Accountabilities: Formulates and administers an accident prevention program which encompasses: (1) Plant inspections to eliminate physical safety hazards. (2) Continuous job performance evaluations to substitute safe practices for unsafe employee activities. (3) Coordination with the training supervisor for continuous employee safety training. (4) Coordination with Safety Directors of other groups.

Job Title: Safety Supervisor   **Job No. 413**

Job Purpose: Occupant of job is accountable for managing the safety program within the division.

Dimensions: Safety budget of $100 thousand. Division sales of $170 million.

Nature and Scope: Reports to the Vice President and Plant Manager, Industrial Machinery Division.

Educational Requirements: High school diploma with either 2 years of college or 4 years experience.

Experience and Training: No experience is required with 2 or more years of college. 4 years of experience required with no college work.

Working Conditions: 90% of time spent working on-site in the plant inspecting and evaluating safety practices and procedures and 10% of time spent on office work.

Special Requirements: Must have taken engineering safety courses in college or completed an engineering safety short course.

Principal Accountabilities: (1) Administers and coordinates safety program set up by the Group Safety Director. (2) Works directly with line department heads to implement the safety program.

Job Title: Shift Chemist   **Job No. 414**

Job Purpose: Occupant of the job is accountable for assisting the Division Chief Chemist in research activities and in managing the laboratory.

Dimensions: Shift payroll of $80 thousand. Sales for Organic Chemicals Division of $130 million.

Nature and Scope: Responsible to Chief Chemist, Organic Chemicals Division. Supervises 8 laboratory technicians, and works with line and staff personnel in achieving plant objectives.

Educational Requirements: Bachelor's degree in chemical engineering or chemistry.

Experience and Training: No previous experience required.

Working Conditions: 90% of time spent in laboratory and 10% of time spent in other departments.

Principal Accountabilities: (1) Assists Chief Chemist in the operation of laboratory. (2) Conducts semicomplex to relatively complex standard quantitative and qualitative analyses to determine chemical and physical properties and composition of materials such as representative samples of raw material, work in process, finished goods, competitors' products, and new products as submitted. (3) Evaluates performance and adaptability of proposed purchases and makes recommendations thereon to supervisor. (4) Assists in investigation and solution of various technical problems. May investigate certain complaints and make recommendations. (5) Trains employees. (6) Prepares technical reports and keeps abreast of pertinent new developments. (Does not perform research functions, which are done by Research and Engineering Department.)

Job Title: Personnel Director   **Job No. 415**

Job Purpose: Occupant of the job is accountable for the personnel management function within the Group.

Dimensions: Department payroll of $200 thousand. Metals Group payroll of $210 million.

Nature and Scope: Reports to the Executive Vice President, Metals Group. Has a staff of 20, with 3 assistants.

Educational Requirements: Bachelor's degree in business administration, personnel administration, psychology, or a related field.

Experience and Training: Minimum of 2 years as an assistant personnel manager in industry or equivalent experience or training.

Working Conditions: Pleasant office and surroundings with adequate lighting. Extensive use of the telephone required. Much time spent engaged in meeting with and interviewing persons.

Special Requirements: Must have a high degree of empathy and ability to deal with people.

Principal Accountabilities: (1) Screens applicants and coordinates the hiring, firing, and recruitment of employees. (2) Delegates the job of training to each department head, keeping overall control. (3) Coordinates the application of basic personnel policy among the divisions. (4) Allocates the use of budget funds assigned to the department.

Job Title: Project Engineer   **Job No. 416**

Job Purpose: Occupant of the job is accountable for assisting the Plant Industrial Engineer in carrying out engineering activities within the division.

Dimensions: Project budgets range from $100 thousand to $500 thousand annually. Sales for Industrial Machinery Division of $170 million.

Nature and Scope: Responsible to Plant Industrial Engineer, Industrial Machinery Division.
Educational Requirements: Bachelor's degree in mechanical engineering.
Experience and Training: Minimum of 3–5 years as an engineering drafter.
Working Conditions: Works on the job site 80% of the time and in the office 20% of the time.

Principal Accountabilities: (1) Directs and coordinates the activities of engineers and skilled crafts workers in the preparation of cost estimates. (2) Directs and coordinates the layout, design, and selection of equipment and systems. (3) Directs and coordinates the preparation of engineering drawings and sketches. (4) Directs the requisition of materials on assigned projects. (5) Trains new employees.

Job Title: Manager of Industrial Engineering   **Job No. 417**

Job Purpose: Occupant of the job is accountable for managing the industrial engineering function within the Group.

Dimensions: Department payroll of $1 million. Metals Group sales of $450 million.

Nature and Scope: Reports directly to the Executive Vice President, Metals Group. Supervises 10 assistants in a department of 100 people.
Educational Requirements: Bachelor's degree in industrial engineering.
Experience and Training: Minimum of 7–10 years experience in industrial engineering with a manufacturing firm.
Working Conditions: Pleasant office and surroundings.

Principal Accountabilities: (1) Administers company policies and procedures in the Group in a manner which will provide management with information and guidance necessary for sound planning and decisions in maintaining effective and economical control of manufacturing operations, reducing costs, and increasing profits. (2) Exercises functional authority over Plant Industrial Engineering units. (3) Coordinates the activities of the Group Industrial Engineering Department with those of other line and staff departments. (4) Participates in Group Management Committee activities as assigned by the Group Executive Vice President.

Job Title: Director of Purchasing   **Job No. 418**

Job Purpose: Occupant of the job is accountable for carrying out the purchasing function within the Group.

Dimensions: Department payroll of $100 thousand. Annual purchases volume for Metals Group of $120 million.

Nature and Scope: Reports to the Manager of Industrial Engineering, Metals Group. Has a staff of 10, with 1 assistant.

Educational Requirements: Bachelor's degree in business administration.

Experience and Training: Minimum of 5 years experience either as a manager in retailing or as a supervisor in supply procurement in the armed services or in an industrial plant.

Working Conditions: Pleasant office and surroundings, with extensive use of the telephone.

Special Requirements: Ability to control costs without sacrificing efficient operations in the organization.

Principal Accountabilities: (1) Is responsible for the purchase of all production materials, supplies, tool and parts, and for the operation of the purchasing office. (2) Supervises the handling of all purchase requisitions. (3) Maintains records of all items kept in stock, as to both quantities on hand and usage rates, to assure that adequate quantities are kept on hand. (4) Acts in an advisory capacity concerning major equipment purchases.

Job Title: Personnel Supervisor   **Job No. 419**

Job Purpose: Occupant of the job is accountable for managing the personnel function within the division.

Dimensions: Department payroll of $50 thousand. Payroll for Rifle and Automatic Weapons Division of $95 million.

Nature and Scope: Reports directly to the Vice President and Manager, Rifle and Automatic Weapons Division (Metals Group), and functionally to the Personnel Director, Metals Group. Supervises 2 assistants and an office staff of 1 secretary and 2 clerical workers.

Educational Requirements: Bachelor's degree in industrial engineering or personnel management.

Experience and Training: Minimum of 3 years experience in industrial engineering personnel management.

Working Conditions: Pleasant office and surroundings.

Principal Accountabilities: (1) Administers company industrial relations policies and programs within assigned operations and provides effective guidance and assistance to the line and staff department heads so as to achieve effective development and utilization of personnel throughout the plant. (2) Exercises direct control over assigned functions and personnel. (3) Coordinates personnel activities with those of other line and staff departments. (4) Maintains relations with appropriate local groups to develop sound community relations. (5) Maintains communications with union representatives so as to contribute to development of a good union-management relationship.

Job Title: Power Engineer   **Job No. 420**

Job Purpose: Occupant of the job is accountable for power plant operations within the division.

Dimensions: Department budget of $60 thousand. Division sales of $170 million.

Nature and Scope: Responsible to Plant Engineer, Industrial Machinery Division. Supervises 1 assistant and 5 boiler room workers.

Educational Requirements: Bachelor's degree in engineering or its equivalent.

Experience and Training: Minimum of 3–5 years experience in a power plant.

Working Conditions: Hot and sometimes dirty work. 50% of time spent in the office and 50% of time spent in the boiler room.

Principal Accountabilities: (1) Directs the operation and maintenance of a high-pressure steam-electric power plant to meet the plant's requirement's of steam, electricity, water, and air. (2) Trains employees. (3) Maintains discipline.

Job Title: Director of Food Services   **Job No. 421**

Job Purpose: Occupant of the job is accountable for the supply of food services to the division.

Dimensions: Department payroll of $500 thousand. Division payroll of $70 million.

Nature and Scope: Reports to the Vice President and Manager, Industrial Machinery Division. Has a staff of 50, with 4 assistants.

Educational Requirements: Bachelor's degree in hotel, restaurant, and institutional operations; agricultural science; business administration; food nutrition; or related field.

Experience and Training: Minimum of 5 years experience in the field of food service operations.

Working Conditions: Pleasant office and surroundings. Majority of time spent in kitchens and dining facilities and in storage and cooling areas. Some travel is necessary to inspect suppliers' facilities.

Special Requirements: Must have thorough knowledge of foods and nutrition and ability to deal with people.

Principal Accountabilities: (1) Is responsible for the plant cafeteria. (2) Sees to the acquisition of top-quality food, determining the quantity necessary to buy at low prices. (3) Plans, with assistants, the menus for the year. (4) Introduces methods into the operation which will maintain quality while controlling costs. (5) Determines the prices to be charged for the various items offered.

Job Title: Plant Industrial Engineer   **Job No. 422**

Job Purpose: Occupant of the job is accountable for plant industrial engineering within the division.

Dimensions: Sales for Industrial Machinery Division of $170 million.

Nature and Scope: Reports directly to the Vice President and Manager, Industrial Machinery Division, and functionally to the Manager of Industrial Engineering, Metals Group.

> *Educational Requirements:* Bachelor's degree in industrial engineering or industrial technology.

> *Experience and Training:* Specialized training in cost accounting. Minimum of 6 years working in an industrial engineering department of a manufacturing firm.

> *Working Conditions:* Pleasant office and surroundings. Position requires 90% office work and 10% on-the-job evaluation.

Principal Accountabilities: (1) Develops and maintains a plant cost control structure to measure and control manufacturing performance. (2) Assists management in attaining economical performance, reducing costs, and eliminating waste. (3) Makes long-range plans for expansion of plant facilities. (4) Coordinates the foregoing activities with the Manager of the Physical Plant.

Job Title: Manager of the Physical Plant   **Job No. 423**

Job Purpose: Occupant of the job is accountable for managing the physical plant within the division.

Dimensions: Department payroll of $500 thousand. Division assets of $288 million.

Nature and Scope: Reports to the Vice President and Manager, Industrial Machinery Division. Supervises 50 employees and has 3 assistants.

> *Educational Requirements:* Bachelor's degree in engineering or related field, including industrial technology, industrial engineering, and industrial management.

> *Experience and Training:* Minimum of 5 years experience in industry in a capacity commensurate with the job description.

> *Working Conditions:* Pleasant office and surroundings, with considerable walking around the plant required. Extensive use of the telephone and participation at meetings and conferences.

> *Special Requirements:* Must have ability to plan and coordinate.

Principal Accountabilities: (1) Is responsible for the physical condition of the plant, including the custodial service, building maintenance, grounds maintenance, and utilities. (2) Coordinates all these activities and makes recommendation for improvements to the Division Manager. (3) Makes budget recommendations and long-range plans for the continued improvement of the overall appearance of the plant. (4) Makes long-range plans for the expansion of physical facilities of the plant in coordination with the Plant Industrial Engineer.

Job Title: Drafter   **Job No. 424**

Job Purpose: Occupant of the job is accountable for carrying out drafting assignments for engineers within the division.

Dimensions: Sales for Industrial Machinery Division of $170 million.

Nature and Scope: Reports directly to the Plant Industrial Engineer, Industrial Machinery Division.

Educational Requirements: High school diploma or equivalent. Knowledge of mechanical drawing desirable but not required.

Experience and Training: 6 months on-the-job training, or 1 year experience in a job requiring extensive use of drafting equipment.

Working Conditions: Work requires 90% sitting or standing at a drafting table. The remaining 10% of time is spent conferring with engineers and in other activities. Position involves some eye strain.

Principal Accountabilities: (1) Prepares detailed drawings of parts, machinery, and structure, including isometric projections and sectional views as needed. (2) Does working drawings of subassemblies or architectural drawings for new buildings. (3) Works on design of improved machinery or new products, working closely with engineers.

Job Title: Chief Chemist   **Job No. 425**

Job Purpose: Occupant of the job is accountable for running the chemical laboratory in the division.

Dimensions: Departmental budget of $240 thousand. Sales for Organic Chemicals Division of $130 million.

Nature and Scope: Reports to Vice President and Plant Manager, Organic Chemicals Division (Chemicals Group). Supervises 3 shift chemists. Works with other line and staff personnel to achieve plant objectives.

Educational Requirements: Bachelor's degree in chemical engineering or chemistry.

Experience and Training: Minimum of 5–7 years experience as a shift chemist.

Special Requirements: Must have ability to supervise people's work effectively and to deal with people outside of department.

Principal Accountabilities: (1) Directs the operation and the maintenance of the laboratory. (2) Coordinates activities with other departments. (3) Trains employees. (4) Prepares technical reports. (5) Requisitions laboratory and chemical supplies. (6) Enforces safety and housekeeping regulations. (7) Maintains discipline. (8) Approves new employees and recommends discharge for cause. (9) Represents company at technical meetings. (10) Keeps abreast of pertinent new developments.

Appendix B   Definitions of Factors for Production Jobs*

1.   EDUCATION OR TRADE KNOWLEDGE

This factor measures the job requirements in terms of the mental development needed to think in terms of and understand the work being performed. Such mental development or technical knowledge may be acquired either by formal schooling, night school, or through equivalent experience.

Trades or vocational training is considered as a form of education and should be evaluated under this factor.

2.   EXPERIENCE

This factor measures the length of time on related work plus job training required to learn the job duties involved and to be able to perform such duties in the minimum acceptable manner. Consider only such time as required to learn to perform the job satisfactorily on the basis of continuous progress rather than elapsed time. Exclude the theory and general mentality required, which are measured under "Education." Fundamental knowledge obtained in the form of trades or vocational training should be evaluated under "Education."

3.   INITIATIVE AND INGENUITY

This factor measures the job requirements in terms of independent action and exercise of judgment, such as devising or developing methods of procedure; analyzing work and adapting methods, equipment, etc., to perform the job; seeing the need for and taking independent action where required; or deciding on matters such as comparison of products with standards. Involves also consideration of the routine or nonroutine nature of the work, rules procedure, or precedents

*Reprinted with the permission of the National Electrical Manufacturers Association, *Job Rating Plan. Definitions of Factors Used in Evaluating Hourly Rated Jobs* (New York: National Electrical Manufacturers Association, 1946).

449

established for performing the work, changes in nature of work, complexity of conditions or facts involved, and type of directions provided.

4. PHYSICAL DEMAND

This factor measures the job requirements which induce physical fatigue by means of exertion required (in weight and duration) and the straining effect of the normal work position involved.

Requires determining the duration involved in handling different ranges of weights (or equivalent exertion, pulling or pushing), or working in different positions.

5. MENTAL AND/OR VISUAL DEMAND

This factor measures the job requirements which induce mental fatigue and/or visual strain in terms of duration of time that mental and/or visual application is required, and the required intensity of such application. It does not relate to the degree of intelligence or mental development but to the quantity and concentration of mental application.

6. RESPONSIBILITY FOR EQUIPMENT OR PROCESS

This factor measures the job requirements for preventing loss through damage to equipment or process. The loss that could reasonably occur from any one probable failure to exercise proper care should be considered. Losses which are possible but highly improbable, or losses inherent in the nature of the job and beyond control of the employee, should not be included.

Equipment is defined as machines, tools, gages, test sets, etc., used in the performance of work. Equipment not used on the job but which is damaged due to collision or similar accidents should be considered. Processes are those such as plating.

7. RESPONSIBILITY FOR MATERIAL OR PRODUCT

This factor measures the job requirements for preventing loss through waste or damage to raw material or product. The amount of loss from each probable occurrence of failure to exercise proper care that can occur before detection and correction should be considered. Cost should include repairs, replacements, additional labor in subsequent operations, and retesting and rehandling, reduced by the salvage value of the material or product. Losses possible but highly improbable, or inherent in the job and beyond control of the employee, should not be included.

Material or product is defined as any item which is processed, fabricated, installed, transported, maintained, inspected, or tested and does not refer to the tools, machines, etc., which are considered as equipment.

8. RESPONSIBILITY FOR SAFETY OF OTHERS

This factor measures the job requirements for safeguarding fellow employees or others who can sustain injury through contact with or proximity to the functions or results of the job. Credit should be allowed for potential injuries sustained by others through employee failure to warn others of probable dangers. Potential injury or health hazards to the employee himself are evaluated under "Hazards."

The use of safety guards or protective devices should be considered in establishing whether or not an injury is probable and whether employee responsibility is thereby minimized.

9. RESPONSIBILITY FOR WORK OF OTHERS

This factor measures the job requirements for assigned nonsupervisory responsibility for instructing, directing, setting up equipment, or maintaining the flow of work.

This factor does not include supervisory responsibilities. Employees may be expected to inform replacing employees of work being performed and stage of completion of work in process.

10. WORKING CONDITIONS

This factor measures the surroundings or physical conditions under which the job must be done and the extent to which those conditions make the job disagreeable. Consider the presence, relative amount of, and continuity of exposure to dust, dirt, heat, fumes, cold, noise, vibration, wetness, etc.

11. HAZARDS

This factor measures the hazards, both accident and health, connected with or surrounding the job, even though safety devices have been installed. Consider the material being handled, the machines or tools used, the work position, and the probability of accident, even though none has occurred.

Appendix C **Definitions of the Factors Used in Evaluating Clerical, Supervisory, and Technical Positions***

1. EDUCATION

This factor evaluates the *job requirements* in terms of the *basic education or knowledge* which an employee should have acquired to do the job satisfactorily. In applying the factor, consider only the requirements of the job. Disregard the individual's formal education or the specific way in which he may have acquired the basic knowledge. *Rate the requirements of the job and not the person's education.*

2. EXPERIENCE

This factor evaluates the time usually required for a person to acquire the necessary ability to do the job. In appraising Experience, it should be correlated with Education. Do not confuse length of service of an individual with experience required to qualify for the job. Experience may have been acquired elsewhere, in whole or in part, by the individual on the job.

3. COMPLEXITY OF DUTIES

This factor evaluates the complexity of the duties in terms of the scope of independent action, the extent to which the duties are standardized, the judgment and planning required, the type of decisions made and the area within which the individual on the job is required to exercise discretion.

4. MONETARY RESPONSIBILITY

This factor evaluates the responsibility for profit or loss to the company as a result of actions or decisions which involve items such as equipment, material, labor,

---

*Reprinted from National Electrical Manufacturers Association NEMA SALARIED JOB RATING PLAN (Clerical, Supervisory, and Technical Positions) (Washington, DC: National Electrical Manufacturers Association.)

452

cost estimates, prices, forecasts, purchase commitments, investments. Consider the extent to which the work is checked or verified, the effect of actions or decisions on operating costs or profits, monetary loss, production delays or effect on employees or customers.

5. RESPONSIBILITY FOR CONTACTS WITH OTHERS

This factor evaluates the responsibility which goes with the job for working with or through other people, to get results. In the lower degrees, it is largely a matter of giving or getting information or instructions. In the higher degrees, the factor involves dealing with or influencing other persons. In rating this factor, consider how the contacts are made and for what purpose.

6. WORKING CONDITIONS

This factor evaluates the conditions under which the job must be done and the extent to which the conditions make the job disagreeable or unpleasant. Consider the presence, relative amount and continuity of exposure to conditions such as noise, heat, dust, fumes. Since the plan includes no factor for physical effort, that phase of the job may be considered under this factor where physical effort is involved.

RATING SUPERVISORY POSITIONS

In addition to the six factors in the basic salaried job rating plan, two more factors are included in the plan *for the rating of supervisory jobs only.* These two added factors—

Type of Supervision
Extent of Supervision

have no application unless the job being rated involves responsibility for some degree of supervision over others.

The degree or kind of supervision exercised is to be evaluated under the first of these two factors—Type of Supervision. In rating a job under this factor, ascertain the place or level of the job in the organization. Refer to an organization chart, if there is one available, to determine this.

The second of these two factors—*Extent of Supervision*—evaluates supervisory jobs in terms of the *number of persons supervised.*

7. TYPE OF SUPERVISION

This factor evaluates the degree of supervision exercised in terms of the level of the job in the organization and the character of the responsibility for directing or supervising other people.

8. EXTENT OF SUPERVISION

This factor evaluates the responsibility for supervision in terms of the number of people supervised.

Appendix D   Wage and Salary Conversion Table

| | | To | | | |
		Hourly	*Weekly*	*Monthly*	*Yearly*
From	Hourly	—	× 40	× 173.33	× 2080
	Weekly	÷ 40	—	× 4.333	× 52
	Monthly	÷ 173.33	÷ 4.333	—	× 12
	Yearly	÷ 2080	÷ 52	÷ 12	—

Note: Assumes 40-hour week and 52 pay weeks per year.

EXAMPLE: Hourly rate is $4.00. Find yearly rate.

$$\$4.00 \times 2080 = \$8,320$$

454

Appendix E   The Federal Government's General Schedule

(1) Grade GS-1 includes those classes of positions the duties of which are to perform, under immediate supervision, with little or no latitude for the exercise of independent judgment—
(A) the simplest routine work in office, business, or fiscal operations; or
(B) elementary work of a subordinate technical character in a professional, scientific, or technical field.

(2) Grade GS-2 includes those classes of positions the duties of which are—
(A) to perform, under immediate supervision, with limited latitude for the exercise of independent judgment, routine work in office, business, or fiscal operations, or comparable subordinate technical work of limited scope in a professional, scientific, or technical field, requiring some training or experience; or
(B) to perform other work of equal importance, difficulty, and responsibility, and requiring comparable qualifications.

(3) Grade GS-3 includes those classes of positions the duties of which are—
(A) to perform, under immediate or general supervision, somewhat difficult and responsible work in office, business, or fiscal operations, or comparable subordinate technical work of limited scope in a professional, scientific, or technical field, requiring in either case—
(i) some training or experience;
(ii) working knowledge of a special subject matter; or
(iii) to some extent the exercise of independent judgment in accordance with well-established policies, procedures, and techniques; or
(B) to perform other work of equal importance, difficulty, and responsibility, and requiring comparable qualifications.

(4) Grade GS-4 includes those classes of positions the duties of which are—
(A) to perform, under immediate or general supervision, moderately difficult and responsible work in office, business, or fiscal operations, or

comparable subordinate technical work in a professional, scientific, or technical field, requiring in either case—

    (i) a moderate amount of training and minor supervisory or other experience;

    (ii) good working knowledge of a special subject matter or a limited field of office, laboratory, engineering, scientific, or other procedure and practice; and

    (iii) the exercise of independent judgment in accordance with well-established policies, procedures, and techniques; or

(B) to perform other work of equal importance, difficulty, and responsibility, and requiring comparable qualifications.

(5) Grade GS-5 includes those classes of position's the duties of which are—

(A) to perform, under general supervision, difficult and responsible work in office, business, or fiscal administration, or comparable subordinate technical work in a professional, scientific, or technical field, requiring in either case—

    (i) considerable training and supervisory or other experience;

    (ii) broad working knowledge of a special subject matter or of office, laboratory, engineering, scientific, or other procedure and practice; and

    (iii) the exercise of independent judgment in a limited field;

(B) to perform, under immediate supervision, and with little opportunity for the exercise of independent judgment, simple and elementary work requiring professional, scientific, or technical training; or

(C) to perform other work of equal importance, difficulty, and responsibility, and requiring comparable qualifications.

(6) Grade GS-6 includes those classes of positions the duties of which are—

(A) to perform, under general supervision, difficult and responsible work in office, business, or fiscal administration, or comparable subordinate technical work in a professional, scientific, or technical field, requiring in either case—

    (i) considerable training and supervisory or other experience;

    (ii) broad working knowledge of a special and complex subject matter, procedure, or practice, or of the principles of the profession, art, or science involved; and

    (iii) to a considerable extent the exercise of independent judgment; or

(B) to perform other work of equal importance, difficulty, and responsibility, and requiring comparable qualifications.

(7) Grade GS-7 includes those classes of positions the duties of which are—

(A) to perform, under general supervision, work of considerable difficulty and responsibility along special technical or supervisory lines in office, business, or fiscal administration, or comparable subordinate technical work in a professional, scientific, or technical field, requiring in either case—

        (i)   considerable specialized or supervisory training and experience;

        (ii) comprehensive working knowledge of a special and complex subject matter, procedure, or practice, or of the principles of the profession, art, or science involved; and

       (iii) to a considerable extent the exercise of independent judgment;

   (B) under immediate or general supervision, to perform somewhat difficult work requiring—

        (i)   professional, scientific, or technical training; and

        (ii) to a limited extent, the exercise of independent technical judgment; or

   (C) to perform other work of equal importance, difficulty, and responsibility, and requiring comparable qualifications.

(8) Grade GS-8 includes those classes of positions the duties of which are—

   (A) to perform, under general supervision, work of very difficult and responsible work along special technical or supervisory lines in office, business, or fiscal administration, requiring—

        (i)   considerable specialized or supervisory training and experience;

        (ii) comprehensive and thorough working knowledge of a specialized and complex subject matter, procedure, or practice, or of the principles of the profession, art, or science involved; and

       (iii) to a considerable extent the exercise of independent judgment; or

   (B) to perform other work of equal importance, difficulty, and responsibility, and requiring comparable qualifications.

(9) Grade GS-9 includes those classes of positions the duties of which are—

   (A) to perform, under general supervision, very difficult and responsible work along special technical, supervisory, or administrative lines in office, business, or fiscal administration, requiring—

        (i)   somewhat extended specialized training and considerable specialized, supervisory, or administrative experience which has demonstrated capacity for sound independent work;

        (ii) thorough and fundamental knowledge of a special and complex subject matter, or of the principles of the profession, art, or science involved; and

       (iii) considerable latitude for the exercise of independent judgment;

   (B) with considerable latitude for the exercise of independent judgment, to perform moderately difficult and responsible work, requiring—

        (i)   professional, scientific, or technical training equivalent to that represented by graduation from a college or university of recognized standing; and

        (ii) considerable additional professional, scientific, or technical training or experience which has demonstrated capacity for sound independent work; or

   (C) to perform other work of equal importance, difficulty, and responsibility, and requiring comparable qualifications.

(10) Grade GS-10 includes those classes of positions the duties of which are—

(A) to perform, under general supervision, highly difficult and responsible work along special technical, supervisory, or administrative lines in office, business, or fiscal administration, requiring—

(i) somewhat extended specialized, supervisory, or administrative training and experience which has demonstrated capacity for sound independent work;

(ii) thorough and fundamental knowledge of a specialized and complex subject matter, or of the profession, art, or science involved; and

(iii) considerable latitude for the exercise of independent judgment; or

(B) to perform other work of equal importance, difficulty, and responsibility, and requiring comparable qualifications.

(11) Grade GS-11 includes those classes of positions the duties of which are—

(A) to perform, under general administrative supervision and with wide latitude for the exercise of independent judgment, work of marked difficulty and responsibility along special technical, supervisory, or administrative lines in office, business, or fiscal administration, requiring—

(i) extended specialized, supervisory, or administrative training and experience which has demonstrated important attainments and marked capacity for sound independent action or decision; and

(ii) intimate grasp of a specialized and complex subject matter, or of the profession, art, or science involved, or of administrative work of marked difficulty;

(B) with wide latitude for the exercise of independent judgment, to perform responsible work of considerable difficulty requiring somewhat extended professional, scientific, or technical training and experience which has demonstrated important attainments and marked capacity for independent work; or

(C) to perform other work of equal importance, difficulty, and responsibility, and requiring comparable qualifications.

(12) Grade GS-12 includes those classes of positions the duties of which are—

(A) to perform, under general administrative supervision, with wide latitude for the exercise of independent judgment, work of a very high order of difficulty and responsibility along special technical, supervisory, or administrative lines in office, business, or fiscal administration, requiring—

(i) extended specialized, supervisory, or administrative training and experience which has demonstrated leadership and attainments of a high order in specialized or administrative work; and

(ii) intimate grasp of a specialized and complex subject matter or of the profession, art, or science involved;

(B) under general administrative supervision, and with wide latitude for the exercise of independent judgment, to perform professional, scientific, or technical work of marked difficulty and responsibility requiring extended professional, scientific, or technical training and experience which has demonstrated leadership and attainments of a high order in professional, scientific, or technical research, practice, or administration; or

(C) to perform other work of equal importance, difficulty, and responsibility, and requiring comparable qualifications.

(13) Grade GS-13 includes those classes of positions the duties of which are—

(A) to perform, under administrative direction, with wide latitude for the exercise of independent judgment, work of unusual difficulty and responsibility along special technical, supervisory, or administrative lines, requiring extended specialized, supervisory, or administrative training and experience which has demonstrated leadership and marked attainments;

(B) to serve as assistant head of a major organization involving work of comparable level within a bureau;

(C) to perform, under administrative direction, with wide latitude for the exercise of independent judgment, work of unusual difficulty and responsibility requiring extended professional, scientific, or technical training and experience which has demonstrated leadership and marked attainments in professional, scientific, or technical research, practice, or administration; or

(D) to perform other work of equal importance, difficulty, and responsibility, and requiring comparable qualifications.

(14) Grade GS-14 includes those classes of positions the duties of which are—

(A) to perform, under general administrative direction, with wide latitude for the exercise of independent judgment, work of exceptional difficulty and responsibility along special technical, supervisory, or administrative lines which has demonstrated leadership and unusual attainments;

(B) to serve as head of a major organization with a bureau involving work of comparable level;

(C) to plan and direct or to plan and execute major professional, scientific, technical, administrative, fiscal, or other specialized programs, requiring extended training and experience which has demonstrated leadership and unusual attainments in professional, scientific, or technical research, practice, or administration, or in administrative, fiscal, or other specialized activities; or

(D) to perform consulting or other professional, scientific, technical, administrative, fiscal, or other specialized work of equal importance, difficulty, and responsibility, and requiring comparable qualifications.

(15) Grade GS-15 includes those classes of positions the duties of which are—

(A) to perform, under general administrative direction, with very wide latitude for the exercise of independent judgment, work of outstanding difficulty and responsibility along special technical, supervisory, or administrative lines which has demonstrated leadership and exceptional attainments;

(B) to serve as head of a major organization within a bureau involving work of comparable level;

(C) to plan and direct or to plan and execute specialized programs of marked difficulty, responsibility, and national significance, along professional, scientific, technical, administrative, fiscal, or other lines, requiring extended training and experience which has demonstrated leadership and unusual attainments in professional, scientific, or technical research, practice, or administration, or in administrative, fiscal, or other specialized activities; or

(D) to perform consulting or other professional, scientific, technical, administrative, fiscal, or other specialized work of equal importance, difficulty, and responsibility, and requiring comparable qualifications.

(16) Grade GS-16 includes those classes of positions the duties of which are—

(A) to perform, under general administrative direction, with unusual latitude for the exercise of independent judgment, work of outstanding difficulty and responsibility along special technical, supervisory, or administrative lines which has demonstrated leadership and exceptional attainments;

(B) to serve as head of a major organization within a bureau involving work of comparable level;

(C) to plan and direct or to plan and execute professional, scientific, technical, administrative, fiscal, and other specialized programs of unusual difficulty, responsibility, and national significance, requiring extended training and experience which has demonstrated leadership and exceptional attainments in professional, scientific, or technical research, practice, or administration, or in administrative, fiscal, or other specialized activities; or

(D) to perform consulting or other professional, scientific, technical, administrative, fiscal, or other specialized work of equal importance, difficulty, and responsibility, and requiring comparable qualifications.

(17) Grade GS-17 includes those classes of positions the duties of which are—

(A) to serve as the head of a bureau where the position, considering the kind and extent of the authorities and responsibilities vested in it, and the scope, complexity, and degree of difficulty of the activities carried on, is of a high order among the whole group of positions of heads of bureaus;

(B) to plan and direct or to plan and execute professional, scientific, technical, administrative, fiscal, or other specialized programs of exceptional difficulty, responsibility, and national significance, requiring extended training and experience which demonstrated exceptional leadership and attainments in professional, scientific, or technical research, practice, or administration, or in administrative, fiscal, or other specialized activities; or

(C) to perform consulting or other professional, scientific, technical, administrative, fiscal, or other specialized work of equal importance, difficulty, and responsibility, and requiring comparable qualifications.

(18) Grade GS-18 includes those classes of positions the duties of which are—

(A) to serve as the head of a bureau where the position, considering the kind and extent of the authorities and responsibilities vested in it, and the scope, complexity, and degree of difficulty of the activities carried on, is exceptional and outstanding among the whole group of positions of heads of bureaus;

(B) to plan and direct or to plan and execute frontier or unprecedented professional, scientific, technical, administrative, fiscal, or other specialized programs of outstanding difficulty, responsibility, and national significance, requiring extended training and experience which has demonstrated outstanding leadership and attainments in professional, scientific, or technical research, practice, or administration, or in administrative, fiscal, or other specialized activities; or

(C) to perform consulting or other professional, scientific, technical, administrative, fiscal, or other specialized work of equal importance, difficulty, and responsibility, and requiring comparable qualifications.

Glossary

Accidental Death and Dismemberment Insurance: Insurance providing benefits in case of loss of life, limbs, or eyesight as the result of an accident.

Accountability: A major dimension used in the Guide Chart–Profile (Hay) method of job evaluation.

Across-the-Board Pay Increase: An identical increase to all employees. Also called a general increase.

Affirmative Action: Requirement that an employer take positive steps to end underrepresentation of minorities and women.

All-Salaried Work Force: Putting all employees on salary to increase motivation.

Annuity: Periodic payment made to a pensioner over a fixed period of time or until death.

Area Differential: Differences in pay for the same job in different geographical areas (either between cities in the United States or internationally between cities in different nations). Differentials may or may not directly reflect cost-of-living differences.

Assessment Center: A form of performance evaluation in which a specialized team does the evaluating using many different techniques and pooling all of the results to achieve a more balanced evaluation.

Average Hourly Earnings: Total wages for the pay period divided by the average hours worked.

Average Straight-Time Hourly Earnings: Straight-time wages (excluding overtime) divided by the hours worked.

Base Country: In international (expatriate) compensation, the country in which the employee is hired.

Base Pay: A wage or salary, excluding incentive premiums, overtime, shift differentials, and so forth.

Bedaux System: A form of individual incentive involving a fixed piece rate.

Behavioral Observation Scale: A performance evaluation method that uses behavioral statements. It attaches to each statement a likelihood-of-observing scale extending from almost never, then from 1 up to 5, and finally to almost always. Points are assigned to scale values and the point values summarized.

Behaviorally Anchored Rating Scale: A scale that uses behavioral descriptions directly applicable to the job being evaluated.

Belly Point: An arbitrary point between the lowest and highest midranges, usually close to the straight (constant percentage) line, that is useful in drawing a pay curve with rising percentage differentials between midpoints of pay grades using the geometric method.

Benchmark Jobs: Jobs used as a standard to compare to other jobs within or outside the organization.

Beneficiary: The person, other than the plan member, designated to receive a medical, accident, pension, or death benefit.

Bona Fide Occupational Qualification: Exception to the usual rules under Title VII of the Civil Rights Act of 1964. It specifies that under certain conditions an employer may require a person to be of a specific sex, race, or religion to fill a particular job.

Bonus: Any direct additional lump sum cash payment made on top of a base salary for either individuals or groups. Bonuses can also be in stock and/or deferred compensation.

Cafeteria Benefits Plan: A plan in which employees have some choice as to benefits received. Usually a common core of benefits is required, but there is a group of elective programs from which the employee may select a set dollar amount. Employees may be provided with additional benefits on a contributory basis.

Call-Back Pay: A guarantee of pay for a minimum amount of time when an employee is called back to work at a time when she would not ordinarily have to work.

Call-In Pay: A guarantee of pay for a minimum amount of time for an employee who reports to work at the usual time but for whom there is no work.

Capitation Payment: A method of paying doctors used in the United Kingdom where a doctor's pay depends on the number of patients.

Check-Off: Provides for deduction of union dues from pay even where a worker does not have to be a union member. This is in effect in many states having so-called right-to-work laws.

Civil Service Commission: See **Office of Personnel Management.**

COLA: See **Cost of Living Allowance.**

Commission: Compensation for the sale of products or services, typically based on a percentage of sales.

Compa-Ratio: Ratio of an employee's pay rate to the midpoints of the pay grade. Can also be calculated for the average of a group of people for budgetary planning.

Comparable Worth: The idea that women who perform work of equal value to that performed by men should receive equal pay. Comparable worth typically relates to internal equity and does not refer to market value.

Compensable Factor: See **Job Factor.**

Compensation: All forms of financial returns, tangible services, and benefits employees receive as part of an employment relationship.

Compensatory Time Off: Time off given in place of overtime. Under the Fair Labor Standards Act, it must be given in the same workweek.

Competitiveness: The extent to which American products and services can compete effectively against the products and services of other nations.

Compression: Reduction of pay differentials between jobs or levels of jobs within an organization.

Computer: An electronic machine for performing logic or mathematical computations. The analog computer projects graphic results while the digital computer produces numbers or letters.

Computer Hardware: The keyboard, the console, the central processing unit, the printer, and other mechanical parts of a computer.

Computer Software: Programs either originating on discs or tape or generated by the computer user. These consist of operating programs that tell the computer what to do or application programs generated by the user.

Constant Dollars: See **Real Wages.**

Constant Percentage Differentials: A fixed percentage difference between the midpoint of one pay grade and the midpoint of the next pay grade.

Consumer Price Index: An index of the cost of living published by the U.S. Bureau of Labor Statistics. It measures the changes in prices of a fixed market basket of goods and services purchased by an average family.

Contributory Pension Plan: A pension plan in which the employee contributes part of the cost.

Correlation: A measure of the relationship existing between two variables such as the heights and weights of a group of students. The height is on one axis and the weight is on the other. A dot is then plotted for each student. If the scatter of dots rises from left to right, there would be a positive correlation between the heights and weights of students.

Cost of Living Adjustment (or Allowance): An increase or decrease in pay according to the rise or fall in the cost of living, usually measured by the Bureau of Labor Statistics Consumer Price Index. In expatriate compensation, it refers to an amount added to or subtracted from base pay to adjust for interarea differences in the cost of living.

CPI: See **Consumer Price Index.**

Craft Union: A union organized along craft lines such as painters, carpenters, plumbers, and the like.

Critical Incidents: Examples of especially good behavior or especially bad behavior on the part of an employee. Such incidents can be useful in formulating scales such as **Behaviorally Anchored Rating Scales** or **Behavioral Observation Scales.**

Currently Paid Bonus: A bonus paid during or shortly after the period for which the bonus is awarded.

Data Base: A collection of information in the computer's memory that typically can be ordered numerically or alphabetically in various ways.

Defined Benefit Pension Plan: A pension plan that specifies the benefits or the method of determination of the benefit but not the level or the rate of contribution.

Defined Contribution Pension Plan: An individual account pension plan in which contributions are specified by formula. The benefits are whatever the amount accumulated in the participant's account will buy.

Degrees: See **Point Method.**

Dictionary of Occupational Titles: A dictionary of job titles and generic job descriptions including more than 20,000 jobs based on more than 75,000 job analyses, published by the U.S. Department of Labor.

Differential: A difference in pay, such as interjob, interarea, shift, or between pay grades.

Direct Labor: Labor that is necessary to the direct manufacture of a product or provision of a service.

Disk Drive: Part of a computer's hardware. It can be either a floppy drive, which uses floppy disks, or a fixed or hard drive, which is built into the computer. The fixed disk can hold more information than the floppy disk.

Dissatisfiers: As contrasted to **Motivators,** job factors to which employees react negatively if they are not present, such as vacation pay or rest periods.

Dividend Unit: Any award made in units analogous to an actual share of stock where the employee receives cash payments equivalent to dividends.

Double-Track System: A framework for professional employees in an organization where two tracks of ascending compensation steps are available, a managerial track and a professional track.

Education Allowance: A benefit often provided to expatriates as an inducement to serve overseas.

EEOC: See **Equal Employment Opportunity Commission.**

Effective Tax Rate: The individual income tax as a percentage of taxable income after deductions but before exemptions. Computations are based on assumptions such as referring to a married couple with two dependents.

Employee Benefits (also called **Supplements to Wages and Salaries):** Nonwage parts of compensation including but not limited to income protection, services, and income supplements for employees provided in whole or in part by employer payments.

Employee Stock Ownership Plan: A plan in which a company borrows money from a financial institution using the company's stock as collateral for the loan. Both principal and interest on periodic loan repayments are tax deductible. With each repayment, a block of stock is released and put into an Employee Stock Ownership Trust for distribution to employees.

Employment Contract: An agreement under which an executive with little seniority gets a fixed yearly payment for a number of years—a better deal than he or she would otherwise get under the company's pension plan.

Employment Shares: The share of employment a particular racial group, nationality, or sex has of the total number of workers in an occupational group. It is a good measure of employment opportunity.

Equal Dollar Intervals: A payment plan in which the difference between the midpoints of adjacent pay grades is a fixed dollar amount.

Equal Employment Opportunity Commission: An agency of the federal government charged with enforcing the provisions of the Civil Rights Act of 1964. It also enforces the provisions of the Equal Pay Act of 1963 with respect to sex discrimination in pay.

Equal Pay for Comparable Work: Under Title VII of the Civil Rights Act of 1964, women can bring suit on sex discrimination in pay involving the principle of comparable worth.

Equal Pay for Equal Work: Equality with regard to the four factors of effort, skill, responsibility, and working conditions. Under the Equal Pay Act of 1963 women can bring suit where the principle of equal pay for equal work is in question. At issue is whether two jobs to be compared are equal with respect to all of the factors.

Equity Bargaining: Collective bargaining based on the relative importance of jobs in the organization rather than on market rates of pay. Used by the California Nurses Association and other groups, especially where questions of comparable worth arise.

Equity Theory: The theory that in an exchange relationship (such as employment) the comparison of outcome/input ratios between two people will determine perceived fairness or equity. If the ratios are unfavorable, the result will be seen as inequity.

Escalator Clause: A provision in a union contract that provides upward or downward wage adjustments according to fluctuations in the BLS Consumer Price Index. See also **Cost of Living Allowance.**

ESOP: See **Employee Stock Ownership Plan.**

Exclusive Recognition: A right enjoyed by some federal government unions where stronger forms of union security are not available under the law.

Executive Compensation: Compensation to executives such as salary, bonuses, profit sharing, and other incentive programs including stock option plans and pension plans, as well as perquisites. Tax considerations are important. See **Total Pay Package.**

Exempt Employees: Employees who are exempt from the overtime provisions of the Fair Labor Standards Act. These groups typically include executives, administrative employees, professional employees, and those engaged in outside sales.

Exercise of Option: The purchase of stock granted under a stock option plan.

Expatriate: An employee assigned outside his or her base country for more than 1 year.

Expectancy Theory: A theory that proposes that an individual will select an alternative based on how this choice is related to outcomes such as rewards. The choice the person makes, then, is based upon the strength or value of the outcome and the perceived probability that his or her choice will lead to that outcome.

Extrinsic Rewards: Rewards a worker gets from sources other than the job itself. Examples are pay, supervision, promotions, vacations, and friendships. See also **Intrinsic Rewards.**

Factor Comparison Check: Used to ascertain the reasonableness of the point values under the point method of job evaluation. This is done by ranking a group of jobs separately on each factor. The results can then be checked against the point values for reasonableness.

Factor Comparison Method: Job evaluation method that differs from ranking in that factors within the job are considered. Individual jobs are ranked by factor. A second ranking is done of the factors within each job. The two rankings are brought into conformity with each other by using either the money method or the percentage method to construct a visual scale using key jobs. Other jobs are profiled visually by comparison with the key jobs.

Factor Comparison Scale: The visual scale used with the factor comparison method of job evaluation.

Factor Evaluation System: A point system used by the U.S. federal government to assign jobs to particular grades under the predetermined grading method.

Factor Weight: A weight indicating the relative importance of a factor in a point system of job evaluation.

Falling Piece Rate: An individual incentive plan in which the rate per piece declines as volume of output increases.

Federal Incentive Awards Program: A program passed by Congress in 1954 and signed by President Eisenhower that includes quality step increases in pay and incentive awards for suggestions from federal employees that result in tangible or intangible benefits to the government.

Fee for Service: The typical method of payment for medical doctors in the United States.

Final Average Pay: A formula used for pensions where benefits are based on average earnings in the last 3 to 5 years of employment before retirement.

Fixed Piece Rate: An individual incentive plan involving a fixed payment per piece as volume of output goes up. This is characteristic of straight piece work.

Flexible Benefits: See **Cafeteria Benefits Plan.**

Flexible Work Force: A concept favored by the Japanese. The idea is to provide lifetime employment but be able to move employees to wherever in the organization they can best be used.

Flexitime: A workweek concept that allows the employee some flexibility in work hours. The employee can choose early or late arrival or departure but on an agreed-upon schedule. Usually part of the time, called core time, is not flexible. This is often time needed to properly operate the business.

Foreign Service Premium: Extra pay to an expatriate for working in a foreign country.

Gainsharing or **Group Incentive Plans:** Incentive plans that are based on some measure of group performance rather than individual performance. Taking data on a past period as a base, group incentive plans typically focus on cost savings (e.g., the Scanlon, Rucker, and Improshare plans) or on profit increases (profit sharing plans) as a standard to distribute a portion of the funds among employees.

Gannt Plan: An individual incentive plan that provides for variable incentives as a function of a standard expressed as time period per unit of production. Under this plan, a standard time for a task is purposely set at a level requiring great effort to complete.

General Increase: See **Across-the-Board Pay Increase.**

General Schedule: The pay schedule used for most employees of the executive branch of the federal government.

GNP Per Capita: For any nation, gross national product divided by population. This ratio is an important indicator of a nation's standard of living.

Green-Ringed Rates: An existing pay rate that falls below the bottom of a pay box when a new pay schedule goes into effect. Such a rate is ringed in green—an indication the rate should be changed to allow the worker to move upward into the new pay box.

Group Medical Practice: See **Health Maintenance Organization.**

Group Permanent Insurance: A benefits plan that usually combines life insurance with retirement benefits and uses the level premium method, under a group contract between the employer and the insurance company.

Group Term Life Insurance: Annual renewable term life (and disability) insurance covering a class (or classes) of employees in accordance with a stipulated schedule of benefits.

GS: See **General Schedule.**

Guaranteed Annual Wage: A plan that guarantees a minimum annual income to employees.

Guide Chart—Profile Method (Hay Method): A method of job evaluation that evaluates jobs with respect to know-how, problem solving, and accountability. It also involves profiling. Used primarily for exempt jobs.

Guideline Method: A method of so-called job evaluation involving pricing a job into a predetermined salary structure (by selecting the midpoint closest to the job price) and then realigning the hierarchy on the basis of relative internal job worth.

Halsey 50—50 Method: An individual incentive plan that provides for variable incentives as a function of a standard expressed in time period per unit of production. This plan derives its name from the shared split between worker and employer of any savings in direct costs.

Hardship Differential: An allowance for expatriates to compensate for difficult working conditions in a foreign environment.

Hay Method: See **Guide Chart—Profile Method.**

Health Maintenance Organization: Prepaid group medical service emphasizing preventive health care.

Hierarchy: The layers of organizational structure and who reports to whom.

Hiring Rate: The beginning rate at which people are hired into a job.

HMO: See **Health Maintenance Organization.**

Holiday Pay: Pay for time not worked on holidays. A worker who works on a holiday may also be entitled to additional premium pay.

Housing Allowance: A differential paid to adjust for differences between overseas housing costs and the costs for similar housing in the United States.

Impasse: Situations in federal government union-management negotiations where the two sides cannot reach an agreement but a strike is not legal.

IMPROSHARE (IMproved PROductivity through SHARing): A gainsharing plan in which a standard is developed that identifies the expected hours required to produce an acceptable level of output. Any savings arising from production of agreed-upon output in fewer than expected hours are shared by the firm and the worker.

Incentive: A motivating influence to induce effort above normal. More narrowly, a reward, financial or other, that compensates the worker for high and/or continued performance above standards.

Incentive Stock Option: A stock option that requires an exercise period of not more than 10 years. The stock must be held for 2 years from the date of the grant and 1 year from the date of exercise. The gain at the time of exercise of the option is not taxed, and the tax upon sale is as a long-term capital gain.

Indirect Labor: Labor that is necessary to support the manufacture of a product or the provision of a service but does not directly enter into the product or performance of the service.

Individual Retirement Account: A defined contribution plan that allows an individual to make a tax-deductible contribution to the individual's own retirement account and also to the spouse's account if the spouse is not employed. Contributions are currently limited to an annual maximum of $2,000 ($2,250 when the spouse is included).

Industrial Union: A union organized on a plant-wide or industrywide basis.

Instrumentality: One of the factors in **Expectancy Theory.**

Intangible Benefits: Under federal government incentive plans, contributions of an employee where dollar savings are hard to measure.

Intercity Cost of Living Allowance: See **Cost of Living Allowance.**

Interjob Differential: Difference in base pay between any two jobs.

Internal Equity: A fairness criterion under which pay rates correspond to the relative value of each job to the organization.

International Compensation: In its broadest sense, international pay comparisons for a number of different nations. In a narrower sense, pay practices for American overseas employees. Foreign services premiums may be paid to cover cost of living and tax differentials. Other incentives are often included.

Interquartile Range: The middle 50 percent of workers if workers were lined up in a continuous rank in order of base pay from the lowest paid to the highest paid.

Interrater Reliability: The extent of agreement among raters rating the same individual, group, or thing.

Intrinsic Rewards: Rewards that are associated with the job itself such as the opportunity to perform meaningful work, complete cycles of work, see finished products, experience variety, and receive feedback on work results.

IRA: See **Individual Retirement Account.**

Job Analysis: A systematic study of the tasks making up a job, employee skills required to do the job, time factors, situation factors such as technology use, physical aspects, information flows, interpersonal and group interactions, and historical traditions associated with the job. Job analysis provides the information needed to define jobs and conduct job evaluation.

Job Classification: See **Predetermined Grading.**

Job Description: A summary of the most important features of a job including the nature of the job performed, specific task responsibilities, and employee characteristics (including skills) required to perform the job (the last known as **Job Specifications**). A job description should relate to the job and not to the person who fills it.

Job Evaluation: The formal process by which management determines the relative value to be placed on various jobs within the organization. The end result of job evaluation is the assignment of jobs to a hierarchy of pay grades or some other hierarchical index of job value. Job evaluation is closely associated with the criterion of internal equity.

Job Evaluation Committee: A committee charged with the responsibility of (a) selecting a job evaluation system, (b) carrying out or at least supervising the process of job evaluation, and (c) evaluating the success with which the job evaluation has been conducted.

Job Factor: Any factor used to provide a basis for judging job value in a job evaluation plan. Most commonly used factors include responsibility, skill required, effort required, and working conditions. Also called **Compensable Factor.**

Job Family: Jobs involving work of the same nature but requiring different skill and responsibility levels (e.g., Applications Programming is a job family; Senior Applications Programmer is a job—a skill/responsibility level—within the family).

Job Obsolescence: Typically refers to outdated job descriptions.

Job Posting and Bidding: A procedure by which job openings in a plant or office are posted so that an interested employee can put in a bid for the job.

Job Pricing: The process of combining judgments regarding external market values and internal job evaluation, typically resulting in a pay structure.

Job Specification: The part of the job description that specifies the individual requirements or qualifications necessary for the individual to perform the job.

Job Title: A label to identify a job.

Joint and Survivor Option: A provision typically applied to a married couple under which a reduced pension is paid to the survivor as long as one of the two is living. The amount of the benefit depends on the age of the survivor.

Keogh Plan: Enables a self-employed individual to establish a qualified tax-deductible pension or profit sharing plan. Contributions are currently limited to the lesser of 15 percent of compensation or $30,000 for profit sharing plans and the lesser of 25 percent of compensation or $30,000 for money purchase plans.

Key Jobs: Used in the factor comparison method of job evaluation. Key jobs should represent differing pay levels and should be both fairly priced on the market and believed to be fairly valued in terms of internal equity. See also **Benchmark Jobs.**

Know-How: A major factor used in the **Guide Chart–Profile (Hay) Method** of job evaluation.

Least Squares Regression Line: A line fitted to a scatter of dots that minimizes the squares of the vertical distances from the line. Mathematically only one such line—the line of best fit—can be drawn.

Liberalization of Benefits: A union strategy where the union gets its foot in the door by first gaining a benefit at the bargaining table and then getting the benefit liberalized—that is to say, getting a more generous benefit. (First, get a dental plan, then get a more generous plan in a later collective bargaining session.)

Lifetime Employment: Practice in major Japanese firms of providing a job for life.

Limit Lines: Diagonal limit lines pass through the midpoints of the tops and bottoms of pay boxes in the process of building a pay structure.

Lincoln Electric Company Plan: The highly successful individual incentive plan developed and used by the Lincoln Electric Company.

Line of Relationship: A line used to indicate the general path of a scatter of dots in a scatter diagram. It need not be mathematical—the "eye squares approach"—but usually the method of least squares is employed.

Local Country Nationals: Citizens of a country in which a U.S. foreign subsidiary is located.

Log-Log Scale: A scale that is logarithmic on both axes—useful in comparing percentage changes in two different series such as sales and salaries.

Long-Term Disability: See **Workers Compensation.**

Lump-Sum Bonus: A way to relate pay to performance on a one-shot basis without necessarily increasing base pay. A merit increase can be a lump sum payment.

Major Medical Insurance: Special protection for large surgical, hospital, or other medical expenses and services. Benefits are paid after a specified deductible is met and are then generally subject to coinsurance. Usually written in conjunction with a basic medical plan and referred to as a supplementary plan.

Management by Objectives: A process in which a superior and subordinate or group of subordinates jointly identify and estabish common performance goals. Success in achieving these goals is later reviewed, again jointly.

Market Pricing: A method of job evaluation that defines a job's worth solely by the going rate in the marketplace.

Maturity Curves: A method of reporting pay for professionals as a function of years since degree or time in the profession. Constructed from survey data, maturity curves are commonly used for engineers, scientists, accountants, and physicians. Some organizations use maturity curves for pricing jobs rather than relying on job evaluation.

MBO See **Management by Objectives.**

Mean (Arithmetic Mean): The result of adding together the base pay of employees in a unit and dividing by the number of employees. For example, if there are five people in a department add together the base pay of all of them and divide by 5. That is the arithmetic mean.

Median: The middle pay rate. If there are five people in a department and you line them up according to base pay from the lowest paid to the highest paid, the individual in the middle is the one with the median base pay.

Mentor: The idea of having someone high in the organization to whom the worker does *not* report who can serve as a career advisor.

Merit Increase: An increase in salary supposedly based on merit.

Merrick Plan: Individual incentive plan that provides for variable incentives as a function of units of production per time period. It works like the Taylor Plan, but three piecework rates are set: (1) high—for production exceeding 100 percent of standard; (2) medium—for production between 83 percent and 100 percent of standard; and (3) low—production less than 83 percent of standard.

Midrange: The point halfway between the high and the low of a pay rate range.

Minimum Wage: A minimum wage level for most Americans established by Congress as part of the Fair Labor Standards Act. As of 1988 the minimum wage was $3.35 an hour. States also have their own minimum wage standards.

Mitbestimmungsrecht (or Codetermination): An arrangement practiced in Germany and some other European nations where unions are given as much as half of the membership on the company's board of directors.

Mode: The item or observation that occurs most frequently. If five employees in a department earn $6, $6, $8, $9, and $10 per hour, the mode for these employees is $6.

Money Method of Factor Comparison: A method that involves ranking jobs by factor and then allocating the total pay rate to the different factors in money amounts. Then an attempt is made to alter the pay data slightly to keep the rankings correct. This typically results in rejection of some of the key jobs. The remaining jobs are then used to construct the visual factor comparison scale.

Motivators: Factors that tend to motivate the employee toward better performance, such as a bonus, favorable attitude of the boss, and so on.

National Consultation Rights: Rights a federal government labor union has in lieu of collective bargaining.

National Labor Relations Board: The governmental body primarily responsible for the conduct of collective bargaining under the Wagner Act.

NLRB: see **National Labor Relations Board.**

Noncontributory Pension Plan: A plan where the employer pays the entire cost of the premiums or of building up a fund from which pensions are paid.

Nonexempt Employees: Employees who are not subject to the provisions of the Fair Labor Standards Act.

Nonqualified Stock Option: Any option that does not meet the requirement of an **Incentive Stock Option.** The executive must pay the ordinary income tax at the time of exercise on the spread between the option price and the market value of the stock on the date of exercise.

OASDHI: See **Social Security.**

Office of Personnel Management: The principal personnel organization for the executive branch of the federal government. Formerly the Civil Service Commission.

Option Price: The price an executive pays for the stock upon exercise of an option.

Overtime Pay: Under the Fair Labor Standards Act, nonexempt employees must be paid one and a half times their normal wage rates for all hours in excess of 40 in the workweek.

Pacific Rim: Refers to nations bordering on the Pacific.

PAQ: See **Position Analysis Questionnaire.**

Pay Boxes: Boxes drawn so the top and the bottom of the pay rate range are at the top and bottom of the box. Width of the box is the point range from low to high or the equivalent.

Pay Curve: A line of relationship between, say, dollars on the vertical axis and points on the horizontal axis. It is not necessarily a curve.

Pay for Skills: The concept of paying the employee more with each new skill acquired.

Pay Grade: One of the classes, levels, or groups into which jobs of the same or similar value are grouped for compensation purposes. All jobs in a pay grade have the same pay range and the same maximum, minimum, and midpoint.

Pay Grade Overlap: The degree to which adjacent pay grades in a structure overlap. Overlap equals the length of the actual overlap divided by the height of the right-hand box.

Pay Range: The high and low of a particular pay box.

Payroll-Based Tax Credit Employee Stock Ownership Plan (PAYSOP): A type of ESOP created in 1983 but discontinued in 1986, under which the employer received tax credits for contributions to the ESOP.

Pay Steps: Steps within a pay grade.

Pay Structure: A graphic portrayal of pay boxes or a line of relationship, between, for example, pay on the vertical axis and points on the horizontal axis.

Pecking Order: Who comes first. For example, in a restaurant chefs have more power than waiters, waiters have more power than busboys, and busboys more power than the dishwashers.

Peer Evaluation: Performance evaluation by others on the same level in the organization as the individual being rated.

Percentage Differential: This refers to the percentage difference between the midpoints of pay grades. The percentage may be fixed or rising.

Percentage Method of Factor Comparison: A method that involves ranking two ways—by job and by factors within each job. The two processes are then mathematically related to develop a system of points from which the visual factor comparison scale is made.

Percentage Pay Increase: Increasing the pay of all employees by the same percentage. This contrasts with the **Across-the-Board Pay Increase.**

Performance Award: An award earned in whole or in part according to the degree of achievement of predetermined performance goals over a specified period (usually 3 to 5 years).

Performance Evaluation (or Appraisal): Any system of determining how well an individual has performed during a period of time. Often used as a basis for determining the amount of merit increases.

Performance Share Plan: A stock grant plan that stipulates achievement of certain predetermined performance goals before the recipient has rights to the stock. The key employee receiving the grant pays a tax on the fair market value of the stock at the time of issuance, and there is no holding period as to when the stock can be sold.

Performance Stock Option: A stock option where the exercise of shares of stock under option is contingent upon the achievement of certain predetermined performance goals.

Performance Unit/Cash Award: An award granted in units or cash. Units may have a fixed dollar payment value with the number of units varying according to performance achievement. Or, a fixed number of units may be granted with the payment value depending on performance achievement.

Perquisite: A benefit tied to a specific key or management level job (for example, a company car for personal use, free meals, financial counseling, or use of company facilities).

Phantom Stock: Any award made in units analogous to shares of stock where, after a specified time, the employee receives a payment equal to the appreciation in value of the stock and often an amount equal to dividends paid during the period.

Piece Rate: Payment based on production by the worker. A payment is made for each piece or other quantity unit of work produced by the worker.

Point Method (or Point Factor Method): An evaluation method in which factors are chosen for

rating jobs, points are assigned for different degrees of each factor (the number of degrees depending on the factor), each job is measured against each factor, and a point total is assigned to each job.

Point Range: The low and high point values that define the width of a pay box in a point plan.

Position Analysis Questionnaire: A job analysis technique that captures 187 aspects of a job. PAQ results can be statistically interpretable directly into points.

Postretirement Deferred Bonus: A bonus paid after retirement.

Predetermined Grading: A method of job evaluation that involves slotting job descriptions into a series of classes or grades.

Premium Pay: Extra pay beyond the regular wage rate for work performed outside of or beyond regularly scheduled work periods (Sundays, holidays, night shifts, and so on).

Prevailing Wage: The amount paid for similar work by others in the same labor market. The concept comes into play under the Davis-Bacon Act and the McNamara-O'Hara Service Contract Act.

Problem Solving: One of the three factors used under the **Guide Chart–Profile (Hay) Method.**

Productivity: Any index measuring the efficiency of an operation—typically output divided by input, such as pounds of product per man-hour.

Profiling: Part of the **Guide Chart–Profile (Hay) Method** of job evaluation.

Quality Step Increase: An increase of one step in the federal government's General Schedule granted on the basis of quality of performance rather than seniority.

Ranking: The simplest method of job evaluation. Each job is compared to every other job. The jobs are then ranked from lowest to highest.

Rating Errors: Errors in judgment that typically occur when an individual observes and evaluates a person, group, or factor (job or performance). Frequent errors include halo (or horns), leniency, severity, and central tendency.

Real Wages: Wages divided by the consumer price index, typically rebased to the most recent year, to translate wages into purchasing power.

Red-Ringed Rate: Rate that is above the maximum rate for a particular pay grade.

Reduction in Force: Layoff based on reduction in the size of the organizational unit.

Reinforcement Theories: Theories such as expectancy and operant conditioned theory which give a prominent role to rewards (such as compensation) in motivating behavior. They argue that pay motivates to the extent that merit increases and other work-related rewards are allocated on the basis of performance.

Relative Pay: How your pay compares with that of someone else. For a more sophisticated idea, see **Equity Theory.**

Reliability: The consistency of ratings either among different raters rating the same person or for the same rater at different times.

Remuneration: Another word for compensation, often used by the SEC in relation to pay of executives.

Restricted Stock Plan: A plan that does not give the recipient of the stock grant the right to full ownership until certain predetermined conditions are satisfied.

RIF: See **Reduction in Force.**

Right-To-Work Law: A law that allows an employee to work without having to join a union.

Ringi-Do: The Japanese communications process in large organizations. An idea may start at the bottom of an organization, be circulated for discussion at that level, then go through the same procedure at the next level up, and so forth until it reaches the top. At the top the idea is usually accepted in its essentials.

Rising Percentage Differentials: Gradually increasing percentage differentials between the midpoints of pay grades.

Rising Piece Rate: An individual incentive plan in which the piece rate rises as the volume of output rises.

Rucker Plan: A group cost savings plan in which cost reductions due to employee efforts are shared with employees. It involves a somewhat more complex formula than the Scanlon Plan for determining bonuses.

Salary: Compensation paid by the week, every two weeks, the month, or the year, rather than by the hour.

SAR: See **Stock Appreciation Right.**

Scanlon Plan: A cost reduction program in which specific cost savings due to employee effort are shared with employees. The Scanlon Plan involves much employee participation, predating quality circles with most of the same techniques.

Scatter Diagram: Used to determine if a relationship exists between two variables. For instance, if the Y-axis is height in inches, the X-axis is weight in pounds, and each dot represents a person, as soon as enough dots are plotted you can tell whether there seems to be a relationship between heights and weights. See also **Correlation.**

SEC: See **Securities and Exchange Commission.**

Securities and Exchange Commission: In this context, the principal federal government agency concerned with the pay of top executives.

Segregation of Jobs by Sex: For example, mechanical jobs tend to be held by men while clerical jobs tend to be held by women.

Self-Evaluation: A method of performance evaluation especially useful for jobs difficult to judge by observation, such as the work of a forest ranger. It is also useful as a supplemental rating for other jobs, such as teacher.

Semi-Logarithmic Scale: A scale where equal vertical distances represent equal percentage differences. It is much used in business as the best way to show trends and fluctuations.

Seniority: Length of time an employee has worked for a particular employer. Narrower interpretations of seniority refer to time worked for a division, department, or in a job.

Seniority Increase: A pay increase based on seniority. To the extent that performance improves with time on the job, the result approximates pay for performance.

SERP: See **Supplemental Executive Retirement Plan.**

Severance Pay (Termination Pay): Payment beyond the normal base pay when a person leaves the organization. In some cases severance pay formulas may be used to creative incentives for a person to leave before normal retirement age.

Shift Differentials: An additional amount paid to a worker for working any shift other than the normal day shift.

Short-Term Deferment: Typically a bonus, a type of award that may be paid out over several years. This is common in the auto industry.

Sick Leave: Pay for time not worked due to employee's illness or injury.

Social Security: Federal old age, survivors, disability, and health insurance system. Beneficiaries include workers, spouses, dependent parents, and dependent children.

Staggered Percent Reductions: A situation in which the highest level of employees may take the largest percentage reductions when pay cuts are carried out, the next layer a somewhat smaller percentage, and the lowest-paid level an even lower percentage cut.

Standard Hours or Time: The amount of time established in a wage incentive plan for performing a specific task. The effect is the same as using a fixed piece rate plan.

Standard of Living: See **GNP Per Capita.**

Starting Rate: See **Hiring Rate.**

Stock Appreciation Right: A right granted in connection with an option where, instead of exercising the option, the executive can get a payment equal to the amount by which the fair market value of the stock exceeds the option price on the date the stock appreciation right is exercised.

Stock Grant: Stock provided at nominal or no cost. It may take the form of restricted stock that is nontransferable or subject to risk of forfeiture until some future conditions are met. The restrictions are often designed to lapse over a period of years, based on continuing service. Dividends on restricted shares may be paid currently or reinvested to buy additional shares, which are paid at the end of the restriction period.

Stock Option: An opportunity to purchse shares of company stock at a stated price (typically the current market value at the date of grant) during a given period of time, often 10 years.

Stock Purchase Plan (Nonqualified): A plan that allows senior managers or other key personnel to buy stock in the business with certain restrictions: (1) the stockholder must be employed for a certain period of time, (2) the company has the right to buy back the stock, and (3) stockholders cannot sell the stock for a defined period of time.

Stock Purchase Plan (Qualified): A plan that allows employees to buy shares of the company's stock, with the company contributing a specific amount for each unit of employee contribution. Stock may be offered at a fixed price (usually below market) and paid for in full by the employee. Benefits are distributed in stock of the employee company.

Structural Unemployment: As contrasted with unemployment due to lack of demand, the disparity between the availability of jobs in one location and the presence elsewhere of people looking for jobs. The unwillingness of people to move to where the jobs are is not caused by overall lack of demand.

SUB: See **Supplemental Unemployment Benefits.**

Subminimum Wage: Authorized under the Fair Labor Standards Act for learners in semi-skilled occupations, apprentices in skilled occupations, messengers, handicapped persons, and students.

Supplemental Executive Retirement Plan: A plan that arose after earlier legislation attempted to put an upper limit on retirement pay of executives to provide executives with higher benefits.

Supplemental Unemployment Benefits: Equalize interstate differences in amount and duration of individual state unemployment benefits.

Take-Home Pay: An employee's earnings less taxes, social security, and other deductions, both voluntary and involuntary, made by the employer.

Tangible Benefits: Relates to federal government incentive awards where the benefits to the government of an employee suggestion can be directly measured by the extent of the savings.

Tax Avoidance and **Tax Evasion:** Tax evasion is deliberately deciding not to pay a tax while tax avoidance is acting within the law to minimize the taxes that have to be paid.

Tax Equalization: A method whereby an expatriate pays neither more nor less tax than the assumed home-country tax on base remuneration. The employer usually deducts the assumed home-country tax from monthly salary and reimburses the employee for all taxes paid in the country of assignment and any actual home country tax on remuneration only.

Tax Reform Act Stock Ownership Plan (TRASOP): A special ESOP that came into existence with the Tax Reform Act of 1976. This act grants businesses the right to cover a specified amount of start-up and administrative costs. Employees have full and immediate vesting in all shares placed in their accounts.

Taylor Plan: An individual incentive plan based on units of production per time period. It provides two piecework rates for production above (or below) standard, which are higher or lower than the regular wage incentive level.

Team Building: An organization development technique in which a supervisor works with anonymous peer and subordinate ratings and negotiates possible changes with a delegation from the rating groups.

Termination Pay: See **Severance Pay.**

Third-Country National: At foreign locations of multinational companies, employees who are citizens of a country other than the host nation or the United States.

Thrift and Savings Plans: The typical thrift and savings plan is designed to help workers achieve savings goals. The most common plan involves a 50 percent employer matching of employee contributions up to a maximum of 6 percent of pay.

Time Span of Discretion: The maximum period of time during which the use of discretion is authorized and expected without review of that discretion by a superior. The time span of discretion has been used as a noneconomic definition of job value in Elliot Jacques' model of pay equity.

Total Pay: A label often used to include salary plus bonuses only. For executives, this concept grossly understates the real total, which must take into account many other benefits. See also **Total Pay Package.**

Total Pay Package: A far more meaningful concept than so-called **Total Pay** including the complete compensation package: all forms of money, stock, benefits, services, and in-kind payments. A borderline part of the package is expense accounts. Under present federal law, union leaders must report such expenses while corporate executives are not required to do so.

Two-Tier Pay Plans: Wage structures that differentiate pay for the same jobs based on hiring date. A contract is negotiated that specifies that employees hired after a certain date will receive lower wages than their higher seniority peers working on the same or similar jobs.

Unemployment Compensation: State administered programs that provide financial protection for workers during periods of joblessness.

Unit Labor Cost: Labor cost divided by units of output. If they include benefits, unit labor costs are a significant indicator of our ability to be internationally competitive.

Valence: One of the variables used in **Expectancy Theory.**

Validity: The quality of a measuring device that refers to its relevance. Does it really measure what it is intended to measure?

Vesting: Typically refers to the time when the employee becomes entitled to employer contributions to a pension plan, even if employment terminates before retirement.

VIE Theory: See **Expectancy Theory.**

Workers Compensation: Laws that provide cash payments for medical care to cover health services for workers injured on the job, partial wage replacement benefits, and rehabilitation services to restore workers to their fullest economic capacity. Benefits are financed by the employer and differ from state to state.

Zero-Overlap Boxes: A method of controlling overlap in developing a pay structure.

Name Index

Subject Index

WE VALUE YOUR OPINION—PLEASE SHARE IT WITH US

Merrill Publishing and our authors are most interested in your reactions to this textbook. Did it serve you well in the course? If it did, what aspects of the text were most helpful? If not, what didn't you like about it? Your comments will help us to write and develop better textbooks. We value your opinions and thank you for your help.

Text Title _____ Edition _____

Author(s) _____

Your Name (optional) _____

Address _____

City _____ State _____ Zip _____

School _____

Course Title _____

Instructor's Name _____

Your Major _____

Your Class Rank _____ Freshman _____ Sophomore _____Junior _____ Senior

_____ Graduate Student

Were you required to take this course? _____ Required _____Elective

Length of Course? _____ Quarter _____ Semester

1. Overall, how does this text compare to other texts you've used?

_____ Superior _____Better Than Most _____ Average _____Poor

2. Please rate the text in the following areas:

	Superior	Better Than Most	Average	Poor
Author's Writing Style	_____	_____	_____	_____
Readability	_____	_____	_____	_____
Organization	_____	_____	_____	_____
Accuracy	_____	_____	_____	_____
Layout and Design	_____	_____	_____	_____
Illustrations/Photos/Tables	_____	_____	_____	_____
Examples	_____	_____	_____	_____
Problems/Exercises	_____	_____	_____	_____
Topic Selection	_____	_____	_____	_____
Currentness of Coverage	_____	_____	_____	_____
Explanation of Difficult Concepts	_____	_____	_____	_____
Match-up with Course Coverage	_____	_____	_____	_____
Applications to Real Life	_____	_____	_____	_____

3. Circle those chapters you especially liked:
   1   2   3   4   5   6   7   8   9   10   11   12   13   14   15   16   17   18   19   20
   What was your favorite chapter? _____
   Comments:

4. Circle those chapters you liked least:
   1   2   3   4   5   6   7   8   9   10   11   12   13   14   15   16   17   18   19   20
   What was your least favorite chapter? _____
   Comments:

5. List any chapters your instructor did not assign. _____

6. What topics did your instructor discuss that were not covered in the text?_____

_____

7. Were you required to buy this book? _____ Yes   _____ No

   Did you buy this book new or used? _____ New   _____ Used

   If used, how much did you pay? _____

   Do you plan to keep or sell this book? _____ Keep   _____ Sell

   If you plan to sell the book, how much do you expect to receive? _____

   Should the instructor continue to assign this book? _____ Yes   _____ No

8. Please list any other learning materials you purchased to help you in this course (e.g., study guide, lab manual).

_____

9. What did you like most about this text? _____

_____

10. What did you like least about this text? _____

_____

11. General comments:

   May we quote you in our advertising? _____ Yes   _____ No

   Please mail to: Boyd Lane
                     College Division, Research Department
                     Box 508
                     1300 Alum Creek Drive
                     Columbus, Ohio 43216

   Thank you!